Hollywood Boozers, Brawlers
and Hard-Luck Cases

ALSO OF INTEREST
AND FROM MCFARLAND

*Hollywood's Hard-Luck Ladies: 23 Actresses Who
Suffered Early Deaths, Accidents, Missteps, Illnesses
and Tragedies* (Laura Wagner, 2020)

Anne Francis: The Life and Career
(Laura Wagner, 2011)

Killer Tomatoes: Fifteen Tough Film Dames
(Ray Hagen and Laura Wagner, 2004)

Hollywood Boozers, Brawlers and Hard-Luck Cases

Fifteen Ill-Fated Actors of the Golden Age

Laura Wagner

McFarland & Company, Inc., Publishers
Jefferson, North Carolina

Condensed versions of some of these profiles have previously appeared in print: Ross Alexander (*Films of the Golden Age* #87, Winter 2016-17), David Bacon (*Films of the Golden Age* #74, Fall 2013), Bruce Cabot (*Films of the Golden Age* #88, Spring 2017), James Cardwell (*Classic Images* #540, June 2020), William Eythe (*Classic Images* #543, September 2020), Billy Halop (*Films of the Golden Age* #101, Summer 2020), Weldon Heyburn (*Films of the Golden Age* #83, Winter 2015-16), Ronald Lewis (*Classic Images* #554, October 2021), Allan Nixon (*Films of the Golden Age* #79, Winter 2014-15), Craig Reynolds (*Films of the Golden Age* #87, Winter 2016-17), Danny Scholl (*Films of the Golden Age* #84, Spring 2016), Lawrence Tierney (*Films of the Golden Age* #83, Winter 2015-16) and Sonny Tufts (*Films of the Golden Age* #99, Winter 2019-20).

:

LIBRARY OF CONGRESS CATALOGUING-IN-PUBLICATION DATA

Names: Wagner, Laura, 1970– author.
Title: Hollywood boozers, brawlers and hard-luck cases : fifteen
ill-fated actors of the golden age / Laura Wagner.
Description: Jefferson, North Carolina : McFarland & Company, Inc., Publishers, 2025.
| Includes bibliographical references and index.
Identifiers: LCCN 2025000307 | ISBN 9781476690117 (paperback : acid free paper) ∞
ISBN 9781476654065 (ebook)
Subjects: LCSH: Motion picture actors and actresses—United States—
Biography. | LCGFT: Biographies.
Classification: LCC PN1998.2 .W327 2025 | DDC 791.4302/80922 [B]—dc23/eng/20250106
LC record available at https://lccn.loc.gov/2025000307

ISBN (print) 978-1-4766-9011-7
ISBN (ebook) 978-1-4766-5406-5

© 2025 Laura Wagner. All rights reserved

No part of this book may be reproduced or transmitted in any form
or by any means, electronic or mechanical, including photocopying
or recording, or by any information storage and retrieval system,
without permission in writing from the publisher.

Front cover image: Actor Tom Neal from the 1945 film *Detour*
(Producers Releasing Corporation)

Back cover image: Lawrence Tierney in a publicity photo
from the 1948 film *Bodyguard* (RKO Pictures)

Printed in the United States of America

McFarland & Company, Inc., Publishers
Box 611, Jefferson, North Carolina 28640
www.mcfarlandpub.com

To James Robert Parish, film historian extraordinaire,
whose work inspired my own.

Table of Contents

Introduction and Acknowledgments 1

Ross Alexander 5
David Bacon 19
Bruce Cabot 32
James Cardwell 61
William Eythe 69
Wallace Ford 91
Billy Halop 120
Weldon Heyburn 132
Ronald Lewis 147
Tom Neal 164
Allan Nixon 195
Craig Reynolds 216
Danny Scholl 229
Lawrence Tierney 245
Sonny Tufts 281

Bibliography 305
Index 325

Introduction and Acknowledgments

"Alcohol is the anesthesia by which we endure the operation of life," George Bernard Shaw once said, and he could very well have been speaking for many members of the Hollywood community in the mid–twentieth century. Of course, alcohol might have momentarily dulled the pain—but it also added to their difficulties. Hollywood and New York nightclubs have historically had their share of boozy brawls, and DUIs were common. Alcohol was not only a social lubricant but also the panacea for mental anguish and frustration, insecurity, undiagnosed bipolar disorders, career doldrums, etc. Once it took hold, it was difficult to shake.

Columnists of the day usually had no sympathy, viewing alcoholism as a weakness, not as the disease we now know it to be. Many an actor has washed his life and career away with the old devil rum. Or Scotch. Or vodka. A classic case: Poor Lawrence Tierney couldn't curb his volatile emotions while under the influence. Writers would preach or poke fun, and the courts would give him second, third, fourth, infinite chances until it was too late. We love Tierney for his air of menace in *Born to Kill, The Devil Thumbs a Ride* and more, but one wonders what his career would have been like had he gotten proper care.

Another bad boy directed by drunken impulses was Ronald Lewis, who had a mean streak a mile wide when he imbibed. A classical British stage actor, he was frustrated by his inability to become a bigger star.

On the other hand, Bruce Cabot didn't care one whit about stardom—he was more interested in drinking, womanizing and having fun, especially with his buddy Errol Flynn (another boozing brawler). By the 1960s, the once trim and handsome Cabot was a shell of his former self and in terrible health. Similarly, Sonny Tufts was a wild man and didn't care who knew it. Although a good actor, he was never taken seriously. Oh, *that*, and he enjoyed a bite or two out of chorus girls' thighs.

Billy Halop's liquor intake stemmed from the tag "Dead End Kid." A successful radio actor before he became a member of the Dead End Kids, Halop envisioned a serious acting career for himself. Instead, he was typecast and treated as a juvenile, even in his thirties. Allan Nixon, as Mr. Marie Wilson, was one of those guys who decided to take advantage of a cushy situation, drink his fill and fight, and not work. That is, until Wilson had *her* fill and gave him the boot. Another wife later assaulted him with a knife. Weldon Heyburn, a name many of you probably won't know, had the disadvantage of looking like a movie star, Clark Gable, while definitely *not* having the same kind of career; he eventually fell into bit parts. James Cardwell, unable to cope with his inability to find acting jobs, killed himself.

Given one look at the breezy, likable Wallace Ford on screen, you wouldn't think he stepped out of a Charles Dickens novel: separated from his parents, put in an orphanage by an aunt, running away from foster homes, taking beatings as a child, becoming a hobo. All that—and Hollywood, too! A dream come true? In terms of money, yes, but he dealt with an alcohol problem and the years-long illnesses of his beloved wife.

With a chip on his shoulder and a short temper, Tom Neal went through Hollywood doing as he pleased. By most accounts, he wasn't a big drinker, but he made up for that with his short fuse, quick fists and impulsive, self-destructive behavior. He almost killed actor Franchot Tone in a fistfight, and later actually murdered his wife (and served a prison sentence).

Singer Danny Scholl endured health problems for years stemming from a blow to his head; Craig Reynolds, a hero in World War II, found that his injuries made life difficult for him and his family when he returned home. A young Warner Bros. actor of the 1930s, Ross Alexander, was traumatized by the suicide of his second wife; his downward spiral robbed us of a talented leading man. Some have speculated about his sexuality and possible double life. Did it factor in his eventual suicide? I have no idea, nor does anyone else. David Bacon's sexual orientation *did* play a part in his mysterious murder, a case unsolved to this day. For whatever reason, William Eythe drank himself to death. Was it because of his love for another actor, Lon McCallister? Or was it something far deeper, an insecurity he couldn't bury?

I have strived to be objective in my reporting on these 15 actors. All of them are among my favorites. I am fully aware that Tierney hurt quite a few people during his drunken rages and that Neal killed his wife in a fit of jealousy—both terrible things. But I try not to judge them, or anyone else. We don't know what the other person is going through, what led to those events. I am here to record the facts and appreciate their work.

Research was done via newspaper archives, quotes from books and interviews with those closest to my subjects. You will notice that I use a lot of primary articles (and gossip columns) from the time when these men were on the town (Tinseltown). I believe this gives a clearer, more accurate picture of how they were perceived at the time. All too often, authors write about their subjects the way they *think* it was, instead of how it *really* was.

If something I have written conflicts with information given elsewhere, it is because I have access to new data, including genealogy records. I have not relied solely on the Internet Movie Database for credits, and have added titles not listed on that site. My timeline in discussing these actors' films is based on shooting dates, not release dates.

I am grateful for the following people for their friendship, support and help: Michael Barnum, Peggy Biller, Lisa Burks, Diane Byrnes, Barbara Feldon, Eve Golden, Ray Hagen, Paul Petro, Fred Olen Ray, Christina Rice, Lou Valentino, Larry and Debra Vichnis, Barry Virshbo, Patricia Wagner and Archie Waugh. Thanks, also, to the late Sandra Grabman, Ruth Prigozy, Charlotte Rainey, Barbara Whiting Smith and Steve Tompkins.

It's been 30 years since I first started writing for the magazines *Classic Images* and *Films of the Golden Age*. I am indebted to editor Bob King for his encouragement, friendship and faith in me. In addition to allowing me to do articles on obscure actors, he made me contributing editor for the two publications. Carol Peterson, now retired from *CI* and *FGA*, is a wonderful, fun lady and one of my best friends.

Tom Weaver assisted with suggestions, corrections and fun trivia. He's a remarkable writer and an infuriating person—and I trust his judgment implicitly. Melanie Young's uncanny ability to uncover facts is unparalleled. She didn't even complain when I needed her to read small print for me on death certificates. Lawrence Tierney's nephews, Tim Tierney and Michael Tierney, provided (very) frank comments about their notorious uncle; Kent Adamson gave me valuable insights on Tom Neal and his relationship with Ann Savage and MGM; Anne Jeffreys, Virginia Mayo and Allene Roberts, all three now deceased, answered my questions about Lawrence Tierney; film historian Greg Mank, whose many books include a Laird Cregar biography, lent his expertise on Cregar's relationship with David Bacon's widow, Greta Keller; Dennis Enfield, the son of Craig Reynolds and Barbara Pepper, was very kind. I know it must have been tough for him to relate that sad time in his and his parents' lives, and I appreciate his openness. John O'Dowd graciously allowed me to quote from his excellent Barbara Payton biography in my Tom Neal chapter.

Thanks to John Antosiewicz for sharing a *Chandu the Magician* photo with me and Tom Weaver for saving my chapter on David Bacon by scanning a great portrait.

Long ago, when I was a teenager, I had a driving teacher named Jerry (I don't recall his last name). I still remember that moment when we both discovered, as I erratically motored down the road, that we both loved Lawrence Tierney and Scott Brady. He was the first person I met outside my family who knew who they were, and it made those lessons more bearable. Thanks, Jerry—wherever you are.

My nephews, Jake and Luke Vichnis, whom I love with all my heart, are extremely important to me. They have put up with their movie-loving aunt all these years and even listen to my often wild tales of my favorites. Luke, a budding writer, was very encouraging and often asked about my progress.

My late mentor, Doug McClelland, gave me a helping hand when I needed it most, shared a love of lesser-known actors, and encouraged me to write about them.

As always, I must thank my amazing brother, Tom Wagner, for standing by me and helping me when I needed it. I don't know what I did to deserve him, but I ain't complaining! I love him very much.

Jackie Jones is my rock, my person, my best friend. She's always there for me with an encouraging word and listens to me when I babble on about obscure actors. I am lucky to have this great lady in my life.

My late mother Fran Wagner had to deal with a teenage daughter who absolutely loved Lawrence Tierney and Tom Neal—and she never understood why. I know she was less than thrilled at my sympathetic approach to their lives. We watched many movies together, something I sorely miss.

This book's dedicatee, James Robert Parish, is familiar to many of you as an author of numerous movie books. He was an early influence in my life and gave me a sense that I could become a film historian as well. It gives me great pride today that he reads my work and comments favorably on some of it. "Made it, Ma! Top of the world!"

Ross Alexander

Today, any mention of Ross Alexander focusses mostly on how he died—a suicide at 29—and his sexuality. Little is said of his sterling stage and movie work, which lasted from 1925 to his 1937 passing. Alexander could play the scene-stealing best friend or the fast-talking lead with an ingratiating personality and charm.

The only child of Alexander Ross Smith, Jr., (1879–1966), a leather goods salesman, and Maude Adelle Cohen (1877–1954), he was born Alexander Ross Smith, Jr., in Brooklyn on July 27, 1907.

At the Brooklyn Dramatic Model School, he studied acting and dancing. He was still a child when he first exhibited high-strung, moody, Jekyll-and-Hyde behavior. In a 1937 *Movie Mirror*, he told interviewer Caroline Somers Hoyt that during his early school years,

> [a teacher] was coaching our class play and I was in it. She was a good sort; worked hard with us. Used to help me with my part after school. Always seemed pleased when we kids took an interest in things. One day we disagreed over the way I was to say some lines. I've always been crazy about acting but I guess I've always, too, wanted my own way about it.
>
> Patiently, she tried to tell me she thought her way was best. I wouldn't listen. I got mad. Tore up the script and threw it at her. Said I wouldn't be in the play and stalked out. As I looked back at her from the doorway, I saw that she was crying. I was sorry about that, terribly sorry. I went to her home that night and apologized. And I tried to give her what was, then, my most cherished possession, a green Eversharp pencil, but she wouldn't take it.

Ross Alexander's "boyish ingratiating personality will endear him to women particularly, young and not so young, and he plays the role of the applesaucer, who believes honeyed words are worth more than gold, with delicate skill and persuasive romantic manner. Part should put him in high demand, especially for pictures appealing to youth," wrote *Variety* (March 14, 1936) of Alexander's performance in *Brides Are Like That*.

She forgave me. I went on in the play and she was as nice as ever. But I've never forgotten what I did, because it was so unnecessary. I think about it every once in a while, even now, and wish I hadn't made her cry.

Alexander attended Brooklyn's Erasmus Hall High School and West High School in Rochester. He was expelled from the latter.

In a 1937 *Movie Mirror* interview conducted by George Madden, he again spoke about his early life:

We weren't very well off. There were lots of things the other kids possessed that I couldn't have; and while that doesn't matter now—and I'm glad for the hard knocks that put me on my own early in life—those things are tough on kids. And so, I kept myself happy by forgetting the things I didn't have and thinking only of those things I would have when I became a rich and famous actor; for I had my mind set on an acting career as far back as I can remember.

In Rochester, Alexander joined Hugh W. Towne's acting group. To pay for private acting lessons with Towne, he worked at several odd jobs. He also took classes in English and psychology in New York City and studied at the Packard Theatre Institute.

Stage star Blanche Yurka got Alexander into Boston's Henry Jewett Repertory Theater, as she needed a juvenile to portray her son in *Enter Madame*. (Also in this company was Peg Entwistle, posthumously famous for her 1932 leap off the HOLLYWOODLAND sign.) Alexander later told columnist Clarke Wales,

[Yurka] took me up to Jewett, so there was no difficulty in getting a hearing. But the Packard Agency in Boston had told me to get $75 a week if I got the job. I had that figure firmly in mind when I went into Jewett's office.

Jewett, a typical old-school actor, adjusted his monocle and looked me up and down. Then he said: "Well, laddie, what experience have you had?"

I lied like a trouper, and then Jewett said: "What is your salary?"

When I said $75, he looked me up and down again and said: "And what, laddie, do I get for $75 a week?"

"Youth and a fair amount of intelligence," I said.

"For that, laddie, I will pay $30."

I gulped and said: "Make it $35 or I won't stay." I went to work for $35 a week.

In December 1925, Alexander made his debut with the company in *Enter Madame*. He also appeared in Jewett's productions of *Snow White and the Seven Dwarfs*, *Mrs. Partridge Presents* (starring and directed by Yurka), *Captain Brassbound's Conversion*, *Loyalties*, *Caesar and Cleopatra*, *Minick*, *The Circle*, *The Wild Duck* and *The Little Minister*. While recalling these days to Wales, Alexander related an anecdote about an experience he had while doing *Much Ado About Nothing*:

I was the villain with a long gray beard…. Everything might have gone all right if a girl in the company [Ethelyne Holzman] who was supposed to sing a romantic song hadn't frozen up with stage fright at the last minute. Jewett adjusted his monocle and looked at me. "Laddie," he said, "can you sing the song?" I said I could. "Very well, then, you will sing it tonight."

Well, I sang the song and played the villain and rushed out to get the papers the next morning. I suppose I expected to be hailed as a combination of Booth and Caruso. But one notice said: "In Mr. Jewett's company are two groups of players, those who seem to know something about Shakespeare and those who apparently have no idea of what they are doing. In the first group are Mr. Jewett, *et al.*, *et al.*, *et al.*; in the second group is Ross Alexander."

After spending almost six months in Boston repertory, Alexander was cast by producer-director Brock Pemberton in the Broadway-bound *The Ladder*. Tryouts revealed problems with this story about reincarnation; before opening in New York, the play had to be extensively rewritten. Alexander utilized the time off to join the Wright Players, a Louisville, Kentucky, stock company that boasted as members Robert Warwick and Helen Flint. In the summer of '26, he was seen in *The Faithful Heart, Two Fellows and a Girl, The Woman in Room Thirteen, No More Blondes, Mamma's Affair, Whispering Wires* and *It Pays to Advertise*.

After more tryouts and more rewriting on *The Ladder*, it finally opened in New York on October 22, 1926. It was not well-received, the *Brooklyn Daily Eagle* blaming playwright J. Frank Davis and Pemberton, who "foisted upon this innocent metropolis a saccharine drama so devoid of substance that its ultimate crumbling was heralded with the curtain descending on the first scene." Pemberton bowed out of the show but the production, now financially backed by oil man Edgar B. Davis, continued to play through new revisions, small audiences, changes in theaters and even free admission. Alexander left the show in March 1928 and its run ended in May.

On March 19, 1928, Alexander married actress Helen Burroughs, five years his senior and "more poised and sophisticated than Ross" (*Movie Mirror*). They reportedly had a daughter, but this is not certain.

Another older man came into Alexander's life to "mentor" him, so to speak: producer John Golden, 54. He hired Ross for his show *Night Hostess* (1928) with Marguerite Churchill. Its out-of-town notices were good; in his autobiography, Golden said that Ross "showed great charm and acting ability."

The *Night Hostess* troupe moved on to Minnesota, with high hopes that their eventual Broadway opening would be a success. But in August 1928, Alexander was struck by a hit-and-run driver (a taxi in some reports). Taken to Polyclinic Hospital, he suffered from a broken jaw—and much more, according to a *Daily Star* reporter. This reporter claimed that Alexander was badly disfigured and that "many expected he would be unable to continue his career." But a plastic surgeon performed what was called "[a] modern miracle." It was later revealed that Alexander had lost almost all his teeth.

In 1940, an unnamed *Brooklyn Daily Eagle* reporter dramatically revisited the unfortunate incident:

> During the two weeks that [*Night Hostess*] played out of town prior to its New York opening, critics hailed Ross as a "find." Then, as these things happen, with his big chance just twenty-four hours away, a speeding taxi careened crazily down a side street—and Ross Alexander lay in a hospital bed, a coin's toss between life and death.

Norman Foster replaced him in *Night Hostess*.

After Ross' discharge from the hospital, he and his wife were strapped for cash. Golden came through with a radio program Alexander could produce (five-minute movie chats) throughout the month of December.

Golden put the actor into *Let Us Be Gay*, which opened on Broadway on February 19, 1929, and signed him to a stage contract. "A young actor named Ross Alexander gives a clean-cut, manly, unadorned performance," wrote Arthur Pollock. It was a hit, but the stock market crash closed it down in December. Alexander subsequently went on *Let Us Be Gay*'s road tour, which lasted until May 1930.

While waiting for Golden's next stage production to start rehearsals, Alexander went to Falmouth, Massachusetts, where the University Players (Henry Fonda, Myron

McCormick, Joshua Logan, James Stewart, Margaret Sullavan *et al.*) were about to start their new summer season. Stage designer Norris Houghton later wrote, "[A]ll summer long [Alexander] lay on the beach, wandered over rocks and dunes, slept at the company men's house, participated in acts in the supper club, and made love to Aleta." Aleta was socialite-actress Aleta Freel (*née* Freile), "charming and pretty with a considerable potential of emotional depth" (according to Houghton). Alexander also helped Henry Fonda paint scenery; the two became best friends.

"All summer long" was actually a month, and Alexander returned to New York to start work on the play *After Tomorrow*. Following a week of out-of-town performances, Golden closed the show and put Alexander into *That's Gratitude*. It ran on Broadway from September 11, 1930, to March 1931, and then went on tour. With *After Tomorrow* substantially altered, Alexander went back to that production. It played on Broadway for 77 performances (August-October 1931).

Critics referred to Alexander as "the typical American boy," with a bright acting future ahead of him, "tall, slender and typically collegiate in type" (Irene Thirer). Columnist John Mason Brown lamented that the "immensely likable" Alexander was not getting the stage vehicles he deserved:

> His touch was light, not heavy. His on-stage spirits were high. His drollery was infectious, his appearance dapper and his manner debonair. Mischief lurked amusingly in his uncommonly bright black eyes and found expression not only in his impish face but in the neat exaggeration of his gestures.... [His technique] is possessed only by natural born farceurs.

Paramount saw him in *After Tomorrow* and came knocking; for that company, he did one picture, the New York–made *The Wiser Sex* (1932). It starred Claudette Colbert, who helped him refine his screen technique, and Melvyn Douglas. Alexander confessed to Katharine Hartley that he signed with Paramount on the proviso that they give him in advance a certified check for $10,000, so he could pay for his divorce from Helen. Another rider in his contract was unique: He would receive a bonus of $1000 every time he stepped in front of a camera.

"I had a good reason for that," he explained to Hartley.

> You see, those contracts require you to do everything—make tests with other players, pose for publicity stills, advertising tie-ups, appear in benefits. From the length of those clauses, you'd think that acting for pictures was the smallest part of it. And I wanted to be sure that when they did put me in a picture, they'd think twice about the kind of part they were going to give me. It stands to reason that if they had to pay me an extra thousand dollars every time they gave me a part, they wouldn't use me in little ones.
>
> The theory was all right, but it turned out all wrong. Instead of thinking twice, they thought three times and didn't use me at all.

Except, of course, in *The Wiser Sex*, which he called "the worst picture ever produced! Ask Claudette if you don't believe me."

Returning to the stage, Alexander acted in *Heavenly Express* (1932), which closed before Broadway, and joined the Monmouth County Players in New Jersey: *Let Us Be Gay* with Alice Brady and Jean Arthur; *Coquette* and *The Greeks Had a Word for It*, both with Aleta Freel; *Holiday* with Freel and Rosalind Russell, and *Love Is Not Important* with Russell. On Broadway during 1932 and '33, he was in *The Stork Is Dead*, *Honeymoon* (directed by Thomas Mitchell), *The Party's Over* (with Claire Trevor) and *Under Glass*. *Variety* wrote of the "lively, loquacious" Alexander, "He's a good-looking juve who has been around for several seasons. Talent scouts somehow passed him up, but after the *Glass* premiere, a flock of 'em went backstage to talk over Hollywood with him."

Alexander accepted an offer from one of them, director Marshall Neilan's Associated Film Productions. With Columbia, that company was co-producing the made-in-Astoria *Social Register*, starring Colleen Moore and Alexander Kirkland. It was released on March 10, 1934, and quickly fizzled.

Nineteen thirty-four started with two short-lived Broadway productions, *The Wooden Slipper* and *No Questions Asked*. About the former, the *New York Times'* Brooks Atkinson wrote,

> It is fortunate for all of us that Ross Alexander plays the part of the inspired cook. For Mr. Alexander has not only an engaging personality, but an infectious sense of humor and considerable skill as an actor. Every scene in which he appears begins to ripple with comedy and expectancy.

The Wooden Slipper lasted only four performances, but Alexander had kudos rained down on him. *No Questions Asked* was not only Ross' last play, it was his final collaboration with John Golden, who had significantly helped his career.

> With the majority of the motion picture producers always on the lookout for new "stars-to-be," how come they've all passed up Ross Alexander…? Alexander, who is by no means bad on the eyes, can out-act most of our present "top" male attractions…. You can thank me for the tip."—Jerry Wald, *The Hollywood Reporter*, February 1, 1934

In February 1934, Alexander and Aleta Freel wed in East Orange, New Jersey, with Henry Fonda serving as best man. The couple moved to California, where both screen-tested for movie contracts. Alexander later told Katharine Hartley,

> Metro signed me on a six-week option at $850 a week…. [T]hey did get around to making a test of me. But even that wasn't until the sixth week. Afterwards, the front office called me in. One of the executives said: "Did you see your test, Mr. Alexander?" I said I had. "Then tell us, if you were a producer, what would you pay that actor?" "About fifty cents a week," I answered. "That's what we think!" he said…. The trouble with them was that they didn't have the heart to tell me what was the matter. I knew, but I wasn't going to tell them. I look like the west end of a horse going east! And don't think I'm kidding when I say that!

Alexander had been insecure all his life, and those feelings intensified after he arrived in Hollywood and found himself surrounded by glamorous actors. He also hated his voice, saying it sounded as if he had a "hot potato" in his mouth; some critics agreed. Alexander was not a conventional actor in looks or manner, which is what made him special. He was "tall and slim," Alice L. Tildesley wrote, "too nervous to be definitely labeled a he-man, although he is athletic and fond of sports."

Dropped by MGM with not a single credit to show for his time there, Alexander next did a test at Warner Bros. He was signed in June 1934. His WB bow came soon after, playing Oscar "Oskie" Berry, the cheerful pal and West Point roommate of Dick "Canary" Dorcy (Dick Powell), in the musical *Flirtation Walk* (1934). Between musical numbers, Oskie serves as comic relief opposite Canary and the gal he loves, Kit (Ruby Keeler).

Filmed next (but released first) was *Gentlemen Are Born*, a drama about the difficult post-college lives of four friends (Franchot Tone, Alexander, Dick Foran, Robert Light). Terming it "depressing movie fare," the *Oakland Tribune*'s Whitney Williams was on target writing, "The picture has its moments but in the main suffers from an undertone of futility." The likable Alexander is the most optimistic of the quartet, and the liveliest, as he aspires to be an architect and makes a life with wife Jean Muir. Nobert Lusk, reviewing Ross' first two films side by side in *Picture Play*, praised Alexander's "magnetic sense of humor" in *Flirtation Walk* and his "glib breeziness" in *Gentlemen Are Born*.

For his first lead role, Alexander again struggled as a young married (opposite Gloria Stuart this time) in *Maybe It's Love*, an adaptation of Maxwell Anderson's *Saturday's Children*. The *Boston Globe* critic opined:

> Mr. Alexander is an amusing purveyor of humor, and his two previous performances in motion pictures have been both refreshing and convincing. But as Rims, the poor boy desperately in love with Bobby [Stuart], who has too many relatives, he is not quite so convincing. One suspects, however, the fault lies not with Mr. Alexander, but with the persons who adapted the play for the screen. It takes a bit of genius to make amusing the plight of two young people very much in love with each other, who are confronted with in-law troubles, jealousy, and financial difficulties.

In 1934, celebrated theatrical producer-director Max Reinhardt helmed a critically acclaimed Hollywood Bowl production of Shakespeare's *A Midsummer Night's Dream*, which came to the screen courtesy of Warner Bros. in 1935. The extravagant, million-dollar adaptation's cast includes James Cagney, Mickey Rooney, Dick Powell, Olivia de Havilland (her film debut), Joe E. Brown, Anita Louise and Victor Jory. Involved in a four-sided love story is Athenians Demetrius (Alexander), Lysander (Powell), Hermia (de Havilland) and Helena (Jean Muir). It's comedically handled business

In *Maybe It's Love* (1935), an adaptation of Maxwell Anderson's play *Saturday's Children*, Ross Alexander (seen here with Gloria Stuart) was given his first film lead.

until finally the couples pair off as they should at the end. The movie, co-directed by William Dieterle and Reinhardt, is a gorgeous display with "magical moments" (*New York Times*) but it received mixed reviews. Graham Greene in *The Spectator* praised the acting as "fresh and vivid" due to its lack of "proper Shakespearian diction and bearing." Alexander disagreed with Reinhardt's approach to the play, but did as he was told.

"Doing as he was told" also meant appearing as the juvenile lead with June Martel in the comedy *Going Highbrow* (1935), in which character actors Guy Kibbee, ZaSu Pitts and Edward Everett Horton ran the show. In *We're in the Money* (1935), he's a wealthy playboy posing as a lowly chauffeur as he romances process server Joan Blondell. ("You might have thought you were romancing with a chauffeur; but you never told me to put on any brakes!") In between these two comedies, there was a request from Paramount to borrow Alexander for two films, *Accent on Youth* and *The Big Broadcast of 1936*. Warners turned them down.

Next on his schedule was another military musical, *Shipmates Forever* (1935), shot partly at Annapolis. As Lafayette "Sparks" Brown, he once more supported Dick Powell and Ruby Keeler, again playing Powell's pal and roommate (and the film's comic relief). "His naturalness, talent, charm and individual sense of humor should stamp him as one of the better Hollywood juveniles," wrote the *Courier-Post*'s Ida Hermann.

Captain Blood (1935) was Errol Flynn's first for Warners, an adaptation of Rafael Sabatini's 1922 novel *Captain Blood: His Odyssey*. A classic pirate swashbuckler, it features Alexander as Jeremy Pitt, a ship's navigator and pal of Flynn's Dr. Peter Blood. One scene has

Joan Blondell gets her man (Ross Alexander), a millionaire posing as a chauffeur, in *We're in the Money* (1935).

become famous to Alexander's fans and admirers: Pitt, strapped spread-eagle to a whipping post, insists to Blood that despite the lashing, he didn't reveal their secret plans. The sequence is extremely well-acted, proving that Alexander could handle dramatics just fine.

"Author" David Bret claims, in his 2000 "biography" of Errol Flynn, that there was a problem on the *Captain Blood* set when the movie's "homophobic" director Michael Curtiz and Flynn got into a row over Alexander's "somewhat exuberant armpits which, Errol declared, 'turned him on like hot twin fannies.'" It gets worse: Bret goes on to write that Curtiz decided that Alexander's hairy underarms, visible in the flogging scene, would get them in trouble with the Hays Office, and he brought a razor to the set, ready to shave the actor's armpits himself. The smitten Flynn objected, took the blade and threatened to cut Curtiz's throat if he "removed so much as one hair from Alexander's 'magnificent oxters,' so the scene was left uncut, and received few complaints."

If there had been an altercation on the set, especially if an actor threatened *anyone* with a razor, it would have been noted in the Warner Bros. production reports. It was not. Interoffice memos were more concerned with the violence of the simulated whipping than Alexander's exuberant armpits.

> Ross Alexander is one of those actors who will achieve a hit some day that will be heard around the world. He did pretty well in *Flirtation Walk* and he has been slowly but surely building himself a public, but the boy so far hasn't had the big break that we all are waiting for. He may get it as Jeremy Pitt in *Captain Blood*, one of the important featured roles.—Louella Parsons, August 6, 1935

Dr. Peter Blood (Errol Flynn) finds that his friend, navigator Jeremy Pitt (Alexander), has been brutally whipped. Alexander's "exuberant armpits" are in full display. *Captain Blood* (1935) was one of three Best Picture Oscar nominees in which Alexander appeared; the others were *Flirtation Walk* (1934) and *A Midsummer Night's Dream* (1935).

"Ross Alexander's faun-like personality saves the role of Rusty. Patricia Ellis's stylized beauty suffices as the torch-singer and Lyle Talbot makes the villainous Lacy agreeable in the story that hasn't much to offer except occasional shots of the colossal dam project." – *Boulder Dam* review in the *New York Daily News*, March 28, 1936. Pictured left to right: Ellis, Alexander and Talbot.

For his good work, Alexander was given leads in two fast-moving Bs: *Boulder Dam* (with Patricia Ellis) and *Brides Are Like That* (with Anita Louise). Florence Fisher Parry (*Pittsburgh Press*) wrote, "Young Ross Alexander has been worked pretty hard lately, and I have seen him in a number of roles, all consistently well played. He is improving rapidly and is being groomed for the juvenile stardom which he shows definite signs of deserving."

Alexander's wife Aleta was not enjoying the success in California she had in New York, and was having difficulty getting roles. Also, Henry Fonda claimed that Ross was a less-than-faithful husband and "enjoyed the company of easy women." Ross' bipolar moods, those extreme highs and lowest of lows, made their lives sometimes difficult. But Aleta didn't want to go back east without him, not trusting her straying husband one bit.

On December 6, 1935, Aleta and Alexander had a "small family spat" (as he called it) at their home on Woodrow Wilson Drive in the Hollywood Hills. Despondent that recent screen tests were unsuccessful, she repeated her oft-heard refrain that she wanted to go back to New Jersey (where her family lived) and return to the stage. A fed-up Alexander snapped at her, "Well, for God's sake, go home, and quit nagging me about it!," and went to bed.

Aleta took the .22 caliber rifle she had in the bedroom and went out to the backyard. After firing a test shot, she put the gun to her right temple and pulled the trigger. Alexander said at the inquest,

> She rushed out of the room and a few seconds later I heard two shots. I ran into the dining room and called William Bolden, the butler, to turn on the yard lights. With Bolden following

me I ran around the house and stumbled over my wife's body, pitching to the ground. Her rifle lay beside her. She was still gasping and I called an ambulance and had her moved to the Cedars of Lebanon Hospital where she died the following morning.

"Whenever I see Ross Alexander," Jimmie Fidler wrote, "his eyes suggest tragedy; since his wife's suicide they seldom seem to join his lips in smiles." An inconsolable Alexander began drinking too much and his behavior became erratic. Henry Fonda later said that Ross "gave up women for port, and drank bottle after bottle. He was rocked, obviously, and he had a real guilt feeling, because I'm sure he knew. I don't think she left a note, but he must have known why she did it."

In mid–January 1936, Alexander was cast in a supporting role in the Pat O'Brien-Josephine Hutchinson film *I Married a Doctor* (based on a Sinclair Lewis novel). In his most dramatic role, Alexander plays a sensitive and unhappy artist who falls in love with Hutchinson. His unrequited passion leads to tragedy.

During production, an "accident" was reported: a "draught blew out a gas heater in his room and he lay breathing in the fumes." According to Harrison Carroll, Ross' bulldog Mr. Watson's "frantic barks saved the day." In March, Alexander was arrested in front of the Trocadero nightclub following an altercation with a parking attendant. Officers said the intoxicated Alexander was violently arguing about whether he was capable of driving. After cooling his heels in the Beverly Hills police station holding cell for several hours, he was released on $100 bail. The following month brought a charge of drunk driving and a suspended license.

He and Beverly Roberts starred in the comedy *Hot Money* (1936), based on a play by Aben Kandel (previously filmed by Warners as *High Pressure* in 1932). In a 1997 *Classic*

Beverly Roberts and Ross Alexander appeared in two 1936 films together, *Hot Money* (seen here) and *China Clipper*.

Images interview conducted by Joe Collura, Beverly said she remembered Alexander quite well: "He was a very complicated and wonderful young man whom I liked and got along with easily. He had a lot of hang-ups, though, so I wasn't that surprised when he had that difficult time that caused him to take his life." In its review of *Hot Money*, the *Albany Evening News* said that as the slick promoter, Alexander "talks and talks and talks…. You could hardly keep count of his words with a split-second watch. He talks his way through an improbable story that is directed at a speed that is meant to cover its fantastic quality." Alexander was certainly at the right studio, fitting in perfectly with WB's other fast-talking contract players.

In 1936, *Movie Mirror*'s Katharine Hartley described how Alexander reacted at a March preview of *I Married a Doctor* when the audience laughed at one of his most dramatic scenes:

> To be laughed at is the worst thing that can happen to an actor. Even though Ross knew it was not his fault—not anyone's—and that that particular scene would be omitted at the final cutting before the picture's release (that is what previews are for) still it hurt. Then, as if that were not enough, Ross was summoned to do the same part on the air for [the radio series] *Hollywood Hotel* [April 3, 1936].
>
> I happened to be there that day. I sat next to him in the control room during rehearsal. The dread of being laughed at again must have been uppermost in his mind. But he never let on. Only his high color, his nervousness, and his pacing up and down gave him away. "Nervous?" someone asked. "Oh no, I've done radio before. I was on *The Collier Hour* steadily several years ago." The boy who had slid down under a seat to avoid recognition only a few days before was now disclaiming any remembrance of the episode.

In April, Ross bought a ten-acre ranch on Ventura Boulevard in Encino. Everyone agreed that it was good for him emotionally to leave the home he shared with Aleta.

Right before he started shooting *China Clipper* in early May, Alexander went on a camping trip in the Canadian woods. He got lost for four days, living on wild berries until a search party located him.

Made with the cooperation of Pan American Airways, and loosely based on that company's history, *China Clipper* was written by aviator Frank "Spig" Wead. Ray Enright directed a typically wonderful Warner Bros. cast of favorites that in addition to Alexander included Pat O'Brien, Beverly Roberts, Humphrey Bogart, Marie Wilson and Addison Richards (and in bit parts Wayne Morris, Anne Nagel, Gordon Elliott and Henry Stephenson). Alexander is good in another friend-of-the-star (O'Brien) role. His character, wisecracking pilot Tom Collins, also has some fun scenes with dimwitted Wilson.

Alexander was seen out with Anita Louise. Many believed they would wed, although she denied such reports. Anne Nagel, seen in supporting roles in *Hot Money* and *China Clipper*, became another frequent date. And in June, she was his leading lady in *Here Comes Carter* (1936) where he played a fast-talking radio gossip commentator who is quick with the quips ("If anybody phones, tell 'em to come up and sue me sometime!"). The *New York Times*' Frank S. Nugent raved: "Mr. Alexander seems to be a younger, sprightlier Jack Benny, with a better gag-man than Jack's and at least as glib a delivery—the ease and self-assurance of his performance having never been exceeded by Mr. Benny himself."

On September 16, 1936, just nine months after Aleta's suicide, Alexander, 29, eloped to Yuma, Arizona, with Nagel, almost two weeks before her twenty-first birthday. He later told George Madden,

Please don't call our marriage a "second chance at happiness," for this is a new adventure Anne and I have just begun—an adventure with a present and a future, but without a past. Our great happiness together is an individual thing that has no relation to anything that has happened to either of us before. We want to keep it that way. We have our eyes and hearts set on the future.

After playing second fiddle to Dick Powell in two musicals, Alexander finally had a chance to win Ruby Keeler in *Ready, Willing and Able* and got to sing two outstanding Johnny Mercer-Richard Whiting songs, "Too Marvelous for Words" and "Just a Quiet Evening"—although he was dubbed by James Newill.

An emergency appendectomy was performed on Nagel on October 14 by Dr. Franklyn Thorpe. Alexander took an adjoining room so he could be near Anne during her hospital stay. Eleven years later, Nagel—now married to her second husband—discovered that Thorpe had "taken out her reproductive organs without her knowledge or consent when he operated on her." She filed suit for $350,000 against Dr. Thorpe and Dr. V.L. Andrews. Thorpe claimed that she knew full well the "nature of the surgery."

The specter of Alexander's dead wife was always between newlyweds Ross and Nagel. Their chauffeur Cornelius Stephenson later testified that Alexander often talked of Aleta and said he "would never find another wife as good." In a posthumously published *Movie Mirror* article, Alexander was quoted as saying that he was trying to make Nagel happy, and then he added ominously,

I haven't made anyone else happy—quite the contrary. I try to tell myself that what is done is done and, honestly, I do love Anne. But I can't forget that if Aleta and I hadn't quarreled that night she—she—. All of the quarrels I ever had with anyone were my own fault.

One wonders how Nagel, already a high-strung, emotional and sensitive person, dealt with Alexander's moodiness and troubling behavior, as he often sat by the fireplace brooding and writing poetry. "When there are dizzy flights to the pinnacle of happiness, there are also the extremes of melancholy and depression undreamed of by normal folk," wrote *Photoplay*'s Gordon Palmer. "Ross Alexander suffered from such flights and falls, and when he had been drinking, sank to the depths of despondency."

According to Stephenson, on the first anniversary of Aleta's death, December 7, Alexander went to their old residence, got "hysterical" and screamed that he wanted to kill himself; Stephenson had to wrestle a gun away from him. This was reportedly just one of several suicide attempts he had made. Palmer revealed, "One night at Victor Jory's Pasadena home, Ross went into suicide mood and his friends had to wrest a gun from him."

Alexander's parents visited the couple, and left for home on New Year's Eve. His mother Maude took with her a sweater that Aleta had been knitting for Ross; Anne had promised him that she would finish it, but his mother thought it morbid. Its loss upset Alexander.

According to Nagel, on the night of January 2, 1937, Alexander was in good spirits as they took down their Christmas tree and he played the guitar and sang to her. Just before dinner, as she sat crocheting, Alexander said he was going out to the barn to "kill a duck" for the next day's dinner. "We heard a shot," the maid said. "And then he did not come back." The cook told the *Boston Globe*'s Mayme Ober Peak,

He used to come in the kitchen often and talk about his other wife, and the things like cream gravy she liked for me to make, but I know he and Miss Anne were very happy and that he loved her. He just didn't know what he was doing sometimes. If he had come out the back door Saturday night, instead of slipping out the front door, I would have headed him off and he would have been alive now. I knew he was drinking, although he didn't always show it. When [his valet] Steve went to call him for dinner and found he was in the barn—and had been there for an hour, my heart went into my boots. Steve came running back, his face was green on one side and black on the other. I said, "You don't have to tell me what happened. I know."

(While the cook claims that Steve the valet went to look for Alexander, all other sources say Stephenson was the one who found him; and that Ross was gone for 15 minutes, not an hour.)

The 29-year-old Alexander was found lying in the barn loft, clutching a .22 caliber target pistol, a bullet through his left temple. He died before the ambulance arrived. A hysterical Nagel fought with officers in an attempt to see her husband's body.

Alexander was interred at Glendale's Forest Lawn Memorial Park. Nagel could not cash in his $35,000 insurance because of a suicide clause. She did, however, inherit his debts.

It was clear to Ross' family and friends that the death of Aleta drove him to this act. Many rumors have surfaced through the years as to the reasons for his demise. In October 1937, columnist Louis Sobol wrote of Alexander's "failure to measure up to the success of Gable, Montgomery, and other male stars." The strangest one came courtesy of the *New York Sun*: In their 1939 obituary of Alexander's former father-in-law, Dr. William Freile, the unidentified reporter claimed that Ross was "killed accidentally on a duck-hunting expedition shortly after his wife's death"!

Author Lawrence Quirk's 1989 Bette Davis biography has muddied the waters considerably: He quotes his go-to guy for outrageous Hollywood stories, publicist Jerry Asher, as saying that Alexander had had sex with a male hobo who then blackmailed him. Since Asher died in 1967, there is no way of knowing if these claims are true; in fact, there's no way of knowing if Asher ever even made these claims. This, however, has not stopped other "historians" from presenting them as fact and even embellishing them. I cannot say whether Ross was bisexual. If he was, it might have added to his feelings of unworthiness and his inability to lead the life he wanted to live. What is known for sure is that he had feelings for his wives.

After playing second fiddle to Dick Powell in *Flirtation Walk* (1934) and *Shipmates Forever* (1935), Ross Alexander finally won Ruby Keeler in *Ready, Willing and Able* (1937).

Warners fretted over Alexander's last movie, *Ready, Willing and Able*, in which he had the leading role. They thought of reshooting his scenes, but ultimately downplayed him in the credits and advertising. When it was released, Ruby Keeler was top-billed, dancer Lee Dixon was elevated to the second spot, and Alexander was billed fifth. The *Hollywood Spectator* wrote of the film, "For Hollywood its gaiety is dampened somewhat by the presence of the late Ross Alexander in the cast, the feeling of regret being accentuated by the fact that his performance is the best he gave on screen. It would have advanced him a long way toward stardom."

1932: *The Wiser Sex.*
1934: *Social Register, Gentlemen Are Born, Flirtation Walk.*
1935: *Maybe It's Love, Going Highbrow, We're in the Money, A Midsummer Night's Dream, A Dream Comes True* (short), *Shipmates Forever, Captain Blood.*
1936: *Boulder Dam, Brides Are Like That, I Married a Doctor, Hot Money, China Clipper, Here Comes Carter.*
1937: *Ready, Willing and Able.*

David Bacon

Between 1942 and '43, actor and socialite David Bacon made five movies and one serial, but if he is remembered today, it is not for his acting but for his death: The brutal unsolved murder of the 29-year-old Bacon has fascinated true-crime and film fans for almost 80 years. The story has sex, blood, multiple suspects, even more blood, contradictory testimony, a double life, and a possible cover-up. The fame David Bacon sought came from the slash of a knife.

Gaspar Griswold Bacon, Jr., was born in Jamaica Plain, Boston, Massachusetts, on March 24, 1914, to Gaspar G. Bacon (1886–1947), president of the Massachusetts Senate (1929–32) and lieutenant governor of Massachusetts (1933-35), and Priscilla Toland (1888–1965). He had two brothers, William (1911–91) and Robert (1919–87). According to Gaspar Sr.'s *Boston Traveler* obituary,

> He was a veteran of both World Wars. He rose from private to major in the field artillery during World War I, and held a major's commission during World War II. He was awarded the Verdun medal and the Croix de Guerre by the French government for his brilliant leadership in the D-Day Invasion of Normandy and in Northern France and the Rhineland with Gen. Patton's Third Army.

Gaspar Sr.'s father, Robert Bacon (1860–1919), was Theodore Roosevelt's Secretary of State for three months in 1909 and then the U.S. ambassador to France (1909–12). Senior's brother, Robert Low Bacon (1884–1938), was a politician and banker, instrumental in creating the Davis–Bacon Act of 1931. Via marriage, Priscilla's sister Matilda became the Baroness de Schauensee; her father-in-law was commander of the Pontifical Swiss Guard in Rome.

Growing up in Barnstable, Massachusetts, the Bacon boys had privileged childhoods because of their prestigious, socially prominent family. Gaspar Jr. counted among his friends John and Franklin D. Roosevelt, Jr. The Bacons were frequent visitors at the White House and FDR's Hyde Park home (although Senior's politics conflicted with that of the president's).

Gaspar was attracted to the theatrical world early. While his brothers fell in line with the family's ambitions for them (William became a doctor and Robert worked for the State Department), Gaspar became a messenger for the University Players in Falmouth, Massachusetts, in the early '30s. In 1944, *New York Daily News* crime reporter Peter Levins wrote about Gaspar's educational record:

> Until he was 12, young Bacon had been privately tutored at home, then he had attended Groton [School] from 1926-'29. In his third year he had failed in five subjects out of seven with the result that the headmaster, Dr. Endicott Peabody, sent for his parents. The family-school

conference resulted in his being removed from Groton and sent to Deerfield Academy at Deerfield, Mass. He remained there until 1933.

At both schools he was given high marks for deportment.

He passed the entrance examinations at Harvard after a heroic studying effort, and lived at the Freshman Dormitories. According to Dean A.C. Hanford, he was an average student. However, in his sophomore year he became a backslider again, but tutors pulled him through. In his junior year, he received three honor grades; in his senior year, he won two B grades and one C grade.

Bacon found his métier in the theatrical projects of the Hasty Pudding Club, soon demonstrating that he had real acting talent. He told friends that he intended going on the stage as soon as he finished school.

Bacon not only acted in the Hasty Pudding Club productions, he co-wrote the books and songs. He was especially adept at his drag roles of "a haughty dowager who strutted through a play which satirized Hollywood and motion picture methods" and a "biddie" named Mrs. O'Shaughnessy (*Boston Globe*). For his work in *Come Across* (1937), he was praised by *Variety* as "the most skilled on stage." The reviewer added, "In the lead role of Lady Lavinia, endowed with most of the snappier lines, Bacon proves himself more than worthy of the assignment. Consistently he sketches a full-length portrait of a fluttery dilettante dowager and whams with a dainty toe dance made utterly silly by his angelic expression that doesn't crack."

The promising film career of socialite-turned-actor David Bacon was cut short by his mysterious murder in 1943 (courtesy of Tom Weaver).

On June 12, 1935, in Falmouth, Massachusetts, he was arrested on a drunk driving charge. His license was suspended for a year and he was fined $50.

According to columnist Mayme Ober Peak, the year Bacon graduated from Harvard, 1937, he "sought a wider horizon by acting in 16-millimeter movies"—although there are no details regarding what was filmed, where or by whom. In New York, he became a master of ceremonies at a silent movie theater. For five months, he studied at the Harvard Architecture School and did summer theater.

During 1938 and part of '39, Bacon was a flying cadet at Randolph Air Force Base, near San Antonio, Texas. He underwent months of training before health problems interfered—Bacon had an "extra vertebrae." According to sciprogress.com, a spinal injury blog,

> the general consensus is that an extra vertebra does not affect either spinal health or the overall health of the individual.... About 10% of people have a 6th lumbar vertebra, which in most cases goes unnoticed. This is a developmental anomaly and typically has very little effect on an individual's health. It's usually discovered when other health issues with the spine such as a lower back pain are being investigated.

Bacon had suffered a back injury while in Texas and this caused him to leave the Air Force (and explains why he was 4-F during World War II). There are reports that have him doing freelance flying in Hyannis, Massachusetts.

On September 9, 1939, in Los Angeles, Bacon was accused of making "improper advances" towards 15-year-old newsboy Curtis D. Larsen. When Larsen came to Bacon's home to collect money due, Bacon answered the door wearing only his pajama top. "He invited me upstairs to see his paintings," Larsen told reporters. "He said he was an artist at MGM studio and he wanted me to see his work. Instead, when we got upstairs, he—" At this point, news reports declined to describe the advance in detail. Larsen continued, "I told him my uncle was waiting for me, and he stopped acting that way at once and asked me if I couldn't come back later in the day." Larsen did come back later—but with the police. While Bacon admitted to the charge, he claimed he didn't know why he had acted in such a way. He was arrested for "contributing to the delinquency of a minor"; his sentence was suspended on the condition that he leave California for a period of three years. Actually, he only got as far as Santa Barbara. (Perhaps his father pulled some strings.) Changing his name from Gaspar to David helped distance himself from the incident.

At the end of 1939, it was stated that Bacon had been signed by MGM—as an actor, not as an artist. "Gossip also has it," wrote the *Boston Globe*, "that the elder Bacon has not yet been informed of his son's ambition to join Hollywood's glamour-lads." The Metro contract announcement was premature; Bacon was not engaged.

Bacon spent the summer of '40 appearing in little theater at the Bass Rocks Theatre in Gloucester, Massachusetts. He had a supporting part in *Caprice* (starring John Lodge and wife Francesca Braggiotti), with the *Boston Globe* stating that Bacon "contributed delightful comedy to a most entertaining performance." *No Time for Comedy* paired him with noted Austrian-born Broadway and movie actress Mady Christians. In Thornton Wilder's *Our Town*, Bacon and Katharine Bard (a seasoned actress who was in the original stage production of *Life with Father*) played the main lovers, George Gibbs and Emily Webb; the *Boston Globe* praised Bacon's "excellent abilities [which] have attracted much professional interest on the behalf of Hollywood." The review continued: "[H]e gives a superb characterization.... He is the personification of the male youth of the village." (This show also featured playwright Wilder himself, as the Stage Manager.)

The Hottentot starred Arthur Treacher, J. Colvin Dunn and Doris Carson. "Post-deb Bella Gardner and Gaspar Bacon Jr. were Boston's share of the cast," the *Boston Globe* reported, "and brother Bob Bacon was in the second row to check on [Gaspar's] good performance."

In late August 1940, at a benefit dance in Magnolia, Massachusetts, Bacon was given a silver cup as "handsomest man," while two debutantes tied for "prettiest girl." At the end of September, it was being reported by Hedda Hopper that Bacon was "testing like mad for the cowboy in Howard Hughes' next picture" (*The Outlaw*). Supposedly, Ginger Rogers was instrumental in getting him the chance.

Nineteen forty-one started with Hopper writing, "Boston's David Bacon tested for *The Outlaw* but his speech was too cultured for Billy the Kid. Howard Hughes liked him so much he's put him under a long-term contract, and now director Sam Wood wants to borrow David for his next picture. Truly, life in Hollywood is wonderful." Well, not *too* wonderful. The Sam Wood picture never materialized, and Bacon "became the star of the Hughes projection room. Whenever there was a test to be made with a young female hopeful, Bacon was called in." The only other thing he did during this time was a summer stock stage production, *Lottie Dundas* (1941), starring Geraldine Fitzgerald and the David O. Selznick Company, at Santa Barbara's Lobero Theatre.

The tall, blond Bacon was hitchhiking to Lockheed one day when he was picked up by a Fox talent scout. "David Bacon is being hailed as a find by 20th Century-Fox," wrote Edwin Schallert.

Fox was in the process of casting *School for Soldiers* (also called *Salute to Heroes*)—soon to be renamed *Ten Gentlemen from West Point*—about the establishment of the U.S. Military Academy at West Point in the early 1800s, and young men were needed to fill the cast as cadets. Bacon, loaned out by Hughes, was given a role vacated by O.Z. Whitehead. At one point, the cadets dress as women to pull a prank; the sequence that surely reminded Bacon of his days on stage at Harvard.

In the film, the U.S. Senate has reservations about the Academy but agrees to fund it for a year. The school's commander is the ruthless Major Sam Carter (Laird Cregar), who relentlessly drives the cadets until there are only ten remaining; his tactic is to have all of them drop out so that the Academy will fail. It almost works when he punishes them by making them sit out in the rain on top of cannons. But Shippen (Bacon), sick with pneumonia, solemnly states that he is not quitting: "I have a debt to pay. My uncle used to be commandant here—General Benedict Arnold." The cadets are later ordered to the Indiana territory where Major Carter is eventually kidnapped by Tecumseh and his Shawnee warriors. The cadets mount an attack to save him, and in the skirmish, Shippen is mortally wounded. Bacon, shown in close-up, has his best screen moment as he lies dying.

Ten Gentlemen from West Point was solid entertainment, but lost money at the box office. Still, at the time, director Henry Hathaway was impressed with Bacon's work, and was quoted by Mayme Ober Peak as saying,

> He's really terrific. He dug into this part as if he were Mansfield in pursuit of the Melancholy Dane. Half the time he drove us nuts, with muttering his lines between takes, brooding over his method of securing the redemption of the Arnolds. He'd take Laird Cregar aside and pump him dry of tricks of acting which might suit his role. Even Maureen O'Hara was not immune from Bacon's energies. When he found out she had been with the Abbey Players in Dublin, it was the beginning of a beautiful friendship, from which he has garnered a good deal of priceless advice.

Mr. Bacon may have annoyed, but he likewise impressed his fellow workers and the studio executives who have seen him in action. He has acquired in the heart of Hathaway a special corner reserved for

In *Ten Gentlemen from West Point* (1942), David Bacon as Shippen, nephew of General Benedict Arnold, is out to prove himself.

Bacon (left) as a submarine lieutenant in *Crash Dive* (1943). Pictured left to right, Bacon, Tyrone Power, Dana Andrews and Harry Morgan.

hard-working youngsters. Net result of this is that when another suitable role comes along, Bacon will get it and it will not go to those who have hidden their talent under a shy and retiring demeanor.

Wishful thinking. Twelfth-billed Bacon showed promise in his few scenes, received a Fox term contract and got some favorable reviews (e.g., the *Los Angeles Daily News*' Harry Mines called his performance "outstanding")—and yet the studio soon seemed to lose interest. In his next Fox assignment, *Crash Dive* (1943), starring Tyrone Power, Anne Baxter and Dana Andrews, he was relegated to an uncredited part as a submarine lieutenant. No character name, no lines, no outstanding moments, no close-ups.

He went straight into PRC's *The Boss of Big Town* (1942). The topical story of food profiteering during wartime boasted a good lead performance from John Litel as the manager of a market who sets out to stop the racket with the help of reporter Florence Rice. Sixth-billed Bacon has the perfunctory role of Dr. Gil Page, who is smitten with Jean Brooks. Grace Kingsley of the *Los Angeles Times* singled him out with a rather embellished notice: "[It] is young David Bacon as a doctor who wins much attention by bringing to the screen a fresh, arresting personality, talent and clean-cut acting, in a greater degree than any juvenile seen lately."

On December 27, 1942, Bacon, 28, wed Austrian-born singer Greta Keller, 39, in a church ceremony at Los Angeles' Chapman Park Chapel. (They had already married secretly in Mexico in July '42.) The couple made their home in a mansion called Castle Hill on Magnolia Drive on Lookout Mountain in Hollywood.

This was Keller's second trip down the aisle: On November 13, 1929, in London, she had tied the knot with American nightclub entertainer Joe Sargent. He, John Barney and Stuart Ross performed as the Three New Yorkers until Sargent and Ross went off as a singing-piano duo specializing in patter songs. Greta joined them for a time on the road and on radio, and they recorded in the U.S. and in Europe. In 1940, she sued Sargent for divorce, charging desertion. (By that time, he was being called a former actor and psychiatrist!) Sargent and Bacon, besides looking alike, were both blond Harvard men (Sargent, class of '22, Bacon, class of '37) and born in Massachusetts.

The elegant Keller's "husky, contralto tones" (Danton Walker) made her a favorite on recordings and in cabarets, and she was a bigger star than Bacon. In the early '30s, she was seen in a handful of German movies. A well-received U.S. airwave appearance on Rudy Vallee's *Fleischmann's Yeast Hour* in 1932 led to a regular spot on Leo Reisman's radio series, and her own show with Sargent and Ross. Hollywood was interested, specifically RKO's Merian C. Cooper, but she waited around without making any screen appearances. "I made no pictures," she told Danton Walker, "but I cooked for half of Hollywood—the Frank Morgans, Chester Morrises, Melvyn Douglases, Walter Connollys, Basil Rathbones, Jimmy Cagneys—everybody. Robert Montgomery once ate nine of my wiener schnitzels at one sitting." Proud of her cooking, she bragged that King Carol II of Romania waited until she was done singing at Paris' Club Casanova one night so he could ask her to make beef Stroganoff. "I sing in three languages," she said, "but I cook in 13." Just before her marriage to Bacon, Keller made her U.S. film debut in a supporting role in MGM's *Reunion in France* (1942).

A rare photograph of David Bacon, 28, and Austrian-born singer Greta Keller, 39, on their wedding day, December 27, 1942.

Based on the story "Prodigal's Mother" by Ben Ames Williams, Republic's *Someone to Remember* (1943) was the poignant tale of elderly widow Sarah Freeman (Mabel Paige), whose home, the Lakeside Towers, has been converted by a university into a men's dormitory. She stays on in hopes that her wayward son—gone for more than 20 years—will find her again. The lonely lady's sweet demeanor and caring nature touches everyone she meets, especially college boy Dan Freeman (John Craven), who she mistakenly believes to be her grandson,

In *Someone to Remember* (1943), Mabel Paige serves tea to (left to right) college boys David Bacon, John Good, Peter Lawford, Tom Seidel and Richard Crane.

and his sweetheart Lucia (Dorothy Morris). Bacon plays the disagreeable Ike Dale, a friend of Lucia's family who thinks he and Lucia should be a couple. Poor Ike, nobody truly likes him, not the other college guys, not Lucia and Dan and not even Sarah, who declares disdainfully that she "doesn't like his brand of humor."

In Universal's musical comedy *Gals, Incorporated* (1943), Bacon played the Marine son of womanizing millionaire Leon Errol and the object of the romantic attentions of Grace McDonald and Harriet Hilliard. Since most of the action centers on Errol's antics and the girls' musical talents, Bacon has little to do, but he does it well. At 6'2", he seems to tower over his fellow actors (Errol was 5'7"). The *Cincinnati Enquirer*'s E.B. Radcliffe felt the talented cast "brightened the gloom of their stale gags and tired and overworked plot ideas." He called Bacon a "personable newcomer."

In 1943, Bacon was handed a top role in the World War II-themed Republic serial *The Masked Marvel*: part of a quartet of insurance investigators seeking to thwart Sakima (Johnny Arthur), a Japanese agent who has instigated a reign of terror on U.S. soil through sabotage. One of the insurance men regularly dons a mask and becomes a Green Hornet–like crimebuster, the Masked Marvel—but which one? Not until the closing seconds of the twelfth and final chapter did viewers know the Marvel's true identity. (In reality, the Marvel was played by none of the four actors: Stuntman Tom Steele was always behind the mask.)

Two weeks after the chapterplay's shooting wrapped: On the morning of Sunday,

September 12, 1943, Bacon and four-months-pregnant Keller argued because he wanted to have sex, but she was not in the mood. Then they planned to go swimming at Santa Monica Beach. "But," Keller later revealed, "after consulting our physician by telephone, it was decided it would be better for me to stay home. David said he didn't want to go without me and I began to write some letters in bed. I dropped off to sleep and when I awakened, he was gone." She pinpointed his departure time as noon, while neighbors said Bacon left about 2 p.m.

Bacon had not taken their three cocker spaniels with him, something he usually did when he went swimming, so police speculated that he may have made an appointment with someone unknown to his wife. Typically, the Bacons visited their friend, socialite-actress Geraldine Spreckels, on beach excursions, but this time he did not.

David Bacon and Grace McDonald are a romantic twosome in *Gals, Incorporated* (1943), a Universal musical comedy.

Later, a witness said that Bacon was seen driving in the beach area with a black-haired man of dark complexion. This mysterious person, who was never identified or found, was either a friend or a hitchhiker that Bacon picked up. (Statements from friends revealed that Bacon "habitually gave lifts to pedestrians.")

Witness Donald Roberts claimed that he was at Los Angeles' Washington Blvd. gas station and saw a man and woman with Bacon: "I saw them pass at 4:30 p.m. Sunday driving toward the beach and return about 35 minutes later." According to Roberts, the man was dark-complected and about 5'4". (A neat trick, estimating the height of a seated passenger in a passing car!) Mrs. B. Watterson said that she had passed the car and had seen only a man sitting next to Bacon. "She noticed them particularly, she said, because the driver appeared to be naked," wrote Frederick C. Othman. "His companion, she reported, was dark-clad." (Neat Trick Part 2: Ascertaining the absence of pants on the driver of a passing car.)

Something happened on that short Washington Blvd. ride. Another witness, 12-year-old Lorraine Smith, said, "I saw the little car wavering along the street. First it nosed into the curb on the south side of the street. Then it went diagonally across the street, over the north curb and into the bean field." Another witness, whose name was withheld, told police that he saw a man leap from Bacon's "undersized British automobile a short time before it careened into the cabbage patch" (*Olean Times Herald*).

The Masked Marvel (1943) **lobby card.**

When the maroon-colored vehicle came to a stop, the shirtless Bacon, dressed in blue denim shorts, staggered about 15 feet before collapsing. The first person to reach the scene, Wayne Powell, noticed blood streaming from a wound in the 29-year-old's back. "He was just lying there between two bean stacks, kicking and squirming. I told him to lie still and save his energy.… He just looked up at me and said, 'Help me! Help me!,' then he died." Before Bacon expired, Powell asked him who had stabbed him, but he couldn't speak.

There was no blood on the outside of the car, no signs of a struggle, but the car interior was saturated with blood. There were many fingerprints in the vehicle—all Bacon's. His bathrobe was also bloodied, but because there were no stab holes, it was concluded that he was not wearing it when he was knifed. Detective Lieutenants Lloyd Hurst and Harry Fremont believed that Bacon was struck without warning as he leaned forward in the car, possibly to release the parking brake. "This theory sounded phony," wrote Frederick C. Othman, "even to the officers who propounded it, and they urged reporters to think up a better one—or page Inspector Queen."

On September 16, the United Press gave the results of a preliminary medical report: "Direction of the wound indicated that the knife was wielded by someone facing the actor" while Bacon was "bending over or leaning forward"—which implies more was going on in that car before Bacon was stabbed. Robbery was not the motive, as he was wearing two valuable rings and had $13 in his wallet. There were no bruises on the body, just the single knife wound, three-fourths of an inch wide and five inches deep, through the back with a stiletto-like blade; it had struck the lower sac of the heart and caused a hemorrhage of the left lung. Dr. Frank R. Webb, county autopsy surgeon, said, "A man with a wound like that might have lived 20 minutes." It was reported that the wound was "made by a stab-knife of the type favored by servicemen assigned to commando-style battle training." The murder weapon was never recovered. Bacon's shorts were dry, "indicating he had not been in the water, but some sand clung to them as though he had been lolling on the beach" (Associated Press).

A heavy, navy-blue crew-neck sweater "thought to be one of those issued to [high] school lettermen in the area six or seven years ago" (*Syracuse Journal*) was found (Powell had placed it under the dying man's head) and was believed to have belonged to the murderer. Another report described the sweater as the type "knitted for Navy and Merchant Marine seamen." Near the collar were a few blond hairs (not Bacon's). Three little feathers were also found on the garment, leading investigators to believe the suspect "may have been employed in a poultry market or on a farm." Poultry markets near the beach were being investigated as it was thought the knife used could be the type "used to kill chickens—a long, narrow blade with which the bird's brain is pierced" (*Los Angeles Examiner*).

"It is logical to assume," said Capt. Thad Brown of the homicide squad, "that whoever stabbed Bacon departed so hastily he left his sweater behind. It certainly does not belong to Mr. Bacon—in fact, it is much too small." Taking the sweater and angle of the knife wound into account, the police were possibly looking for a 5'8", 140-pound, left-handed blond culprit. (Greta Keller, trying to be helpful, told police, "David liked tall blond boys best." His family was probably horrified when this statement went public.)

The police investigation, soon to be referred to as "The Masked Marvel Murder Mystery," took a lot of weird turns, uncovering a double life for the socially respected Bacon. It subsequently was revealed that he had recently rented a "canyon hideaway" about a mile from his home. He told Greta that it was for a man who he was going to hire as a gardener-handyman.

Radio producer Harry Frazee had found the apartment through an advertisement, and lived there in exchange for several hours' work per day at Bacon's home. "I was between jobs and thought it would be a grand way to rest up and also find a nice spot to live," Frazee said. "But after four days I obtained a position with an aircraft company with a radio future, and took it. Then the O.W.I. offered me this other position. I moved out without notice." Frazee left some of his belongings behind.

On the Friday before Bacon's death, September 10, the hideaway's landlord, Dr. Charles Hendricks, claimed that he (Hendricks) came by the duplex apartment to collect rent money. "There was another man with Mr. Bacon. He was dark and slight, foreign looking, and his face was flushed like he was angry. All the time I was there, he never spoke a word, nor did Mr. Bacon introduce me to him…. His only explanation in renting the little place was that it was for a friend." The description of the man with Bacon that night matched that of Bacon's passenger on the day of his murder.

Actor Leslie Denison, who lived in the upstairs half of the duplex, said that the place had only been occupied twice that he knew of, that Friday and the Sunday that Bacon was killed. "I believe someone was there Sunday because I have the water heater for both places, which is slow acting, and Monday morning it was cool like most of the hot water had been run out." When officers searched the apartment, they found coffee, spaghetti, dirty dishes, several women's purses and cigarette holders (left by Harry Frazee's friend, radio scriptwriter Phyllis Parker), monogrammed towels (from Frazee's friend Wilfred Buckland, Jr.) and the books *Delilah* by Marcus Goodrich and *To Step Aside: Seven Long Short Stories* by Noël Coward (both were owned by Buckland). In Bacon's wallet when he died was the key to the front door.

Keller told police that her husband had "religiously" kept a secret diary written in code which he "would never allow her to read" (*Endicott Daily Bulletin*). Attempts by the FBI to decipher the journal failed. She also gave detectives a page torn out of a ledger; there were references to streets in Boston, San Francisco, Washington, D.C., and Santa Barbara—all in code.

Several suspects and leads were investigated. Twenty-three-year-old bad boy Charles R. While was arrested after he confessed to the murder twice while intoxicated; he was released when he recanted his statements and it was found that he actually knew no details of the crime other than what he had read in the newspapers. Between those two confessions, the troubled youngster was detained for attacking a man with a butcher knife.

On September 20, Blakely Clifford Patterson, 22, called variously a band singer, actor and hospital orderly, gave an interview to the *Los Angeles Examiner* about a possible extortion note. He alleged that he and Bacon met while swimming at Santa Monica Beach and that he had known the actor for two months. Patterson declared that a few weeks earlier, he and Bacon met a man at a downtown hotel and, on the morning of his death, Bacon had asked Patterson to go with him to see this man again. Patterson claimed Bacon said, "Pat, I received a threatening note from ____ (the man Patterson had met with Bacon) demanding money. I don't know what to make of it."

"I feel sure that Mr. Bacon was going to meet the man who sent him the note," Patterson told the *Examiner*. "He was nervous and tense and obviously very worried." Patterson said he was unable to accompany Bacon to his appointment.

A day after Patterson made these claims, he confessed that he had made up the story to get publicity. "I thought I could get into the movies if I had my picture in the paper," he said. He was sentenced to ten days in jail for giving a false report and was then ordered to return to his home in Hibbing, Minnesota. Is it possible that Patterson was telling the truth, but was either scared or persuaded to recant? The *Los Angeles Examiner* said that Patterson had given the newspaper the name of the man who supposedly threatened Bacon—a lead they never followed up on.

Glenn Erwin Shaum's name was found in Bacon's personal telephone book: The actor had hired Shaum as his live-in gardener on September 3, 1943, then kiboshed the deal a few days later. Shaum was ruled out as a suspect when his alibi checked: On the day of the murder, he was with his wife. No one ever explained why, if Shaum was married, he accepted the live-in job. It turned out that the 20-year-old was in trouble with naval authorities because he had deserted the Navy at San Diego that past August 24, two weeks after having been drafted.

Three weeks before the murder, the canvas top of Bacon's Cadillac had been slashed with a knife by persons unknown but he never reported it. Keller could not get a straight answer from her husband about it. First, he told her he was in the car when the slashing occurred; then he claimed it happened when he was at the studio and he knew nothing about it. The authorities felt Bacon had subsequently gotten rid of the Cadillac because "some enemy or enemies knew it was his, and he wanted to be driving a different car to throw this enemy or enemies off the track" (*New York Daily News*).

Amid all these tumultuous events, the pregnant Greta Keller was bedridden, using sedatives to cope with her grief; it was reported that she was suffering from shock. An old friend, actress Pola Negri, stayed with her during this time. David's brother William, an obstetrician and resident physician at Boston Lying-in Hospital, came out and attended to his sister-in-law; he told the police that they "positively could not question her any more because of her condition." (David's other brother and their father were both in the military and could not come to California.) Sent to the hospital, Keller suffered a miscarriage. William said the baby had been conceived outside the uterus, and "it never had a chance to be born normally." Other sources say Keller gave birth to a stillborn baby.

David Bacon had been close friends with Laird Cregar, who had appeared in *Ten Gentlemen from West Point* with him. Bacon was wrapping up his performance as the Masked Marvel about the same time that Cregar was playing Jack the Ripper in *The Lodger*. Cregar's biographer, Gregory William Mank, says that Laird

> felt such sympathy for Greta Keller after her husband's murder and their baby's death, that he took her for a time into his Coldwater Canyon cottage. As platonically kind as Cregar was to her, it must have been emotionally draining for her to reside with a man who came home from 20th Century–Fox every night after having played a murderer who also was never apprehended ... and whose choice of weapon was a knife.

Bacon's handwritten will, dated June 14, 1943, left his estimated $100,000 estate to Keller, including all his holdings in the J.P. Morgan Co., the New York Guaranty Trust, any savings from Boston's Seamen's Institute and the First National Bank of Boston, all cash in the Bank of America, all real estate in his name, and also the title to his "little house in Woods Hole [Massachusetts], whether or not it's in my name."

Bacon's body was embalmed before detectives could view it or order tests that might have helped in the investigation. (His cremains were subsequently interred at Woods Hole Village Cemetery.) The murder case hit many such roadblocks and was never solved; all relevant Los Angeles Police Dept. and FBI files for the case were reportedly destroyed. Lack of concrete details and a possible cover-up of Bacon's homosexuality or bisexuality have led to some wild stories from so-called biographers. One is that a camera was found in the back seat of Bacon's car; when the film was developed, it showed a nude Bacon on the beach, the photographer possibly his murderer. Another far-fetched claim was that Bacon and Howard Hughes were lovers, and that Bacon was blackmailing him by threatening to publish a tell-all book about their relationship. Both of these stories and other elaborations on the case sound less like fact than fiction.

More believable is the scenario Peter Levins described in the *New York Daily News*, one that other reporters shied away from:

> During the investigation late in the Winter, a curious sort of call house was unearthed in Venice. Instead of girls being sent out, as is the usual order, this house sent good-looking young boys. They all gathered around a bath house half way between Venice and Santa Monica.
>
> The stabbing could have taken place at that spot, the police said. They were convinced that his wound was acquired during some kind of altercation of which he was ashamed, since he did not call for help but drove in the direction of home. As suggested, he apparently hoped desperately to reach a physician with whom he need not be embarrassed. It is believed that he might have saved his life if he had gotten help in time to stop the bleeding.

Bacon was known to frequent the area around the bath house on many occasions. Author Jeffrey Stanton wrote that Santa Monica's beachfront, "attracted numerous drifters, hustlers and petty criminals. But it was the runaways and perverts that were attracted to its famed Muscle Beach that worried city officials and the police department the most." ("Perverts" was the term used back then for homosexuals.)

In 1956, a thrill killer by the name of Stephen Nash was arrested for knifing a ten-year-old boy under the Santa Monica Pier. Described by police as a "sexual pervert and a psychopath," the bushy-browed, toothless transient had blood-encrusted hands and was carrying a blood-stained hunting knife when he was apprehended. Eventually, it was discovered he had killed a total of 11 men and boys between 1955 and '56. In 1957, Thad Brown, chief of city detectives, revealed that he had questioned Nash about the Bacon murder of 14 years earlier. "Nash could have done it," Brown told Lee Belser. "He was in the vicinity at the time and there was a merchant seaman's sweater found in Bacon's car. Nash was in the Merchant Marine." Not mentioned was that Nash was the same size as Bacon, 6'2", 180 pounds, and the sweater would not have fit him. Anyway, Nash denied knowing Bacon—and the case went cold again. Nash walked the last mile to the gas chamber in 1959.

"I can't rest until I find the murderer," Greta Keller told a reporter almost ten years after Bacon's death. "David was just a big, lovable kid. Nobody could help liking him. And how could anybody kill him? ... I have had the feeling that [it was] somebody from his former life. Someone who had a kind of power over him." Keller died of liver cancer on November 11, 1977.

The Masked Marvel remains popular with serial fans, many of whom are aware of "the Masked Marvel jinx": Actor Rod Bacon (no relation to David), who played another insurance investigator, came forward after David's killing in an attempt to help police—and then, five years later, he, too, died under mysterious circumstances. There's also the strange anecdote of how stuntman Tom Steele, who played the Masked Marvel throughout the 12 chapters, was going to be rewarded with top billing, but ultimately went completely *un*credited due to an oversight.

Another macabre twist: In the midst of the David Bacon investigation, Republic made Chapter 1 of *The Masked Marvel* available to theaters—and Saturday matinee audiences thrilled to a pottery factory fight scene in which a baddie (actor-stuntman Fred Graham) charges at Bacon with a knife. Bacon struggles to disarm him and—on film, at least—he prevails.

1942: *Ten Gentlemen from West Point, The Boss of Big Town.*
1943: *Crash Dive, Gals, Incorporated, The Masked Marvel, Someone to Remember.*

Bruce Cabot

Nobody'll remember anyone in the picture except the big ape.

In 1933, when Bruce Cabot made that prediction to columnist Robbin Coons, he had just finished playing the hero in *King Kong* and had no idea the impact the film would have on audiences—and on his career. *King Kong* cemented his place in movie history and remains his best-known credit.

Cabot was also known for something else: for being a heel, on-screen and off-. True, he did some questionable things throughout his life, but what movie star (for example, his longtime cohort Errol Flynn) hasn't? Cabot was a drinker, brawler and womanizer, like Flynn. But, like Flynn, he tempered all that with a nicer side. How many people know that, during the Vietnam War, Cabot visited wounded soldiers on his own time, without regard to publicity?

Of French and Irish descent, he was born Étienne de Pelissier Bujac, Jr., in Carlsbad, New Mexico, on April 20, 1904; his mother, 39-year-old Julia Armandine Graves, suffering from tuberculosis, died that May. His father was a decorated military officer (the Spanish-American War and the Philippine-American War) turned attorney. The year after Étienne Jr. was born, Étienne Sr. married Jane Geraldine Robinson. (The rumor was that he first asked Jane's *mother* to marry him; when she declined, he proposed to 23-year-old Jane the next day.) They had a daughter, Adele (1906–98). Starting in 1909, Étienne Sr. commanded the New Mexico National Guard (Infantry) in Carlsbad, and during World War I, he led the 144th Machine Gun Battalion. Not long after, he was relieved of duty, some say due to asthma, others blaming his dependency on alcohol.

On Christmas Day, 1916, 12-year-old Étienne Jr. was out driving with two friends

Bruce Cabot was a drinker, brawler, womanizer and well-dressed cad who excelled at playing villains in films.

when their car tipped over at a turn and Étienne was pinned under the vehicle. A cut along his left calf, down to the bone, was 10 to 12 inches long, with the ligaments all torn loose. His left arm was crushed and unjointed at the elbow, and it was thought at first that he would lose the limb. According to the *Carlsbad Current*, "The flesh wound, while very painful now, will in all probability cause him very little pain in the future, but the arm may prove a handicap through life."

Étienne Jr. attended Sewanee Military Academy, New Mexico Military Institute, the University of New Mexico, University of the South, and the University of Tours, France—but he didn't last long in any of them. The fun-loving, restless Étienne planned to be a lawyer like his father, but got sidetracked. Dropping out of college, he drifted around, working as a sailor, salesman, reporter, mechanic, boxer and realtor. When he worked in the oil fields, he was nicknamed "TNT" because Étienne is pronounced A-T-N.

In 1926, in Carlsbad, at 22, he met Grace Mary Mather-Smith, 17-year-old daughter of Charles Frederic Mather-Smith (who owned a paper manufacturing business, grove properties and mines) and socialite Grace Mather-Smith of Highland Park, Illinois, and Orlando, Florida. (Some sources erroneously claim that Grace Mary was the African American actress Grace Smith.) The two were set to marry at Orlando's St. Luke's Cathedral on New Year's Day, 1927. Future brigadier general John A. McEwan, then attending Virginia Military Institute, laughingly told the *Orlando Sentinel*'s Jean Yothers, "I remember those parties before the wedding. It was constant partying every night until dawn." Étienne did things in a "grandiose style, practically taking over the San Juan Hotel to entertain," McEwan added. "He rented separate rooms just for the wraps and liquor."

Grace Mary's mother wrote in her book *My Darlings: A Memoir*, "Oakland was agog for a week before the ceremony and on [their wedding day] their entourage was escorted through Orlando behind a detail of motor police, while fire bells and whistles welcomed them along their way." The Reverend P.C. Wolcott and the Reverend Cameron Mann, bishop of South Florida, presided over the Episcopal ceremony.

Calling it a "notable social event," the *Orlando Sentinel* described the service:

> The chancel was banked with palms, evergreen and floor baskets filled with white and yellow chrysanthemums, and lighted cathedral candles were in floor candelabras. Down the center aisle at each pew were the lighted candles in white post holders and white chrysanthemums tied with white bows of tulle.

The wedding cake was cut with a silver sword. During the wedding breakfast, the Fort Pitt Orchestra played for the guests. The newlyweds honeymooned in Cuba.

The couple made their home at Chicago's Lake Shore Drive Hotel, and Étienne worked as a broker. On December 6, 1927, their daughter Grace Julie (Jennifer) was born.

It's easy to imagine that Étienne quickly grew restless with his new, restricted life. They divorced in June 1929. In July, Walter Winchell wrote, "Frances Williams' new baby-talker is a nobleman tagged Etienne de Plessie de Bujac, 2d, recently divorced and in the golf supply racket in L.A. She'll show you the ring." They had met that past April in Chicago when the blonde Williams was appearing in *George White's Scandals*. A musical-comedy star on Broadway and in vaudeville, she had been engaged at least five times in the past six months. This time, however, she said, "it's serious." It wasn't.

Dividing his time between Carlsbad, New York, and Los Angeles, the now renamed

Jacques de Bujac entered into a business deal with restaurateur Eddie Brandstatter, who ran the Sunset Inn, the Café Montmartre and the Embassy Club. The latter was exclusively for movie stars when it opened in 1929 on Hollywood Blvd., next door to the Montmartre. By 1931, Brandstatter was having financial difficulties, which is where Bujac came in. Bujac was in charge of the Embassy's adjoining roof garden and acted as host and master of ceremonies for a short time. The general public was now welcomed, and the place lost its exclusivity. Brandstatter declared bankruptcy in 1932.

Now running with a Hollywood crowd, Bujac dated such actresses as Dorothy Burgess. Making the rounds of the studios, he landed some uncredited parts. At a party, he met RKO producer David O. Selznick. He talked about their meeting to Irene Thirer in 1936:

> We talked, and I told him I had had stage experience. Of course, it wasn't true, as he must have found out when he gave me my first screen test. It was terrible!

Bruce Cabot and Fay Wray react to *King Kong* (1933) in this publicity shot.

But Mr. Selznick had hopes for me. My second test wasn't too awful. The third was pretty good. And then he signed me to an RKO contract. My real name is Jacques de Bujac, which of course wouldn't do. Mr. Selznick suggested John Bruce or Charles Cabot. And I said: "Why can't it be Bruce Cabot?" So we settled on that. I've been Bruce Cabot ever since—but not legally.

The new RKO contractee assisted in screen tests and became the pupil of acting teacher Josephine Dillon, ex-wife of rising superstar Clark Gable. To get some publicity for her new student, Dillon told reporters, "Women love Clark Gable, but they adore Bruce Cabot." No one took this seriously until Bruce was cast as the bad guy in 1932's *The Roadhouse Murder* (his first billed part) and attracted "considerable fan attention" (*Los Angeles Times*). An *Indianapolis News* reporter singled out the "adorable Cabot" as a "tall, athletic youngster with a shock of bright blond hair and belligerent underlip. He has an excellent voice and something else, which, to be discreet, will be termed 'audience appeal.' …He may be another Gable."

On April 12, 1932, back in Carlsbad, Cabot's 64-year-old father died from a 30–30 rifle bullet to the heart. His friend Sheriff W.L. McDonald was the first on the scene:

> I could not say positively whether it was accidental or suicide, but from all indications, and my personal knowledge of Colonel Bujac, I really believe the death was accidental. Members of the family said he had gone into the yard to shoot birds. He had been sitting on a bench in the yard and it is entirely possible that the rifle was accidentally discharged when he leaned it against the bench. I knew Colonel Bujac … and I am quite sure there is no truth in reports that he had previously attempted to kill himself.

The colonel's nephew, assistant district attorney James N. Bujac, agreed and said no inquest was necessary. The bullet entered just below the heart, traveling upwards, and powder burns indicated that the gun was fired at close range. Bujac had been in poor health for quite some while, spending most of his time at the William Beaumont Veterans Hospital in El Paso, Texas, and a local hospital.

Cabot screen-tested to play Constance Bennett's leading man in *What Price Hollywood?* (1932). While auditioning for the role of Count Zaroff, the psychotic big game hunter in *The Most Dangerous Game* (1932), he came to the attention of producer Merian C. Cooper. While Cabot didn't get the part of the count, the test led to him being cast as *King Kong* hero Jack Driscoll. Third-billed Cabot is girl-shy and tongue-tied around the lovely Ann Darrow (Fay Wray) except when she's in danger, and then he's a tiger rushing to her rescue, first when she's carried off by Kong on Skull Island and climactically when she's in Kong's hairy paw as he climbs the Empire State Building. *Kong* was in production for more than a year, but the actors worked off and on for about half of that time, May to October 1932.

Lucky Devils was shot after *Kong* but released first. In his small part, Cabot portrayed Happy, a member of a group of Hollywood stuntmen headed by Bill Boyd and William Gargan; we later learn via dialogue that Happy was killed doing a fire stunt. At the end of '32, Cabot had a supporting part in *The Great Jasper* (1933) and played himself in *Scarlet River* (1933). In the former, he depicted someone quite like himself, a drunken, irresponsible ladies' man who seduces his half-brother's fiancée. The product of one of his dad's (Richard Dix) long-ago affairs, he's a chip off the old block. *Flying Devils* (1933), directed by publicist Russell Birdwell, cast him in a self-sacrificing role as flying circus stunt pilot Ace Murray. When his brother (Eric Linden) falls in love with a married woman, Ace protects him from her irate husband, the carnival owner. Around this time, Cabot tested for the lead opposite Greta Garbo in *Queen Christina*, but John Gilbert was hired.

In *Disgraced* (1933), a loan-out to Paramount, heartless playboy Cabot seduces Helen Twelvetrees with promises of matrimony. When she realizes that he has no honorable intentions, that he thinks of her simply as one of his many "knick-knacks," she confronts him—gun in hand. Beautiful and stylish Adrienne Ames enacted the lady that Cabot intended to marry all along.

Off-set, Adrienne had "permission" from her rich New York–based husband Stephen Ames to "go places" with Cabot. "Adrienne Ames is teaching Bruce Cabot a new step," wrote Dan Thomas, as the gossips tittered.

RKO gave him the lead in *Midshipman Jack* (1933), set at the Annapolis Naval Academy, and then cast him as Captain Lafe Resnick, a World War I officer who seduces, impregnates and abandons Irene Dunne aka *Ann Vickers* (1933).

In August '33, the Ameses announced a trial separation, citing Adrienne's sustained interest in movies as the problem. They both denied that Cabot had come between them. "Mr. Cabot is a friend of the family and Mr. Ames has no objections to us being companions at social gatherings," Adrienne insisted. Their no-divorce edict was thrown out, columnist Dan Thomas reported, after Ames paid an unannounced call on his wife. "Just what occurred he refuses to say, but he visited his attorneys immediately upon leaving her home." When Adrienne left for Reno in September, plans for her and Cabot's nuptials were already underway. Meanwhile, Cabot was at Columbia on loan-out for the quickie *Shadows of Sing Sing* (1933) with Mary Brian.

On October 31, 1933, four days after *Sing Sing* wrapped and one day after she legally split from Ames, Adrienne wed Cabot in his hometown of Carlsbad.

Bruce Cabot and Adrienne Ames on their wedding day, October 31, 1933.

Shades of *Ann Vickers*: Cabot's nice-guy intern gets the leading lady, this time Frances Dee, pregnant—with different results—in *Finishing School* (1934); he's a suspect in the slaying of a teacher in *Murder on the Blackboard* (1934), the second Hildegarde Withers mystery; and in *His Greatest Gamble* (1934), he's in love with Richard Dix's daughter (Dorothy Wilson).

Cabot was not happy playing second fiddle to Slim Summerville and ZaSu Pitts in the James Cruze–directed *Their Big Moment* (1934)—but what did he expect? He was the bad guy. Wrote Louella Parsons, "Cabot, it seems, has Clark Gable ideas and Radio has other plans." Those plans included loaning him out to Poverty Row: He played leads in Monogram's *Redhead* (1934), Majestic's *Night Alarm* (1934) and Liberty's *Without Children* (1935). Dorothy Lee, who was in the latter, told author Jamie Brotherton, "Bruce Cabot was a big jerk who thought he was God's gift to women. Maybe he was, but I never bothered to find out." Toward the end of shooting, Lee's character was in bed recovering from a gunshot wound. Cabot leaned over her "and he's practically drooling. He looked at me like he wanted to jump on top of me right then and there. I told him, 'Knock it off! You're supposed to be my father, you ass!'"

In August '34, Cabot asked for and received his release from RKO, claiming "he was not being spotted in suitable parts by the company," according to *Variety*. His first as a freelancer was the Columbia crime quickie *Men of the Night*, written and directed by Lambert Hillyer. As Detective Sergeant "Stake-Out" Kelly, he and his partner (Ward Bond) go after a gang of jewel thieves.

Nineteen thirty-five was the year Cabot came into his own. In early February, he was signed to a term contract by MGM (and unsuccessfully tested for *Anna Karenina*), but it was two loan-outs which turned the tide for him. While the handsome actor was a more-than-acceptable hero, he found his forte as a heavy, which was perfect for his brusque style. His matter-of-fact underplaying registered well on camera.

Reliance's *Let 'Em Have It* was part of a cycle of federal man crime dramas then in fashion. Cabot plays Joe Keefer, dissatisfied son of servants, working as a chauffeur, who becomes the ringleader of a gang of crooks and murderers. He wants a million dollars so he can have all the advantages he never had growing up, a relatable character during these Depression times—until he guns down neophyte G-man Eric Linden in cold blood. To evade the law, Keefer undergoes plastic surgery to change his face. In the film's most memorable moment, the bandages come off and we see the doctor's handiwork: He has carved Keefer's initials into his face. Cabot's anguished reaction is priceless, as is his whole performance: He snarls, shoots and slugs his way through the film. "Bruce Cabot as the gang chief gets a chance to prove that he is a first-string player of genuine ability that ranks him with the best heavies Hollywood has seen in years," wrote *The Film Daily*. "He easily dominates the film with the sense of power and menace that he creates."

Cabot was even more ruthless in Twentieth Century–Fox's *Show Them No Mercy!* (1935). The screenplay was co-written by Polish-born Kubec Glasmon, a specialist in stark, hard-hitting stories (*The Public Enemy*, *Three on a Match*). Cabot plays Pitch, one of a gang of kidnappers encountered by a husband and wife (Edward Norris and Rochelle Hudson) and their baby during a rainstorm. The crooks' leader (Cesar Romero) is more level-headed than the depraved Pitch, who has a compulsion to kill the couple. He does shoot their dog. Andre Sennwald of the *New York Times* wrote,

> In the character of Pitch, Mr. Glasmon paints a primitive gunman with a shocking accuracy of detail that rarely finds its way to the screen under its present kindergarten management.

Treacherous, mean and icily savage, he suggests the murderous Vincent Coll, who was called the Mad Dog during his brief reign of terror in the New York underworld. His whims run to such sadistic practical jokes as that in which he sets fire to a newspaper covering one of his sleeping confederates. When he is driven back to the hideout after quarreling with his chief, he effects a truce and then coolly shoots the man down the moment he turns his back. His own demise a few moments later is a fine example of cinema delusions.

Sennwald added, "Bruce Cabot gives a terrifying performance as a surly killer who is transformed by liquor and nerve into an irresponsible madman."

Nicer roles came in *Robin Hood of El Dorado* (his first at Metro) and *Don't Gamble with Love* (a lead at Columbia, with Ann Sothern).

Life at home was tumultuous as Cabot was an unrepentant womanizer. In July 1935, Ames filed for divorce; he said marriage interfered with his movie work, he disliked her relatives, and he preferred "a career as a bachelor to that of a husband." The divorce was granted, but before it became final, they reconciled.

Seven months later, Ames was back in court with more serious charges, alleging that Cabot would come home from drinking sprees, curse and threaten her, and fly into "uncontrollable rages" resulting in broken furniture. Even more disconcerting: An enraged Cabot would make like Tarzan, ripping open his shirt and screaming. "I wish to determine whether I can divorce myself from him mentally before I divorce him actually," she said. She also claimed she attempted to "wean him from the liquor bottle," but got a hall clock thrown at her head for the effort. Adrienne was guaranteed $125 a week "until she finds a new husband," newspapers reported. This time there was no reconciliation.

According to a *Hollywood Reporter* item, Cabot tested for the lead in MGM's mega-production *San Francisco* (1936), ultimately a Clark Gable-Spencer Tracy starrer and Best Picture Oscar nominee. Instead, MGM cast him in light roles as a con man in *The Three Wise Guys* and a reporter-turned-lawyer-turned-detective in *Sinner Take All*. In Fritz Lang's *Fury*, he reverted to villainous form as a mob agitator who leads the charge to burn down the prison housing Spencer Tracy, wrongly accused of kidnapping.

The rest of his 1936 schedule consisted of loan-outs. Made to order for the actor was the role of the treacherous Huron Indian Magua in Edward Small's adaptation of James Fenimore Cooper's 1826 novel *The Last of the Mohicans*. Reputed to be one-sixteenth Cherokee (his friends nicknamed him "Indian"), Cabot definitely (and defiantly) looked the part with his high cheekbones, protruding, surly lower lip, scalp lock and deep tan. Acting-wise, one couldn't ask for a more brutal, powerful enemy for good guys Randolph Scott (as Hawkeye) and Henry Wilcoxon (as Major Hayward). "I played villains and heroes about 50–50," Cabot said in 1971, "but my best films—like *The Last of the Mohicans*—were when I was a baddie. I think I was something new in badmen: I wasn't well-mannered and there was something about me that suggested I might take off and do something very physical."

Cabot was set to portray another Native American, Painted Horse, in Cecil B. DeMille's *The Plainsman* (1936), but was replaced by Hungarian-born Victor Varconi. Sheilah Graham's far-fetched explanation was that, although Cabot looked the part, his "interpretation was too gangster-like." Columnist Harold V. Cohen simply stated that Cabot was "dissatisfied" with his role and withdrew from the picture.

RKO's *Don't Turn 'Em Loose* (1936), an "impassioned plea against the undiscriminating release of convicts through the parole system" (*New York Daily News'*

Kate Cameron), allowed Cabot to show two sides of his screen personality in the Jekyll-and-Hyde role of brutal murderer Bat Williams, who hides his criminal activities from his small-town family (which includes father Lewis Stone and sister Betty Grable). Cameron praised the film's no-frills style, which made "no attempt to sentimentalize or romanticize convicts and racketeers," and called Cabot the "personification of the egotistical and cruel criminal...." He is particularly effective near the conclusion, challenging his father.

As an actor, Cabot was often dismissed ("Honestly now, have you ever seen Bruce Cabot give a really good performance?"—Harold V. Cohen), which, in the words of his teacher Josephine Dillon, made him oversensitive and resentful of criticism. But he had every reason to be proud of his sterling notices for *Don't Turn 'Em Loose*. The *Detroit Free Press*' Grace Wilcox wrote,

> Life presents some strange contrasts and contradictions in Hollywood. For instance, where else could one go to a preview to see Katharine Hepburn in *A Women Rebels* and come away with the memory of one of the finest performances of the year turned in by Bruce Cabot in *Don't Turn 'Em Loose*? Yet this very thing happened to me, when I remained for a few moments after the Hepburn picture in order to avoid being caught in the crowds.
>
> Never having heard of *Don't Turn 'Em Loose*, I expected nothing of vital importance, but from the first moment of the story, I found myself following Cabot and the twists of the plot with absorbing interest. Here, my friend, is an actor. His portrait of a gangster-killer, who is a cold-blooded fiend, but who comes of a good family, is one of the really great pieces of acting I have seen on the screen.
>
> ...When Cabot, in one of the most unsympathetic roles ever done on the screen, can hold you fascinated, absorbed and enthralled, what could he do in a part in which his sincerity and engaging smile could be used to elicit your sympathy?

Clarke Wales in the *Democrat and Chronicle* also raved about his "expert portrayal":

> The screen has presented many a rat; there is one in nearly every picture. But Cabot in *Don't Turn 'Em Loose* becomes the most notable rat in my recollection. He is, without overplaying or caricaturing his part, the most consistently vicious criminal I have seen on the screen.
>
> Most striking is the fact that he presents his viciousness more by acting than by action. True, there is plenty of overt villainy—murders, robberies, sluggings. But far more expressive is the fleeting expression of contentment that crosses his face as he lies down for a nap, knowing that he has just killed with a time bomb the only witness to his last previous murder, that of his sweetheart.
>
> ...The conflict between [Lewis] Stone and Cabot, after the father learns that his son is a murderer, is made much better than usual screen drama by the exceptional portrayals of the two players.

RKO's *The Big Game* (1936) was a football story adapted by Irwin Shaw. Cabot had a supporting part as a first-class jerk who wises up by the end. Columbia's *Legion of Terror* (1936) was based on the same real-life case as Warners' better-known *Black Legion* (1937). As its postal inspector hero, Cabot infiltrates a Ku Klux Klan–like organization to learn who sent a time bomb to a U.S. Senator.

Nineteen thirty-seven got underway with a loan to George A. Hirliman and Grand National for *Love Takes Flight* (1937), directed by actor Conrad Nagel. It's not been recorded how Cabot felt about being demoted from MGM to an indie, playing leading man to Louis B. Mayer's girlfriend Beatrice Roberts, also on loan. It was, nevertheless, a cute romantic comedy of an airline pilot who becomes a movie star, and an air hostess who becomes a record-setting aviatrix. This was a combination of two topical subjects: the making of airline pilot John Trent into an actor and the popularity of Amelia Earhart.

The now-single Cabot attacked the Hollywood social whirl with a vengeance. He was known for his polychromatic sports coats; it was not unusual to see him wearing (say) orange or green suits, green- or orange-striped shirts and loud ties or purple bowties, and suede shoes with his initials in silver on the front. He was considered one of the town's best-dressed men. His interests included golf, swimming, hunting, riding, tennis, backgammon and gambling. He had a pilot's license and a Boxer Bulldog who wore a bib in the house because he drooled. Cabot loved fast cars and even faster women.

"Bruce Cabot has been very obliging to charming ladies, whose husbands are too busy to night-club it," wrote Walter Winchell. "Liz Whitney and Paulette Goddard, frinstance." He was often joined in these escapades by Errol Flynn; together they cut a wide swath through the bevy of eager starlets, stars and socialites in Hollywood and New York. Cabot once famously gifted Flynn with a chorus girl wrapped in cellophane, ribbon—and not much else.

It wasn't all play. Cabot never forgot his friends in Carlsbad, and he often spent time there seeing old pals, haunts and his family (his stepmother and half-sister still lived there). During a January '38 trip, he stopped at the Alvarado Hotel for breakfast. "Cabot is embarrassed by praise," the *Albuquerque Journal* reported. "Told by a bystander that his pictures were hugely enjoyed, the movie actor hung his head with a bashful, country-boy grin, and said, 'Uh—. It's very nice of you to say so.'" When someone mentioned his illustrious father, he replied, "I believe he was a much better actor than I am. He could really 'sell' those juries. Pretty tough audience, what?"

In his last two MGM pictures, *Bad Guy* and *The Bad Man of Brimstone* (both 1937), he played disreputable and despicable characters. "Conspicuous among [*Bad Guy*'s] supporting cast is Bruce Cabot, who used to be the Clark Gable type (turtle-neck sweaters and all) but now is one of the screen's most competent villains," wrote John Kinloch of the *California Eagle*. "*Bad Guy* was made to order for Bruce Cabot," said the *New York Daily News*' Kate Cameron. "Not since he played the ruthless killer in *Show Them No Mercy* has he had a role that enabled him to swagger about the screen and be as tough as he pleased...." Edward Norris, who played his half-brother in the picture, told interviewers Tom and Jim Goldrup that filming on the B picture was delayed because of an intoxicated Cabot:

> I had finished my work an hour or so previously, and now I was in the same car with Bruce, drinking out of the same bottle with him. The director [Edward L. Cahn] came to me and said, "Eddie, get out. Beat it. You're finished with your part. Don't sit here. You're going to get blamed for it." To make a long story short, the word got out and that was strike three [for me at MGM].

And probably for Cabot as well. Right after *The Bad Man of Brimstone*, he was looking elsewhere for work. At Universal for James Whale's *Sinners in Paradise* (1938), he had a good role as Robert Malone, known in the underworld as "The Torpedo," who is running away from his former gangland friends with $150,000 when he and others get stranded on an island. As a mob lawyer in RKO's *Smashing the Rackets* (1938), he was elevated to underworld czar. Tough law enforcement leads came in Republic's *Tenth Avenue Kid* (1938) and Columbia's *Homicide Bureau* (1938), the latter with Rita Hayworth as his forensic scientist leading lady.

Nineteen thirty-nine, legendarily Hollywood's greatest year, had its most exciting Western in Warners' Technicolor *Dodge City* with Errol Flynn as a soldier of fortune, partnered with roisterers Alan Hale and Guinn "Big Boy" Williams in the Old West's newest answer to ancient Babylon, the lawless Dodge City, Kansas. The role of *Dodge City*'s main baddie was intended for Charles Bickford but Cabot got a break when he inherited the plum assignment. Highlights include the mother of all barroom brawls, fun for everybody but the bar's crooked owner Jeff Surrett (Cabot), who later surveys the wreckage and pronounces, "Somebody's gonna pay for this and it ain't gonna be with money." It's Cabot and his goons vs. Flynn and his boys throughout, culminating in an edge-of-the-seat shootout in the blazing mail car of a speeding train.

During this period, wherever Errol Flynn went, Brucie (as he was called) was sure to follow, often with their pals Hugh "Bud" Ernst and Guinn Williams, chasing women, drinking and brawling in nightclubs. Cabot was then involved with socialite Liz Whitney, aka Mrs. Jock Whitney, who had tested for the role of Ruby, the saloon singer, in *Dodge City*. Although Cabot coached her, she lost the part to Ann Sheridan (another Cabot girlfriend). On December 11, 1938, Cabot, Flynn and Ernst were at a cocktail party hosted by Liz at her Beverly Hills home. Between drinks, Aidan Roark, an Irish-born polo player and assistant to Fox's Darryl F. Zanuck, made some snide remarks to Flynn about his ancestry and acting ability. Cabot and Ernst tried to keep them apart, but

Two movie men about Hollywood: Errol Flynn and Bruce Cabot straighten their ties as they vie for a dance with starlet Flo Hall. Cabot and Flynn were best pals for years before their falling out in the 1950s.

punches were thrown, Cabot got knocked out and Flynn lost a tooth. Hit three times, Roark had to be revived by a doctor. A poloist friend of Roark's, who had tried to help his pal, was taken away, the worse for wear. "According to all reports," wrote H.H. Niemeyer, "it was one of the best battles staged in the movie set in some time. Mrs. Whitney can usually be counted upon to furnish unusual entertainment at her parties...." Roark later claimed that Cabot held him in position for Flynn to score the KO.

> Get Bruce Cabot and Errol Flynn to tell you about the other night when they wandered into a country club where a sorority dance was in progress. The two stars just wanted to get a drink in the bar, but the young ladies spotted them and staged a rush. Flynn and Cabot thought it was fine until they got their bar check—$36 [more than $700 today!].—Harrison Carroll, December 22, 1938

> Errol Flynn and Bruce Cabot will bachelor in New York for the purpose, to quote Mr. Cabot, "of catching up with our homework."—Sheilah Graham, January 3, 1939

When Cabot and Flynn were on location in Modesto, California, for *Dodge City*, 22-year-old bellhop Jimmy Bugg ran errands for them. Cabot pledged to help him: "[Jimmy] was a personable chap and came around every day while we were shooting scenes. He wanted to break into the movies. When we came back to Hollywood from Modesto, I brought him along with me. I [tried to get] him a Guild card and employed him as my valet until I could find a job for him in pictures." On January 9, 1939, Bugg repaid the actor's kindness by stealing from Cabot's Riviera Country Club apartment jewelry, clothing, a silver flask (with the initials B.C.) and watches. A night clerk stated that Bugg had told him that Cabot had given him permission to enter the apartment while he was away. The following day, a policeman came upon an intoxicated Bugg on a street corner wearing Cabot's overcoat, his loot stuffed in the pockets. Bugg was eventually given three years' probation, with the first 90 days spent in the county road camp.

Meanwhile, Cabot was preparing to go on a hunting trip with Flynn and his wife Lili Damita. Plans were changed when he reported to work at Universal for the lead in one of producer Irving Starr's Crime Club films, *Mystery of the White Room* (1939). In it, he was a surgeon solving a murder at a hospital between operations, with nurse Helen Mack as his romantic interest. It was based on James G. Edwards' 1935 novel *Murder in the Surgery*.

> Bruce Cabot, film actor, is en route to Charlottesville, Va., for a week of fox-hunting with Franklin D. Roosevelt, Jr.; from Virginia he will go to Miami and then to Bermuda, where he will visit Brenda Frazier, the publicized debutante.—United Press, February 24, 1939

In Virginia, Cabot stayed at Carter Hall, the estate of Gerard B. Lambert, president of the Gillette Safety Razor Co. Bruce has often been vilified, especially by Errol Flynn fans and biographers, as a mere hanger-on, a sycophant, using Flynn to meet people. In fact, Cabot did all right by himself. With his socialite background, he knew many influential persons, and his engaging personality attracted the rich and famous.

On May 1, 1939, Cabot's car collided with one carrying four Pasadena Junior College students at Sunset Blvd. and Charing Cross Road, Holmby Hills. He came out of it with slight bruises and abrasions; the students were not as lucky. The most seriously injured was John Lucas, the son of actor-director Wilfred Lucas and writer-actress Bess Meredyth, and stepson of *Dodge City* director Michael Curtiz. The passengers all eventually sued Cabot for reckless driving with their own separate damage suits: Lucas

($25,827), Katherine Cuppett ($25,670), Paul G. Darrow ($3000) and Ernest Sloman ($2500). The following year, Cabot settled all four cases out of court.

Cabot's injuries delayed the starting date of Republic's *Mickey the Kid* (1939) with Tommy Ryan (from *Tenth Avenue Kid*) and Ralph Byrd. He and Ryan played criminal father and son whose flight from the law is complicated by a snowstorm and a bus full of children; it was inspired by a true story.

> The Bruce Cabot-Brenda Frazier dueting last week was hero-worship on the parts of both. His real girl, however, wasn't amused at all.—Walter Winchell, June 19, 1939

Not long after the publication of the above item, Cabot and Franklin D. Roosevelt, Jr., walked into the New York nightclub La Conga and spotted Frazier at the table of *New Yorker* artist Peter Arno. What happened next was colorfully described by the *Los Angeles Times*:

> The gong—and if ever a fight needed a gong this one did—sounded about 3:30 a.m. and the ringside tables were well filled.
>
> Arno entered the arena first with Miss Frazier on his arm. They went directly to a prominently placed table and sat down to wait.
>
> About two hours later, Cabot entered with the younger Roosevelt. Cabot disclosed to a waiter that he was looking for Miss Frazier, who has so far been very negative about talk of appearing in a picture with him.
>
> "Brenda told us to come down," Cabot said.
>
> Miss Frazier was by no means inconspicuous in a white ermine jacket. Cabot approached, looking supremely confident, as befits a movie actor in the presence of a lady. He bent over the table and made as if to sit down.
>
> It was noted that Arno and Cabot did not shake hands. Arno's face was flushed a deep red. He threw Cabot a dirty left look but the Hollywood hotshot shook it off and shuffled in for more.
>
> "Go sit at your own table," Arno said, leading again.
>
> That ended the first round and Cabot retired to an opposite corner, where Roosevelt joined him. Cabot looked fresh.
>
> After a brief rest, he was up again, having thought of something to say, and advanced directly to Arno's corner, who was a little late getting up.
>
> When he did get up, the artist was sculpturing his fist into a mess of knuckles. For a second or two it looked as though something dreadful might happen.
>
> But nothing did. Hoot Gibson, that hard-riding, straight-shootin' cowpuncher, entered the saloon, looked around and sized up the situation at a glance. There wasn't any bar to vault over but he pushed a couple of waiters aside and came between the two. He separated them by saying, "Now, now, fellows."

The International News Service presented another take on the altercation:

> Words—recriminations—and Peter's artistic fist flew in the general direction of beautiful Bruce's jaw. Brenda screamed. Club promoter Mario Tosatti intervened. Franklin Jr. (only an innocent spectator) apologized. Hoot stepped up and ordered drinks all 'round and everything was calmed down.
>
> All this Arno admits, adding: "I pushed him away but before any real blows were struck Mario stopped me."
>
> Bruce denies all.
>
> Brenda denies all.
>
> Mario's press agent confirms everything and denies everything.
>
> Broadway consensus: The winnah, and still champion, Peter Arno.

Cabot tested for the role of the Ringo Kid in John Ford's *Stagecoach* but lost out to John Wayne. A role in *Allegheny Uprising* (1939) with *Stagecoach* stars Wayne and Claire Trevor was on Cabot's itinerary, along with a two-month cruise with Mr. and Mrs. Roosevelt Jr. Instead, Cabot elected to go to England to star in the espionage thriller *Traitor Spy* (1939). Again, Cabot is a disreputable cad, trying to sell stolen naval blueprints to the Nazis. French actress Marta Labarr plays the wife he cheats on—until the exciting, fiery conclusion when they stand by each other in a doomed embrace. The *New York Daily News*, reviewing it under the evocative title *The Torso Murder Mystery*, called it "satisfactorily horrendous and suspenseful. And being topical increases interest. It is well done, as are most English thrillers, with the gory atmosphere that adds excitement."

When Cabot got back to the States, he went to Columbia for the crime drama *My Son Is Guilty* (1939). He plays Ritzy, another bad egg who causes his father (this time Harry Carey) no end of grief. Just out of prison after a two-year stretch, Ritzy rejects his policeman father's advice to settle down and hooks up with a girl crook (Wynne Gibson) and her gang. Glenn Ford, in his second feature, portrays the nice guy who loves the nice girl (Jacqueline Wells) whom Cabot desires. The *New York Daily News'* Kate Cameron knew the score:

> From the moment Bruce Cabot was assigned to the role, poor Ritzy was doomed and the moment he made his appearance on the screen the audience knew that Ritzy would turn out to be a heel. Cabot is always assigned to the bad boy type of role, so his presence in this, or any other film, is the tipoff that he is ready to betray his mother, or father, as in the current adventure, for the sake of some easy money.

At the beginning of filming, Cabot's salary was attached by deputy sheriffs. He owed ex-wife Adrienne Ames $5950 in back alimony.

> Brenda Frazier has a $250 wager with Bruce Cabot (and he has one with her) that they won't fall off the wagon until New Year's. She drinks nothing containing over 12½ percent alcohol.—Walter Winchell, November 29, 1939

Cabot might not have had money to give his ex but, a fixture at many of the Hollywood and New York nightclubs, he wined and dined a revolving door of ladies that included Hedy Lamarr, Miriam Hopkins, Cobina Wright, Jr., Wendy Inglehart (*Harper's Bazaar* writer), Pat Wilder, Gloria Spreckels, Marjorie Leigh, Eleanor Burns, Norma Hall, Mary Rogers (Will's daughter), June Lang, Carole Landis, Mignon Woideman, Gloria Vanderbilt (who called him "Cousin Brucie"), Mimi Baker, Frances Robinson, Frances Farmer, Dorothy Lamour, Doris Duke, Diana Barrymore—and the list goes on…

> Errol Flynn, Big Boy Williams, Bruce Cabot and three cronies almost broke up the show at the Folies Bergère by taking seats in the front row and producing opera glasses.—Harrison Carroll, December 6, 1939

> Errol Flynn, Cary Grant and Bruce Cabot, the three best-looking men in Hollywood, have joined forces and are doing the gay spots and nightclubs together—which is unfair to disorganized females. Sheilah Graham, December 9, 1939

> Errol Flynn, Bruce Cabot, Howard Hughes and James McKinley Bryant are known by the ladies of Hollywood as "The Pack"—because they do their hunting together…—Sheilah Graham, December 29, 1939

Pat DiCicco (Thelma Todd's ex) and his cousin Albert "Cubby" Broccoli were two of Cabot's frequent pals around town. Another good friend was Fred Astaire.

Nineteen forty began with two rejections: Cabot lost roles in the Errol Flynn vehicle *The Sea Hawk* and Cecil B. DeMille's *North West Mounted Police*. (In the latter, he was up for the role of a half-breed, but Technicolor revealed his blue eyes and he was replaced.) He did get good supporting parts in MGM's *Susan and God* and Hal Roach's *Captain Caution*. The last stars Victor Mature in a seafaring adventure based on Kenneth Roberts' novel. Cabot is a double-dealing slave trader who comes between sailor Mature and Louise Platt, who is seeking to avenge the death of her captain father at British hands during the War of 1812. Donald Kirkley of the *Baltimore Sun* wrote that Cabot played his role with "such spirit [that he] overshadows the somewhat phlegmatic Mr. Mature." The critic added, "[T]heir positions should have been reversed in the casting." In fact, Roach originally wanted John Wayne for the lead.

Cabot was the sort to play jokes. On one set, he slipped ice cubes down the gown of his leading lady. When Warner Bros. premiered their Errol Flynn Western *Virginia City* (1940) in Reno, Cabot was right there, ready to have a ball. Lucius Beebe of the *New York Herald-Tribune* gave his readers the scoop:

> First to arrive and very likely the last to go was handsome and amiable Bruce Cabot who arrived in a flying machine a full day ahead of time, was made a member of the police department by Chief Andy M. Welliver, changed to frontier attire and was in the Bank Club in a kitchen midden of roulette chips within an hour. Although not implicated in the film itself, Mr. Cabot was probably the favorite character of a dazzled and admiring audience and was patently public favorite No. 1 throughout the weekend.
>
> Humphrey Bogart, who actually acted in *Virginia City*, was also received with suitable glad cries and disorders, but since, whenever their appearance was solicited at receptions, in parades or other spectacles, Mr. Cabot contrived to insinuate himself between Mr. Bogart and his public, effectively masking him out with perhaps six inches of stature and proportionate breadth, any decibel count would have given Mr. Cabot the palm.

Beebe also revealed that Cabot circulated a rumor that Bogart was giving away silver dollars with every autograph, "a circumstance which, when it was definitely proved to be not so, tended to estrange Mr. Bogart's public."

> Bruce Cabot and Phyllis Brooks, garbed "strictly formal," gulping hamburgers at a drive-in before starting the nite-spot rounds.—Jimmie Fidler, May 20, 1940

> Liz Whitney has shelved Bruce Cabot because he was "too wild," according to her intimates' giggles.—Dorothy Kilgallen, June 24, 1940

During the summer of 1940, Cabot did the play *One Sunday Afternoon* in Cedarhurst, New York, and Gloucester, Massachusetts. He unsuccessfully tested for roles in RKO's *A Girl, a Guy, and a Gob* and Paramount's *I Wanted Wings*.

> Bruce Cabot and millionairess "Liz" Whitney feeding peanuts to the monkeys in front of Grauman's Egyptian…—Jimmie Fidler, July 11, 1940

> Bruce Cabot slugged it out with a guest at a swank coast party given by the Ray Dodges the other evening, but the event was hushed.—Dorothy Kilgallen, October 9, 1940

That punchfest was probably a picnic compared to his brief relationship with Leonore Lemmon, a wild party girl whose claim to infamy was for being the first woman thrown out of the Stork Club for fistfighting. In October 1940, columnist Danton Walker wrote that Lemmon "was so mad because Bruce Cabot failed to meet her, as arranged, at the Café Pierre, that she carved her name in the $5000 bar, so as to remind him next time he came in." Leonore is best-known today for being George Reeves' fiancée at the time of his mysterious 1959 death.

Cabot claimed he was making more dough doing personal appearances than making movies, so he pretty much stayed away from California for the rest of 1940. The New York night spots, and the society ladies, welcomed him with open arms.

> I have discovered that … when Bruce Cabot drinks champagne it brings out the Indian in him.—Dorothy Kilgallen, November 17, 1940

> Bruce Cabot, dancing with Fernanda Munn last night, accidentally fell to the floor—and tore his partner's shoulder strap.—Leonard Lyons, November 18, 1940

On November 25, Cabot, Betty Furness, Mary Brian, Hugh O'Connell and Dennie Moore started their pre–Broadway run of the play *Off the Record* in Wilmington, Delaware. The political satire was written by Parke Levy and Alan Lipscott. "Bruce Cabot is on the wagon for a month, to win a $500 bet that he won't bend the elbow until *Off the Record* gets on the boards," Danton Walker wrote on November 28, 1940.

In December, they performed *Off the Record* at the McCarter Theatre in Princeton, New Jersey, and Washington's National Theatre. Jay Carmody of the *Washington Evening Star* blasted the play as "dizzily inept," dubbing the playwrights a "couple of screwballs" and the production the "worst play of the season"—so far. Carmody continued:

> The things that these people are called upon to do and say are baffling not only to the audience, but to themselves. There is one girl, for instance, who spends most of her time saying "I'm going to leave," which would be the brightest thought of the evening if it ever produced any results."

As for Cabot, Carmody considered him one of the "two semi-decent persons about whom the action swirls continuously." The show did better in Philadelphia, playing to appreciative crowds. *Off the Record* never reached New York.

> Bruce Cabot back from the east staging it at Ciro's but it won't be for long.—Louella Parsons, December 30, 1940

> Ye ed doesn't like butting into such things, but if he didn't make the warning public, so they could see it—and it happened to them—he'd never sleep. So this is to warn Bruce Cabot and "Bunty" Bacon about a heavyset man (about 255 pounds) who is going to knock all their teeth out.—Walter Winchell, January 31, 1941

After years of toplining second features, Cabot was handed a golden opportunity when Universal cast him as Marlene Dietrich's leading man in *The Flame of New Orleans* (1941), French director René Clair's first Hollywood film. Hedda Hopper had doubts: "You can expect fireworks on the *Flame of New Orleans* set. Joe Pasternak said he'd scoured the town for a leading man, then signed Bruce Cabot. Bruce is all right, but I don't think he's Dietrich caliber. However, I can be convinced. But I'll wait till the picture's finished." Pasternak was certain Cabot had what it took, and Clair was quoted by Robbin Coons as saying that Cabot's test "was the best. And it seems to me it is good to give actors a chance to do different things. We need new leading men. We cannot all have Cary Grant and Clark Gable."

> [Now] that Bruce Cabot has been signed as Marlene Dietrich's leading man … look for the usual hokum about him being Marlene's latest "flame."—Danton Walker, January 6, 1941

Definitely hokum. He and Dietrich clashed immediately; she later called him

> an awfully stupid actor, unable to remember his lines or cues. Nor could René Clair, who didn't speak a word of English, lend him a helping hand. Besides, Bruce Cabot, in contrast

Cabot had a golden opportunity as Marlene Dietrich's leading man in *The Flame of New Orleans* (1941), but he antagonized the star by not knowing his lines. They sure looked great together, though.

> to John Wayne, was very conceited. He wouldn't accept any help. I finally resigned myself to paying for his lessons, so that he would at least know his lines during the shooting.

It must be remembered that Dietrich resented Cabot for being cast instead of John Wayne, and that screenwriter Norman Krasna didn't even want *her* for the lead.

Cabot, handsome and jaunty with his mustache and unruly hair, does what he can with the role of sea captain Robert LaTour, who falls for fortune hunter Claire Ledeux (Dietrich); one minute he's a cocky risktaker, the next bashful and modest, and back again. It seems inconceivable that either Wayne or Cary Grant (Krasna's selection—of course) could have pulled off the part.

Patrick McGilligan asked Krasna about the film's censorship problems:

We finished the picture, and the Hays Office said, "Keep it, it's dirty." We couldn't get away with the sex stuff. A small studio like Universal can't keep a picture. Things were changed in the storyline. They found that by dropping the middle two reels, it could still be released. The picture is missing two reels.

Bruce Cabot, who doesn't rate very high with a lot of locals, can't persuade Marlene Dietrich to do the town for publicity—he's her current leading man—but definitely not OFF the lot.—Marshall Ames III, February 1, 1941

The Flame of New Orleans did not do well at the box office—or make Cabot an A-list star, as predicted.

Bruce Cabot is going to Mexico after his chore with Marlene Dietrich in *The Flame of New Orleans*. When asked why, Bruce replied, "To meet some nice people."—Sheilah Graham, February 28, 1941

Bruce Cabot called the Mocambo from Dallas, Texas, insisting that six pals there listen to a girl (his Dallas date) sing to each in turn over the phone; the place was in hysterics.—Jimmie Fidler, May 8, 1941

Producer Walter Wanger liked Cabot's *Flame of New Orleans* performance, and what Louella Parsons called his "definite he-man personality with a Gable appeal," and signed him to a three-picture deal that started with Henry Hathaway's *Sundown* (1941). *Photoplay* griped that the picture, set at a government outpost in British East Africa,

at times almost loses itself in a whirlwind of shooting, spying and gun-running. Still, with George Sanders, Bruce Cabot, Joseph Calleia, Reginald Gardiner and Gene Tierney to inject some fine acting, *Sundown* emerges a worthwhile epic.... Cabot as commissioner of the post steals most of the honors.

Back in '36, Jimmie Fidler revealed Cabot's "love for siestas in the sunshine. Bruce enjoys nothing more than a lazy snooze in a spot where he can absorb the full effect of the sun's rays." This lazy dozing obviously extended to the soundstage. Hathaway labeled him a "playboy," complaining years later, "He was insolent, he was drunk all the time, he was sleeping on the set, he'd lie down in his clothes and sleep. He never knew his lines."

Bruce Cabot, who declares his heart belongs to Liz Whitney, has found romance in the bull ring. The little gal's name is Conchita Cintrón. She has slain more bulls than Cabot has thrown—and brother, that's bull!—John Truesdell, July 30, 1941

Wanger loaned Cabot to Warner Bros., where he played the title role in *Wild Bill Hickok Rides*. Cast opposite Constance Bennett (playing a lady gambler), he does a nice job as he battles land-grabber Warren William and his gang. A Pincher Creek, Alberta, Canada, exhibitor opined in *Motion Picture Herald*,

This was made with the obvious intention of eliminating triple-bills by the simple expedient of incorporating into one picture all the clichés known to the business, and maybe a few ideas never thought of before, although it all happened so fast I couldn't say for sure. Starting with the Chicago Fire, it warmed up from there at a pace that had my action fans pop-eyed for fear they would miss a killin.' Very good business.

Aside to Bruce Cabot: Think twice before spending another evening appropriating the other nite-spot wolves' Little Red Riding Hoods—the boys are plotting revenge.—Jimmie Fidler, August 14, 1941

SIGHT OF THE WEEK: Barbara Hutton buying sweaters for Cary Grant, with Bruce Cabot trying them on for size.—Erskine Johnson, October 16, 1941

I have the word of Milton Berle that he recently met a beautiful young actress who: 1. Never had a date with Bruce Cabot or Franchot Tone; 2. Never has been to Ciro's; 3. Wears a sweater only to keep warm.—Paul Harrison, November 10, 1941

Bruce Cabot got into a spat at El Morocco the other night for which apologies have been forthcoming from the coast all week.—Harold Conrad, December 3, 1941

BRUCE CABOT: It's all right to come back. That man who claims that you hit him is willing to forget and won't sue.—Leonard Lyons, December 3, 1941

Those two debs in New York who kept Errol Flynn and Bruce Cabot waiting for an hour and then stood them up have captured the hearts of all Hollywood.—Hugh Dixon, December 12, 1941

Bruce Cabot, just back from Mexico City, regales with his witty stories of playing gin-rummy with ex–King Carol [II of Romania] and his Magda [Lupescu].—May Mann, April 1, 1942

Another loan, to MGM: the fun *Pierre of the Plains* (1942), with Cabot as, yes, a villain.

Obtaining his release from Wanger, the actor accepted a contract with Paramount, where he was promised big things. One project mentioned was Dashiell Hammett's *Red Harvest,* to star Paulette Goddard and Brian Donlevy; "If it does for Bruce what *The Maltese Falcon* did for Humphrey Bogart," noted Louella Parsons, "he will really be on his way." How could it lead to anything? It wasn't as if the studio was going to star him; he was to play the bad guy.

Paramount loaned him out for two roles which had him playing third fiddle: producer Harry Sherman's *Silver Queen* (1942), starring George Brent and Priscilla Lane, and Warners' *The Desert Song* (1943) with Dennis Morgan and Irene Manning. Critiquing the latter, the *New York Times'* Bosley Crowther, a hard man to please, called Cabot a "swaggering French colonel who sneers and leers magnificently."

Funniest of the recent nightclub fights never hit the papers at all. Among those involved were Bruce Cabot, Johnny Meyer, Alexis Thompson and several of the visiting Argentines. The argument (more comical than serious, though blows were struck) lasted for hours and ranged over two different clubs.—Harrison Carroll, July 22, 1942

Bruce Cabot and Errol Flynn (Damon and Pythias) have had a falling out.—Jimmie Fidler, August 6, 1942

Some local bistros are "refusing" to serve Bruce Cabot alcoholic drinks under the "no hooch to Indians law" (Cabot is part Indian). It's a rib by Bruce's cronies.—Jimmie Fidler, August 11, 1942

The girl who caused the Errol Flynn-Bruce Cabot feud is [18-year-old] Faith Dorn [Domergue], who once wore Howard Hughes' ring.—Jimmie Fidler, August 13, 1942

Bruce Cabot and Errol Flynn patched their feud before it broke into open fireworks.—Jimmie Fidler, August 29, 1942

Cabot was considered for Paramount's *Hostages* (1943) and Warners' *Edge of Darkness* (1943), but got neither. On radio's *CBS Playhouse*, he enacted the role of "Mad Dog" Roy Earle with Nancy Kelly in an adaptation of the 1941 film *High Sierra*.

Bruce Cabot's broken hand came from playing tennis with John Perona.—Dorothy Kilgallen, September 15, 1942

Bruce Cabot has a black eye. He says he received it while playing tennis. Or did he receive it during a fist fight in a Hollywood nightclub? I'm only asking.—Erskine Johnson, September 21, 1942

> Marie McDonald has been nursing Bruce Cabot's black eye, which he claims he got from bumping into the proverbial doorknob.—Tedwell Chapman, October 3, 1942

In late September, Cabot and Constance Bennett went out selling war bonds. Columnist Ed Sullivan marveled at Bennett's fortitude on the tour while still looking chic. "She is the swellest girl I ever met," Cabot remarked. Bennett responded, "Coming from the leader of the wolf pack, that is the nicest compliment I ever received." Sullivan noted that Cabot "actually blushed." A *Poughkeepsie Journal* reporter wrote, "Both celebrities were modest in revealing the success of their current tour. But from another source it was learned that together they have sold more than $2,000,000 worth of bonds in the past week, not including the $102,275 total which they sold here yesterday." (That would be a total of more than 36 million today.)

> Bruce Cabot and Phil Ammidon practicing jiu-jitsu in the foyer of El Morocco.—Dorothy Kilgallen, October 14, 1942

> What happened to the beautiful Bruce Cabot-Errol Flynn friendship?—Dorothy Kilgallen, October 17, 1942

> Bruce Cabot and Alexis Thompson holding hands at Le Coq Rouge—they are merely twisting one another's arms to see who is the strongest while their lady friends place bets on the outcome.—L.L. Stevenson, November 5, 1942

Louella Parsons mentioned that Cabot was sorry he was going to "miss the best role of his life" in Cecil B. DeMille's *The Story of Dr. Wassell* (1944)—although it's not clear what role that would be—because he was going to join the Army. "But," Cabot interjected, "there will be lots more roles when we win the war."

> Bruce Cabot is cramming 10 days of the high life into five in Manhattan before he reports for a fitting for khaki at the Army barracks.—George Ross, November 19, 1942

On December 9, 1942, Cabot was sworn in at Camp Blanding in Florida. Columnist John Truesdell wrote, "The howl of the Hollywood wolf pack has hit a high C. The boys are yelping in agony because one of their foremost leaders has left to join the air forces. Bruce Cabot, who reigned as king of the pack for the last several years, resigned to serve Uncle Sammy...." In March 1943, after Cabot graduated from Officer Candidate School in Miami, he went through Combat Intelligence School in Harrisburg, Pennsylvania. That May, Lt. Cabot was due to spend part of his leave in Hollywood—at Errol Flynn's. "He'll probably run me ragged," Flynn told Harrison Carroll. "I wired him back, if he'd just not stay with me, I'd get him a suite at a hotel." Cabot spent most of the time with Ann Sheridan.

> Bruce Cabot is now stationed in Washington, D.C.—as if Congress didn't have enough to worry about!—Dorothy Kilgallen, June 9, 1943

Earning a commission, the second lieutenant was shipped to Tunis, Tunisia. As an operations officer in the Air Transport Command, his duties included briefing the pilots, keeping them on schedule, monitoring the weather, making sure the ships were oiled and gassed, and getting messages through.

> Quentin Reynolds and Lt. Bruce Cabot slugged it out in Algiers—but then shared a hotel room and became friends.—Leonard Lyons, August 16, 1943

There were vague gossip column references about what Cabot was doing in the service. ("Lt. Bruce Cabot, victim of vicious, baseless rumors from overseas, was actually cited for being a good soldier," wrote Walter Winchell.) As early as February 1944, there

Lt. Bruce Cabot didn't let a little thing like a war interrupt his love life. Ann Sheridan, obviously smitten, was his frequent date into the late '40s.

was talk that he was confined to a jail cell for some unspecified reason, but all the columnists pooh-poohed the idea. Lt. Alexis Thompson, Cabot's millionaire sportsman friend, wrote columnist Ed Sullivan,

> Delighted to read the column in which you came to Bruce Cabot's defense. Cabot didn't have to enter the service—he'll be 40 next birthday, but he had an abiding hatred for the Germans—which is why he requested overseas service. I have no facts, but I can state, without fear of being wrong, that the rumors about Bruce being in a serious Army jam are wrong, and that he was not in the mess described. Bruce, as you know, was pretty good at getting into minor scrapes, but he was always a lot smarter than people gave him credit for being. He's always in the position of being the guy that always gets the blame, and some have taken great pleasure in knocking him. Personally, I've met few to equal Cabot's instinctive kindness and generosity. Thanks for giving him the benefit of the doubt.

Sullivan also received a letter from a Major Matthew J. Faerber, who also wanted to thank him

> on behalf of myself and the large number of officers and men in this overseas area who really got to know [Cabot]. As Thompson said, Bruce enlisted as a buck private when he was over 38. How many of those envious, small-time critics who didn't even know him, can match that record? Let me say that we who have really known him and lived with him are unanimous in our verdict that he is a top guy, and we all stand ready to have it out, face to face, with any of the back-fence gossipers who don't know what the hell they're talking about. So thanks from the Yanks, Ed, again for standing up for a right guy.

Cabot obviously had very good friends, ones with money who might have helped him out with his troubles. The truth was, he *was* arrested. According to Colonel L. Fletcher Prouty of the U.S. Air Force, Cabot was the "key cog in one of the world's greatest gold smuggling operations." Prouty announced:

> The Hitler SS troops ransacked Europe for gold and set up an ingenious smuggling line from Germany, through the Balkans, into Turkey and from there into the hands of American teammates in Egypt and North Africa. That stolen European gold was shipped, as aircraft parts, etc., from Cairo to Dakar via our own Air Force, Air Transport Command, and from Dakar to Natal, Brazil. There the Germans had set up a connection to Argentina. It was an enormous gold ring.

It was Prouty who put the finger on Cabot after seeing him in Adana, Turkey. "He was charged with the crime and convicted. Because of the war, he was kept in Africa and transferred to the isolated air base we used at Atar in the desert, just north of Dakar. He was held there until the end of the war." The colonel assumed Cabot had Nazi sympathies because Cabot's bestie Errol Flynn was alleged to be "closely connected" with them (which he was *not*).

The simplest explanations are usually correct, and in this case, that explanation would be that Cabot considered it easy money and thought he could get away with it. Which he did, to an extent. And the public didn't know. Dorothy Kilgallen even wrote in her column, "Lt. Bruce Cabot back from Africa and wearing campaign ribbons, confides that the startling rumors about him which flew across the Atlantic a few months ago were started by a superior officer. The officer was broken, he says."

In June 1944, Cabot, on terminal leave, showed up in New York. "Quite a verbal to-do in 21 the other evening between Lieutenant Bruce Cabot (on one side) and Colonel 'Butch' Morgan and Sergeant Broderick Crawford," Kilgallen wrote.

Cabot was officially discharged on July 19, 1944. That August, on vacation in Mexico City, he was detained by police relating to the disappearance of a $50,000 emerald brooch belonging to Mrs. Valentina Asterman Garcia de Olay, wife of the Spanish ambassador to Cuba.

Returning to Paramount, Cabot was immediately cast—as a bad guy, what else?—in director Raoul Walsh's *Salty O'Rourke* (1945), in which he's a bookmaker putting the screws to race track gambler Alan Ladd. It wasn't much of a part, but at least he was in a popular movie. Jimmie Fidler remarked, "Studio workers are agog at the change Army life wrought in Bruce Cabot—for the better." Kilgallen stated that Cabot, "who used to be something of a cut-up, is the best-behaved boy in the studios since his army career."

> When Bruce Cabot enlisted in the Air Force two years ago, his Filipino houseboy and his boxer dog, Fritz, also went into the service. Now Bruce is out of the Army and making a picture (*Salty O'Rourke*). The houseboy has received a discharge and only the dog remains in the war. "He turned out to be a better soldier than either one of us," says Bruce.—Harrison Carroll, October 17, 1944

> Bruce Cabot examining the glamour gallery at El Morocco with a lean and hungry look. —Dorothy Kilgallen, November 8, 1944

From pioneer British aviator Claude Grahame-White, Cabot leased a spacious Sunset Blvd. home that had once belonged to actress Pauline Frederick. On March 13, 1945, he was the victim of another high-profile robbery. The culprit was Allen T. Sturges II, whose parents were wealthy (and gave him an allowance of "only" $100 a week), and his estranged wife was an heiress to the Tiffany jewelry fortune. He got into Cabot's residence by telling the maid he was a good friend of Cabot's and then, left alone, helped himself to three sets of diamond cufflinks, a cigarette case (reportedly with the inscription, "To the most unpleasant ... I know—Jock") and a few other items valued at $1600. Apprehended, Sturges admitted to being in possession of the items and pawning them (for $310), but denied stealing them. At the time of the theft, Sturges was already facing charges of forging a $3000 check and writing his own bad ones. Cabot said he knew Sturges slightly in New York and that on several recent occasions Sturges had visited him at his Beverly Hills home when Pat DiCicco was a guest. Sturges was fined $500 and given five years' probation.

Cabot was cast in the leading male role in Monogram's *Divorce* (1945), starring (and co-produced by) Kay Francis. The predatory and much-married Dianne Carter (Francis) returns to her hometown and zeroes in on her childhood friend Bob Phillips (Cabot)— who is happily married (to Helen Mack). But not for long. Dianne worms her way into his life, tearing him away from his family. Some reviewers found the story too obvious, with Dorothy Masters in the *New York Daily News* writing, "No less subtle than story presentation is Kay Francis' performance as siren. She stops short of actual bludgeoning, but bears so heavily on intimidation by gesture and dialogue that both she and Bruce Cabot look ridiculous."

At Twentieth Century–Fox, he was seen in two supporting roles. In *Fallen Angel* (1945), he's one of the men involved with Stella (Linda Darnell), who is later murdered; he subsequently gets beaten by policeman Mark Judd (Charles Bickford). (*Des Moines Tribune*: "Bruce is beginning to creak. He looks beat up before Bickford lays a glove on him.") As the good-for-nothing brother of Fred MacMurray in *Smoky* (1946), he lets Fred go to jail for him, mistreats horses, rustles cattle and forges his brother's name to an IOU.

Pat DiCicco, acting as president, formed Imperial Productions (with his cousin "Cubby" Broccoli as vice-president) and their first—and last—film was *Avalanche* (1946), directed by Irving Allen and written by Edward Anhalt. Cabot starred as a Treasury agent who goes to an Idaho mountain ski lodge (actually Alta Lodge in Utah) to make an arrest; he is met with murder, double crosses and the title disaster. Walter Winchell called *Avalanche* "an acceptable felon fable with Bruce Cabot supplying muscles the scenario lacks."

Cabot moved out of the Frederick mansion and Claude Grahame-White immediately hit him with a damage suit for $3000, alleging that the actor left the property in a "filthy, damaged and uninhabitable" condition: furniture soiled and damaged, carpets and floors ruined, kitchen utensils "burned beyond use," etc.

Angel and the Badman (1947) began Cabot's long personal and professional association with John Wayne. (Wayne told Erskine Johnson that Cabot "can play a villain without screwing his face out of shape.") In June 1947, Louella Parsons informed her readers:

> [F]or six weeks, Bruce Cabot steadily has been losing his voice. Ever since he made a movie on location in Arizona [*Angel and the Badman*], where he breathed in sand and dust, he has suffered an irritation of his left vocal cord that is growing more and more serious.
>
> So, on June 19th he will go into the hospital for an operation which Dr. Joel Pressman (Claudette Colbert's husband) will perform.
>
> I doubt if this would have come out about Bruce if he had not done a swell thing and turned down a big role in an Edward Small picture because he did not want to take a chance of having to quit in the middle of the film—and cost Eddie a lot of money.

Since he couldn't speak for five weeks after the surgery, Cabot very Cabot-ishly hired a pretty girl to go around with him, to take notes and to "interpret." That September, Harrison Carroll wrote that Cabot was going to stop in Detroit to "advise" a young boy who had the same throat ailment.

Cabot and John Perona, owner of the El Morocco, became good friends with the maharajah of Cooch-Behar, Jagaddipendra Narayan, and they helped him buy farm equipment; they also did the nightclubs together, and hunted. Perona was always up for some fun with Cabot and whoever else decided to tag along. One night, they were cruising around with millionaire Bob Topping when they decided to help the police locate two hold-up men who robbed the Hotel Sutton Plaza at two in the morning.

In other bad-guy movie roles from that period, Cabot took on Randolph Scott in *Gunfighters* (1947)—reportedly using guns that his own father wielded during the Spanish-American War; William Elliott in *The Gallant Legion* (1948), and Forrest Tucker in *Rock Island Trail* (1950). He portrayed outlaw Cole Younger in *Best of the Badmen* (1951). With Bob Hope and Lucille Ball, he appeared in *Sorrowful Jones* (1949) and *Fancy Pants* (1950). In the late '40s, Cabot was devoting most of his time to the oil business. Alexis Thompson sold him a share in the Philadelphia Eagles pro football team.

> Hollywood visitors keep gabbing about a swing Esther Williams allegedly took at Bruce Cabot in the Mocambo recently.—Dorothy Kilgallen, September 27, 1946

Cabot continued to wheel and deal: He part-owned a Miami nitery called the Spa and a night spot, the Tampa Club; invested in Oklahoma oil wells with his friend Ray Ryan; and invested in neons, ballpoint fountain pens, soft drinks and barbecue pits. He also sought to produce movies, but found himself buying stories and reselling them to others at a profit ("The Regal Rustler," "Hacienda in Hawaii," "Blackjack," "Hialeah"). Barton MacLane and Cabot produced *Listen, Kids*, a film about juvenile delinquency; shot in color on 16mm, it cost around $15,000 and was made available to schools and churches. During a night in August 1949 when Cabot was squiring Ann Sheridan to Ciro's, his house was robbed—again. He lost three pairs of shoes, five suits, jewelry, slacks and sports jackets, to the tune of $2390.

"Bruce Cabot turned down some real dough offered him by a national magazine to write an article about his pal, Errol Flynn," Hedda Hopper revealed. In a similar vein, he turned down a proposed Broadway show called *Make Mine the Tall One* because he claimed it was a burlesque on Flynn. Despite a few spats, their friendship was still strong; in fact, Cabot admitted to Hopper that he was "lost without Flynn." As for Errol, he considered Bruce the brother he never had. Both were perfectly imperfect men prone to do the wrong thing every once in a while and happily played jokes on each other. When Flynn's wife Nora returned from Jamaica, she found their swimming pool filled with fish.

> Bruce Cabot was at the El Morocco last night, cursing the Hollywood agents and their treatment of the beautiful young ladies who aspire to movie careers. "Do you feel this way about agents because they don't get jobs for these girls?" Cabot was asked... "No," he explained. "It's because the first thing they tell the girls is 'Don't go out with Cabot.'"—Leonard Lyons, July 6, 1948

He spent most of 1949 and '50 acting as a $500-a-week greeter at Houston's Shamrock Hotel, which was owned by pal Glenn McCarthy.

On September 17, 1950, the man columnists described as "the wolves' idea of a wolf" and the "big dame hunter" married for the third time, to Francesca De Scaffa, a beauty almost 30 years his junior. She wasn't Portuguese as everyone thought, she told Louella Parsons. "My mother, she is French and Chilean. I was born in Venezuela and educated in Paris. My father, he is Hindu." Parsons asked, "What does that make you?" Francesca replied, "Well, not Portuguese." When she first showed up in Hollywood, De Scaffa was called an Indian princess. The wedding ceremony was initially going to take place at oilman Lenoir Josey's Cypress, Texas, ranch, but Cabot's half-sister complained that the Texas wedding was "undignified"; Cabot and De Scaffa ended up being married by the justice of the peace at the Santa Barbara home of Cabot's nephew. He had two best men, Mike Romanoff and Pat DiCicco (Flynn was out of the country).

Three months after the wedding, De Scaffa had a miscarriage.

True to form, there were problems. In May 1951, De Scaffa filed for divorce saying he left her alone too much, spending most of his time in New York. "I tried my best," she said, "but Bruce should never have married anyone." They reconciled weeks later. The following month, he appeared on a telethon for the City of Hope's new cancer hospital in Duarte, California, describing his own recent bout with the disease. Many applauded his decision to step up to inspire others. In August, he was arrested for drunk driving and crashing into a tree (fined $100 and treated for a cut over his left eye); September saw De Scaffa locking him out of the house when she caught him kissing another woman when they were dining at Romanoff's. October was a busy month: He was in hot water for writing five bad checks totaling $1150 to Wilbur Clark's Desert Inn, and De Scaffa again wanted out of the marriage because she claimed he called her names in French ("foul and evil words"), hit and kicked her.

After obtaining an interlocutory decree, they were back together by December. Harrison Carroll told his readers that the crowd at Ciro's admired Cabot for the way he held his temper when a heckler annoyed him and De Scaffa. And Louella Parsons praised Cabot in her column: "I heard something very nice about Bruce. During a recent trip around the country, he went on his own to visit hospitals in San Francisco, Denver and St. Louis, and didn't try to get any publicity out of it."

Cabot complained he was getting little work, although it didn't seem to affect his socializing. He did *Lost in Alaska* (1952) with Abbott and Costello, and was seen on TV's *Lux Video Theatre, Armstrong Circle Theatre, Stars Over Hollywood, Gruen Guild Theater, Pantomime Quiz, Tales of Tomorrow* and *The Pepsi-Cola Playhouse*. In 1951, he starred in an unsold pilot based on *The Virginian*. He and Errol Flynn appeared together on *The Colgate Comedy Hour*. "Abbott and Costello present a couple of he-men (creaking slightly but he-men) on their Sunday TV stanza," wrote the *Brooklyn Daily News*' Al Salerno. Cabot also had a supporting part in *Kid Monk Baroni* (1952) as boxer Leonard Nimoy's unscrupulous manager.

De Scaffa was again pregnant but Cabot left her, traveling to New York, Oklahoma and Miami Beach; she was unable to reach him when she again decided to start legal actions. French author Pierre La Mure (*Moulin Rouge*) let her stay with him during her pregnancy. "Mrs. Cabot, along with many locals, can't understand Brucie-boy's attitude—even under their estranged circumstances," wrote Edith Gwynn. "She's about to become a mother." There was a warrant out for his arrest in California for not supporting her or providing pre-natal care for the baby.

> You can find him around El Morocco Club in New York, where he is giving champagne parties.—Attorney Jerry Giesler, September 13, 1952

The Cabots' daughter, Alphonsine, was born October 3, 1952—without Bruce ever seeing her. De Scaffa hocked her jewels, accepted loans from Cabot's friends, appeared on TV and in movies (Hugo Haas' *Edge of Hell*) and became a secret tipster for *Confidential* magazine to make ends meet. At one point, she was threatened with deportation. All while Cabot golfed and chased girls.

By mid–1953, Cabot had relocated to Italy, where he acted with Errol Flynn in the movie *The Story of William Tell*, which Flynn was producing. Financing fell through and they couldn't finish the movie or pay the actors. Cabot, who had a reputation for borrowing money from Flynn and others and never paying them back, wanted to be paid—he needed the money. He attached several of Flynn's personal items and brought suit against him, demolishing their long friendship. (Flynn, in a nice gesture, later gave Cabot's estranged wife $1000 to help her out with the baby.) In 1954, when Sheilah Graham told Cabot that she "saw your friend Errol Flynn" in London, Cabot corrected her: "ex-friend." He added, "We were pals for 18 years. But now I've had it." He didn't elaborate.

Cabot mainly remained in Europe, where he appeared in print ads for Norelco electric razors; raced cars; partied and dated Hedy Lamarr, and avoided De Scaffa and their child. He also took up with Danish-Swedish model Laila Stocking. At the end of 1953, he was reported seriously ill in a Switzerland sanitarium for a "recurrence of an old lung ailment." But he still planned, or so he said, to marry Stocking. Back in California, De Scaffa was still seeking a settlement. ("He gave me a bad time. I may just give him one in return," she told Harrison Carroll.) Cabot, ordered to pay $450 a month, refused to do so. De Scaffa claimed he told her via mail that he still loved her, but he couldn't afford her. "Even if he could afford me," she told Carroll, "I wouldn't even look at him."

Cabot also made movies in Italy. In *Il mantello rosso* (1955), aka *The Red Cloak*, he plays a governor terrorizing the sixteenth-century Pisa and trying to wed lovely Patricia Medina. Enter a Zorro-like hero to save the day. "[The] part of the villain is entrusted to the redoubtable Bruce Cabot, a bit older now, of course, but still spirited and zestful," wrote *Boxoffice*. As a member of a group seeking German Field Marshal Erwin Rommel's treasure in *Il tesoro di Rommel* (1955), his co-stars included British Dawn Addams, Swiss Paul Hubschmid (aka Paul Christian) and Italian Isa Miranda. As a gangster in the comedy *Totò lascia o raddoppia?* (1956), he bets with Rocco D'Assunta on the outcome of a TV quiz show.

[The] bad feeling between Errol Flynn and Bruce Cabot spilled over into a fist fight in Rome last week.—Sheilah Graham, March 14, 1955

De Scaffa fed columnists tidbits about Cabot, notably that he fathered a son, Brucie, with Stocking and that he was going to marry Lady Sylvia Ashley (widow of Douglas Fairbanks and ex-wife of Clark Gable); both were gleaned, De Scaffa claimed, from a May 9, 1955, phone conversation with him. "There are many among us who feel Lady Sylvia Ashley Gable and Bruce Cabot, who are talking about a merger, dearly deserve each other," Mike Connolly wrote sarcastically. De Scaffa claimed that Cabot told her he was making big bucks in Europe and had "no intention of returning to Hollywood. He said he was living in style in a palace in Rome." This is doubtful. A judge issued a bench warrant for Cabot on contempt charges for non-payment of $4950 in child support—giving Cabot yet another reason not to come back to the U.S. From Rome, Cabot said,

> For two years I have been quiet while Miss De Scaffa told story after story about me. Now I read that she says I talked to her on the trans–Atlantic phone on May 9, that I told her I was in love with a Lila Sterling, and that I have had a son named Brucie by this Sterling.
>
> I am going to the United States consulate in Rome and swear out a statement that I did not talk to my wife on May 9, that I do not even know Miss Sterling, and that the only child I ever have had was born in 1929 by a previous marriage.

Cabot charged that she "dreamed up" the name of the woman he allegedly had a baby with. Well, she *did*; the name was Laila Stocking, *not* Lila Sterling—and that his marriage intentions with Lady Ashley were "just as phony as the present charge."

De Scaffa was furious over him denying paternity of Alphonsine—as Laila Stocking *should* have been, for the sake of Brucie. He and De Scaffa finally divorced in 1957, putting an end to their drawn-out gossip-columns battle.

Diana Dors and Vittorio Gassman starred in the Italian horse-racing comedy *La ragazza del palio* aka *The Love Specialist* (1957), with Cabot in a minor role. Other modest-sized parts came in U.S. productions filming overseas: a tough foreign correspondent in *The Quiet American* (1958), a gunfighter in *The Sheriff of Fractured Jaw* (1958) and a seaman in *John Paul Jones* (1959). In *Guardatele ma non toccatele!* (1959), a silly military comedy starring Ugo Tognazzi, Cabot got special billing as a colonel. He was more at home as the merciless Alboino, king of the barbarians, up against Steve Reeves as Emiliano (aka Goliath), in *Il terrore dei barbari* (1959). In the U.S., where it was titled *Goliath and the Barbarians*, the *New York Times*' Bosley Crowther wrote that Cabot and Livio Lorenzon "loll and leer with villainous enjoyment, all in color and Totalscope."

When Cabot wasn't acting, he was part-owner of a travel agency and a hotel, wrote special nightclub material for various singers, and served as the exiled King Farouk's social secretary. Denying he was in self-imposed "exile," Cabot told Gabriel De Sabatino that he was in U.S. two years earlier, "and I'm going back next fall. The reason I stay here is because I like it, I like the country, its climate and its people. I've made Rome my headquarters, but this doesn't mean I've moved in for good. Plans are always subject to change."

Lauren Bacall's steady date abroad is Bruce Cabot. (Steady for a day?)—Walter Winchell, July 20, 1959

In 1960, Cabot returned to the States to appear in *The Slowest Gun in the West*, a pilot for a proposed series starring Phil Silvers. The comedian surrounded himself with an impressive collection of Western character actors, headed by Cabot as the owner of the town saloon, and the town itself—until Fletcher Bissell III, the Silver Dollar Kid, becomes sheriff. On *77 Sunset Strip*, Cabot played mobster Silk Cipriano, and he did his first John Wayne film of the 1960s, *The Comancheros* (1961), as a major in the Texas Rangers. In Wayne's *Hatari!* (1962), he was Indian, a member of Duke's crew, capturing wild animals in Africa for transfer to zoos; he gets gored by a rhino. On that set, Cabot told the *London Guardian*'s Tom Hutchinson,

> Duke said we shouldn't drink together so much, because there was a German actor and a French actor on the picture, and he was worried about international morale.
>
> I said, "Shit to morale!" and went off drinking with the crew. Eventually, he came over and he drank whiskey and I drank vodka through the night and I said, "Whatever happened to international morale?" We finished up at four-thirty in the morning and the call for filming

was at five o'clock. Mind you, we'd sweated out the liquor, it was so hot. Not that I've ever been late, even with a hangover; I'd shoot myself rather than be late. Same with Duke.

In July 1962, Louella Parsons asked Cabot about his love life, "which used to be considerable." Cabot replied, "Haven't time for that now. I'm off to Honolulu for *Donovan's Reef,* also with Duke Wayne. But," he laughed, "I may just check the beach at Waikiki." Cabot did not appear in *Donovan's Reef.*

It's unknown whether Cabot had trouble getting acting jobs or if he had just become lazy and didn't try. He relied on his friends to cast him in films; Wayne rarely let him down, giving him supporting roles in *McLintock!* (1963), *In Harm's Way* (1965), *The War Wagon* (1967), *The Green Berets* (1968), *Hellfighters* (1968), *The Undefeated* (1969), *Chisum* (1970) and *Big Jake* (1971). "Duke's a great guy," Cabot told John Bustin, "but you don't kid around on his pictures. He's a perfectionist, and he doesn't have much patience with you if you don't know your job. He pays you to know what you're doing." Producer A.C. Lyles cast him in *Law of the Lawless* (1964), *Black Spurs* (1965) and *Town Tamer* (1965). He also played the sheriff in *Cat Ballou* (1965) and Jane Fonda's unpleasant stepfather in *The Chase* (1966).

In 1963, his experience working on *Choque de Sentimentos* might have turned him off working with unfamiliar filmmakers. Cabot, Fay Spain, Tom Hernández and Minda Guild were stranded in Rio de Janeiro when the Italian producer ran out of money. Cabot speculated, "Maybe he didn't get enough money from his backers. Or maybe he just spent it all. I understand he's still in Rio, though."

Close friends and drinking buddies, John Wayne (middle) and Bruce Cabot (left) appeared together in 11 movies between 1947 and 1971. They're joined by Rock Hudson (right) in this shot from 1969's *The Undefeated.*

Cabot didn't enjoy working in television but he guested on *Burke's Law, Bonanza* (a stellar performance as a drunken sheriff trying to relive past glories) and *Daniel Boone* (one of his most cold-hearted bad guys), and was part of the Bob Hope special *Have Girls, Will Travel* (1964). His old friend (and romantic partner) Ann Sheridan wanted him to play a regular part on her TV series *Pistols'n'Petticoats*, but that deal fell through. A spot as a villain on TV's *Batman* also never happened: Cabot told columnist Donald Freeman, "The producer called me and said, 'Bruce, we don't have a script yet. We don't have much past the basic idea. But you'll play a heavy whose name is King Kong.' Sounds great to me."

For a couple of years, he was more interested in a liquor business in which he was partnered with John Wayne and Howard Hawks. Cabot made sure bars and hotels were stocked up with their product when they were out on location and when he was on the road promoting the films. He was also part-owner of boxer Sal Algieri's contract.

Errol Flynn died in 1959; in '65, Cabot went after Flynn's estate for monies still owed him from *William Tell*. He also wrote his memoir, *Hollywood Went Thataway*, which was well-publicized—but never published. In between acting jobs, Cabot served as a VIP greeter and goodwill ambassador for Universal Studio Tours. "I also sweep the floors," he joked to Harrison Carroll.

In *WUSA* (1970), starring Paul Newman and Joanne Woodward, he wore a replica of a Tom Mix costume playing old-time cowboy hero King Wolyoe "with bravado," wrote the *Atlanta Constitution*'s Bob Geurink. Reviewer Emery Wister wrote, "John Wayne may frown because Bruce Cabot's aging, flag-waving cowboy star seems to be cut from his mold."

His last film appearance came via his friend "Cubby" Broccoli in the Sean Connery James Bond adventure *Diamonds Are Forever* (1971). "I got to work in Las Vegas, Palm Springs and, now, London," he told the *London Guardian*. "That's pretty high on the hog for me. I usually end up outside El Paso, living in a tent and eating box-lunches." During filming, he reminisced about his career with Tom Hutchinson of the *London Guardian*, who, of course, asked him about Errol Flynn. Cabot's response:

> He was a better actor than his publicity gave him credit for. I shared his house, his fights, his liquor and his girls. He was a real man with terrific looks. What happened to him, of course, was that he took to the dope—in fact, he was registered over here in England as an addict—and that destroyed him. God, if he were alive today, do you realize that he would be 61 ... and probably still a star.

After *Diamonds Are Forever*, Cabot was admitted to California's Loma Linda University Medical Center for surgery and radiation treatment for cancer of the lungs and throat. John Wayne was a constant visitor. In December 1971, he was discharged and went to recuperate at the Motion Picture Country House and Hospital in Woodland Hills. In April 1972, he fell and broke his left hip and arm.

On May 3, 1972, 68-year-old Cabot died at the facility. His friend Ray Ryan was the informant on his death certificate. He left his entire estate of $22,080 (almost $149,000 today) to his teenage son Bruce, living in Sweden with his mother, finally acknowledging the boy as his own. Cabot's body was buried in Carlsbad Cemetery in his hometown of Carlsbad.

1931: *Heroes of the Flames* (uncredited), *Confessions of a Co-Ed* (uncredited).
1932: *Lady with a Past* (uncredited), *The Roadhouse Murder*.

1933: *Signing 'Em Up* (short), *Lucky Devils, The Great Jasper, King Kong, Disgraced, Flying Devils, Midshipman Jack, Ann Vickers, Shadows of Sing Sing.*
1934: *Finishing School, Murder on the Blackboard, His Greatest Gamble, Their Big Moment, Redhead, Men of the Night, Night Alarm.*
1935: *Without Children, Let 'Em Have It, Show Them No Mercy!*
1936: *Don't Gamble with Love, Screen Snapshots Series 15, No. 5* (short), *Robin Hood of El Dorado, The Three Wise Guys, Fury, The Last of the Mohicans, Don't Turn 'Em Loose, The Big Game, Legion of Terror, Sinner Take All.*
1937: *Tenth Avenue Kid, Bad Guy, Love Takes Flight, The Bad Man of Brimstone.*
1938: *Sinners in Paradise, Smashing the Rackets.*
1939: *Homicide Bureau, Screen Snapshots Series 18, No. 9* (short), *Mystery of the White Room, Dodge City, Mickey the Kid, My Son Is Guilty, Traitor Spy.*
1940: *Susan and God, Captain Caution, Girls Under 21.*
1941: *The Flame of New Orleans, Sundown.*
1942: *Wild Bill Hickok Rides, Pierre of the Plains, Silver Queen.*
1943: *The Desert Song.*
1945: *Salty O'Rourke, Divorce, Fallen Angel.*
1946: *Smoky, Avalanche.*
1947: *Angel and the Badman, Gunfighters.*
1948: *The Gallant Legion.*
1949: *Sorrowful Jones.*
1950: *Rock Island Trail, Fancy Pants.*
1951: *Best of the Badmen.*
1952: *Kid Monk Baroni, Lost in Alaska.*
1955: *Il mantello rosso, Il tesoro di Rommel.*
1956: *Totò, Lascia O Raddoppia!*
1958: *The Quiet American, La ragazza del palio, The Sheriff of Fractured Jaw.*
1959: *Guardatele ma non toccatele, John Paul Jones, Il terrore dei barbari.*
1960: *The Slowest Gun in the West* (TV).
1961: *The Comancheros.*
1962: *Hatari!*
1963: *McLintock!*
1964: *Law of the Lawless.*
1965: *Choque de Sentimentos, In Harm's Way, Black Spurs, Cat Ballou, Town Tamer.*
1966: *The Chase.*
1967: *The War Wagon.*
1968: *The Green Berets, The Moviemakers* (short), *Hellfighters.*
1969: *The Undefeated.*
1970: *Chisum, WUSA.*
1971: *Big Jake, Diamonds Are Forever.*

JAMES CARDWELL

From the Camden, New Jersey, *Courier-Post*:

The hometown screen debut of James Cardwell, who hit the film jackpot in role of the oldest brother in the stirring picture *The Sullivans*, was acclaimed by hundreds of his former associates and fellow high school students at the Savar Theatre last night.

In honor of the Woodrow Wilson school graduate, Mayor Brunner proclaimed the week beginning yesterday as "Jimmie Cardwell Week."

Camden's premiere of *The Sullivans* in 1944 was a big deal—a way to honor one of their boys who made good. James Cardwell never forgot their kindness and remained loyal to his hometown, visiting often and writing home every chance he got. His career in Hollywood might have been, by some standards, lackluster and spotty but to Camden residents, he was a star.

He was born Albert Paine Cardwell in Camden on November 21, 1921; he had a sister, Jeannie (1933–83). Their World War I veteran father Raymond worked as a gas station attendant and then as a clerk. Mother Bessie was a librarian and later a hospital ward clerk.

Cardwell was interested in a writing career, but also played sports while attending Alfred Cramer Junior High and Woodrow Wilson High School. After suffering an ankle injury, he switched to the drama and debate clubs and was president of the dramatic society. His drama teacher Jean C. Welsh later remembered the first time Cardwell performed, at an assembly program in commemoration of Abraham Lincoln:

The boyishly handsome James Cardwell had great potential when he was signed by 20th Century–Fox in 1943.

"Unassuming, quietly, but with poetic fervor rare in a high school boy, he read Homer Hoch's lines written in appreciation of the Great Emancipator."

Cardwell was elected president of the Camden Junior Recreation Commission and helped in an effort to "make Camden flourish with playgrounds and to take action as would help the young of the city to have breathing spaces within the municipality" (*Courier-Post*). In 1940 and '42, he was commentator in the "Golden Youth" program of the Cultural Olympics of the University of Pennsylvania.

He acted with the Camden Drama Guild and the Merchantville Players. Evaluating Cardwell's performance in *Death Takes a Holiday*, the *Courier-Post* wrote that his "poise stamps him as a juvenile with ability" and praised his "fine work."

After graduating with honors, Cardwell worked as a clerk at the Iron Rock Golf Course and bookkeeper at a real estate office. Joining the Hedgerow Theater Group in Moylan, Pennsylvania, he acted in *Macbeth, Turpentine Boy, Family Portrait, Saint Joan* and other plays.

He was employed in RCA Victor's shipping department when he met secretary Esther Borton (who was voted "prettiest girl" in her high school). On June 20, 1942, they married at the Holy Communion Lutheran Church in Berlin, New Jersey. The couple lived with Esther's parents in Watsontown.

A Paramount scout spotted the boyishly handsome Cardwell in the Hedgerow Theater parking lot, but a resultant screen test in New York was a failure. In 1943, 20th Century–Fox was looking for unknown young actors to play the five Waterloo, Iowa, Sullivan brothers who served together during World War II and who all went down with their ship in the South Pacific. Fox saw Cardwell's test and re-tested him in Los Angeles. He won the role of eldest brother George Thomas Sullivan in *The Sullivans* (1944)—and was also signed to a Fox contract.

Early studio publicity claimed that Cardwell owned and operated the largest silver fox farm in New Jersey and that it would account for his "sudden popularity with the fair sex." They didn't continue with that false storyline.

Based on his first movie, Louella Parsons called the renamed James Cardwell a "real find." Fox rewarded him with the lead opposite Linda Darnell in *Sweet and Low-Down* (1944), where he played a Chicago factory worker who gets a chance to play trombone with Benny Goodman's orchestra and lets it go to his head. Edwin Schallert wrote that the studio was "booming" him. *Modern Screen*'s Virginia Wilson advised her readers that the "newcomer [will] definitely send you" and "you'd better get your fan mail in ahead of the rush."

During pre-production on *Claudia and David* (1946), it was announced that Cardwell would play a prominent role opposite Dorothy McGuire and Robert Young. But when Fox finally got around to shooting it, John Sutton had the role. Cardwell had a supporting role in the war movie *A Walk in the Sun* (1945).

Big things seemed on the horizon, with the studio grooming him for John Payne–type roles. But when Payne came back from war service, Cardwell asked for and got his release from Fox at the end of 1944. *A Walk in the Sun*'s producers, Lewis Milestone and Samuel Bronston, each expressed interest in signing him, and Bronston won out.

Newspaper columnists were printing letters asking about Cardwell and there was a lot of buzz surrounding him—but no studio to exploit it. He had a tough guy quality calling to mind John Garfield and James Cagney, and an accent to match. Bronston didn't have the clout to get Cardwell the roles he should have been getting. It was early enough in the actor's career to build on his promise, but it did not happen.

After two years of marriage, Esther got fed up with Hollywood and returned to New Jersey. The two eventually divorced.

Cardwell and Joan Barclay had the romantic leads in the Monogram Charlie Chan mystery *The Shanghai Cobra* (1945) with Cardwell "turning in an engaging portrayal of a novice sleuth" (*Motion Picture Herald*). In *Voice of the Whistler* (1945), Columbia cast him as nice-guy doctor Fred Graham, who is engaged to nurse Joan Martin (Lynn Merrick). She hatches a plan to marry terminal John Sinclair (Richard Dix) and inherit a fortune upon his imminent death; Graham is horrified and she calls him "soft." She loves him but remembers her struggles growing up and wants a better life for her future children. When Sinclair lives longer than expected, Joan resorts to a murderous scheme, with Graham playing along.

Freelancer Cardwell worked mostly at the Poverty Row studios, where his roles were typically supporting. At Monogram, he was in two of Kane Richmond's Shadow films, *Behind the Mask* and *The Missing Lady* (both 1946). The former did a better job of showing Cardwell off: As blackmailing columnist Jeff Mann, he dominates the first ten noirish minutes of the film. Through dark, rainy slick

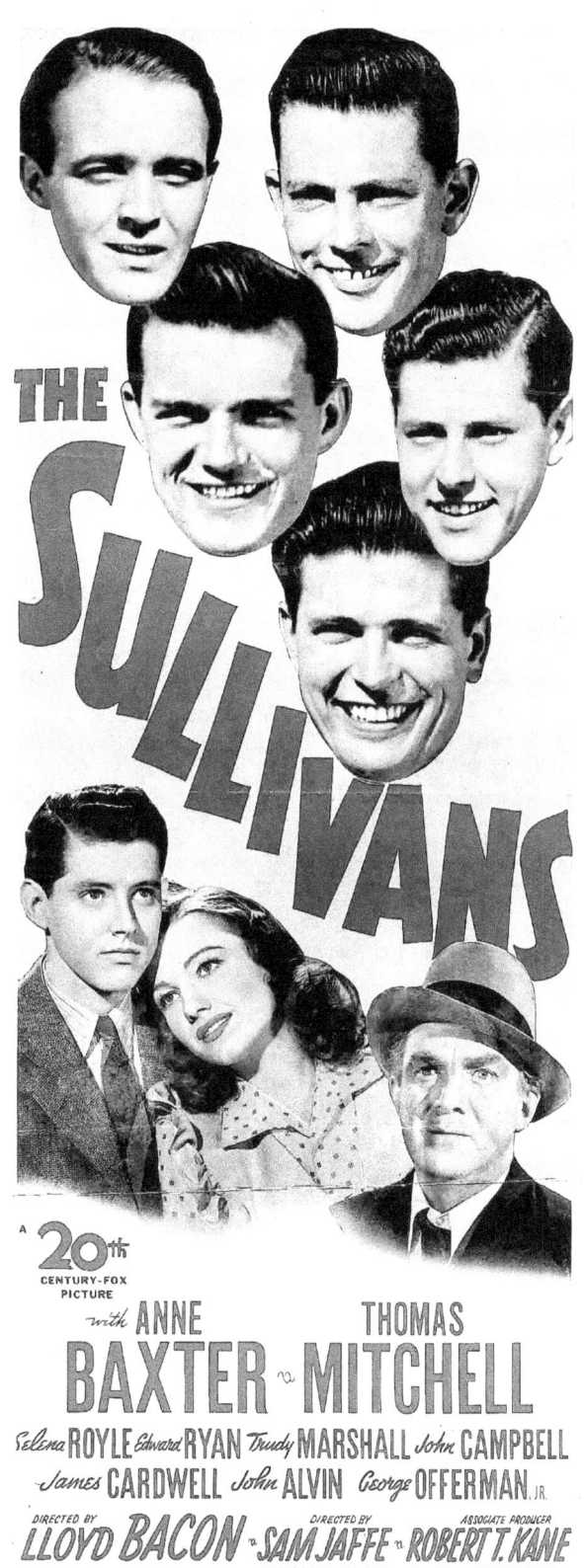

Poster for the World War II drama *The Sullivans* (1944), the story of the ill-fated Sullivan brothers of Waterloo, Iowa.

Cardwell with his *Sweet and Low-Down* (1944) leading ladies Lynn Bari (left) and Linda Darnell.

streets, Mann confronts his marks and he develops all the necessary qualifications of a B-movie murder victim.

In 1946, Cardwell took pre-med night classes at UCLA, but this did not last.

He was fourteenth-billed in *Canyon Passage* (1946), a major Walter Wanger Western, but it was a small role with minimal dialogue as he and Virginia Patton marry and later die at the hands of Indians. Cardwell's best chances were in the Bs, where he excelled at playing thugs. One of his most atypical roles came when he replaced William Bishop in *The Return of the Whistler* (1948). This eighth and final Whistler (the only one without Richard Dix) had Ted Nichols (Michael Duane) trying to save his fiancée Alice (Lenore Aubert) from her late husband's treacherous family. Is she a widow as she claims or is she crazy? A mustachioed and polished Cardwell portrays the man who claims to be Alice's very-much-alive husband. Or is he her husband? He had an excellent (if brief) supporting part in a movie well-regarded by film noir enthusiasts, Eagle-Lion's *He Walked by Night* (1948). As a police sergeant paralyzed in a shootout, Cardwell had some good moments showing off his dramatic chops.

In the late 1940s, most of Cardwell's appearances were in support or uncredited bit parts, but he did get one last lead: Republic's *Daughter of the Jungle* (1949). His

Poster for the Charlie Chan whodunit *The Shanghai Cobra* (1945).

The secretary (Christine McIntyre) to blackmailing columnist Jeff Mann (Cardwell) seems to be the only one of his co-workers who likes him in *Behind the Mask* (1946), a Shadow mystery.

resemblance to Tom Neal allowed the studio to pad out the 69-minute feature with footage from Neal's 1941 serial *Jungle Girl*. Although Harry Medved and Randy Dreyfuss included the movie in their 1978 book *The Fifty Worst Films of All Time*, *Daughter of the Jungle* is not a stinker. The cast is excellent, Cardwell is a stalwart, husky hero, Lois Hall a pretty, charming heroine and there's action a-plenty.

Since acting gigs were scarce, Cardwell looked for other means of support. He owned an interest in a Beverly Hills interior decorating business. Stage work included a supporting part in the Pasadena Playhouse production of *Laura* (1946); in 1949, he appeared in *Light Up the Sky* (1949) at the Honolulu Community Theatre in Hawaii. The latter was a change of pace from Cardwell's usual toughie roles, and the *Honolulu Star-Bulletin*'s Clarice B. Taylor appreciated the way he played his part in a "delightful, extravagant manner." His stay in Hawaii was extended by the popularity of *Light Up the Sky*, and at Christmastime he appeared in the radio presentation "The Story of the Birth of Christ." He stayed through the new year of 1950 to star in *The Silver Whistle* at the Honolulu Community Theatre and to play the villain in *The Drunkard* at the Waikiki Tavern Orchard Room.

In May '50, Cardwell joined Joe E. Brown's six-month touring production of *Harvey*; the group played Australia and New Zealand. In November, he was back in Australia for the play *Babes in the Woods* and he began dating 20-year-old cast member June Croker. He remained in Australia into 1951 and was seen judging beauty contests and giving a "humorous" monologue that "kept the huge crowd at the Journalists' Ball amused" (*Sunday Times*).

Crooks Michael Whalen (middle) and Cardwell (right) don't stand a chance against undercover Federal agent Michael O'Shea in Eagle-Lion's *Parole, Inc.* (1948).

Paul Reeves (Whit Bissell, middle) is questioned by police sergeants Cardwell (left) and Scott Brady (right) in the classic film noir *He Walked by Night* **(1948). While his part is small, Cardwell gives one of his best performances.**

While Down Under, Cardwell was approached by Maurice Colleano, who had a comedy-acrobatic dance act. By this time, Cardwell and June Croker were engaged and he arranged for her to join him in the Colleano act.

Before that happened, she had to fulfill a nightclub engagement at the Celebrity Club. As she made her way to the stage, a spirit burner set her dress afire. Cardwell acted quickly, tearing down a curtain and wrapping it around Croker to extinguish the flames. June still suffered severe burns about her face, body, arms and legs. Plastic surgery fixed her face, but her body was scarred. Croker told the *Mirror* that her career was ruined; she became withdrawn and went to live with her mother. She successfully sued the nightclub. Croker said that Cardwell "wanted me to follow him to England and then to America, but I decided to let him go his own way. I didn't want to be a millstone."

Cardwell toured with the Colleano troupe. From London, they ended up at the Thunderbird in Las Vegas in 1952. He got good notices for his clowning and gags.

Since 1950, he had been off movie screens. Television should have offered some possibilities, but Cardwell had trouble finding employment. *City Detective* was one of the few TV series to cast him. After a blink-and-you-miss-him bit in *Them!* (1954), he wrote his parents that he was doing "fine," especially on television. He made sure to regularly visit his family in New Jersey, send flowers to his mother and let his family know he was doing okay.

But he wasn't doing okay. With no acting work forthcoming, he suffered from depression, He fell behind in his rent, and his Screen Actors Guild membership dues were several months overdue.

At around ten p.m. on January 31, 1954, the 32-year-old Cardwell borrowed pilot-actor Archie Twitchell's car. Parking in a West Hollywood parking lot, he shot himself in the right temple with a .45-caliber pistol. His body was found a few hours later, slumped over the steering wheel. His suicide took place a short distance from the two-room bungalow where he resided. In Cardwell's possession was a letter from his landlord, possibly an eviction notice.

Services were held at the Murray Funeral Home in Camden on February 6, and he was interred at nearby Harleigh Cemetery. After his death, friends claimed that Cardwell often said in the past year that he was "going to be an actor or nothing."

1944: *The Sullivans, Sweet and Low-Down.*
1945: *The Shanghai Cobra, Voice of the Whistler, A Walk in the Sun.*
1946: *Fear, Behind the Mask, Canyon Passage, The Missing Lady.*
1947: *The Devil on Wheels, It Happened on Fifth Avenue* (uncredited), *Robin Hood of Texas.*
1948: *The Return of the Whistler; King of the Gamblers; Daredevils of the Clouds; Harpoon; Parole, Inc.; He Walked by Night; Trouble Preferred.*
1949: *Daughter of the Jungle, Down Dakota Way, San Antone Ambush, Tokyo Joe* (uncredited), *And Baby Makes Three* (uncredited).
1950: *The Arizona Cowboy.*
1954: *Them!* (uncredited).

William Eythe

> Bill Eythe is a young fellow, by the calendar, but he speaks with such a sense of sureness and experience, that it's easy to get the impression he's older than his 26 years. He likes the colorful things in life and would try anything, he says, for fun or adventure, if it wasn't illegal. He's a marked individualist.
>
> —Rosalind Shaffer in 1945

If mentioned today, William Eythe gets the typical "He never became a star because he didn't click." That might apply to some actors, but it is not true of Eythe. He *did* click at 20th Century–Fox and had a devoted bobbysoxer following. But, being the individualist that he was, he wasn't happy with movie stardom. He wanted to be his own man and live his life the way he wanted. He preferred the stage to film. On the verge of stardom, he left Hollywood for New York. A complex, conflicted man, he found a measure of success and happiness on the East Coast that he didn't have in the movie capital.

William John Joseph Eythe was born on April 7, 1918, in Mars, Pennsylvania, to Carl Sebastian Eythe (1886–1956), a Harmony Short Line railroad conductor, and Kathryn A. Walsh (1885–1970), and grew up in Pikesville and Franklin. A brother, Howard, and two sisters, Kathryn Jr. and Ruth, preceded him. When Bill was three months old, his eight-year-old sister Kathryn died after a brief illness. Father Carl later had his own contracting business.

Young Bill was sensitive and insecure, traits that would intensify. His brother Howard (nicknamed Dutch) was charismatic, popular, and an all-around athlete. During Howard's years at Pittsburgh's Carnegie Tech, he played varsity football and basketball and was an all–American baseball player. After graduation, he taught and coached at McDonogh School for more than 40 years. Having such a successful sibling might have cast a large shadow over Bill. He was not athletic but artistic—and also sickly. As a baby, he reportedly had a serious ear infection which never went away: Its effects included earaches, a buzzing sensation and slight dizziness, resulting in many sleepless nights.

When Bill was nine, he appeared in a school play as Peter Rabbit. Although he did it to please his mother, he found that he enjoyed acting. But his earliest ambitions were to be a director and a writer. An 11-year-old Bill could be found in the hills near his home making imaginary Westerns. Holding a shoebox (for a camera) and a megaphone, he directed his actors in stories he had written. When he tried to leap from one tree to another, he fell and broke both legs. He later converted an old barn into a theater where he presented his own plays.

He didn't see a professional play until he was 17: Maxwell Anderson's *Winterset* with Burgess Meredith and Margo, during its pre–Broadway run. "I'd been studying art at the Pittsburgh Art Institute, but the show intrigued me," Eythe later told Earl Wilson. "I was a pretty direct guy, so after the show I just busted backstage to see Margo and Meredith. I asked them how to get into show business." They suggested the School of Drama at Carnegie Tech.

In 1937, Eythe enrolled at his brother's alma mater Carnegie Tech, where he studied scenic design. He later credited teacher Edith Warman Skinner with correcting his long-time stammer, which made it possible for him to study acting and to be featured in many of the school's theater productions. He also took special acting classes from actress Mary Morris. In his sophomore year, he wrote and directed a series of 15-minute plays for the Dock Players at Point Chautauqua, New York.

In the summer of '40, Eythe was one of the Fox Chapel Players. Under Robert Gill's direction, the company performed in a renovated barn in Fox Chapel, a borough in Allegheny County, Pennsylvania. Each production ran Tuesday through Friday every week. The plays presented were *Room Service; The Last of Mrs. Cheyney; Post Road; Yes, My Darling Daughter; Liliom; Penny Wise; The Bat; Goodbye Again; You Can't Take It with You* and *Invitation for a Murder*. Regarding the latter, the *Pittsburgh Sun-Telegraph*'s Herb Kubly wrote, "[As] the typical dastardly charmer, Mr. Eythe proves his flair for sophisticated decadence and occasionally tends to overplay his hand."

Columnist Harold V. Cohen wrote, "There are a couple of young fellows with the Fox Chapel Playhouse, William Eythe and Carl Betz, who show plenty of promise." (Betz, then a Carnegie Tech student, went on to TV fame as the husband on *The Donna Reed Show*.)

In 1941, when the local Kaufmann's department store put on the musical revue *Take a Tip*, Eythe had the lead opposite Broadway and Hollywood actress Polly Rowles, a Carnegie Tech alum. (She had also done *The Last of Mrs. Cheyney* and *You Can't Take It with You* with Eythe at Fox Chapel.) During *Take a Tip*'s run, Eythe had to do double duty when Carl Betz, playing the lead in the Carnegie Tech play *The Beggar's Opera*, was taken to the hospital with a severe throat ailment. Eythe spent the night before cramming for the part and did the two shows back to back.

In April 1941, Eythe appeared in the Pittsburgh Playhouse's *Lend an Ear*, which featured sketches and songs by Charles Gaynor and was directed by Fred Burleigh. Bill was also a member of a theater group called Scotch and Soda which produced musicals at the college; he wrote songs and designed sets and costumes.

20th Century–Fox hired William Eythe for his resemblance to their top star, Tyrone Power.

After he graduated from Carnegie Tech, Eythe, with the help of Mary Morris and Fred Burleigh, got a spot with the South Shore Players in Cohasset, Massachusetts. He was in such plays as *Ladies in Retirement, The Male Animal, George Washington Slept Here* and *Lend an Ear. Variety* said of the latter,

> William Eythe, a good-looking versatile juvenile who makes his work outstanding, can sell a romantic or comic song equally well, he can dance and his dramatic work here in previous productions this summer has demonstrated acting talent. Eythe is definitely a new personality for Hollywood and Broadway inspection.

The local press also predicted stardom for him. "Slender, handsome, curly haired, he may make the movies," wrote the *Berkshire Eagle*.

Harold V. Cohen called Eythe the "acting sensation along the straw hat circuit." Jane Cowl was interested in him as a leading man, the South Shore Players wanted him as an assistant director, and agents enticed him with Broadway offers. (He read for Eddie Cantor's *Banjo Eyes*, but didn't get it.)

With Ruth Chatterton, Eythe toured Canada and New England in the play *Caprice* in 1941. According to Eythe, he was nervous and read badly at his audition in front of Chatterton, and so confused that he bowed himself off stage saying, "Thanks very much! I've been delightful." Chatterton was amused and gave him the part. She praised Eythe's "natural ability.... He knows instinctively the right thing to do."

Producer Oscar Serlin cast him in Ferenc Molnár's *The King's Maid* (1941), but it closed out of town and never reached Broadway. Eythe was an announcer at New York television station WNBT, where he emceed a variety show. On his own show, *Radio City Matinee*, he interviewed notables visiting the city.

Serlin signed Eythe for *The Moon Is Down*, which opened on Broadway on April 4, 1942. Adapted by John Steinbeck from his novel, it was about Nazis occupying a small Norwegian village. Eythe had the intense role of neurotic Nazi Lt. Tonder, lonely and love-starved, who gets himself killed by the girl with whom he wants to spend time. Reviewers praised the newcomer but thought his part tangential to the main story. During one scene, a hysterical Eythe was slapped by a fellow officer; the nightly blow caused further damage to his eardrums. (During World War II, he was classified 4-F because of his eardrums.) Not long after the show opened, Eythe was heard on Kate Smith's radio show doing a vignette from the play.

Before the *Moon Is Down* run ended in June '42, Darryl F. Zanuck bought the screen rights and signed the darkly handsome Eythe to a contract—some say because of his resemblance to the studio's top star Tyrone Power, who was then in the Marines.

For his screen debut, Eythe was given the supporting part of Gerald Tetley in director William Wellman's *The Ox-Bow Incident* (1943). Based on the novel by Walter Van Tilburg Clark, it centered on a posse's search for men who rustled cattle and killed a man. Incited by Major Tetley (Frank Conroy), the group finds and lynches three men they believe to be guilty. In Clark's novel, the major's son Gerald was "always half sick, kept to himself and the big library as much as his father would let him, hated the ranching life and despised yet feared the kind of men Tetley had to deal with now." The major, only interested in "power and cruelty," is ashamed of his gentle son and eventually forces him to participate in the hanging. "I'll have no female boys bearing my name," Tetley says to his reluctant son. "You'll do your part, and say nothing more." One character in the novel muses that Gerald is "passionate and womanish, but with a man's conscience and pride...." In the novel, that conscience leads Gerald to take his own life (he does not commit suicide in the movie). Eythe says few words in the film, relying more on expressions, until the conclusion when he finally stands up to his father, calling him depraved. It's his big moment and he makes the most of it.

It was expected that Eythe would recreate his stage role of Lt. Tonder in the screen version of *The Moon Is Down*. But it began filming in November '42 with German-born Peter van Eyck assigned to the part. Nothing came of the suggestion that Eythe be loaned to Sam Goldwyn for *The North Star* (1943), even though he was available at the time.

It would be a while before Eythe was cast in his next picture, *The Song of Bernadette* (1943). Based on the Franz Werfel novel, it tells the true story of Bernadette Soubirous (Oscar-winner Jennifer Jones), who is not believed when she claims to have seen visions of the Blessed Virgin Mary at the Massabielle grotto in Lourdes. Michaela O'Harra of the *Arizona Daily Star* praised Eythe's "fine performance" as Bernadette's friend and admirer Antoine Nicolau, calling it "unobtrusive but heartwarming." The tender scene where Antoine hands flowers to a departing Bernadette and says goodbye is beautifully played by both actors. While his part is smallish, he was lucky to be in such a distinguished and popular movie.

During the filming of *Bernadette*, Eythe began dating Alicia Díaz, daughter of the Honduras treasury chief; she played a small role in the film. They briefly contemplated marriage in June 1943. He was also seen around town with Anne Baxter, Dorothy

Jennifer Jones and Eythe in *The Song of Bernadette* (1943). Jones won the Best Actress Oscar for her performance; Eythe was awarded top-billing.

McGuire, Ann Corio, Madeleine LeBeau, Nancy Kelly and Carol Thurston. Baxter was pegged as a serious contender and the press was always guessing whether wedding bells would ring.

Eythe turned down the lead in *Immortal Sergeant* because he thought it would typecast him in weakling roles, even though the character in that film (ultimately played by Henry Fonda) overcomes his fears and becomes a hero.

In October 1942, Maxwell Anderson's World War II play *The Eve of St. Mark* with William Prince and Mary Rolfe premiered on Broadway. A hit, it attracted Hollywood's interest. *Life* magazine wrote, "Spiced with the crisp soldier dialog of Anderson's *What Price Glory?* this play has more mood than plot, is warmer in emotions, embraces the home front as well as the foxholes." The title refers to the legend that ghosts of persons slated to die are seen on the eve of St. Mark (April 24). Fox bought the screen rights for $300,000 and cast some of the Broadway performers, notably Michael O'Shea. Eythe and Anne Baxter played the William Prince and Mary Rolfe roles. Screenwriter George Seaton had to be careful adapting the play, as some situations and dialogue were deemed inappropriate by the Production Code.

The Eve of St. Mark is broken up into three sections: the romance of Pvt. Quizz West and Janet Feller, who grew up on neighboring farms; Quizz and his fellow soldiers at Camp Grace, where they joke about gambling and women; and the same soldiers holed up in a cave on a Philippines island fighting the Japanese, malaria and each other. While the trio of stories don't exactly jell, each is well-acted and holds interest. Quizz has less depth than the other characters, but Eythe's thoughtful performance as the idealistic dreamer in love with Baxter's Janet is sincere and well-played. He and Baxter have wonderful chemistry, and their love scenes have "exquisite tenderness" (*Motion Picture Herald*).

The play ended with the boys' sacrifice on the island. The movie's preview audiences were not happy with this outcome, so it was changed to imply that they survived and would soon be coming home. This negated the title and the

Anne Baxter and Eythe appeared together in two films, *The Eve of St. Mark* (1944) and *A Royal Scandal* (1945). In between, they almost did *Sunday Dinner for a Soldier* (1944), but Eythe was injured and replaced with John Hodiak.

legend, but it appeased the romantics and families with boys in the service, who didn't need a depressing reminder of the toll the war was taking.

The Eve of St. Mark put Eythe on the map—and in the fan magazines—as someone who was definitely going places.

"None of 20th Century–Fox's new male finds is getting a greater build-up than William Eythe," wrote Edwin Schallert. "In fact, the promotion of his career reminds of Tyrone Power's in an earlier day at the studio. He is definitely winning the 'breaks.'" These "breaks" included roles in *House of Chedworth* with Ida Lupino and *The Story of a Guy*. Neither movie came through.

Wilson (1944), a biopic of President Woodrow Wilson, was Darryl F. Zanuck's expensive pet project—and a box office flop. Regardless, it was nominated for ten Academy Awards and won five. Its story begins in 1909 when Wilson (played by Alexander Knox), president of Princeton, is in the football stands with his family watching Princeton play Yale. Wilson brags to his daughter about George Felton (Eythe), who then proceeds to fumble the ball. (Jim Wheeler doubled Eythe on the football field.) After Princeton loses, a dejected Felton passes by Wilson, who reassures him with a kind word. From there, we see Felton acting as a cheerleader in Wilson's campaigns for governor and president; then at a White House reception and at a party when Wilson is elected to a second term. Felton is silently sitting by Wilson's wife when the Great War is declared. Publicity materials describe Felton as a friend of Wilson's but with very little dialogue, he fails to stand out in his fleeting scenes. In the character's only sustained moment, he visits Wilson to say goodbye before going to war; it's a good scene for Eythe, but since a friendship between the men had not really been established, it falls somewhat flat. We never do know what happens to George Felton after he goes to war.

Eythe was interested in portraying drunkard Johnny Nolan in *A Tree Grows in Brooklyn*, but it was not to be. Fox announced him for the leads in *Irish Eyes Are Smiling* with June Haver and *Don Q, Son of Zorro*. The latter had been meant for Tyrone Power as a follow-up to his *The Mark of Zorro* (1940). *A Tree Grows in Brooklyn* didn't make it onto Eythe's schedule, and *Don Q* wasn't made at all.

Instead, he replaced Randolph Scott in *Wing and a Prayer: The Story of Carrier X* (1944). Months after the Pearl Harbor attack, an American carrier is sent on a decoy mission to deceive the Japanese into thinking the U.S. fleet is scattered all over the Pacific. This eventually leads to the Battle of Midway. The film's stars were Don Ameche and Dana Andrews; third-billed Eythe had one of his best roles as ex–movie star Hallam Scott, nicknamed Oscar because of the Academy Award which he carries around for good luck. At first, Ensign Scott is egotistical, craving the spotlight, but he quickly learns to be a team player. Eythe is at his best reacting to the death of his buddy Gus (Richard Crane), silently packing Gus' belongings to be sent home. His teary restraint makes the scene one of the film's highlights. Eythe also has a fun moment describing to other crew members what it's like kissing a glamour girl in the movies. Columnist E.B. Radcliffe wrote, "One William Eythe, who reminds you of a Tyrone Power on the stocky and rugged side, plays a movie actor who makes good as a flier after an unimpressive start. Willie has plenty of personality."

Eythe was in demand. He was announced for *Take It or Leave It* and *All-Out Arlene* (with Dorothy McGuire), and was sought for the male lead in the Broadway show *Bloomer Girl*. (Fox said no and David Brooks got the stage role opposite Celeste Holm.)

At the beginning of May 1944, Eythe was cast in *Sunday Dinner for a Soldier* with

Dana Andrews (left) and Eythe in *Wing and a Prayer: The Story of Carrier X* (1944). Eythe is packing up his dead buddy's belongings.

Anne Baxter, about a lonely soldier and the poor family that spends time with him. His first scenes were shot at Drew Field in Tampa, Florida, while the rest of the location work took place in Sarasota. "This is my first trip to Florida," he told the *Tampa Tribune*, "and I am certain I shall feel right at home because California looks much like Florida."

Two weeks into filming, Eythe was in a car accident: His vehicle left the highway and crashed into two palm trees. Suffering minor facial lacerations and broken ribs, he was sent back to Hollywood to recover. John Hodiak replaced him in the movie (and, two years later, married Anne Baxter).

In September 1944, Eythe went before the cameras as leading man to Tallulah Bankhead in *A Royal Scandal* (1945). Adapted from the play *Die Zarin* by Lajos Biró and Melchior Lengyel, the sparkling comedy of the hussy and the hussar was produced by Ernst Lubitsch and directed by Otto Preminger. Eythe's character of Alexei Chernoff was first envisioned for Charles Boyer, but Bill got the part and pleased Lubitsch with his performance. According to Hedda Hopper, Lubitsch viewed the rushes and called Eythe "the greatest star material I've run into in twenty years." No doubt this was mere publicity hyperbole, but it had to mean something to the actor to hear such praise.

Overenthusiastic, naïve and devoted, Alexei becomes the object of Catherine the Great's (Bankhead) desire and she quickly promotes him to commander of the palace guards. Things are complicated by Alexei's fiancée, Countess Anna Jaschikoff (Anne Baxter), who is Catherine's favorite lady-in-waiting, and by a simmering revolution. Eythe's portrayal of the idealistic lieutenant is excellent and he's absolutely gorgeous (especially with his mustache and beard). "You look simply divine in that uniform," an infatuated Tallulah growls. "[I]f you haven't taken William Eythe seriously before, you will now as the empress' flame," wrote the *Spokesman Review*. "And when you see him in his white Russian army uniform, you are apt to get as excited about him as the empress did."

Eythe later called *A Royal Scandal* the movie he most enjoyed making. He told Earl Wilson,

> We had so much fun that it's a wonder the picture ever got made. For some reason I struck Tallulah funny. The simplest thing I said made her fall on the floor laughing. She'd give that husky laugh and tell me, "Ahahaha, darling, say that again, ahahahaha!"
>
> She'd laugh so hard her eyes would puff up, and they'd have to stop work to put ice on them so we could go on. If you print that I'll be shot.

(Eythe was known around Hollywood and Broadway for his outrageous sense of the absurd.) The actor split his skin-tight pants twice when he bent over to pick Tallulah up.

Eythe was considered for a role in *State Fair* (1945) with Jeanne Crain but lost out to Dana Andrews. There was some buzz around the studio that Fox would buy the screen rights to W. Somerset Maugham's *The Razor's Edge*, and Eythe wanted the lead badly. But he had no chance; Darryl Zanuck waited for Tyrone Power to be discharged from the Marines and cast him in the role.

Charles Coburn was one of the main players in *A Royal Scandal* and Eythe commented at the time what a great actor Coburn was and what an inspiration he had been to him. Coburn headlined *Colonel Effingham's Raid* (1946) as a retired Army man who

A Royal Scandal (1945) was Eythe's favorite, and Tallulah Bankhead became one of his closest friends.

returns to his hometown of Fredericksville, Georgia, gets after the politicians to restore a historic courthouse, and tries to give a boost to the townspeople's civic pride. Effingham's cousin, newspaper reporter Al Marbury (Eythe), initially does not stand behind him in his efforts. Quarreling with Marbury throughout is society editor Ella Sue Dozier (Joan Bennett), who acts as his conscience and eventually becomes his romantic interest. After Marbury enlists in the National Guard, there's a nicely played scene where Effingham tells him how proud he is of him and gives him his watch.

The story is set in 1940 and there's a lot of war talk. It started filming in December 1944, but was not released until February 1946. Critic Harold V. Cohen thought it "lightweight," and that Eythe "deserves a little more encouragement than this, especially from his own Twentieth Century–Fox bosses. For the movie ... is a minor thing the major lots usually reserve for a loan-out from some other studio."

At the beginning of 1945, Eythe was in New York when Fox called him back to do *Dragonwyck*. "Seems like they can't do without this attractive youngster in Hollywood," wrote Sheilah Graham. Producer Ernst Lubitsch wanted Eythe for the role of Dr. Jeff Turner, a rather dull secondary part compared to the star Vincent Price. Ultimately, Glenn Langan was cast in the role.

Four months later, Eythe was assigned the movie for which he is best remembered: *The House on 92nd Street* (1945). Produced by Louis de Rochemont and directed by Henry Hathaway, the movie, per the opening written prologue, was "adapted from cases in the espionage files of the Federal Bureau of Investigation. Produced with the FBI's complete cooperation, it could not be made public until the first atomic bomb was dropped on Japan."

Told in semi-documentary style (with Reed Hadley's resonant narration), the movie details the FBI's efforts to round up Mr. Christopher and his nest of German foreign spies, who are attempting to get Process 97—the secret ingredient of the atomic bomb. The film was based on two separate FBI cases.

Bill Dietrich (Eythe), an American college student of German ancestry, is approached by the German American Bund to train in a German spy school for undercover work in the States. Dietrich contacts the FBI and becomes a double agent. His character was based on German-born William G. Sebold (1899–1970), who helped the Feds get the goods on the Duquesne Spy Ring.

Eythe spent about five months in New York's Greenwich Village while *The House on 92nd Street* was being shot on location. Sheilah Graham claimed that his three most frequent visitors were Tallulah Bankhead, Greta Garbo and Ruth Chatterton. It didn't take Bill long to get irritated by bobbysoxers who followed him around the city. Various incidents were reported, included the story of a group of girls who ripped his coat to pieces and stole his watch.

"William Eythe's option picked up at 20th Century–Fox for another year," Sheilah Graham reported in July 1945. "Bill has quite a following since he wore those tights in *A Royal Scandal*."

The lead (opposite Vivian Blaine) in the musical *Doll Face* was going to be Eythe's next, but it didn't happen. Graham was glad it didn't: "They made him grow a Hitler mustache for the role. It didn't suit him. His face is too round for such goings on. Bill came back from New York with a dark tan—says he got it on the balcony of his Greenwich Village apartment."

In September 1945, Eythe was named a Star of Tomorrow by theater owners in the

Charles Wagenheim, Alfred Linder, Eythe and Lydia St. Clair in *The House on 92nd Street* (1945).

Motion Picture Exhibitor. That same month, he started filming the Jerome Kern musical *Centennial Summer*. It revolved around two sisters (Jeanne Crain and Linda Darnell) competing for the same man (Frenchman Cornel Wilde) during Philadelphia's 1876 Centennial exposition. On the sidelines of this triangle is obstetrician Ben Phelps (fourth-billed Eythe); he loves Edith (Darnell) and wants to marry her, but she delights in keeping him on a string. Eythe's role is decidedly secondary, but he's handsome and charming in what he's required to do. ("[He has] little to do through the picture but pout between his sideburns"—Gene Handsaker.) He gets to sing parts of "All Through the Day" and "In Love in Vain"—but he is dubbed by David Street.

Nineteen forty-five saw Eythe seriously dating singer Margaret Whiting. "Bill and I thought we were head-over-heels in love," Margaret remarked in her autobiography. She went on:

> We were very romantic. We went to premieres and parties and spent a lot of time alone at his house. Bill was bright enough to know that he would never be Tyrone Power. Bill was an extremely sexual person and he was a sweet and tender lover, but there was something missing. He said he loved me, but I could never put my finger on the dissatisfaction.

Margaret later put her finger on it when Eythe "discovered, or admitted, that he actually preferred men."

One of those men was actor Lon McCallister. The two had a lot in common, including a love of animals, traveling, writing and painting (some of Eythe's work was exhibited). Lon had been typecast as shy boy-next-door types, roles that fit the real-life clean-cut Lon perfectly, as he neither smoked nor drank. By 1944, Eythe had a serious alcohol problem, one that would worsen as time went on. McCallister would remain a constant, faithful companion to Eythe for the rest of Bill's life. They were very discreet with their romance. In fact, when Margaret Whiting's *It Might as Well Be Spring: A Musical Autobiography* was published in 1987, McCallister was livid that Whiting had "outed" Eythe—so angry that he threw her book in the river near his home.

Fan magazines such as *Modern Screen* played up the Eythe-McCallister friendship in their pages, showing the two at the beach, hanging around each other's houses, being together at parties. The most notorious layout (nowadays) was called "Terrific Trio!," which dealt in part with Bill, Lon and their friend Ray Sperry and the time leading up to McCallister's entrance into the military. Marcia Daughtrey wrote in *Modern Screen*,

> One night shortly before Lon was inducted, Ray had a date, so Bill Eythe and Lon went out to dinner in duo instead of the usual triplicate. Offhandedly, Bill produced a small box. "Here's something to remember me by," he said. "Aw, nuts, don't look at me like that—this isn't anything much. It'll turn green in ten days unless you paint it with your mother's finger polish."
>
> The box contained a friendship ring—a wide gold, very masculine band. "I'll wish it on," Bill said gruffly as he pushed it into place on Lon's finger. "Don't take it off until you get to your basic training camp. And—er—when you take it off, well, then you can read the inscription on the inside."
>
> Lon looked hard at the handsome ring. Then he shook hands with Bill. "Gosh, the things you do find in dime stores," he kidded, but there was no kidding and no superficiality in the long, steady look he exchanged with the man who has been his fellow-dramatic struggler and fellow prankster for many precious years.

Reportedly, Darryl Zanuck read about Eythe slipping a ring on McCallister's finger, hit the roof and demanded that the two never again be featured together in print. The trouble with the report of Zanuck's outrage is that it's belied by the fact that Eythe and McCallister *were* subsequently featured together in print. In 1944, the sweet story above came across as entirely innocent and it's a given that Zanuck approved it and would not have been shocked by it. Many twenty-first century "film historians" like to put their own spin on stories like this and interpret them using current sensibilities.

Eythe had a serious romance with Italian-born Patrizia Cobb Chapman, known as Buff Cobb. An aspiring actress, under contract to Fox and doing bit parts, she was the daughter of opera singer Frank Chapman and playwright Elizabeth Cobb; her maternal grandfather was author and humorist Irvin S. Cobb and her stepmother was mezzo-soprano Gladys Swarthout. Buff was newly divorced from attorney Greg Bautzer when she started dating Eythe.

Eythe appeared on radio with Tallulah Bankhead (*This Is My Best*) and in an adaptation of *The House on 92nd Street* on *This Is Your FBI*. At the end of '45, he was having eye trouble stemming from his accident in Florida the year before; glasses, rest and eye exercises were prescribed.

In December, at a benefit in Chicago, Eythe felt that he and the other stars were not being treated nicely and he made "the shortest benefit speech on record," reported Dorothy Kilgallen. She went on: "When introduced as the actor who took such a terrific beating in *The House on 92nd Street*, he went to the mike, said: 'It wasn't as bad as the beating I'm taking here tonight' and walked off."

Meanwhile, Fox announced him for a remake of *Seventh Heaven* with Jeanne Crain and the part of the villain in *Methinks the Lady* (which would later become *Whirlpool*). He was also considered for a supporting role in *13 Rue Madeleine* (1946).

But he wasn't cast in anything. MGM tried to make a deal with Fox to get Eythe under contract. Zanuck nixed the offer, giving Eythe a new contract and more money. Yet Bill spent the first half of 1946 not working on screen. He did some radio, notably joining Gene Tierney and Clifton Webb on *Hollywood Star Time* in an adaptation of *Laura*. In March, he was hospitalized with pleurisy.

It was decided that Eythe would go to England to do *Meet Me at Dawn*, set to start shooting in June 1946. Produced by Marcel Hellman at London's Dunham Studios, the film would be distributed by 20th Century–Fox. Eythe was the first Fox actor to be involved in a film lend-lease deal and he was given a bonus of $50,000 (all taxes paid) to do the picture. He also obtained visas to visit several places in Europe.

Meet Me at Dawn, set in 1900 Paris, is Eythe's most obscure credit today, but it was one of his best chances to show off his light comedy skills. He plays an expert duelist who makes a career out of fighting duels for others. His life is turned upside down when he falls for a mysterious woman (Hazel Court).

Some sources claim that Zanuck sent Eythe out of the country to end his relationship with Lon McCallister. Then, these sources contend, Zanuck was enraged when Lon joined Bill on location, and the two traveled to Paris after the shooting was over. This scenario has no basis in fact. There is, obviously, a record of Eythe leaving the country (to make the movie in England) but there is none for McCallister. In fact, when Eythe left the U.S., Lon was finishing up *The Red House* and then immediately started *Bob, Son of Battle* (aka *Thunder in the Valley*), which continued filming until late September '46. He enrolled in art classes at Chapman College in Orange, California, and then in November he made personal appearances in New York.

Meanwhile, Eythe finished making *Meet Me at Dawn* and did some traveling. In October, he was back in England to represent Fox at a command performance before the king and queen. He returned to the U.S. in November for the New York premiere of *The Razor's Edge* (McCallister was also there). He then spent Thanksgiving with his family in Mars. In no hurry to get back to Fox, Bill spent part of Christmas with James Mason and his family in Greenwich, Connecticut.

Throughout 1946, Eythe had grown restless, fed up with some of his film roles and the unwanted fan attention which he saw as an invasion of privacy. He wanted to get back to the stage and considered his deal with Fox a sort of bondage. (Because of his Fox contract, he missed the chance to appear with James Mason on Broadway in *Bathsheba*.)

After seven months away from Hollywood, he returned in January 1947 and asked for and received a release from his Fox contract. He detested the romantic parts given him, and wanted more character roles. "I am no Tyrone Power or any other glamour actor," he remarked to Lawrence Perry, "I am not romantic."

Others have claimed that Zanuck, still angry with Eythe for defying his order to stop seeing McCallister, fired both when they returned from overseas. This does not jibe with the facts. McCallister, who was under contract to producer Sol Lesser, was cast in Fox's *Scudda Hoo! Scudda Hay!*, which started filming the month after Eythe was released. Only after Lesser cancelled McCallister's contract in November did the actor's deal with 20th Century–Fox come to an end.

Eythe later told Marjory Adams another reason he wasn't happy in Hollywood:

It isn't the acting I mind, but the living up to what the publicity men expect of you. It's like swimming around a goldfish pool. You have to be seen with the right stars, especially at previews, and you must own a swimming pool if you amount to anything at all. Everywhere you go you must manage to be photographed with important people, no matter who your real friends happen to be.

Your home, your automobiles, your girlfriends and even your dogs must be photogenic. Eventually you begin to lose all your sense of humor and find yourself believing what the papers print and what the publicity men have built you into. By then you haven't a life or an idea of your own—you are just what they have forced you into being.

Eythe told friends, "There must be a better life than being an actor in the films," and began contemplating play offers. He also did radio.

On June 2, 1947, he married Buff Cobb. They planned to spend their honeymoon doing plays—separately. On June 30, he began a week-long run of Tennessee Williams' *The Glass Menagerie* (as the son) at the County Theatre in Suffern, New York. He had arranged with Tallulah Bankhead to take Buff under her wing and give her a role in her touring engagement of *Private Lives*. Eythe supposedly said, "Give her the works, Tallu. If she comes through a summer with you, still loving the theater, we'll look around for a play with which to open on Broadway [together]."

Eythe and Buff were reunited when he went to Westport, Connecticut, to star in the comedy *French Without Tears* on July 7. Don Peters and Virginia Gilmore co-starred. He then did *Dear Ruth* at the Ivoryton Playhouse.

While Eythe was in Connecticut, Jimmie Fidler wrote in his column: "Actors in need of a good role to bolster fading prestige: William Eythe." Little did Fidler know that Eythe couldn't have cared less; he was currently in his element.

He acted again in *Dear Ruth* in Princeton, New Jersey, at the McCarter Theatre, with Doris Dowling as his leading lady. *The Glass Menagerie* became a favorite of Eythe's and he did three straight summer engagements of it in Beverly, Massachusetts, at the Beverly Summer Theatre; Cohasset, Massachusetts, with the South Shore Players (the group with which he had started), and at Connecticut's Ivoryton Playhouse. Then it was on to *Dear Ruth* with the Van Wyck Players at the Roosevelt Theatre in Beacon, New York.

Finished with his summer stock commitments, Eythe starred on the radio series *Exploring the Unknown*, playing an aeronautical engineer in "Crash Detective." He was going to do an East Coast tour of *The Last Rose*, but was persuaded to come back to Hollywood by producers Pine-Thomas to replace Richard Arlen in *Hard to Kill*.

Hard to Kill, eventually renamed *Mr. Reckless* (1948), covered familiar territory: Crazy-tempered café owner Gus (Nestor Paiva) is engaged to waitress Betty (Barbara Britton) but she's in love with Gus' friend, oil rigger Jeff (Eythe). The fated-to-end-badly triangle has been done to death on celluloid. The rest of *Mr. Reckless* is typical Pine-Thomas: comedy relief and a fair amount of action, especially at the conclusion. While the affable Eythe is the leading man, he is overshadowed by the character actors in the cast.

The rumor mill had the Eythes expecting a baby in November '47, but both denied it. In the six months they had been married, they saw very little of each other. Buff was in Chicago with Tallulah in *Private Lives*. Pine-Thomas wanted Eythe to do *Captain China* for them. (The production was delayed and when it finally went before the cameras in 1949, John Payne starred.)

In January 1948, Buff filed suit for divorce in Chicago, alleging that on September 28 and 30 of the previous year, Eythe had struck her with "great violence."

On February 18, *The Glass Menagerie* began a limited engagement at Los Angeles' Las Palmas Theater. Eythe produced (with Franklin Gilbert), staged and starred as the narrator and the son. Joan Lorring, Leif Erickson and Mary Perry rounded out the cast. A critical and box office success, the production moved to the Coronet Theater on March 30. (Paul Lambert and then John Hubbard replaced Erickson.) It broke all house records and was extended until April 18.

By March, Buff Cobb had left the cast of *Private Lives*. She had been ill; some sources claim she was recovering from an unspecified major operation, others say that she had strep throat. All agreed that she and Bill had reconciled and were together in Los Angeles.

The Glass Menagerie's success impelled Eythe to next do the revue *Lend an Ear* (which he had done in his pre–Hollywood days), this time with new material by composer Charles Gaynor. Eythe produced (Mars Productions) with Franklin Gilbert, directed and performed. Choreography was by Gower Champion. The cast included Anne Anderson, Carol Channing, Hal Hackett, Gene Nelson, Al Checco, Dorothy Babbs and Linda Ware. "It is a revue without a message or social significance," Eythe remarked, "and I hope that because it is unique in this and numerous other respects it will be entertaining." The only similarity between this and Eythe's previous *Lend an Ear* was the title and a couple of songs.

Perhaps as a way to make some money for this new venture, which was to open in June at the Las Palmas, Eythe accepted a movie role. By day he worked on Pine-Thomas' *Special Agent* (1949); at night he rehearsed and fine-tuned *Lend an Ear*.

Special Agent harkened back to *The House on 92nd Street*, complete with narration (by Truman Bradley). A departure for Pine-Thomas, it told in semi-documentary style the story of brothers Paul and Edmond Devereaux (George Reeves and Paul Valentine), who steal a train payroll and kill three men. Eythe plays the main railroad detective on their trail and does a "crisp and engaging job" (*Pittsburgh Post-Gazette's* Harold V. Cohen). He is especially effective in the quiet scene where he consoles Lucille Peters (Laura Elliott) after the murder of her father.

The reconciliation between the Eythes didn't last and Buff moved to Chicago. By early June '48, she had retained her ex-husband Greg Bautzer to handle her divorce—a move Harrison Carroll called "typical Hollywood news."

Lend an Ear opened at the Las Palmas on June 16. The *Los Angeles Times'* Edwin Schallert called it "top-flight ... the cleverest little show to hit the town in many a month. It is a little show that turns into a big show before it is through, one that looks like a sure-fire hit." Singled out as standouts by Fred Broomfield of the *Valley Times* were Anne Anderson ("with her peculiar and infectious brand of comedy"), Al Checco ("excellent comedian with a refreshing delivery style") and Eythe ("good quality performance in diversified parts"). Others raved about newcomer Carol Channing. An instant hit, *Lend an Ear* played to capacity audiences. "I have a chip on my shoulder," Eythe told Aline Mosby. "I want to show Hollywood how to produce. It can be done efficiently and effectively." Hedda Hopper quoted Raymond Massey as calling it "such darned good theater." Bob Thomas noted that in one skit, Eythe "gets in a few jibes at his former boss, Darryl Zanuck." So popular was *Lend an Ear* that Eythe planned to take it to Broadway: The original cast would go to New York while another company stayed at the Las

Palmas. Several Broadway producers wanted a piece of *Lend an Ear*, with William R. Katzell (co-producer of *Finian's Rainbow*) outbidding all the others.

Eythe's run of successes was spoiled somewhat in mid–November: Edith Gwynn reported that Buff Cobb was considering her current divorce and seeking an annulment instead, alleging that their marriage was never consummated. This must have been embarrassing for Eythe, since he was very much in the closet at the time.

Lend an Ear's two-week tryouts began in Boston on December 2, 1948, with Hal Gerson taking over as director from Eythe. Added to the cast were William Tabbert and Jenny Lou Law. (Law, along with Al Checco, was at the Pittsburgh Playhouse with Eythe in the early '40s.) The Beantown critics and audiences loved it. Cyrus Durgin of the *Boston Globe* called it a "honey" and "completely fun," and was sure it would be a "Broadway clickeroo."

It sure was. *Lend an Ear* bowed at New York's National Theatre on December 16, to more raves. "It is so good," wrote the *New York Daily News*' John Chapman, "it does not need any names to carry it—but it should make some. The first-nighters were enchanted to the point of cheering." In particular, Chapman predicted success for Carol Channing, Yvonne Adair and Gene Nelson. Kaspar Monahan wrote that Eythe "reveals himself as a song-and-dance man and a jester of no mean ability in a number of the sketches...." Most reviewers singled out his skits "Neurotic You and Psychopathic Me" and "The Gladiola Girl." "He is not spectacular as a singer or dancer," wrote Donald Kirkley of *The Baltimore Sun*, "but he is clever, versatile and at ease in all the revue departments. And he has a candid, friendly, cheerful attitude which wins the audience from the first."

Buff Cobb changed her mind about her annulment and decided she wanted to reconcile with the talk-of-the-town Eythe. Hedda Hopper quoted him as remarking to Buff, "Thanks, Honey, but it's too late now." On February 12, 1949, in Chicago, she received an uncontested divorce after reiterating that Eythe had struck her twice in September '47. A month later, Cobb wed radio announcer–actor Mike Wallace. (They did *Mike and Buff*, a radio and TV talk show, together. Years after they divorced, Wallace became famous for his long stint on TV's *60 Minutes*.)

While doing *Lend an Ear*, Eythe also performed on radio (*Theater Guild on the Air*, *The Cavalcade of America*) and TV (Ed Sullivan's *Toast of the Town*, *Philco Television Playhouse*).

In July 1949, Eythe took a ten-day vacation from *Lend an Ear* (Hal Hackett was his replacement). En route to Hollywood by car, he and Lon McCallister met five girls in Valparaiso, Indiana, and spent about two hours telling them about Hollywood while their car was being serviced. Bill and Lon ate at a Valparaiso restaurant. "They were just wonderful," one girl gushed. "You would never dream they were movie stars unless you recognized them from pictures and their work on the screen. They were more like old friends."

While Eythe was in Hollywood, he was offered a play called *Danny Larkin* by James Vincent McGee. He wanted Joan Lorring to do it with him; she was too busy, so he turned it down.

He returned to New York and *Lend an Ear* just in time to be featured with the whole cast on the TV series *Tonight on Broadway*. The innovative show took cameras to the theaters where the shows were appearing and filmed excerpts for home audiences.

On September 18, 1949, Eythe starred as detective Philip Marlowe in a *Philco Television Playhouse* adaptation of Raymond Chandler's newest novel *The Little Sister*. Harold

Lon McCallister and Dorothy Babbs (a member of the cast of the play *Lend an Ear*) confer with Eythe. The two men had a longtime romantic relationship that ended with Eythe's death.

V. Cohen thought Eythe "wasn't too bad" as the famous private eye, but deemed the episode a shambles: "The show was pretty poorly produced and directed, too; several times the people were on the screen seconds before the action started." Another mishap: In rehearsal, Eythe apparently kissed his leading lady Patricia Breslin too hard and broke one of her front teeth!

In October, *Lend an Ear* lost Carol Channing, an important part of the show; her unique style wowed them every night. She and Eythe were great pals, and he often took her to parties. It wasn't long before she caught the attention of other producers—and Eythe encouraged her to branch out. Channing went right into Broadway's *Gentlemen Prefer Blondes*, which made her a star. She and Eythe remained friends and she always credited him with giving her a break; she called *Lend an Ear* her favorite show. She wrote in her autobiography,

> Bill and I worked beautifully together, and we shared … a theater experience which amounted to a spiritual journey, or so it seemed to us. I didn't know I was being used as a "beard" for him and Bud [McCallister], but it doesn't matter, because Bill and I instinctively protected each other. He was an excitable child at heart. That heart was pure. He was so proud of every last person involved with his *Lend an Ear*, including me.

In November 1949, Eythe decided to leave *Lend an Ear*. He wanted more money, but his co-producers, William Katzell and Franklin Gilbert, turned thumbs down. John Beal took his place. Eythe remained as producer, albeit from afar at times.

He took an option on the play *The Valentines* by Richard Houghton Hepburn (Katharine's brother) and hoped to premiere it on the West Coast and then bring it to Broadway. There was a lot of talk but it eventually fell through.

On November 6, Eythe appeared on radio in the drama "The Traitor" for *Theatre Guild of the Air*—with Tyrone Power, the actor with whom he was always compared. Nina Foch was also featured. A week later, with Kim Hunter, he did another *Philco Television Playhouse* episode, "The Promise." ("Eythe did a bang-up job … in fact, it was one of the best TV performances that's ever come through here."—Harold V. Cohen.)

Beginning production in November '49, the film *Customs Agent* was another semi-documentary with more than a passing resemblance to *The House on 92nd Street*. As disgraced customs agent Bert Stewart, Eythe joins a gang smuggling a diluted form of streptomycin into Shanghai. The story was topical: Streptomycin was then being used to treat tuberculosis, meningitis and bacterial infections, and the black market took advantage of the need for this "miracle drug." In August '49, a Japanese black-market ring was caught selling baking soda as streptomycin. That same month, a Chinese freighter was seized with $200,000 worth of contraband, which included streptomycin. With this as a takeoff point, Columbia got Russell S. Hughes and Malcolm Stuart Boylan to fashion a screenplay based on a story by Harold Jacob Smith. Eythe does his typical solid job and it's a good movie, but he had to be wondering when the semi-docs would end.

After *Customs Agent*, Columbia offered him a term contract. Eythe turned it down. He preferred to remain independent and able to pick and choose.

In April 1950, Eythe was hired to replace Dennis Harrison in the lead role of the play *The Liar*, then in Philadelphia and headed for Broadway. Singer-actor Alfred Drake co-wrote the book, which was a musical adaptation of Carlo Goldoni's *Il bugiardo*, and also directed. Eythe was brought in on short notice and had to learn the part and the songs in the week before the New York opening. It was then decided to delay the opening another week so that he could have extra time to familiarize himself with the role out of town. Eythe's singing voice wasn't on par with Harrison's so, despite being the lead, he had no solo numbers.

His character, Lelio Bisognosi, was a man who can't help stretching the truth as he pursues numerous ladies in sixteenth-century Venice. Eythe tried his best but his notices were mixed. The *Pittsburgh Press*' Jack Gaver wrote, "William Eythe has rather a field day in the role of the Italian youth…. He gives an engaging performance, one that Drake himself might envy except in the vocalizing department. Drake, of course, is a real singer. Eythe is an actor getting by as a singer." Richard Watts of the *New York Post* saw it differently, saying that Eythe was "competent enough" but lacked "the proper romantic style and humorous flourish…. [H]e strives manfully to fabricate an air of satirical bravado that is not forthcoming."

The *New York World-Telegram and Sun*'s William Hawkins felt Eythe would have conquered the part in time because he had "the flourish, the stamina and the charm" necessary. But Hawkins noted that Eythe's "cocky banter" and "zany range" suggested "Carol Channing doing an imitation of Ronald Colman." The role was written by Drake for a Drake type—but there's only one Alfred Drake, and Drake didn't play it.

The show opened on Broadway on May 18, 1950, and was set to close four days later;

it was given a reprieve until May 27 and then packed up. Blame cannot be placed on Eythe; the show was having problems out of town and they were never satisfactorily resolved. Many felt the musical was a disorganized mess and the book had long stretches of boredom. Louis Sheaffer wrote,

> In my next-morning review of *The Liar*, I was rather unfair, I'm now thinking, to William Eythe. A good song-and-dance trouper, a likeable personality, he was faced with a grueling role and he had to keep smiling about it. It would take a combination of Danny Kaye, Alfred Drake and Douglas Fairbanks Sr. to have played the role properly.

Eythe's reviews were good enough to get him a lot of new offers. The King Bros. wanted him for the lead in the movie *Southside 1–1000* (yet another semi-doc) but he rejected it in favor of staying in New York. He did radio (*Cavalcade of America*, *Theater of the Air*), and NBC wanted to sign him to an exclusive five-year TV deal. Eythe considered the pact restricting and he declined. He cherished his freelance status.

In July 1950, at Connecticut's Ivoryton Playhouse, he was on hand to help direct the college comedy *The Poor Nut* starring Lon McCallister. Then it was onto Matunuck, Rhode Island, to stage *Break It Up*, which starred Nancy Andrews and David Burns and had music by Robert Wells and Mel Tormé. Then to Ogunquit, Maine, to star in *The Silver Whistle*.

In Chicago to oversee the *Lend an Ear* company, Eythe was arrested on September 3, 1950. The charge made by Buff Cobb was non-payment of the two-year-old divorce settlement of $2500. He was taken to Cook County Jail on a "no-exit writ" and his bond was set for $5000. After a few days in jail, Eythe was able to settle the matter with Buff and he was released.

Eythe was supposed to resume playing his original role in *Lend an Ear* on tour, but he instead returned to New York and did a *Lights Out* TV episode, "Sisters of Shadow." He then accepted the lead in the Broadway musical *Out of This World*. It had some excellent musical talent attached to it: actor-singers Charlotte Greenwood, George Gaynes, David Burns and Priscilla Gillette, staging by Agnes de Mille and a Cole Porter score. Tryouts began on November 4, 1950, at the Shubert Theatre in Philadelphia, and then moved to the Shubert in Boston on November 28. The book, adapted from a Latin comedy called *Amphitryon*, was essentially a sex comedy featuring Olympian gods and mortals.

George Abbott was brought in to fix the production and he ended up cutting some good songs, including "From This Moment On," an Eythe-Gillette duet. There were two reasons given for the deletion: Abbott needed to tighten the show and Eythe couldn't vocally handle the song. Even if the latter was true, the song could have been assigned to someone else—and it wasn't. (It turned up later in the 1953 film version of *Kiss Me, Kate* and became one of Porter's enduring standards.) Another one of Eythe's songs was also cut, "We're on the Road to Athens," which he was to do with Gillette and William Redfield. Second-billed Eythe ended up music-less.

So why was so-so singer Eythe cast? Selma Tamber, who worked with Cole Porter, told author William McBrien that Porter saw Eythe on the street one day and found his looks "appealing." Tamber also noted that she considered Eythe "a bad boy who chased [boys] too much."

This reportedly got him in trouble days before the New York premiere. It's been alleged that Eythe no-showed for an evening's rehearsal, and the producers later learned that he had left the theater in the afternoon and went to a subway men's room where he was arrested for "indecent conduct." Charles Schwartz wrote in his Cole Porter biography, "There was thus the horrible possibility that not only would the news get out—to the detriment of the show—but that Eythe would not be able to perform as scheduled. Fortunately, the charges against Eythe were quietly squashed, reportedly through payoffs to the 'right' people." No newspaper covered Eythe's alleged misadventure. (The arrest has become notorious but, in the retelling, many have dramatically pushed up the date to the day of the Broadway opening.)

Out of This World opened to mediocre reviews at the New Century Theatre on December 21, 1950. Porter's score did not generate much excitement at the time (it took years before it was appreciated), with "Nobody's Chasing Me" being the standout number and Charlotte Greenwood stealing the honors. It closed on May 5, 1951, after 157 performances.

It was announced that Eythe and Jenny Lou Law would do *Lend an Ear* on the subway circuit for five weeks and then take the show out on a stock tour for another five. Instead, Eythe acted in episodes of TV's *Studio One, Armstrong Circle Theatre*, Faye Emerson's *Wonderful Town* (a tribute to Pittsburgh), *Lux Video Theatre, Lights Out*, etc. One of his most interesting small-screen credits was *Tales of Tomorrow's* "The Invader." The claustrophobic, intense story is set on Dr. Burroughs' (Edgar Stehli) research boat where he and his crew take samples from the sea. His son Roy (Eythe) wants to help but is dismissed as less than a man. When a strange glowing object falls into the ocean, Roy volunteers to go down and investigate. Is it a meteorite or a UFO? Eythe starts the episode as an uncertain son looking for approval, but when he returns from his dive, he is a changed man. The live broadcast is a fine example of the kind of work Eythe could do on TV and the stage. His passion drives the offbeat tale and he is at his best as the arrogant alien lifeforce menacing the crew.

He acted in a lot of TV and later remarked that it "takes a lot out of an actor. I wound up at the end of the series [of appearances] with a near-breakdown." Yet he considered TV his favorite medium. "It combines all of the features of movies and the stage. You've got to watch out, though, that you don't fall into the old stock tricks. Then television can be as lousy as any Grade C picture."

Starting on January 29, 1952, Eythe and Gale Storm starred for a week in the comedy *Gramercy Ghost* at St. Louis' Empress Theater. The *St. Louis Post-Dispatch's* Myles Standish called it a "weak-as-water" comedy, with even weaker performances. But he commended Eythe as the only cast member "to do a thoroughly competent work. He had spirit, verve and style."

After doing a *Schlitz Playhouse of Stars* and *Hollywood Opening Night*, Eythe briefly kept Lon McCallister company on his stock tour. Lon was appearing in theater-in-the-round at Birmingham, Alabama's Belmont Hotel in Philip Barry's *The Youngest*. The producer was Bill and Lon's friend Allen Draper. They began talking about doing a movie in Alabama; Lon would star, Bill would direct, and Draper would produce. All they needed was a good story set in Alabama. Evidently, they never found one because it never got made.

On June 3, 1952, at least five people contacted police reporting that a man was erratically driving his convertible up and down the Pacific Coast Highway. It took an hour for officers to stop the car and Eythe was arrested after he failed a sobriety test. He insisted they drive him home instead of arresting him, but he was booked on a drunk driving charge. He told reporters at the station, "I can't remember a thing since two o'clock [yesterday] afternoon."

It was back to stock in *Petticoat Fever* and *The Live Wire*. The latter, at the Evanston Showcase Theater in Illinois, was acclaimed by Ray Tudor of the *Chicago Tribune*:

> Under the spell of the dynamic Eythe, the Evanston players breathed life into the comedy of witty dialog, stock characters and contrived plot. The players rose above the script at times with a sense of timing which until now has been missing on the Evanston stage this season.... Eythe, stage and movie star, as the unscrupulous and overly ambitious Leo Mack, commendably fused a pleasing charm with the villainous elements of the character."

Eythe planned to produce and direct legit plays in a defunct movie theater. "TV has forced the closing of dozens of theaters," Eythe told the *Arizona Republic*. "The medium itself has caused a resurgence to live plays." In 1948, Eythe had had the same plan; neither time did it reach fruition.

By this time, Eythe and McCallister had been living together in Malibu for several years. Lon gave up acting in 1953 and went into real estate and a new business with Eythe: The two went on a working vacation to South America, where they shot film of the various locales they visited, so they could eventually sell it for use as stock footage for news broadcasts and film libraries.

He and McCallister formed Aries Productions. They spent many months looking for investors to stage Charles Gaynor's new revue *Between Friends*, which like *Lend an Ear* started at the Pittsburgh Playhouse. They wanted to take it to Broadway. In December '54, they ran through the show for Joshua Logan, who liked it so much that he agreed to act in an advisory capacity. When millionaire Huntington Hartford put a little money into it, it was decided to premiere *Between Friends* at Hollywood's new Huntington Hartford Theater. Eventually, they could only raise half of what they needed. They reimbursed their investors and dropped their option on the play.

On May 13, 1955, Eythe was set to act on TV's *Omnibus* in the play "A Different Drummer" with Martha Scott, John Alexander, Margaret Hamilton and Jack Dempsey. During rehearsals, he collapsed and was carried unconscious off the set by a fellow actor and brought to the hospital. The excuse given in print for his illness was an ulcer.

The next month, he was back with McCallister, roaming Rome and Istanbul filming exotic places and news events. Like Lon, Eythe had now stopped acting. When Earl Wilson asked why, McCallister answered, "Bill's too fat and I'm too old." It was then explained that because of his ulcer, Eythe had started to drink milk—and gained 25 pounds. The pair then went to Madrid and Africa to film scenes. Eythe said that his mother still phoned him from Pittsburgh asking, "When are you going to come home and go back to work in Kaufman's Department Store?"

In March 1956, back in the States, they were contacted by producers Huntington Hartford and Ray Golden to help out with the struggling stage revue *Joy Ride*, then in its fourth month at the Hartford Theater. (Hartford's money kept it going although few people came to see it.) Bill and Lon assisted in revising the show for its hoped-for transfer to Broadway. On June 4, 1956, it landed in Chicago at the Shubert Theatre. "Even though L.A. and Chicago critics panned *Joy Ride*," wrote Danton Walker, "Huntington Hartford is going to bring his revue to New York." No, he wasn't. The show closed with a whimper in Chicago on June 23. "*Joy Ride* flopped at the box office here and folded completely Sat. night," wrote Herb Lyon. "Instead of going to New York City, the cast took a sad ride back to the coast."

Eythe always had something brewing, such as the Stephen Longstreet story "Beach House," which he wanted to produce with Joan Blondell on Broadway. There was also *Strategy for Murder*, a satire about Nero and Satan in Hades, which he was to direct in Los Angeles in January 1957; it was then to go to San Francisco, Philadelphia and Broadway.

But by this time, Eythe had become seriously ill with hepatitis. He suffered with it for five weeks before he entered Good Samaritan Hospital in Los Angeles in January 1957. Critically ill, he lapsed into a semi-coma. McCallister contacted Carol Channing, telling her that Eythe was dying. "As soon as I got the call, I dropped everything … even Ethel Barrymore … to be with Bill," Channing remembered in her autobiography:

> Long after *Lend an Ear* we stayed close. During that period Bill had several times predicted the scene of his own death to me, even the room he would be in. Now, years after the prediction, when the doctors told me, "He's not going to make it," I was stunned to see the exact room Bill had described. He said, "The room is all white. There's a window to my right, almost behind me. The sheer white curtains are billowing. The head of my bed is wrought iron. You're there, Carol, sitting next to my bed holding my hand."

On January 26, 1957, a little over a week after being admitted to the hospital, 38-year-old Eythe died. Channing claimed that when the moment came, she was the only one with him: "The next day in all the papers they said I was the only one with Bill when he died. Bud [Lon McCallister] was nowhere around when Bill died, and I know he wanted to be." In fact, all of Eythe's newspaper obituaries reported that McCallister was the only person at his side when he passed. (On Eythe's death certificate, "Herbert A. McCallister" was the informant.) In addition to acute hepatitis, Eythe also had Laennac's cirrhosis, a disease with which he had been afflicted for about ten years.

A high mass was conducted at Hollywood's Blessed Sacrament Church, where he was a member, and he was interred with his father (who died in February 1956) and sister Kathryn Jr. at Saint Peters Cemetery in Butler, Pennsylvania. Mother Kathryn joined them there in October 1970. After Eythe's death, McCallister took on the task of editing the footage they shot. In the '60s, he briefly returned to acting, then went back to traveling the world before retiring. He died in 2005 at the age of 82.

Pittsburgh Sun-Telegraph columnist Karl Krug wrote that Eythe had "died far too young at 38." Krug continued:

> He was an actor of intelligence and perception, and he refused to appear in motion pictures in which he had no faith. He was a credit to both the stage and screen, and his future was really ahead of him.
>
> It was a privilege to have known Bill, who came up the hard way, working for the education that later resulted in fine performances in *The Eve of St. Mark, The Moon Is Down, The Ox-Bow Incident, The House on 92nd Street*, etc.
>
> They'll bury Bill Eythe on Thursday in Butler. But the memory of his *Lend an Ear*, especially that show's "Gladiola Girl" number, in which he participated, will endure as one of the Theater's monuments. It was a minor classic that owed much to Eythe.
>
> Playhouse director Fred Burleigh had a great early faith in Bill Eythe. It was a faith that was to be justified many times.

1943: *The Ox-Bow Incident, The Song of Bernadette*.
1944: *The Eve of St. Mark, Wing and a Prayer: The Story of Carrier X, Wilson*.
1945: *A Royal Scandal, The House on 92nd Street*.

1946: *Colonel Effingham's Raid, Centennial Summer.*
1947: *Meet Me at Dawn.*
1948: *Mr. Reckless.*
1949: *Special Agent.*
1950: *Customs Agent.*

WALLACE FORD

Likable, fast-talking Wallace Ford wasn't matinee idol–handsome, but projected a more realistic "regular guy" persona that was appealing and easy to identify with. "He possesses personality," wrote Scoop Conlon of the *Detroit Free Press*, "with a breezy, natural way of playing a role that makes the audience forget it is being acted." His "naturalness, simplicity and earnestness" (George L. David, *Democrat and Chronicle*) and the little touches he gave his characters endeared him to audiences, which led to a long career.

Looking at the wisecracking, easygoing Ford on film, you wouldn't think that he had once lived a Dickensian life of orphanages, foster homes, beatings, a hobo existence at the age of 11, on his own, riding the rails. He found success and comfort in Hollywood, but also a drinking problem that resulted in multiple arrests. Yet he enjoyed a happy family life, was a devoted Catholic, farmer, and a friend to everyone.

He was born Samuel Grundy Jones in Bolton, Lancashire, England, on February 12, 1898, to Samuel Grundy, an Irish bootmaker, and Catharine Jones, a housemaid and street singer; it appears likely that his parents were unwed at the time. Publicity in the 1930s and '40s skirted this issue or just denied it. "I never knew whether I had a legitimate father," Ford told Frederick C. Othman in 1937. "When people called me names, whether joking or not, I always feared that some of those names fitted me. I was glad to learn that my mother and father were respectable married folks, and that I was sent to the orphanage after my father died and my mother was too sick to care for me."

Who *was* his father? When he was mentioned at all (which was very rarely), he was said to have died a short time after his son's birth. A few claim he was killed in India fighting in the British Army, which sounds a bit fanciful. Anyway, no reporter ever dwelled on the subject. With his mother destitute and unwell, and his father out of the picture, the infant Sam was taken in by his maternal aunt Mary, a laundress, and her husband Alfred Beddows, who worked as a joiner, in Birkdale, Lancashire. Money was tight—the Beddows had six children ranging from two to 14—so Mary decided to send Sam to one of Dr. Thomas John Barnardo's homes for foundlings.

In 1905, seven-year-old Sam was one of a group of 163 children who was shipped out of England on the *SS Southwark*, arriving in Canada on July 1. He lived in Barnardo's Toronto boys' home and was placed with at least 17 different foster families, but he kept running away. When Ford later became a name in Hollywood, stories were sent out about his time at the home: "Officials at the Barnardo Home, which has taken care of 50,000 children entering Canada, still talk about Sammy Jones," reported the *Brantford Expositor*. "Even in his early life at the home he showed historic ability and was the leading spirit in arranging school plays, they said."

Eventually adopted by a doctor and his wife who lived near Ingelow, Manitoba, Sam was still unhappy: "They didn't want to adopt a child, they wanted a slave—a child slave," he later told columnist J.B. Woodside. "One that they could abuse and beat and keep as ignorant as a pig."

Running away yet again, Buster Jones (as he was now known) became involved with the Winnipeg Kiddies and the Winnipeg Permanent Players, playing bit parts and working backstage. In later life, the actor took great pride in relating that he never attended a day of school. He was taught to read and write backstage by other actors.

Taking to the road and rails, Sam struck up a friendship with a man named Wallace Ford, well-educated but a born hobo. "This Wallace Ford sort of took me under his wing, and I stayed with him for about a year," he explained to Lee Belser. "I worked in coal yards, as a dishwasher and sold newspapers to get enough to eat. I guess you'd call us a couple of bums. We cooked our food over campfires near the railroad tracks and found shelter wherever we could." They were on a freight train when Ford accidentally fell off and was crushed by the wheels. In honor of his dead pal, Sam changed his name to Wallace Ford. "It was half sentiment," he told the United Press' Ernest Foster, "and half dislike of that undistinguished handle, Sam Jones."

He continued to find menial jobs wherever he could, and began getting work as an actor with the Morgan Wallace Players (Sioux City, Iowa), the Fletcher Stock Company (Sabetha, Kansas) and Edward Dubinsky's company (St. Joseph, Missouri). His debut with the latter, *Common Clay* (1918), was praised by the *St. Joseph News-Press*: "[Ford brings] the part of a butler into the limelight for several moments by his unusual ability." In 1919, he briefly served with the U.S. Cavalry at Fort Riley, Kansas. In later interviews, he claimed that he was underage at the time and was discharged after 30 days because he was found out; not true. But his service *was* short and uneventful.

During these early years, Ford performed extensively on the legit stage (*Seventeen*, *Abraham Lincoln*), in stock and in vaudeville, and spent time with stock companies in Indiana and Pittsburgh. He appeared in such Broadway shows as *The Poppy God* (1921), *Broken Branches* (1922) and *Abie's Irish Rose* (1922–23). Ford got the lead in the latter after the show's original leading man, Robert Williams, was arrested for accidentally running down and killing a seven-year-old boy. Martha Haworth, who played one of the six bridesmaids in the production, was the daughter of actor-playwright William

A young Wallace Ford when he was playing likable leads in B movies.

Carnival performers Ford (left) and Leila Hyams (right) flank 18-inch-tall Johnny Eck, one of the sideshow *Freaks*. Reviewing director Tod Browning's 1932 shocker, *Harrison's Reports* raged, "Anyone who considers this entertainment should be placed in the pathological ward in some hospital."

trapeze artist (Olga Baclanova) marrying a midget (Harry Earles) with the intention of fatally poisoning him for his money. Ford, playing a clown, is the audience identification figure as he bonds with many of the human oddities and tries to run to the rescue in the film's riotous final reel.

This macabre publicity item appeared in April 1932: "Wallace Ford, the one actor in Hollywood who scoffs at all superstitions, purchased the entire wardrobe of the late Robert Williams and uses it on the screen." The 37-year-old Williams, whom Ford had replaced in 1922 in Broadway's *Abie's Irish Rose*, had recently died of peritonitis.

Ford might not have been superstitious, but he found that life at Hollywood's biggest studio wasn't bringing him any luck. MGM gave him supporting roles in the 1932 releases *The Wet Parade*, *Are You Listening?* and *Skyscraper Souls*. Leads came when he was on loan to Mack Sennett for *Hypnotized* and to Warner Bros. for *Central Park*. In the latter, he played a role for which romantic leading men Charles Farrell and Douglas Fairbanks, Jr., had been considered, and did a good job.

In March '32, under Leo McCarey's direction, Ford had the juvenile lead (alongside Anita Page) in the Marie Dressler-Polly Moran comedy *Prosperity*. Louis B. Mayer and Irving Thalberg did not like the finished product and called for retakes. Retakes soon turned to rewriting and then reshooting the whole movie, with Sam Wood taking over as director and Norman Foster playing the character played by Ford on the first "smacks of a flavor of the Ghetto." John Scott of the *Los Angeles Times* thought Ford typified a New York boy, "[o]r a typical boy of any other city for that matter. He is the easy-going not-interested chap who cannot be told anything about anything. Yet under the self-satisfied exterior, he is the earnest, anxious-to-please type."

The 33-year-old Ford told Scott,

> I've been playing juveniles and youthful character parts for some time now, and this is the first time I've been able to just be myself. The boy in *Bad Girl* doesn't have to act all over the place. He gets a lot of laughs, but they come legitimately, without any undue mugging at the audience.

> Another New York stage actor has arrived in our midst, and by arrived I mean he has the picture producers and directors talking about him over the luncheon table. Wallace Ford is the young man's name and when not appearing at a local theater in *Bad Girl* he is going from studio to studio to talk business and make tests.—Eileen Percy, *Los Angeles Evening Express*

Ford told the *Los Angeles Times*' John Scott,

> Of course, every stage actor who comes out here is anxious to make a picture. I'm no exception. But the stage is a pretty good breadwinner. It will never die. A fellow can't just sit around and wait for film producers to fall on his neck. He would starve for sure. But changing off between the screen and the stage would be swell.

On June 29, *Bad Girl* moved to the Geary in San Francisco. Sometime during that month, director Clarence Brown saw Ford on stage and thought him perfect for a movie he was doing at MGM: *Possessed,* starring Joan Crawford and Clark Gable. Lenore Coffee's screenplay was adapted from Edgar Selwyn's Broadway play *The Mirage*. Marian (Crawford) is a small-town factory girl who wants more out of life. Co-worker and childhood friend Al Manning (Ford) resents her ambitions and unwillingness to marry him. She eventually gets to New York and hooks up with lawyer Mark Whitney (Gable). Ford has a difficult role as the likable common guy who finally shows his true, mercenary colors. Mona Cannady (*New York Daily News*) wrote of Ford, "He isn't good looking, he talks a little out of the side of his mouth, and in [*Possessed*] he plays the role of a 'heel.' But Hollywood seems to be going for him."

Metro signed Ford to a seven-year contract, reported to be the first such long-term deal. They then promptly loaned him to the Poverty Row outfit Tiffany for *X Marks the Spot* (1931). The "X" signifies where the dead body of a chorus girl was found in her apartment. Winchell-esque Broadway columnist Ted Lloyd (Ford) is the number one suspect. Scripted by Warren Duff and Gordon Kahn, the film provides an atmospheric, colorful look at the inner workings of a newsroom. It's one of Ford's best early roles, as he's torn between saving himself or turning in the real killer who years before did him a good turn. Mordaunt Hall of the *New York Times* appreciated the film: "It is unpretentious in production, but much of it is vivid and all of it interesting. And in the final scenes, with a condemned murderer loose in a courthouse, it rises to a breathtaking climax."

Ford played his best two MGM roles at the same time. In the gritty *The Beast of the City* (1932), police chief Walter Huston's detective brother (Ford) allows the coarse charms of bad girl Jean Harlow to sway his morals and sense of duty. His dramatic supporting performance was singled out as an "excellent piece of work" by the *Philadelphia Inquirer,* an assessment echoed by many other critics. In director Tod Browning's notorious *Freaks* (1932), Ford topped a cast dominated by real-life Siamese twins, armless girls, a pinhead, a human skeleton (and more) in a sordid story of a glamourous circus

In 1944, when actor Ralph Bellamy was interviewed by Lawrence Perry in the *Indianapolis Star*, he put an ominous coda on this story (while changing the amount of lost loot from $10 to $800):

> Wally happened to know one of Capone's leading henchmen, to whom he related his experience. This man, whom I'll identify merely as "Spike," frowned and said nothing. Two days later, Wally was asked to get into a handsome sedan and take a ride to a country club where he had a date to play golf. On the way the car stopped. The chauffeur got out and pulled aside a clump of underbrush, revealing a dead body. "Was that skunk one of the men who held you up?" he asked. Wally, trembling, said it was. Returning to the car, the driver pulled a cloth off the rear seat, revealing another body. "Was that the other guy?" he asked. "Yes," moaned Wally. "All right," said the chauffeur. "Here's your $800." And he handed Wally a roll. "Now you can go and play golf." But Wally leaped out of the car and started running and did not stop running for a long time.

On October 14, 1929, *The Nut Farm* premiered on Broadway (minus Lowell and O'Brien). "Wallace Ford is a very large but very youthful Willie, with a habit of talking lines through the nose," wrote the *New York Daily News* critic. The show ran only 40 performances, closing that November. The following month, Ford tried out the farce *Junior* with a Greenwich, Connecticut, stock company which included silent star Betty Blythe and Lysle Talbot (soon to become Lyle Talbot).

In 1930, Ford went to work at Warner Bros.' Vitaphone studios in Flatbush. His first screen efforts were the shorts *Absent Minded* and *Fore*. *Film Daily* said of the first, "An amusing reel has been built up here on the idea of a chap who is more than ordinarily absent-minded. Wallace Ford, of the legitimate stage, plays the principal part and makes it an interesting as well as laugh-provoking characterization. Will please most anywhere."

On May 18, Ford replaced Douglass Montgomery ("compelled to retire from the company to undergo a surgical operation"—*Chicago Tribune*) in the Chicago play *Many a Slip*. Ford was praised for his ability to portray "brisk young American lads with an alert sense of comedy" (*Chicago Tribune*) and his participation was eagerly anticipated. "[The] patrons of the Cort [Theater] have a strong affection for Wallace Ford, whose debut in *Many a Slip* will be worth watching." Not this time. The show abruptly closed on May 31. Ford had better luck in Detroit appearing with Marjorie Peterson in *Young Sinners* (1930–31) for nine successful weeks at the Lafayette Theater.

Nineteen thirty-one saw Ford joining St. Louis' Grand Central Players in *Broadway* and *Jonesy* (the latter with Claire Trevor and Lyle Talbot). He and Marjorie Peterson reunited in Detroit for *Bad Girl*, based on Viña Delmar's bestselling novel and Broadway play. Like their previous collaboration, this did boffo box office. The two stayed together at the Lafayette for a week's engagement in *The Nut Farm*, then went to Cleveland for *Young Sinners* and then on to Los Angeles to duplicate their success in *Bad Girl*. William Keighley directed the L.A. production at the Belasco.

Opened on June 15, 1931, the show changed Ford's life and career. California audiences had never seen him before—and they liked him. "Wallace Ford does a remarkable thing with the part of Eddie," wrote Llewellyn Miller of the *Los Angeles Evening Post-Record*. "He has hardly a gleam of sympathy in his lines, yet he manages to convey his concern, his hidden sweetness to the audience from the start. And all in some of the toughest, most clipped dialogue spoken around here in many a day."

The *Illustrated Daily News*' Eleanor Barnes criticized his diction, which she felt

Haworth and niece of actor Joseph Haworth. Martha, previously in stock and vaudeville, was also a writer and sculptress—and, according to many, a dead ringer for the elegant Ann Harding. On November 22, 1922, she and Ford married in Cleveland. Their daughter Julia died at birth on October 20, 1923. They later had a daughter named Patricia (1927–2005).

Ford continued on Broadway in *Nobody's Business* (1923), *Gypsy Jim* (1924), *Nancy Ann* (1924) and *Pigs* (1924–25). He did a *Pigs* road tour with his New York co-star Nydia Westman until the summer of 1926. Ford then played in the military comedy *Americans All* (1926) with Mayo Methot. It was to open on Broadway, but closed after two nights in Stamford, Connecticut. It was back to the tried-and-true *Pigs* with Una Merkel in Boston, Philadelphia, New Jersey, Connecticut, Vermont, Washington, D.C., and Baltimore. Starting in April '27 and into '28, Ford headed one of six road companies for the show *Broadway*. In it, he portrayed New York nightclub hoofer Roy Lane, a "slangy, wise-cracking, egotistical yet wistful boy" (*Kansas City Times*) in love with a chorus girl. When the production landed in Kansas City, Missouri, in January 1928, the *Kansas City Times* reviewer called Ford "capital" in his part:

> He plays the light and the heavy scenes with equal skill and he never drops his "small time" actor air, the talking out of the side of his mouth, the remark that "Jack Donahue isn't so good—he just got the breaks," the cocky self-assurance that has been the property of every "song-and-dance man" since the beginning of time. His scene when he is arrested in the second act is a pretty thrilling bit of dramatics for a minute, but he snaps right back to his lighter bits later without missing a cue. Mr. Ford is a gentleman who is on his way somewhere in the stage world, we would wager.

In May 1928, Henry Hull was scheduled to star with the Lyceum Players in a Rochester, New York, stock production of George M. Cohan's *The Baby Cyclone*, but was replaced by Ford. This last-minute change, reported the *Rochester Democrat and Chronicle*, was done when Hull, who had rehearsed the role for three weeks, was "ordered to take a two to three weeks' rest by his physician, because he was on the verge of a nervous breakdown from overwork." For the rest of 1928, Ford went back to the play *Broadway* in Buffalo; appeared in the sketch *Decision* at the Palace in Chicago; and starred in *Excess Baggage* (with Miriam Hopkins and Frank McHugh), *Cradle Snatchers* and *Tommy* in Rochester. In Great Neck and Brooklyn, New York, and in Pittsburgh, he acted in Maxwell Anderson's *Gypsy*, "[an] extraordinary play beautifully acted" (*Brooklyn Daily Eagle*). The show opened on Broadway on January 14, 1929, closed in March, and then played in Flatbush and Yonkers.

With a cast headed by Ford, Helen Lowell and Pat O'Brien (one of Wally's best friends), the comedy *The Nut Farm* (1929) was tried out in Chicago for more than five months. During this successful run, Ford was one of a few actors around the city who fell victim to shakedowns. Two men went around to various theaters claiming they were members of the West Side Sporting Club looking for contributions. Ford told a reporter (quoted by the *New York Daily News*) that "two dapper youths called on him in his dressing room. He believes that both were armed. Ford told them that he had little money but, frightened by their threats he left for the stage, telling them to help themselves to the money he had in a coat pocket. They took $10 and left." The *Sioux City Journal* put a lighter spin on Ford's encounter, writing that he laughed and characterized them as "overgrown kids" who "posed to him as sluggers and told him he needed protection while in rough Chicago." Other actors who fell victim were Richard Bennett and Mae West, who lost at least $3000.

go-round. Some newspaper ads and publicity stories carried Ford's name when the picture was released that November. By that time, the actor and MGM had called it a day.

Ford's first as a freelancer was Universal's *The Big Cage* (1933) starring Clyde Beatty, the World's Greatest Animal Trainer, in his feature film debut. If we are to believe press reports, Ford was passing by the cage that housed Jiggs, a black leopard, when the animal reached out and "severely" clawed his arm and hand. After that, cast member Andy Devine nicknamed him "Leopard-bait." Ford ended 1932 at Warners in *Employees' Entrance* (1933), where he and Loretta Young, playing secretly married store employees, cope with store manager Warren William's cutthroat "profits over people" attitude.

Calling Ford "one of our best freelance players," columnist Eileen Percy continued, "[He] has been doing more roles since his departure from Metro than at any time during his contract period there." She likened his appeal to that of James Dunn, who became a star after being cast in the movie version of *Bad Girl*. While Dunn had a Fox contract, Ford had to rely on his own persuasive talents—and it seemed to be working. In 1933, he made ten movies; most were supporting roles in big-studio offerings, e.g., *Three Cornered Moon, Goodbye Again* and *Men in White* (the latter released in 1934). Len G. Shaw of the *Detroit Free Press* wrote that Ford stole *My Woman*, "mak[ing] the egoistical Chick thoroughly detestable, which is as good a tribute to him as an actor as could be paid."

Wally's first of five films for director John Ford, *The Lost Patrol* (1934), told the harrowing World War I story of a small group of British soldiers stranded in an oasis in the vast Mesopotamian desert, and being picked off one by one by unseen Arab snipers in the sand dunes around them. The cast is small, and gets smaller with each reel: Coping with the terror of an "invisible" enemy are patrol leader Victor McLaglen, Boris Karloff, Reginald Denny, Alan Hale (*et al.*) plus Ford as Morelli, a former music hall performer. The temperature in the desert near Yuma, Arizona, was triple-digit (one day it came close to 130 degrees) and several heatstroke victims in the crew were sent home. The *New York World-Telegram*'s William Boehnel called the results "breath-taking," "certainly one of the finest [films] that have come out of Hollywood."

Ford did back-to-back films for Bryan Foy Productions, both directed by Benjamin Stoloff and released by Columbia. Bela Lugosi was top-billed in *Night of Terror* but Ford, "breezy and dynamic" (*Crowley Daily Signal*) drew more notice as a "fast-moving police reporter [who] infects the role with his effervescent personality. At the same time, he provides some pleasant romantic moments with attractive Sally Blane." His competition in that department was mild-mannered scientist George Meeker, who devises a way to survive without oxygen for extended periods; to prove this, he asks to be buried alive. While all this is going on, a killer known as The Maniac is on the loose, Hindu servants skulk around, and a mix of spookiness and comedy prevails. In Ford's other film for Foy, *Swellhead*, he plays a baseball player with serious ego issues. For whatever reason, the film's release was delayed until 1935.

East of Fifth Avenue, about love, infidelity, suicide and death in a boarding house, was another lead at Columbia: Ford marries Mary Carlisle but is responsible for Dorothy Tree's pregnancy. It's a shame Ford couldn't have secured a contract with Columbia; it would have given direction to his career. Monogram cast him as a boxer in love with a movie star (Marguerite De La Motte) in the zippy *A Woman's Man*, based on a *Cosmopolitan* story by Adela Rogers St. Johns. "Wallace Ford never gave a more human performance unless it was in *Bad Girl* on the Belasco theater stage," wrote *Hollywood Filmograph*.

In the midst of all this activity, Ford was hospitalized. A manicurist cut his finger and infection spread to his wrist, elbow and as high as his armpit. It was probably an exaggeration that the "loss of the arm seemed imminent," but he did lose about a week of work.

Nineteen thirty-four started with enjoyable performances in two independent movies. *I Hate Women* has Ford as newspaper reporter Scoop McGuire, who helps a lady (June Clyde) falsely accused of killing her husband. Mary Eunice McCarthy's screenplay has equal doses of mystery, comedy and romance and Ford proved once again what a well-suited fit he was to these surroundings. A tad milder was *Money Means Nothing*, a rich girl-poor boy story minus the usual clichés.

These indies may be entertaining, but at the time the only things they did for Ford was keep him busy and diminish whatever standing he'd have as a lead actor in major studio pictures. "Luck did not come his way in Hollywood" was how the *Los Angeles Times'* Edwin Schallert put it. The tonic for this was a return to the stage after *Money Means Nothing* wrapped in late March '34. In Cleveland, he spent two weeks in *Sailor, Beware!*, a risqué comedy that was at the time still enjoying a successful run on Broadway.

In September, Ford was back in Hollywood, as busy as ever, acting in four films in quick succession: *The Man Who Reclaimed His Head* (1934), *The Mysterious Mr. Wong* (1934) (in his frequent role as a reporter), John Ford's *The Whole Town's Talking* (1935) (as another reporter) and *The Nut Farm* (1935), reprising his lead from the Broadway production.

The following year was just as active: He was top-billed at Columbia in *In Spite of Danger* (as a race car driver who loses his nerve) and *Men of the Hour* (teamed with Richard Cromwell as newsreel cameramen), plus a terrific supporting part in *She Couldn't Take It* with George Raft and Joan Bennett. On Poverty Row, he played leads in Mascot's *One Frightened Night* and Mayfair's *Get That Man* (in a dual role). Ford also had secondary parts in Paramount's *Mary Burns, Fugitive* (1935) and RKO's *Two in the Dark* (1936). Speaking of RKO: Although Brian Donlevy was billed first in *Another Face* (1935) as a ruthless crook who changes his face and goes Hollywood, it's Ford who saves the day and gets Phyllis Brooks at the fade.

Another John Ford assignment, another Hall of Fame motion picture: RKO's *The Informer*, set in the foggy Dublin slums of 1922, with Victor McLaglen as a hard-drinking, swaggering lout tempted by the £20 reward on the head of his friend Wallace, a wanted member of the underground Irish Rebel Army. McLaglen tells the British Army where to find him, and find him they do, and at the end of a furious gunfight Ford is machine-gunned as he dangles by one hand (literally by his fingernails) from an upper-story window of his mother's house. Now other rebels get on the trail of the informer. For their work in this powerful drama, McLaglen, director Ford, screenwriter Dudley Nichols and composer Max Steiner received Oscars.

In June 1935, Ford provided police with a letter he received from Mary Beddows, who "claimed to be his aunt." The missive told him that his mother Catherine Jones was living in England. Ford had been searching for many years for his parents, and this was his first real clue. He placed advertisements in London newspapers and, according to Paul Harrison, he received a number of responses, "most of them obviously from people whose imaginations have been stimulated by the knowledge that Wallace Ford, orphan, is making a lot of money in Hollywood." Ford was quoted by *Sunday Mercury*:

In 1922 Dublin, Ford's Frankie McPhillip is the elusive Irish rebel with a £20 bounty on his head—enough to tempt *The Informer*. Director John Ford's masterpiece was a 1935 Best Picture nominee.

> I want you to know that my story isn't a sob story, although like every man who's worth his salt, I've had some hard slugging in my time. Well, I've taken the rough with the smooth, and I've got no kick coming.
>
> I took the name Wallace Ford as a stage name. My real name is Samuel Jones, and I keep one of my bank accounts in it.
>
> Whoever my parents were, I inherited from them one characteristic for which I'm grateful—thrift. I own my homestead, and my life is insured for £20,000 [£1,125,735.53 today, or $1,354,709.01 in U.S. money].
>
> I left the Barnardo orphanage and went to its branch at Toronto in June, 1905, when I was seven—I know the date because the people at the home gave me a Bible with my name and the date on the fly-leaf. I've still got it.

Although Ford insisted that his life was not a sob story, it's interesting that one writer who interviewed him in 1935, Whitney Williams, described him in passing, "High-spirited one moment, he can descend into the lowest pit of despair the next." His drinking, mentioned frequently in stories about him, would worsen as he got older.

In 1934, in the *Los Angeles Illustrated Daily News*, columnist Eleanor Barnes painted a personal sketch of Ford, who lived on a six-acre San Fernando Valley farm raising chickens and vegetables:

> Wally has become one of Hollywood's favorite colorful personalities. He is dynamic, but paradoxical.
>
> He is an actor's actor on and off. He loves to go everywhere, the fights, races, previews, golf; but particularly does he like to sit up all night swapping wisecracks and plotting "ribs." Fellow troupers say he is the best audience in Hollywood.
>
> Withal, he is a devoted family man. If he sits up all night with the boys, he takes Martha

and Patty Ann out the next. He is crazy about his daughter. Has been known to play "hookey" with Patty, keeping her out of school for a day at the beach. He craves the childish amusements he never enjoyed as a boy.

He is a devout churchgoer, yet he can't break himself of a weakness for shooting craps and playing poker, any time, any place—and he seldom wins.

He smokes about 16 cigars a day. He never smokes cigarets because when he was a kid some man told him that only sissies did.

He rivals Jack Oakie as the "old clothes man" of Hollywood. Has a compete wardrobe of brand-new suits, which he seldom wears except in pictures. He prefers turtleneck sweaters and sweatshirts. His favorite garb is an old tweed sportscoat and light gray trousers which once belonged to his pal, the late Robert Williams.

Speaking of Ford's pals: When his actor-friend Vince Barnett was arrested on a drunk and disorderly charge in July 1935, Ford testified in court on his behalf. He was out with Barnett and his wife Genevieve on the night in question, and told the judge,

> Barnett had not been drinking. He was perfectly sober when police accosted him and his wife in a parking lot near a downtown theater.
> The police approached them in the parking lot and then I saw Barnett on the ground and heard Mrs. Barnett cry, "You've hit my husband."
> I saw one of the officers hit Mrs. Barnett and Bill Casper, a friend of the Barnetts. It looked like they were going to lick everybody, so I left.

The parking lot pandemonium had started when autograph hunters converged on Barnett and his wife. They stepped on his toes and pushed elbows in his stomach. One person even slugged him in the eye. Then the police came—and blamed Barnett.

On Monday, December 16, 1935, at 9:30 a.m., actress Thelma Todd was found dead of carbon monoxide poisoning in her automobile. Martha, Mrs. Wally Ford, told police (and repeated at the grand jury trial) that the day before Todd's body was discovered, she (Martha) got a phone call at four in the afternoon. The caller identified herself as Todd, confirmed that she was coming to a party Martha was hosting that day, and asked if she could bring a guest. Asked who the guest was, the caller said it was a surprise; she wanted to see the look on Martha's face when they arrived. "Just wait till I walk in—you'll fall dead," she said.

No one had seen Thelma after her chauffeur delivered her home from the Trocadero at 3:30 a.m. on Sunday morning, and police said she was dead before that telephone call. Also, phone records revealed that *no* calls had been placed from Todd's residence at that time. "I know Miss Todd's voice," Martha insisted, "having talked with her frequently, and I can say definitely it was she who spoke to me." Martha's testimony added just another shadowy element to the notorious, still unsolved mystery. Some sources believe the Mob was responsible, and it would be easy to view the January '36 poisoning death of the Fords' Saint Bernard Mary as payback for Martha's testimony. However, at that time, there was a string of dog poisoning deaths near Laurel Canyon.

Martha became seriously ill from pleurisy and pneumonia. By late February 1936, this infection had cleared up, but she then suffered a nervous breakdown. Martha went to recuperate at Furnace Creek Inn in Death Valley, California. As a consequence, Wally made fewer movies in 1936 than in past years. His first of '36 was the quickie murder mystery *The Rogues Tavern*, made by Mercury Pictures. Detective Ford and his prospective bride Barbara Pepper stop at an out-of-the-way inn populated by a group of people getting bumped off by what they think is a wolf dog.

Irene Hervey and Ford in MGM's *Absolute Quiet* (1936). "Even though this show is a Metro program number," wrote *The Film Daily*, "it is mighty good entertainment for those who want something lively. For a *Grand Hotel*–like affair which is loaded with talk, it is surprising what a great amount of action and suspense has been injected."

After supporting in MGM's *Absolute Quiet* (1936) and Paramount's *A Son Comes Home* (1936), Ford sailed for England in July '36 to make *O.H.M.S.* (short for On His Majesty's Service), a comedy-adventure directed by Raoul Walsh. Ford, an American gangster on the run, takes a dead man's papers and ends up in the British Army. Ford even got to do a song-and-dance with Grace Bradley to "Turning the Town Upside Down" (written by Samuel Lerner, Al Goodhart and Al Hoffman). "Wallace Ford really makes this film," wrote the *Sunday Sun* reviewer. "As the tough guy in New York, as the rebellious talkie, as the trained soldier, he's great, and John Mills as his rival acts right up to his level, with charming Anna Lee doing a grand job of work." It was released in the U.S. as *You're in the Army Now*.

Ford remained overseas for two other pictures, *Jericho* (1937), a Paul Robeson starrer partly shot in the Sahara Desert, and *Stardust*, with Lupe Velez and Ben Lyon, which was released in 1938.

Ford's search for his mother ended in December 1936: She had been living in Northwich, England, for about 30 years. On March 1, 1926, she had wed Daniel Maxted, a match seller and rag-gatherer known as "Blind Dan." (An accident at the Winnington Chemical Works had cost him his sight.) Catherine, around 69 years old, was known to locals as "Mam Kit." She and Daniel were living in an old circus wagon near the River Weaver under poor conditions. "He is my son Sammy," she remarked when she and Ford saw each other face to face for the first time in many years. "He has got my family's gray eyes and our mouth. At last, we are united like a fairy tale come true."

Writer Ann Pinchot described the scene further:

> [When] his mother came in [the room], he knew her immediately—the same short figure, the same nose, the same barrel chest. When reporters fired questions on her past, the old woman got mad and threatened to use a poker over their heads. "Of course, I was married to my son's father! What do you mean by asking me questions like that?"
>
> She never told Ford why she committed him to the institution. But she did say hesitantly, "I did not treat you right, son…" to which Wallace answered lightly, "Let's forget it, Mother. Let's think of the future—"

Ford told the press, "I'm going to see that my mother gets what she wants, that she'll be comfortable for the rest of her days. What she seems to want most is a little cottage, so that she can leave the old caravan. She shall have that. I am glad the search is over. My mind is at ease."

He added quietly, "She has had a hard life."

Ford arranged with James Lynch, a scrap-iron merchant responsible for finding Catherine, to supervise the future of his mother and her husband. Less than a month after the reunion and before they could move into their new home, Daniel died of pneumonia.

"I have enjoyed working in England," Ford told the *Daily Province*'s Joan Littlefield in May 1937, "but I shall be quite glad to get back to my home in Hollywood in July. I'll have been away a year, and that's quite long enough. I shall see the Coronation [of George VI and Elizabeth], of course, and then I want to travel to Scotland and Ireland."

> Wally Ford suffered a badly wrenched ankle when he slipped on a gangplank boarding a boat in New York for home via the Panama Canal, according to a radio message to friends. He's returning after a long absence in England.—Read Kendall, *Los Angeles Times*, July 1, 1937

Back in the movie colony, Ford signed a deal with Grand National to do a series of comedies centering on gobs Pete Kelly and Husky Stone. The first, *Swing It, Sailor!* (1938), featured Ford as Pete and Ray Mayer as Husky. If we are to believe publicity, Clara Bow was being enticed to come out of retirement for the female lead but, according to Harriet Parsons, "the salary Clara's asking is a little rich for G.N.'s blood and may mix up the deal." It either did or she really wasn't asked, because Isabel Jewell was cast instead in this seafaring love-triangle comedy. Wally was in the middle of filming *Swing It, Sailor!* when he received word that his mother had disappeared from the home he had bought her. Sending inquiries to friends in England, he hoped to find her again.

Harrison Carroll claimed that MGM contacted Ford to help out with story suggestions for their new Freddie Bartholomew movie *The Perfect Gentleman* (retitled *Lord Jeff*), which was dedicated to the memory of Dr. Thomas John Barnardo and dealt with a boys' home similar to Barnardo's.

Ford went to Republic for another B lead, *Exiled to Shanghai* (1937), where he and Dean Jagger are rival newsreel reporters vying for schoolteacher June Travis. R.B. of the *Honolulu Star-Bulletin* wrote, "Wallace Ford, one of the better comedians who has slipped to second-rate studios, shows his old-time skill as a wisecracking newsreel cameraman, whose battles with his bosses land him on his uppers."

Read Kendall gave the *Los Angeles Times* various (and vary*ing*) accounts of an incident that took place during production:

An engaging *Exiled to Shanghai* (1937) publicity still of June Travis and Ford.

Wallace Ford broke a rib trying to find the bathroom in the dark and the next day he had to start work at Republic in a picture which called for him to fistically battle for his life.—October 11, 1937

Wallace Ford is having a difficult time speaking his lines because of those cracked ribs he suffered in a bathtub spill.—October 15, 1937

Laurels for being a real trouper justly go to Wallace Ford. While filming *News in the Air* [*Exiled to Shanghai*] for Republic, Wally slipped in his bathtub and cracked half a dozen ribs. Wrapped up in court plaster, he continued with his part. Two days ago, he slipped on the set while carrying a newsreel camera. The poor chap fainted with the pain from his re-fractured ribs, but went on after a rest of several hours.—October 22, 1937

The Kelly-Stone series did not continue after *Swing It, Sailor!* (although James Dunn was named as a possible substitute for Ford). Grand National's David Diamond let Ford out of his contract so he could do Broadway's *Of Mice and Men*, a role Wally got over such names as Spencer Tracy, Lee Tracy and James Cagney. Louella Parsons wrote, "Wally Ford ... leaves broken ribs and all Sunday night [October 24, 1937] for New York to start rehearsals in *Of Mice and Men*."

Of Mice and Men was John Steinbeck's own stage adaptation of his novella. The play's two main characters, George Milton and Lennie Small, are described in the book thusly:

The first man was small and quick, dark of face, with restless eyes and sharp, strong features. Every part of him was defined: small, strong hands, slender arms, a thin and bony nose. Behind him walked his opposite, a huge man, shapeless of face, with large, pale eyes, with wide, sloping shoulders; and he walked heavily, dragging his feet a little, the way a bear drags his paws. His arms did not swing at his sides, but hung loosely.

Ford played the shrewd George and Broderick Crawford his simple-minded friend Lennie, field hands living itinerant lives, not unlike Ford's own adolescence. In this case, though, the two have been run out of the last place they worked due to Lennie's fondness for petting soft things (and sometimes killing them): He touched a girl's dress, she screamed and they were chased by a mob. While George calls Lennie a "crazy bastard" and "a lot of trouble," he also is protective and affectionate towards him. As the play begins, they are on their way to another ranch, where another set of troubles await them in the form of the boss' son Curley, Curley's Wife (no name in the play) and Lennie's inability to control his strength and emotions.

Directed by George S. Kaufman, *Of Mice and Men* opened at the Music Box Theatre on November 23, 1937, to raves for all concerned. Ford got the best notices of his career and found a part that fit him perfectly. According to the *Cincinnati Post*'s George Ross, Ford had the first night audience on its feet, "cheering for the heartrending quality of his work." Other reviewers on their feet included Donald Kirkley of *The Baltimore Sun*:

> Broderick Crawford is exactly right as Lennie, but the chief acting credit goes to Wallace Ford as George. In Hollywood, where he has been wasting his time for several years, Mr. Ford was typed for the most part as a brash, flip, wise-cracking fellow. As the unkempt, forlorn, kind-hearted wanderer in *Of Mice and Men*, he has established himself at one stroke as a character actor who can vie with the best.

Robert Francis of the *Brooklyn Daily Eagle*:

> [Ford] returns to the stage after a lapse of seven years in pictures, and after last night I trust that he will be here with us for a long time to come. He plays George with deep feeling, and in the last scene, which could be easily ruined by overplaying, he puts just the right restraint to make it absolutely convincing.

George Jean Nathan of the *Atlanta Constitution Sunday Magazine*:

> Ford in particular has proved a great surprise, for if ever there was a ham actor it was this same Ford in previous plays—to say nothing of in all the movies to which he contributed his presence. But here in *Of Mice and Men* he suddenly reveals himself an understanding, sensitive, well-poised and touching actor.

And Annie Oakley of the *Windsor Star*:

> Wallace Ford's George has been cheered by the critics as a marvel of patience, courage and grief—casual and sincere.

It was announced in January 1938, while Ford was still on Broadway, that D.W. Griffith wanted to cast him as the Little Colonel in a remake of his controversial *The Birth of a Nation*. This racist character, played by Henry B. Walthall in the 1915 original, would have been quite a stretch for Ford. During the making of *The Lost Patrol*, Ford actually attacked and chased a cook who refused to serve a black crew member. Due to protests, Griffith's remake was never made.

Of Mice and Men closed in May 1938 after 207 performances. Ford had an offer to go to London to star in a movie for British International, but canceled his trip to screen-test along with Sam Jaffe and George E. Stone for the title role in RKO's *Gunga Din*. "Ford has long been relegated to Class B stuff, but with fame resting on his brow, he's said to be due to merit new respect in Hollywood," wrote S.M. in the *Cedar Rapids Gazette*.

In California, Ford was visiting friends in September when his car was stolen. Two weeks later, Harrison Carroll reported, "Wally Ford's stolen car was found and the thief must have read Wally's moans over losing a jar of bread and butter pickles made by the mother of Pat O'Brien. The pickles were left in the car. Clothes, golf clubs, everything else was taken."

In October '38, Ford began work on producer-director William K. Howard's crime drama *Back Door to Heaven*. Filmed at Paramount's Astoria, Queens, studio, it tells of Frankie Rogers (played as a kid by Jimmy Lydon) and the path his life takes as he grows up and makes criminal choices. Released from prison, he returns to his hometown to see an old schoolteacher (Aline MacMahon) and finds that many things have changed while he was away. The John Bright-Robert Tasker screenplay was based on Howard's story "Picket Fence," which was loosely based on *his* childhood in St. Marys, Ohio, and his friendship with Jim Tully (later to become a writer) and Charles Makley, who years later joined Dillinger's gang and was killed attempting to escape from Ohio State Penitentiary. In a 2009 article in *LA Weekly*, French journalist Philippe Garnier wrote that Ford "gives a haunting performance that makes Henry Fonda's felon in Fritz Lang's *You Only Live Once* seem fake by comparison." Ford was proud of the picture, as well he should be. An unnamed reviewer for the *Hartford Courant* called *Back Door to Heaven* "powerful and thought-provoking," a "pretty grim" film that "will grip you." As for Ford, "here [he] establishes himself as one of the screen's finest character actors." *Back Door to Heaven* was unlike other movies of the era, and many audiences didn't know what to make of it. It was not a success.

When Ford was on Broadway, it was predicted that his stock as an actor would rise considerably and that major leads would follow. *Back Door to Heaven*, a low-budget affair, proved that wrong. Offers for him to top-line a British movie about George Washington and a William K. Howard–produced play, wherein he'd portray an unbalanced character, led to nothing. Sidney Kingsley denied that Ford was going to star in his adaptation of *The Outward Room*. "Ford," he told Burns Mantle, "is a splendid actor—but the part calls for a man about twice his size" (Ford was 5'8").

Ford told Ann Pinchot of the *Atlanta Constitution Sunday Magazine*, "I don't want to be a star. I know my limitations. I can act only those roles which I can feel. Put me in a drawing room comedy and I'm a flop."

Ford bought a racehorse and called it Agitator. "In the east I read all about the thoroughbreds [that] Hollywood actors, producers and movie execs were buying up, so I thought you had to have a horse of your own to be anything in filmland this season." Also, he liked to go to the races with his buddies, particularly Pat O'Brien.

In December 1938, Ford, along with George Burns, Jack Benny and Jack Pearl, became involved with "blond, buttery" (*Time* magazine) Albert Chaperau, who was charged with conspiracy, smuggling, faking a passport and fraudulently claiming U.S. citizenship. Indicted with him was Elma N. Lauer, wife of New York Supreme Court Justice Edgar J. Lauer, for colluding to smuggle $1833 worth of "Paris finery" into the U.S.

"I blame it all on Adolf Hitler," Chaperau remarked.

At a dinner party that October 21, Mr. and Mrs. Lauer, Chaperau and guests were having a heated discussion about Hitler when the Lauers' new maid, Rosa Weber, reportedly declared, "Ladies and gentlemen, I am a true German. I love Adolf Hitler. If you don't stop talking against him, I will stop serving the dinner right now. It is up to you." Justice Lauer fired her immediately. As she left the house, Rosa vowed revenge.

A trip to Customs authorities did the trick.

During the grand jury investigation, Chaperau's attorney David Garrison Berger stated that he would "summon Burns, Benny, Pearl and Ford as character witnesses for my client. The reason the government became interested in these stars was because their names were found in Mr. Chaperau's effects when agents raided his suite at the Hotel Pierre."

Chaperau explained that he liked to give gifts to his friends. *Time* magazine quoted him cracking, "I smuggled in a dwarf for Snow White, a wig for Shirley Temple, shoes for Garbo, size 9, a necktie for Charlie McCarthy, a rattle for Mickey Mouse and a corncob pipe for Popeye."

Ford took it all in stride, making a joke out of it when he was threatened with indictment. "[It's] a big laugh," he told Frederick C. Othman:

> The federal agents called me in to see what I knew about the charges. They said they understood I had some neckties smuggled from France. I didn't. All I had was a tie Chaperau had given me—and I happened to be wearing it when I called on the G-men.
>
> I didn't know it was smuggled. I didn't know anything about it. Chaperau gave it to me as a gift and I appreciated it. He seemed like a nice little guy to me. I met him in Bill Silver's tie shop in New York. He didn't try to sell me anything. I liked him. I'd like anybody who'd make a gift of a tie like this one [deep red with white spots].
>
> Odd thing about the whole case is how all the folks involved—most of whom I've known for 20 years—all want to get me in the corner and talk about their troubles. When one of 'em hails me, I sort of get a kick out of replying, "Hello, how's the smuggler today?"

George Burns, admitting to paying Chaperau for jewelry worth almost $5000, pleaded guilty, claiming he didn't know the items were smuggled. Fined $8000, he was given a suspended sentence. Benny received a suspended sentence and a $10,000 fine. The judge scolded him, "Sometimes men who are prominent in pictures and radio are just easy marks for smart people. But you should have been smart enough not to fall in with such a plan." Elma Lauer was fined $2500 and served three months in prison, while her husband resigned from the New York Supreme Court. Chaperau was sentenced to five years in federal prison, but was pardoned by President Roosevelt after he helped nab other smugglers. The Nazi maid was paid for informing on the group; and Ford was given a good story to tell his friends and acquaintances.

More "trouble by association" came at the beginning of 1939 when Franklin Schaum, 24, was arrested in Detroit. A former valet who had served Ford, Boris Karloff, director Alfred Santell and others, he was accused of stealing two dozen shirts, three dozen ties and an expensive camera from Santell. Detroit police said that Schaum, using the alias Roland Connell, admitted to them that he had worn out the clothing and pawned the camera in Los Angeles. As for a wallet with Ford's name on it, Schaum alleged that the actor gave it to him because he liked his (Schaum's) work. Also in the man's possession were three unregistered pistols. He was acquitted of the latter charge because the detectives had found the stolen items during an illegal search. According to the *Detroit Free Press* article "Ex-Valet to Actor Freed of Gun Possession Count," Schaum's attorney said that police had gained entrance to Schaum's place "by a ruse, attempted because they had information that Schaum might have stolen several items from Ford when he left the latter's employ to come to Detroit a year ago."

Ford told reporters he would produce and star in the screen version of *Of Mice and Men*. Even though he had befriended John Steinbeck, Wally's plans were cut off when director Lewis Milestone and writer Eugene Solow obtained the option to the film rights. To insure that he got the role of George, Ford invested his own money in a West

Coast limited-run stage version to show everyone in Hollywood that he was the only actor who could portray the character. Broderick Crawford and Claire Luce from the original were too busy to participate, so Ford replaced them with Lon Chaney, Jr., and Isabel Jewell. Frank Coletti, George S. Kaufman's assistant, directed, and Sam H. Harris, from the New York production, co-produced with Ford.

Steinbeck had never attended any of the Broadway performances but, maybe out of friendship to Ford, agreed to take a look at rehearsals—and he wasn't happy with what he saw. As Steinbeck wrote to a friend (quoted by author Jackson J. Benson), "Wally is an actor. He wants to yell and posture. They are screaming their lines. No Kaufman to hold them down so they're just playing their heads off. The hell with it. I've asked Wally to keep his voice down three times but he's an actor." The *Los Angeles Times* quoted him in a more positive mood: "I have seen enough to know that my play is in most capable hands—and am very happy about the prospects of its success on the West Coast—I'd just be in the way if I stayed."

He never returned to rehearsals or attended any of the performances.

On April 6, 1939, *Of Mice and Men* opened at the El Capitan Theatre, with *Variety* calling it one of the "finest acted dramatic performances of recent years.... Typical first night turnout of picture people rose to their feet at the final curtain and gave the cast a reception rare in local theatre annals." Chaney was singled out from the cast.

It was on to the Geary in San Francisco on April 24, for a two-week run. H.M. Levy of the *Oakland Tribune* went on at length about Ford's performance:

> If Steinbeck's [play] is authentic, then Wallace Ford's George is accurate in the same degree. There's little left of Ford's old cinema technique in his translation of the rough but gentle wanderer; only a trace, now and then, of the unwelcome staccato that used to mark many of his film roles. His is a well-rounded and veracious character; a rolling stone who longed to gather the moss of economic independence to be found in his own few acres; a battered and worldly little hulk who knew what he wanted but refused it with a grand gesture for devotion to a helpless, idiotic friend.

Of Mice and Men was back at the El Capitan on May 15, 1939, for a one-week return engagement. The *Oakland Tribune*'s Wood Soanes credited Ford's "magnificent aplomb" with making *Of Mice and Men* "one of the most soul-searing dramas of the decade."

After he closed in the play, Ford went right into *Isle of Destiny* (working title: *Trouble Over the Pacific*), the only feature filmed in the Cosmocolor process. (Prints today are in black and white.) William Gargan and Ford play Marines stationed on the island of Palo Pango (really Santa Catalina Island) who comically and daringly deal with gun smugglers and a lady pilot (June Lang). The original plan was for Grand National to distribute the picture, but after that company's bankruptcy, RKO handled its release in 1940.

In June 1939, Ford received the news that Burgess Meredith would be cast as George in the movie version of *Of Mice and Men*, to be directed by Lewis Milestone at Hal Roach Studios. An even harsher pill to choke down was that Lon Chaney, Jr., whom Ford had coached and helped, was to be the screen Lennie. On June 27, 1939, Ford was arrested for speeding (55 in a 20-mph zone) and driving through a stop sign on Hollywood Boulevard. His wife Martha said that Ford had been brooding over the loss of the coveted role and he seemed to be "taking it out on the car." After the police ran him to the curb, Ford refused to sign the citation because he claimed he didn't understand what the charges were. According to the officers, Ford asked them, "Don't you know who I am?"

"No," chorused the officers.

"Well, I'm Wallace Ford, the actor, and you can't give me a ticket."

It didn't work: they took him to Lincoln Heights jail. "The cops were rude and slapped me," he alleged. Fined $55 for the traffic violation, he denied in court that he had been insulting to the officers. "The booking officer started to put his hands in my pockets and when I protested, he knocked me down," Ford alleged.

Busying himself with other things, Ford discovered Horace McCoy's 1935 novel *They Shoot Horses, Don't They?*, which focused on a dance marathon during the Depression. Ford wanted to produce a play or a movie based on it and offered the lead to Judith Barrett. He got Dudley Murphy to write an adaptation called *Give Us a Break*.

> Wallace Ford, who produced and financed [*Of Mice and Men*] and appeared in the star role, failed to improve his screen status…. He's still looking for a celluloid sponsor, and if it isn't forthcoming by fall, will go back to a Broadway show.—Harold Heffernan, September 1, 1939

On December 26, 1939, at Maxine Elliott's Theatre, Ford returned to Broadway for *Kindred*, a drama written by Paul Vincent Carroll ("…and not his best by a long shot"— Arthur Pollock). He appeared in the prologue as mad painter Dermot O'Regan, who seduces his maid. When he learns she is pregnant, he kills himself. In the two acts that follow, Arthur Shields (who also co-produced) portrays O'Regan's fiddler son. Others in the cast include Aline MacMahon and Barry Fitzgerald. The show lasted only 16 performances, closing on January 6, 1940.

> Unkempt, his heavy mane dripping to his shoulders, a familiar figure stalks past on Fifty-Second Street…. Wally Ford, one of the unhappy heroes of the unhappy *Kindred*.—Louis Sobol, "The Voice of New York"

Ford should have gotten an honorary press card for the number of times he played a newspaper reporter. In the Poverty Row mystery *Murder by Invitation* (1941), he and his girlfriend (Marian Marsh) find themselves in the middle of a family dispute involving an inheritance— and, of course, murder.

Progress was announced on *They Shoot Horses, Don't They?* Hedda Hopper claimed it was definitely going to Broadway, with Ford starring. After calling Ford "one of Hollywood's best actors," she added: "I'm hoping Wally will prove himself to our boys who hand out the fine parts." He wouldn't be proving it in this vehicle. Perhaps Horace McCoy's story was ahead of its time; it wasn't adapted for the screen until the highly praised 1969 film directed by Sydney Pollack.

"That stuff about movie people going back to Broadway to be re-discovered is a lot of bunk," wrote Harold V. Cohen. "Wally Ford won raves in Manhattan in *Of Mice and Men* and has waited until now (*Two Girls on Broadway*) to get a picture break again. He's good, too, which makes his infrequent screen appearances all the more mystifying."

Nineteen forty was the beginning of the character actor phase of Ford's career, with supporting parts in *Two Girls on Broadway, Love, Honor and Oh-Baby!* and the Dead End Kids' *Give Us Wings*. At least in *The Mummy's Hand* (1940) he shared hero honors with Dick Foran. Kate Cameron in the *New York Daily News* described his character as comedy relief and continued, "The role of Babe Jenson seems hardly suited to Ford after his fine dramatic performance in *Of Mice and Men*, but Hollywood has always been a series of ups and downs for its actors and Ford must take the downs occasionally in order to come up again." In fact, the role of Babe, loyal sidekick to Foran's archaeologist Steve Banning, was one of Ford's best. He gives a snappy, lively performance in a fun monster picture.

Of the six movies he made in 1941, two were leads as newspaper reporters: Monogram's *Roar of the Press* and *Murder by Invitation* (Ford replacing Roger Pryor in the latter). Ford liked *Roar of the Press*' screenplay, written by Albert Duffy, so much that he spent a couple of years trying to adapt it for the stage and wanted to use two other members of the cast, Jean Parker and Jed Prouty.

By 1941, Ford had apparently reestablished contact with his mother: The *Hollywood Citizen-News* wrote in April that Ford "received a letter from his mother who lives just outside London, in which she says that she would rather take her chances with bombs than the 'wild life' in America."

For two weeks starting on October 27, 1941, Ford was in Miami co-starring with Grant Withers in *Here Come the Marines* for producer George A. Hirliman and Colonnade Studios. Toby Wing, living in Miami with her flyer husband Dick Merrill, came out of retirement to romance Marine Michael Doyle in the picture. Ford and Withers are Marines who drink, battle spies and each other, and spar over singer Sheila Lynch (alias of model Violet Lynch aka Choo Choo Johnson). Jack Kofoed, who worked on the script, wrote, "This is the first of seven action pictures to be produced within the next 12 months by Colonnade, a distinct contribution to the importance of Miami as an amusement center, and a potential secondary Hollywood."

Making movies wasn't as easy as the Floridians thought. When a year had passed and the film hadn't been released, Kofoed lamented that he wasn't entirely paid for his script doctoring, the movie was made in too much of a hurry, and the screenplay was pared down as they operated on a limited budget. "I've written this," he said, "to keep from explaining to several hundred people what the devil ever happened to *Here Come the Marines*." Colonnade never made another movie. One of the actors, Don Lanning, had a 16mm print and showed it in the dining room of his Miami tavern in July '42.

According to Erskine Johnson, Ford's wife was seriously ill in 1941 and confined to a wheelchair. "The medicos have ordered a year's rest for Wally Ford's missus," added Ed

Sullivan. When they celebrated their nineteenth wedding anniversary in November of that year at Charley Foy's Supper Club, it was, said columnist Lida Livingston, her "first visit to a nightclub in more than a year, due to illness."

Wally made another half-dozen films in 1942, notably PRC's *Inside the Law*, in which he leads a gang who have second thoughts about robbing a bank and want to go straight. "No picture in which Wallace Ford plays the lead can be entirely bad," wrote Grace Kingsley of the *Los Angeles Times*; "but it must be admitted that Wally looks a bit bewildered at moments in some of the highly improbable scenes—even for a comedy—of *Inside the Law*.... But the story has exciting moments and some comic ones, and is made palatable by the appearance and acting of Ford...." *The Mummy's Tomb* (1942) was a 30-years-later sequel to *The Mummy's Hand* in which Ford, made-up to look like an old man, pays the ultimate price for defiling an Egyptian temple (in *Hand*) when the Mummy (Ford's *Of Mice and Men* co-star Lon Chaney, Jr.) catches up to him in America.

In the Alfred Hitchcock suspenser *Shadow of a Doubt* (1943), Joseph Cotten starred as the killer of wealthy widows, with undercover police detectives Macdonald Carey and Ford on the trail, passing themselves off as a pollster and his photographer. Another hero role came Ford's way that year in *The Ape Man*, with Bela Lugosi in the title role. "Wallace Ford was very nice, a very special man to work with," his leading lady Louise Currie told Tom Weaver in *Comics Scene* magazine. "He was an actor who had been around and working a lot longer than I had, but he was very helpful and cooperative. He made things easy and fun."

On July 11, 1942, Ford was a last-minute substitute for Alan Ladd on radio's *Stars Over Hollywood*, in writer Roger Quayle Denny's story "His Rightful Heritage." Radio columnist Ben Gross approved: "Ladd's many recent radio chores have proved his ability, but had he appeared as scheduled he couldn't have topped Ford's performance. As a city tough guy regenerated by rural life, Wally was perfectly cast."

"It's nice to see Wally Ford getting a lot of work again," Harold V. Cohen wrote at the beginning of '43. The only film the actor made that year, however, was MGM's *The Cross of Lorraine* (1944), a serious war drama that shot from April to July. In it, he played one of a group of French soldiers in a German POW camp. For his role as Pierre, Ford grew a beard. When he went to a restaurant and was asked who he was, the actor replied, "Monty Woolley's stand-in."

Here Come the Marines was finally released in the summer of 1943 when Astor bought it from Colonnade and renamed it *The Marines Come Thru*. Reviewers thought it was new—and not very good. Dorothy Masters wrote in the *New York Daily News*,

> That the Leathernecks should take such a shellacking from anybody is a tragedy; from the home front, it's also sabotage, and high time Hollywood put an end to such quickies as undermine various branches of the armed forces.... Dialogue is badly written and spoken, direction is terrible and story worse. The best to be said of the players is that they look slightly ridiculous.

Variety reviewer "Wear" noted, "They laughed at the wrong time or hooted this one in Brooklyn—and it's no wonder." All this for a harmless, amusing comedy made pre–Pearl Harbor. In 1951, the film's staunchest critic, Jack Kofoed, wrote in his column that a friend saw it on television. "Sin never really can be hidden indefinitely ... but if TV has fallen to the depths of using *Here Come the Marines*, it has no more future than the horse and buggy."

Nineteen forty-three was an eventful year, even without a lot of movies, as Ford finally received his final citizenship papers and legally changed his name to Wallace Ford. On March 1, he began work at North American Aviation on the swing swift.

> Someone asked Sam Goldwyn, "What do you think of Wally Ford?" "No one thinks of Wally Ford," said Sam testily, "except when they think of George Washington and the Revolution!"—Sheilah Graham, July 8, 1943

On August 16, 1943, Ford was arrested and booked at the Van Nuys jail as "drunk in auto." At Balboa and Genesta in the San Fernando Valley, he had parked diagonally in the middle of the intersection and gone to sleep, "resisting all efforts to awaken him." Ford denied he was drunk, telling officers he was working on a real estate transaction in the area; then, "simply overcome by the heat," he went to sleep. In court, however, he admitted that he had been drinking and pleaded guilty. He was originally ordered to serve 90 days, but the judge suspended two-thirds of it and sentenced him to 30 days. His driver's license was suspended for six months.

"The actor served his sentence weekends at the Van Nuys jail," wrote the *Van Nuys News*, "where he proved himself a good trusty and entertained other prisoners at intervals, police officers say." The newspaper also claimed that Ford subsequently wrote to the sentencing judge:

> Since my release last Monday, I have become aware of the fact that my well-intentioned friends have had considerable to say regarding my sentence in your court.
> I write to assure you that I did not have nor will I have any part in that—I shall not support any statements detrimental to you or any criticism of the treatment accorded me while I was serving the sentence given me.
> I have only to say, having pleaded guilty, you were fair and just to me and it is my most earnest desire to join your crusade in persuading those I come in contact with to take not the smallest chance of endangering their lives or those of others.

Ever since Ford and Pat O'Brien appeared together on stage, they were buddies. Paramount's *Secret Command* (1944), their first movie together, was about sabotage in a shipping yard; O'Brien the lead, Ford as his friend who comes to a bad end. In the PRC comedy *Machine Gun Mama* (1944), Ford teams with El Brendel as Brooklyn truck drivers who transport an elephant named Bunny to Mexico and then get mixed up with a carnival, the fiery Armida and loan sharks. On radio's *Lady Esther Screen Guild Theatre* (July 10, 1944), Ford, Charles Bickford (replacing Victor McLaglen), Reginald Denny and Isabel Jewell enacted a half-hour version of *The Informer.*

In the summer of '44, Ford was bicycling back and forth working on two films at once, *The Great John L.*, playing boxer John L. Sullivan's manager, and Hitchcock's *Spellbound*. About the latter, columnist Paul Jones wrote that Ford provided one of its brightest moments "when he appears momentarily as a drunken stranger in the hotel lobby." His last of the year was as a reporter in the James Cagney vs. Japanese wartime drama *Blood on the Sun*. "Wallace Ford's performance is so vivid and honest," wrote Boyd Martin, "that we regret the script called for his early demise."

It was announced at the beginning of 1945 that Monogram was "hot" (Lowell F. Redelings) after Ford to headline four crime pictures for them. Instead, he accepted an offer to appear in John Ford's *They Were Expendable*, a true story based the United States PT boat unit Motor Torpedo Boat Squadron Three. Ford played a bearded, pipe-smoking Navy chaplain, and supposedly had a substantial part. A scene between Wally and an atheist in a foxhole was one of the director's favorites—but it was cut, along with most of the rest of Wallace's footage. John Ford blamed MGM, but the movie *was* over two hours, and maybe studio executives thought Wally was truly expendable.

More supporting parts came in *On Stage Everybody*, *A Guy Could Change*, *The Green Years* and *Crack-Up*, the latter again with Pat O'Brien. Ford's daughter Patricia had a bit in *A Guy Could Change*. It was reported that she was being pursued for film roles, radio singing spots and a contract at RKO in 1945. Several columnists mentioned that she made her screen bow in an uncredited bit in 1940's *Swiss Family Robinson*. Any serious ideas the 18-year-old had about a showbiz career ended with her marriage to Zeno Zachary, 28, on June 26, 1945.

In 1944, Frank Fay scored a comeback hit as Elwood P. Dowd in the Broadway show *Harvey*, named after Dowd's imaginary(?) friend, an invisible rabbit over six feet tall. The play was so successful, multiple road companies were being sent out in '45 while the production was still playing in New York. Columnist George Bourke wrote in July '45 in the *Miami Herald*,

> [W]e met the only actor besides Fay to whom we'd entrust the role if it was our dough that was paying the production bills: Wallace Ford. Now that the matter of road companies of *Harvey* is being discussed we'd like to nominate that likable Wally for the job. If the film moguls took one look at Ford in the part, I'm afraid Fay's stock would drop.

Louella Parsons agreed, saying that Ford would be "swell" in the road company.

Ford was too busy to even consider the job (if he was even offered it), as he had movies to make. "Wally Ford's star is apparently shining again," Maxine Garrison wrote at the end of '45. "After a long period of eclipse, Wally's been making himself felt in roles which, though small, stand out mightily as portrayed by him."

"Eclipse" is hardly the word to use for any point in Ford's career. Never ambitious, he simply enjoyed the work, savoring the character parts and not worrying if he was starred or not. It was a plan that actually extended his life in Hollywood. In 1946, he became a grandpa when Patricia gave birth to Peter Nicholas Zachary. Pat O'Brien was Peter's godfather. Granddaughter Stephanie was born a couple of years later.

The year wasn't all work (four films) and rattles. During the making of Humphrey Bogart's *Dead Reckoning*, Ford became seriously ill with a kidney ailment. Always on the go, he recovered quickly and even went into talks about a new play, which didn't pan out. *Academy Award Theatre* (May 25, 1946) rounded up some of the original cast of *The Informer* (Victor McLaglen, Margot Grahame, Ford, J.M. Kerrigan) for another half-hour airwave version. On March 18, 1951, on Hedda Hopper's local KFI radio program, Ford and J. Carrol Naish did scenes from the movie. *The Informer* followed Ford his whole career and beyond.

On January 3, 1947, at 12:30 a.m., at Ventura Blvd. and Canoga Avenue in Woodland Hills, Ford's pick-up struck 18-year-old Silvers A. Foster's car. After swerving into the mud, Ford asked Foster to help him out, but all Foster wanted was his name and particulars. Wally refused. When the police arrived, they found Ford wandering down the road. He told them he was a rancher and insisted that his nowhere-to-be-seen hired man Sam Billings had been driving. He also denied he had fled the scene: He claimed that he was trying to locate his "valuable" German shepherd, which had jumped out the car window. Foster, suffering from a possible ankle fracture, stated that a "very drunk" Ford was definitely behind the wheel and alone except for the dog. Ford was arraigned on a hit-and-run felony charge and his bail was set at $1000.

At the preliminary hearing (January 16), the hit-and-run felony was dismissed. Ford would, however, have to answer to drunk-driving charges. That April he was in court, pretty much making a mockery of the justice system and the note he had sent the judge in his previous trial. Newspaper photos from the time of his arrest showed him clean-shaven, but now he was bearded—and actually looking like Monty Woolley's stand-in—and he told a new tale: The wind had blown his "whiskers" in his eyes, causing him to hit Foster's car! Deputy District Attorney Joseph L. Carr sarcastically applauded Ford for his "beautiful piece of courtroom acting."

Foster and a police officer testified that an intoxicated, non-bearded Ford was "weaving around" after he got out of his truck and then made his getaway when he heard police sirens. Wally claimed that right after the accident, Foster asked him for $40 to fix his smashed fender; when Ford refused, the police were called.

Two of Wally's pals, his stand-in Johnny Breen and actor–café owner Ted Wray, testified that they were with Ford a few hours before the accident and he wasn't drinking. Ford himself admitted he had one bourdon highball and a "sip" of straight whiskey and he "was at a loss as to why he was under arrest" (*Los Angeles Times*). Superior Judge Walter S. Gates, "unable to decide whether whiskey or whiskers caused Wallace Ford to have an automobile accident" (*Hollywood Citizen-News*), recessed the trial so he could visit the crash scene. The judge ultimately acquitted Ford, saying there was "considerable doubt in his mind that Ford was under the influence of liquor" and that he (the judge) was bound to give Ford the benefit of this doubt. Before you cry "Bribe!," be aware that Judge Gates was acquitted of bribery charges in 1932.

This little bump in the fender didn't affect Ford's employment. Less than a week after the trial, he began playing the first of two Eagle-Lion roles in *Man from Texas*, complete with whiskers. His next for the small studio, the noir classic *T-Men* starring Dennis O'Keefe, is one of his best-remembered. Ford gave a weasely performance as The Schemer and had a memorable death scene in a steam room. According to Michael Baron of the *Winnipeg Tribune*, "Wally spent three days in a 'steam room' just for one little scene. They used smoke instead of steam so that the camera lens would not fog over. Wally's eyes were infected. He went to the hospital for three weeks." The *Philadelphia Inquirer*'s Mildred Martin wrote,

> Wallace Ford, who has come into his acting own with the years, and who is undoubtably one of Hollywood's best, though perhaps least appreciated character players, does an outstandingly fine job as the one-time big shot whittled down to size by scornful superiors and finally murdered when he undertakes to cash in on his "ticket to life."

Ford then went to Columbia for the Randolph Scott Western *Coroner Creek*. By this point, Ford's trim, attractive leading man looks had given way to a stockier, sometimes grizzled, craggy-faced appearance that served him well as a supporting player.

On January 27, 1948, Ford directed a limited-run *Of Mice and Men* at the El Patio Theater in Los Angeles, and also played the role of the one-handed ranch worker Candy who befriends George and Lennie. The cast for this engagement is impressive, at least to film buffs: Douglas Fowley as George, Forrest Tucker as Lennie, Shelley Winters as Curley's Wife. Lloyd L. Sloan (*Hollywood Citizen-News*) complained,

> The assumption would be that a vehicle as well-known as *Mice and Men* would be rather simple stuff for a group of capable actors.
> Unfortunately, this is not the case. With all due allowances for first-night problems, and

there were many, the over-all production does not have the polish or pace necessary to draw crowds to a boxoffice selling tickets to a play many people have seen before. Such a show must be exceptionally well-staged, and at the El Patio it is not.

Shed No Tears, an Eagle-Lion film noir, was the last movie in which Ford was toplined. It was a rather different kind of role for the aging actor: He is married to the younger June Vincent, and they plan to fake his death and collect the insurance money. But Wally doesn't reckon on his wife's mercenary nature and an extramarital affair. Warner Bros.' romantic crime drama *Embraceable You* gave Ford a solid part as a police detective who makes sure wheelman Dane Clark takes care of the lady (Geraldine Brooks) he accidentally hit with his car. In *Red Stallion in the Rockies*, Ford as ex–circus performer "Talky" Carson helps out at a ranch and assists in saving a wild stallion. Ford played a "seedy drunk" (*Pittsburgh Post-Gazette*) in *Belle Starr's Daughter* and a small role in the boxing noir classic *The Set-Up*.

Since Ford found his mother in 1936, his contact with her had been sporadic as she disappeared at least twice, even though he had bought her a cottage and taken care of her living arrangements. (One source said there was no cottage, that she went to live with relatives.) In December 1948, some news came out of England, courtesy of the *Manchester Evening News* and a columnist known simply as Mr. Manchester:

> Sitting up in bed in Ormskirk County Hospital, silver-haired 72-year-old Mrs. Catherine Maxted learned from me that her film-star son, Wallace Ford, from whom she had not heard for years, had been trying to find her and was offering her a home in Hollywood. "I would love to go," said Mrs. Maxted, eagerly game though infirm.
>
> I found Mrs. Maxted after an exhaustive search, following an appeal from Mr. Ford's agent in London. I told Mrs. Maxted that all her son's letters to her during the last few years had been returned to him.
>
> Mrs. Maxted explained that during that period she had been in two hospitals and at different addresses in Manchester and Southport.
>
> Mrs. Maxted, who is now a widow, told me she would look forward to a letter from her son—and she hopes he will enclose a photograph, as the two she had have both been lost.

In February–March 1949, Wally was included in an all-star stage benefit tour of *What Price Glory?*, which played around California. The cast included John Wayne; Gregory Peck; Maureen O'Hara; Pat O'Brien (as Sgt. Quirt); Ward Bond (as Capt. Flagg); Robert Armstrong; George O'Brien; Harry Carey, Jr.; Alan Hale; Oliver Hardy; etc. It was co-directed by John Ford and Ralph Murphy. Everyone waived their fees to help the Motion Picture Chapter of the Military Order of the Purple Heart. The proceeds went to building a clubhouse for paraplegic vets.

On June 9, 1949, at 2:30 in the morning, Ford was arrested by patrolmen after he smashed his car into a parked car on Ventura Blvd. and kept right on goin'—fleeing the scene again. He was charged with a hit-and-run misdemeanor. The *Van Nuys News*, who took almost a week to report the accident, called him a "screen idol of the silent films era." It seems this arrest held no interest for newspaper editors and its outcome caused not a ripple. (To add insult to someone else's injury, Ford was featured in advertisements for Wax Seal for automobiles. "Just wipe Wax Seal on and rub it off," Ford says in the ad. "You'll get a glaze that protects the car surface for about three months"—or until someone barrels into your vehicle and leaves the scene.)

The "ex-silent idol" acted in only two movies that year, the Westerns *Dakota Lil* and *The Furies*. He was supposedly on the list of candidates for the lead opposite Shirley

Booth in the upcoming Broadway show *Come Back, Little Sheba* by William Inge; when it opened the following year, the Daniel Mann–directed drama had Sidney Blackmer in the role of Doc, the recovering alcoholic. It became a landmark play and both Booth and Blackmer received Tony Awards.

Four months later, it was learned that Peter, Ford's three-year-old grandson, was in the hospital with polio. At one point, doctors wanted to put him in an iron lung. Louella Parsons, sympathetic to all that Ford had been through in his life, wrote, "Poor Wally, he's certainly had his share of trouble." (Peter eventually regained his health and even became a strapping football high school hero!)

On October 24, 1949, Ford, alongside pal Pat O'Brien, made his television debut on local KTTV on Bob Purcell's public service program about the battle against polio. Ford ended the year as he often did: impersonating Santa Claus at children's hospitals and orphanages, and at Archbishop J. Francis McIntyre's special Christmas party in the Crystal Room of the Beverly Hills Hotel.

Ford was hit hard in January 1950 when actor Alan Hale and Ted Wray died one after the other. The latter, owner of Hollywood's Ivarene Café and sometime-actor, had gone with Ford to Big Bear Lake, where Wally was to crown the queen of a snow festival. The two were staying at the El Paraiso Lodge. One afternoon, Wray went into his room to take a nap. According to the *San Bernardino County Sun*, "Ford looked in on him at 8:30 p.m., and became alarmed at Wray's appearance." Wray, 41, had died, presumably from a heart attack.

Supporting roles came in John Garfield's last two movies, *The Breaking Point* and *He Ran All the Way*, the latter as Shelley Winters' father; and he was a bearded, pipe-smoking cavalry private named "Irish" Potts in the action-packed Western *Warpath* starring Edmond O'Brien. Another "comeback" was touted when he essayed the comic taxi driver in the film version of *Harvey* with James Stewart; reportedly, he got a round of applause from the preview audience.

The coveted dramatic role of Doc Delaney in *Come Back, Little Sheba* might have been lost to him in 1949, but come July 3, 1950, he was given the nod when Sidney Blackmer decided to leave the show. Doc, wrote author Ralph F. Voss, is a "deeply frustrated and disappointed man, an alcoholic … who now struggles daily to stay sober and make the best he can of his situation." When he was a young med student, he married his pregnant girlfriend Lola (Booth), and then she lost her baby; he dropped out of medical college, sacrificing a promising career,

As Ford got older, his heavier frame and whiskers served him well in character parts like this one, Private "Irish" Potts in *Warpath* (1951).

and became a chiropractor. "Although Lola is just as important in *Sheba* as Doc is," continues Voss, "it is Doc's frustration that gradually builds, and it is Doc who eventually gets drunk and forces the dramatic action. Indeed, Doc is one of Inge's relatively few male characters who is truly realistic and powerfully compelling." When the show closed on July 29, the *Baltimore Sun*'s Donald Kirkley called Ford's performance "one of the best things [he] has done on stage or screen." A tour was planned, but Booth refused; she did the movie version in 1952 instead.

That September, Ford received a cable that his mother had died in Southport after a lengthy illness. Her funeral at Duke Street Cemetery was well-attended by family, *sans* Ford. He might have longed for a relationship with her, but it never seemed to happen. One wonders how Catherine felt about being found after all those years and why she resisted the idea of coming to live with him.

In February '51, while acting in *Painting the Clouds with Sunshine*, Ford fell at home and broke his left arm in two places; reports differed as to where the accident took place (ranch steps, bathtub, tripped over dog, etc.). The *Daily Clintonian* claimed that Wally was "four hours on the operating table. He has a plate in his shoulder and pins holding the bones together." On the *Painting the Clouds* set, Ford told Darr Smith, "I broke it falling off a chair that wasn't there. And it's got six plates in it. I mean six screws in it. I mean it's got two plates and six screws to hold it all together. I must have a screw loose somewhere." He added to Smith that *Painting the Clouds* director David Butler insisted he should go directly home at night after filming and "was absolutely not to stop off to have a fast one with any of his happy friends." Explaining why he didn't go to a party in Texas that past weekend for the second anniversary of the Shamrock Hotel, Ford stated, "I'd get down there, and I'd get loaded, and I'd get in a fight with somebody and first thing you know the arm would be broken again, and then what would I say to Butler?"

> Wallace Ford is in Queen of Angels Hospital to undergo reconstructive surgery on his left arm, which he broke in a fall last February.—"In the News," *Los Angeles Evening Citizen News*, May 31, 1951

A stock tour of *Come Back, Little Sheba* with Una Merkel was postponed. He entertained various offers from playwrights for possible Broadway shows. His own play, about Irish patriot Michael Collins, was optioned. Writer William Danch wanted to create a television series centering around Wally. None of this happened. He ended the year in two pictures, *Rodeo* (as washed-up rodeo performer Barbecue Jones) and *Flesh and Fury* (as the manager of deaf boxer Tony Curtis). Clyde Gilmour of the *Vancouver Sun* wrote of the latter, "[O]ld-timer Wallace Ford again proves that he can do more with one silent flick of his shaggy brows and over a fresh-lit match than the average screen actor can do with five minutes of conversation."

Ford's wife Martha's health, always precarious, declined; in November '51, it was revealed that she had suffered her second heart attack in two months. This could be why Ford only acted in one movie in 1952, *She Couldn't Say No* (released in 1954). He made up for it in '53, with roles in *The Boy from Oklahoma*, *The Great Jesse James Raid* and *The Nebraskan*. ("[Ford] seems to have inherited all the Gabby Hayes grizzly roles"— *New York Daily News*.) He was also seen in the TV series *Dude Ranch* (subbing for Leo Carrillo on a local KTTV show), *General Electric Theater*, *Armstrong Circle Theatre*, *Death Valley Days*, *Goodyear Playhouse*, *The Motorola Television Hour*, *Campbell Summer Soundstage* and *Juke Box Jury*. Earl Wilson quoted Pat O'Brien as wiring Ford about one of his recent TV appearances: "There is undoubtedly a warrant out for your arrest for stealing every scene so beautifully." Ford also directed (but did not act in) a production of *Of Mice and Men* at Hollywood's Ivar Theater, starting on March 2. The cast was made up of unknowns, with co-producer Robert Nelson as George and John Mooney as Lennie. The *Hollywood Citizen-News*' Ridgely Cummings credited Ford's staging and called it a "moving experience," adding, "Mr. Ford understands Steinbeck's intentions to the core…. His direction is psychologically sound, extracting the best from his cast…."

In 1954 and '55, Ford had a particularly busy period of activity. Most of his movie roles were in Westerns: *Destry*, *The Man from Laramie*, *The Spoilers*, *The Maverick Queen* and *Johnny Concho*. He was the head of the *3 Ring Circus*, which starred Dean Martin and Jerry Lewis. In June 1954, he had another mishap at home requiring medical attention; Jimmie Fidler reported that Ford "objected to the presence of a housefly in the kitchen. He charged the buzzing nuisance with a swatter. Missed, and his left arm collided with a butcher knife. Sequel, some mumbled remarks, and five stitches. The fly? It vanished and has not returned."

Television continued to supply more work, as he guested on *Studio One*, *Inner Sanctum*, *The Whistler*, *Jane Wyman Presents the Fireside Theatre* (with Victor McLaglen in 1955's "Big Joe's Comin' Home," directed by Blake Edwards), *Screen Directors Playhouse*, *Playhouse 90*, *Father Knows Best*, *Whirlybirds*, etc. When Jim Jordan and his wife Marian decided (or had it decided for them) not to reprise their Fibber McGee and Molly characters on TV, Ford and Grace Hartman were just one of the couples to unsuccessfully test in 1954.

In a 1955 adaptation of "The Ox-Bow Incident" for *The 20th Century–Fox Hour*, Ford portrayed town bum and posse member Monty Smith. It had quite a cast: Robert Wagner, E.G. Marshall, Raymond Burr, Hope Emerson, Cameron Mitchell, Michael Ansara, etc. *Climax!* cast him in another movie adaptation, "Champion," adapted by Rod Serling, starring Rory Calhoun as boxer Midge Kelly, with Geraldine Brooks, Tommy Cook and Wally Brown. "I think Rory Calhoun's vidversion of the Ring Lardner story far surpassed Kirk Douglas' movie portrayal," wrote TV critic Maggie Wilson. "And Wallace Ford as the champ's inebriate father who didn't understand his kids maybe far surpassed Calhoun's dramatics. Camera angles, including some overhead shots of the kayoed champ, added to the dramatic impact. Surely this one will be in the running when the Television Academy hands out the Emmys next year."

"[TV is] a young industry and chaotic," Ford told Erskine Johnson; then, exaggerating a bit, he added, "It takes a little time to get used to a director with a crew haircut and college lingo but it has the fresh breath of youth and it's alive. I like it." Ford had harsher words for the new movie actors; he told Hedda Hopper they would "come and go," adding:

> Personalities will never take precedence over acting ability. In today's pictures you're as good as your part. Most older actors came to pictures with a solid stage background. It shows on the screen. Newcomers scratch their ears, pick their noses, and scratch under their arms. They try to get a feeling from some outside source—modern acting schools teach them to stand in a corner and pretend they're a rock. They don't realize they can't project unless there's feeling inside. Real actors don't move their hands like windmills. They put their character across with voice and real feeling of conviction that comes from the soul.

At home, Martha was still very ill. She was hospitalized in 1955 (after suffering a stroke), 1958 and 1960.

You see a lot of Wallace Ford these days, and for a reason. He's one of the best and most versatile talents in the business.—Bill Summers

In 1959, Ford began a recurring role as Silver City, Arizona, Marshal Herk Lamson on the NBC-TV Western series *The Deputy*. Henry Fonda starred as Chief Marshal Simon Fry of the Arizona Territory, with Allen Case his deputy Clay. Read Morgan, who guested in a Season One episode and joined the series as a regular character in the second season, told author Glenn A. Mosley that Ford was a "wonderful guy, a fun guy. He had a tremendous body of work and a million stories." Ford appeared in 24 episodes, leaving the series in 1960, reportedly because he and the producers could not come to terms. On a guest shot on *Tales of Wells Fargo* that year, he played another marshal, one a lot tougher than Lamson.

On December 14, 1960, Ford was honored with a plaque by the Los Angeles County Nursing Home Association for his "community activity on behalf of the aged," particularly at the Motion Picture Relief Home.

Ford was slowing up in the early 1960s, doing mostly television appearances on *Klondike, Peter Loves Mary, The Barbara Stanwyck Show, The Dick Powell Theatre, Wide Country, The Great Adventure, The Magical World of Disney* (as Bristle Face), *The Travels of Jaimie McPheeters, Lassie* and *The Andy Griffith Show* (as one of Aunt Bee's old beaus who comes a-courtin' again). He did at least three pilots, *The Glass Palace* (1963), *Three Wishes* (1963) and *Hey, Teacher!* (1964). The latter starred Dwayne Hickman as a teacher whose first day of school turns to chaos when a student's pet snake gets loose in the classroom. Ford played the school "jokester and janitor" (*Kokomo Tribune*) Lester Tinney. The *Akron Beacon Journal* said that after watching *Hey, Teacher!*, "you're likely to appreciate all the [regularly shown] programs you've been criticizing."

Ford only made two features in the '60s. In *Tess of the Storm Country* (1960) with Diane Baker in the title role, farmer Ford feuds with the family that sold land in their rural area to a chemical company that contaminates the river. Ford's final film was the indie *A Patch of Blue* (1965) with Elizabeth Hartman as a teenager accidentally blinded in childhood by her trampy, heartless mother (Shelley Winters), and now living with Winters' abuse in a tenement apartment along with Winters' aged, alcoholic father (Ford). Winters and Ford's pathetic "Old Pa" bicker and snap at each other throughout, and even get into an extended fight that leaves no piece of bric-a-brac unbroke and brings all their neighbors to the door. A well-regarded movie that received multiple Oscar nominations, it was a good showcase for Ford as he neared the start of his final year. "[Winters and Ford] give the plot its realistic roots," wrote Judith Crist of the *New York Herald-Tribune*.

On February 9, 1966, while Ford was still gathering laurels for his *Patch of Blue* performance, his beloved wife Martha passed away. In early March, Ford was signed to appear on the *Daniel Boone* episode "Cibola," but illness forced him to withdraw (Royal Dano took the part). He entered the Motion Picture and Television Country House and Hospital in Woodland Hills on March 21. On June 11, the 68-year-old Ford died of advanced heart disease and cirrhosis of the liver. At his funeral at St. Martin of Tours Roman Catholic Church in Brentwood, his pallbearers included Pat Buttram, Anthony Caruso, Frank Faylen, Jimmy Lydon, Frankie Thomas and Keenan Wynn. Ford is buried next to Martha at Holy Cross Cemetery in Culver City.

In 1950, when asked what he wanted on his tombstone, he replied, "At Last I Get Top Billing." As of this writing, his grave is unmarked.

In his "Voice of Hollywood" column, Abe Greenberg wrote:

So Wally Ford's gone to the Great Beyond … and what can anyone say but that we'll miss him sorely … but none more than that fine broth of a buddy, Pat O'Brien, who, until he left on tour, paid Wally a daily visit to comfort his last days at the Motion Picture Home.… Rest easy, Wally, knowing you leave friends like Pat to keep your memory bright.

- **1930**: *Fore* (short), *Absent Minded* (short).
- **1931**: *Possessed, X Marks the Spot.*
- **1932**: *The Beast of the City, Freaks, The Wet Parade, Are You Listening?, Skyscraper Souls, Central Park, Hypnotized.*
- **1933**: *Employees' Entrance, Night of Terror, The Big Cage, Three-Cornered Moon, Goodbye Again, My Woman, Headline Shooter, East of Fifth Avenue.*
- **1934**: *A Woman's Man, The Lost Patrol, Men in White, I Hate Women, Money Means Nothing, The Mysterious Mr. Wong, The Man Who Reclaimed His Head.*
- **1935**: *The Whole Town's Talking, In Spite of Danger, The Nut Farm, The Informer, One Frightened Night, Swellhead, Men of the Hour, Get That Man, She Couldn't Take It, Mary Burns, Fugitive, Another Face.*
- **1936**: *Two in the Dark, Absolute Quiet, The Rogues Tavern, A Son Comes Home.*
- **1937**: *You're in the Army Now, Jericho, Exiled to Shanghai.*
- **1938**: *Stardust, Swing It, Sailor!*
- **1939**: *Back Door to Heaven.*
- **1940**: *Isle of Destiny; Two Girls on Broadway; Love, Honor and Oh-Baby!; Scatterbrain; The Mummy's Hand; Give Us Wings.*
- **1941**: *A Man Betrayed, Roar of the Press, Murder by Invitation, Blues in the Night, All Through the Night.*
- **1942**: *Inside the Law, The Mummy's Tomb, Scattergood Survives a Murder, Seven Days' Leave.*
- **1943**: *The Marines Come Thru, Shadow of a Doubt, The Ape Man, The Cross of Lorraine.*
- **1944**: *Secret Command, Machine Gun Mama.*
- **1945**: *Blood on the Sun, The Great John L., On Stage Everybody, Spellbound, They Were Expendable* (uncredited).
- **1946**: *A Guy Could Change, The Green Years, Lover Come Back, Rendezvous with Annie, Black Angel, Crack-Up.*
- **1947**: *Dead Reckoning, Magic Town, T-Men.*
- **1948**: *Man from Texas, Shed No Tears, Coroner Creek, Embraceable You, Belle Starr's Daughter.*
- **1949**: *The Set-Up, Red Stallion in the Rockies.*
- **1950**: *Dakota Lil, The Furies, The Breaking Point, Harvey.*
- **1951**: *He Ran All the Way, Painting the Clouds with Sunshine, Warpath.*
- **1952**: *Rodeo, Flesh and Fury.*
- **1953**: *The Great Jesse James Raid, The Nebraskan.*
- **1954**: *She Couldn't Say No, The Boy from Oklahoma, Destry, 3 Ring Circus.*
- **1955**: *Wichita, The Man from Laramie, Lucy Gallant, A Lawless Street, The Spoilers.*
- **1956**: *The Maverick Queen, The First Texan, Johnny Concho, Thunder Over Arizona, The Rainmaker, Stagecoach to Fury.*
- **1958**: *Twilight for the Gods, The Matchmaker, The Last Hurrah.*
- **1959**: *Warlock.*
- **1960**: *Tess of the Storm Country.*
- **1965**: *A Patch of Blue.*

Billy Halop

The *Daily Gazette*'s reviewer wrote of Universal's *Little Tough Guy* (1938), "Billy Halop deserves better than to be bracketed with the other five kids as simply one of the [Dead End] gang for he plays a long feature role with passionate intensity and strong feeling. This young actor has the makings of a star and was well chosen for a stellar part in this film."

There was a time, back in 1938, when Halop was considered a potential breakout film star. Success came early for him on radio and when he was on Broadway and on film in *Dead End* as one of the Dead End Kids. He had the skills but in Hollywood that meant little if you were typecast. For many years, up until he was a gray-haired 50-something, Halop's name would always be preceded by "Dead End Kid" and he was most identified as juveniles. "It's horrible, a great drawback," he said in 1976. When he was on a lunch break from playing his recurring role on an *All in the Family* episode, he auditioned for a part on the TV series *The Rookies*. "I'm trying to read my lines, and here's this director jumping up and down saying, 'Billy Halop! Boy! I never thought I'd be in the same room as *him*!!!' All he wanted to hear was Dead End. I read the lines, and he kept looking at me, like he was fascinated. I didn't get the part."

William Halop Cohen was born in Brooklyn on February 11, 1920, the oldest of three children to Lucille (a Russian-born dancer) and Benjamin (a lawyer whose parents were born in Hungary). His sister Florence (1923–86) went on to become a character actress, his brother Joel (1934–2006) a civil engineer. "My Joel wanted no part of acting," Lucille told the *Long Island Star-Journal*, "although all my children have plenty of natural talent."

Grandfather Jack was a Russian violinist who was given a medal by the czarina in recognition of his "meritorious performances" (*Hartford Courant*); according to another story, he got the medal because he was a member of the Queen's Guard. Another relative was an opera singer.

The family moved to Jamaica, New York. While in kindergarten, five-year-old Billy was such a hit in a school playlet that he was encouraged to go on the radio. Using Halop as his professional surname, he was soon an in-demand actor in the medium (*Coast to Coast on a Bus*, *Let's Pretend*, *The NBC Children's Hour*, *Home, Sweet, Home*, *March of Time*, etc.). In 1929, he and his sister performed together on their own radio show over Brooklyn's WSGH. He portrayed Puck on the airwaves in *A Midsummer Night's Dream* and Romeo in *Romeo and Juliet*.

In 1933, Billy began playing the lead role of Bobby Benson (taking over from Richard Wanamaker) on the very popular *The H-Bar-O Rangers*, working with sister Florence and future screen cohort Huntz Hall. As Bobby, he performed with the "real

A pensive portrait of Billy Halop. He longed to become a serious actor but got typecast as a Dead End Kid.

cowboys" in the W.T. Johnson Circus Rodeo and Ringling Bros. and Barnum & Bailey Circus. Radio star Halop was earning more than $700 a week over the air. He attended Children's Professional School and then McBurney's School for Boys (which he claimed expelled him).

In 1935, he accepted the part of the leader of a gang of kids in Sidney Kingsley's Broadway play *Dead End*. His mother had misgivings because of "the nasty language in the script," but she ultimately relented. *Dead End* centered on a group of people, notably several young boys, surviving in the New York City slums during the Great Depression. The adult stars were Theodore Newton, Joseph Downing, Elspeth Eric, Sheila Trent, Margaret Mullen and Marjorie Main. The show was a success and brought a lot of attention to the kids: Halop, Bobby Jordan, Gabe Dell, Huntz Hall, Leo Gorcey and Bernard Punsly.

Leo later remembered, "[A]ll the kids shared one dressing room, with the exception of Billy Halop. He was the leader of the gang, and his parents were not about to let anybody forget it. Billy had his own private dressing room." According to Gorcey, Halop "did not associate with us underlings. After all, as I said, he was the star." This was the start of the contentious relationship between Halop and Gorcey. Leo resented that Halop was the leader of the boys and later, when they were making movies at Warners, he wanted to be the group's leader.

Burns Mantle thought the actors playing the gang were "amazingly natural and enthusiastically shrill." Willard Keefe, who called Halop a "genuinely gifted boy," said that the play would have been "helpless" without Billy. So effective was Halop's acting that columnist Don Sutton said he saw audience member Joan Crawford "clutch tightly the arm of Franchot Tone during that brutally realistic third-act scene when the boy-gangster Tommy [Halop] is about to slit the throat of his enemy 'Spit' for squealing to the cops."

For a while, Halop also continued portraying radio's Bobby Benson and made other airwave appearances. In 1936, his parents went to court to legally change their surname from Cohen to Halop.

MGM and Paramount looked to sign Halop to a contract. After Samuel Goldwyn purchased the screen rights to *Dead End*, Halop went to Hollywood at the beginning of 1937 to reprise his stage role along with Gorcey, Hall, Dell, Punsly and Jordan (plus Marjorie Main). Lillian Hellman adapted Kingsley's script (and cleaned it up for the screen) but it still captured the essence of the play. "[William] Wyler's keen direction and Gregg Toland's … photography of the urban vignettes gives the picture a stunning, artistic ambiance," wrote critic Howard Thompson. And the other members of the cast couldn't be better: Sylvia Sidney, Joel McCrea, Humphrey Bogart, Claire Trevor (Oscar-nominated), Allen Jenkins and Wendy Barrie. "The narrative is moved with simple directness and intense sincerity for distinguished theatrical achievement," wrote *Variety*, "keeping in mind at all times the balance of fascinating detail and the social significances behind the surface play." As on Broadway, the kids stole the show. They were a hit and Goldwyn contemplated casting them in another film, but didn't.

Taking over Halop and Jordan's contracts, director Mervyn LeRoy brought them and the other guys over to Warner Bros., where the Dead End Kids made *Crime School*

Tommy (Halop) is arrested by Mulligan (James Burke) while his sister Drina (Sylvia Sidney) vows to stand by him in *Dead End* (1937). Tommy's pals (left to right) are T.B. (Gabriel Dell), Milty (Bernard Punsly), Angel (Bobby Jordan) and Dippy (Huntz Hall).

(1938). Halop was serious about his work but the other kids were rambunctious, playing pranks on the set and creating havoc just as they had done during the filming of *Dead End*. *Crime School* was set at a reform school where the boys dealt with a sadistic warden (Cy Kendall) and a reformer (Humphrey Bogart) out to create a better environment for the boys.

After filming ended, Warners dropped the boys' options and Halop went to Universal for 1938's *Little Tough Guy* (with Hall, Dell, Punsly, David Gorcey and Hally Chester). Again, as in most of these films, Halop was, according to George Turner, "the most sympathetic member of the group, whose tearful screen mother [more often sister] was always telling the judge that 'Tommy is really a nice boy.'" Unlike the other boys who had names like Spit, Ape, Pig and String, Halop almost always had a normal name like Tommy or Billy.

The *Democrat and Chronicle's* George L. David spent most of his *Little Tough Guy* review raving about Halop, saying (in part) that he "submits a strong, sometimes vivid and always highly intelligent performance. It is a study of the potential boy criminal that comes close to matching the best that Humphrey Bogart or any of his adult equals have accomplished. Halop ... is an unmistakably gifted youngster." Many critics praised his realism and commented that Halop would soon outgrow the group.

Warners saw the great returns of *Crime School* and welcomed back the boys. While the four other kids were given new $250-a-week contracts, Halop received $750. (At the time, he told Sheilah Graham that his radio and movie earnings were in a trust fund and that when he turned 35, he would receive $100 a week for life.) Graham reported that his spending allowance was $1 a day (about $21 today)—"or as much as I want when I go out," he told her. The columnist wrote that Halop

> likes parties. But does not like Hollywood. He says, "There's nothing to do here." He lives with his mother. Billy's opinion of the local girls coincides with Gorcey's—"they're not intelligent," he says. Exception number one is Judy Garland.... Favorite sports—swimming, bowling, and billiards.... Ambitions—to be a director and to undo the "tough" reputation of the boys.

Graham asked Halop about his mother's opinion of Hollywood, and he replied, "How can she be happy when Pop's in New York?" While Lucille chaperoned Billy, her husband did not find it necessary to move his practice to California at that time. He was also working as an executive for the Trunz meat processing plant in Brooklyn. Lucille would periodically commute to see her husband until the marriage went on the rocks. They divorced in August 1940, but remarried on December 10 of that same year. "Billy was so happy over the whole thing he tossed a big party for them at Charley Foy's supper club," wrote Louella Parsons.

Under their new contract, the Dead End Kids made the two Warners films for which they are now best known. In *Angels with Dirty Faces* (1938), Soapy (Halop) and the Kids are devoted to both New York gangster James Cagney and compassionate priest Pat O'Brien; O'Brien is slowly losing the battle for the minds and souls of the kids, who are more interested in fast money and thrills than in their ultimate salvation. While Leo Gorcey tried to upstage Cagney (getting a cuff to the face and a warning for the attempt), Halop had great respect for the star. "[He] taught me a lot," Halop said in 1974. "He told me to get a bag of actor's tricks. He told me to pick up tricks and put them into my bag to use whenever I really needed them."

They Made Me a Criminal (1939) isn't a sequel but Dead End Kids–wise it plays

In the classic *Angels with Dirty Faces* (1938), the boys (Gabriel Dell, Bobby Jordan, Huntz Hall, Leo Gorcey, Bernard Punsly and Halop) can't believe that their gangster hero Rocky "broke" on his way to the electric chair. In the background, priest Jerry Connolly (Pat O'Brien) observes the boys' reactions.

like one: Here they're tough "New Yawk" youths sent to rehabilitate on an Arizona date farm, thanks to a fund set up by a kindly priest who recently died. Their character names are all different (as is the name of the late priest) but they're the same old Kids, constantly clowning and bullying one another, and this time gravitating to a New York boxing champion (John Garfield) posing as a hobo while on the run from the law.

Off camera, the kids were still troublemakers, but tolerated due to their popularity. Halop was considered the one with the most potential. Halop's best role, without the other kids, was with Humphrey Bogart in *You Can't Get Away with Murder* (1939). "This solo acting opportunity," wrote the *Waterloo Courier*, "serves to reveal young Halop as a youth who is well on the road to achieving his declared ambition, which is to be, when he matures, such an actor as Paul Muni." He was getting thousands of pieces of fan mail a week, with one columnist (dubiously) claiming he was second only to Errol Flynn on the Warners lot.

In 1938, his father and trustees of Billy's savings invested part of his money in a new business venture: a series of five super-service gas stations. (A couple of years later, he bought an apartment house. None of his investments paid off.)

Halop never got another solo chance at WB after *Murder*; he went back to being a member of the gang in four more Warners films (*Hell's Kitchen, The Angels Wash Their Faces, Dust Be My Destiny* and *On Dress Parade*). In June 1939, Warners let the boys' options drop. Two reasons were given: They had grown up and were no longer, in the studio executives' eyes, kids anymore; and their troublemaking and pranks had become

In *They Made Me a Criminal* (1939), Detective Monty Phelan (Claude Rains, left) has finally tracked down Johnnie Bradfield (John Garfield, middle) who is wanted for murder. Tommy (Billy Halop) is prepared to help Johnnie escape and go on the run with him.

In a rare 1930s non–Dead End Kid appearance, Billy Halop (left) is caught up in the criminal activities of Humphrey Bogart and Harold Huber in *You Can't Get Away with Murder* (1939).

too much. They were going to keep Halop, but did not want to raise his salary when option time came up. That was fine with Halop, who left to freelance and explore the acting field.

He directed a one-act play called *It Could Only Happen Here*, produced by the Footlighters Workshop in Hollywood. His movie stand-in Bob Cagle (who also wrote songs with Halop) and sister Florence starred.

Universal signed Halop and Huntz Hall for *Call a Messenger* (1939), advertised as a Dead End Kids and Little Tough Guys mash-up—although Leo Gorcey, Gabe Dell, Bernard Punsly and Bobby Jordan were absent. The Little Tough Guys were made up of Hally Chester, Billy Benedict, David Gorcey and Harris Berger. Halop professed to be happy that the core group had broken up: "It gives me a chance to do something bigger and better," he told Sheilah Graham.

He continued to do radio and had a supporting part as a bully in RKO's *Tom Brown's School Days* ("Billy Halop of the Dead End boys surprises everyone by bursting out with a beautiful English accent"—*Silver Screen*). Halop directed a trio of plays at the Laurel Avenue Workshop Theater, attracting yet more attention. "Mark Billy down as a future director and a good one," wrote Cal York.

Universal had Halop and Hall and now they signed Dell, Punsly and Jordan. The Dead End Kids (minus Leo Gorcey) were reunited in 1940's *You're Not So Tough*.

Halop and Jordan and a supporting troupe were sent out in a Dead End Kid vaudeville act. Dorothy Kilgallen mentioned that Halop and Jordan were especially unfriendly to each other, to the point of fisticuffs.

Halop flew solo (i.e., without the other boys) in Universal's serial *Sky Raiders* (1941)

Cop Frank Conroy (Dick Foran) wants to make sure Tom Barker (Billy Halop) doesn't turn to a life of crime in *Mob Town* (1941), a mash-up of the Dead End Kids and the Little Tough Guys. Pictured left to right, Victor Kilian, Halop, Foran, Anne Gwynne and Darryl Hickman.

and then in Warner Bros.' *Blues in the Night* (1941). He was particularly pleased about the latter and the cast that included Jack Carson, Priscilla Lane, Richard Whorf, Betty Field, Lloyd Nolan and Elia Kazan. "It's like a stage show packed with stars," he told Paul Harrison. "Everybody working hard, like on opening night, and every character different.... If I don't learn a lot out of this, I oughta go back to the circus or something." ("It's a pleasure to see him holding his own in fast acting company," the *New York Post*'s Arthur Wilson said of him in *Blues*.) Halop also told Harrison, "I've always felt like some sort of freak until lately. Now that I'm not cute anymore, or precocious, I can just be an actor. And with this mug, I'll never have to worry about being a leading man."

But the popular Dead End Kids comedies kept coming: features and serials (notably *Junior G-Men* and *Junior G-Men of the Air*). Hollywood saw him as a juvenile and he accepted because he wanted to work.

"When I go out, I try to date the best-looking gal in town and we go to Ciro's and close the joint," he said. In addition to dating Judy Garland, he squired Helen Parrish, Virginia Hill (mob courier), Helen Kilgallen (Dorothy's sister) and Georgiana Young around to all the nightclubs. Loretta Young, the latter's half-sister, disapproved of Halop—and no wonder: "Freddie Bartholomew used to play sissy types in pictures," Halop told Nancy Anderson in 1974, "but he wasn't like that at all. We used to cruise up and down in a Cadillac and pick up broads." (Georgiana later wed Ricardo Montalbán and they remained married until her death 63 years later.)

Billy was thrilled to be cast in Warner Bros.' *Blues in the Night* **(1941) and enjoyed the ensemble. Left to right, Peter Whitney, Richard Whorf, Priscilla Lane, Jack Carson, Billy and Elia Kazan.**

Halop organized a theatrical company called the Glen Group Players which put on his play *Joe Hale* as their first production.

Billy's last with the kids was *Mug Town* (1942). When the others (plus Leo Gorcey) went to Monogram to begin a series of East Side Kids comedies, Halop was not involved. ("We don't speak," Gorcey told Erskine Johnson.) Halop had wanted to break away for a long time, and this caused tension between him and the others. Halop was announced for a role in the Universal serial *Gang Busters* (1942) but ultimately was not featured.

In 1942, Halop joined the Army Signal Corps. Corporal Halop was an instructor at New Jersey's Camp Wood. He also directed local U.S.O. productions and acted with Constance Bennett in a radio dramatization of *Days of Glory* on *Saturday Night Bandwagon*. Transferred to England, Halop did a three-times-a-week broadcast called *The Army Speaks*. He also toured U.S. army bases in Europe in *Golden Boy*. (Halop later reprised the part, his favorite, at Maine's Rangeley Lakes Summer Theatre.)

In 1946, Halop was honorably discharged as a sergeant and, wrote columnist Danton Walker, he planned to "go in for serious stage and radio work." But he soon found that his career had hit a real dead end. "When I came back to California in 1946, no one remembered who I was," he said in a 1974 interview. He wanted to steer away from the delinquent roles he had done previously, even turning down offers that were a reflection of that image. Radio remembered him, and he got some work over the airwaves.

On May 30, 1946, Halop, 26, married Helen Tupper, 23, in Las Vegas. She was referred to as a stage actress but it appears that she did nothing more than to entertain the troops during the war.

Halop was in his mid–20s but could not escape his juvenile image. There was an attempt by PRC to do a series similar to those of the Dead End Kids, East Side Kids and Bowery Boys. Halop did just the inaugural film, *Gas House Kids* (1946).

By August 1946, wedded bliss had ended. Halop won an uncontested divorce in January '47 when he claimed that Tupper was "disinterested in keeping house," never had any food in the house, and that he was "forced to cook dinner for himself and his guests."

After he got the lead in Sol M. Wurtzel's *Dangerous Years* (1947), Halop told Louella Parsons that he was "desperately trying to shed the name of Billy": He wanted to be William Halop, actor, not Billy Halop, Dead End Kid. Yet in the film, he treaded the same ground as before: He played a hoodlum with a vulnerable streak. The only reason the film is still remembered is because Marilyn Monroe made her debut in a bit as a waitress. "No, I never thought she'd be a big star," Halop said later. "It took her two days to do one scene."

On February 14, 1948, Halop wed radio singer Barbara Van Brunt (eight years his senior) in Ensenada, Mexico; they re-tied the knot a year later in Palm Springs. Barbara was the ex-wife of actor Kirby Grant.

The new movie career he envisioned never emerged. He continued to do radio (*Broadway Is My Beat*, *This Is Your FBI*, *Suspense*, etc.) and, starting in 1949, television, but he didn't get enough work to live on.

In January 1950, the Economic Cooperation Administration, a U.S. government agency set up to manage the Marshall Plan, hired him to work as a radio producer, writer and actor in France. By June, he and his wife were back in the U.S.; he had developed pneumonia, she bursitis.

Acting work was scarce, and Halop became a part-time electrical appliance salesman in Hollywood. "I spent over four years in the army," he remarked to Hedda Hopper, "and have done three pictures in five years since my return. It's pretty disheartening after 26 years as an actor not to be able to get to talk with a producer. I'm a salesman. I'm not ashamed of it. But my job is acting, and it's sad to be washed up at 31." Months later, he was general manager for a furniture company. (So much for his trust fund, which was squandered on bad investments.)

In 1952, Halop was quoted as saying that he was nixing all bad boy roles to escape the Dead End Kid "stigma." Throughout the 1950s, Halop got only one movie role, a supporting part in *Air Strike* (1955). Eighth-billed, he has very little to do (or say) and just seems to be there with no real character. At one point, he's aboard his plane checking in with squadron commander Richard Denning, and his voice has been replaced by another actor.

He got TV work in dribs and drabs: *The Bigelow Theatre, Racket Squad, The Unexpected, Boston Blackie, The Cisco Kid*. "They don't see me as a mature individual," Halop later complained to Richard Lamparski, "they see me as a child actor and I'm not."

His alcoholism hindered most of his chances. Television spots continued to come, including some substantial roles, but more often menial parts as unnamed characters. "My rejection in Hollywood made me feel unwanted. I started drinking to escape. One morning ... I woke up and didn't know who or where I was. The next thing I knew, I was in a state hospital and had two series of shock treatments. That brought my memory back." It was his wife Barbara who had him committed to the state mental hospital at Camarillo. Halop remarked, "I became a schizophrenic because of booze."

On May 31, 1954, Halop called the West Los Angeles police telling them, "I've just taken some [Benzedrine] pills." When the cops arrived, they found Halop sprawled out on his front porch and arrested him on a drunk charge. He later admitted, "I've been drinking wine because my wife left me." Halop was okay (the hospital found no trace of pills) and he was given a five-day suspended jail sentence. In June, he and his wife reconciled. Two years later, he suffered a nervous breakdown.

One of his better TV roles came in 1957's *Telephone Time* where he played real-life army chaplain (and parachutist) Raymond Hall, who was known as the "Jumping Parson" during World War II.

To supplement his meager acting income, Halop worked as an electric dryer salesman for the Leonard Appliance Company. At the beginning of 1959, he filed for divorce from Barbara (they had been separated since March of the previous year), listing as community property two automobiles and furniture.

By the mid–50s, his father Benjamin had finally moved to California and he and Lucille opened a children's dress shop. Benjamin died in September 1959. In March '67, Lucille married Aubrey Malin Moore in Mexico City.

Original Dead End Kids Halop, Leo Gorcey, Bernard Punsly, Bobby Jordan and Huntz Hall were reunited on TV's *About Faces* in 1960. The next (and last) time they were all together was at Jordan's 1965 funeral.

Halop married again on December 17, 1960. Soon after, bride Suzanne Roe learned that she had multiple sclerosis. In taking care of her, Halop decided to go back to school and get a medical degree. He was discouraged from taking this step but went ahead anyway, becoming a registered nurse and finding work at St. John's Hospital in Santa Monica. He dealt mostly with geriatrics, alcoholics and drug addicts. He and Roe divorced in 1966. "Billy Halop is trying to remarry his ex-wife, Suzanne Roe," wrote Harrison

Carroll. "She got the decree because she has multiple sclerosis and didn't want to saddle him with a cripple."

His career bumped along in the 1960s. Uncredited movie roles came as an elevator operator, milkman, subpoena server and taxi driver. He was seen on TV's *Wanted: Dead or Alive; 77 Sunset Strip; Wagon Train; The New Breed; The Fugitive; The Adventures of Ozzie and Harriet; Perry Mason; The Andy Griffith Show; Gunsmoke; Gomer Pyle, U.S.M.C.; Land of the Giants*; etc. In a 1969 episode of *Adam-12*, he played a judge.

On November 21, 1966, he eloped to Las Vegas with Hazel Tedrick, a nurse co-worker.

Halop took one of his periodic breaks from his nursing to work at a haberdashery. "They'll let me off to take acting jobs," Halop remarked to John L. Scott. "Nursing, especially taking care of old people, is a worthy profession, but recently two of my patients died and I've had it right up to there." Despite the other jobs he took to survive, acting remained at the forefront: "It's my main purpose in life, and I'll take practically any role to keep my foot in the theatrical door.... I'm also very much interested in becoming a director. I know the business from A to Z. You know, now and then I run into the newer breed of director who couldn't even direct traffic successfully."

In January 1967, he and Tedrick separated. That November, he filed for an annulment, claiming he had "sobered up from a six-week drinking binge to realize the wedding was a horrible mistake." Halop told the judge, "I have an alcohol problem. I do things I wouldn't do otherwise when I'm drinking." He also testified that he had no knowledge of his wife's current whereabouts.

By 1970, Halop had suffered two heart attacks. He underwent open heart surgery the following year. He talked of writing his autobiography, called *There's No Dead End*, with author Jerald Albarelli. During these years, he lived with his second wife Barbara, although they did not remarry. Now out of the nursing profession altogether, he was a chef at Ted's Rancho in Malibu.

He got a break when he became a regular on TV's *All in the Family* in 1971, playing Burt Munson, a pal of Archie Bunker (Carroll O'Connor), for $500 a day. He eventually appeared on ten episodes, the last airing on February 9, 1976. "I am happy. It's a wonderful experience, the closest thing in Hollywood to Broadway. And Carroll O'Connor is a gem. They all cater to him, but when it's your scene, he gives it to you."

In his later years, Halop spoke bitterly about his association with the Dead End Kids, saying that the only one he got along with was Gabe Dell. The others, Halop claimed, were jealous of him because he was paid more than they were. As successful as he was during the Dead End Kid years, Halop did not relish mentioning them. "I was wealthy at 21. We all were. But then things went awry. I don't know if the fame came too soon for us or what, but a lot of the guys had personal problems their whole lives."

Two days after suffering another heart attack, 56-year-old Halop died in his sleep on November 9, 1976. He is interred with his parents Benjamin and Lucille (she died in 1982) in Los Angeles' Mount Sinai Memorial Park.

"In his youth, Billy appeared exceptionally talented," wrote the *San Bernardino County Sun*'s Buck Biggers, "yet beyond the Dead End format, success remained elusive. Thus, the announcement of his death … seemed doubly sad. It spoke of unfulfilled promise."

1937: *Dead End.*
1938: *Crime School, Little Tough Guy, Angels with Dirty Faces.*

1939: *They Made Me a Criminal, You Can't Get Away with Murder, Hell's Kitchen, The Angels Wash Their Faces, Dust Be My Destiny, On Dress Parade, Call a Messenger.*
1940: *Tom Brown's School Days, You're Not So Tough, Junior G-Men, Give Us Wings.*
1941: *Sky Raiders, Hit the Road, Mob Town, Sea Raiders, Blues in the Night.*
1942: *Tough as They Come, Junior G-Men of the Air, Junior Army, Mug Town.*
1946: *Gas House Kids.*
1947: *Dangerous Years.*
1949: *Challenge of the Range, Too Late for Tears* (uncredited).
1955: *Air Strike.*
1962: *Boys' Night Out* (uncredited).
1963: *The Courtship of Eddie's Father* (uncredited), *For Love or Money* (uncredited), *The Wheeler Dealers* (uncredited).
1964: *A Global Affair* (uncredited).
1966: *Mister Buddwing* (uncredited).
1967: *Fitzwilly* (uncredited).
1974: *The Phantom of Hollywood* (TVM).

WELDON HEYBURN

"Weldon Heyburn ... didn't choose to resemble Clark Gable," Mollie Merrick wrote in 1932. Back in the 1930s, plenty of men would have killed to look like Gable—tall, dark and handsome, with a virility that was hard to match. For an actor, however, it was a liability. "[If] it weren't for the fact that duplicates of other people never register in Hollywood, I'd feel fate gave me a lucky break when I resembled him," Heyburn told Merrick. "But as things are, I'd rather forget it, if it's possible." He continued:

> But you've got to be yourself in life and the most unfortunate thing that can happen to you is to be a weak echo of someone who already has impressed his personality and attainments on the public mind.
>
> I'd rather play comedy if that were possible than to attempt what this profession calls "Clark Gable roles." In that way I keep away from the rubber stamp "a second Gable."

Try as he might, Heyburn could never get away from that tag. In a 25-year career, he played varied stage parts and more than 60 movie roles but was never allowed to forget who he looked like. In 1951, his obituaries commented that he "acted in a number of films but his Hollywood career was handicapped because of his marked resemblance to film star Clark Gable."

Weldon Heyburn Franks was born in—take your pick—Washington, D.C.; Selma, Alabama; or Delaware City, Delaware (the latter according to baptism records), on September 19, 1903. Weldon was the only son of Wyatt Golson Franks (1872–1940) and Marie Pierce Moore (1878–1929); he and his two younger sisters, Kathryn and Jessie, grew up in Washington, D.C. Their father, an

In the early 1930s, there was no one hotter than Clark Gable, the reigning King of Hollywood. Weldon Heyburn was lucky enough to look like him, but unfortunately, he did not possess that certain *something* that Gable had. For a time, the Poverty Row outfits appreciated him.

accountant, entered the military in 1898, fought in the War with Spain and the First World War.

While in junior high, Weldon was a swimming champ and a Boy Scout. He studied law at George Washington University and the University of Alabama; at the latter, he was a member of the Blackfriar Players. "Spanny" to his friends, he found himself spending more time in the campus theater than hitting the books, and dropped out in his senior year. Shortening his name to Weldon Heyburn, he acted with the John B. Mack Players in Lynn, Massachusetts, and with stock companies in Pittsburgh; he also did *What Price Glory?* on the road. The young actor shared the stage with such notables as Florence Reed, Marjorie Rambeau and Chrystal Herne.

On October 6, 1924, Heyburn, 21, wed British-born Phyllis Connard, 24, in Lynn, Massachusetts, where they acted together in the John B. Mack Players. They had obtained a waiver of the five-day law (as Heyburn was leaving to do stock in Windsor, New York) and were married at the rectory of the St. Stephen's Episcopal Church by Reverend William A. Lawrence.

In 1925–26, when he toured with *Abie's Irish Rose,* the *Fremont Evening Tribune* called him "an artist of unquestioned merit." The *Idaho Statesman*, however, felt he "looked a little too much like Jack Dempsey to be a perfect Abe Levy, likable chap as he was."

During this time, he tried to promote himself by claiming that his uncle was Senator Weldon Heyburn (1852–1912). He laid it on thick, telling the *Idaho Statesman*,

> My acquaintance with my uncle is not very clear in my mind. I am told it consisted chiefly of his trotting me on his knee and often putting me to sleep. It was decided by my family, who are of the genuine old Quaker type of Philadelphia, that I should follow in my distinguished uncle's footsteps and I took the law course at the University of Alabama, where I was graduated.

Other reports had him practicing law for a brief time. Of course, this is untrue. Senator Heyburn's niece denied he was a relative, and told the *Spokane Daily Chronicle* that the actor was "an impostor if he persists in his claims." Other members of her prestigious family also wrote to newspapers to expose his lie. This didn't prevent this biographical "fact" from popping up in his later publicity. He also alleged that he had played a number of roles in silent films.

Phyllis Connard was granted a divorce on October 15, 1926.

In 1926 and 1927, Heyburn was employed as leading man with the Wright Players in Lansing, Michigan, and appeared in *Adam and Eva*, *The Goose Hangs High*, *Smilin' Thru*, *The First Year*, *In Love with Love*, *Applesauce*, *The Green Beetle*, *The Alarm Clock*, *Peg o' My Heart*, *The Old Soak*, *Laff That Off*, *Kick In*, *The Brat*, *Why Men Leave Home*, *Three Live Ghosts*, *The Patsy*, *The Show-Off*, *Crooks Square*, *The Best People*, *White Collars*, *Pigs*, *The Love Test* and *Some Girl*. "LADIES—An Autographed Photo of Weldon Heyburn Will Be Presented to Each Lady Next Wednesday Matinee," promised ads for *The Brat* in 1926. Joining the Anne Bronaugh Players in Winnipeg, Canada, Heyburn was seen in the productions *Madame X, Applesauce, Rain* (making "an awful mess" of the part of fanatical Reverend Davidson—*Winnipeg Tribune*), *Fair and Warmer* and more. He made his Broadway bow in *The Mystery Man*, a drama which opened January 26, 1928, co-written by actor Morris Ankrum. About a month later, Heyburn was replaced by Gordon James.

He became a heartthrob for his leading roles in two Syracuse, New York, stock companies, the Temple Players and the Syracuse Theater Guild Empire Players, and in the Mae Desmond Players in West Philadelphia. One *Syracuse American* columnist remarked that Heyburn "causes all the 'Oh's' and 'Ah's' from the female members of the audience whenever he steps on the Temple stage." He toured in vaudeville with Jeanne Eagels doing scenes from *Her Cardboard Lover* and *Rain*.

In September 1928, five months after *Skidding* premiered on Broadway, Heyburn briefly took over the role of Wayne Trenton III from Walter Abel. Not long afterward, he was one of four actors given screen and voice tests at the Famous Players Studio in Astoria for the part of Michael in Mary Pickford's upcoming *Coquette* (1929); he lost out to Johnny Mack Brown. (Heyburn's publicity declared that he roomed with Brown at the University of Alabama and that he was a member of the 1925 Alabama Crimson Tide football team. Both claims are false.)

At Werba's Flatbush, he supported star Mary Boland in *Mrs. Cook's Tour* (1929); it closed for some rewriting and never reopened. His next Broadway show was *Troyka* (1930), adapted from a Hungarian play, starring Zita Johann. The *Brooklyn Daily Times'* Rowland Field called it an "unhappy production that fails lamentably in its attempt to present a somber story of Russia on the stage." It closed after 15 performances. Heyburn proceeded to (briefly) become the "It Boy" of Pittsburgh's Sharp Players.

Heyburn was cast as the virile, aggressive bootlegger Dingo Mike in Lenore Ulric's *Pagan Lady* (1930), which was in out-of-town tryouts. Franchot Tone played the main male lead. When Dudley Digges was hired to polish up the production before its October 20, 1930, New York premiere, he replaced Heyburn with Russell Hardie.

Weldon's first known screen appearance was in the filmed-in-New York Vitaphone short *Compliments of the Season* (1930). A young lady (Lenita Lane) is saved from suicide by a recently released crook, Jimmy "Fingers" Dugan (Eric Dressler), on Christmas Eve. While Dugan is hounded by a police detective (Pat O'Brien), he holds up a man on the street (Heyburn) so he can get a meal for himself and the girl. Things turn around in an unexpected way.

In December 1930, Franchot Tone left the *Pagan Lady* cast and Hardie assumed his vacant part—and Heyburn got his old role back. After a five-month run on Broadway, Ulric and company took the show on the road. In 1931, Heyburn was involved in the pre–Broadway run of *Nikki*, based on John Monk Saunders' series of *Liberty Weekly* short stories, "Nikki and Her War Birds," his novel *Single Lady* and the film *The Last Flight* (1931). The title role was played by Saunders' then-wife, Fay Wray.

Many thought the dark, good-looking Heyburn resembled Clark Gable, who was then making an impression as an MGM leading man. "Gable-less studios aren't exactly looking for more Clark Gables," said columnist Hubbard Keavy, "but they would like to have dark-complexioned he-men with soft voices and menacing eyes." The six-foot, husky Heyburn fit the bill, and in August 1931, Fox signed him. "He is decidedly the Gable type: An Antithesis. He has strong, determined eyes and a soft, convincing voice," Keavy continued. "You get the idea, looking at him, that he could be either hero or villain, or both. That's what you think when you see Gable and that's the reason he panics the women folk." (Heyburn shared something else: In 1928, he was headlining a stock company whose "character woman" Josephine Dillon was then Mrs. Gable.) Despite Heyburn's resemblance to Gable and acting experience, he lacked a crucial element: Gable's charisma and star power.

In a blatant attempt to connect Heyburn to Gable, this Fox press release went out before he was even seen in a movie:

When Weldon Heyburn, leading man, came to Fox Studio, he was accepted with certain stipulations. Two of these reservations involved Weldon's ears, which stood out at angles calculated to cause considerable wind resistance.

Well, Weldon's ears have [been] revised and since they now lie flat against his cranium in a fashion delightful to Fox execs, he'll get busy on some roles under his long-term contract.

Fox believed he had the potential to be a top star. "I am told on the Fox lot he is being pushed ahead," Louella Parsons wrote. Heyburn's first was *The Silent Witness* (1932), based on a play by Jack De Leon and Jack Celestin. When Anthony (Bramwell Fletcher) confesses to his parents that he has killed his mistress, gold digger Nora Selmer (Greta Nissen), his father, London barrister Sir Austin Howard (Lionel Atwill in his talkie debut), takes the rap to save his son. A third-billed Heyburn—wearing a mustache and looking and sounding a *lot* like Gable—is the "beaming and scoundrelly" (*Philadelphia Inquirer*) heavy Carl Blake who is married to Nora. Affected and stiff in his first scenes, Heyburn gets much better near the conclusion when he drops all pretense and roughs up Nissen. His overly polite cad might have gone over well on stage, but it was only partially successful on film.

Norwegian-born Nissen thought he was hot stuff, and on March 30, 1932, they eloped to Tijuana; Justice of the Civil Court Ricardo Gilbert officiated. Weldon's father

"Greta Nissen, film actress, and Weldon Heyburn, actor, who were married March 30 [1932] at Tia Juana, Mexico, are shown here in an intimate scene of homelife as they appeared before the camera just before they flew from Hollywood to the scene of their wedding."

and Tijuana newsman William Clay Silver acted as witnesses. News reports called Weldon Nissen's "caveman" and related the "sweet story" of how their love affair began: "They met in a picture which called for Heyburn to choke Miss Nissen. At the first rehearsal of the choking, according to [Nissen], so kindly did [he] pretend to throttle her that affection developed." Born Grethe Rüzt-Nissen, she started out as a ballet dancer. After dancing on Broadway in *Beggar on Horseback* (1924), she was discovered by Paramount. The advent of sound put a serious crimp in her career. Howard Hughes' *Hell's Angels* began shooting as a silent film, with Nissen playing Helen; but in the middle of production, the release of the part-talkie *The Jazz Singer* (1927) prompted the decision to start *Hell's Angels* again, this time with sound. Nissen was replaced by Jean Harlow.

It's a wonder the Heyburns made it to their first anniversary: Their on again-off again relationship made the newspapers regularly, as they were always on the verge of divorcing. His jealousy was a problem. At a June 1932 party, an intoxicated Heyburn thought Nissen was flirting with someone, got into his car and, wrote Mollie Merrick, "drove madly away from it all and right over a sixty-foot embankment smashing the car to tiny bits but hurting himself practically not at all." According to *Variety*, he suffered a dislocated collarbone.

Hubbard Keavy mentioned in his column that Heyburn resembled German boxer Max Schmeling, an apropos comparison considering an October 1932 incident wherein Heyburn took a swing at director Dudley Murphy at a Hollywood nightclub called the Club New Yorker for dancing with Nissen. Quite unlike Schmeling, Heyburn was a bust: "One blow was used," wrote the *Los Angeles Times* of the encounter. "It was delivered by Heyburn and was intended for Murphy's chin, or eye, or something. But it missed its mark." Solidifying his caveman rep, Heyburn picked Nissen up and carried her out of the nightclub.

Instead of starring him as they had stated, Fox put Heyburn in character support: Mexican Jito in *The Gay Caballero* (1932), socialite golfer Jud Carey in *Careless Lady* (1932), the evil sheik Abdullah in *Chandu the Magician* (1932) and Native American Ronasa in *Call Her Savage* (1932). Except for *Careless Lady*, none of them traded on his similarity to Gable. "Mr. Heyburn is disconcertingly like Mr. Gable," opined M.B. of the *Spokesman Review* about *Careless Lady*, "a Gable who is more robust and more brawny and more smiling." The *Detroit Free Press*' Ella H. McCormick felt the similarity was only in the profile and the speaking voice. "The moment the Heyburn countenance faces the camera it loses all likeness of the Gable features. Clark photographs well at any angle—Weldon only in profile. In proof, watch Mr. Heyburn in *Careless Lady*." A *Kansas City Star* reviewer sarcastically called Heyburn

> [a] performer who looked and talked exactly like Warner Baxter but who now is made up to resemble Clark Gable and to sound like him. In view of other recent movie successes, it seems an even break between Mr. Heyburn's impersonating Jackie Cooper or Marie Dressler in his next picture. All of which adds suspense and zest to going to the movies.

By October 1932, Heyburn had left Fox and was being enticed by Mary Pickford to sign up to be her leading man in the Frances Marion–written *Shantytown*—and offered a long-term deal with United Artists. "Every young man in this village with the slightest claim to ability was after that role in *Shantytown*," wrote Mollie Merrick, "and this is a triumph for the stage actor who could have had a happier experience at Fox studios than he did." Ultimately, Pickford couldn't decide whether she wanted to do *Shantytown*

Edmund Lowe's Chandu (left) battles to save Irene Ware from baddies Bela Lugosi and Weldon Heyburn in the stylish sci-fi–fantasy *Chandu the Magician* (1932). (Photo courtesy of John Antosiewicz.)

or *Secrets*. The latter won out. Heyburn was to do *Secrets* and, at a later date, *Shantytown*. His hopes were way up, but his triumph was short-lived: He was considered "not the type," and Leslie Howard got *Secrets*. After Pickford retired, *Shantytown* and Heyburn's contract with UA were gone with the wind.

Heyburn found himself at Monogram for the quickie *West of Singapore* (1933) starring Betty Compson—his first leading man role on screen. *Variety* opined,

> Not a bad picture for the small spots, providing, of course, *Red Dust* hasn't preceded it. In such a case it will disappoint through repetition and subsequent comparison. Story is virtually a dupe on the Jean Harlow-Clark Gable picture, but with less attention devoted to production. Characters have been altered somewhat, but not sufficiently to hide identity.

As for Heyburn, who was obviously there for his resemblance to Gable, they added that his "grimacing spoiled an otherwise good performance, and brought occasional chuckles from the preview audience."

In August '33, he and Nissen were still having marital troubles when they co-starred in the indie *Hired Wife* (1934). Filmed at Sun Haven Studios in St. Petersburg, Florida, it was directed by George Melford, who had also helmed Valentino's *The Sheik* (1921) and the Spanish-language *Dracula* (1931). Harold Ballew of the *Tampa Bay Times* claimed that Heyburn handled all his wife's business, and then quoted Heyburn as saying, "I was in New York rehearsing a play when this Florida matter came up. My wife was in Hollywood."

Many critics considered Monogram's *West of Singapore* (1933) with Heyburn and Margaret Lindsay a rip-off of MGM's Clark Gable-Jean Harlow starrer *Red Dust* from the previous year.

> Somehow, the offer didn't appeal to me at all—until they agreed to let Miss Nissen star in the picture. With great anxiety I closed the deal for both of us, not knowing that my wife had committed herself to British pictures and was planning to leave for London tomorrow, the same day that shooting was to start here on *Hired Wife*.
> God bless dear old London. With many excuses, Miss Nissen will make pictures in Florida.

All this sounds rather fishy. If Heyburn *really* took care of Nissen's business, he would have known she was leaving for England—and, no doubt, wanted her to stay in the U.S. As for the producers agreeing to "let" her star in the movie, it was probably the other way around; Nissen was the draw here, not Heyburn.

About the Sun Haven Studios, Heyburn remarked, "The studio here is fine. The equipment is the most amazing for a studio of its size either of us has seen. We anticipated working in a barn and on arriving in St. Petersburg we find a progressive organization that should in no time be a great credit to Florida."

The following month, September, the Heyburns were a picture of wedded bliss. Not. "Here's the latest on the Weldon Heyburn-Greta Nissen marriage complications," reported Walter Winchell. "Although they were photographed 'sailing together' last week—he didn't. There was a stormy scene at the pier, and this time the bust-up is definite." Nissen bolted to England.

In New York, he did the Vitaphone shorts *Masks and Memories* with Lillian Roth; *Darling Enemy* with Gertrude Niesen; *The Winnah!* with Arthur Lake, Florence Lake and Dorothy Dare; and *The Mysterious Kiss* with Jeanne Aubert. But acting work was so scarce that he also worked as an actors' agent. Meanwhile, Nissen, in London making movies, announced for the umpteenth time that she was seeking a divorce. "Mr. Heyburn and I prefer to sacrifice our matrimonial tie in the hope of preserving our friendship. We have no horrible accusations to hurl at each other."

While Nissen was dating artist Jacques Darcy, Heyburn was involved with Pola Negri and touring with her in the duolog "For All We Know." On June 25, 1934, he replaced Lester Vail in Broadway's *Are You Decent?*, and received more than 200 mash notes from female admirers during the week he was in it. He took a short break from the show to make *Convention Girl*, portraying a square-shooting gambler who wants to marry cabaret hostess Rose Hobart. She refuses unless he goes into some other line of work. Directed by Luther Reed, it was shot in Atlantic City and at the Photocolor studios in Irvington, New York, and it premiered on September 10 at Steel Pier. The movie is notable today for featuring Shemp Howard in a serious role as a blackmailer who tries to kill Hobart's nephew.

Are You Decent? closed on September 29, 1934. Heyburn was then engaged to play the leading male role in the Broadway-bound *Sexes and Sevens* on October 15 at Philadelphia's Chestnut Street Opera House with Margot Grahame. It was the American premiere of this French farce, written by Anthony Prinsep and Alfred Savoir. According to the *Philadelphia Inquirer*, Heyburn "early captured the audience and his work throughout was sparkling." After a little more than a week, the show closed for extensive revisions—and never reopened.

Nineteen thirty-five was tough for Heyburn. The only movie he made was *Highway Patrol* for the Hope Rubber Co. with Eve Farrell, Jane Steel and Walter Gilbert. It was produced with the cooperation of the Pennsylvania state police in the interests of safer driving. (The film was reissued in 1938 as *Dynamite Delaney* and in 1941 as *The Fighting Chump*.) Heyburn was now in a "destitute financial condition."

On September 16, 1935, Nissen signed a petition in London for annulment, claiming that they tied the knot in Tijuana without following Mexican law: They went through with the ceremony without establishing legal residence, without getting physical examinations, and without qualified witnesses, and therefore their marriage was not legal. The action was filed on October 19. "Mexican marriages and divorces seem to be very convenient," wrote a *Los Angeles Times* reporter. "If either the Mexican marriage or the divorce does not happen to suit, one can always go into court and get either set aside.... It seems strange it would take her so long to discover the marriage was illegal."

Broadway's *Good Men and True* (with Heyburn in a top role) was a flop, and yet it led to a screen test and contract at MGM. But first, he was committed to another play, *I Want a Policeman!*, which opened on December 26, 1935, in Philadelphia and on January 14, 1936, on Broadway. Edgar Price of the *Brooklyn Citizen* considered Heyburn "manly and good looking" as the main detective on the murder case. Critic Arthur Pollock called the play "amiable, friendly, amusing and quite often thrilling," and said that Heyburn looked a "good deal like Jack Dempsey." (Another fitting description, especially since Heyburn once got into a nightclub brawl with ex-boxer Jack "Doc" Kearns, Dempsey's manager.)

In February, Heyburn left *I Want a Policeman!* and was on his way to Hollywood. Louella Parsons wrote, "[He] is going into picture-making in a serious way.... Heyburn is good-looking and he may really do something in pictures. In fact, he is on the Gable type, which right now is so popular with the women."

Speed (1936) didn't give him much of a chance to show off that type. Set around an automobile factory, it featured one of those love triangles then favored in Hollywood: Brash, cocky test driver and inventor Terry Martin (James Stewart) and steady, nice-guy engineer Frank Lawson (Heyburn) compete for publicist Jane Mitchell (Wendy Barrie). Will Martin get the financing to perfect his new carburetor? Can he hold his temper long enough for Jane to win him? At least Heyburn gets to fall back on secretary-turned-executive Josephine Sanderson, played by the wonderful Una Merkel. Filming took place from March 20 to April 7, 1936, and it was sped into release in May. This was Stewart's second lead role (after the same year's *Next Time We Love*).

After finishing *Speed*, Heyburn filed for bankruptcy, listing as liabilities $2050.96, which he claimed were Nissen's obligations. Later that month, April 29, the annulment became final, their stormy marriage finally dissolved. The press reported that Nissen was "as pleased as a kid with a lollipop," and she told reporters, "It's been a long wait. Three years and five attorneys. I am very glad."

Heyburn was, too. Before you could say "Me Weldon, you Jane," he had found his Jane: Cleveland-born society girl Jane Eichelberger, the daughter of an attorney (and, allegedly, a cousin of Tallulah Bankhead) and the ex-wife of tennis player Morton Bernstein. Eichelberger was infamous for dressing in fur and walking her pet ocelot on a leash in Central Park.

On May 5, 1936, Heyburn, 32, and Eichelberger, 24, married in the garden of his Brentwood home. The ceremony was performed by Reverend Gordon C. Chapman,

Inez Courtney was a wonderful screen cohort for Heyburn in *The 13th Man* (1937), one of his best movies.

pastor of the Westwood Methodist Episcopal Church. Edwin L. Marin, who directed Heyburn in *Speed*, was supposed to be best man, but he didn't show up and no one could find him; broker Frank Clinton took his place. Among the small gathering of friends was actresses Wendy Barrie and Nancy Carroll.

While the Heyburns honeymooned in Ensenada, Mexico, Weldon's home was looted of $1000 worth of silverware (almost $20,000 today)—gifts from their wedding. The heist was believed to be the work of a gang of "honeymoon burglars." The theft was reported to the police by the bride's mother.

At the end of October, showgirl Lillian Land brought suit against Heyburn for $2336. She charged that between September 15, and November 30, 1935, he had borrowed money from her with the promise of marriage, and then reneged. The case was settled out of court.

For Heyburn, life at MGM was not what it could have been. *Speed* was his only film for Metro; after spending many months there, he was let go. In 1940, Heyburn vaguely stated to director John Cromwell (subbing for Walter Winchell), "A studio paid me $25,000 to stay off the screen for 12 months so there'd be no mix-up with Clark [Gable]. I was plowed under, but here I am again."

In 1937, the Poverty Row studios were more than willing to have their very own pocket Gable. *Git Along Little Dogies*, a Gene Autry starrer, was Heyburn's first for Republic. He played a supporting role as a seemingly respectable citizen who is really up to no good. For Monogram, he starred in one of his best films, *The 13th Man*, as radio commentator-newspaper reporter Swifty Taylor, investigating the murder of a district attorney with the help of his secretary (Inez Courtney). An *Independent Exhibitors Film Bulletin* reviewer thought it was done in a "bright, snappy style.... Nor is there lack of suspense. This chap Heyburn is a comer, or we miss our guess."

Republic's *Sea Racketeers* was a "buddy" movie featuring Heyburn and Warren Hymer as Coast Guardsmen who battle J. Carrol Naish's gang of fur smugglers. As a side occupation, they fight over women, in this case Jeanne Madden and Dorothy McNulty (aka Penny Singleton). For the *Motion Picture Herald*'s "What the Picture Did for Me" column, a Fort Worth exhibitor wrote,

> This action picture received the heartiest patron approval of any Republic production we have played, the Gene Autry films excepted. Several of our patrons who are alert to the technical side of the business commented upon the good sets, photography and sound, and noted that the picture was apparently budgeted at a higher figure than usual. The cast, while not exceptional, is more than adequate and manages to make some of the obvious situations seem less so. We consider ourselves fortunate in having played this film."

> While Hobe of *Variety* thought Heyburn "even more kittenish than usual," he was far less enthused over leading lady Madden: "[She] has about as much life as a department store clothes dummy."

In May '37, aviator Dick Merrill and his co-pilot Jack Lambie made the first commercial transatlantic round-trip flight (dubbed the "Coronation Flight"). Two months later, Monogram signed them to appear in *Atlantic Flight*, where the two were seen "repeating" the feat in the same plane—a Lockheed Model 10E Electra called *Daily Express*. Merrill and Lambie were no actors, so Monogram "spun a likable melodrama" (*Film Daily*) around them, with Heyburn, Paula Stone, Ivan Lebedeff, Milburn Stone, Gertrude Messinger and others taking up the acting slack. Heyburn acquitted himself well in one of his best roles as a plane designer who romances Paula Stone. Also for Monogram, Heyburn had the lead with Anne Nagel in *Saleslady* (1938).

Weldon Heyburn and Anne Nagel play a married couple in *Saleslady* (1938).

On August 19, 1937, audiences at San Francisco's Curran Theatre saw the return to the stage of Marjorie Rambeau after an absence of a few years. William Hurlbut's *Story to Be Whispered* was set in the bonanza mining days of the 1870s with Rambeau as a madam and Heyburn as a mining man. Ada Hanifin of the *San Francisco Examiner* wrote that Weldon "has charm and conveys a crude boyishness and naïveté that courts the audience as well as Rose Grandee [Rambeau]. An actor, who by virtue of his looks and manners, could easily become a matinee idol." Although the acting was praised, most reviewers were disappointed in Hurlbut's treatment of a familiar story, and the play never reached its intended destination of Broadway.

Heyburn had a brief, uncredited role in the Paramount comedy *Every Day's a Holiday*, where, looking slick with a mustache and tux, he danced with star Mae West.

Those in the "know" were convinced that Heyburn and Eichelberger's union would be one of the most colorful mergers of the decade—but what did they know? From the start, the match was not a good one, as she had no intention of mingling with Heyburn's friends—and vice versa. Eichelberger left him on October 12, 1937.

The years 1938 and '39 were slow ones for Heyburn, and also the period when he made the transition from hero to heavy, notably playing the duplicitous head guard in the Dead End Kids vehicle *Crime School* (1938). The Zane Grey Western *The Mysterious Rider* (1938) gave him a different kind of villain to play: As the hot-tempered son of a rancher, Heyburn fights his old urge to cattle-rustle but can't help feeling jealous and violent when the girl he wants to marry (Charlotte Field) fancies another (Russell

Hayden). At the conclusion, Heyburn almost redeems himself when he goes after the killer of his father.

Seen around nightclubs with Nancy Carroll, Eda Hedin, Adrienne Ames and Virginia Field throughout 1938, Heyburn kept his marital problems on the down-low, and the press didn't even report his filing for divorce. That all changed when Walter Winchell wrote in January 1939 that Heyburn alleged that Eichelberger "prefers Nassau, Nantucket and New York to his Fox, Metro and Warner films." On charges of "willful desertion," he was granted a divorce by default on March 15, 1939.

The 36-year-old Heyburn eloped to Tijuana with 21-year-old Maryland debutante Virginia Maggard on September 9, 1939. They had first met a few years earlier when he was acting in *I Want a Policeman!* and she was attending Gardner's Finishing School. How could this marriage possibly go wrong?

On December 22, he played opposite Charlotte Greenwood at Los Angeles' El Capitan in *She Couldn't Say No*, a "laugh riot" (*Los Angeles Daily News*). The two-week engagement ran into the new year of 1940. In January came rumors that Heyburn and ex-wife Greta Nissen would reconcile. Virginia, his bride of only four months, wasn't mentioned at all. It took Nissen three months to deny the stories. "It is very embarrassing," she told Harrison Carroll. "I have another commitment." (Her 1941 marriage to executive Stuart Eckert lasted until her death in 1988. They had a son.) His marriage to Maggard kaput, Heyburn dated Christine McIntyre and Stephanie Bachelor.

Variety called Heyburn a "good he-man type which tailors best for cop, saddle hero, athletic or similar roles" at a time when he found himself a character actor, often unbilled. He carved a nice niche for himself as a Western baddie. "Weldon Heyburn oozes villainy from the first moment he appears," wrote *Showmen's Trade Review* about his performance in the Three Mesquiteers' *The Trail Blazers* (1940). Harry Sherman, who had produced *The Mysterious Rider*, also cast Heyburn in *The Round Up* and the Hopalong Cassidy movies *In Old Colorado* and *Stick to Your Guns* (all 1941).

Through the years, it was often mentioned that Heyburn's likeness to Gable had stopped his movie career before it had begun: "Audiences don't want to see anybody that looks like Gable. They want to see Gable," he told director John Cromwell. By the 1940s, however, hard drinking had taken a toll on Heyburn's once handsome face. In fact, in 1940, Jimmie Fidler wrote, "One look at *North West Mounted Police* rushes, showing Weldon Heyburn with a mustache, and C.B. DeMille ordered his scenes re-shot. He looked too much like presidential candidate Tom Dewey!" When he appeared in the 1943 Western *Death Valley Manhunt*, it was reported that he was wearing one of Gable's *Gone with the Wind* costumes.

On September 24, 1940, Heyburn was seen in the West Coast premiere of Elmer Rice's *Two on an Island*, a "fable about life in Manhattan" (*New York Times*), at Los Angeles' Wilshire Ebell Theatre. The leads were Terry Belmont (aka Lee Bonnell) and Renee Haal (who became Renee Godfrey after marrying director Peter Godfrey). In the role of hard-boiled stage producer Lawrence Ormont, Heyburn "gave an expert, finely modulated performance, bringing color and excellent comedy to the scene" (the *Los Angeles Times*' Katherine Von Blon).

For a week, starting November 12, 1941, he had the leading role in William Anthony McGuire's *The Divorce Question*. "Weldon Heyburn, lately of the New York stage, was welcomed home by a fine audience at the [Guy Bates] Post Theater," wrote Von Blon. On May 18, 1942, he entered the U.S. Army Signal Corps. Not long after, he was honorably discharged and went to work in an aircraft factory. He was in Washington, D.C., when it was alleged that he impersonated an Army sergeant. On May 8, 1943, he was given a suspended sentence of a year and a day by Federal Judge W.A. Keeling in San Antonio, Texas.

Back in Hollywood, he went back to appearing mostly in Westerns. An exception was Monogram's Charlie Chan stanza *The Chinese Cat* (1944), in which he was seen as a police detective unable to solve a locked-room murder. In the film, Heyburn, 40, was also the romantic interest of Joan Woodbury, 28.

Heyburn—"and goodness, I haven't heard of him in years," exclaimed Louella Parsons—and Marta Mitrovich had the leading roles in the American premiere (October 17, 1943) of *Immortal Girl* at the Wilshire Ebell Theatre. Written by Marianne Rieser, it was a "satirical drama of a timeless love story laid in Alexandria during the days of early Christian persecution," wrote the *Los Angeles Times*. "The parallel to modern times is said to be arresting." It was meant to transition to Broadway, but that never happened.

In 1945, radio work included a regular stint on the five-days-a-week serial *Right to Happiness*. The play *Dinner for 3* opened on March 19 in Delaware, on March 22 in Philadelphia and on April 2 in Boston. The cast also included Harry Ellerbe, Miriam Seegar, Stanley Logan, Marjorie Lord, Les Tremayne and Anne Francine. It was produced, written and directed by Tim Whelan, Hollywood director and husband of Seegar. While the comedy entertained receptive audiences, it never got to New York.

The Charlie Chan whodunit *The Chinese Cat* (1944) gave Heyburn a fair-sized role as a police detective at a time when he was mostly doing bits. Pictured left to right: Joan Woodbury, Heyburn, Sidney Toler and Benson Fong.

That September 8 in Philadelphia, Heyburn was in the supporting cast of *Emily*, a psychological thriller starring Simone Simon as a "nasty, neurotic" invalid with revenge on her mind. It closed on September 22 for major revisions. "Simone Simon, out of town with the Shubert show *Emily*, is having trouble with actors in the cast who don't give her 'the right inspiration,'" Dorothy Kilgallen reported. *Emily* never reopened.

At this point, Heyburn was again having trouble finding work. His last really good movie role came in Charles Starrett's Durango Kid Western *Frontier Gunlaw*, his only 1946 release, as a wheelchair-bound newspaper editor who is actually the head of an outlaw gang. In August '46, he acted at the Pompton Lakes Summer Theater in *Outward Bound* with Ruth Altman. The *Paterson Evening News* wrote, "In the portrayal of Mr. Lingley of Lingley, Ltd., Weldon Heyburn is a poised businessman who exploits his charm and stage presence with professional skill."

Western actor Pierce Lyden, who appeared in *Death Valley Manhunt* with Heyburn, called him "one of the handsomest actors with whom I worked. Great things were expected of him. Some thought he might be a challenger to Clark Gable, but he was a heavy drinker, and the word got around. The last time I saw him [1946], he seemed disillusioned, discouraged and down on his luck."

"Weldon Heyburn, once under contract to MGM for $1000 a week, is at the Birmingham hospital facing surgery," Harrison Carroll reported on October 26, 1949. "Doctor may let him out to play a part in [a] Joan Crawford picture before the operation. Weldon would like to hear from some of his old pals." He was able to play an uncredited bit as a butler in the Crawford movie *The Damned Don't Cry* (1950). In November '49, a plea was sent out via Edith Gwynn's column: "[Heyburn] knows he probably can't get well from his illness and asks help from the producers in making the most of what's left him." No acting jobs came through. (His last movie, 1950's *The Great Jewel Robber*, was filmed prior to his surgery.)

He spent a year at the Veterans Administration Hospital in Los Angeles, suffering from terminal bronchopneumonia, cancer of the mouth, and metastases to adrenal and kidney. The 47-year-old died there of pneumonia on May 18, 1951. He is interred next to his father at Arlington National Cemetery.

1930: *Compliments of the Season* (short, uncredited).
1931: *The Last Parade* (uncredited).
1932: *The Silent Witness, The Gay Caballero, Careless Lady, Chandu the Magician, Call Her Savage*.
1933: *West of Singapore*.
1934: *Hired Wife, Masks and Memories* (short), *Darling Enemy* (short), *The Winnah!* (short), *The Mysterious Kiss* (short).
1935: *Convention Girl, Highway Patrol* (aka *Dynamite Delaney* and *The Fighting Chump*).
1936: *Speed*.
1937: *Git Along Little Dogies, The 13th Man, Sea Racketeers, Atlantic Flight, Every Day's a Holiday*.
1938: *Saleslady, Crime School, The Mysterious Rider*.
1939: *Panama Patrol, Should a Girl Marry?, Fugitive at Large*.
1940: *Emergency Squad* (uncredited), *Women Without Names* (uncredited), *North West Mounted Police* (uncredited), *The Trail Blazers*.

1941: *Flight from Destiny, The Round Up, In Old Colorado, Redhead, Caught in the Draft* (uncredited), *Criminals Within, Stick to Your Guns, Jungle Man, They Died with Their Boots On* (uncredited), *You're in the Army Now* (uncredited).
1942: *Code of the Outlaw, Rock River Renegades.*
1943: *Blazing Guns, Overland Mail Robbery, Death Valley Manhunt, Death Valley Rangers.*
1944: *Westward Bound, My Best Gal* (uncredited), *Charlie Chan in the Chinese Cat, Man from Frisco* (uncredited), *The Yellow Rose of Texas, Bordertown Trail, When Strangers Marry* (uncredited), *Code of the Prairie, The Princess and the Pirate* (uncredited), *Here Come the Waves* (uncredited), *She Snoops to Conquer* (short).
1945: *Incendiary Blonde* (uncredited).
1946: *Frontier Gunlaw.*
1948: *A Southern Yankee* (uncredited).
1949: *Alias Nick Beal* (uncredited), *Samson and Delilah* (uncredited).
1950: *Perfect Strangers* (uncredited), *The Damned Don't Cry* (uncredited), *The Great Jewel Robber* (uncredited).

Ronald Lewis

For a time in the 1950s, Ronald Lewis was considered a star in the making, with the potential to be a great stage actor. Personal demons ate away any chance he had of achieving that fame. He was a complicated man consumed by anger. When he drank too much, which was often, he had a violent temper. There were several instances where he seriously hurt others. Then, also, there were times when he was charming and showed a gentle side to his personality. Lewis was constantly on the go, pushing himself, trying to prove himself. It is not surprising that he burned out so quickly.

Ronald Glasfryn Lewis was born on December 11, 1928, in Port Talbot, Glamorgan, Wales. When he was seven, the family moved to London; a few years later, they returned to Wales. At the all-boys Bridgend Grammar School in South Wales, Ronald made his acting debut, playing Bassanio in the school production of *The Merchant of Venice*. His desire to become a professional actor was cemented after he saw Ann Casson in the play *Saint Joan*. The family relocated to London for good, and that is where Ronald attended high school. (After Ronald's death, his first wife Norah Gorsen told *The Daily Mail* that he had a strict Welsh chapel upbringing, a home where drink was banned, and a stern accountant father who disapproved of acting and wanted his son to become a linguist.)

In April 1946, 17-year-old Lewis, a member of the Student Players of Toynbee Hall, was in a production of *Hamlet*. *The Stage* opined, "[He] created an arresting portrait of Claudius in spite of not quite being able to disguise his youth." Toynbee Hall was an institution dedicated to charitable ventures; they put on *Hamlet* to help the Reunion Theatre Association for ex-service actors and actresses. Yugoslavia's King Peter and Queen Alexandra attended one performance and said they were quite impressed.

Ronald Lewis was a complicated man, full of anger and contradictions. His career never reached the heights it might have.

Lewis enrolled at London's Royal Academy of Dramatic Art (RADA). On August 3, 1949, students performed George Bernard Shaw's *Arms and the Man* at the Stanford Hall People's Festival. The *Nottingham Journal* singled Lewis out, saying he "gave a good performance, light but convincing, and was possibly the most effective in 'pointing' his lines" (placing emphasis on certain words and phrases). Less than a week later, the *Nottingham Journal*'s Carole Findlater complained about most of the other students' stilted speech, but praised Lewis for his "intelligent and effortless acting." Act 2, Scene 2, from *Cymbeline* was performed at a RADA matinee on March 28, 1950, with Lewis as Iachimo; a reviewer for *The Stage* wrote that he gave a "delightful impression of impish humour without once raising his voice beyond a whisper...."

By the following month, Lewis was a member of the Overture Players (with Alan Bridges, Margaret Diamond, Andrée Melly, Frederick Treves, Charles Morgan and Alan Robinson) at the Connaught Theatre. He had supporting parts in *Anna Lucasta, Bright Shadow* and *Random Harvest*. Some of the Overture Players, including Lewis, then joined the new Worthing Theatre Company. Lewis was in their *Master of Arts, The Purple Fig Tree, The Family Upstairs, Dear Evelyn, What Anne Brought Home, Room for Two, If This Be Error, September Tide, Queen Elizabeth Slept Here, The Case of the Frightened Lady, Black Chiffon, We Proudly Present, A Lady Mislaid, The Bridge of Estaban, The Third Visitor, Three Wise Fools, Mrs. Warren's Profession, Too Young to Marry* and *Gathering Storm*. Of his performance in the latter, the *Worthing Herald* declared, "Ronald Lewis' simple-minded grandson, a difficult part, is a skillful creation." He was also singled out in the paper's review of *The Late Edwina Black*: "[A]lthough rather a lightweight for the part of the husband, [Lewis] tackles it gamely and gives quite a persuasive reading of it, making the fellow the sort of weak young man a wealthy woman might have married."

Lewis had his first lead with the company in *Romeo and Juliet*, with Carol Marsh as his Juliet. *The Worthing Herald* wrote, "Lewis' Romeo is particularly well-spoken and outstanding. His Romeo is young, vigorous and intelligent." Most of his parts were supporting, and reviewers commented that he came across too youthful, but the *Worthing Herald* noted that he had an "instinct for character" and often got "right inside" his roles.

In January '51, the *Worthing Herald* reported that Lewis was leaving the Worthing Theatre Company: "He has ambitions which point towards work for the films." But movies were not in the cards for him just yet; he returned to the Overture Players and also worked with the County Players, the Playhouse Company and the Bankside Players. During this phase of his stage career, he performed in *The Merchant of Venice, The School for Scandal, A Midsummer Night's Dream, Captain Carvallo, Night Must Fall, The Vigil, Home or Away, As You Like It et al*.

While performing Christopher Fry's *The Boy with a Cart* at the Regent's Park Open Air Theatre, he met his future wife, actress Norah Gorsen. She said in the abovementioned *Daily Mail* article, titled "Tragedy of the Nearly Man," that she sensed "something tearing away at him inside" but she couldn't figure out what. They wed in 1953 and divorced in 1956.

On September 29, 1952, at Brighton's Royal Theatre, Lewis opened in Ralph W. Peterson's boxing drama *The Gladiators*. By the time it reached London's Lyric Hammersmith on October 21, the title had been changed to the more suitable *The Square Ring*. Set entirely in the boxers' dressing room, the play focused on various stock types of pugilists. According to the *Western Mail* newspaper, "Eddie Evans [Lewis' character], a young Welsh tyro emerging from the amateur to the professional class, alternating in over-confidence and timidity, [was] brilliantly played." In Eddie's first—and only—pro fight, he learns a hard lesson when he goes against a dirty fighter who rubs resin in Eddie's eyes.

The Square Ring was a critical and commercial success. Nineteen fifty-three saw Ealing Studio putting the play onto celluloid, with Basil Dearden directing. It starred Jack Warner, Robert Beatty, Maxwell Reed and, reprising their stage roles, Lewis (his character's name changed to Eddie Lloyd), Bill Owen, Bill Travers and George Rose. Screenwriter Robert Westerby's adaptation added characters (played by actresses Joan Collins, Kay Kendall and Bernadette O'Farrell) to open up the story.

Lewis was seen on stage in William Douglas Home's *The Bad Samaritan* (1953), a comedy-drama of sex, love, sacrifice and religion, which enjoyed success on the road. "Two young players, Virginia McKenna (21) and Ronald Lewis (23), contributed performances of infinite promise and sound intuition," opined the *Portsmouth Evening News*. The *Western Mail* added, "He has much in his favour: a fine presence, a rich and well-controlled voice and a rare gift of natural acting. He should go far."

Lewis had a small part in the movie *The Beachcomber* (1954) as a native boy, complete with brown makeup and pidgin English ("Come, please. My father wish see you"). Filmed in Rome in 1954 but not released until 1956, the epic *Helen of Troy* featured Lewis as Trojan hero Aeneas, the one true friend of his cousin Paris (Jack Sernas). Also set during the Trojan War, *The Face of Love* (1954) was a BBC-TV adaptation of Shakespeare's *Troilus and Cressida*. Playing the warrior Diomedes, Lewis got to act with such fine actors as Mary Morris, Laurence Payne, Peter Cushing and Donald Pleasence. He appeared as a doctor on another BBC show, *Fantastic Summer* (1955), in which a woman (Fay Compton) finds she has second sight. *The Stage* called it a "melodramatic trifle."

In the controversial BAFTA-nominated *The Prisoner* (1955), acting heavyweights Alec Guinness and Jack Hawkins go toe to toe as prisoner and interrogator respectively. Lewis played the guard who has romantic troubles with the married Jeanette Sterke. According to Doreen Turney-Dann of the *Bradford Observer*, this subplot was meant to "relieve the tension" of the intense main storyline.

On June 9, 1955, *Mourning Becomes Electra* began its seven-week run at the Arts Theatre. Eugene O'Neill's retelling of the Greek tragedy *The Oresteia*, it featured Lewis as Orin, a sensitive, tormented man controlled by his mother and sister. From the *Western Mail*:

> We watched Ronald Lewis with a fascinating interest, in all the changing emotions of his great part, the alternations of his mood and attitude towards his mother, and still more impressive, the oncoming madness which springs from his guilt. [His performance] has placed him in the front rank, winning the approbation of the critics and of the other sophisticated folk who crowd into the Arts Theatre.... To undertake such a role in such a place, and with such brilliant and experienced actresses as Mary Ellis and Mary Morris, would be an act of courage for anyone.

Lewis' performance commanded attention and *The Stage* believed it earned him a "permanent place in the West End theatre. His acting shows so many fine, sensitive qualities, and his style has such virile conviction that he stands out among actors of his age."

The theater might have been where Lewis' heart was, but the real money came from the movies. Signed to a contract by London Films, Lewis first played a supporting part in *Storm Over the Nile* (1955), a CinemaScope remake of *The Four Feathers*. In mid–1955, the *Manchester Evening News* reported that Lewis and George Baker (an Associated British contract star) "are being tested for the lead in MGM's mammoth remake of *Ben-Hur*."

When Lewis wasn't acting, he played tennis and studied languages. "He enjoys translating from the Russian," noted one publicity item.

A Hill in Korea (1956), a "much belated tribute to the work of the British Army in that tragically inconclusive war" (Anthony Carthew, *Daily Herald*), gave Lewis his first chance to show his stuff on screen. Lewis' Private Wyatt has a bad attitude and is disliked by his fellow National Servicemen. He shows arrogance, poor judgment (he throws away their only radio because he no longer wants to carry it), cowardice, hysteria—and finally bravery. The *West London Observer's* Ray Willis: "Ronald Lewis, a young actor of considerable ability, depth of feeling, and intelligence, gives the character depth and in so doing forces one to pity rather than despise him."

Back on June 6, 1955, Lewis appeared in a TV version of Philip King and Falkland Cary's play *Sailor, Beware!* The following year, he, Peggy Mount and Cyril Smith reprised their roles in a big-screen adaptation (released in the U.S. as *Panic in the Parlor*). Lewis "played engagingly" (*Leicester Chronicle*) the role of sailor Albert Tufnell, who is set to marry his sweetheart Shirley (Shirley Eaton)—*if* they can survive the wedding preparations and the meddling of Shirley's mother Emma (the loud and bombastic Peggy Mount).

A behind-the-scenes candid of Vivien Leigh and Lewis when they acted on stage in Noël Coward's *South Sea Bubble*.

When first-choice Peter Finch turned down the role because of a film commitment, Lewis got the opportunity to act on the stage opposite Vivien Leigh in Noël Coward's *South Sea Bubble*, which opened at the Lyric on April 26, 1956. Taking place on the mythical Isle of Samolo, the comedy focused on Lady Alexandra and the native Hali Alani, "with whom she gets amusingly tangled" (Edwin Hall, *Worthing Herald*). The play itself got mixed reviews but Lewis was praised, and it upped his standing in the theater. "Ronald Lewis ... scores as the native male charmer, using his handsome mien, flashing teeth and an attractive broken accent to spout his oddly-constructed sentences," wrote *Variety*. "His beach-house flirtation scene with Miss Leigh is neatly done."

In June '56, after Lewis' movie contract was sold to Rank, he replaced Anthony Steel in *The Secret Place* (1956) with Belinda Lee. His character, a diamond thief, seems at first to be a genial guy in love with Lee, but he shows his true colors when he tries to kill the young boy who finds the stolen gems.

With Vivien Leigh leaving the cast of *South Sea Bubble* that August (she was pregnant), Lewis found himself on a grueling schedule: He had to rehearse with Leigh's replacement Elizabeth Sellars during the day and then, after evening performances of *Bubble*, shoot night scenes for *The Secret Place* at Pinewood. Lewis told the *Motherwell Times*, "At least the nights are short at this time of the year. We finish shooting at dawn, so I get a couple of hours sleep before going to the theatre." In September '56, the BBC brought in cameras to film *South Sea Bubble*'s second act. On October 7, he did "The Hollow Crown" on TV's *Armchair Theatre*.

After a total of 276 performances, *South Sea Bubble* closed on Christmas Day, 1956.

At the beginning of 1957, Lewis took riding lessons for his upcoming role as a bushranger (i.e., a thief living in the bush) in *Robbery Under Arms*. "I am enjoying the training for this," he told the *Western Mail*, "as much as I did my boxing lessons for *The Square Ring*, which gave me a big chance in London." Part of the movie was filmed in Australia. Brothers Dick and Jim Marston (Lewis and David McCallum) rustle cattle and rob coaches with their father (Laurence Naismith) and the notorious Captain Starlight (top-billed Peter Finch). During a fight scene, stuntman-actor Laurence Taylor "smashed two of Lewis' ribs" which, reported the *Peterborough Advertiser*, "turned into a real-life slug-as-you-please session." Taylor replied, "No hate about it, though, whatever they say. It was just a good fight scene. I was acting all the time. Perhaps the temperature—110 degrees in the shade—put an edge on our tempers." John Fraser—an actor not in movie—said in his autobiography, without revealing his source, that Lewis, a "bruiser and a bully," attacked and beat up David McCallum on the set.

Emlyn Williams adapted his play *Night Must Fall* for a 1957 episode of TV's *Hour of Mystery*, in which Lewis starred as baby-faced killer Danny. Betty Hardy was the old woman he befriends and murders. Lewis was to play the title character in another TV production, *El Bandido*, that year, but was replaced at the last minute because his face was swollen from an impacted wisdom tooth (or so they say). His replacement was Charles Gray. "I was sorry to learn that Ronald Lewis was indisposed and unable to appear in the play," wrote the reviewer for the *Liverpool Echo*. "But he was fortunate to be spared this dreadful charade."

In a 1957 *Armchair Theatre*, Lewis played Oswald in "Ghosts," with Marie Ney as his mother and Basil Sydney as the pastor. Ney had done the first TV adaptation of the Ibsen drama in 1937, and Sydney had played Oswald on stage in 1917.

Shot on location in India, the romantic World War II drama *The Wind Cannot Read*

(1958) told the love story of British Flight Lieutenant Michael Quinn (Dirk Bogarde) and his Japanese language instructor Suzuki San (Yôko Tani). Lewis got special "And" billing for his fairly small role as the smug Squadron Leader Fenwick. He goes through most of the movie with a chip on his shoulder, and disliked by his comrades; life imitated art as, off-camera, Lewis did not endear himself to his castmates, particularly supporting player John Fraser:

> Ronnie Lewis [was] hailed at that time as a great actor in the making. He had tiny eyes, inexpressive like a bear's, a jaw like the bumper of a truck and a dangerous quality, for the good reason that he was. Extremely dangerous. I found out later that he had thrown his live-in girlfriend out of a first-floor window, breaking her skull and several ribs....
>
> Ronnie hated India. He hated the heat and the multitude and the poverty and the erratic plumbing, and he was blind to the beauty on every side. He spent his free time by the pool drinking Pimms or brandy sours, and by the evening he was often morose. He could "haud 'is boattle," as my Aunt Gatty would put it. He didn't slur his words or bang into things or fall over; his drunkenness was dogged and depressed.

Fraser found out firsthand one night that Lewis' temper and alcohol were a volatile mix. Lewis began needling Fraser about his homosexuality, yelling at him, "Come on, you yellow fucking pansy bastard. I'll show you what a man can do to a fucking Nance." Concerned about how onlookers would perceive him, Fraser decided to stand and fight.

> But the factor that I had failed to take in account in this struggle was that my opponent was insane. Sexual jealousy and envy and resentment boiled in his brain, already inflamed with drink, to make an already miserable and angry man demented. As soon as I was facing him, he charged me like a maddened bull at the matador's cape and with one swing of his fist he felled me and broke my jaw. Not one other blow was exchanged. The diners, galvanized at last by his savagery, came to my rescue, preventing him from killing me.

As a result of one of his molars being knocked out, Fraser had lasting impairment to his sinuses. He submitted to two surgeries in an attempt to fix the damage. He declined to sue due to the notoriety the case would have attracted.

On May 3, 1958, on the BBC-TV program *The World Our Stage*, Lewis and Peggy Cummins acted in David Whitaker's ten-minute playlet *The One Day a Year Man*, which was filmed on the grounds of Longleat House, home of the Marquess of Bath.

In *Bachelor of Hearts* (1958), a German exchange student (Hardy Kruger) tries to fit in at Cambridge. Most of the comedy derives from his attempts to adapt to the British way of life. Lewis, again relegated to support, plays an overgrown schoolboy who is a member of a group of undergrads known as the Dodos. Edwin Hall of the *Worthing Herald* recounted an incident involving Lewis on the set: "He had to run out of one of the colleges, wearing only a bath towel, and scale a wall. When he got to the wall, a gust of wind took hold of the towel. The film unit people shut their eyes. But they needn't have— Lewis had forgotten to tell them he was wearing shorts." When Lewis later told friends this story himself, he finished by looking at himself in a mirror afterwards and remarking, "I am getting on for 30. It's high time I started taking myself seriously."

Not long after, Rank dropped Lewis from their contract list, possibly at the actor's insistence. "I have never been happy there," he said. "I have never been satisfied with the films they have given me to do." The *Worthing Gazette*'s Peter Dean called this an "unfortunate quote" and implied that Lewis (and others like him) were ungrateful for the chances that movie studios gave them. Maybe, but Lewis considered himself, first and foremost, a theater actor.

In the summer of 1958, Lewis was signed as one of the principal actors at the Old Vic. They opened the season on September 17 with *Mary Stuart*, with guest stars Irene Worth as Stuart, Catherine Lacey as Queen Elizabeth and Ernest Thesiger as the Earl of Shrewsbury; Lewis portrayed Sir Edward Mortimer. In October and November, he played Mark Antony in *Julius Caesar*, prompting the *Birmingham Daily Post*'s J.C. Trewin to declare, "Ronald Lewis' Antony has presence and voice without exercising special subtlety in the oration." Audiences cheered Lewis and Flora Robson when they performed Ibsen's *Ghosts*, with Lewis enacting a "remarkably sensitive and convincing [Oswald]" (*The Stage*).

On New Year's Day 1959, Lewis was to deliver the lecture "From Studio to Stage" at the National Student Drama Festival. He did not make it. He also walked out on rehearsals at the Old Vic, and stayed away from the theater for two days. "I just could not face going on the stage," he remarked afterwards. "I did send a message saying I was not fit to work."

"He has gone away to rest in the country for a month," his agent Kenneth Carten told a *Western Mail* reporter. "I cannot say where he is. All I can say is that Mr. Lewis' doctor has told him to have four weeks' rest. It is simply a case of nervous exhaustion. He has worked solidly for six years without a holiday." The *Western Mail* asked if Lewis would return to the Old Vic after his rest. "No," Carten stated, "they cannot wait for him."

Lewis' first acting job after his break was *Armchair Theatre*'s "The Fabulous Money Maker" (March 1, 1959), in which he took on the role of Swedish match king Ivar Kreuger. *The Stage* reported that his "transformation from a thirty-year-old actor to a man of fifty is a great compliment to the makeup department. Also, the inflections and tonal changes of his voice really gave the impression that he was actually born in Sweden and was able to speak excellent English."

On March 16, 1959, Lewis started a three-week run at the Connaught Theatre in Charlotte Hastings' *The Captives*. Interviewed during rehearsals by the *Worthing Herald*, he repeated a line he had said while making *Bachelor of Hearts*: "I'm getting on for 30. It's high time I started taking myself seriously." He then added, "I don't want to be a glamour boy or a beefcake boy or spend my time being interviewed. I just want to act. If I cannot make a living out of my ability to act, I'll quit the profession, and I am prepared to be stubborn about it." Betty Gardiner of the same newspaper remarked a few days later that Lewis' stage career "has recently been interrupted by the accident of a string of bad films."

From April 6 to May 2, 1959, Lewis was back at the Old Vic with Flora Robson and Donald Wolfit in *Ghosts*. Then the three went off on a provincial tour of the show, which ran into June. For *Armchair Theatre*, he did "The Grandma Bandit" and "Lysette." The latter was written by his *Square Ring* castmate Bill Owen and its premise was bizarre—and derivative: A puppeteer's (Lewis) doll, made in the image of an ex-girlfriend, gets jealous when he marries. "This play is not for the squeamish," Owen warned. St. John Roberts (*The Stage*) thought otherwise, calling it an "embarrassing hour."

Filmed in Italy, *Conspiracy of Hearts* (1960) was a poignant and suspenseful World War II story of nuns saving Jewish children from a concentration camp. Based on true wartime incidents, it was shot at a monastery four miles south of Florence. Lewis played Italian Major Spoletti, under the yoke of the Nazis but sympathetic to the nuns and the partisans in the hills. Lewis' role was subordinate to those of Lilli Palmer, Sylvia Syms,

Yvonne Mitchell and the other actresses portraying the nuns, but he was very proud of the film and his performance. When the BBC featured him on the program *Spotlight*, about Welsh actors in show business, he requested that they use scenes from this movie.

Nineteen sixty started with Lewis acting in *Armchair Theatre*'s "Fifth Floor People" with Billie Whitelaw. He was scheduled to join Jack Hawkins in John Hall's *The Lizard on the Rock* at the end of February. It was to be Hawkins' return to the stage after several years. But during rehearsals, the production was shelved owing to Hawkins' throat infection.

Instead, Lewis headlined *The Full Treatment* (1960), "one of the most compulsive, powerful and suspenseful films in years" (so said publicity). Based on Ronald Scott Thorn's 1959 novel, it was co-scripted by Thorn and the film's director, Val Guest. On their wedding day, newlyweds Alan (Lewis) and Denise Colby (Diane Cilento) get into a car accident. Alan sustains a traumatic head injury that leaves him with no memory of the crash. He acts erratically and has an urge to strangle his wife. Denise seeks help from psychiatrist David Prade (Claude Dauphin), but gets more than she bargained for. Lewis, taking over for the originally cast Stanley Baker, turns in one of his finest performances. His character is hardly a likable sort—he's surly, jealous and short-tempered—but he elicits a sympathetic response from the viewer. His best scenes come during his hypnotherapy sessions, as he struggles to remember what happened before the accident. It's Lewis at his best. Val Guest thought so, too, telling the *Leicester Chronicle*, "The trouble is that he has been shamefully neglected by our producers. He is a highly gifted actor. Like the equally talented and gifted Diane Cilento, he should have been a world star years ago. But he's never been given the continuity of work or the roles that would have spotlighted that talent and given it real impact."

In *The Full Treatment* (1960), Lewis and Diane Cilento play newlyweds with a slight problem: He wants to strangle her.

The movie's title was changed to the more exploitable *Stop Me Before I Kill!* when it arrived in the U.S. the following year. The *New York Times*' Howard Thompson called it a "snug, tautly-strung little thriller.... [Its] dialogue has a nice, cutting edge, the tempo and photography are crisp." Most praised the location shooting in the French Riviera and the neat widescreen camerawork.

Reporting from the *Full Treatment* set, *Sunday Mirror*

columnist Jack Bentley remarked, "I sympathise with actor Ronald Lewis in his failure to become a big film name," to which Lewis responded, "I have always steered clear of the typecast label. On the stage, in films, and on TV I have played everything from comics to neurotics. But the public can't seem to keep track. Everyone knows my face, but not my name." Val Guest believed that *The Full Treatment* would finally bring Lewis international stardom. But it was wishful thinking.

For *ITV Television Playhouse*, Lewis appeared in "Tomorrow" and "Penelope" (both 1960), the latter starring Maggie Smith in the title role.

Supporting player Christopher Lee called *Taste of Fear* (1961) "the best film that I was in that Hammer ever made," explaining, "It had the best director [Seth Holt], the best cast and the best story." Screenwriter Jimmy Sangster felt the same, claiming it was the favorite of his work. Quoted in Howard Maxford's *Hammer Complete: The Films, the Personnel, the Company*, Sangster said,

> Even now, after 40 years, it holds up well. It's exciting, suspenseful, scary, and it has more twists than most other movies of its type. If that sounds like I'm blowing my own trumpet, I am. And why not? I have little enough to say about most of the movies I wrote and/or produced and/or directed and, for me, this one stands out.

Ann Todd thought otherwise, and told author Chris Fellner, "[It] was a terrible film. I didn't like my part, and I found Susan Strasberg impossible to work with—all that 'Method' stuff." It helped that it was hugely popular, even in the U.S., where it was renamed *Scream of Fear* (a title driven home by a poster that featured leading lady Susan Strasberg letting one rip).

This stylish thriller features Strasberg as Penny, the prodigal daughter returning to her father's estate after ten years and being told that he is away. Her stepmother Jane (Todd) is cool but friendly, and the hunky chauffeur Robert (Lewis) all too helpful. Penny's problem: She keeps seeing the obviously dead body of her supposedly alive father in the strangest places. Is she going mad? Lewis' role is attractive, but doesn't give him much to work with until near the end. For all his talk about not wanting to be a glamour or "beefcake boy," in one scene Lewis wears a bathing suit that leaves little to the imagination.

"Ronald Lewis has just left for his first taste of the Hollywood treatment, thanks to a sound performance in *Taste of Fear*," wrote Dick Richards of the *Daily Mirror*. "He has earned his break." The movie was producer-director William Castle's *Mr. Sardonicus*, fifth in the horror film series that made Castle famous as Hollywood's "No. 1 Shock Expert" (and No. 1 purveyor of outrageous gimmicks). In a period setting (Central Europe in 1880), Lewis played a London doctor lured to the medieval castle of Baron Sardonicus (Guy Rolfe), whose paralyzed face resembles a grinning skull. The baron is as ugly inside as out, vowing to deform his own wife (Audrey Dalton) if Lewis refuses or fails to make him presentable again. The sadistic Sardonicus has the upper hand throughout, until the surprise ending that wipes the smile off his face but good. *Sardonicus* reviews ran the gamut but few critics found fault with the acting, the *Hollywood Citizen-News*' Nadine M. Edwards commending Lewis for giving "a highly creditable performance, the film's best."

In October and November '61, Lewis starred in Aeschylus' *The Oresteia* with the Meadow Players at the Oxford Playhouse and the Old Vic. "Mr. Lewis, with his flashing eyes, bold yet controlled action and beautiful speaking and indefinable aura of an

Lewis (left) and Guy Rolfe (right) confer with producer-director William Castle behind the scenes on *Mr. Sardonicus* (1961).

inspired actor, is altogether memorable," *The Stage* wrote of his performances at the Old Vic. *The Stage*'s R.B. Marriott opined:

> Talking with Ronald Lewis soon makes it clear that he has by no means shifted his interest mainly to films. On the contrary, I have rarely met a young actor with such a deep love and respect for the theatre. Or one who takes such pleasure in playing in a production that makes real demands, and from which he can derive something of that rich, lasting satisfaction for which all genuine artists long.

According to Lewis,

> When I had the chance to go to the Oxford Playhouse for *The Oresteia*, I was thrilled. Here was something I could get my teeth into. A good, worthwhile film part may come along occasionally, but most of the time the work is trivial, making no great demands on one as an actor, at least, not in the way a fine stage part does.
> ...I wish there were more theatres doing work like the Meadow Players at Oxford. Such companies offer an ideal opportunity for playing great parts in great plays, or of trying out worthwhile new ones. This is a new trend in the theatre which I think cannot be over-estimated in its importance, and which should be given every possible encouragement. Perhaps one day there will be similar production companies scattered throughout the country.

In 1962, Lewis had three films released. *Twice Round the Daffodils* was a comedy-drama based on Patrick Cargill and Jack Beale's play *Ring for Catty*. (The 1959 movie *Carry on*

Nurse was also adapted from it.) Juliet Mills is Catty, head nurse of a tuberculosis ward where the "romantic and brooding" (*Films and Filming*) Lewis is being treated. After his childhood sweetheart (Nanette Newman) breaks up with him, he relapses but eventually finds love with the caring and dedicated Catty. Lewis and Mills displayed a lot of chemistry—more than any other Lewis–leading lady combo.

Lewis' character in *Billy Budd*, Maintopman Enoch Jenkins, was in and out in the first 45 minutes of the Herman Melville naval tale. Still, while he's on screen, Lewis has a first-rate role as a disagreeable shipmate of Budd's (Terence Stamp). Jenkins has a fight with Budd and then comes to respect him. Peter Ustinov produced, directed, co-adapted the screenplay and co-starred in this prestigious production. Lewis' third picture of '62, director Val Guest's *Jigsaw*, was a good murder mystery with Jack Warner and Lewis top-billed (with "Guest Star Yolande Donlan," Mrs. Guest, right behind). But Lewis as police sergeant Jim Wilks, Warner's partner, has little to do.

The following year, Lewis did the plays *Jackie the Jumper* and *Poor Bitos*; the TV shows *ITV Television Playhouse* and *Armchair Theatre*, and the movies *Nurse on Wheels* and *Siege of the Saxons*. The former paired him again with Juliet Mills, to terrific effect. The scene where he lets her drive his car with him in the passenger seat is hilarious. Lewis showed a different side to Mills. In 2019, she told an interviewer, that Lewis "was a charming man, and I worked with him quite a bit in those days…. Ronnie was a very good actor and a gentle person to be with…. He was a nice man with a gift for light comedy."

In *Billy Budd* (1962), Terence Stamp (left) and Lewis battle it out as their shipmates look on.

Siege of the Saxons was made by Hollywood producer Charles H. Schneer back to back with another picture, *East of Sudan* (both were directed by Nathan Juran). In a *Starlog* interview, Schneer said, "Columbia had a lot of unused footage in their library. If ten percent or less of a film made in the United Kingdom was comprised of stock footage, you received a government subsidy. I decided that would be a good commercial opportunity, so I made both pictures that way. I took the big action sequences out of Columbia's library." Much of the library footage in *Siege of the Saxons* came from the British Alan Ladd starrer *The Black Knight* (1954); Lewis wore a costume similar to Ladd's, but looked a lot beefier. Other clothing and props came from *Lancelot and Guinevere* (1963). Lewis, as the Robin Hood–like Robert Marshall, helps King Arthur's daughter (Janette Scott) claim her rightful place on the throne. Lewis did a good job in this atypical assignment.

In 1963, he wed actress Elizabeth Marlow; they had two daughters. This marriage, too, did not last, and he was reportedly devastated by the break-up. "He left their idyllic country home in Essex for a rootless existence of changing girlfriends and flats," according to *The Daily Mail*'s "Tragedy of the Nearly Man" article. Marlow, quoted in that article, said, "Ronnie didn't believe in himself—that was his only stumbling block."

At the beginning of '64, he and Donald Pleasence started a six-month run in *Poor Bitos*. In March, they appeared on the TV show *Tempo* to talk up the production and act out some scenes.

Siege of the Saxons (1963) with Lewis and Janette Scott (pictured) was a low-budget actioner with so much stock footage from the 1954 Alan Ladd starrer *The Black Knight* (1954) that Lewis had to wear the costume Ladd wore in the original.

The year ended with Lewis playing in his third and last Hammer film, the actioner *The Brigand of Kandahar*. The setting was India's North West Frontier in 1850 and the story was the old one about a mixed-blood officer (top-billed Lewis, dripping with brown makeup) coping with prejudice at a British outpost (*à la* King in *King of the Khyber Rifles*). Eventually he's driven to join the other side, a band of savage bandit raiders led by laugh-a-minute maniac Oliver Reed. Reed's sister Yvonne Romain is dubious about the newbie, asking Reed, "You trust this man?"

> **REED:** Like my own brother.
> **ROMAIN** (*taken aback*)**:** You killed our brother!

Like *Siege of the Saxons*, *Brigand of Kandahar* was a modest production which, in the homestretch, is made to look like a million bucks by the inclusion of impressive stock footage of battles from a past picture, in this case *Zarak* (1956). Among the highlights of *Brigand*: A lengthy Lewis-Reed fight scene, which starts with the men holding a sword in each hand. Among the "lowlights": an image of Lewis bouncing back and forth as if on a rocking horse, matted into a stock footage *Zarak* shot of men on charging horses. It wouldn't have taken much re-writing to turn the entire script into a Western, with the lead character half–American Indian rather than half–Indian. This hypothetical task would be especially simple when it came to Lewis and Romain's death scene, an obvious homage to the epic Western *Duel in the Sun* (1946)!

Supposedly, the failure of *The Brigand of Kandahar* ended Lewis' film career. But he still had stage and TV to keep him busy.

One of the highlights of *The Brigand of Kandahar* (1965) was the fight scene between Lewis and Oliver Reed (right).

On May 21, 1965, businessman Joseph Pigg attempted to take Lewis' car keys away from him as Lewis tried to drive home, "obviously the worse for drink." Lewis attacked Pigg, who hit back and gave him a black eye. After Lewis somehow got back to his home in Stafford Clays-Road, Grays, that night, his "distressed" wife arrived at the local police station. Policeman James Hughes was sent to the actor's residence, where Lewis attacked him. Lewis soon found himself knocked to the ground and sporting another black eye. Lewis admitted to driving while "unfit through drink," assaulting a police officer, and being drunk and disorderly. He was fined £65 and banned from driving for a year. Some sources report that this incident resulted in Lewis not getting any more acting work. That is untrue. He was a big drinker, but so were many actors back then; and some of the others had similar, more frequent public episodes.

On television, he acted on *Armchair Mystery Theatre* and the futuristic *Out of the Unknown*. The latter's production design was by Ridley Scott. In 1965 and '66, Lewis was with the Daniel Mayer Company at the Scala with Sylvia Syms in *Peter Pan*, which got excellent reviews. (When *Peter Pan* landed at the Grand Theatre, Wolverhampton, the *Birmingham Daily Post* wrote, "Ronald Lewis gives a splendidly villainous study of Captain Hook.") This was followed by *Happy Family* at the Hampstead Theatre Club and an episode of *Thirteen Against Fate*.

In July 1966, he joined Juliet Mills, Isabel Jeans, Wilfrid Hyde-White and Coral Browne in a pre–London tour of *Lady Windermere's Fan*. The production was directed by Anthony Quayle with scenery and costumes by Cecil Beaton. "From Ronald Lewis there is a sensitive, convincing, brilliantly composed study of Lord Darlington," wrote *The Stage*. It arrived in London on October 20, 1966, and continued until March '67. During the run, Lewis did another episode of *Out of the Unknown*.

He co-starred with Anna Massey in two plays: *First Day of a New Season* (1967) and *The Flip Side* (1967–68), the latter also filmed for television. Ronald Millar's comedy *They Don't Grow on Trees* (1968–69), with Lewis and Dora Bryan, ran in the West End and on tour. He stopped long enough for two more TV gigs: *Armchair Theatre* and *ITV Sunday Night Theatre*.

On July 29, 1969, motorist Lewis struck a parked car in King's Road, Chelsea. He then reversed his car and drove off, while two men banged on his vehicle to get him to stop. Lewis was charged with hit-and-run and failing to report an accident. In court, he testified that he did stop, about 15 yards from the accident. A man who said he was the damaged car's owner inspected the damage and said he would accept £2. At the man's request, Lewis made a check out to cash. But Lewis had been scammed: The man did not own the car. The hit-and-run charge was dropped, but Lewis was fined for not reporting the accident. The magistrate said that the ersatz car owner "saw a grand opportunity to make a bit of easy money—not uncommon in King's Road. Unfortunately, Mr. Lewis is much too trusting and fell for it." After setting Lewis' fine, the judge joked, "Do you want to pay that by check?"

Irene Coates' *This Space Is Mine* (1969), presented at the Hampstead Theatre Club, again paired Lewis with Anna Massey. *The Stage* looked on the bright side, claiming the play would be practically unbearable without Lewis and Massey's "brilliant" performances: "Both make unconvincing, banal characters take on a semblance of life, and absorb one by the delicacy of their art and the fineness of their technique." Lewis portrayed with "slippery-tongued bravado" (J.C. Trewin, *Birmingham Daily Post*) a prison mogul in *Insideout* (1969), and he tried "valiantly to make [his character] into someone worth bothering about" (*The Stage*) in Carson McCullers' *The Square Root of Wonderful* (1970). The *London Observer*'s Ronald Bryden wrote of the latter that Lewis had some difficulty with his Georgia accent, "but his performance goes to the heart of the character, glittering with brazen neurosis. It confirms him as one of the strongest players of his generation."

In January 1970, Lewis was in court to face charges that on October 21 previous, he "had dined late and rather too well," drove "with excess alcohol—116 milligrams—in his blood" (*Chelsea News and General Advertiser*) and went through a red light. The actor pled guilty. His license was suspended for three years and he was fined £105.

Lewis performed on TV in *W. Somerset Maugham*, *Armchair Theatre* and *Tales of Unease*. He also starred in his own TV series, *His and Hers*, about a married couple; she works outside the home, he (a writer) is a stay-at-home. Lewis' "Her" was first played by Sue Lloyd and then Barbara Murray. It lasted until 1972.

Lewis was now in his early forties and living a hard lifestyle. His drinking continued unabated. A functional alcoholic, he was still capable of giving brilliant performances. Producers obviously felt he was worth the trouble, his talent still shining, especially on the stage. He ended 1970 with an appearance on BBC Radio 4 in "An Ideal Husband" with Noel Johnson and Jane Wenham.

He had a supporting part as the father of Sean Bury in the movie *Friends* (1971), and reprised the character in the sequel *Paul and Michelle* (1974). He also acted on TV's *Hine* in the episode "The Old School Noose" with Barrie Ingham and Michael Goodliffe, and did *The Man of the World* for the Prospect Theatre Company.

Robert Chetwyn's production of *Hamlet* for the Prospect Theatre Company, starring Ian McKellen, opened at the 1971 Edinburgh Festival, played at the Cambridge in London and then toured Europe. According to Ronald Bryden of the *London Observer*, "The best supporting performance is Ronald Lewis' Claudius; burly and saturnine, with a basso which rides like a rock amid the light voices of most of the cast. This is an actor in his prime."

Chetwyn told McKellen biographer Mark Barratt that Lewis

> announced that he wanted equal billing with McKellen at the Cambridge. The management wouldn't have it. Ronnie had been something of a film star, and was a good actor, but he was a very delicate kind of guy. I think he felt he should have been in Ian McKellen's position. He had that kind of start. He was a Richard Burton type and he kept doing wonderful work but not quite top league.

Years later McKellen wrote on his website that the "doughty" Lewis "occasionally took an unexplained night off" and that Lewis' understudy, newcomer Tim Pigott-Smith, often had to go on for him. Pigott-Smith described in his autobiography one instance during the 14-week tour: "Ronny had met an old girlfriend, had gone on something of a bender and had not recovered sufficiently to perform that night."

On television, Lewis did *The Rivals of Sherlock Holmes* (playing an Austrian detective), *Harriet's Back in Town*, *Crown Court*, *Nightingale's Boys*, *Public Eye*, *Warship* and *Z Cars*, and he had recurring roles on *Big Boy Now!* and *The XYY Man*. In 1976 and '77, he worked on Radio 4 in *Saturday Night Theatre*'s "Footnote to the Conspiracy" by Bruce Stewart, based on the true story of the trial of a Protestant pastor (Lewis) accused of plotting to kill Hitler; Doris Lessing's "The Grass Is Singing," and the 26-part "Vivat Rex," narrated by Richard Burton, with Lewis voicing King John of France.

Lewis appeared on stage in Alun Richards' *The Snowdropper* (1974); Alan Ayckbourn's

How the Other Half Loves (1974); *Macbeth* (1975) with the Welsh Drama Company; Andrew Carr's *Hanratty in Hell* (1976), and Ibsen's *The Wild Duck* (1976) with Dawn Addams and the Welsh Drama Company. *The Stage* wrote of the latter, "Ronald Lewis plays Hjalmar Ekdal with real awareness of the comic possibilities of the weak and foolish inventor."

Lewis put his own money into *The Snowdropper* at the Hampstead. He told the *Aberdeen Evening Express*,

> The big managements had all rejected the play, but I knew they were wrong. Audience and critics' reaction proved me right but they still didn't want to know. It is very difficult to find a decent play in the West End. Shows are being cancelled all the time and you have to go into the provinces to find good plays.

Lewis felt that the entertainment industry was catering to the lowest common denominator. "The audiences are treated as unintelligent. I can see it getting worse until there is a reversal of values and ideas. The whole industry is in a dreadful state." The *Aberdeen Evening Express* added that Lewis "experienced the malaise of the film industry," to which he responded, "There are only a few films I remember with pride including *Taste of Fear*, *Bachelor of Hearts* and *Conspiracy of Hearts*."

In February 1977, while in rehearsals with the Actors Company at the Warwick University Arts Centre Theatre for John Osborne's *The Entertainer*, Irish actor Patrick O'Connell decided to give up acting to become an artist. On short notice, Lewis took on the role of music hall performer Archie Rice and got respectable reviews. He stayed with the Actors Company to do *The Amazons* and another engagement of *The Entertainer*. In October, Lewis starred in a production of Peter Shaffer's *Equus* at the Watford Palace Theatre. "Ronald Lewis plays the vast role of the psychiatrist with a compelling panache," wrote Nick Carter of the *Harrow Observer*. With the Welsh National Theatre, he did, among others, Dylan Thomas' *Under Milk Wood* (1978) at the Alexandra Theatre. His last screen role was in the Australian television movie *The John Sullivan Story* (1979).

September 13, 1979, was opening night of the two-week run of Anthony Shaffer's play *Sleuth* at Coventry's Belgrade Theatre. Its star Lewis collapsed in his dressing room minutes before he was to go on. Cast member Terry Wale was on his way to Lewis' dressing room when he heard a crash. There, he found Lewis had fallen and hit his head. "He seemed to have been a little off-colour over the last few days of rehearsal," Wale told Peter McGarry of the *Coventry Evening Telegraph*. "I thought he was probably under a bit of strain." As Lewis was taken to Walsgrave Hospital, the performance was cancelled and everyone in the near-full auditorium got their money back; Lewis was replaced. It was discovered that he was suffering from a mild form of epilepsy.

Lewis never seemed to regain his health, and he was unable to work other than a 1980 appearance on Radio 4 in "Sitting Duck." (The *London Guardian* wrote that he played his role with "magnificent relish.") The actor now lived on Social Security. In July 1980, he was in London Bankruptcy Court, telling the judge that he had no assets to pay debts amounting to £21,188. He blamed this on his "naivety, lack of guile, and office acumen, over-generosity, trusting people too much and neglect of tax affairs."

In early January 1982, 53-year-old Lewis checked into the Astoria Hotel, a £6-a-night boarding house in Pimlico. On the 11th, he gave the unemployed waiter who lived in the room next to him some money and told him, "Here, get yourself something to eat." These were perhaps the last words he ever spoke. The next day, he was found lying on the bed, his past-due rent money on the blanket next to him. Two uneaten sandwiches and a carton of milk were sitting on the windowsill and an unopened pack of

Players cigarettes was on the nightstand. On the floor were several empty bottles of aspirin and Scotch. His death was considered a suicide by drug overdose.

Lewis' actor friend Kenneth Williams wrote in his diary the day after the incident, "The paper says Ronald Lewis has taken an overdose! He was declared bankrupt last year! Obviously nobody offered him work & he was driven to despair. I remember Ronnie ... and that drinking session at the White Horse all those years ago ... he was a kind boy & people used him."

John Fraser, who went through life one molar lighter after eating a punch from Lewis, had a different reaction to the news. He wrote in his autobiography, "I have never hated anyone. But when Ronnie Lewis killed himself, I felt not a twinge of sorrow or regret."

The Stage's R.B. Marriott paid tribute to Lewis:

> [The] theatre has lost one of its finest actors. He was only 53 and in recent years unfortunately had obtained little work and had financial difficulties, including bankruptcy.... Lewis was successful and in demand, and it seemed he would become a player of uncommon distinction, in the class, say, of Paul Scofield. He had good looks, a fine voice, a deep sense of poetry, dramatic power and a facility for creating a character richly while giving an impression of perfect ease and naturalness. He was intelligent and likable.
>
> Although he achieved much, opportunity and advancement seemed to fall away from him and recently he was practically a forgotten actor. He will be greatly missed by his colleagues and friends.

The writer of *The Daily Mail*'s "Tragedy of the Nearly Man" article pointed out that none of the other Astoria Hotel residents knew of Lewis' acting achievements because, by the end, "Lewis had chosen anonymity. He had no friends to trust with his personal tragedy." It continued:

> Yet when news of his death broke, there were millions who mourned, if only for a memory. To the cinema and theatre-going public, Lewis was an idol of their youth, a handsome debonair actor with aristocratic looks and distinctive flared nostrils. To countless directors, producers and fellow-actors, he was a major talent who inexplicably faded from the scene.
>
> On the surface, his life seems to have flitted by like a clichéd, third-rate Hollywood film. But the script—"big star dies friendless in seedy bedsit"—does him scant justice.

- **1953**: *Valley of Song* (uncredited), *The Square Ring*.
- **1954**: *The Beachcomber, The Face of Love* (TVM).
- **1955**: *Fantastic Summer* (TVM), *The Prisoner, Sailor Beware* (TVM), *Storm Over the Nile*.
- **1956**: *Helen of Troy, Sailor Beware, A Hill in Korea*.
- **1957**: *The Secret Place, Robbery Under Arms*.
- **1958**: *The Wind Cannot Read, Bachelor of Hearts*.
- **1960**: *Conspiracy of Hearts, The Full Treatment*.
- **1961**: *Taste of Fear, Mr. Sardonicus*.
- **1962**: *Twice Round the Daffodils, Jigsaw, Billy Budd*.
- **1963**: *Nurse on Wheels, Siege of the Saxons*.
- **1965**: *The Brigand of Kandahar*.
- **1971**: *Friends*.
- **1974**: *Paul and Michelle*.
- **1979**: *The John Sullivan Story* (TVM).

TOM NEAL

"Fate, or some mysterious force, can put the finger on you or me, for no good reason at all."—*Detour* (1945)

Thomas Carroll Neal, Jr., was born in Evanston, Illinois, on January 28, 1914. He was the youngest of the three children of Thomas Carroll Neal, vice-president of the Central Trust Company of Illinois, and Mary Lambie Martin. The likely lad attended Lake Forest Academy and Evanston Township High School. In 2015, Tom Neal, Jr., told interviewer Tom Weaver,

> My dad's father was a banker and they lived pretty well, even during the Depression. My dad had two sisters [Mary and Dorothy aka Dot] and when they all turned 16, they all got their own cars and everything. That was unheard-of back then; in those days, a lot of families didn't own a car. So my dad's dad had some money. But my dad kind of did his own thing and he was kind of the black sheep of the family.

Tom's nephew Walter Burr (Mary's son) told author John O'Dowd,

> Even before he sold all his bank stock in 1934, my grandfather was worth over one million dollars on paper. His best friend was accounting giant Arthur Andersen, who for many years came over to my grandparents' house for breakfast every Saturday morning, to talk about their various investment deals.
>
> My grandfather was very low-key about his good fortune, but then again, he was always very stoic, in general. He and my grandmother were not flashy types; they were just nice, decent people. Tom's father was a member of the Westmoreland Country Club and the family lived in a beautiful, ten room house, but that's about as much "flash" as they ever showed.

Tom Neal could be likable or he could be a cad—off-screen, as well.

At Northwestern University, Tom majored in mathematics. (Many sources erroneously claim he got a Harvard law degree.) Starting in 1932, he competed in amateur boxing matches (mostly in Cambridge, Massachusetts) and in the Golden Gloves tournament. His boxing record was said to be 44–3, 41 of those wins knockouts in the first or second rounds. The drama club became a growing interest, and he appeared in the school's theater productions. Dropping out of Northwestern, he acted in stock in Chicago.

The family spent winters in Florida and Arizona. Tom spent time at the Fort Lauderdale beaches where he and sister Dot gave parties. Tom was a lifeguard and proud of the physique he had acquired through bodybuilding. He also sang with several local orchestras.

If we are to believe MGM publicity, Neal struggled with no help from his family during these early years. Some of it *could* be true; maybe his father expected him to pay his own way if he wasn't going to stay in college. Or perhaps Neal wanted to be out on his own. Neal told *Silver Screen*'s Leon Surmelian,

> I went up to Michigan and worked as a stripper and cutter in a lumber camp. When I had saved $275, I went to New York to see the theatrical agents. But it took me nine months before I got my first job on the stage. My money didn't last long in New York. So I tried to break into the modeling racket, posed for *Physical Culture* and other magazines, but it didn't get me anywhere. I went to work for the subway on Sixth Avenue as a day laborer. I emptied buckets at the driller for $4.80 a day.
>
> It was good money for a guy who was broke, but I found out I couldn't go around to the theatrical agencies anymore, and I was missing a lot of calls. So I got a job as a lineman with the Bell Telephone company. My hours were from 6 p.m. to 3 a.m. My next job was writing radio scripts at $65 a week, and I had a good chance to develop as a writer in the radio business, but I still wanted to be an actor.

According to publicity, Neal played semi-pro ice hockey with the Chicago Seals, before a broken knee cap (or arm or dislocated hip) ended his skating days.

In July and August 1935, he was an assistant stage manager and bit player with the stock company at the Beach Playhouse in West Falmouth, Massachusetts; among the players there were Tyrone Power and Rita Johnson. According to Leon Surmelian, every Saturday night Neal and Power "painted the town red" together. In New York, Neal studied dramatic art.

In September '35, Tom's brief romance and engagement to the notorious Inez Norton became public. Gangster Arnold Rothstein's mistress at the time of his 1928 murder (and a major benefactor in his will), she had a teenage son from a long-ago marriage. Newspaper reports gave Neal's age as 24 (wrong) and Norton's as 32 (maybe). The two had met the year before on a plane to Havana and became inseparable. Since Tom would be an heir to a trust fund (close to $1,000,000) when he turned 25, he needed his father's permission to wed. "He is opposed," Tom said, "but I am confident I can console him around to it when he gets here. I think he will give in when he gets to know Inez." His parents were now residents of Washington, D.C.; the senior Neal was doing government work. When he heard that his son was itching to walk down the aisle, he got on a plane to New York. After a "heart to heart," Senior convinced him to wait. "We talked it over and decided I ought to get a job first and show I was able to get along in the world first," Tom said. "We decided to postpone the wedding. That is, Dad decided it." His father rightly thought Tom was too young and inexperienced, and might "squander" all his money. "So I'm starting out tomorrow to try and establish myself in New York. Miss

Norton is very much upset. She may take a trip to Bermuda. But the wedding is definitely not 'off.' It's just postponed."

It didn't take long for Tom to announce that the engagement *was* off. "I am beginning to see the wisdom of not marrying a woman so much older than I am"—a statement that probably rankled the matronly Norton. The *Fort Lauderdale News* reported: "Sister Dot Neal says that was only a publicity gag about Tom Neal planning to marry Inez Norton ... and that her brother received stage and movie offers after the story had been spread in the papers."

Twenty-one-year-old Tom got his first known acting part on Broadway in the Theatre Guild's *If This Be Treason* (September-October 1935), playing a diplomat. It ran for 40 performances. At least one '40s publicity item claimed that Neal was then in another Theatre Guild production, *Love Is Not So Simple* (1935), which closed out of town, but his name is not listed in that production's playbills.

For the rest of 1935 and part of '36, Neal was back relaxing with his family in Florida. From August to September 1936, he was on Broadway in the Philip Barry flop *Spring Dance*, produced by Jed Harris. This was followed by another bomb, *Daughters of Atreus* (1936), where he played Hippolytus. Others in the cast included Olive Deering, Edmond O'Brien, Cornel Wilde, Maria Ouspenskaya and Gale Gordon.

In 1937, on a Florida beach, Neal was serving as a lifeguard when his muscles attracted the attention of a talent scout for Samuel Goldwyn, and he was put under contract. At Goldwyn, he did nothing, although he almost secured the lead in director John Ford's *The Hurricane* (1937); he lost the choice part in the exotic adventure to Jon Hall. "It was the perfect part for me," Neal later remarked to Leon Surmelian. "It required not only acting but athletic ability. Losing it was a bitter pill to swallow."

In May 1937, while claiming to be attending Columbia University, Neal answered a newspaper ad placed by Heloise Martin (*College Humor*'s Shower Girl) looking for two college boys to kiss her four times a day on the Loew's State Theatre stage for $30 a week each. He and Patrick O'Shaughnessey were selected and their pictures ran in newspapers across the country. "I picked the two most personable," Martin told reporters. "With Granny's approval." (Granny was the revue's producer, N.T. Granlund.) Martin described what the boys had to do:

> They're "plants" in the audience. Then they come on the stage and a roller-skating act spins them around. This is after I do my tap dance on toes. While I change my costume and come back in an evening gown, the boys pretend to be dizzy and play football with a hat. I'm supposed to kiss the one who walks a straight line after the roller-skating team finishes with them. But I don't really.

At this point, Granlund interjected, "Of course you do. Say, if the roller skating don't ruin them, the kiss does." Martin replied (or "snapped," as newspapers put it), "Remember, I'm engaged to Bus Bergmann, my boyfriend at Drake University. They don't kiss me."

At the beginning of 1938, Neal was in the play *June Night* in Philadelphia. It was headed for Broadway, but closed out of town. He then toured in the show *Brother Rat*. He explained to Virginia Irwin (*St. Louis Post-Dispatch*) what happened next: His best friend Jack Carlton, a trapeze artist, was hurt in a fall and planned to go to California to recuperate. "[O]f course, I couldn't let him go alone. I knew there was plenty to do out here—no sandhogging or lumberjacking maybe, but being a lifeguard can be exciting, too."

In Los Angeles, Neal worked the nightshift at Helms Bakery and made the rounds of the studios during the day. At this time, he was sharing a beach house with Carlton (who would later change his name to Clayton Moore). They both lucked out with MGM contracts that September.

Neal's screen debut came in *Out West with the Hardys* (1938). The part of a young tough being sentenced in Judge Hardy's court at the beginning of the movie was small, but it was a start.

> Metro-Goldwyn-Mayer is apparently planning a build-up for Tom Neal, 23-year-old Broadway actor, much along the same lines as that which boosted Robert Taylor to the top.—*Hollywood Citizen-News*, October 11, 1938

Neal was next given an interesting—and unique—role: Father Joseph Damien de Veuster (1840–89), aka Father Damien, a Belgian priest who worked at the Hawaiian island of Molokai's leprosy settlement. Produced and narrated by Carey Wilson and written by Morgan Cox, the short *The Great Heart* (1938) showed off Neal as Damien completely disguised by makeup and facial hair and wearing the same soutane Spencer Tracy wore in *San Francisco* (1936) and *Boys Town* (1938). "This will be the first time any actor other than the Academy Award winner has ever donned the cassock," wrote Ina Sullivan.

Smallish parts came in the 1939 releases *Burn 'Em Up O'Connor* as a hotshot, tough-talking race car driver who gets killed on the track; *Four Girls in White* as a doctor asking nurse Florence Rice for a date ("I get chills just looking at her," he tells another doctor); and ambulance drivers in *Honolulu* and the short *Money to Loan*. For *Fast and Loose*, the second film in MGM's Joel and Garda Stone detective series, the studio shot scenes with Neal in the second lead for two days, but he was "found to be not the type," wrote *Variety*. He was replaced by Anthony Allan (aka John Hubbard). With a lot of other newcomers, Neal tested for *Golden Boy* at Columbia.

Neal had his first lead in *They All Come Out* (1939). Directed by Jacques Tourneur, it was originally intended to be an entry in MGM's *Crime Does Not Pay* shorts series, but it was expanded to feature-length. The story is about the rehabilitation of prisoners, in particular Joe Cameron (Neal) and former moll Kitty Carson (Rita Johnson).

Within the Law, a 1912 play by Bayard Veiller, was filmed several times, including *Paid* (1930) with Joan Crawford. Now it became Neal's second leading role at MGM, although the real star is Ruth Hussey as Mary Turner, a shopgirl framed and sent to prison for shoplifting; she vows to avenge herself against the store owner, Mr. Gilder (Samuel S. Hinds). After she is released, she leads a gang of thieves and plays up to Gilder's son Richard (Neal). Czechoslovakian Gustav Machatý directed *Within the Law*. The film *Ekstase* (aka *Ecstasy*) (1933) made both him and Hedy Lamarr famous, and they were both contracted by MGM. *Within the Law* was his first American feature. (And Neal was dating Lamarr at the time.)

Also in '39, Carey Wilson's short *Prophet Without Honor* had Neal as Matthew Fontaine Maury (1806–73), a naval officer who, after a crippling accident, devotes his life to charting winds and currents. He was called the "Pathfinder of the Seas." (A statue of Maury in Virginia, which was erected in 1929, was removed in 2020, following local protests after the death of George Floyd. "A crowd of more than 100 onlookers cheered as a crane lifted the statue of Matthew Fontaine Maury from its base and onto a flatbed truck," wrote Vernon Freeman, Jr., at CBS 6 News, Richmond. Maury dedicated his time

Little does Samuel S. Hinds (left) know but ex-con Ruth Hussey has plans to exact revenge against him and his son Neal. *Within the Law* **(1939) was one of Neal's best MGM films.**

to helping all people, but his service in the Confederacy has soured his legacy. He had actually unsuccessfully tried to stop the Civil War by going to Europe for help.)

In 1939, MGM sent out publicity in which Neal supposedly said that his greatest ambition was to "be box office, to be hot and be liked by everyone." There were various "news items" reporting that Neal saved several people from drowning; that he became an expert diver off the rocks of Malibu Beach; how he "spends a great deal of time diving for abalone"; his new hobby was throwing boomerangs; he had the urge to climb random steep cliffs; he enjoyed building boats and sailing them; he went fishing for swordfish; and he was a "steady competitor in the marksmanship trials held for studio policemen."

The *Fort Lauderdale News* stated that Neal had a "nice, juicy part" in *6,000 Enemies* (1939), but actually he merely played a prisoner who is glimpsed only occasionally. *Stronger Than Desire* (1939) had him as a reporter. Director Fred Zinnemann led him and Jo Ann Sayers through the *Crime Does Not Pay* short *Help Wanted* (1939), about an employment agency scam; he was the sweet, loyal guy in love with Virginia Grey in *Another Thin Man* (1939), and a good-for-nothing in *Joe and Ethel Turp Call on the President* (1939).

By now, it was fairly obvious that Metro was *not* building Neal up as they had Robert Taylor. Around this time, the studio's casting director Fred Datig described Neal to columnist Lucie Neville as a "nice young Gable type who might go places"—somewhat less than a ringing endorsement. And it's doubtful that Neal's supporting role in Clark

Gable–Joan Crawford's *Strange Cargo* (1940) would have led to stardom—*if* it had happened. The real reason he was taken off the picture has been blurred through the years, so it is difficult to determine what went wrong, and if it resulted in long-term career problems. A reporter for the *Bonham* (Texas) *Daily Favorite* wrote, "Tom Neal was gypped out of a wonderful career because he looked too much like the great Gable...." Far-fetched, but stranger things have happened.

Strange Cargo star Crawford has long been blamed for Neal's exit from that picture and his MGM contract. Kent Adamson, who was later Ann Savage's manager and authorized biographer, said,

> Tom Neal claimed to his son that he had a frequent sexual relationship with Crawford in the late 1930s. Joan claimed they never did. Crawford was certainly on his list as he attempted to work his way through many of the women on the MGM lot.
>
> Ann Savage told the story on tape and in her live appearances that Tom broke social rank and approached Crawford out of the blue, saying to her, "I want to fuck you." Though this story rings partially true, as told to Ann at a later time by Tom, it is far from the entire story. Tom did set Crawford off on many levels, beginning with being approached brazenly by a lowly contract player. By making his intentions base, direct and unromantic, Neal far, far overstepped his bounds and was punished for it. Tom also defied her will by his persistence, social obviousness and loud troublemaking. Whatever their romantic and sexual involvement had become, Crawford sought to minimize it, Neal sought to publicize it.

Tom's nephew Walter Burr told John O'Dowd that Neal was carrying on with both Crawford and a studio executive's wife. "When Crawford learned he was two-timing her, she did her own complaining to [Louis B.] Mayer, who wound up blasting Tom."

What is agreed upon is that Crawford took a serious dislike to Neal, enough to lobby Mayer to cancel his contract. But the fact is that MGM did not fire Neal after his dismissal from *Strange Cargo*.

Off-screen, Neal was indeed a ladies' man, dating up a variety of models and actresses that, in addition to Hedy Lamarr, included Florence Rice, Dixie Dunbar, Margaret Roach, Jo Ann Sayers, Jean Parker and Dona Drake. "Hollywood reporters completely missed the furious fracas between Diosa Costello and Eleanor Troy at the Swing Club out there," reported Ed Sullivan at the beginning of 1941. "Fists, hair, chairs and plates were flying.... All over Tom Neal." One who didn't want to be associated with Neal was the feisty Maureen O'Hara, who denied all connection with him to Sheilah Graham: "What's all this tommyrot about me and Tom Neal? It's been in two columns and on the radio that Tommy Neal and I are having a romance.... I have never been out with Tommy Neal in my life."

A *Fort Lauderdale News*' column, "The Palm Leaf Fan," kept tabs on Neal because his family spent a considerable amount of time there. In November 1939, after the supposed incident concerning *Strange Cargo*, the unnamed columnist wrote:

> Latest news from movie headquarters at Hollywood has Tom listed fifth or sixth on the MGM fan mail accumulation! He's been assigned to Greta Garbo's dressing rooms, if you please ... one of them all mirrors which must make Tom snicker a bit. Another room in the suite is said to have wall sketches done by Garbo herself. Tom just now is busy working in *New Moon* along with Jeanette MacDonald and Nelson Eddy.

Word went out that Neal's newly formed fan club had close to 13,000 members.

Neal was not in *New Moon*. For 1940 release, Metro cast him in the *Crime Does Not Pay* short *Jack Pot* (as a victim of a slot machine racket and extortion), as a pilot in the

Nick Carter series entry *Sky Murder*, as himself in the short *Rodeo Dough*, and as one of the Hellcats Squadron members in the Robert Taylor starrer *Flight Command*.

Better was a loan-out to RKO: *The Courageous Dr. Christian*, second in the Jean Hersholt–starring series. The plight of the residents of Squatterstown, in particular Dave Williams (Neal) and his two siblings, rekindles the doctor's plan to get them affordable housing and to change the attitudes of the citizens of River's End. When he gives the cynical Dave a job as his chauffeur, Dave develops an interest in Christian's nurse (Dorothy Lovett).

> DAVE: What's a guy have to do around here to get a little ... nursing?
> JUDY: Break a leg.
> DAVE: Hard to get, eh?

An epidemic of spinal meningitis changes everyone's perception. While Neal gives "a good imitation of John Garfield hating the world" (Leo Simon, *Los Angeles Daily News*), his is not a one-note or overdone performance. He allows his softer side to come through, especially in his scenes with the kids and Lovett.

In April 1940, Neal had "just completed a role" (columnist Bill Moore) in *Andy Hardy Meets Debutante*, playing Cecilia Parker's love interest. There were also a few publicity items that said he was on the set. When *Debutante* debuted that July, Neal was left behind on the cutting room floor, along with almost all of Parker's footage. This was also the end of reports that he was going to portray her boyfriend in two additional Hardy pictures.

At the time of the Andy Hardy picture, Neal was dating cast member Diana Lewis and they were even reported to be engaged. Kent Adamson revealed,

> She dated Neal briefly, but dumped him to marry MGM star William Powell, almost twice her age. Characteristic of Tom, he loudly, publicly protested what he perceived as romantic betrayal and a broken engagement by Diana Lewis, and also confronted William Powell. Perhaps more than the protests of Crawford to Louis B. Mayer's ears, the embarrassment Neal had stirred up for a longtime, major A-list star like William Powell, finally sealed Tom's fate at the studio and resulted in his dismissal at MGM.

Lewis and Powell remained married until the latter's death in 1984.

It has frequently been alleged that getting the boot from MGM resulted in Neal being blacklisted. It would seem not. Nineteen forty-one started with Neal appearing in the two-reeler *Wings of Steel*, a Warner Bros. Technicolor special for the U.S. Army Air Corps. It follows the training of a group of young men headed by Douglas Kennedy, who thinks he knows all the answers. Neal, a tough upperclassman, tells him otherwise.

As a freelancer, Neal landed the lead in Columbia's Edward Dmytryk–directed exploiter *Under Age* (1941), which catered "to the rougher type of patron" (*Harrison's Reports*). Then came starring parts in PRC's boxing drama *The Miracle Kid* and the Republic serial *Jungle Girl*, both 1941. The latter, a 15-chapter barn-burner set in unexplored Africa, starred Frances Gifford as Nyoka (a distaff Tarzan) and Neal as an adventurous pilot, sharing such dangers as "Death by Voodoo," a "River of Fire," "Jungle Vengeance" and "Tribal Fury" (chapter titles). Exceeding the length of *Gone with the Wind*, *Jungle Girl* was shot in 45 days.

There was a period during 1942 when Neal did a series of smallish parts in such movies as *Ten Gentlemen from West Point*, *The Pride of the Yankees*, *Flying Tigers*, *No Time for Love* (as a sandhog, a profession he knew well), *China Girl* and *Air Force*. At

Monogram, Neal shared the screen with the lot's resident bogeyman Bela Lugosi in the crime-horror melodrama *Bowery at Midnight*, with Lugosi as a bespectacled university instructor by day and the ruthless leader of a criminal gang by night. Neal underplays his role as one of Lugosi's hoods, who takes advantage of his own gun-crazy rep and intimidates fellow gang member Wheeler Oakman. (Oakman nervously calls out, "Don't get gay, kid, just because you're handy with the heater!")

In November 1942, Columbia signed Neal to a contract. He started off modestly as Jinx Falkenburg's leading man in the musical *She Has What It Takes* (1943) and as Jess Barker's scheming rival for Claire Trevor in *Good Luck, Mr. Yates* (1943). According to Kent Adamson, Tom "annoyed tough studio boss Harry Cohn by refusing assignments in routine pictures not to his liking. Cohn allowed him to work [on loan-out], which got him off the Columbia lot, where he was considered a troublemaker."

Neal's first for Columbia: *She Has What It Takes* (1943), as Jinx Falkenburg's leading man.

Borrowed by RKO, the actor got a good role in *Behind the Rising Sun* (1943), inspired by foreign correspondent James R. Young's book about his years in Japan. The movie was the work of director Edward Dmytryk and screenwriter Emmet Lavery, the team behind the same year's surprise hit *Hitler's Children*. At the time, Dmytryk told Robbin Coons,

> This isn't a hate picture. It's an attempt to show the Japs [sic] as they really are—the kind of human beings they are, influenced as they are by the militaristic regime. We're taking this Japanese boy who goes to [Cornell] and gets an American point of view. Then we take him back to Japan where the army gets him. We show how, step by step, he becomes brutalized. It isn't a quick process. At first, he is horrified, but silent, over the things he sees done in China. Then he becomes less horrified. Finally, he is completely changed—becomes the one who gives the orders. But he is never the stock villain. He's a person.

In the role of Taro Seki, an American-educated Japanese who returns to his homeland in 1936, Neal was given a real character part, one that finally showed off his acting skill. When he comes home to his family, they notice that he has taken on the demeanor and slang of America. Taro slowly changes as the army hardens him, making him cold and cruel until he betrays his American friends and his fiancée Tama (Margo). Neal's performance is not overstated and is quite good, once one gets past the yellowface. A writer for the Los Angeles newspaper *The Tidings* wrote,

Would Hollywood dare use any established romantic hero to impersonate a Jap [sic]? Dollars to doughnuts against it. It is argued you would never again accept him as a romantic screen personality. So, they cast Tom Neal, once set by MGM as a likely successor to Clark Gable. That plan didn't quite click, so Tom almost slipped off the screen. Now, at last, he gets a chance to play a character instead of playing himself....

When *Behind the Rising Sun* became one of the most talked-about hits of the year, Columbia began "boosting Neal actively" (Edwin Schallert, *Los Angeles Times*). The company cast him in a series of Bs that showed him off to good advantage. In *There's Something About a Soldier* (1943), he's an egotistical Officer Candidate School hopeful who has to learn to work well with others. His scenes with Evelyn Keyes, especially when they first meet, add a spark to the proceedings. *Klondike Kate* (1943), while ostensibly about Kate (Ann Savage), actually centers on the rivalry between dance hall owners Jefferson Braddock (Neal) and "Sometime" Smith (Sheldon Leonard). The screenplay is muddled, but the actors do their best under the trying conditions. Neal, with his mustache and gray-streaked hair, is dashing, and he works well with both Savage and Glenda Farrell (who calls him "Handsome" throughout). Hedda Hopper wrote, "Tom has been called 'The Road Show Clark Gable' but he's beginning to forget the captain [Gable was then an Army Air Forces captain] and give out with that old Neal personality."

Klondike Kate was Neal's first pairing with Ann Savage, and on-screen they were simpatico. It was the start of a long, complicated relationship. According to Kent Adamson, Savage's manager and friend, Neal and Savage knew each other well from 1943 through 1955:

> Though they started off badly (Ann knocked Tom down at their first encounter on set), they grew to respect and enjoy each other over the three movies they made for the Columbia B unit. Ann began to appreciate Tom as a versatile actor of talent and they became friends. Though they didn't publicly date, they saw each other off screen and warmed slowly into a heated affair.

Neal portrayed *The Racket Man* (1944), who undergoes a change in attitude when he is drafted and in charge of breaking up a black-market gang. The Neal-Savage combination was repeated in two 1944 patriotic actioners: *Two-Man Submarine* (with Neal as a scientist on a remote island with a secret penicillin formula sought by the Japanese) and *The Unwritten Code* (as a sergeant who suspects that a wounded British soldier is actually a Nazi).

During night shooting on *Two-Man Submarine*, Savage became sick in the freezing studio tank and developed a serious case of pneumonia. Said Adamson:

> Ann called in sick for several months and was put on suspension without pay by Columbia. Ann said that Tom and her actress-model girlfriend Ann Lester were the few who inquired and looked after her. They helped Ann and her mother out during Ann's long illness. Ann's friendship with Tom persisted actively through other film projects, their marriages and relationships to other people, and their dislocation from Hollywood.

In between the two pictures with Savage, 30-year-old Neal eloped to Las Vegas with 18-year-old Dublin-born actress Vicky Lane on May 27, 1944. They were accompanied by Neal's best friend Eddie Hall, a stand-in and bit actor, who wed Patricia Stengel a half-hour later. The following month, Edwin Schallert wrote:

> Swank Hollywood affair was the reception for Tom Neal and Vicky Lane, recently married, held at the home of her parents in Bel-Air, even to the butler in tails who smilingly greeted

Pictured left to right: Neal, Hugh Beaumont and Anthony Caruso bring the beefcake in Columbia's *The Racket Man* (1944). Neal plays a gangster who joins the Army, reforms and cracks his old black-market ring.

arriving guests. Flashing prominently as personalities in the assemblage were Lana Turner and Esther Williams, who stayed for both the afternoon and evening phases of the party. Numerous other stars and prominents of Hollywood were present.

At the time, Lane was under contract to MGM, which explains the presence of Turner, Williams and other players from that studio.

A writer for the *Cumberland News* concluded, "If there ever were any doubt in the minds of Columbia Pictures executives that they had discovered a versatile and fast-growing star when they signed handsome Tom Neal to a long-term contract, that doubt should now be completely dispelled after the variety of his most recent roles and the deft manner in which he has handled them." About four months after this was written, Columbia dropped Neal. To add to his troubles, a luggage shop he owned in Atlantic City burned down.

"Tom Neal, problem child. Mr. Neal, always prone to adopt in real life the hobbies suggested by his screen roles, has left a trail of dislocated joints and strained muscles in his wake since playing a jiujitsu devotee in *Behind the Rising Sun*." This vague item, written in July 1944 by Jimmie Fidler, omits who Neal supposedly beat up (never mind that he didn't do jiujitsu in *Rising Sun*).

Fidler again: "When Tom Neal saw his actress wife, Vicky Lane, in her makeup for *The Ape Woman* [*The Jungle Captive*, 1945], he wanted to strangle Universal executives. 'Gorilla' warfare?"

Harrison Carroll reported in late 1944, "Nice work by Tom Neal getting homes for 19 discharged war dogs." Both Neal and Vicky loved animals; he even took a veterinary course. They had a kennel of dogs, with Clark Gable gifting them with an Afghan hound. They also entered their dogs in shows, oftentimes nabbing first prize. On the equine front, Neal had the lead in Republic's *Thoroughbreds* (1944) as an ex–U.S. Cavalry sergeant who trains a horse for a big race.

Neal might have thought he hit rock bottom when he went to work on three pictures for PRC and associate producer Martin Mooney, but today they're among his best-known credits. *Crime, Inc.* (1945), based on Mooney's 1935 book, cast him as a reporter breaking up a crime syndicate while falling in love with a nightclub singer (Martha Tilton). Raymond L. Schrock is credited as screenwriter for *Club Havana* (1945), but its director Edgar G. Ulmer later claimed that most of the story was made up by him and the actors as they went along. The drama takes place at the Latin-flavored Club Havana, where hospital intern Neal is dining with his date (Dorothy Morris). PRC managed to corral an impressive cast: Margaret Lindsay, Don Douglas, Isabelita (aka Lita Baron), Gertrude Michael, Paul Cavanagh, Marc Lawrence, Pedro de Cordoba and John Dehner, plus Kristine Miller and Linda Christian as cigarette girls. Neal's pal Eddie Hall also had a role; it was one of ten movies in which both appeared.

For Universal, Neal was the hero in two back-to-back Bs, both produced by Ben Pivar and co-written by George Bricker: *The Brute Man* (1946) and *Blonde Alibi* (1946). The former, starring real-life acromegaly victim Rondo Hatton as the Creeper, was sort of a prequel to Hatton's earlier *House of Horrors* (1946) and shows how he became a deformed murderer. Universal later sold the film to PRC, and that company put it into release. A reworking of 1934's *The Crosby Case*, *Blonde Alibi* with Martha O'Driscoll was called a "tight melodrama, with enough comedy to lighten the suspense" (Jimmie Fidler).

> A studio that's not noted for dramatic gems, turns out one [*Detour*] any producer would be proud of—Jimmie Fidler, November 3, 1945

The high spot in Neal's career was PRC's *Detour* (1945). If ever a role fit him, it was Al Roberts, a hard-luck cynic who just can't catch a break. Based on Martin M. Goldsmith's "grim, raw, restless" (*Norfolk Ledger-Dispatch*) 1939 novel, it was adapted by Goldsmith with uncredited help from Martin Mooney and the film's director, Edgar G. Ulmer. The novel told two separate stories, each with its own protagonist: Alexander Roth, a classical violinist playing in a nightclub, and his girlfriend, Sue Harvey, who goes to Hollywood in search of fame. The moviemakers chucked Sue's story to concentrate on the renamed Al Roberts, now a pianist, who hitchhikes to California to be with Sue. Along the way, he is picked up by a pill-popping Charles Haskell, Jr., who accidentally dies en route. Roberts, certain that the authorities will jump to the conclusion that he killed Haskell, does what any noir hero would do: He trades identities with the dead man. Continuing west, he picks up a hitchhiker, Vera, and introduces himself as Haskell. Bad luck!: Vera knew Haskell! "What did you do with the body?" she spits accusingly. "What'd you do, kiss him with a wrench?" From that moment on, Roberts is in her mercenary clawhold as she blackmails and threatens him. Playing the hard-boiled Vera

Neal's best-known movie role came in director Edgar G. Ulmer's *Detour* (1945) with his frequent co-star and friend Ann Savage. For Neal, the bleak film noir could also be called prophetic.

is the remarkable Ann Savage, the most ferocious of femme fatales and a long way off from the Columbia pictures she did with Neal.

Ulmer claimed in a 1970 *Film Culture* interview conducted by Peter Bogdanovich that most of his PRC films were shot in only a week. In fact, *Detour* was filmed in 14 days, from June 14 to June 29, 1945. Still an impressive achievement. The *Los Angeles Times* called it "one of the most poignant and disturbing stories to reach the screen in any year…." And columnist Hugh Dixon wrote, "Tom Neal does a terrific job in PRC's *Detour*. In a major studio movie, it would put him in the Academy talk. He's a fine actor, somebody's going to discover before very long." The movie's reputation has grown through the years, and in 1992 it was selected for the National Film Registry by the Library of Congress as being "culturally, historically, or aesthetically significant."

RKO again called on Neal to put on Asian makeup for *First Yank into Tokyo* (1945), hoping box-office lightning would strike twice. Produced and written by Mexican-born J. Robert Bren (from a story by Bren and wife Gladys Atwater), it concerns pilot Major Steve Ross (Neal), who believes that his girlfriend, nurse Abby Drake (Barbara Hale), was killed on Bataan. As he was raised in Japan and speaks the language, he's asked to undergo plastic surgery to look Japanese and go on a special mission. Since he has nothing to live for with Abby dead, he agrees. He is to contact POW scientist Lewis Jardine, who has the formula to build an atomic bomb. Through a series of contrivances, Sergeant Tomu Takishima (as Ross is now called), ends up at Jardine's POW camp where, lo and behold!, Abby is also working. *And* where Ross' college roommate, Hideko Okanura (Richard Loo), is in charge. It doesn't get more coincidental than that! Most thought

Neal acted with conviction, despite the absurd plot and makeup. *The Tidings* wrote, "[T]he disguise provided for him by the Hollywood plastic surgery wizards succeeds in making him look uncannily like Boris Karloff's Frankenstein monster. Certainly, no Japanese could have been deceived by any such device.... It is dime-magazine trash from beginning to end. Too bad the artists had no better material, for performances are nicely turned...." The *Los Angeles Times'* Philip K. Scheuer thought it "written and acted artfully enough to entrap all but the wariest spectator, and if you are not careful you will find yourself taking the bait—not whole or for long, but for exactly the length of time it is dangled before you." Scheuer did *not* like the inclusion of the atomic bomb in the narrative and the newsreel footage shown at the conclusion: "This strikes me as the grossest kind of exploitation." In fact, it was a last-minute addition; in the original, Jardine had plans for a new type of gun, but just before the film was released, atomic bombs were dropped on Japan and RKO producers saw the chance for a "first."

There was enough Neal without makeup in *First Yank into Tokyo* to interest Miriam Hopkins, who was looking for a leading man for her stage production of *Laura*. She was to play the title role, Laura Hunt; Tom essayed Detective Lt. McPherson, described in the play as "in his early thirties, a shrewd young man, guarded in his manner, but with a dry sense of humor. He is not handsome, but attractive in a lean, vigorous, masculine way. He limps slightly." Otto Kruger portrayed the sophisticated and snippy Waldo Lydecker. Vera Caspary had originally written it as a serial for *Collier's*, "Ring Twice for Laura," in 1942, followed by a novel (1943) and a classic movie (1944). Then, with the help of George Sklar, Caspary adapted it into a play. Starting in April 1946, it commenced a road tour with the ultimate goal of Broadway, playing Wilmington (Delaware), Philadelphia, Boston, Baltimore, Detroit, Washington and Chicago. There was trouble on the road, with producer Hunt Stromberg, Jr., contemplating replacing director Michael Gordon and actor Walter Coy. (In the role of Shelby Carpenter, Coy hurt Kruger during a fight scene.) Neal was a target of rumors, with the producer thinking Michael O'Shea would be better as McPherson.

Neal stayed on with the limping production. An unnamed *Baltimore Sun* writer reported that in that city,

> a growing crowd of bobby soxers will sigh happily at [Neal's] departure from the villainous roles that have typed him on the screen.... Neal's role in *Laura* still is that of a tough guy, a detective, but he believes he has made considerable strides in the right direction. Box office receipts, which are showing an increasing volume of sales to bobby soxers who do not ordinarily go to the more elaborate mysteries such as *Laura,* are bearing him out.

Perhaps. The production did well in a couple of places, including Washington, but apparently not well enough. Reviews were respectable—except in Chicago, where the *Tribune*'s Albert Goldberg ripped the performances (particularly Hopkins') and wrote that Neal could "improve a likable job if he were to sustain the part's essential wryness and give up his incessant smirking." The *Chicago Tribune* wasn't done with the play—and Neal—yet. Another *Tribune* reviewer, Claudia Cassidy, also panned the play, calling Neal "a reasonably competent, reasonably attractive but obviously incompatible leading man."

Laura closed in Chicago on July 6, 1946, with Stromberg claiming it would open on Broadway in the fall. A new company was organized the following year (K.T. Stevens, Hugh Marlowe and John Loder, the latter soon replaced by Otto Kruger), and *Laura* ran on Broadway for 44 performances.

Meanwhile, Neal was having some career doldrums. "Although he hasn't reached his own goal—stardom, Tom isn't allowing himself to grow sour," observed the *Shamokin News Dispatch*, which then quoted Neal: "I'd like to see my name billed above the title, but if that never happens to me, I'll still be happy! Some of us get the breaks, and others don't." How very optimistic—*if* true—but, really, how could he be happy that Flame the Dog was billed over the title *and* him for *My Dog Shep* (1946)? Made by Robert Lippert's Golden Gate Pictures in nine days, it gave Neal very little to do to earn his second billing; the story centered on Shep (Flame), Danny (Lanny Rees) and Carter (William Farnum), all unwanted until they find each other.

Filming ended on *My Dog Shep* in late August 1946. Neal didn't get another screen job until March of the following year when he was cast by Lippert's Screen Arts Corp. in the role of detective Russ Ashton in two short films, shot back to back and released by Screen Guild: *The Hat-Box Mystery* and *The Case of the Baby Sitter* (both 1947), both directed by Lambert Hillyer and featuring Pamela Blake, Allen Jenkins and Virginia Sale. In the first, talking directly to the camera, Neal introduces himself, his secretary-fiancée Susie (Blake), his dimwit assistant "Harvard" (Jenkins) and "Harvard"'s girlfriend Veronica (Sale). After this novel opening, the rest of the credits play. The series stopped with these two, which is a shame, as the likable players worked well together and they were involved in tight mysteries. *Hollywood Review* wrote of *Baby Sitter*, "Pic sensibly is terse, loaded with action, corn comedy and competent ham, all wrapped up neatly in 40 minutes."

In July '47, Neal starred in "Solid Citizen," a 15-minute episode of the radio series *The Unexpected*; Neal's ex-con character is blackmailed by a past cellmate. His narration was reminiscent of Al Roberts' in *Detour*. That November, he got a major studio assignment, Paramount's *Beyond Glory* (1948). Neal's role of West Point grad Captain Harry Jason Daniels, the commanding officer and best friend of "Rocky" Gilman (Alan Ladd), is important to the plot, but gives him very little screen time. In combat in World War II Tunisia, Gilman believes that his cowardice resulted in Daniels' death, and he is haunted by guilt even after the war; he eventually contacts the captain's widow (Donna Reed), becomes a West Point cadet and gets into a mess of trouble. We hear more about Neal's character than we see him, unfortunately.

Again, many months elapsed before Neal was cast in another picture. In August 1948, he started work on the 15-chapter Sam Katzman–Columbia serial *Bruce Gentry, Daredevil of the Skies,* based on an aviation comic strip by Ray Bailey, with location shooting at Lone Pine and Kernville. Charter pilot Gentry goes up against "agents of a certain foreign power" (led by super-villain The Recorder) who have kidnapped a scientist to work on their deadly remote-controlled flying discs. The low budget almost ruins an action-packed serial. Instead of the practical special effects Republic used, Katzman & Co. went with badly drawn animation for their flying discs; a couple of times, a parachuting Neal himself is animated in place of using a stuntman. The sheer force of Neal's brash, manly personality and his gung-ho attitude in the fight scenes makes this one of Columbia's most exciting chapterplays.

Amazon Quest was his only feature made in '48. Filmed at Charlie Chaplin Studios in December, it had "the shortest shooting schedule of the year, totaling 4 days on the set and one on location, and nobody is talking about its budget" (*Independent Exhibitors Film Bulletin*). Neal plays Thomas Dekker, Jr., who goes to Brazil to clear his father's name and prove his family has a share in a successful rubber company. A part–Portuguese girl, Teresa (Carole Mathews), guides him through the jungle. Most of the 75-minute running time is stock footage from the 1938 German film *Kautschuk* starring Luxembourgian actor René Deltgen. This serves as flashbacks telling of the senior Dekker's adventures and it works because of Deltgen's resemblance to Neal. "Quite lengthy and drawn-out, with the jungle scenes commanding interest, this will find its niche on the lower half," wrote *The Exhibitor*. "It has exploitation possibilities, and the acting and direction are both adequate." Mandel Herbstman (*Motion Picture Daily*) also praised its exploitation value: "Most of the jungle footage has a documentary-like authenticity, and as such makes good film fare. However, the dramatic narrative that was built around the jungle scenes runs pretty much in conventional style." *Variety* felt that Neal "walks through his paces energetically but without much conviction." Director Steve Sekely got credit from *Motion Picture Daily* for keeping "things constantly on the move," but Austrian Eduard von Borsody, who helmed the original, deserves the kudos.

On March 12 and 13, 1949, Neal and wife Vicky were among the select group of tennis players competing in the Beverly-Wilshire Hotel invitational mixed doubles tournament. That July 4, appropriately Independence Day, she filed for divorce. They continued to live together until they both could find apartments. "We are still friends but this isn't one of those trial separations. It's over and final between us," Vicky was quoted by the *Minneapolis Morning Tribune*. There was no community property and Lane did not ask for alimony.

> Tom Neal has lost so much weight worrying about the breakup of his marriage of five years that his friends are worried about him.—Louella Parsons, July 12, 1949

In August, a divorce court judge heard Vicky Lane's complaints: "I couldn't even go down to the corner to get a pack of cigarettes without being accused of seeing other men." Yet, she said, Neal would often go out without her. "We never went out evenings together. We sat at home and that was that." If any of her friends came over, "he'd storm out." She was awarded an uncontested divorce. In November, Lane was in Las Vegas establishing residency for a quick divorce. She did not want to wait for her decree to become final in August '50, as she was in love with minor league baseball player Jim Baxes. Something happened to her plans, love and otherwise, and she left Las Vegas and waited for the final decree.

Neal had a friend in producer Robert L. Lippert who between 1949 and '51 cast him in ten pictures, including *Red Desert*, *Apache Chief* (both 1949), *Radar Secret Service*, *I Shot Billy the Kid*, *Train to Tombstone* (all 1950) and *Danger Zone* (1951). All but the comedy-musical *G.I. Jane* (1951) featured Neal in support—and some had him as a dirty heavy, which he did well. Producer-director Ron Ormond, who worked with him at Lippert, put Neal in two Lash La Rue Westerns, *King of the Bullwhip* and *The Daltons' Women* (both 1950). At Monogram, he played bad guys in *Joe Palooka in Humphrey Takes a Chance* (1950), *Call of the Klondike* (1950) and *Let's Go Navy!* (1951); and was the lead in the seven-day quickie *Navy Bound* (1951), as a Navy boxer who helps save his family's fishing boat. Some critics considered the latter a sleeper. On television, Neal was on two 1950 episodes of *The Gene Autry Show* as baddies.

When bandleader Xavier Cugat and his estranged wife Lorraine were going through a contentious divorce, Neal's name was dragged into the fight. A typewritten letter, dated January 25, 1950, was sent to Hedda Hopper, signed by Lorraine:

Dear Hedda,

Rather than have you hear it from any other sources, I would like to say that as soon as my divorce with Cugie is final, I will marry the actor Tom Neal.

This may come to you as a surprise but we have been in love for some time. Hopeing [sic] to see you personally soon, I remain

Sincerely,
Lorraine Cugat

Hopper wrote in her column, "First, she isn't divorced; she has no settlement from Cugie, and why should she jeopardize both by sending in such news? I checked with her, and she swears the signature on the letter is a forgery, and she's turning it over to the postal authorities for investigation." At least one other columnist got the same letter. The soon-to-be-ex–Mrs. Cugat and her lawyer took Hopper's note to Assistant U.S. Attorney Vincent N. Erickson. "Naturally, I didn't write these letters," Lorraine told him. "I only met the actor referred to in the letters at a party once about a month ago. There is no romantic attachment and marriage to anyone is the farthest thing from my mind at the present time." She wanted the forger found and federally prosecuted; Erickson said he would investigate when new evidence came to light. By October '51, the Cugats were still battling it out and Xavier named Neal in his divorce suit—and with recorded conversations. So much for Lorraine not being romantic with Tom.

Mike McCauley, a play about American GIs in wartime Italy to dynamite a bridge, opened in Santa Barbara on January 26, 1951. Neal had a featured role in the production, which starred Don DeFore (as Mike) and Isa Miranda. In the article "*Mike McCauley* Features Neal as Fem Heartthrob," a *Santa Barbara News Press* writer predicted, "Feminine hearts should flutter violently in the confines of the Lobero Theatre … when Hollywood's soi-disant gift to the fair sex, Tom Neal, makes his first entrance in the comedy-drama, *Mike McCauley*…." The show then played a limited engagement, starting on January 29 at San Francisco's Geary Theater. ("Tom Neal registers strongly as a small operator traitor."—Hortense Morton, *San Francisco Examiner*.) In Chicago, it opened on February 15 at the Harris—and promptly tanked. "Broadway can forget about … *Mike McCauley*," wrote Harold V. Cohen. "Lambasted by the Chicago critics, it quickly folded there on Saturday night (Feb. 17). The authors intend to revise the script this summer and perhaps try again."

Meanwhile, in March '51, Neal went to Arizona to support Mickey Rooney and Jane Nigh in the comedy *Sailor, Beware!* at the Sombrero Playhouse. Also in the cast was William Phipps, who told Tom Weaver in 2015:

At one point in the play, as part of the action, [Neal] restrains me, he grabs my arms and shoulders and holds me. Every performance he used to do it much, much too roughly, as if to say, "Look how strong I am," "Look what I can do," "If you're not careful, I'll break your back!"—that was the implication. That used to piss me off. He was psycho, and I recognized that. Neal restraining me—it was only a few seconds' action on stage and then it was over, so I used to just ignore it and walk away from it. I wouldn't say anything to him, I wouldn't even say hello or goodbye, I'd never talk to him. 'Cause I realized that he was a powderkeg.

Columnist Buddy Mason wrote,

One of the most versatile young players in Hollywood today is Tom Neal. A hard-working, studious young man, Tom keeps polishing his many talents. He's never quite satisfied with anything he does and continually seeks to improve. He constantly amazes everyone by showing skills in a variety of little-known arts.

Versatile, yes; in demand, no. He guested on *Hollywood Theatre Time* with Sheila Ryan.

> I don't know whether they were kidding or on the square but Denise Darcel and Tom Neal were having hot words at the Mocambo.—Harrison Carroll, July 16, 1951

Neal's relationship with Darcel was nothing compared to what he got himself into with another actress.

In July '51, 23-year-old blonde bombshell Barbara Payton was under contract to producer William Cagney and Warner Bros., where she had lead roles opposite Gary Cooper, James Cagney and Gregory Peck. She was not yet divorced from her second husband, John Payton (the decree would be final that September), but she was engaged to urbane actor Franchot Tone, twice her age at 46. Despite her strong start at WB, Payton was now on loan-out to producer Jack Broder for a jungle-horror exploitation film, writer-director Curt Siodmak's *Bride of the Gorilla*.

While Tone was in New York, his fiancée grew lonely and went to a pool party at the Sunset Plaza Apartments. It was there, wrote *Exposed* magazine's Kenneth Grange, that she spied Neal, "displaying his masculinity" in a bathing suit. "Honey, I took just one look at him and I absolutely flipped!" Payton later recalled. "It was love at first sight. Because I saw him in a swimming suit. He looked so wonderful in his trunks I knew he was the only man in my life." At the time, the 37-year-old Neal was in peak physical condition and, added Grange, the "memory of whatever Tone resembled in his undies was blurred by strutting Tom's conspicuous bulges."

Sidney Skolsky's report that Neal and Payton "seem to have gone but overboard ever since they met at a party two weekends ago" was an understatement. Within days, they were living together. Barbara's friend Tina Ballard told Payton's biographer John O'Dowd,

> I noticed that his clothes and personal belongings were strewn all over the house and Barbara was just gaga over him. He had kind of a rough exterior but Tom was really a nice guy. And I could tell by the way he looked at Barbara that he was just crazy about her.
>
> I asked Barbara, "What about Franchot?," but she just waved her hand and said she would deal with it later.

Neal's nephew Walter Burr told O'Dowd,

> With Barbara working at Warner Bros. and Tom freelancing at Lippert and Monogram, I'm sure she was doing a lot better financially than he was. I could definitely see my uncle shacking up with her right away, especially if she asked him. When given the chance, Tom played the

Neal's association with actress Barbara Payton was the definition of "complicated relationship." She later famously gushed of him, "Tom was a beautiful hunk of man. He had a chemical buzz for me that sent red peppers down my thighs."

part of the "resident stud" very well. He had no problem at all letting a lady foot most of the bills, especially since he was usually stone broke between films.

According to Payton, within four minutes of meeting, they decided to marry. "She is very young," Tone told Dorothy Manners, "and youth attracts youth. If she says she is sincerely in love with Neal—she means it. This isn't just an impulsive thing."

Or was it? Payton found herself in a dilemma: Did she want the security Tone could give her or the excitement Neal promised? Maybe she herself didn't know that answer.

> Harriet Ames is another torch-toter as a result of Tom Neal's decision that Barbara Payton was the girl for him. (The string of broken hearts Tom left behind put him in the What-a-Man class.)—Dorothy Kilgallen, August 8, 1951

> Barbara Payton is another whose sudden yen to be Mrs. Tom Neal had her reeling last week. She couldn't wait to fly to Mexico and say the words that would make them one. Now she thinks she'll hang around until her divorce from John Payton is final so she can be married in the U.S.A.

> I'm laying odds that by the time she gets her final decree she won't even be speaking to Neal, much less giving him her heart and hand. Wonder if the kid wasn't trying to needle Franchot Tone into slipping a plain golden ring on her finger?—Florabel Muir, August 8, 1951

About two weeks later, Gloria Grant (*West Los Angeles Independent*) and others were reporting that Tone wasn't going to take "no" for an answer and was attempting to change Payton's mind—and succeeding. The merry-go-round had begun. For the next couple of weeks, Payton kept breaking up with one or the other and it was never clear who was going to be her next groom.

Columnists didn't take it all seriously and, of course, put the blame on Payton. In a "personal" letter to Barbara, Dorothy Manners called it all an "endless string of silliness": "Scenes and quarrels may be part of your youth, as Franchot seems to believe, but there is such a thing as personal dignity which you had better learn about if you're really going somewhere except 'down' in your career." Harrison Carroll called Payton a "very mixed-up girl." No more mixed-up than Tone and Neal, supposedly mature men who eagerly played with Payton's emotions.

It all blew up on September 14, 1951. Barbara had finally decided to marry Tom, but the night before the wedding she went out nightclubbing with Franchot. In Barbara's apartment, Neal sat and waited for them to return—seething, drinking, complaining to friends he had invited over, ready to confront the couple.

At 1:30 a.m., Tone and Payton finally arrived and the two men went nose to nose in a heated argument. Tone made a critical mistake when he remarked, "Let's settle this thing outside." Neal related later that when they got outside,

> Tone swung on me. I ducked the punch and then hit him very hard, knocking him about ten feet. Then I landed on him like a cat and hit him three or four more times. He went out cold. At this point Barbara came screaming at me and I pushed her aside. I saw them carry Tone into the house, all bloody, and still unconscious. Then I left.

A neighbor, Judson O'Donnell, claimed he saw the scrap from his window and told police the beating was a "methodical, sickening thing" of about 30 blows. He added, "It sounded like a prizefighter in a gym beating the bags. It was one of the bloodiest fights I've ever seen."

When the dust settled, the "frail, underweight" (*Los Angeles Daily News*) Tone was in a semi-coma. He had suffered a serious concussion and fractured facial bones (a smashed cheekbone, broken right upper jaw and broken nose) that required him to get plastic surgery. His doctor told reporters, "In a general way, it's reasonably certain he'll look like Franchot Tone, but as for closeups, who knows?" Payton sported a black eye, also courtesy of Neal. Tom, nursing swollen hands and ripped-raw knuckles, said he was sorry that Tone was in such serious condition, and even offered to give him a blood transfusion, if needed. Days later, Payton snuck into Tone's hospital room via the fire escape.

While Tone's memory was hazy, he had a distinctly different tale to tell about the fight. He told Lee Ferrero,

> I didn't throw the first punch. As a matter of fact, we went outside to talk over our differences. My face was turned the other way when Neal hit me, although we had been arguing inside on whether or not he should leave. I remember being knocked down, and my head hit the steps; then I put my hands up to cover my face and passed out. That's all I remember.

Payton adamantly agreed that the "vicious" Neal struck first and "showed no mercy." She told Ferrero,

> I love Franchot Tone. I love him more now than ever.
> Tom Neal is a brute. I hope Franchot has him arrested. I'd be his witness if he wants me to. I should have married him long ago, and I don't know whatever possessed me to break off with him and plan to marry Neal.
> The fight was horrible. Franchot certainly did not swing first, and I love him more than ever.

On September 17, it was announced that Payton and her victimized lover would marry, but they were waiting for his face to heal. Neal was quoted as saying, "I was very much in love with the girl, and still am today. I hope she and Tone will be very happy."

The front-page drama of the Tone-Payton-Neal triangle was the most reported news of the time. Everyone had an opinion, even evangelist Billy Graham, who told 5000 followers at the Hollywood Bowl (September 16) that the only salvation for sinners was the return to the teachings of Christ:

> The need of the hour in Hollywood is a great revival of religion in the hearts of its people.
> The real problem in Hollywood is sin—S-I-N—one little word. Sin is at the root of all your troubles.
> I would like to say to Franchot Tone, Barbara Payton and Tom Neal, that one minute united in Christ would solve any problem they have ever known.

The *Los Angeles Mirror* quoted Barbara as insisting she never wanted to see Neal again. "My whole concept of him has changed. Y'know, when I first met him, I thought he was a real gentleman. But now—well, I'm not even goin' to bother thinking up names to call him. He's just a vicious man who I once thought was a nice guy."

But an irresistible one. Three days after asserting that she would marry Tone, Payton was seen out with Neal—dancing at Ciro's, at a party at Jackie Coogan's house and at her apartment. Tone's lawyer admitted that they knew of the reunion, and a nurse said that when Franchot heard the news, he groaned from his hospital bed. Publicly, Tone did a turnaround and, according to Florabel Muir, he didn't believe Barbara was seeing Neal and "thinks she's a victim of a sensation-seeking press." Muir added, "Love does funny things to a guy or gal and how it pulls the wool over eyes bedazzled by a pair of red lips or the curves of a so-called form divine."

Tone couldn't make up his mind whether he wanted to file a felony assault charge against Neal, or an assault-and-battery misdemeanor. District Attorney S. Ernest Roll called the three principals into his office to tell their versions of the "Love Brawl." Payton backpedaled and said that she wasn't sure who threw the first punch; she was now protecting Neal, whom she admitted seeing since the fight, but only on "business." The following day, per Florabel Muir, Payton—"torn between two loves"—took an overdose of sleeping pills, but was saved by friends. On September 26, Payton left Los Angeles for her hometown of Cloquet, Minnesota, to spend time with her aunts.

Whether there was a connection between her o.d., her trip and Franchot's decision to call off any legal action against Neal, we will never know. On September 27, Tone told the district attorney that he had reconsidered the matter "and I feel the best interests of my family, my friends and my profession dictate my discontinuing any prosecution of my application for a complaint...." (Walter Winchell: "Franchot Tone decided not to bring Tom Neal into court. It'd only make him nervous to see Tom raise his right hand again.") That same day, he left to join Payton. That night, Neal was seen on TV in an episode of *Racket Squad*, his first on-camera job since the Love Brawl.

On September 28, Payton and Tone married at her aunts' home in Cloquet. Barbara Flanagan of the *Minneapolis Morning Tribune* covered the wedding and claimed that among the crowd outside the house was a group of teenage girls, who "weren't at all sure they'd have picked Tone." One 13-year-old said, "Franchot's nice, but he's not cute. Tom Neal's cute." Three other girls agreed with her.

Back in Hollywood, Neal was asked what he thought of the nuptials. He wished Franchot and Barbara happiness and added, "As far as my plans are concerned, marriage is the farthest thing from my mind—there are so many beautiful women in the world, and so little time." His new girlfriend was Russian-born French-American socialite-actress (and later Buddhist nun) Countess Zina d'Harcourt (aka Zina Rachevsky).

> At a showing of *Drums in the Deep South* t'other night, you should have heard the hoss-laffs when James Craig and Guy Madison have a slugging match over, pardon the expression, Barbara Payton. Consensus of opinion seems to be that Franchot Tone, with his background and intelligence, will come out of the current mess as a figure to be "more pitied than scorned"—unless he suddenly snaps out with lots of extra sense; that Tom Neal, with his braggadocio printed statements; his (also printed) crude moral indictment of a gal who'd already indicted herself with cheap talk, can only emerge as a figure of contempt. We've had a deluge of mail—the writers mostly wondering why these people are given more and more printer's ink and obviously wishing they'd be faded out of the picture (and pictures) entirely. But, in answer to many a "tirade" received, we want to quote a confrere who so very rightly itemed, "Hollywood has no more bums than any other town. But here, they're famous!"—Edith Gwynn, September 30, 1951

Neal bragged to Alice Mosby that his "sex appeal rating" went up after he thrashed Tone and he claimed that he was being offered "dates with movie stars" and $5000-a-week personal appearance tours. He declined the latter because "I think that cheapens not only the person, but the affair." He also said he felt that the Tone incident "may help my career. After all, I didn't do anything wrong like being named a Communist. I just fought for the woman I loved." He claimed to be sorting through movie, stage and TV offers and that soon he would be a "romantic lover in A epics." Walter Winchell wrote that Neal's lawyer insisted that Tom would "accept only leading roles" from then on.

In actuality, for the remainder of '51, Neal acted in no films or theatre; he appeared in only two documented TV episodes, both of them *Boston Blackie*s. His boasting about his big-time career was just bluster—and very sad. In a rare reflective moment, quoted by Erskine Johnson, Neal revealed why he hadn't made "the big star grade" in Hollywood, and of course he placed none of the blame on himself:

"Movie queens." …

"I get involved with them," Tom grunted. "I had a great chance at MGM but a certain actress on the lot killed it for me. The same thing happened at RKO. I loused myself up. If The Lady is with you, your career goes. If The Lady's not with you, you don't go."

Meanwhile, after seven weeks, the Tone marriage was already crumbling. Franchot was not happy that Payton was contemplating a movie with Tom. "I've got to work," she explained. "I must earn a living." Tone accused her of not being able to forget Neal.

> New Yorkers close to the Franchot Tone-Barbara Payton mess believe Barbara will marry Tom Neal, the other member of the triangle, when her divorce from Franchot is final. They now talk openly about the theory many held when she married Tone: that she did it simply to keep him from prosecuting Neal—whom, even then, she would have preferred to marry. Franchot, having refused to take action against Neal at the time of the assault, cannot reopen the case at this late date.—Dorothy Kilgallen, November 28, 1951

By December, the Neal-Payton film project was dead, the producer having been unable to raise the money. "Good!" columnist Ed Sullivan bluntly wrote in the *New York Daily News*. And although the trio was having trouble getting film jobs, supposedly exhibitors were profiting from reissues of their old pictures due to the "clamor" (Erskine Johnson). When Neal's oldies were advertised in 1951 newspapers, he was sometimes called "The Franchot Tone Slugger!," "Franchot Tone's Rival" and "Tom Knockout Neal." Jimmie Fidler thought it was all "nauseating."

Worse, the "once gentlemanly" (Fidler) Tone was in court charged with spitting in columnist Florabel Muir's face, kicking her shins and trying to choke her at Ciro's. He didn't like how she reported on the Love Brawl and accused her of listening in to telephone conversations between him and Payton. Fidler surmised the reasons for Tone's drastic change in demeanor were obvious: "Barbara Payton and vodka for breakfast." According to Muir, "Tone's actions were so peculiar that they suggested the acts of someone who might be 'narcoticised.'" Writer Leo Katcher called Tone a "Hollywood hooligan."

Soon it was being reported that Neal and Payton were together again, but just as fast, she reconciled with Tone. "Tom Neal has disappeared from his familiar haunts," wrote Harrison Carroll. "Pals say he took off for somewhere in his car." When he materialized at the London House in Chicago, in the company of Payton, he told photographers: "Don't you realize Barbara's still married to Franchot Tone? We can't be posing for pictures. The way you guys follow me around you'd think I murdered someone." Clenching his fists, he added, "I use these"; then he calmed down to say that Barbara was "a wonderful woman—the greatest woman I've ever known.…We can't even go out and have a quiet drink together without you guys trailing us."

Around this same time, Neal tried to get Vicky Lane's mother to back a play starring him, Payton and Vicky. It did not happen. Vicky was one of the few who stuck by him during his difficulties in 1951 (which included his mother's death on November 5). "Tom Neal's ex, Vicky Lane, tells friends she thinks Tom's an awfully nice feller despite all the bad press," wrote Herb Stein. Neal sought TV work in Chicago, and in California shared living space with friends Jackie Coogan and Mickey Rooney.

Reporters relentlessly insisted that Neal and Payton were going to elope to Juarez, Mexico. "Where do these columnists dream up these fairy tales?" Payton wanted to know. Maybe from Neal: Florabel Muir claimed that Neal himself "bragged" to patrons in a barbershop, as the barber "trimmed his manly head," that they were going to Mexico. "Neal has insisted that he was blonde Barbara's true love ever since he busted Tone on the beezer on her front lawn last September," wrote Muir.

That was January '52. The following month, Neal was in the news again "visiting" wealthy Ruby Stroud at her Palm Springs residence. Before he arrived, so say the police, the home was burglarized of $11,000 in furs and jewels. Neal wasn't considered a suspect. Stroud was friends with Payton and, in fact, was to be one of the bridesmaids at the Neal-Payton wedding that never happened. Payton was reportedly unhappy that Neal was seeing Ruby.

In March, Tone revived his divorce suit against Payton, citing Neal as the reason. Barbara denied reports that *she* had to be revived when she swallowed sleeping pills in a "fit of frustration and despondency" over the pending divorce. She also denied that she and Tone had a knockdown-dragout fight in their hotel room. Edith Gwynn wrote,

> The biggest and most shocking of all current Hollywood gab concerns the set of photos that Barbara Payton and Tom Neal supposedly posed for recently! We haven't seen them but copies are said to be soon available by the hundreds. Disgusting—but EVERYBODY in town is talking of little else at the moment!

They certainly didn't pose for *these* photos. Tone had hired someone to take incriminating pictures of Barbara with Tom and other men and even went so far as to mail them anonymously to her friends and family.

In March, Neal appeared on *Adventures of Wild Bill Hickok*, doing a good job with his tough, ambiguous character.

Tone sought to amend his divorce suit to include charges of adultery. The press had a field day describing Neal and Payton's nighttime meetings as reported by private detectives hired by Tone. Barbara countered that, because Tone threatened to kill her, she had asked Neal to stay with her and act as a bodyguard. Columnist Buck Henshaw wrote, "Barbara's million $$$$ settlement demand was tossed out of court when Tone submitted actual flash photos of his 'bride' with muscle boy actor Tom Neal. Yes, I saw one of 'em. No comment."

Finally, the opposing lawyers convinced all concerned to "postpone the fireworks" and settle. Payton got an undisclosed sum of money, and Tone got an uncontested divorce.

The damage, however, had been done: The reputations of Payton and Neal were in tatters. "Pay no mind to the many who'll tell you or infer that a 'full-length feature' featuring Barbara Payton and Tom Neal is making the rounds of the Beverly Hills 'private projection room circuit,'" wrote Edith Gwynn. Pay no mind, but here it is, another sordid item about the couple.

"The story is over," Tone remarked after he received his divorce from Payton. Maybe for him; he could move on and was wealthy enough to weather any career problems, but Neal had trouble getting acting jobs. In July '52, he was on a *Dick Tracy* episode buying a stolen car from juvies, and he did two five-minute episodes of the local Los Angeles series *Gaines Little Theater*, one with Ann Rutherford, the other with Elena Verdugo.

> Barbara Payton waits outside the State Unemployment Office while Tom Neal picks up his $25 check. But in a Cadillac!—Mike Connolly, June 18, 1952

Payton flew to England to star in two films, *The Flanagan Boy* (1953), also called *Bad Blonde*, and *Four Sided Triangle* (1953). She claimed that Neal acted as her manager and negotiated excellent deals for her. To save face, Neal stated that he would join Payton, "to see about some offers of work he received from London, Paris and Rome." There were no offers. Erskine Johnson wrote that before Barbara left for England, she "confided to a pal that she hocked her minks and that Tom Neal sold his car to survive the depression that followed her divorce from Franchot Tone. The famine's over now that Babs and Tom have movie assignments in Europe."

There was again talk that the couple would do a movie together, but they didn't. Neal was primarily in England on "business for an engineering firm he heads," according to the *San Bernardino County Sun*. "He said the firm owns a revolutionary new camshaft which will enable a tank to do 100 miles an hour. He plans to show it to British manufacturers." His partners were Travis Kleefeld (aka singer-actor Tony Travis) and Bill Garland, Jr.

"Tom Neal and Barbara Payton are startling conservative London with their violent fights," wrote Earl Wilson in October '52.

Erskine Johnson reported that Neal was telling everyone he would be Hedy Lamarr's co-star in the Italian-made TV series *The Great Love Stories*, to be directed by Edgar G. Ulmer. Eventually, it became the feature film *L'amante di Paride*, aka *Loves of Three Queens* (1954), with Neal nowhere in sight.

> Whatever Happened to Tom Neal?—Mike Connolly, November 18, 1952

> Stopped at the traffic light at Sunset and Fairfax, we spotted Tom Neal in a top-down convertible, with Babs Payton at the wheel. Tom was reading the want ads.—Sheilah Graham, December 5, 1952

In mid–December, Payton started filming the comedy *Run for the Hills* with Sonny Tufts. Producers were still trying to find a suitable vehicle to team Neal and Payton to capitalize on their notoriety. A war story and a film noir were variously in the works but fell through. Instead, Lippert, a company always good to Neal, got them as a package deal and cast them in the AnscoColor Western *The Great Jesse James Raid*, which began shooting in April '53. Robert L. Lippert, Jr.'s, first producing credit, it was directed by vet Reginald LeBorg. Willard Parker had the lead as Jesse James, who organizes a gang to steal a gold shipment. Neal is one of his pals, murderous gunfighter Arch Clements. Payton is a world-weary dance hall girl whom the men fight over (of course), but she and Neal are not a couple in the film—in fact, Neal grabs her at one point as she yells, "You rotten, low-down, rummy piece of muck!" Betrayal and cold-blooded murders are the name of the game here, and the eight-day wonder made money for Lippert.

> The season's most pregnant summer stock note: Barbara Payton and Tom Neal will co-star for the barn theatres, and Franchot Tone with Betsy von Furstenberg will be playing the same straw hat circuit. (Bandage, anyone? Iodine? Ambulance?)—Dorothy Kilgallen, May 11, 1953

Starting in July 1953, in Norwich, Connecticut, Barbara and Tom did a summer tour of *The Postman Always Rings Twice*. James M. Cain, author of the original novel, was involved with this production. When it was first performed, it was considered a "ponderous bore," and Cain went about revising, cutting scenes and making some changes to the story. As it headed to Pennsylvania, he felt he had licked the problem. "With Barbara Payton and Tom Neal in the leading roles," Cain told the *Hartford Courant*'s Bob Zaiman, "I think we have the proper combination. She is the type of woman a man would commit murder for and Neal is just the sort of man who would do it." He added, "He's got the fire it needs."

Before the play opened, M. Oakley Stafford made some astute observations about Neal in her column:

> Tom Neal looks like the middle-weight fighter he once was.... His black eyes are slanting, a little, and very intense.... His teeth shine out against a tanned skin so that you cannot avoid noticing how white and straight they are.... Neal, you get the idea, acts first and thinks afterward.... [He] has an intensity and vitality about him which made it still more of a puzzle.... He looks the type a girl would never leave, and he would have to fight to free himself of, rather than fight to win.... So, I am wrong again, because he had to battle for Barbara Payton and risked a great deal in doing so....

Jim Haas (*Evening Herald*) felt that the play, then in its second week at John Kenley's Lakewood Theater, was "still in the throes of doctoring. Its Broadway possibilities look pretty good, providing Mr. Cain, the novelist, permits a professional play doctor to step in and pull up some loose ends."

> Those noises you hear backstage in the touring company of *The Postman Always Rings Twice* are Tom Neal and Barbara Payton acting like Tom Neal and Franchot Tone.—Lee Mortimer, August 26, 1953

On September 28, 1953, *Postman* began its planned national tour at Pittsburgh's Nixon; the *Pittsburgh Post-Gazette*'s Harold V. Cohen remarked that the play's modest success during the summer gave the producers a "false sense of security," and all he felt watching the play was a "sense of waste" and how the revisions had weakened it, made it less potent, the characters mere stereotypes:

> Miss Payton and Mr. Neal are striking visual illustrations of the doomed couple Mr. Cain introduced so vigorously in his novel, but their performances stay on the surface. That is perhaps because they can go nowhere else as written. There are some small compensations late in the third act when Miss Payton climbs into a one-piece bathing suit and Mr. Neal into swimming trunks for a brief beach scene. The Nixon will long remember the resulting cheesecake and beefcake. Very little else about the beginning of the 1953–54 season is ever likely to be recalled, though.

Kaspar Monahan of *The Pittsburgh Press* concurred, calling it a haphazard production which "woefully lacks cohesion and sustained drive." He liked the stars, though: "As the brash hobo, muscular Tom Neal is equal to the varying emotional demands of his part—pleasantly 'wolfish' at the outset, exhibiting gradually the pangs of conscience as the sordid affair continues, then nervous fears as the foul plot nears realization, ultimately distrust of his partner-in-crime."

It was then on to Detroit, St. Louis (where one critic thought Neal looked like a "muscular Bob Hope with curly hair") and Chicago. "To the surprise of practically nobody," wrote Harold V. Cohen, "[*Postman*] closed in Chicago Saturday night [October 24] after being on the road only four weeks." Don Hope sniped that Neal and Payton "scored a big NOTHING in Chicago [in *Postman*]. Some in Hollywood are snickering over one critic's remarks which contained the observation: 'This crude dramatization suggests that if the theater isn't dead, someone should arrange a mercy killing!'"

In November '53, columnist Louis Sobol reported that the couple had "pooled their resources" to build a deluxe hotel with a swimming pool in La Paz, Mexico. This was a way-out claim considering that they had trouble paying their hotel bill in St. Louis. It was said that Neal was contemplating a play called *Blaze of Glory*.

> Those explosions from 'way down in Texas are just Barbara Payton and Tom Neal staging battles—the like of which haven't been seen in the Lone Star State since the Alamo.—Dorothy Kilgallen, March 6, 1954

Shortly after the above item ran, the couple broke up—this time for good. According to several reports, Neal had become a police officer in either Evansville, Indiana, or Evanston, Illinois, but wasn't happy and wanted to return to Hollywood. In fact, Neal had recurring roles on the live weekday Chicago television soaps *Hawkins Falls: A Television Novel* (as the warden of a boys' correction farm) and *A Time to Live*. It's possible that he was hanging around with police while in Evanston (where his sister Mary lived) because he had written a script called *4:20 A.M.* ("loaded with Mickey Spillane–ish dialog—only better"—Herb Lyon, *Chicago Tribune*), which he wanted to make locally and direct. Car dealer Joe Saporito was interested in being the producer and Chicago Police Captain Tom Harrison was to be technical adviser. That same month (May '55), Sheilah Graham wrote that Neal had passed his bar examination and was going to join the F.B.I. In July, Sidney Skolsky referred to Neal's screenplay as *4:30 A.M.*—it gained ten minutes—and said it was "filled with bop talk."

> Tom Neal is back in town. He'll continue acting, but I hear he also has an interest in a wash rack on Wilshire Boulevard.—Harrison Carroll, August 19, 1955

> Tom Neal is back in Hollywood—if anyone cares. He hopes to break back in movies.—Louella Parsons, September 8, 1955

> I've been asked by several people if that darkhaired gentleman running the gas station on Wilshire Blvd. in Beverly is Tom Neal. I'll have to get out to that station at the right hour and have a look.—Sidney Skolsky, September 26, 1955

> Tom Neal ... is part owner of a gas station on Wilshire Boulevard, Los Angeles, and is working there.—Danton Walker, October 5, 1955

In October 1955, Neal reunited with Ann Savage on the TV series *Gang Busters*. Directed by W. Lee Wilder, the episode, "The Red Dress Case," featured him as William Harlan Crain, just out of San Quentin after a five-year stretch for armed robbery. His high-strung girlfriend Juanita (Savage) is waiting for him with his two old gang members and she decides to be boss and call the shots. They let her—would *you* tell Ann Savage no? But things go wrong fast when her insistence on knocking over a dress shop so she can have a red dress leads to murder.

At the beginning of '56, according to Louella Parsons, Neal was "turning all his so-called charm" on 70-something oil heiress Elsinore Machris. "Personally, I hardly can believe that Elsinore, who does so many wonderful things for charity..., can be serious about Neal, who, I'm afraid, might be another heartbreak for her." They were seen for a few weeks around Palm Springs where, according to Harrison Carroll, the crowd at the Racquet Club "almost fell off the bar stools" when Machris walked in on Neal's arm. Machris told reporters that Tom had given up acting to concentrate on his writing. Neal also became the maître d' at the Doll House, a popular Palm Springs restaurant. Mike Connolly quoted Neal as saying that his "biggest cross" to bear on his new job was when guys from the bar came over to him and remarked, "I don't think you're so tough!"

In July 1956, Neal married airline stewardess Patricia Fenton.

Wanting to learn the restaurant business, Neal acted as host at Sea Wolf and the Town House, and was part-owner of a short-lived Italian restaurant, Dominick's. By the end of the year, he had started his own landscaping business, Neal's Nursery, in Palm

Springs and got his landscape architect's license. The couple had a son, Tom Patrick, born on March 14, 1957.

Reporter Lee Belser called the Neal home in August '57; Tom wasn't there but Pat was, and she told him that her husband "has no interest in getting back into films." His business was doing very well and he was "working very hard to make a living." Belser said that Neal had been served a subpoena to testify in the *Confidential* magazine libel trial about stories relating to him, Tone and Payton. "He doesn't want to testify," Mrs. Neal responded. "All he wants is to be left alone."

Robert Lippert, Jr., and his father owned apartment rental units and hired Neal to design the property. Lippert, Jr., told John O'Dowd,

> No one can ever say that Tom was afraid of hard work. He was a very talented landscaper who put in long hours and always did a very exceptional job for us. Even in his 40s, Tom maintained his muscular build and seemed to be in excellent physical condition. He worked out with weights all the time, and he was a strong son of a gun. But he was always a little bit testy. If you looked at him sideways, or caught him on an off day, you were asking for trouble.

Talking with Vernon Scott of the United Press in November '57, Neal said his life changed for the better after he moved to Palm Springs. "It was tough work at first under the broiling desert sun, but it was worth it. I really found myself—for the first time in my life." He did so well, he was able to hire several employees. "I wouldn't go back to acting for anything," he insisted:

> I'm outside all day long. I'm my own boss, and I don't have to worry about waiting for a call to work. No agent shoves me around, and there's no stretching the bank account between pictures. I'm a very fortunate man. I've found religion [he was studying Christian Science], a good wife and work I can be proud of.

But as quoted in *Detour* (1945), "That's life. Whichever way you turn, Fate sticks out a foot to trip you." On March 11, 1958, three days before their son's first birthday, Neal's wife, only 29, died of cancer. The contentment he had found further crumbled with financial woes. That October, he returned to acting in "Faster Gun," an episode of *Tales of Wells Fargo*. As ruthless outlaw Johnny Reno, he outdraws Dale Robertson's Jim Hardie and robs banks and stagecoaches. Three months later, Neal was framing *Mike Hammer* for murder on that Darren McGavin TV series. Neal's polished, gritty acting could have served him well as a character actor, but he returned to Palm Springs.

In the early '60s, in Chicago, he was a business consultant for a life insurance company. He also signed with Chicago talent agent Shirley Hamilton to do local radio and TV work. He was still doing landscaping in Palm Springs. His son often stayed with his aunt in Evanston.

On June 7, 1961, after knowing each other only three days, Neal, 47, and Gail Lee Kloke, 25, a receptionist at the Palm Springs Racquet Club, wed in Las Vegas. Tom Neal, Jr., recalled, "I always had the feeling that Gail, well, she didn't hate me, but she just couldn't be bothered with children. She wanted to go out and have a good time. But I was part of the package, I guess."

In this new marriage, Neal's jealousy was aroused more than once and he tired of Gail's desire to party. She, in turn, got fed up with him and his accusations. Neighbors often heard yelling and arguing from the house. Gail filed for divorce on March 11, 1965. On March 31, at 5:30 p.m., Neal came home from visiting his son in Evanston. Realtor Frank Seyferlich was there to give Gail copies of a letter of recommendation she had asked for. In an insistent manner, Gail asked Seyferlich to stay, but he declined because he felt that she and her husband had things to talk about.

On April 1, sometime between 2:45 and 6 p.m. at the Neal residence at 2481 Cardillo Road, a .45 caliber bullet tore through Gail's right ear, passed through her head, came out the left side and became embedded in a pillow on the oversized living room sofa. Not long afterwards, a rambling, disturbed-looking Neal went into The Tirol, an Idyllwild restaurant run by his friends Robert Lawrence Balzer and James Willett. While spending at least six hours there, Neal allegedly confessed to them that he had shot his wife as she napped: "She had become my whole life and I could not live without her." Thinking it a bad April Fool's joke, Balzer and Willett didn't believe him, but he insisted: "I shot her, I shot her. Pow! Pow! Like that."

Beverly Hills lawyer James Cantillon was called, and at 6:30 the next morning, police met him and Neal at an intersection about a block from the Neal home. When police entered the house, they discovered Gail's body half-covered by a blanket on the sofa, her green pants ripped and pulled down. The spent .45 caliber shell was underneath the coffee table, but the gun could not be located; the cops did find an identical bullet in Neal's pocket. The couple's bedroom was in disarray with papers and clothes strewn about. On the bedroom wall was a gag barometer with the question "How is my darling today?" The barometer, which could be set to give various answers, was adjusted to read, "He—Affectionate. She—Cold."

A brown leather wallet and a coat were found; they were later identified as belonging to insurance man Steve Peck, who had taken over the northeast bedroom in the house and paid half the rent. At the time of Gail's murder, Peck was in Phoenix.

During their investigation, the police revealed that while Neal was away in Evanston, several men had visited Gail and that a triangle might be a motive for murder. Gail's mother asserted that her daughter was not promiscuous, that she was faithful to Neal, but frightened by his temper. Gail's co-workers claimed that she told them, "I filed for divorce. My husband told me if I ever divorced him, he'd kill me."

Neal was held without bail on suspicion of murder. Arraigned on April 5, he was transferred to Riverside County Jail where he asked for Christian Science reading materials and a Bible. Detective Sgt. John Herrera stated, "He's as cool as a cucumber. You'd think he was here for a rest cure." On the basis of restaurateurs Balzer and Willett's disclosures, Riverside County District Attorney William Mackey sought a murder indictment against Neal on April 9.

After Cantillon bowed out of the case, Neal said he could not afford another attorney. Public defender James Kellam was assigned. Neal pleaded not guilty on June 3.

Tom Neal, Whose Trial Starts Aug. 23, urges his friends to write him care of the jail in Indio, Calif.—Walter Winchell, July 20, 1965

Auto dealer Glenn Austin set up a fund to raise money to hire a new attorney for Neal. Contributors included Mickey Rooney, Blake Edwards and Franchot Tone. "If true," wrote Dorothy Kilgallen, "Franchot is not only a gentleman but approaches saintliness in his ability to forgive." A new mouthpiece, Leon Rosenberg, was retained. A grateful Neal wrote in a note to Austin, "You my friend, have swept away dark clouds that were threatening to engulf me."

Rosenberg tried to get a change of venue because he didn't think Neal would get a fair trial in Palm Springs. The motion was denied. The murder trial began in Riverside County Superior Court on October 11. Roland Wilson, Riverside County Deputy District Attorney, sought the death penalty in what he described as a cold, calculated execution-style murder. Jury selection took a few days, ending up with ten women and two men.

The prosecution's most important witnesses were Balzer and Willett. Balzer testified that Neal told him he brought the (still-missing) gun with him from Chicago. Weeping on the stand, he maintained that he was not happy about testifying. He remembered that he had told Neal: "The problems of life are as a tiger at the door."

Neal replied, "I am that tiger."

On October 25, it was reported that veteran MGM director Clarence Brown was present in court that morning. At one point, he approached Neal and shook his hand. He left before reporters could talk with him.

Starting on November 2, Neal took the stand; this was the first time he gave his version of what had happened that fateful day: The Neals returned home after dinner. A gun was on the coffee table, Tom said, because Gail was afraid of being alone and had asked him to load it and take the safety catch off for her. When she rebuffed his sexual advances on the couch, he accused her of infidelities, adding, "I bet you didn't even draw the color line." Suddenly, he alleged, she stated, "I'll kill you, you s.o.b.," and the pistol was being pressed against his head. Neal claimed that when he shoved the automatic [sic] away with both hands, it unexpectedly discharged, killing Gail instantly. Probably giving his lifetime-best performance, Neal tearfully related,

> I couldn't believe what I saw. I realized from looking at Gail that she had been hit along the side of the head. You're dumbfounded in a situation like this. I prayed. I took her hand. I called her name, "Gail, oh, God, Gail."

According to Neal, he then held her hand and said over her, "Talitha Cumi," which is interpreted as "Fair maiden arise, for thou art whole." Next, Neal testified (with a straight face, one hopes), "She seemed to raise up a little bit." When he tried to continue quoting Bible passages, the prosecution objected.

Neal claimed he didn't know what became of the gun and suggested that perhaps a third person made off with it. He also questioned the disorder in the bedroom, as he had kept that space tidy; he seemed to be implying that someone else *had* to have been there. As for the two restaurateurs, he insisted that they had misunderstood him: He had not confessed to the shooting, he had said that Gail had been shot "and I feel that I am to blame because if I hadn't come back, she'd still be alive."

Two firearms experts testified that the pistol couldn't have discharged the way Neal described. And the blood spatter on the inside of the lampshade near the couch proved she was lying down when she was shot, not sitting up as Neal claimed.

The jury took only two days to deliberate. On November 18, a verdict of involuntary manslaughter was reached. "It's been a long, tough road," a teary Neal said in the courtroom. Rosenberg added, "His deep religious faith carried him through." On the 24th, he was freed on a $2750 bond. According to Kent Adamson, "Tom contacted Ann Savage to reunite onscreen for a movie project he was working on while out on bail."

On December 10, Neal was sentenced to state prison for one to 15 years. Neal, who had believed that he would get probation and a suspended sentence, was visibly upset. He said that he had been railroaded, without going into specifics. "He has no history of any prior arrest, he has never had a brush with the law in his 51 years," Rosenberg said, conveniently forgetting the Tone-Payton fight. "He has a history of being a useful citizen of society. The tragic circumstances of April 1, 1965, came as a culmination of a period of marital instability." Prosecutor Wilson responded by saying that he still felt that Neal was guilty of first-degree murder: "The fact that the jury brought back only an involuntary manslaughter verdict is as big a break as Mr. Neal deserves."

"There would be no sense in putting me back [in jail]," said Neal, who had already spent about seven months behind bars and didn't realize—or care—how he had lucked out. "My atonement is complete. I've seen the light." He added, "There will always be those who will believe that I willfully murdered Gail. But in my heart and in God's knowledge I know differently."

Neal's nephew Walter Burr told John O'Dowd:

Calling prison a "bad scene," Neal was released in 1971. The years behind bars wreaked havoc on his good looks.

> There was never any doubt in our family that Tom killed Gail—and not in self-defense, either. He was my uncle and I cared about him, but I have to be honest here. Tom was a loose cannon for many, many years and I think his intense jealousy of Gail just built up until it finally put him over the edge.

Neal was sent to the California State Prison in Chino. Superior Court Judge Merrill Brown and District Attorney William Mackey recommended to the State Adult Authority that Neal should serve the full term: "Regardless of the jury's verdict, this was a cold, deliberate killing of the defendant's wife who had filed divorce proceedings."

> Friend of Tom Neal tells me he is assigned at Chino to the prison receiving and releasing department known as Mahogany Row. He still hopes to go through with the appeal on his conviction in the death of his wife.—Harrison Carroll, February 11, 1966

On July 29, Neal's appeal was dismissed. D.A. William Mackey said that Neal "filed notice of appeal but never hired an attorney and filed no briefs although he was warned by the 4th District Court several times of this necessity."

After leading a difficult life away from acting (drunkenness, prostitution, passing bad checks), 39-year-old Barbara Payton passed away on May 8, 1967. She had attended court and had written Neal while he was in prison, their strong connection still there even though they hadn't seen each other in years. Several reporters noted that the two waved briefly to each other in court, which, if true, is a bit heartbreaking.

The other part of the legendary triangle, Franchot Tone, died on September 18, 1968, of lung cancer.

Neal was denied parole in 1969. His lawyer said he spent his time in stir doing a lot of writing and landscaping. Tom Jr. lived at first with his Aunt Mary, and then with Mary's daughter Nancy and her family.

In November 1971, Neal was moved to a state-run halfway house as part of Chino's work-furlough program. A month later, he was paroled. Looking older than his 57 years, with white Bobby Troup–style hair, an unrecognizable Neal remarked that prison was a "bad scene."

He landed a job as associate producer of a local Saturday morning TV series called *Apartment Hunters*, and had a job with a construction and real estate firm. While on a pre-parole furlough, he had seen his old agent and wanted to get back into acting. "I've lived a lot. I've got more character now than in the old days. And I've mellowed. When I see a fight nowadays, I walk away from it." The agent suggested filming Neal's life story and Neal was "willing to go along with that." Ann Savage also contacted him, wanting to work with him on a TV movie project.

Neal and his 15-year-old son moved into a second-floor apartment at 12020 Hoffman Street in Studio City. "During that [time], I got to know my dad better than the whole seven years I had spent with him in the years before prison," Neal Jr. told *Filmfax* magazine's David Houston. "We were buddies. We went to the beach, to movies, to restaurants, to visit friends"—friends that Neal had made in prison.

On August 7, 1972, the teenage Tom went into his father's room at 7:30 a.m. to wake him, and found him unresponsive. Junior went next door to get Neal's friend, old-time bit actor and sometime-stuntman Jimmy Noel. Noel called paramedics, and they pronounced the elder Neal dead. The night before, Neal had complained of heartburn and went to sleep at 11. Death was attributed to a heart attack.

His lookalike son, using the name Tom Neal, Jr., had a starring role in a remake of *Detour*, made in Kansas City, Missouri, and released in 1992. (Ann Savage was asked to play a supporting part, but turned it down, and Susanna Foster was cast instead.) "[Junior] had striking good looks and the persona of the classic 1940s movie star with a striking resemblance to his father," said the new *Detour*'s producer-director-writer Wade Williams. In 1988, when Junior began filming the movie, he was the same age—31—his dad was when he did the original. In a weird twist of fate, both father and son died at the same age, 58, Junior passing away of cancer on August 24, 2015.

Tom Neal followed a difficult path and had more than his share of ups and downs until he finally found peace. "Dad and I could both be cynical, negative about things," Neal Jr. summed up. "He faced life as a film noir movie. And I agree. It can be a real bitch with more bad than good in it."

1938: *Out West with the Hardys, The Great Heart* (short, uncredited).

1939: *Burn 'Em Up O'Connor, Four Girls in White, Honolulu* (uncredited), *Money to Loan* (short, uncredited), *Within the Law, Prophet Without Honor* (short, uncredited), *6,000 Enemies, Help Wanted* (short), *Another Thin Man, Stronger Than Desire* (uncredited), *They All Come Out, Joe and Ethel Turp Call on the President*.

1940: *Jack Pot* (short), *The Courageous Dr. Christian, Sky Murder, Rodeo Dough* (short), *Flight Command* (uncredited).

1941: *Wings of Steel* (short), *Under Age, Jungle Girl, Top Sergeant Mulligan, The Miracle Kid.*
1942: *Ten Gentlemen from West Point* (uncredited), *One Thrilling Night, The Pride of the Yankees* (uncredited), *Flying Tigers, Bowery at Midnight, China Girl* (uncredited).
1943: *Air Force* (uncredited), *No Time for Love* (uncredited), *The Rear Gunner* (short), *She Has What It Takes, Good Luck, Mr. Yates, Behind the Rising Sun, There's Something About a Soldier, Klondike Kate.*
1944: *The Racket Man, Two-Man Submarine, The Unwritten Code, Thoroughbreds.*
1945: *Crime, Inc., First Yank into Tokyo, Detour, Club Havana.*
1946: *Blonde Alibi, The Brute Man, My Dog Shep.*
1947: *The Hat-Box Mystery, The Case of the Baby Sitter.*
1948: *Beyond Glory.*
1949: *Bruce Gentry, Daredevil of the Skies; Amazon Quest, Apache Chief, Red Desert.*
1950: *Radar Secret Service, The Daltons' Women, Joe Palooka in Humphrey Takes a Chance, I Shot Billy the Kid, Train to Tombstone, The Du Pont Story, Call of the Klondike, King of the Bullwhip.*
1951: *Fingerprints Don't Lie, Navy Bound, Stop That Cab, Danger Zone, G.I. Jane, Varieties on Parade, Let's Go Navy!, All That I Have, The Valparaiso Story.*
1953: *The Great Jesse James Raid.*

ALLAN NIXON

"It is fame I am talking about. *Fame* is the bitch goddess! Pursue her and she'll take you down to hell and damnation. Like every bitch, she'll emasculate you one way or another, kill you...."

This passage, from Allan Nixon's 1977 novel *Nikki*, could well have been Nixon's "take" on life. Few had it rougher in Hollywood, but he brought on his own troubles with alcohol and women ... rather like the weak-willed male protagonists in his later novels. Success as an actor was not to be, no matter how much he desired it. Marriage to star Marie Wilson didn't help. She meant well, wanted to protect him and make him happy, but as a result of their relationship, he took no responsibility for his own life and actions.

Of Scottish-English descent, Allan Hobbs Nixon was born in Boston on August 17, 1915, to Arthur Allan Nixon, a decorated fireman, and Mary Elizabeth Hobbs. Seven years later, his sister Ruth (1922–88) was born.

When he was younger, acting was of no concern to him; he was first and foremost an athlete. While playing for the Jamaica Plain High School football team, he was chosen as All-City pivotman. "He was a great high school center," wrote the *Richmond News Leader*'s John Oliver in 1935,

and great things were predicted for him in college. In 1932, Nixon enrolled at Kent's High Academy and the coach there tried him at tackle and end, but with little success. He entered the University of Richmond last year [1934] and was tried at tackle and end on the freshman team, but again he failed to come through.

Before becoming an actor, brawny Allan Nixon was a football player and wrestler.

That changed in 1935 when the Richmond Spiders' coach Glenn Thistlethwaite put Nixon into a game to replace an injured center. "He delivered in such successful fashion, he played out the game and now he is the regular Spider center," Oliver wrote. Assistant coach Russ Crane told the *Richmond Collegian*, "Allan Nixon is developing into a good defensive center, but he has a long way to go before he can be called an excellent offensive center." Nixon, "particularly brilliant as a defensive player" (*Richmond News Leader*), eventually proved to be a versatile and important member of the Spiders. At the university, Nixon also participated in boxing tournaments, studied journalism (he wanted to be a newspaper sportswriter) and worked on the school literary magazine, the *Richmond College Messenger*.

In 1936, Nixon competed with Ed Schaaf for the first-string center position on the Spiders. "Nixon is bigger, more rugged than Schaaf, though not as fast," opined Chas. Hamilton of the *Richmond News Leader*. "With classical features, the Boston boy picked up considerable spending money working as an artists' model last year. However, he can forget his movie profile and go into action when the occasion arises."

In the summer of '36, financial difficulties prompted Nixon to leave the university. In New York, he became a commercial model, appearing in ads and magazine stories; he played end and center for the Lawrence Collegians in the New England Football League, and was picked as center for the league's all-star team; he worked as a bouncer at a café; he was signed by the Washington Redskins (but didn't make the team after the exhibition season); he worked as a newspaper and hotel publicity man in Boston; and wrestled in New England under the ring names "Kid Galahad" and "Tiger." He also managed to work in a June 19, 1937, elopement to Elkton, Maryland; Annette was (or had been) a model.

At the beginning of 1938, the *Richmond Times-Dispatch*'s Jimmy Jones printed a letter from Nixon telling of his recent experiences as a Warner Bros. contract player:

Dear Jimmy—Since straying from the flock at Richmond, I have gone to Hollywood, where I had a six months' contract with one of the major studios. For six months, I sat around, accumulating corns (you can guess where) while waiting for a part. I collected 100 iron men each week—but no part.... I swam daily at Malibu Beach, spent my hard-earned money foolishly at the Trocadero, and wound up back in New York with $300 saved out of a possible $2000.... I was tested for 13 leading roles while in the studio school, and as they say out there, I certainly managed to "stink up plenty of footage." I guess the fumes of some of my acting efforts are still smoldering out there. I photograph like a million and act like two cents. I was signed up in New York after I had posed for commercial ads. A scout saw my mug in an Ironized Yeast ad and tested me (with about 10 others) for the role in *Kid Galahad*.... Wayne Morris got the part, as you noticed. But I got a fat contract that would have run for seven years if they had taken up the option. I told them I couldn't act and they sneered. I got out to the studio and when I reached the gate and told the special cop who I was, he just said, "Oh, yeah?" It took me two days to get inside, then two more weeks to get in the school.... Glenn Thistlethwaite wrote me and told me he had seen my leering face in a few ads and stories and tells me I'd take the ride of my life if I showed up in Richmond before the stigma of my adventures had died down.

As for *Kid Galahad*, Nixon also claimed at the time that he was the artist's model for the drawings of the boxer featured in Francis Wallace's six-part *Kid Galahad* serial in *The Saturday Evening Post* (April 11, 1936, to May 16, 1936).

Back in Boston in August 1938, Nixon joined the Marshfield Players, acting in the plays *Pursuit of Happiness* and *Murray Hill* (the latter with Jacqueline Susann). But he longed to get back into football, telling John Oliver, "I am in shape at 190 pounds and rarin' to go." He subsequently played in the Dixie League with the Richmond Arrows and the Norfolk Shamrocks.

The brawny Nixon, now up to 210 pounds on his 6'6" frame, also went back to wrestling. "He's a fine-looking boy and with his popularity here he should be a great drawing card," promoter Bill Lewis told Oliver. Oliver added,

> Nixon has the physique of an Adonis and his regular features are topped by a head of wavy, brown hair.

His ambition is fired with the desire to help his family and he sends money to his home in Boston whenever he can.

"With football, acting, working and, I hope, wrestling, I ought to be able to do all right," he said.

For his first wrestling match for promoter Lewis (October '38), Nixon beat George Wilson. According to the *Richmond Times-Dispatch*:

> Allan Hobbs Nixon, who gained football fame at the University of Richmond, made his debut here with a vengeance as he rammed head first into George Wilson, knocking him completely out and doing some damage to himself. The bout lasted only four minutes and it was Nixon's bull-like rush which brought victory. Incidentally, the loss proved very costly to Wilson for he lost a complete set of bridgework which had just been put in his mouth.

(In Nixon's novel *The Last of Vicky* [1966], Mitch "Cowboy" Hurley slams into a bad guy's "gut head-first with a bull-like rush." Later, another character, in another fight, loses his bridgework: "The empty space where the bridge had been combined with the sagging upper lip gave him the look of some prehistoric bird.")

Alternating between football and wrestling couldn't have been a physically easy task. In December '38, Nixon had to withdraw from a wrestling tournament due to an injury sustained in a football game.

June 1939: "Allan Nixon, the wrestler, has become a John Powers pretty," wrote Dorothy Kilgallen. The modeling brought him to the attention of MGM, and after a silent test, he was signed. Nixon was up for the role of Otto von Rohn in *The Mortal Storm* (1940); he was deemed too tall, and the part went to Robert Stack. Nixon was cast in a small, uncredited part as a college student turned Nazi (with a thick Boston accent) who attacks Martin Breitner (James Stewart). "I remember the director Frank Borzage on *Mortal Storm* gave me a complicated line and I was so nervous I couldn't do it," Nixon told Tom and Jim Goldrup. "He asked me where I came from and how did I get here. I told him I had a silent test. He said, 'Well, if silent pictures ever come back, you're in business.' He was a nice guy; he was just making fun." James Stewart helped Nixon through his jitters: "I got nervous and he said, 'Come over here and sit with me.' He took a script out and said, 'Just read it to me.' I read it and he said, 'Now you got it.' Then I missed it again, but I did it finally."

The Metro pact didn't last. Later recalling this period for the *Los Angeles Mirror*'s Dick Williams, Nixon admitted it wasn't the studio's fault: "I was only 22 [actually 25] and looked 16. I couldn't act. I looked like a model. I wasn't ready."

According to the *Richmond Times-Dispatch*'s Chauncey Durden, Nixon was to be groomed as a cowboy at Republic, "provided he learns to ride a horse." Which leads to a story Nixon told when he was a guest columnist for the *Richmond Times-Dispatch*. It's probably not true, but it's amusing and shows his budding storytelling skill:

Was just thinking of the time Robert Sterling, then unknown; Craig Stevens, even more so, and myself were rigged out in cowboy suits by Republic Studios to do an audition for George Sherman's Red Ryder series.... Instead of a test, we were shoved into a studio bus and driven to the Republic Ranch out in North Hollywood.... To our collective dismay, we saw a couple of Western pintos frisking very energetically on the greensward to our right. "You guys can ride for us first," we were told. I noticed Stevens blench visibly.... You see, none of us had ridden.... There was a general hanging back among us when the director told us to each ride a horse around a sort of runway and holler "Whoop-dee-doo" and wave our ten-gallon hats with personality.... No mention was made of how to mount or hang on, which was the main issue to us three, I am sure.... Sterling's pinto rose high on his hind legs in a Heigh-o Silver pose, did an about-face, and galloped into the barn.... Stevens' little gem leaped a wagon with Craig hugging its head (with personality) and disappeared into a thicket far beyond.... Hired hands recovered the lost actor an hour later, and led him and horse back on foot.... I will skip Nixon....

On March 28, 1940, Nixon was divorced by his wife Annette. According to Mrs. Nixon, it was hardly a marriage: She alleged that, a week after their "I do"s, "he blackened both her eyes, and continually accused her of flirting with other men." His temper (and strength) was so ferocious, she said, he tore a closet door off its hinges and threw it on the floor. Two months after they wed, he left her.

Nixon was free, but not for long: On October 8, 1940, in Los Angeles, he married Opal Hendley, a private nurse. This union, too, was short-lived. In April '41, he appeared in the two-character play *Jealousy* at Los Angeles' Musart Theatre with Dianne Joyce. Chauncey Durden kept Richmond readers up to date on their adopted son:

> He lives at the Knickerbocker Hotel, makes a good living between modeling, athletic coaching and working in a couple of [radio] serials. I talked to his personal manager who is certain Allan is leading-man material, and THAT is something that every studio is looking for. He has been going to dramatic school in what little spare time he has and, after talking with him and seeing that he certainly has the looks and build for leading roles, I do believe Richmond has hatched another potential star.

Wishful thinking. Talk of future big roles was just that—talk, from Richmond writers who wanted Nixon to succeed. Being tall and handsome does not make you a shoo-in for stardom, as Nixon found out. When it came to his movie parts, "blink and you miss him" was the norm. Edith Lindeman, a faithful *Richmond Times-Dispatch* columnist and booster, looked on the bright side about Nixon's part in *Rookies on Parade*: "If you look sharply enough, you'll recognize Allan Nixon saying two lines and serving as handsome background for many of the crowd scenes." But, Nixon told Dick Williams, he "didn't want to get tied up as a bit player; like Marie said—you might as well be out of it as be a bit player."

Marie was Marie Wilson, a blonde, buxom actress who had a featured part in *Rookies on Parade*. She had made her screen debut in the early 1930s and became known via her roles at Warners and her image as the dumb blonde with the innocent delivery. Marie was in a long-term relationship with the more-than-20 years older Nick Grinde, who had helped her with her career and directed her in a couple of features and a short. Nixon was attractive and needed mothering, and Marie responded to that immediately.

On April 27, 1942, Allan and Marie got hitched in Las Vegas, but agreed to keep it a secret until she could break the news to Grinde. It didn't take her long to regret her decision. That June, Louella Parsons painted a pretty sad and confusing portrait of where Marie was at mentally during this time:

Marie Wilson and Allan Nixon were married from 1942 to 1950. It was a tempestuous union, and Wilson put up with *a lot*. "Better the devil you know than the devil you don't," Marie told Sheilah Graham. The couple, flanked by two unknown men, are seen here at a 1949 cocktail party at Hollywood's Ciroette Room.

Last April pretty Marie Wilson and Allan Nixon … were married in Las Vegas. No word was said about this very secret marriage, which did not come out because Marie was wed under her stepfather's name of White. The surprising part is Marie has been in love with Nick Grinde, motion picture director, for several years and everyone supposed they were engaged. Well, Marie is still in love with Nick and her marriage to Nixon was apparently on the impulse of the moment. When I talked to her, she burst into tears and said she loved Nickie and the secret marriage was all a mistake. One moment she would admit she had married Nixon, with whom she has been seen on various occasions, and the next she would become hysterical and say her life would be ruined if it were made public. Finally, she said she probably would seek an annulment.

Not long after this column ran, Marie was again out and about with Grinde, who had "forgiven" her (according to Louella), and she was burbling about severing ties with Nixon. By November, that idea was forgotten: "Marie Wilson's husband, Allan Nixon, is a buck private in the Army," Louella wrote, trying to keep up, "and if this marriage has not turned into a very happy one, they certainly were fooling diners at Mike Lyman's."

Wilson's career received a huge boost when Ken Murray signed her for his Los Angeles stage show *Blackouts of 1942*, a vaudeville-type success that ran for years; Marie continued to appear in it while also doing movie and radio jobs. Meanwhile, Nixon, who was studying still camera photography at RKO, was in the Signal Corps reserve and expected to be called for active duty within a few months. But Wilson, who obviously knew the right people, saw to it that he didn't have to serve overseas.

He appeared in several training and propaganda films for the First Motion Picture Unit operating out of Hal Roach Studios. "My shining hour of the war came when Navy Commander John Ford arrived at Roach to direct a training film as a favor to the Armed Forces," Nixon told the Goldrups.

> He called me for an interview, cast me. Ford! I was elated. I had never been able to meet him as an actor in civilian life. My heart raced all night. I was unable to sleep, hardly able to wait to report to makeup as ordered at six a.m. I recall it now as though it were yesterday. Sitting in the makeup chair in the chill dawn. The shock of hearing the sergeant in makeup telling me to drop my pants, wondering, "What now?" Then, aghast, watching him apply warts and hideous lumps to my penis. My role in the film was explained in the script which was, as you may have guessed, a VD film: As a flight surgeon indicates the blackboard with a pointer, his voice comes over: "This is the condition in which this man returned to camp"—insert my penis—"after a night in town." …The makeup job they did should have deterred all but the bravest of men from straying into strange and forbidden territory.…The picture [*Sex Hygiene*] might as aptly have been titled Allan Nixon in *A Private's Privates*. I was, I guess, chosen as the typical American prick.

Corporal Nixon was also on permanent guard duty:

> Today, when memories are blurred and I am asked where I served during the Second World War, I truthfully say: "I spent a lot of time at a little Coral Island and it pains me to talk about it." It is true, because there was a bar in Culver City near Roach called the Coral Island, and it pains me to talk about it because I was arrested by the M.P.s there on a drunk and disorderly charge at a time I was supposed to be on guard duty at the post.

The Nixons' marriage was rocky due to Allan's drinking and volatile nature. On August 31, 1945, a day after columnists were writing of the couple's "vacation" together at the Beverly Hills Hotel, it was announced that Marie had filed for divorce. She claimed that her career and his Army life created differences of opinion that led to their separation. She added, "It was just another case of a stage career interfering with a perfect home life." Wilson was still in *Blackouts* (now called *Blackouts of 1945*) and had established a record of more than 2000 consecutive performances. On September 10, Nixon told Dorothy Manners that Wilson had withdrawn the divorce: "It was all just a silly quarrel that took place while I was in camp, and before I could talk to Marie, she filed suit. I knew the minute we had a chance to get together and talk things over, she would change her mind. We are as much in love as we were the day we married." Wilson, without any sentiment, told Sheilah Graham, "Better the devil you know than the devil you don't." She gave a softer response to the *New York Daily News*' Rosaleen Doherty: "We changed our minds. You know"—looking longingly at Nixon—"he's kind of cute. I mean, he's really handsome. I couldn't stay mad at him very long."

After his discharge, Nixon was added to the road tour of Mae West's *Come on Up* (1946), co-written by Miles Mander. When it played in Boston, Cyrus Durgin wrote, "Any supporting role in a West show is not an actor's dream, since all hands must play straight man to Mae's comedy. Nevertheless, Michael Ames is a handsome leading man, and Allan Nixon and Harry (The Hipster) Gibson as the sailors and Joe McTurk as the taxi driver shine by their own capers." Reviewer Herbert L. Monk singled Nixon out as one who "pleased the spectators."

When the show reached the end of the road (Los Angeles) in February '47, writer Bob Thomas made the prediction that Nixon would be "snapped up by a studio." Not exactly, but independent producer Maurice Conn did give him a one-scene, 13th-billed part as pilot Lt. Ashley in *Dragnet* (1947), a murder mystery concerning jewel thieves. Thanks to his wife, Allan got a negligible role as a cop in Eagle-Lion's comedy *Linda, Be Good* (1947) starring Elyse Knox, and with Marie as burlesque performer Margie LaVitte.

On April 11, 1947, Wilson hit paydirt when she began starring on radio's *My Friend Irma*, the role with which she would forever be identified. Wilson was the chief (i.e., *only*) breadwinner in the family. Nixon did not find himself in demand, but occasionally work did trickle in—though not as fast as the alcohol he consumed. In between limited runs on the Los Angeles stage in *Free for All* (1947) and *The Stone Jungle* (1948), Nixon was employed as a leg man for a Hollywood writer. He also was tested by producer Sol Lesser to replace Johnny Weissmuller in the role of Tarzan; he was passed over in favor of Lex Barker.

On June 29, 1948, Nixon was at the Laguna Beach Playhouse with Nancy Kelly, Robert Armstrong and Jane Darwell in Aben Kandel's *You Twinkle Only Once*. Based on a 1943 short story first published in *Story: The Magazine of the Short Story* (and a 1946 out-of-town stage flop), it was about an aging, conniving actress who covets the lead in an upcoming movie already cast. She marries the leading man to get the role, but soon realizes he is stealing the picture from her. After she deliberately undercuts his part with actor tricks, he is fired due to his heavy drinking and they separate. It was a plot that Nixon would later borrow (and embellish) for a section of his novel *Nikki*. Kandel's show did not get to Broadway, but leading man Nixon got nice notices.

Also noticing him: director John Brahm, who was working on the Maria Montez–Jean-Pierre Aumont movie *Siren of Atlantis*. It had originally been filmed at the beginning of 1947 under the direction of Arthur Ripley. Trouble with the Breen Office and a disastrous test screening added to the budget and to producer Seymour Nebenzal's headaches. In June '48, Brahm was hired to oversee two weeks of reshoots and additions at Sam Goldwyn Studios.

French Legionnaires André Saint-Avit (Aumont) and Jean Morhange (Dennis O'Keefe) are abducted and brought to the lost city of Atlantis in the heart of the Hoggar Mountains. There they meet the lusty and fickle Queen Antinea (Montez), who has had a long line of romantic partners. One of them is Lindstrom (Nixon), a tormented Swede driven to drink by his obsession with the queen.

Nothing Nebenzal did could save *Siren of Atlantis*: At a cost of $1,800,000, it only grossed $335,000 when released in 1949. Since neither Ripley nor Brahm wanted credit for the final film, *Atlantis*' editor, Gregg G. Tallas, took the rap. (In Nixon's 1969 novel *The Bitch Goddess*, his actress protagonist DeDe O'Dell signs a contract to do a movie called *Eve of Atlantis*: "Playing a mythical queen of the lost Atlantis, she would go through a succession of lovers in myriad costumes, all diaphanous, many almost nonexistent.")

"Everybody is raving about the drunk scene Allan Nixon plays," wrote Harrison Carroll. Years later, Nixon ridiculously remembered to the Goldrups that he was "reasonably close to getting nominated for Best Supporting Actor" for his *Siren of Atlantis* performance, but that he "had no chance" because the film flopped. "I played a hopeless drunk who kills himself over a woman, and I was also told that characters that die tragically always get noticed. Like Red Buttons in *Sayonara*." Yes, that's right, *exactly* like Red Buttons in *Sayonara*. His mumbling Lindstrom has very little screen time and his suicide, shown in a long shot, is so obscured by darkness that it is difficult to see what he's doing.

On December 14, 1948, Nixon was caught jaywalking in front of the El Capitan Theatre (where Wilson was appearing in *Blackouts*) by two policemen and detained on a drunk charge. During his struggle with the boys in blue, Nixon growled, "I used to be an MP. You can't arrest me!" and broke off a pair of handcuffs. Wilson pleaded with the officers, to no avail. As Nixon was being put in his cell at Hollywood Jail, one of the officers stated, "You ought to be proud. This is the same cell Errol Flynn once occupied." According to Hedda Hopper, Nixon replied, "Get me out of here. Flynn's a phony—I'm really tough." Wilson posted the $20 bail. As the couple left the station, Nixon muttered, "Talk about the Gestapo." "He was just jaywalking when the police came up," Wilson later told the *Los Angeles Times*. "He didn't like the way they treated him. He wasn't drunk."

Two weeks after the jaywalking incident, Wilson—trying to smooth things over—told Harrison Carroll, "Isn't he strong? His birthday is coming up … I think I'll get him a pair of cufflinks inscribed, 'Handle with care, darling'!"

Seymour Nebenzal signed Nixon to a contract and "plans to do something special with him as the result of his good work in *Siren in Atlantis*," wrote Louella Parsons. He was being considered for the lead in a proposed remake of 1926's *The Son of the Sheik*.

On January 28, 1949, the Nixons separated. Wilson filed for divorce days later, blaming temperament and "two careers in one home" as the issues. "She asked for no alimony—nothing," the *Los Angeles Daily News* wrote. "She said there is no community property. Everything she has is hers." They neglected to say that everything *he* had was *also* hers. A week later, the sweet-tempered Wilson gave in when Nixon left their Yorkshire terrier Hobbs at her apartment with a note attached to his collar, which could have been referring to him:

> Dear Mother: My father can't keep me in the manner to which I am accustomed. When he explained this to me, he cried. I would have cried too but dogs don't cry. I haven't eaten or drunk all day. I don't even enjoy a passing lamp-post. I'm very lonesome so I guess I'm all yours. (Signed) Hobbs.

Wilson told Hedda Hopper: "I love him. I'm lonesome; I'm not one to tear around. It scares me to go out with new men. I'm no good to anyone unless I'm happy, so when I saw Allan at Ken Murray's party after a week's separation, I just threw myself in his arms and started to cry."

Nixon's contract with Nebenzal yielded nothing and, "pending acting jobs" (Harrison Carroll), the discouraged Nixon became a publicity man.

In mid–July 1949, Nixon and Ann Dvorak did an Eastern straw hat tour of *Anna Lucasta*. At the beginning of August, Florabel Muir reported that Nixon was in New York, "suffering a nervous breakdown after a successful stage engagement." She quoted Wilson as saying, "Poor boy. He doesn't know how to take care of himself when I'm not around. He doesn't eat right."

But chances are, nothing got in the way of his drinking—except maybe two longshoremen. On August 5, Nixon was in a bar in Lower Manhattan when John P. Brady and James M. Carney approached him and asked, "You're an actor, ain't you?" When he replied in the affirmative, the men attacked him with a broken beer bottle and a table leg—or so the story goes. Nixon defended himself, in Wild West style, with chairs and tables, but ended up with bruised knuckles, cuts on his face and a nasty gash on his chest that took 17 stitches to close. The men were arrested and charged with assault, and later with robbery when it was learned that they held up the bar earlier in the evening. Wilson, taking care of Nixon after he was discharged from St. Vincent's Hospital, told reporters that he was "doing fine—it isn't contagious." Dorothy Manners told her readers:

> You have to take off your hat to Marie Wilson, the gal who soared to fame playing "dumb," like a fox, she's dumb. After that knifing scrape her husband, Allan Nixon, got into in New York (two men attacked him in a bar), Marie was distraught.

But she went out of her way to be charming to the press and to counteract any bad effects of the publicity. The press fell for her and went all the way along with her in her attempt to clear up the muddle.

> The press agents in the Paramount New York office—and believe me, those boys know—call her the most cooperative star they have ever worked with.

Nixon's earliest known TV appearance was on *The Silver Theatre*'s October 10, 1949, presentation of "'Til Death Do Us Part," starring Faye Emerson and John Loder.

Aben Kandel tried again with *You Twinkle Only Once*, revising it and renaming it after the title character, Kitty Doone, when it opened at the Circle Theatre on December 6, 1949. It was directed by Jerry Epstein; Charlie Chaplin contributed to the staging. Ellanora Reeves (*née* Ellanora Needles, soon-to-be-ex-wife of George Reeves) starred, and Nixon was cast again as Gene Morton, the actor who's too good for his own good. Others in the cast included William Schallert, Sydney Chaplin, Cecil Elliott and Robert Knapp. Philip K. Scheuer of the *Los Angeles Times* opined,

> [The] writing was superior to the usual Coast effort, the staging—considering the Circle's cramped quarters—surprisingly smooth and the acting uniformly crisp and efficient. In at least a couple of instances it was better than that. The taste of Hollywood is bitter in Kandel's mouth....[It] is best described as a comedy-drama and its mood as one of no-punches-pulled realized.

As for Nixon, Scheuer thought he had "just the right ingenuousness for the boy, a difficult and not completely realizable part at best."

Kitty Doone continued to be performed on stage and on television, but it never reached Broadway. "The press agent in the play says what I'd want to say," Kandel told the *Los Angeles Daily News*' Ezra Goodman, "when he remarks of his own corruption: 'But this job keeps me in choice cuts and old alcohol, supports two feeble bookies and a couple of fragrant concubines.' I don't know if anyone in Hollywood will be mad about my play and I honestly don't care." It was an experience that influenced Nixon. His new attitude toward Hollywood jibed with Kandel's and would influence his later writing.

Wilson appeared at almost every rehearsal with food and refreshments for the cast. "You couldn't find a sweeter gal," remarked columnist Lloyd L. Sloan.

Hal B. Wallis, who had produced a number of Wilson's movies, was impressed when he saw Nixon in *Kitty Doone*. "Hal thinks Allan has something as a screen bet and made tests of him for two days before giving him a contract," wrote Louella Parsons. Could it be that Wilson had a hand in the sign-up? Oh, and "incidentally," added Louella, Nixon's first for Wallis "will be *My Friend Irma Goes West* [1950], in which he will get a chance to emote opposite his wife, Marie."

> The New York D.A.'s office has subpoenaed Allan Nixon to go back and testify against the two men who beat him up in a café.—Harrison Carroll, February 7, 1950

> On the first day that Allan Nixon testified against those two men..., somebody stole his overcoat right out of the courtroom—Harrison Carroll, March 2, 1950

Nixon was to play a transport pilot in *My Friend Irma Goes West*, but he probably realized that the part wouldn't have been as big as Tamba the chimp's. He relinquished it in favor of an assignment in *Pickup* (1951), character actor Hugo Haas' first American feature as producer-director-star. In it, Allan played Steve, the young guy who falls for Jan Horak's (Haas) wife Betty (Beverly Michaels).

> Hugo Haas is directing and playing a lead in *Pickup*, and because Hugo favors himself so much, Allan Nixon, another lead, says Haas should call the picture *Close-Up*.—Sidney Skolsky, March 27, 1950

Hal B. Wallis sought to cast Nixon in a small role in *Dark City* (1950), but again Nixon balked. Dropped by Wallis, Nixon accepted an offer from producer Albert J. Cohen to play the lead in *Prehistoric Women* (1950) in "hazy Cinecolor" (*Oakland Tribune*). Yes, he gave up working at Paramount with Hal Wallis to portray a caveman. Cohen had seen Nixon's Tarzan test and felt he had just the right amount of animal appeal. Erskine Johnson wrote:

> Anatomy is paying off all the way around in the Marie Wilson-Allan Nixon family now

In *Pickup* (1951), Nixon and Beverly Michaels are an adulterous pair.

that Allan is making pikers of Vic Mature and Alan Ladd by unveiling his chest in *Prehistoric Women*.

Marie swells with pride—no mean trick, that—when she listens to hubby talk about his career.

"For years, people used to say, 'Aw, he's just Marie Wilson's husband,'" Allan told me. "'Nice guy, but just a husband.'"

"That's right, dear," Marie chimed in.

Allan is hoping that the caveman epic will do for him what *One Million B.C.* [1940] did for Vic Mature.

"At least," he said, "it will show that my wife is not the only one in the family with a chest."

"Yes, dear," said Marie.

"It was no great thing," Nixon remarked to the Goldrups about *Prehistoric Women*, "but it was good for me. They had flying dragons and that sort of stuff. The dialogue was all spoken like caveman talk. There were no real words, but the audiences were supposed to pick up on the meaning of the words as you grunted them." Actually, the action is described by narrator David Vaile (at the time a television newscaster).

When a small female tribe, headed by Tigri (Laurette Luez), comes across a group of men in the jungle, they kidnap and enslave them—and plan to marry them, to ensure their tribe's future survival. The robust Nixon, playing Engor, discovers fire and battles a panther, a flying dragon and the giant Guadi (7'8" Johann Petursson), while Tigri and Arva (Mara Lynn) fight over him. It was the kind of cut-rate picture that critics love to pan—especially when its producer remarks that the movie is "about 50 percent historically authentic."

Nixon turned down a role at Paramount to portray a caveman in *Prehistoric Women* (1950) with Laurette Luez.

The girls wear false hair cascading down their backs and animal skins with plunging necklines that were approved by the Johnston office. They also are equipped with clubs, an expression of burning desire crossed with a leer, and make-up like they were man-hunting from ringside tables at the Mocambo. One of the men they're after is Marie Wilson's husband, Allan Nixon. He wears a leopard skin and pats his shaggy curls between scenes.—Aline Mosby

Although not billed as a comedy, *Prehistoric Women* is really a very funny film and gets many more chuckles than most more sophisticated and deliberate [recent] comic efforts….—Theresa Loeb

Whether [*Prehistoric Women*] is intended as a colossal joke we wouldn't know. But viewed straight or sidewise it is hilarious as a

> half-dozen fur-wearing primitive maids—who look far more like ladies of a burlesque ensemble—prance and prowl the woodsy locales in search of mates, giving off screeches and little shrieks and scaring the wits out of every available male in the neighborhood.—Mildred Martin

> It all ends with four of the girls getting husbands. Before which, however, two gals with a yen for the same muscular guy stage a forerunner of rassling women. But not one of the prettily painted lips is disturbed.—A.S. Kany

Since *Prehistoric Women* did well at the box office, Cohen was going to make something called *Riviera Girl* with Nixon, but those plans evaporated. On June 7, 1950, Allan joined wife Marie, William Schallert, Sydney Chaplin, John O'Malley and Naomi Stevens in a five-week engagement in the Circle Theatre's *The School for Scandal*, a comedy of manners by Richard Brinsley Sheridan. While Marie got most of the attention (being *the* star of the show), Nixon got a crumb from the *Los Angeles Times*' Edwin Schallert (cast member William Schallert's father): "[Nixon made a] notably good impression." Ezra Goodman of the *Los Angeles Daily News* focused mostly on references to Wilson's bust, but stopped for a second to mention that Nixon "delivers his dialog rather colloquially."

A summer theater organization offered Wilson and Nixon $3000 a week to tour in *The School for Scandal*, but at this point Marie had too much happening professionally (particularly her *My Friend Irma* radio series) to consider going on the road. Besides, the Nixons were arguing more than usual, even doing it openly on the Las Vegas junket for *My Friend Irma Goes West*. Edith Gwynn tattled,

> Lotsa people think Marie Wilson and Allan Nixon tiff like they do because his mark as an actor hasn't equaled her screen success. But, actually, Nixon is a frustrated writer, believe it or not—and his chums say he should scribble his way to the top. His imagination and ability being what they are.

Columbia and 20th Century-Fox were both interested in signing Nixon, with the former winning out. Nixon definitely felt discouraged that his acting career hadn't advanced since he first had screen aspirations in the 1930s. It didn't help that he turned down several lead roles in—what he considered—"run-of-the-mill" films after *Pickup* and *Prehistoric Women*. Wilson had supported him since they married and no matter how much in love they were and how tolerant Marie was, resentment was only natural—especially since Nixon was an alcoholic. It was alleged that Wilson had trained their dog to bark every time Nixon took a drink. Nixon said he regretted the way that his drinking affected his career, and said that if he had it all to do over again, he would have watched his "conduct in public more carefully—no heavy drinking."

The day the above-quoted interview (conducted by Dick Williams) was published, came news of another arrest.

On September 25, 1950, Nixon was in the Hollywood Jail drunk tank waiting for his wife to bail him out. Police had found him intoxicated, slumped over the wheel of his new vehicle. He had crashed into a parked car, bumping it into another automobile and causing a lot of damage. When he was arrested, a cool Nixon remarked, "Sure, I was driving, but I don't know what all the fuss is about." This time, Wilson did not come to the station to bring him home; Jerry Epstein from the Circle Theatre showed up. Wilson had sent over $20 for the bail. If, as the newspapers claimed, the bail was $100, then Epstein shelled out the balance.

On October 4, *Three Out of Four*, a quartet of one-acters, opened at the Circle, starring Wilson and featuring Nixon, Naomi Stevens and William Schallert. Nixon appeared in two of the playlets, "Sparkin'" and "Suppressed Desires." "Allan Nixon gave a surprisingly good account of his talents," wrote Edwin Schallert. "He has advanced since *Kitty Doone*." Wilson wasn't featured in *Suppressed Desires*, but one of its supporting players would later prove important to her: Robert Fallon.

The following month, Wilson headed for Reno for a divorce. To her credit, she never badmouthed Nixon—even if she definitely had cause to. And she never publicly complained about his drinking. The closest she came to a criticism of him was calling herself a "tennis widow." Harrison Carroll quoted Nixon as humorously replying, "If the judge sees me play, her case is shot." According to Hedda Hopper,

> The chief difficulty between Allan and Marie Wilson lay in their careers. While she worked almost constantly, he was trying to establish himself as an actor, and occasionally went off the deep end when his frustration got the better of him. Too bad that they should have decided upon a divorce just as Lady Luck began to smile on Allan.

Hedda credited Lady Luck for Nixon's engagements in a Broadway show with Nancy Coleman, *Tonight's the Night*, and the romantic lead in the movie *They Sell Sailors Elephants*. At times, Lady Luck has a very unlady-like way of running out—and she gave Nixon the brush, as he wasn't in either project. *They Sell Sailors Elephants*, renamed *A Girl in Every Port* (1952), was made with Groucho Marx, William Bendix, Don DeFore and ... Marie Wilson.

Dorothy Kilgallen got straight to the point: "Marie Wilson's intimates say gambling-and-highballs was the combination that wrecked her marriage to Allan Nixon. In the past year he piled up a formidable record of brawls and arrests for drunken driving."

Before the divorce became final at the end of December 1950, Nixon was dating bit player–dancer Judy Landon, one of his *Prehistoric Women* co-stars. She later married Brian Keith.

"It didn't work out too well at Columbia, some special circumstances came up," Nixon told interviewers Tom and Jim Goldrup vaguely. "Before the first six months were up, I was out of business there." It's been speculated that Harry Cohn blacklisted him due to "a conflict over an actress." More plausible is Nixon's assertion that he was asked to play small roles in Bs, and he rebelled. "[Cohn] put me on suspension and then finally told me I would never work at the studio unless it was the way he wanted, and as long as he was there, I wouldn't work anywhere else," Nixon told the Goldrups. "I stayed on suspension for about three months. Eventually I asked for my release."

While it was being (erroneously) reported that Nixon was engaged to stripper Betty Rowland, he was still hoping for a reconciliation with Wilson.

> Marie Wilson, and believe it or not, Allan Nixon, her ex, sipping champagne together at the Macayo restaurant. Is there still a spark there? Or does Marie feel sorry for him?—Louella Parsons, February 10, 1951

In fact, Nixon and actor Robert Fallon had gotten into a scuffle over Marie. Nixon might have won Round 1, but soon it was Fallon squiring Wilson around town. Round 2: Columnist Johnny Masgay wrote, "The Hollywood news hounds, with yours truly in pursuit, are having a field day trying to locate the man who gave Allan Nixon a black eye when he (Allan) was prowling around ex-wife Marie Wilson's home during the mystery man's visit."

After leaving Columbia, Nixon found no acting jobs. "I thought I was going to do better, but found out that it was a small town and that they all stuck together in the top studios and he [Harry Cohn] had blacklisted me.…My agent couldn't get me a job." Without Wilson to support him, he worked as a longshoreman.

Louella Parsons mentioned Nixon's situation on her radio program, and it caught the attention of stage director Jus Addiss. He wired Louella: "As a result of your broadcast I am casting Nixon in the lead opposite Gladys George in *Rain* opening July 1 [1951] at the [Deauville Beach Club] theater in Santa Monica. Allan needs and deserves this break." Edwin Schallert was not particularly impressed by the production, especially since James Logan (as Reverend Davidson) went up on his lines and at one point left the "stage inopportunely, as there are no prompters in central staging." Gladys was praised for her "vivid, picturesque" Sadie Thompson, and Schallert called Nixon "consistently good in his work as Sgt. O'Hara."

"Marie Wilson's ex, Allan Nixon, tells intimates that the reason he is acting in *Kind Lady* at Laguna is to make money with which to win Marie back. It isn't money that interests Marie," Sheilah Graham wrote on August 27, 1951. Also at Laguna, Nixon did *Miranda* (1951) with Peter Adams and Felippa Rock.

> Allan Nixon, Marie Wilson's ex-husband, has friends depressed. They say he's gone to pieces since the divorce.—Dorothy Kilgallen, October 31, 1951.

In November 1951, Nixon was hired by producer Ron Ormond for *Outlaw Women* (1952), Howco Productions' first picture. In one of his best roles, he portrayed Bob

Nixon uncorks a powerhouse punch on this *Outlaw Women* (1952) lobby card.

Ridgeway, a doctor who is abducted and brought to Las Mujeres (Spanish for "The Women"), a town run by Iron Mae McLeod (Marie Windsor) and mostly populated by the fair sex. The Larabee sisters, Beth (Carla Balenda) and Ellen (Jacqueline Fontaine), both fall for the husky doctor. Meanwhile, Iron Mae, all the girls in the town and Mae's old flame Woody Callaway (Richard Rober) find themselves up against outlaws Frank Slater (Richard Avonde) and Sam Bass (Leonard Penn). The movie had two directors, with Ormond handling the actors and Sam Newfield the actresses. Although Nixon is not the main hero (that's Rober's job), he does get to scrap with two outlaws near the end—his shirt flying open, hairy chest exposed and fists flying.

"Last year everything blew up," Nixon told Erskine Johnson. "Marie Wilson divorced me and there was no work for me. I couldn't get a job. I think this is the turning point at last."

No matter what Nixon did, even promising Wilson that he could be a "good boy," he could not win her back. She had become engaged to Robert Fallon, now a television producer. Sheilah Graham claimed that Marie had Nixon's "blessing" for her December 14, 1951, wedding to Fallon—as if it mattered. "I'm glad Marie is marrying Bob," Allan supposedly said. "She's now out of my mind, a closed book. We were seeing each other too much." Erskine Johnson wrote that Nixon would not be sending congratulations to the couple, as there was a "sizzling feud on between the boys." However, a couple of days after Marie became Mrs. Fallon, columnist George Fisher said that Nixon told him that the stories of bad feelings between them were "nonsense," and that he had sent flowers to the newlyweds.

On January 7, 1952, Nixon opened at the Coronet Theater in the play *Heir to the Flesh* with Marta Mitrovich, Helen Noyes and Glen Vernon. A convoluted drama about artificial insemination, it was deemed talky and predictable by Grace Kingsley of the *Los Angeles Times*. She did, however, call Nixon's playing "magnetic and forceful." Arizona's Sombrero Playhouse staged *Lady in the Dark* with Nixon as movie star Randy Curtis, about whom one character exclaims, "My God, girls, what a beautiful hunk of man! And he's got a voice that goes through you like a pound of cocaine!" He did a silent bit as Carolyn Jones' brother at the beginning of the Bob Hope-Bing Crosby-Dorothy Lamour comedy *Road to Bali* (1952).

When director Herbert Tevos' 1951 sci-fi cheapie *Tarantula* proved to be unreleasable, Howco bought it and put Ron Ormond to work directing additional footage, including short framing scenes featuring Nixon. He's second-billed in the eventual movie, retitled *Mesa of Lost Women* for its 1953 release, but appears only in the frame: In a field hospital, he and others try to get Robert Knapp, a man found sunburned and dehydrated in the desert, to tell them how he got into that fix. Knapp babbles about giant spiders and a mad scientist, creating the impression that he's out of his head, but a smiling, amused Nixon suggests to the others, "Let's listen to his story anyway. What do we got to lose?"—and with that, the movie segues into Tevos' *Tarantula*. Other *Outlaw Women* players brought aboard for the Ormond footage: Jackie Coogan, Paula Hill, Dolores Fuller and Lyle Talbot.

Ormond also directed Nixon as Lemuel Gulliver in the unsold TV pilot *Gulliver and the Little People* (1953), produced by roller derby entrepreneur Leo A. Seltzer. "It was updated so instead of landing in a ship," Nixon told the Goldrups, "he landed from an airplane with a parachute." Another unrealized project: the lead in a biopic of war correspondent Floyd Gibbons. On TV, Nixon appeared on *Death Valley Days*,

Fireside Theatre, Adventures of Wild Bill Hickok and more.

In June '53, Louella Parsons said she was "touched" by a "courageous letter" Nixon had sent her:

> Six months ago, I joined Alcoholics Anonymous, thanks wholly to the efforts of a kind, good friend—Ron Ormond, who believed in me despite my severe "emotional disturbances."
>
> Since joining A.A., I have not had a drink, and I know I am on the way to complete rehabilitation.
>
> I can never express my complete gratitude to Ormond....Thanks to A.A. and a wonderful friend, there's a whole new life ahead for me.

In late 1953, a Nixon comeback hit a snag—or more precisely, wrote Harrison Carroll, something hit *him*:

> [Nixon] has been released from the Veterans' Hospital at Sawtelle after a frightening experience. When the acting business got slow before the holidays, Allan took a temporary job with a construction company. He was hit on the head by a falling plank. Didn't think much of it until he began to have headaches. Several weeks later, he went to a doctor and found he had been suffering from a concussion and a slight skull fracture! He's okay now.

Allan Nixon, looking totally demoralized, and Tandra Quinn in a *Mesa of Lost Women* (1953) publicity photo.

Nineteen fifty-four started with a supporting role in a Los Angeles stage production of *Tobacco Road* with John Carradine—but little else. Thanks to Arthur Kennedy, one of the stars of *Crashout* (1955), Nixon had an uncredited part as Frank, a motorcycle cop; *Hollywood Reporter* indicates that he may have had a bit in *Not as a Stranger* (1955). But other than those, there were no other screen jobs in 1954 or '55. He supplemented his income by becoming a tipster for *Confidential!*, supplying dirt on several people, including Marie Wilson, a situation that came out during the magazine's notorious 1957 libel court case. At one point he was given $25 by *Confidential*'s publisher because he was broke. The memory of his past problems with alcohol lingered. "Whenever my name is brought up for a part," he told Paul V. Coates, "they just dismiss me as a lush."

On August 7, 1954, in Las Vegas, he wed Alma Christina Hammond. Eleven days later, she asked for an annulment, alleging that Nixon "secretly intended" to be her husband "only in form" and wanted her solely for financial and moral support. She claimed he refused to live with her and "never intended to."

Ron Ormond came through again, more or less, with *Untamed Mistress*; he incorporated footage from a television pilot called *The Black Panther*—minus the scenes featuring its star, Sabu—and a trio of topless girls dancing with gorillas to add "spice" to the hodgepodge. In addition to starring, Nixon also did some uncredited directing. Three writers, Orville H. Hampton, Ormond and Paul Leslie Peil, concocted the story of Velda (Jacqueline Fontaine), who was "reared by the gorilla tribe, mothered by baboons." Her fiancé Jack (John Martin) doesn't want to hear this—well, *naturally*—or that someday "her soft caresses could turn into hairy steel claws around [his] throat." Nixon is Jack's brother, a doctor who takes them on a safari into gorilla country to search for the answer to an "ageless question: Could evolution have any basis, could it influence the mating instinct of a girl whose life had been half gorilla and half civilized?"—knowing it would put all their lives in jeopardy. Way to go, doc! ("His smile was as false as the plagiarized plot of *Untamed Mistress*," reads an out-of-left-field line in Nixon's 1968 novel *The Actor*.)

In 1956, more TV roles came Nixon's way: *Brave Eagle*, the unsold pilot *The Phantom* (capably playing a drunken doctor) and multiple episodes of *Tales of the Texas Rangers* and *Judge Roy Bean* (in one, he portrayed Black Jack Ketchum).

In July '56, Nixon told Paul V. Coates, "A few months ago I tried to get a job driving a truck and delivering bottled water. Just so I could get enough for food and rent. But the personnel manager told me a man with my theatrical background wouldn't be satisfied with such menial work. I guess I couldn't convince him I was no longer thirsty. I was just hungry." Maurice Miller, owner of the Casablanca Hotel, gave him a job: Nixon swept out the bar and collected towels before Miller made him the desk clerk. Eventually he became the hotel's assistant manager and publicity director.

This didn't stop him from getting into trouble. "That big noise outside at a Cienega

Poster of *Untamed Mistress* (1956).

late spot was Allan Nixon and David Street in jealous row over Sharon Lee," wrote Harrison Carroll in August '56. After the brawl was over, the trio had dinner—together—at the Luau.

In Tijuana, on February 15, 1957, Nixon took as his fifth bride model Velda May Sievers; they remarried in a church ceremony in Hollywood on May 17. It seems prophetic that her name was the same as the Velda in *Untamed Mistress*.

Nixon had bit parts in the movies *Apache Warrior* (1957) and *The Buccaneer* (1958). The latter was a remake of producer-director Cecil B. DeMille's same-name 1938 film. In 1957, DeMille was not well and entrusted his big-budgeted Technicolor-VistaVision epic to his son-in-law, actor Anthony Quinn (Quinn's only movie as director). Yul Brynner starred as French pirate Jean Lafitte, in love with governor's daughter Annette Claiborne (Inger Stevens), and fighting alongside Major General Andrew Jackson (Charlton Heston) in the Battle of New Orleans. Nixon had no character name, was uncredited and barely noticeable, playing an American lieutenant. After the production wrapped, his friend Quinn wrote him a note:

> Dear Allan—It's always been a pleasure being with you whether it was at tennis or cutting up a few, but I must say that having you on *The Buccaneer* was a great pleasure and I can only tell you that your contribution will be a definite factor in making the picture a great success. I am preparing a picture to do this fall and certainly hope to find something adequate for your talents. Affectionally, Tony

Alas, *The Buccaneer* flopped and, as far as we know, Nixon didn't work with Quinn again. But Nixon gave him a shout-out in his 1979 novel *Shadow of a Man*. He wrote that Quinn befriended a writer, not "for professional reasons," but because he was an "outgoing, genuine man."

On the small screen, where Nixon was typed as shady characters, he performed on *The Silent Service, The Alcoa Hour, Gunsmoke, Highway Patrol et al.* On January 18, 1958, two days before the latter aired, Nixon was in the hospital, a victim of a domestic quarrel with wife Velda. "A statuesque brunette was held in jail today, charged with carving up her actor husband with a pair of steak knives he gave her for Christmas," read one report. She was booked on "suspicion of assault with intent to commit murder."

The fight started when Nixon learned that Velda had visited her old flame Burt Lancaster, who was in the hospital recovering from an appendectomy. "My husband read a meaning in the visit that wasn't there. He became angry. He was jealous. It was exaggerated out of all proportion. [After he] cuffed me a few times, he accused me of things that were not true. I grabbed a steak knife and let him have it." Nixon sustained wounds to his shoulder, forearm, leg and arm.

Velda told the police that she went after Nixon twice, once at the "height of the argument" and a second time when he came back to get some clothes. "I knew that in his mood I wouldn't be able to defend myself. Allan is a former football player and he prides himself on the fact that he has never laid a hand on a woman—he just kicks them." Asked if his wife had "succeeded in frightening him," Nixon replied, "I am afraid of her now." Despite the wounds, the two lovebirds were ready to forgive and kinda forget. She called him an "overgrown child," adding, "I'm awfully sorry I hurt him. I'm sure we'll get back together."

Nixon did not sign a complaint against her because he was "concerned" what effect a court trial would have on his career. What career, exactly? That February, after he recovered from Velda's knifework, he acted on an episode of *Sergeant Preston of the Yukon.*

On September 19, 1958, 31-year-old Velda went into the bathroom of their Hollywood home, to light a cigarette. A gas leak caused a terrific explosion, and she suffered burns on 75 percent of her body. Without regaining full consciousness, she died in the hospital on September 30. Nixon perversely incorporated Velda's cause of death into his first novel, 1963's *Blessed Are the Damned*:

> Norma had run into the hall, her clothing and hair aflame, screaming. By chance, the man in the apartment two doors down had been coming out at that moment, and had ripped off his topcoat, with which he smothered the flames.
>
> The blast of a gas explosion which had rocked the building, the commotion in the hall, and Norma's whimpering cries had drawn other tenants on the floor to the scene.
>
> They had all stood around horrified and helpless waiting for the Hollywood Police Emergency Ambulance. Norma, they told me, had sat on the floor, her back to the wall, naked except for tattered remnants of her clothes and the burned topcoat, and waited for the ambulance.

As *Blessed Are the Damned* continues, doctors tell Norma's husband, Mitch "Cowboy" Hurley, "If, by some outside chance she should live … they would have to amputate her feet and hand, so intense were the burns to her extremities." A suicide attempt is suspected, but Hurley is adamant: "It was an accident. She hadn't tried to kill herself. It was those god-damned heaters. There should be a law." In fact, Norma's death *was* a homicide, but he is unable to prove it.

Screen work remained sparse for Nixon. In November '58, he did an episode of *Union Pacific* and the following month he started a run as a regular on the local Los Angeles series *Emergency Ward*. Dorothy Kilgallen gave out the news that Nixon was spending his Sundays as a tour guide, conducting "bus excursions that take in movie stars' homes and a picnic feature."

Old Army pal William T. Orr, a former actor, now a Warner Bros. producer, put Nixon under contract and gave him small parts in the Warner Bros. series *Maverick, Sugarfoot, Hawaiian Eye, Bronco, Cheyenne, 77 Sunset Strip, Lawman, Surfside 6, Colt .45* and *The Alaskans*. His last known TV appearances were on two episodes of *Rawhide* in 1960 and '61, although there could have been more uncredited roles after that. Hopalong Cassidy producer Harry Sherman's daughter Lynn Sherman wanted Nixon to star in a TV Western as *Jingle-Bob Jones*, but the idea did not sell.

On March 18, 1960, the 41-year-old Nixon wed wife #6, model Maria Magda (aka Meg Lecours), 34, in Riverside, California.

In 1962, Nixon decided to leave acting, telling columnist William S. Murphy, "I became tired of waiting for the phone to ring, and besides, the calls were becoming infrequent. I originally started in journalism in college.… I thought I'd try a book." His first, *Blessed Are the Damned*, was labeled a "novel of intense consuming passion, of murder, lust, love and hate." Its publisher, Paperback Library, called Nixon a "writer with the powerful male drive and authority of a new James M. Cain. [His] first novel blazes with passion, drama and explosive force."

Robert Taylor optioned *Blessed Are the Damned* and planned to make a movie version in Portugal with Senta Berger, director Byron Haskin and producer Hall Bartlett. In June 1969, Taylor died and the picture was never made. Haskin was a good friend of Nixon's; he was mentioned in Nixon's 1968 novel *The Actor,* and the 1977 novel *Nikki* is dedicated to him: "For Byron Haskin: Confidant, Mentor and, most importantly, FRIEND."

Nixon dedicated *Blessed* to his wife Meg, "who told me I could do it." They divorced in 1964.

Nixon's success as a writer encouraged him to pen more books, regularly sleazy and with frequent Hollywood backdrops: *Nobody Hides Forever* (1964), *The Last of Vicky* (1966), *Malibu Pick-Up* (1966), *The Bitch Goddess* (1969), *The Scavengers* (1969), *The Gold and Glory Guy* (1970), *Power Man* (1972) and *Shadow of a Man* (1979). (In the latter, he used the names of two ex-wives, Annette and Opal, for the characters of a comedian's kept mistresses.) Three detective novels—*Get Garrity* (1966), *Go for Garrity* (1970) and *Good Night Garrity* (1969)—focussed on Tony Garrity, "half Aztec, half Irish, convicted killer of two—and the wildest new private eye on the Coast!" To the October 1976 issue of the digest *Mystery Monthly*, Nixon contributed the story "Garrity's Gamble."

He also wrote books under the pseudonym Nick Allan: *Divorce Bait* (1965), *The Love Trap* (1965), *The Meal Ticket* (1966), *Dynasty of Decadence: Hollywood's Lavender Casting Couch* (1966) and *The End Zone* (1967). Under the name Don Romano, Nixon co-wrote, with Oscar-winning screenwriter Ernest (*The French Connection*) Tidyman, the novels *Mafia: Operation Porno* (1973), *Mafia: Operation Cocaine* (1974) and *Mafia: Operation Hit Man* (1974).

A "natural storyteller" (William S. Murphy), Nixon wrote about what he knew: alcoholism, sex, Hollywood and football. His books share a common denominator of unlikable characters who are jaded, unhappy, desperate, unfaithful and ambitious to a fault. Nixon's disdain for Hollywood is fairly obvious, as actors are used and abused, especially sexually, in their quest for stardom. He writes about explicit sex of all types—straight, gay, incest, pedophilia, bestiality and miscegenation. There's lots of homophobia ("Perverts like to party"), particularly in *Dynasty of Decadence* where he writes supposedly true stories of Hollywood notables with names omitted. He even claims to have "interviewed" psychiatrists of the rich and famous, who all willingly talked about their patients' hang-ups, and the "queers" themselves. This is undoubtedly Nixon's worst book, trading on his so-called inside knowledge of Hollywood.

"I made enough from my writing to buy my house," Nixon told the Goldrups, "which I didn't do as an actor because, unless you're kind of big time in acting, I don't think you come up with as much money as some people might think."

In 1964, he started dating DeDe West. This relationship proved to be his most lasting; there is no evidence that they made their union legal. At the beginning of *Power Man*, he called her a "[l]oving and Loyal Companion, who shares the author's growing pains, fulfillments and long silences with a spirit perpetually blithe." *Shadow of a Man* was dedicated to "all the wonderous things she is, and for her devotion to my work beyond the call of duty." It looks as if Nixon finally found happiness.

Near the end of his life, Nixon remarked to the Goldrups about his acting career: "Things went wrong, just put it that way. I'm not bitter. I enjoyed it. I enjoyed the people I met and the fun I had."

The 79-year-old died of emphysema in Los Angeles on April 13, 1995.

1940: *The Mortal Storm* (uncredited), *Escape* (uncredited), *Gaucho Serenade* (uncredited).
1941: *Rookies on Parade* (uncredited).

1942: *The Bugle Sounds* (uncredited), *Thunder Birds (Soldiers of the Air)* (uncredited), *Sex Hygiene* (short, uncredited).
1943: *Margin for Error* (uncredited), *Three Cadets* (short, uncredited).
1944: *Ditch and Live* (short, uncredited).
1947: *Dragnet*; *Linda, Be Good.*
1949: *Siren of Atlantis.*
1950: *Prehistoric Women.*
1951: *Pickup.*
1952: *Outlaw Women, Road to Bali* (uncredited).
1953: *Mesa of Lost Women.*
1955: *Crashout* (uncredited).
1956: *Untamed Mistress.*
1957: *Apache Warrior.*
1958: *The Buccaneer* (uncredited).
1963: *Wall of Noise* (uncredited).

CRAIG REYNOLDS

Craig Reynolds began acting in the 1930s and enjoyed steady employment into the early '40s. In B pictures, particularly those at Warner Bros., he played lead roles and supporting parts. While never a star, he projected masculinity and easily transitioned from good guy to bad. Come World War II, he was one of the first actors to join up, serving valiantly as a Marine in the hellish fighting on Guadalcanal. One of the few survivors of his platoon, he came back to Hollywood badly wounded, and landing movie roles became more difficult. But he forged on for the sake of his family—until tragedy struck.

Harold Hugh Enfield was born on July 15, 1907, in Anaheim, California, the second of three sons. His parents were Oscar Enfield (1878–1953), a math teacher who later became the principal of the Los Angeles Progressive School, and Leila Goold (1884–1965), a homemaker. While his brothers Rollin (1906–84) and John (1913–82) followed their father into the educational field, Hugh wanted something else—and that something did not include going to college.

Actor and war hero Craig Reynolds.

After graduation from Franklin High School, he made the rounds looking for Little Theater jobs and debuted at the Drama Art Workshop. "I know my paternal grandparents were not happy with my father being an actor," Hugh's son Dennis Enfield told me in 2007. "He went to Los Angeles; he wanted to be an actor. He was kinda disowned from the family." To support himself, Hugh shingled roofs, was a parking attendant, and drove a lumber truck.

On March 7, 1926, he married high school sweetheart Elizabeth Jean Robertson; months later, on September 19, the couple had a daughter, Andree. The marriage lasted only three years. (Andree died on April 3, 2002.)

At some point, Hugh worked as an assistant manager of a lumber yard, but after six months he realized the job was taking time away from his search for acting gigs—so he quit. Supposedly, he joined a school friend in operating a hamburger stand, which gave him more time for theater work.

This ended when he met Josephine Marie Dowler, who persuaded Hugh to join her acting company. A few months later, he was a member of the Pasadena Community Theatre; during his two years there, he appeared in *Jack Straw, If* and *Spring Song*. The latter brought him in contact with actress Vera Gordon, who selected him to accompany her on a year-long vaudeville tour. After this, he did some shows with Lucille La Verne, including *To What Red Hell*.

He was acting at the Spotlight Theater in Hollywood when Ivan Kahn took one look at the handsome, 6'2" 180-pound, gray-eyed Hugh Enfield and thought he was screen material. ("His eyes were very catching. Everything stops when you look at him," Dennis told me.)

In 1933, after a screen test, Enfield was signed by Universal. His first assignment was the 12-chapter serial *The Phantom of the Air* starring Tom Tyler. A gang of smugglers, headed by LeRoy Mason, is out to steal William Desmond's invention, the Contragrav, but Border Patrolman-expert flyer Tyler is hot on their trail. Mason is the "brains heavy" but newcomer Enfield got more footage as the "dog heavy," engaging in fisticuffs on the ground and gun battles in the air.

Enfield's character in the serial *Gordon of Ghost City* (1933), a duplicitous ranch hand, was less prominent. Uncredited parts came in 1933's *Don't Bet on Love, Saturday's Millions* and *Only Yesterday*. Publicity made much of Enfield being in the cast of the latter, even going so far to say that director John M. Stahl personally selected him, but Hugh was completely lost in the shuffle and is not readily visible.

He had better luck with his next assignment: the male lead in the serial *Perils of Pauline* (1934) with Evalyn Knapp. For the occasion, the Universal front office decided to change his name to Robert Allen, which was a combination of his grandfathers' first names. "Universal … sponsored the name change," wrote the *Los Angeles Times*' Edwin Schallert, "because exhibitors said Enfield doesn't mean anything. Nothing, anyway, except a rifle!"

The studio was happy with his "rough and ready" (*Saskatoon Star-Phoenix*) performance in the cliffhanger and considered casting him in a boxing drama. This didn't happen, but they did change his name back to Hugh Enfield. Universal never built him up, instead putting him in small, often uncredited parts in *Cross Country Cruise, I'll Tell the World, Let's Be Ritzy, Love Birds* and *Million Dollar Ransom* (all 1934). Despite the size of Hugh's roles, fan magazines and critics noticed him. In its *Love Birds* review, the *Austin Daily Texan* opined, "Besides the stars and little Mickey Rooney, another actor who has only an infinitesimal part deserves attention for good character portrayal. That person is Hugh Enfield, who plays the part of the bus driver."

On the *Love Birds* set, Hugh forged a friendship with 14-year-old Rooney. When Mickey was later hospitalized with a broken leg, Hugh bought him a model airplane. This was the start of Craig's fascination with miniature airplanes, which continued the rest of his life. His friendship with Rooney came to mean a lot to Enfield when times were tough.

If Universal wasn't giving him important assignments, local theater was. In April 1934, Enfield replaced George J. Lewis as a conceited movie star in *Biography* with Alice Brady at the Biltmore Theatre. Also in the cast: Vera Gordon, one of Enfield's early cheerleaders. He stayed with the company when they moved to San Francisco for an engagement at the Columbia Theater.

Universal dropped his option and, in September '34, he headlined the cast of a new play by Claire and Paul Sifton dealing with German life under the Hitler regime, *Blood on the Moon*, at the Mayan Theatre. In it he played a Nazi officer who falls in love with a Jewish girl (Lenita Lane). The *Los Angeles Times* rated the drama average and said it was too talky, but thought that Enfield was "exceedingly fine," handling his role with "fine fervor." Columnist Eleanor Barnes added that she thought he looked "like a younger Clark Gable."

On November 1, 1934, at El Capitan Theatre, Enfield played a dimwitted boxer in the West Coast premiere of *The Milky Way*, starring Hugh O'Connell (as a milkman-turned-prizefighter) and Jean Dixon. When Paramount set in motion their plan to bring the property to the screen in late '34, it was expected that Enfield would reprise his part and that Jack Oakie would be tapped to star. None of this came to pass: When it reached screens in 1936, it starred Harold Lloyd, with William Gargan in Hugh's boxer part. The studio did cast Enfield in their 1935 films *Rumba, Four Hours to Kill!* and *Paris in Spring*, but the roles were of little consequence.

In May 1935, Enfield did a brief tour in the play *Coquette* with Mary Pickford. This brought him to the attention of Warner Bros., and he was put under contract. With his new pact came another name, Craig Reynolds. "He is dark, handsome and powerfully built," according to one publicity blurb. "The new name seems to fit and he is much pleased with it."

Craig Reynolds had his first feature lead in *Jailbreak* (1936). Opposite him is June Travis.

At Warners, he was essentially a supporting player, but he was being used more often and in more visible roles than he had been at Universal and Paramount. He was particularly adept at portraying bad guys. In the Dick Foran Western *Treachery Rides the Range* (1936), Reynolds "smartly supplies chief menace as defiant head of hide firm invading Indian reservation and tricking redskins into breaking treaty" (*Variety*).

There were a few missed opportunities and might-have-beens. Leads in the Bs that were announced for him (*The Law in Her Hands, Bengal Tiger, Talent Scout*) went to others whether because of scheduling difficulties or because of illness. It was reported that WB bought for him the properties *March or Die* (a Foreign Legion story) and *Get It First* (a newspaper yarn), but both of these fell through.

He was given his first feature lead in *Jailbreak* (1936), a Big House murder mystery which the *Los Angeles Times*' Barbara Miller described as "lusty as a wrestling match, spotted with violent death, brawls, relentless officers of the law bent on getting their man." She added that Reynolds was "very blithe as the reporter," a quality he brought to many of his roles.

More supporting parts finally gave way to a lead in *The Footloose Heiress* (1937), a "frivolous, exaggerated farce.... Largely silly, incredible, with a laugh now and then: some suggestiveness" (*The Educational Screen*). In this film, he was billed over an up-and-coming Ann Sheridan. It was basically *The Taming of the Shrew*, with wealthy man posing as hobo (Reynolds) putting flighty heiress (Sheridan) in her place. Publicity quoted him as saying, "I've become so used to being a meanie that I have to watch myself in love scenes with Ann Sheridan to keep myself from snarling and grabbing her in true villain style." (Actually, he does get rough with her in the movie, but still comes off as a likable character.)

Sheridan introduced Reynolds to her good friend, actress Barbara Pepper. Reynolds had been dating singer Gertrude Niesen (it was regarded as his most serious relationship) but in late 1937, Pepper took over as his main squeeze.

Born May 31, 1915, in New York City, Pepper was an ex–Broadway showgirl who got into the movies in the early 1930s as a Goldwyn Girl. At that time, she met Lucille Ball, who was also just starting out, and they became great friends. The blonde Pepper excelled at playing snappy, wisecracking floozies, dance hall girls, showgirls, waitresses and assorted party girls. While she typically did small roles (playing characters with

"Right this way," says headwaiter Stuart Holmes to a party of five in *Melody for Two* (1937). Pictured left to right: Dick Purcell, Gordon Hart, Patricia Ellis, Harry Hayden, Reynolds, Holmes.

such names as Honey, Bubbles, Mamie, Belle, Budgie, Flossie, Goldie, Francie LaRue, Maizie, Speedy, Boxcar Annie and Big Bertha), she had good roles in *Let 'Em Have It* (1935), *Mummy's Boys* (1936) and *The Westland Case* (1937). In *Our Daily Bread* (1934),

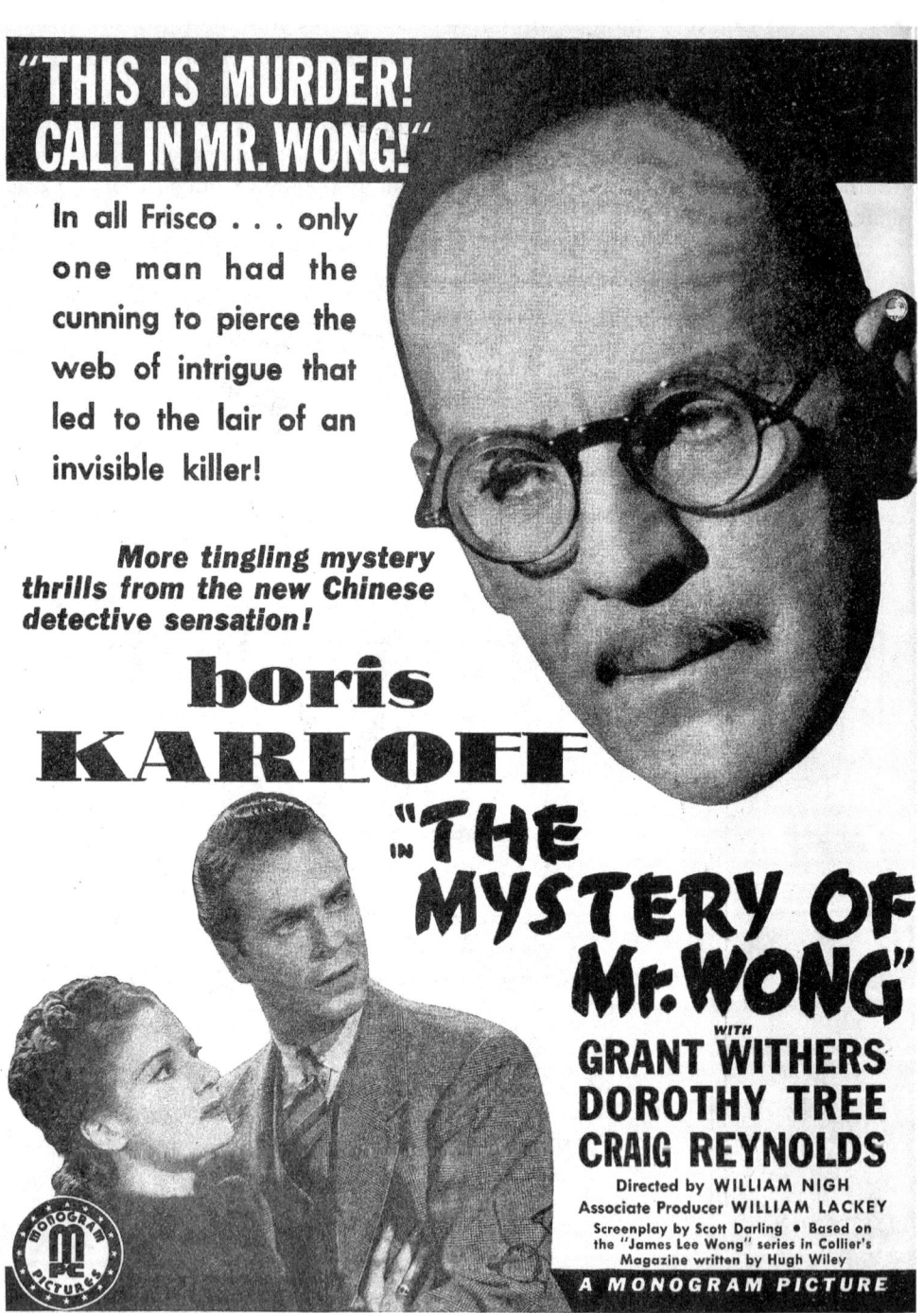

Magazine ad for *The Mystery of Mr. Wong* (1939).

her role as Sally, a platinum blonde floozie who threatens the marriage of John and Mary Sims (Tom Keene and Karen Morley), is especially memorable.

Reynolds' last for Warners was the Technicolor musical short *Romance Road* (1938) starring Walter Cassel and Anne Nagel, in which he plays a ruthless character.

As a freelancer, he was employed by the Poverty Row outfits, again mostly as a supporting actor, although he did headline the indie *Slander House* (1938) with Adrienne Ames. In PRC's *I Take This Oath* (1940), his last movie for a long while, Reynolds brought an affecting touch to his secondary part. His last moments, after taking a bullet meant for star Gordon Jones, are especially well-acted and some of the best emoting he ever did in films.

Although America was still neutral, World War II was underway, and on October 8, 1940, Reynolds became one of the first actors to join the Marines. "I could see the war coming," he told Marine Corps Correspondent Sergeant Edward Burman. "I decided to get into the service and prepare myself for the future. In school I had gained some military experience, but my training really started in the Corps and since that time things have happened pretty fast."

Completing Officer Candidates School, Reynolds was commissioned a second lieutenant. On August 7, 1942, American and Allied forces went on the offensive in the Guadalcanal Campaign, and Reynolds and his unit were among the first to enter the struggle to wrest control of the islands of Florida, Tulagi, Gavutu, Tanambogo, Macambo and Guadalcanal from the Japanese. "One night things were plenty hot," Reynolds told Burman. "One of our machine gun platoons in the front lines was attacked by a sizable Jap [sic] force. Twenty-five men, weapons and ammunition were rushed up and the attack was beaten off. I was in the group. Next morning, we counted 35 dead Japs [sic]." The unit was under attack for 65 days.

In December '42, while in a tent being interviewed by Burman, Reynolds was asked if he had planned ahead for the postwar world. "[H]e was reluctant to look ahead too far, and make predictions," wrote Burman. "To him, the job at hand was more important than any personal conditions. He's that kind of a guy." There was a bit of looking ahead when it was reported that Reynolds and Barbara Pepper were engaged and would marry when he was out of the service.

When the commanding officer of his 75-man unit was killed, Reynolds took over. "It was basically a battlefield promotion," Dennis noted.

In mid–January 1943, a bomb blast tore up Reynolds' left leg and killed eight of his men. Dennis later met a man named Pat who had been in the Marines or the Navy, and he talked to Dennis and his brother about Reynolds' service on Guadalcanal. Dennis recalled,

> My dad obviously did the altruistic thing of trying to shield a platoon member and a mortar exploded and that's how he got a bad leg. Pat told us that he and Craig bonded because Craig and the other guys were trying to help the Seabees [U.S. Naval Construction Forces] not get killed by the Japanese. So, I think he was wounded more than once.

In March '43, Reynolds was transferred to the Marine hospital in San Diego. Paralyzed from the knee down, he had to wear a steel brace. He had hopes it would come off in about five years. "I'm beginning to be able to wiggle my toes a little," he told Robbin Coons. "I never expected to be back here, but now that I am, I want to get back to work." He received a Purple Heart and two presidential citations.

Barbara Pepper's mother had been opposed to their match before Reynolds enlisted, but now she was all for the union. "I don't want them to wait," Mrs. Pepper told Harrison Carroll. "They've wasted too much time already." Reynolds was still in the hospital when he and Pepper wed on April 24, 1943. Actress Evelyn Venable (who had appeared in 1938's *Female Fugitive* with Reynolds and *Hollywood Stadium Mystery* with Pepper) served as matron of honor and her husband, cameraman Hal Mohr, was best man.

Reynolds and his mother-in-law "got along famously," Dennis remarked. "I remember them singing together. She wrote an unpublished novel about the South Pacific, but she had never been to the South Pacific, so they also connected on that level because he was writing his memoirs." Reynolds' book *I Came Back*, written with help from novelist-screenwriter Guy Endore, was also never published.

During military leave, Craig visited Warner Bros. and ran into his old friend (and his co-star in *The Footloose Heiress*, 1937), Ann Sheridan.

Acting work for Reynolds was not forthcoming; instead, he spoke at women's clubs and bond rallies. Coons asked Reynolds how realistic Hollywood war movies were, specifically *Guadalcanal Diary* (1943). "Did they begin to approach the realities of jungle war?" Coons inquired. Reynolds responded that that was hard for a picture to do: "You have to see it before you get an idea what it's really like. I saw the pictures of the landing at Tarawa, made by Capt. Louis Hayward and crew, and those are what I'd like the American people to see—without cuts. That'll give them the idea."

With Pepper and Charlotte Wynters, Reynolds starred in a Los Angeles staging of *Lady Chatterley's Lover* directed by actor Ian Keith. When Louella Parsons heard of the production, she was skeptical: "I don't see how they can make a play of D.H. Lawrence's very censorable *Lady Chatterley's Lover*.... It's certainly a story that needed vacuum cleaning in the original form." The ads proclaimed that it had a "Sexceptional New York cast" and that it was "saucy, spicy shockingly funny....Daring romance of a woman Who Craves Love!" When it premiered at the Belasco Theater on New Year's Eve, 1943, the *Los Angeles Times* called it a play that has "neither gloss, polish, not even much purpose," although they praised the cast who "do probably as well by it as can be anticipated." It was a bit weird for Reynolds to be associated with the production, as the plot concerned Sir Clifford Chatterley (Donald Kirke), a paralyzed war vet, whose wife has an affair with Reynolds. On January 16, 1944, it moved to the Geary Theater.

In 1944, Reynolds signed a contract with RKO, which resulted in a small part in *Nevada*. "I'm always glad to report that the men who have been in the thick of things are coming back to good breaks," wrote Louella Parsons. "I think it means a lot to all the boys to hear that their old jobs, or better, are waiting for them back home." Not so fast. He was announced to "co-star" with Rosalind Russell in *Sister Kenny*, but that did not come through, and he was released from his contract.

Leaving Pepper in California, Reynolds went to Boston with the play *Black Limelight* (1945), which was headed to Broadway. If it was a success, his family was going to move to New York with him. "And won't it be ironic if Reynolds makes a hit!" wrote Harrison Carroll. "He hasn't had much luck since he was wounded and discharged from the Marines. Universal gave him a small part in [*The Strange Affair of Uncle Harry*], but the going in general has been very tough." Alas, the show died out of town.

Also in 1945, inspired by his own troubles getting acting parts, Reynolds and radio writer William A. Holmes devised a radio show called *Veterans' Canteen*, to help discharged servicemen return to show biz. *Variety's* Jack Hellman called it

> one of the worthiest projects that has joined the parade of summer candidates, and unless we're off the beam, will get a ready reception and a fast sale....It is show biz's way of taking care of its own, which is now more realistic than sentimental-sounding and will get the backing, actual and otherwise, of every performer in the game.

Nothing happened after a test recording. Later that year, however, Reynolds filed a $100,000 damage suit, accusing the sponsors of Ginny Simms' radio program of appropriating his idea. For the next several years, Reynolds was in and out of courtrooms seeking justice, but he was never successful.

Screen roles trickled in, mostly supplied by friends. Producer Jeffrey Bernerd gave him a secondary part in Monogram's *Divorce* (1945) and promised if he made good, he would co-star Reynolds with Kay Francis in *Allotment Wives*. He did well, but was not cast in *Wives*.

Reynolds was having a difficult time with his recovery. His leg hampered his movements, he was in constant pain, and he began drinking too much. Also, he was suffering recurring bouts of malaria, for which he took Quinine. "During one of his malarial bouts, he went to the grocery store about a block from our house," Dennis related. "The produce person was Asian and my dad flipped out and attacked him. They had to break that up."

He and Pepper had two children, Dennis (born November 17, 1944) and John (October 26, 1946—July 5, 2005), and money was tight.

A couple of unbilled parts came in *The Lost Weekend* (1945) and *Just Before Dawn* (1946), a Crime Doctor starring Warner Baxter.

Among Dennis' other memories of his father:

> The thing I remember specifically was the brace on his leg, and he did walk with a limp. I remember playing with him in the front yard of our little tiny house. He would pick me up and hug me and he had a bristly little black mustache. We would horse around. He would take me to a restaurant and I rode on the back of his motor scooter....I got to have a Shirley Temple [drink] and I remember sleeping in one of the booths for a while, waking up and Dad carrying me back on the scooter.

In 1946, Reynolds had star billing in the Los Angeles stage production *All Women Are—*. *Variety* reported,

> If there was any mystery attached to the title of the show which opened at the Belasco last night, the audience soon found out the answer. "All Women Are—" gabby. Not only is the

Reynolds with his wife Barbara Pepper and son Dennis.

Al York play composed of a wordy series of set-tos among a group of dull characters, it is remarkably silly. What is billed as a psychological mystery is merely a story about a faithless wife who gets slipped a lethal mickey. It takes almost two acts to kill her, after establishing, by means of tedious verbiage, just how really smart and upper crust everyone is in the cast.

Praise did come Reynolds' way from *Variety*'s man on the aisle: "[He] tried valiantly and appeared to be the only professional on stage." The reviewer concluded, "[The play] should be hurried back to the warehouse or else handed over to the not-so-tender mercies of the backwoods little playhouses ... it doesn't belong on the commercial stage."

"It is gratifying that one of our boys who served in the war is getting a break," Louella Parsons reported of Reynolds' casting in PRC's *Queen of Burlesque* (1946). "I think it is wonderful that good old Mother Nature, plus lots of courage, have brought him to the point where he can play any type of part no matter what the physical demands." The "first-rate whodunit" and "highly suspenseful melodrama" (*Variety*) concerned murders at a burlesque house. His role was strictly a supporting one, with newcomer Carleton G. Young and Evelyn Ankers in the top spots. *Variety* thought Reynolds gave a "genuine performance" as a "harassed burley operator."

But it was still a struggle to obtain acting roles. *My Dog Shep* was his only other 1946 appearance.

Parsons wrote in December 1946,

> More credit to Craig Reynolds, who under his own name of Hugh Enfield, is delivering Christmas packages for the Los Angeles post office. But not more credit to the movie industry who hasn't given this war hero, wearer of the Purple Heart, and former leading man a job. Why isn't there some place for him in his own profession? He has two sons, and he's man enough to want to support them and his wife....[Pepper] says Craig just refuses to sit down and do nothing.

Parsons and Hedda Hopper were both in Craig and Barbara's corner and boosted them in their columns during these lean years. "Mom called Louella Parsons 'Lollie' and they evidently went back a long way together," Dennis said.

After the birth of her two children, Pepper was also finding it hard to get jobs. Friend Warner Baxter gave her a role in the *Crime Doctor* mystery *The Millerson Case*, but that was her only 1947 release.

Mary Pickford and Charles "Buddy" Rogers hired Reynolds as dialogue director of their production *Stork Bites Man* (1947). Longtime pal Mickey Rooney filmed a screen test of Reynolds for him to take around the studios, but he had little luck. After Reynolds played a small role in *The Fabulous Texan* (1947), Republic optioned him for a contract. This was great news and there was hope for steady employment. Bryan Foy announced that Reynolds would have a good part in *He Walked by Night* (1948), but he was not cast. After 1948's *The Man from Colorado*, in which he played a small part as a nasty character, Reynolds saw the writing on the wall and gave up seeking movie parts. He was employed as an iceman and drove for the Yellow Cab Co. in Beverly Hills. "Mom told me he was pissed, he did not like having to take that job," remarked Dennis.

Louella Parsons again got on her soapbox:

> Hollywood, usually so quick to help, seems to me not to be giving Craig Reynolds the helping hand he so well deserves. Craig, who is a veteran, still has a very bad leg....Surely there must be a place in this great industry of ours that will give him work that can keep him at home with his wife and two babies. Not that Craig is complaining. He's very brave, but he's still crippled, and he was one of the real heroes.

Hedda Hopper got in the act, commenting about his stint as a taxi driver: "[I]f that doesn't bow some heads here, nothing will."

At the beginning of October 1949, Pepper left Reynolds to live with her mother. Reynolds was making $250 a month driving a cab and he gave Pepper half of that to

Reynolds (middle) looks like he's up to no good in *The Man from Colorado* (1948)—unbeknownst to (left to right) Ray Collins, William Holden, Glenn Ford and Jim Bannon. It was Reynolds' last film.

support his sons; she found work in a laundry. Although she didn't want to, she started divorce proceedings.

On October 17, 1949, Reynolds was riding his motor scooter on Santa Monica Blvd. and Poinsettia Place. A motorcycle coming from the opposite direction caught its wheels in some car tracks and swerved into Reynolds. Reynolds was taken to French Hospital suffering from a skull fracture. A week later, the 42-year-old died. He was interred at Forest Lawn Memorial Park.

Pepper, informed of his death, became hysterical and collapsed. Dennis said that Lucille Ball took over immediately and helped Barbara and the kids out with money and groceries. The chauffeur's union gave her a $500 insurance check and Reynolds' father also pitched in. "My agent has helped too," Pepper told Harrison Carroll. "He called and said there is going to be a bit for me in a Twentieth Century–Fox picture [*No Way Out*]. I need to lose weight and I am going to Terry Hunt's health salon here. He is so sweet. He refuses to accept any payment."

According to Dennis, Pepper had never really gotten along with Craig's parents:

> She did not communicate much with Leila and Oscar and when we did it was very formal, very civil. I only remember Leila and Grumpy (as we called him) after my father died because we went to visit them a couple of times. Looking at it through the eyes of five or six years old, I remember he was very frail, he laughed and I think we joked and called him Grumpy because he reminded us of that movie, *Snow White and the Seven Dwarfs*.

Every year at Christmas, Leila sent Dennis and John tiny cards with ten dimes. Shortly after Reynolds' death, Dennis and John were sent to stay for a week with

Craig's brothers, Rollin and John. Contact with their uncles, however, was limited. "In the '60s, I lost contact with them because Mom just didn't get along too well with Dad's family. And so, when Leila and Oscar died, we pretty much lost track of them except every once and a while we would get a call from one or two of the brothers or their kids."

Returning to the subject of his father's passing, Dennis said,

> I don't even remember my emotional state. I do know that, according to my mom, almost immediately after my dad died, I was hospitalized. They thought it was meningitis. I had a high temperature they couldn't bring down and they put me in the hospital and after four or five days I had recovered.

Barbara, Dennis and John lived with Pepper's mother in a two-bedroom house. "Mom was working in a diner off Melrose and La Cienega Boulevard, maybe a block from where we were living. She was also working in a dry-cleaning plant there. I remember she was tired and sad a lot. My maternal grandmother really helped my brother and me. It was a neat extended family just making it in the '40s and early 50s." In 1967, Pepper reflected to Erskine Johnson, "It's funny, when you ask for a job, even in a drugstore, saying you are an out-of-work actress, the answer is no."

Pepper never got over Reynolds' death. She suffered from alcoholism and depression and let her weight get out of hand. Regardless, says her son, she never let it affect her ability to be a good mother. "She was a wonderful, caring, loving mom. She was also a very devoted friend. I am a very lucky man."

Lucille Ball knew that Pepper was a proud woman who had trouble accepting what she thought was charity. "I have wonderful recollections of Lucy," Dennis remarks. "What a woman! I liked Desi, but he was more distant, although he was always so warm and kind. Little Lucy and Desi were so much fun to play with."

Once *I Love Lucy* became a TV hit, Ball was in a position to cast Pepper in various parts in many episodes ("I couldn't have gone on without Lucille's help," Pepper told Erskine Johnson). Ball's initial idea was for Pepper to play Ethel Mertz, but Pepper's drinking problem made that a risky proposition.

Despite her drinking, Pepper was always professional, said Dennis. Friends Preston Foster, Jack Benny, Jerry Lewis and Raymond Burr were also a big help to Pepper during these difficult years, always finding roles for her in their projects. Harry Brownfield, owner of the grocery store where Reynolds had attacked the produce boy, held no grudge; in fact, said Dennis, "He was always helpful to Mom. He floated her for as much money as she needed to feed us, he was great."

Dennis started his own acting career in 1955 (as Dennis Pepper). "I kept him away from acting as long as I could," Barbara told Erskine Johnson at the time. "Now it's obvious he inherited a flair for it." He did mostly television: *Stage 7, The Jack Benny Program, Leave It to Beaver, The Adventures of Ozzie and Harriet, Petticoat Junction, The Beverly Hillbillies, My Three Sons* and *Green Acres*.

> I had a chance [at getting a recurring role as Linda Henning's boyfriend] on *Petticoat Junction*, but I didn't get it. Then I got hooked on the stage after I graduated from high school. Mom was always supportive. I helped her with her lines, she always helped me memorize mine. I went to New York and I realized I wasn't going to make it. But I gave it a good shot, came back home and became a drama teacher.

Dennis married and had two children.

His brother John had a rougher passage. He was married twice, his first resulting in an annulment when he was still a teenager. Dennis continued:

John went into the Marine Corp for a while, in the reserves, came back and did some odd jobs. He got involved with alcohol, that was a problem, but he overcame that through Alcoholics Anonymous and then joined the Masonic Lodge in Hollywood. Basically, he was a caretaker who facilitated AA meetings for about 20 years. He lived a very solitary life. After years being sober, he died of a heart attack, alone; they didn't discover his body for days.

The brothers did not have a close relationship and saw each other only occasionally; they mostly communicated through letters. "When we were growing up, I was the one who got the accolades and John did not. So, as we got older, that was something that was a problem." John was the father of two daughters.

In 1964, Barbara Pepper began earning a steady income when she was cast as Doris Ziffel on *Petticoat Junction* and then the following year on *Green Acres*. She continued with *Green Acres* until 1968, when she had to withdraw because of declining health; she was replaced by Fran Ryan. Pepper's last movie was Jerry Lewis' *Hook, Line and Sinker* (1969), in which she had an uncredited part. Also in '69, she appeared in an unsold sitcom pilot, *Houseboat* with Arthur Hill. On July 18, 1969, in Panorama City, California, the 54-year-old Pepper, suffering from multiple health issues, died from a coronary thrombosis. She is interred at Hollywood Forever.

After thinking a bit about his father's legacy, Dennis told me, "I would want my dad remembered as a man of principle, who did what he believed in. And he was a good hugger. To me, he was a loving man who lived by his ideals."

1929: *Coquette* (uncredited).
1933: *The Phantom of the Air* (uncredited), *Don't Bet on Love* (uncredited), *Gordon of Ghost City*, *Saturday's Millions* (uncredited), *Only Yesterday* (uncredited), *Perils of Pauline*.
1934: *Cross Country Cruise*, *Love Birds*, *I'll Tell the World*, *Let's Be Ritzy*, *Million Dollar Ransom* (uncredited).
1935: *Rumba* (uncredited), *Four Hours to Kill!*, *Paris in Spring*, *The Case of the Lucky Legs*, *Man of Iron*, *Dangerous* (uncredited).
1936: *Ceiling Zero*, *The Preview Murder Mystery* (uncredited), *Boulder Dam* (uncredited), *Treachery Rides the Range*, *Times Square Playboy*, *Sons o' Guns*, *The Golden Arrow*, *Jailbreak*, *Stage Struck*, *The Case of the Black Cat*, *Here Comes Carter*.
1937: *Smart Blonde*, *The Great O'Malley*, *Penrod and Sam*, *Melody for Two*, *The Go Getter* (uncredited), *The Case of the Stuttering Bishop*, *Slim*, *Talent Scout* (uncredited), *The Footloose Heiress*, *Back in Circulation*, *The Great Garrick*, *Under Suspicion*.
1938: *Romance Road* (short), *Making the Headlines*, *Female Fugitive*, *Romance on the Run*, *Gold Mine in the Sky*, *Slander House*, *I Am a Criminal*.
1939: *Navy Secrets*, *The Mystery of Mr. Wong*, *Wall Street Cowboy*, *The Gentleman from Arizona*.
1940: *The Fatal Hour*, *Son of the Navy*, *I Take This Oath*.
1944: *Nevada*.
1945: *The Strange Affair of Uncle Harry*, *Divorce*, *The Lost Weekend* (uncredited).
1946: *Just Before Dawn* (uncredited), *Queen of Burlesque*, *My Dog Shep*.
1947: *The Fabulous Texan* (uncredited).
1948: *The Man from Colorado* (uncredited).

Danny Scholl

"Danny *who*??," you wonder. That's understandable. Even back in his 1940s-50s heyday, he was only a moderately successful singer-actor, although he had the voice to go further. If Hard-Luck Cases had a poster boy, it would be Danny Scholl: robbery victim; multiple strokes and brain operations; paralysis in his legs, arms and mouth; cancer; blood clots; a heart attack; family and divorce drama. He faced it all courageously, using his talent not to reach for fame but for the betterment of others. A true inspiration.

Born in Cincinnati on July 2, 1921, Daniel Scholl was of German descent: the oldest child of Arthur Victor Scholl (1895–1969), a tinsmith and World War I veteran, and Kate Maxwell (1892–1963). According to the *Cincinnati Enquirer*'s Alice Hornbaker in 1983, Danny and his siblings, Louise (1922–88) and Arthur (1926–2001), were rejected by their parents, especially their father, and they "spent more time in foster homes than in their own home." Scholl told another writer that he was orphaned at 11. In a 1953 article by the *Los Angeles Daily News*' Marie Mesmer, he said he was placed in a children's foster home by a social worker. "Being unloved and unwanted is a feeling that is hard for anyone to take," he told Mesmer,

> but especially so for a youngster. At the home, I worked on a farm plowing the fields. We only had one battery radio set for entertainment. My big day was Sunday when I was permitted to attend a movie. I walked 22 miles to the nearest theater, but it was worth it. I was enraptured with the movies and Bebe Daniels was my screen sweetheart.

What is interesting about his conflicting stories is that he is always alone, never mentions his siblings. Whether any of the above is true, the reality seems much worse: On August 25, 1929, after an argument between an intoxicated Arthur Sr. and his wife got physical, she was minus her right

Danny Scholl had a great career ahead of him as a singer, recording artist, movie and stage actor when health problems intervened.

eye. He was arrested, but she did not press charges. She filed for divorce the following year, asking for custody of the children and alimony, but it appears that the divorce was never finalized. The Scholls were in the news again in 1932 when she swore out a warrant on him for "abusing his family," in particular *her*. The *Cincinnati Enquirer* reported:

> Mrs. Kate Scholl ... carried a small tombstone with her when she appeared in Municipal Court to prosecute her husband, Arthur Scholl, for abusing her yesterday. The stone, made from a golf course marker, was inscribed in pencil with "In Memory" on one side and "John Barleycorn" on the opposite side.
>
> Mrs. Scholl testified that her husband handed her the stone Friday [August 5] night and told her to prepare to die. She said that he then attacked her [with a table leg] and she struck him on his head with a water pitcher. Scholl was treated for [deep lacerations] on his scalp.
>
> Judge Landon L. Forchheimer placed Scholl under a peace bond. He warned Scholl that he would be given a jail sentence if he violates the peace bond.

Danny was eight and ten years old respectively when these two incidents occurred, and it's doubtful these were isolated episodes. One wonders how his parents' fighting and drinking affected him.

And the family drama wasn't confined to his parents. On April 14, 1932, a "free-for-all" brawl at an apartment house on Cincinnati's Vine Street resulted in several arrests, with Danny's mother, Uncle Harry and Aunt Helen finding seats in the paddy wagon. It had all started with Helen and Kate trailing Harry to the apartment of his friend Michael Berry where, Helen said, he "loitered a great deal" (*Cincinnati Enquirer*) instead of supporting her and their children. A fight broke out, with Berry using a blackjack in the scuffle. Things got worse when police arrived. Several individuals suffered cuts and bruises, including the cops, as hundreds of spectators congregated in front of the building. The women were fined.

Perhaps one of the ways Danny learned to cope was to pretend. In later years, he told fanciful and contradictory stories about his life. He "recalled" for Alice Hornbaker,

> When I was a tough kid growing up in the slums in Cincinnati's West End, I fought Golden Gloves bouts in the ring because that was my way to gain recognition, acceptance and, yes, even respect. The only guy who ever beat me was a national champion, Ezzard Charles. I was always big for my age and I could punch—hard.... I found it was much easier to gain acceptance by singing than by punching, so I decided to become a singer.

In another interview, he said he boxed to get money for singing lessons.

When Danny was around 16, he went to live with his father's sister Louisa and her husband, Andrew Rub, in Roselawn, Ohio. He attended Reading High School and Rosedale Dance Academy; at the latter, he was taught voice by Betty McMahill.

In a 1940 radio contest sponsored by a local music store, the Rudolph Wurlitzer Company, Scholl was one of six singers picked out of almost 500 to appear at the Shubert Theatre with Paul Whiteman and his orchestra. The 18-year-old eventually won first prize: a week's engagement at the Shubert with Shep Field. They were heard over radio station WLW.

Scholl received a music scholarship from the Cincinnati Conservatory of Music, where he briefly studied voice under Robert Powell. While continuing at the conservatory, he was signed by orchestra leader Deke Moffitt (who had heard him at the Shubert), and they played a run at Kentucky's Beverly Hills Country Club. The teenage Scholl was sharing the bill with the likes of Gertrude Niesen, Ella Logan and Billy De Wolfe.

In October 1941, Scholl left Cincinnati to become a featured vocalist on tour in *Earl Carroll's Vanities*. In February of the following year, they were in Philadelphia. Mildred Martin of the *Philadelphia Inquirer* thought the *Vanities* was a "generally shoddy show containing shopworn gags and costumes." She did, however, include Scholl among those "who work hard with unrewarding material." When the company was in Canada, *Ottawa Citizen* reviewer W.P.M. wrote that Scholl's "voice was stirring even over the [Auditorium's] loudspeaker system."

By May '42, Scholl, billed as "Cincinnati's Own Tenor," was back with Deke at the Glenn Rendezvous in Newport, Kentucky. He and Deke even wrote some songs together.

Scholl was inducted into the Army on July 22, 1942. Two months later, the *Cincinnati Enquirer* gave readers an update on "Private Dan Scholl, son of Mrs. Andrew Rub": "Stationed at the Atlantic City Basic Training Center of the Army Air Forces Technical Training Command, Scholl frequently is a principal on the center's radio programs and takes singing roles in programs at the post auditorium." Supposedly, he also briefly sang with Glenn Miller's Army Air Force Band. He had a role in Broadway's *Winged Victory* (1943–44), and was called upon to appear in the 1944 20th Century–Fox film version. According to columnist Ray Lanning, "When *Winged Victory* comes to the Cincinnati screens, you'll see a close-up of Danny singing the 'Silent Night' number." The only problem with that statement is that opera singer John Tyers is the one who performs the song. Scholl *could* be in the film, but with hundreds of servicemen in the cast, I was not able to spot him. The original *Winged Victory* cast, Danny included, brought the show to Cincinnati's Taft Theatre in January 1945.

After winning his gunner's wings, Scholl twice ferried cargo to an island base. June '45 brought a new show: *Winged Pigeons*, the "first all–GI Air Forces variety show to be organized for soldier morale building in the Pacific forward areas" (*Honolulu Advertiser*). The troupe, which would tour island installations, consisted of Sgt. Danny Scholl, Sgt. Peter Lind Hayes, Sgt. Jerry Adler (harmonica player), Sgt. Joe Bushkin, Corp. Walter Long (ballet-tap dancer), Corp. John Tyers, Corp. Julian Stockdale (jazz guitarist) and Corp. Jack Morgan (pianist). Managed by Sgt. Gant Gaither, they performed on Oahu, Eniwetok, Guam, Iwo Jima, Tinian, Saipan and Okinawa. Scholl was awarded a Bronze Star.

Out of the service in 1946 and back in Cincinnati, Scholl was heard over the airwaves on the radio program *Supper Serenade* with Burt Farber and his orchestra. Al Jolson and producer Mike Todd, developing a musical show entitled *Oh, Susanna*, wanted Scholl to portray composer Stephen Foster. But then Scholl's friend, singer-actress Jane Kean, introduced him to her agent, who got him a part in a Broadway revue instead—a lucky break, since the Todd production fizzled. *Call Me Mister*, which opened on April 18, 1946, was produced by actor Melvyn Douglas and Herman Levin, with songs by Harold Rome. "The program bills no stars," wrote the *Meriden Record*, "but Betty Garrett and Jules Munshin are topnotchers at comedy.…[Scholl's] minor notes are unforgettable with their hint of tragedy." The production's big song was "South America, Take It Away," which made Garrett a star. Scholl did "Along with Me" (with Paula Bane) and "His Old Man," which Lee Evans called a "pensive ditty [sung] over the crib of his infant son." Evans called Scholl "an effective sentimentalist."

By the end of '46, Scholl was getting offers from Hollywood studios. When *Motion Picture* magazine polled its readers on the country's top singers, Scholl placed seventh on the resultant top ten list. "Yeah, I had to think twice, too," wrote columnist Jack O'Brian, "and I'd seen him in a show, *Call Me Mister*....He won his curiously high place on the list despite never having had a radio show or picture credit." Well, he was guesting on radio, for instance *Hollywood Jackpot*. In a peculiar decision for someone currently co-starring in a hit Broadway show, he appeared as a contestant on *Arthur Godfrey's Talent Scouts* (August 25, 1947) singing "Time After Time." The winner of each show was determined via an audience applause meter. He won and appeared on Godfrey's morning radio program on September 1.

Call Me Mister closed on January 10, 1948, after more than 700 performances. The handsome and husky 6'4" Scholl was tested by 20th Century–Fox as a possible replacement for Dick Haymes in their musicals and at Paramount for a spot in a Bing Crosby movie, but nothing happened. He later told columnist John Rosenburg,

> I starved out there [Hollywood] for a year and a half, just begging for a chance. It was like yelling at the moon. Everyone gave me the brush-off and the same line: "Get a name for yourself."
>
> They don't care about talent. All they judge anyone by is his press clippings. I spent all the money I had saved; exhausted my unemployment insurance, and then worked part-time in the Los Angeles post office so I could eat.
>
> Every studio I went to told me the same thing. "Sure, you did a fine job in *Mister*, but the show's closed now and you can't make a name for yourself in one show even if it is a hit."

"Danny Scholl, out of the Broadway show *Call Me Mister*, has been signed for an Arthur Freed musical at MGM," reported the *Los Angeles Daily News*' Darr Smith. "Betty Garrett, out of the same show, was signed by Metro some months ago and her great talents have been allowed to lie fallow." There was no Freed musical forthcoming. Danny played the Bombay in Palm Springs and the Bar of Music; did the radio show *Piano Portraits* with Annette Warren; and unsuccessfully tested at Columbia for a part in *Anna Lucasta* (1949) with Paulette Goddard.

During late 1948 and early '49, Scholl was seen around town with 22-year-old MGM starlet Janet Leigh—more of a publicity combo than a serious romance. But it indirectly led to a life-changing incident in February 1949:

> **Harrison Carroll:** Little Janet Leigh, MGM star, just missed a terrifying experience. Singer Danny Scholl took her to a movie and then to Sherry's for a midnight snack. After he drove her home, he was held up in Cahuenga Pass by three men. When he put up a fight, they beat him brutally. His lips are swollen and his head is bandaged like a mummy's. Pretty tough for a guy who is supposed to go on every night at the Bar of Night.
>
> **Sheilah Graham:** The money clip given by Janet Leigh to Danny Scholl was among the articles stolen when Danny was robbed and beaten a few nights ago. Danny says that is what hurts the most. The boy is being gallant—he really took a beating.
>
> **Jack Lait, Jr.:** The thugs who beat and robbed filmtown singer Danny Scholl recently knew what they were doing. Danny had just been paid for the week.
>
> **Sheilah Graham:** Janet Leigh stopping by at the *Tongue in Cheek* rehearsals, to say hello to Star Danny Scholl. Danny is still in bandages from the beating he took from hoodlums recently. He says he will be all right for the play's opening.

The revue *Tongue in Cheek* opened at the Las Palmas Theater on March 21, 1949. In addition to Scholl (who sang "Girl in the Window"), the cast included Ross Hunter (who co-produced), Frances Irvin, Sandra Gould and Peter Marshall. The songs were written by Earl Brent. Scholl left the cast in April (replaced by Warde Donovan) and the show continued on into the summer.

Janet Leigh and Scholl at the West Coast premiere of *The Stratton Story* (1948) at the Egyptian Theatre.

Producer Joe Pasternak saw *Tongue in Cheek* and offered Scholl a part in the MGM musical *Nancy Goes to Rio* with Jane Powell. Filming took place between mid–June and early August 1949. Pasternak thought he looked too young for co-star Ann Sothern and ordered him to wear a mustache and sideburns in their big production number, "Time and Time Again." He was to have a bigger part and another number but, as he later told Marie Mesmer, "practically everything I said in the picture landed on the cutting room floor. I really wasn't ready to make a movie. I had just gotten out of the Army and emotionally and mentally I was still 'GI.' When Joe Pasternak said I needed more experience, I know the guy was right."

That October he was on the 15-minute television program *Mohawk Showroom* (starring Roberta Quinlan), and accepted the romantic lead in the Johnny Mercer-Robert Dolan Broadway musical *Texas, Li'l Darlin'.* It premiered on November 25, 1949, at the Mark Hellinger Theater, which was owned and operated by *Texas'* producer Anthony Brady Farrell. Kenny Delmar (known for his Senator Beauregard Claghorn on Fred Allen's radio show) was the main star, with Mary Hatcher as Scholl's love interest. Scholl's numbers were "A Month of Sundays" (with Hatcher), "Hootin' Owl Trail," "The Big Movie Show in the Sky," "Horseshoes Are Lucky" and "It's Good to Be

Scholl and Ann Sothern in the big production number "Time and Time Again" from *Nancy Goes to Rio* (1950). Since Danny looked too young for Sothern, he had to wear a mustache and sideburns.

Alive." The book, a political satire by John Whedon and Sam Moore, was considered the show's weakest element. It ran a modest 293 performances, closing on September 9, 1950. Scholl was praised for his good singing and "comedy sense" (UP's Jack Gaver). Mercer regarded it as one of his favorite shows.

During the run, Scholl performed on radio (*Theatre Guild of the Air*) and did the midnight show at the Shelburne Lounge. At the end of 1949, he received a special scroll from the Sister Kenny Foundation for his fundraising efforts.

In 1950, he signed a contract with National Records and waxed his first commercial songs, "Open, Parachute!" and "Our Love Story." The former came about when Scholl told songwriters Buddy Kaye, Ralph Care and Bill Harrington that he had to bail out of a "blazing plane" in the South Pacific. Columnist Inez Gerhard quoted him as saying, "I prayed, and I guess the good Lord made that parachute open."

There was talk again of movie offers, but Scholl was not eager to accept due to his previous Hollywood experiences. "So far," he told John Rosenburg, "the dollar signs haven't been big enough, nor have they offered me a role....I've adopted the attitude that if they want me, they can come and get me. And to get me, they'll have to make a pretty fair offer."

Scholl acted as host of the daytime TV series *Make Me Sing It* and *Wishbone Party*, and guested on *The Morey Amsterdam Show, Star Time, Talent Parade, Meet Buddy Rogers, The Ed Sullivan Show* and *The Steve Allen Show*. He also appeared in *Musical Comedy*

Time's adaptation of "No! No! Nanette" with Jackie Gleason and Ann Crowley; one of its highlights was Scholl's duet with Crowley, "I've Confessed to the Breeze (I Love You)."

In 1946, comedian Bobby Clark starred in the short-lived Broadway show *The Would-Be Gentleman*, which he had adapted from Molière's *Le Bourgeois Gentilhomme*. The show came to TV on the February 18, 1951, *Colgate Comedy Hour* with a cast that included Clark, Basil Rathbone, Sarah Churchill, Walter Abel, Mary Boland, Fran Warren and Scholl. The *Boston Globe*'s R.F. McPartlin: "*The Would-Be Gentleman*, a farce with music, combining the wit of Molière with gags from Broadway, may have baffled some television viewers last evening when it was presented.... Nevertheless, the program deserves to be listed with the better productions of the season."

From July 9 to 22, 1951, at Dallas' Fair Park Auditorium, Scholl revisited *Texas, Li'l Darlin'* with Jack Carson, Susan Johnson and (from the original) Fredd Wayne.

Touted as a rising star (again), he got a recording contract with RCA Victor, and his "Shrimp Boats" was a minor hit. "Scholl at 28 is still young," wrote Stewart George. "And youth together with the unaffected delivery displayed in his version of 'Shrimp Boats,' won't hurt his career a bit." Hunt Ryan of the *Baltimore Sun*: "[There's] more to his voice than most of the fellows who put forth tunes of the moonlight-and-romance type. He is not just a crooner. There is quality in his tones, and the smoothness is not too cloying."

At the beginning of '52, Scholl took over Lindy Doherty's role as Judy Lynn's love interest in Broadway's *Top Banana* starring Phil Silvers and Rose Marie. In February, WNEW disc jockey Martin Block named Scholl as the most promising singer of 1952. When *Top Banana* went on tour, Silvers, Scholl, Lynn, Kaye Ballard (replacing Rose Marie) and Johnny Coy went with it.

In 1953, he tested for the role of Curly (opposite Florence Henderson as Laurey) in the screen version of *Oklahoma!* "It looks pretty good for me," he told Marie Mesmer, "unless they decide on a bigger name." They did; the part went to Gordon MacRae.

The last stop on the *Top Banana* tour was Los Angeles' Biltmore Theatre. Marie Mesmer wrote on June 16, 1953, "

> Danny Scholl is tall, dark and good looking. And Danny also has a dandy voice which should take him places. And he's the featured male singer in *Top Banana*....
>
> But the real news, girls, is that Danny is not married—and gives

"Danny Scholl, singing star of the new movie *Top Banana* [1954], which comes to Boston on February 22, is seen here with orchestra leader Abbey Albert, who is currently holding forth at the Hotel Stadler in Boston."

every appearance of being footloose and fancy free. The bobbysoxers have already spotted him and nightly they gather at the Biltmore backstage for just a glimpse and an autograph.

The following month, Scholl was in the cast of a 3-D color film version of *Top Banana* made by the Broadway producers. It was filmed in a week as a play on a specially constructed proscenium stage at Hollywood's Motion Picture Center Studios. When interest in the tri-dimensional process waned, it was released flat.

In March 1954, Scholl told William Collins of the *Cincinnati Enquirer* that he had signed for a regular role on TV's *Your Show of Shows* ("next season"), he would be at the St. Louis Municipal Opera that summer and he would marry in September. The bride-to-be was Elise Weber, New York socialite. "She can cook and sew, and that's important for me," Danny said. "I bet her $5 she couldn't turn out a chocolate cake. Just before I left New York last week, she baked the most delicious one I've ever tasted." He also claimed he had become a "private eye on the side": a partner in a firm called Certified Detective Agency on Long Island, New York. "We've got cars equipped with telephones. I had to pass tests—shooting and so on. It's a sideline." Newspaper writers really had to like Scholl to print such baloney. As for the marriage, Miss Weber was never mentioned again; she faded from his imagination as quickly as he had conjured her up. And *Your Show of Shows* didn't see a "next season."

He did appear at the St. Louis Muny Opera in *Panama Hattie* (with Mary McCarty and Martha Stewart) the week of July 26, 1954, and in *Where's Charley?* (with Gil Lamb and Martha Stewart) starting on August 2. During these two engagements, he was on the local radio program *Summer in St. Louis* with soprano Betty Winsett.

In late August, Scholl was dropped from Betty Hutton's upcoming TV special *Satins and Spurs*. The absurd reason, according to Earl Wilson: He was "too tall and too handsome." He started 1955 with *Max Liebman Presents*, which featured a jazz version of the comic opera *H.M.S. Pinafore*. Desperate for work, he even went on Dennis James' talent show *Chance of a Lifetime*, where he won a thousand dollars. On TV's *Omnibus* (March 6, 1955), he starred in William Schuman's original opera *The Mighty Casey* (based on "Casey at the Bat").

In June 1955, Scholl had a two-week run in *Oklahoma!* at the Fox Valley Playhouse in St. Charles, Illinois. His Laurey was Sybil Lamb, and Ado Annie was played by a young Lee Remick. Claudia Cassidy of the *Chicago Tribune* wrote,

> I always did like *Oklahoma!* The Fox Valley version is pint size, of course, with the Rodgers score cut down for about nine strings… [T]he production is fresh, it moves briskly, and once you get out of the realm of Agnes de Mille, it has its share of spirit and charm.
>
> It has several pieces of genuine casting luck. Danny Scholl's Curly is a big, personable fellow whose good baritone pours the cream of the Rodgers and Hammerstein songs.

At the same venue in July, Scholl starred in *Show Boat* with Carol Bruce, Etta Moten and Brock Peters. Near the end of '55, he joined the headed-for-Broadway musical-comedy *Delilah* starring Carol Channing. When he was replaced in previews by Robert Rippy, Scholl sued the producers for $100,000 since he had done several auditions to raise money for the show. The title was changed to *The Vamp* during its short New York run.

He kept busy singing on local TV shows, recorded for Unique, continued to do nightclubs, and had a supporting role in *Producers' Showcase's* "Bloomer Girl" (1956). On June 16, 1956, his uncle Andrew Rub, 74, who with his wife raised Scholl, was

On the March 6, 1955, TV series *Omnibus*, Scholl starred as "The Mighty Casey," William Schuman's original opera adapted from "Casey at the Bat."

killed. He had been inspecting the front of his parked truck when it was hit from behind. The *Cincinnati Enquirer*: "The impact of the rear-end collision turned his vehicle completely around and threw him to the sidewalk." Suffering leg, ankle and rib fractures and a head injury, he died at the hospital. Earl Wilson wrote, "Singer Danny Scholl's under medical care after his father's accidental death in Cincinnati." It was a typo, but it said much about how Danny felt about Andrew Rub, the only father he had ever really known. Mrs. Rub went to live with Danny. He had been set to star with Mary McCarty in *Annie Get Your Gun* at the Boston Music Festival, but because of his uncle's death, he bowed out and Wilton Clary took his place.

In 1957, he performed at the Riviera in Las Vegas and tested for the role of Lt. Cable in the movie version of *South Pacific*. (The part went to non-singer John Kerr, who had to be dubbed.) He also did a *Frankie and Johnny* album for MGM with Mary Mayo; played in *Damn Yankees* at the St. Louis Muny Opera; brought *Texas, Li'l Darlin'* into Dallas for two weeks with Jack Carson, and starred in *The Pajama Game* at the Westchester Music Theater in Rye, New York.

But then he had trouble finding work. Jack Paar came to the rescue, booking him more than 40 times on his *Tonight Show*. "Jack is such a wonderful person," Scholl told

Earl Wilson. "He is one performer who likes to give another guy a break." His work with Paar got Scholl a recording contract with Decca. In the summer of 1958, he did *Roberta* in Palm Beach with Marion Marlowe and in St. Louis with Bob Hope (who was reprising his character from the original 1933 Broadway show). Scholl became good friends with Hope and his family. Hope grew up in Cincinnati, so he and Danny had that in common. In Dayton, Scholl was again in *Roberta* and followed that up with productions of *The Pajama Game* with Betty Jane Watson and *Damn Yankees* with Albert Dekker and Cathryn Damon.

On November 27, 1958, Scholl was in rehearsals for a Paar episode when he collapsed and was sent to New York's Roosevelt Hospital. The stroke paralyzed part of his left side. By January '59, he was able to walk with a cane and was on his way to recovery. In April, it was reported that he would tour with Betty Hutton in *Annie Get Your Gun*, but it didn't happen.

Scholl was back in action in August as *Li'l Abner* at the Lyric Circus in Ithaca, New York. *Philadelphia Inquirer* columnist Burt Boyar made a perplexing comment in September: "Jack Paar's Hate Parade includes comedian Danny Scholl who was paralyzed on the star's TV show."

While Scholl didn't tour in *Annie Get Your Gun* with Hutton, he did star in a five-week production at the Paper Mill Playhouse in Millburn, New Jersey, starting on November 3, with Helena Seymour. The *Bergen Evening Record* said he "matches his 6 foot 4 frame with a clear, sweet, free-flowing baritone voice of far-reaching proportions, and he looked every inch one's image of a Frank Butler."

On April 18, 1960, Scholl made his dramatic acting debut on TV's *The Texan*. The episode, "The Nomad," was written by the series' star, Rory Calhoun. "It's really a good role for an actor," Scholl told columnist Luke Feck. "I get to do just about everything, even with my bum leg....I had to use crutches and a cane for a while. Now I get along with just a leg brace, and I'll be done with that before long." This interview was the first to add a Jeep to the narrative about Scholl's injuries: "Danny's leg was paralyzed by a case of muscular neuritis last November," wrote Feck. "When he was in the Army, a Jeep overturned and pinned his leg. It didn't bother him until a Thanksgiving night rehearsal for *The Jack Paar Show*."

Scholl also told Feck, "There are four producers who have series lined up for this fall, and they all have me in mind. I'm looking for the right one." He must not have found it. One project mentioned was *The Wedded Blisses*, a domestic comedy series with Lita Baron (Rory Calhoun's wife). Sheilah Graham asserted that Danny and Lucille Ball were dating, but if anything, she only wanted him to audition for her upcoming Broadway show *Wildcat*. Meanwhile, Scholl toured in *Girl Crazy* (1960) with Christine Norden and Harvey Lembeck. This updating of the Gershwin musical did not meet with critical approval.

Scholl was romantically linked with British-born actress-singer Norden, who was about to divorce her fourth husband. Columnists speculated that Danny would be her fifth ride on the marriage-go-round. On December 26, 1960, the *New York Daily News*' Charles McHarry reported some downtown doings:

> Cigar-smoking Christine Norden, who plays the madam in *Tenderloin* [a 1960 Broadway play], wasn't keeping very good order in the house the other night, but then it wasn't her house. The place was Ralph's, a theatrical hangout, and the disorder centered around Danny Scholl and [dancer] Ron Stratton.... They started slugging each other over Christine's favors

and both got mussed up a bit before being separated by other guests. Christine, declining to take sides, puffed a stogie during the fracas and later exited with a third guy.

Betty Hutton was slated to appear in *Calamity Jane*, a new stage musical based on the Doris Day-Howard Keel 1953 movie, with Scholl as Wild Bill Hickok. Again, she bowed out. Deedy Irwin was enlisted to take her place, but vacated the role due to illness. Betty O'Neill ended up playing Jane to Scholl's Wild Bill. The premiere took place on May 27, 1961, at Fort Worth, Texas' Casa Mañana. The score featured all the Sammy Fain-Paul Francis Webster songs from the movie (including their Oscar-winning "Secret Love") plus new ones by the songwriters. Columnist Elston Brooks of the *Fort Worth Star Telegram* liked the whole cast, but thought Scholl's "baritone is the best voice in the house, and especially fine on 'Higher Than a Hawk' and 'Adelaide.'" With his performance of the former tune, the *Shreveport Times'* Pericles Alexander wrote that Scholl "brings glory to himself."

After the show closed on June 17, Scholl went to Denver for two weeks in *Carousel*. He told Fort Worth reporters that he had spent "several weeks in Hollywood, where he filmed a TV episode for *Westinghouse Playhouse*, which was written especially for him by award-winning Rod Serling" (*Fort Worth Star Telegram*)—although no such thing happened. From July 31 to August 12, he co-starred with Don Wilson in *Texas, Li'l Darlin'* at the Casa Mañana. According to reviewer Sydney Rose, Scholl "just about stole the show. He was remarkably good as a slow-thinking, drawling Texan, with an excellent singing voice." Scholl implied to Elston Brooks that when he was finished with *Texas, Li'l Darlin,'* he was going back to Hollywood to *star* in the new *Dr. Kildare* series with Raymond Massey, and that he had also gotten a part in a new Fox movie. More bushwa.

Polish designer Princess Marusia Toumanoff was seen frequently with Scholl. In 1961, she opened the Peppermint West dance club in Hollywood, and Danny was a manager. It wouldn't last long.

"All you guys and dolls who enjoyed the singing and acting of Danny Scholl ... might drop him a line," wrote E.B. Radcliffe in July 1962. "He is in Veterans Hospital, Dayton, Ohio. Been battling pneumonia and paralysis. Two guys who worked with him in movies and TV didn't forget. Danny's recent phone callers were Rory Calhoun and Bob Hope."

By October '62, Scholl had undergone three operations. On February 12, 1963, he was seen in a supporting role in the *Dick Powell Show* episode "Luxury Liner" with his friend Rory Calhoun. By February 17, he was back in the hospital, unable to move his right leg or arm. In May, he was recuperating from phlebitis, inflammation of a vein in his leg. Despite all this, he was on *The Dick Van Dyke Show*'s November 27 episode "The Ballad of the Betty Lou," playing a sailor.

In 1964, the *Cincinnati Enquirer*'s E.B. Radcliffe related all that Scholl had recently endured:

> He has survived a long-odds, two-year battle for life; one that included a brain and two abdominal operations; a lung collapse, and temporary total paralysis of one arm and one leg.
> Danny was 6 feet 4, weighed 215 (not fat), and was going strong in New York when he collapsed suddenly from a clot on the brain a couple of years ago. He is still 6 feet 4; back up to 180 (he was down to 150). The lung hasn't recovered completely, and he has to wear braces below the knee of both legs.
> Nevertheless, he is back in there pitching in the entertainment world.

Scholl told Radcliffe that he was planning a variety series and TV guest shots, and was at work promoting a song he had published, "October," written by former silent screen actress Corinne Griffith. "I tire easily, but I feel I'm getting my strength back. And I take nine pills a day to keep my blood thin."

Scholl told Eve Starr that friends such as Griffith, Calhoun and Hope kept his spirits up. "It was the prayers of all these people that really brought me through. Look, I've knocked around a lot in my life and thought people were corny or something with this prayer stuff, but now I'm sincere when I say there must be something to that business. My whole outlook has changed."

His mouth was partially paralyzed, and doctors told him he would never sing again—but he defied them: "Lying in my hospital bed, I rolled marbles around in my mouth, squeezed a rubber ball in my hand and prayed to God," he told Carole Valentine. "I promised God that if He restored my speech, I would spend my life lecturing, entertaining and encouraging the handicapped."

He added, "I said to God, if He would restore my voice, I would devote my life to aiding those in my own condition." God did do some fix-up on his voice, and Scholl sang on local TV and radio shows.

On February 17, 1965, Scholl's life took a bizarre detour when he became the fourth husband of wealthy Corinne Griffith, 27 years his senior. Louella Parsons told her readers:

> You could have knocked me over with the postage stamp when the card arrived announcing the marriage of Corinne Griffith to musical comedy singer Danny Scholl. Seems the happy event took place in Alexandria, Virginia. Since then, the newlyweds have been in Washington, D.C., being wined and dined. Corinne used to be a queen bee of Washington....
>
> Scholl ... made medical history when he was pronounced dead on five occasions only to come back to life. *Ben Casey* is doing a TV show based on his astounding experience.

The world still awaits that *Ben Casey* episode.

In March, Griffith told reporters that Scholl had left her to move in with Rory Calhoun and his wife. "He hasn't been feeling well," she said. "He's had [three] brain operations—and he hasn't been well lately."

He and Rory went into the catering business at Marina del Rey, but Scholl also wanted to continue singing. He was presented by Calhoun on an episode of *Hollywood Talent Scouts*, and his valiant performance was a highlight. Unfortunately, his condition was worsening and his chances of reactivating his career were getting slim.

In December '65, he and Griffith went to court to end their 35-day marriage. Although Scholl explained that he had undergone three brain operations and was still partially paralyzed, Griffith complained that he "failed to fulfill his promise of being a loving and affectionate husband." Scholl said he had been existing on $120 a month in disability insurance. Griffith was ordered to pay his attorney and court fees and $200 a month in support. The case went before a Superior Court the following year, a humiliating and stressful eight-day experience for Scholl when Griffith accused him of being impotent. At one point, Scholl started to have convulsions, crying, trembling and slapping the witness stand for about ten minutes. He was helped into another room to lie down.

The proceedings took another weird turn when Scholl's attorney accused Griffith of falsifying her age at the time of the marriage. Even weirder, she denied *being* silent screen actress Corinne Griffith, claiming she was actually Griffith's stand-in and that she had taken Griffith's place and name upon the famous star's death. "I don't know my age," she remarked. "I don't give my age because it's part of my religion." Her claim of not being Griffith was shot down by a 74-year-old friend from childhood and actresses Betty Blythe and Claire Windsor.

Scholl said that Griffith expected him to be her bodyguard and that she had asked him to beat up a columnist who printed their ages. "I told her that, with clamps in my brain, I couldn't afford to get into any free-for-alls."

When the dust settled, Griffith was awarded a divorce. The judge said that he didn't feel either was "misled in the marriage and their treatment of each other was not conductive to amorous activity." Scholl's request for $1000 a month in alimony was denied. The marriage that began on a Valentine's Day ended on a Friday the 13th.

In September and October, he suffered both a stroke and a heart attack and developed a blood clot in his right leg. He spent months at Sawtelle Veterans Hospital. When he was well enough, a still partially paralyzed Scholl moved back to Ohio to be near his family. There, he was hired by state auditor Roger Cloud as a public relations representative; he gave speeches about his health struggles, lectured about the "Power of Prayer and Guts," and also sang for civic and fraternal organizations. He recorded his theme song, "No Man Is an Island," and all royalties went to organizations helping the handicapped. Visiting other disabled persons in hospitals, he encouraged them to overcome their troubles. "Never give up. Never be discouraged," he said.

He also claimed that as a "singing soldier," he was on Iwo Jima and "singlehandedly captured seven enemy soldiers and in the process sustained a broken spine" and two curvatures of the spine, after crashing the Jeep he was using to deliver the prisoners. (Crowded Jeep! No wonder it crashed.) In 1972, the *San Francisco Examiner*'s Dick Alexander went into more detail in an interview with Scholl, although it didn't follow the standard story the singer had been peddling:

Dissolve to Iwo Jima—1945.
On Mount Suribachi he went into a cave looking for souvenirs but found instead eight starving Japanese soldiers. On a narrow mountain road, he tied his prisoners to a Jeep, lost his footing and fell over the hillside, impinging the nerve in his spine.
Found by some Seabees, he was taken to a hospital at Hickam Field, Hawaii, and eventually discharged in "pretty good shape."

Scholl claimed that doctors traced his later strokes to his wartime injury. There is no evidence to support his stories that he suffered a back injury in the war. More likely his problems started with the 1949 beating.

Scholl served as special events chairman for the local National Foundation–March of Dimes campaign. He appeared multiple times on Bob Braun's TV show and was Ronald Reagan's official campaign singer when he ran for governor of California. The Footlighters, a community theater group, gave him the opportunity to direct musicals.

On April 23, 1970, Scholl was named Handicapped American of the Year by the President's Committee on Employment of the Handicapped. "I believe that God let me live for a reason, and that reason is to help somebody else."

Scholl was one of the final guests on *Life with Linkletter*, his episode airing September 14, 1970. "Art broke down in tears when I finished singing," Scholl told the *Cincinnati Enquirer* of the show's (August 25) taping. "The audience would not stop applauding and then I broke down, too. We both stood there and could not continue. Art's such a wonderful guy! He treated me royally."

Then–vice-president Spiro Agnew (right) gives Danny the Handicapped American of the Year Award in Washington, D.C., on April 23, 1970.

Throughout the '70s, Scholl appeared on local TV and radio and continued to lecture and sing around Ohio. Aunt Louisa, who had stood by Danny through the years, passed away on June 30, 1971. Her obit called her "beloved mother of Danny Scholl." For a short while, he lived in California. Back in Cincinnati in 1973, he was named deputy sheriff in charge of youth resources in Hamilton County. At the end of that year, he was one of five men on the Blue Ribbon Committee for the aid of the handicapped, and represented the Midwest area. Scholl's old friend President Richard Nixon wrote him: "I have just learned that you are honored by your fellow Ohioans for your patriotism and love of God and country. From all reports, the reward given you was indeed well deserved and I just wanted to add my heartiest congratulations to the many you have already received."

In 1974, he sang the song "Thanks America" in the Ted V. Mikels–directed *Alex Joseph and His Wives*, the true story of a polygamist (playing himself) who founded his own southern Utah town. That same year, he appeared in the Cotton Follies production *Hooray for Hollywood*, singing his anthem "No Man Is an Island." The annual Cotton Follies benefited the Redwood School and Rehabilitation Center for those with cerebral palsy. Scholl was the director of the Vince Lombardi National Youth Football League for eight- to 16-year-olds.

A movie on Scholl's life was being planned, he said, and he claimed that Alan Alda would portray him. News to Alda! The *Cincinnati Enquirer* quoted him as saying, "I have not seen a script or any written outline about such a project. I can't consider it at this time ... I just don't have the time for any movies."

In 1976, Scholl guested on TV's *The Hour of Power* hosted by Reverend Robert H. Schuller. His singing got a standing ovation. At the Veterans of Foreign Wars Convention in New York, he was given the Gold Medal Award for his patriotism and "spirit of great accomplishment." A local Ohio TV special, *An Evening with Danny Scholl*, aired on Christmas Eve 1977, and his next, *With a Song in My Heart*, ran the following summer. His appearance on the syndicated TV series *To Tell the Truth* (January 10, 1978) had him as one of the mystery challengers. Scholl was the notable and two other guys "impersonated" him.

While Scholl was in California, another stroke laid him low on January 4, 1979; both legs and his left arm were paralyzed. When he was transferred from Sepulveda's Veterans Administration Hospital to the Wadsworth Veterans Hospital in L.A., he claimed to be leaving behind more than 7000 get-well cards and letters. In mid–April, he was moved to a Cincinnati veterans hospital, and thence to a Fort Thomas, Kentucky, nursing home. The wheelchair-bound Scholl's speech improved and he began to contemplate performing again. "I was on the Bob Braun television show the other day," he told the *Dayton Daily News* in September, "and when I saw those women [in the audience] in tears, I broke. It wasn't just that, but when they played my record, I was thinking, 'Will I be able to sing like that again?'" The idea of a Scholl biopic was mentioned again (although probably only by Scholl); this time around, it would star Chad Everett. This was probably news to Chad too.

By 1983, he had regained his singing voice and recorded the album *No Man Is an Island* for Rayvel Records. He also traveled around in a specially equipped van to make personal appearances. A party for Scholl was planned for July 3 at Beverly Hills' Wilshire Ebell Theatre; the guest list included Milton Berle, Janet Leigh, Ed Asner, Bob Hope and Loretta Young. "I'm more alive than I have ever been," he told Alice Hornbaker. "My appearance there will prove it." The show, he said, would reaffirm to people that if you believe and work hard, you can overcome handicaps:

> I've got 14 clamps in my brain; suffered four strokes and lived through a cancer operation two years ago on my throat. Each time doctors wrote me off. Said I couldn't walk or talk again. Well, I'm talking. I'm singing. And maybe someday I'll walk again, too. But I'm definitely back. This month on Bob Braun's television show I sang again, too; live—for the first time in four years.

On Thursday, June 16, 1983, Scholl and his friend and personal aide Richard Eyerman returned home around 12:30 p.m. and Eyerman began lowering the van's wheelchair ramp. Somehow Scholl's wheelchair tipped backwards and he fell on the concrete and hit his head.

Doctors told Scholl's brother that Danny wouldn't live past Friday night. "We're just hoping that he can snap out of it and regain consciousness," Eyerman said. "Doctors last night [Friday] didn't give him half the night to live. But he's made it."

Four days later, on Tuesday, June 21, 1983, the 61-year-old died at Cincinnati Veterans Hospital. He is interred at Rest Haven Memorial Park in Evendale, Ohio.

In 1993, Cincinnati's Xavier University began awarding a Danny Scholl Memorial Music Scholarship.

After's Scholl's death, his friend Jeanne M. Stophlet, National President of the Service Star Legion, wrote the *Cincinnati Enquirer*:

As a friend who was with him on many of his struggles, I know that we of Greater Cincinnati and across the nation can learn many things from Danny's life. He was a giving and caring human being and, time after time, he would step or wheel forward to someone's cause. "No Man Is an Island," and Danny really lived that song. He loved people and he had friends from all walks of life.

In 1979, with his last stroke, he was housed at Fort Thomas Veterans Administration Hospital, and he brought a very special something to the patients as he touched their lives. We placed a star on his hospital door.... And, although he was touched by the gesture, he reminded us with a friendly voice that all veterans are stars.

I was there as he struggled to walk, as he struggled to speak and, oh, how he struggled to sing. A man who stood tall, now was surrounded by this iron machine they call a wheelchair. This was the way my friend would come on stage, still smiling, still giving of himself; and, thanks to God, he sang again live on stage.

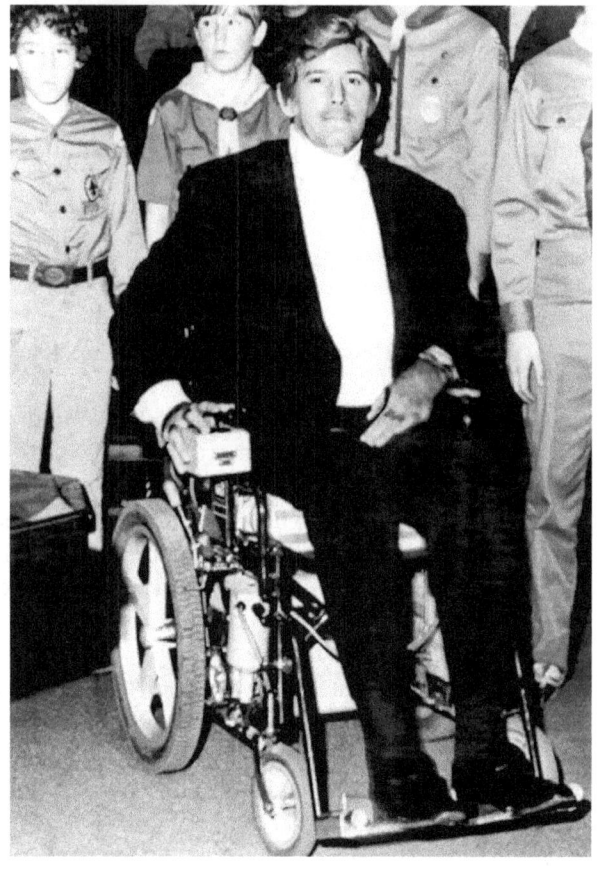

The wheelchair-bound Scholl near the end of his life.

Danny loved his flag and loved his country and, oh, how he loved people. The stage is quiet now and lights have gone off on Danny, center stage. But he lives on in our hearts. He lives on in his music. His records are the strength of his struggle, his faith in God and his hope for the tomorrow. Thanks, America, for our star that shone so brightly.

1944: *Winged Victory* (uncredited).
1950: *Nancy Goes to Rio* (uncredited).
1954: *Top Banana*.
1977: *Alex Joseph and His Wives* (voice).

LAWRENCE TIERNEY

In the February 1952 *Modern Screen* article "Hollywood's Most Tragic People," Louella Parsons wrote, "I do not consider that Lawrence Tierney [is the responsibility] of Hollywood. Poor Tierney, an emotionally ill boy, would be his own worst enemy in any walk of life, anywhere." Called the *enfant terrible* of the screen, Tierney soared to fame in 1945 by playing gangster John Dillinger in a movie. The role fit the actor like a pair of custom-made brass knuckles. This casting was apt considering Tierney's multiple scrapes with the law; he was eventually arrested in real life more times than the real Dillinger, Public Enemy #1.

In 1947, Tierney also made an impression in the classic *films noir Born to Kill* and *The Devil Thumbs a Ride*, portraying hard-core killers without consciences. His tough acting had a ring of authenticity; his steely-eyed verve, good looks and charisma made everything he did believable. His screen success, however, was hampered by personal demons hyper-fueled by a volatile mix of alcohol and blind rage. Tierney had many chances to climb higher on the Hollywood ladder, but these opportunities were all washed away. Hedda Hopper remarked in 1950, "Lawrence Tierney might well have turned into another Burt Lancaster if he'd joined Alcoholics Anonymous in time."

The eldest son of Irish-Americans Lawrence Hugh Tierney and Marion "Mary" Alice Crowley, Lawrence James Tierney was born in Brooklyn on March 15, 1919. Both his brothers became actors: Gerard, better known as Scott Brady (1924–85), had the best Hollywood career of the three; Edward (1928–83) had the briefest

Despite Lawrence Tierney's numerous brushes with the law, he was a very well-read, intelligent man and a good actor.

245

run. When Lawrence Sr. was young, "he was an artist and traveling salesman," says his grandson Tim Tierney. "Later, through family connections, he was appointed to be commissioner of the Aqueduct Police and turned out to be very capable in that role, especially during World War II."

As a child, Larry was influenced by his maternal grandfather Timothy Francis Crowley, a "a real tough guy who taught Larry how to fight." In 2011, Larry's nephew Michael Tierney (Edward's son) told Gary Sweeney,

> I sometimes say that Scott and Eddie were more Tierneys and Larry was more of a Crowley. Because it seems like the madness comes from the Crowley side: our grandmother, Mary Alice Crowley, the daughter of Timothy Crowley. A lot of the alcoholism seems to come from that side of the family, a lot of the violence, whereas I see that Lawrence Hugh Tierney, our grandfather, and Scott and Eddie seem to be a little more stable and consistent.

On October 1, 1939, 68-year-old Timothy died from injuries sustained in a bar fight.

In high school, Larry won awards for track and field. He entered Manhattan College on an athletic scholarship; dropping out two years later, he used his father's connections to land a job as a laborer on the New York Aqueduct. (In his last film, 1999's *Evicted*, Tierney ad-libbed some dialogue about working on an aqueduct as a young man.) His other jobs included catalogue model for Sears, Roebuck.

Larry began acting with the New Rochelle, Blackfriars and American-Irish theater groups. After his opening night performance with the latter in the play *War Wife*, its author, Father Will Whalen, took the stage and, referring to Tierney, announced to the audience, "Tomorrow, I want all movie scouts to come here. We have Errol Flynn, years younger and without a yacht."

Eventually, Tierney *was* spotted by a scout. Signed by RKO in 1943, he started out with uncredited parts in *Gildersleeve on Broadway*, *Government Girl*, *The Falcon Out West* and *Seven Days Ashore*. He also went unbilled in producer Val Lewton's melodrama *The Ghost Ship* but appeared in the movie's most unforgettable scene: After getting on the wrong side of a ship's megalomaniac captain (Richard Dix), sailor Louie (Tierney) is accidentally(?) sealed in the anchor chain locker by the captain, and crushed to death when the enormous links of the chain pour back into it. (The captain, getting a glimpse of what must be the crushed-to-a-pulp body, casually orders a subordinate, "Better get a coupla men down here and get that cleaned up…")

Tierney got on-screen billing for the first time when he played a supporting role in Lewton's *Youth Runs Wild* (1944). The screenplay by John Fante, about unsupervised children running amok during wartime, was ostensibly based on a *Look* magazine photo essay, "Are These Our Children?" Lewton was not happy with the slant demanded by RKO: They wanted exploitation, "appealing only to the sensational," and nothing more, while Lewton sought realism, seeing this as an opportunity to make a serious statement about a social issue. The March 29, 1944, test screening went poorly. The movie was now subjected to extensive reshooting and editing and whole subplots were eliminated.

Essaying his first substantial film role, Tierney is a standout, seething with seamy charm. He hangs around the neighborhood leading local lambs astray. In an interview, he recalled that his character peddled drugs, although that plot element didn't make it into the final cut. It's to Tierney's credit that he suggests much with body language and tone of voice, giving his character an edge.

Tierney did not serve in the war. The "official" studio-released story was that he'd hurt his hand working in a shipbuilding yard. The injury was actually the result of some childhood roughhousing with brother Gerard, aka Scott Brady. Gerard's son Tim Tierney says,

> The story I got from my dad was that Larry was a rotten older brother who regularly beat him up. One day my dad was fleeing from him through the house and slammed a door behind himself with an inset window that Larry thrust his forearms through. He lacerated himself deeply enough to cause nerve damage that later rendered him 4-F for military service. Larry was very angry with Scott about being kept out of the military.

In October '44, Tierney was picked by the King Brothers (Frank and Maurice) to headline their Monogram film chronicling the life and crimes of the notorious John Dillinger (1903–34). In the belief that casting an established actor as the gangster would "destroy the illusion," the Kings were looking for an unknown. They got the newcomer from RKO for a paltry $100 a week. "He is six feet tall, 25 years old and considerably better looking than the late Dillinger," wrote Louella Parsons.

Philip Yordan's *Dillinger* screenplay, which was Oscar-nominated (surely a first and last for the King Brothers), was a mostly fictional take on the notorious bank robber. In flashbacks, we watch the rise of a two-bit thief to leader of a mob to Public Enemy #1. Tierney takes control of the screen right away, even overshadowing more experienced actors such as Edmund Lowe. He is by turns menacing, cocky and charming, the latter

John Dillinger (Tierney, far left) and his gang (left to right, Elisha Cook Jr., Edmund Lowe, Eduardo Ciannelli and Marc Lawrence) in 1945's *Dillinger*. The King Bros.–Monogram production made Tierney a star.

especially in his scenes with Anne Jeffreys who plays his eventual downfall, the Woman in Red. Tierney's physical attractiveness was key to his success in the part: Like a coiled snake, he appears "harmless" one moment and then ready to strike the next. Particularly memorable is the scene where, projecting an expressionless, seething menace, he suddenly attacks a waiter who had once refused him service. The violence (a broken beer mug to the face) is off-camera but Tierney's facial expression will chill the viewer.

Tierney's deadpan, low-key delivery gave his portrayal a quietly sinister feel; *Variety* pegged him as a "youthful Bogart." The style would serve Tierney well throughout his career, even in films in which he portrayed a good guy.

Released in March 1945, *Dillinger* was banned in Chicago; in a letter to the Production Code Administration, noted director Frank Borzage denounced *Dillinger* and asked for the "total elimination of the glamorized gangster movie." *Dillinger*, a tale "written in bullets, blood and blondes," was Monogram's first attempt at a big-budget film sold on a percentage basis. It was a major success, reaping millions, and Tierney became an overnight star. "A year ago, I was building billboards," he told Harrison Carroll. "Now my picture is on them. I guess anything can happen in Hollywood."

But stardom was a mixed blessing: He was so awesome and authentic as the Depression-era gangster that the role stuck to him—on-screen and off-. Anne Jeffreys echoed many when she laughingly stated, "Larry thought he *was* Dillinger." While she liked him, she was wary of him; she described his conduct on the set as erratic. Jeffreys told me that during one scene, she and Tierney were standing on a narrow scaffold high above the set when he looked at her menacingly and quietly said he was going to push her off. A gaffer working above heard the threat and warned him, "You do, and I'll have to drop this light on your head."

The King Brothers planned to borrow Larry again for their psychological mystery *Payment Due*, but this time RKO set his loan-out fee at $35,000. "It seems to me that Tierney's bosses might have shown a bit more gratitude to the independents who had made them a valuable property," wrote columnist Jimmie Fidler. (*Payment Due* was never made.)

It wasn't as if RKO was capitalizing on what they had. In 1945, they assigned him supporting roles in *Those Endearing Young Charms*, *Back to Bataan*, *Mama Loves Papa* and *Sing Your Way Home*.

On July 27, 1945, Tierney was charged with being drunk and disorderly (for the third time in as many months) and sentenced to ten days in jail. Even at this early stage in his career, alcohol was a real problem. In November, Jimmie Fidler wrote, "We hear that Lawrence Tierney's pals are urging him to see *The Lost Weekend*—and think about its moral." He apparently did not heed the advice.

Filmed from September to October '45, the Randolph Scott starrer *Badman's Territory* gave Tierney a thirteenth-billed role as outlaw Jesse James. He was somewhat lost in the shuffle among all the other actors playing famed Western bandits in the movie. *Badman's Territory* was one of RKO's most successful pictures of 1946.

Much better for Larry was *Step by Step*, which began shooting in December '45. In his first lead role at RKO, Tierney plays a good guy, ex–Marine Johnny Christopher, who goes on the run with secretary Evelyn Smith (Anne Jeffreys), dodging Nazi spies and also the police, who think they are killers. Tierney carries this one in fine style, cool and charming with a bit of good-natured humor; when the situation calls for it, though, he is handy with his fists. The Tierney-Jeffreys chemistry was as potent as it had been in

Dillinger, and they made a likable couple. The final waterfront brawl where Tierney goes *mano a mano* with the spies is rousing—and even Jeffreys helps a bit.

But it was nothing like the free-for-all that broke out on the night of January 18, 1946, during a party at the home of artist John Decker. The fuse was lit when William Kent, the stepson of Mocambo owner Charlie Morrison, accused Tierney of insulting his (Kent's) girlfriend. "[H]e was ill-mannered and rude," Kent told reporters, post-fight. "He said to me, 'Oh, you want to fight, huh?' and I told him, 'No, I had enough fighting during four and a half years with the R.A.F. and the U.S. Army.' …[He] waited for me outside and then jumped me." Kent's summation: "I guess he thinks he's Dillinger off the screen, too."

Tierney sang a different tune:

> Kent was insulting and obnoxious to me. He told me that "anyone who likes Errol Flynn is no good." I didn't particularly like or dislike Mr. Flynn. I just met him for the first time that night. He was at the party, too. I didn't strike Kent, but I wish I had now. Anyway, he taunted me as I was leaving the party and then he struck me. We came to grips and rolled around on the ground.

Actress Frances Robinson said that after Anthony Quinn pulled Kent off Larry, Tierney went berserk and there were flying fists galore. At one point, according to Diana Barrymore, "that perfectly awful Tierney" hit Ethel Barrymore's son Sammy Colt:

> When I saw Sammy covered with blood, I got furious. Tierney had pulled his own shirt off and was standing there like Tarzan. I went up to him and said, "You are hitting everybody so why don't you hit a woman?" Then I slapped him across the face as many times as I could [witnesses counted eight slaps]. I'm sorry it had to happen but when he hit Sammy I had to go after him.

The melee spilled out into the street. The biggest loser that night: Jack La Rue, who tried to break up the ruckus. Partygoers said he "collided with a haymaker," fell and hit his head against a parked car. Deputy sheriffs found the bloodied actor lying in Decker's driveway. Asked if alcohol had contributed to the brawl, Decker exclaimed, "Drinking? Of course, there was drinking! What kind of a party would it be without drinking?" No charges were filed. Decker referred to it as "just another party and another fight," adding, "There are always fights around here—I don't pay any attention to them anymore. Somebody's always fighting at my parties."

Anne Jeffreys co-starred with Tierney in two pictures, *Dillinger* (1945) and *Step by Step* (1946), and they complemented each other well.

On February 21, 1946, French-born bit actor–novelist Paul de Loqueyssie brought a $7600 suit against Tierney, alleging that Larry had recently attacked him in front of Vetry's Den and given him a black eye. "Mr. Tierney followed me and a young lady [Hungarian actress Hella Crossley] out from the nightclub and attempted to get into her car to obtain her address and telephone number. I tried to humor him as you would a lunatic but he became aggressive. He struck me from behind." Crossley also claimed that Larry tried to punch her dog as she and de Loqueyssie drove away. (De Loqueyssie was later awarded $600.)

On March 9, Tierney went Round 2 with William Kent at the Mocambo and he was arrested on another drunk charge. While a full-scale brawl was avoided, Larry and a bouncer scuffled before the actor was carted off to jail. Larry said he was the target of "abusive remarks" from Kent, but the latter denied that he spoke to the actor: "I'm awfully bored by that man," he remarked. Tierney was fined $100, but his 90-day sentence was suspended on the condition he report to a probation officer once a month.

Larry said he had joined Alcoholics Anonymous—a step ordered by RKO. Although RKO was profiting from his off-screen escapades, the studio bosses weren't happy about them. Jimmie Fidler came to Tierney's defense: According to Fidler, Larry was emotionally ill-equipped to handle his sudden fame:

> He was thrown into a world about which he knew nothing, except that it was loaded with glamour. His preparation for the life of a star did not include the knowledge that making motion pictures is a serious business and that its much-publicized glamour is only part of the superb salesmanship that goes into the marketing of films. He had no way of knowing that a movie star is just another citizen, with responsibilities equal to any other American.

Larry vowed to clean up his act. His father came to California to have some "heart-to-heart talks" with him. In Hollywood, a club called "The Defense of Lawrence Tierney" was formed.

The King Brothers wanted Tierney to star in *Suspense* with Belita, but when he asked for a $10,000 advance bonus, they gave Barry Sullivan the part. "[T]hey promised me a bonus when I made *Dillinger* for them," Larry told Sheilah Graham, "and I didn't ever get it." Perhaps a little miffed by the money request, Maurice King joked from the set of *Suspense*, "Lawrence Tierney has joined Alcoholics Unanimous!"

In May '46, Tierney got back in front of the camera to headline the hard-edged film noir *Born to Kill*, an adaptation of James Gunn's novel *Deadlier Than the Male*. The movie more than lived up to Bosley Crowther's *New York Times* assessment that it was "morally disgusting" and "malignant ... a cheap and unsavory tale of a hard-hearted murderer's fascination for a self-seeking divorcee." Crowther didn't mean this as a compliment, but those qualities are exactly why *Born to Kill* is considered a classic today.

Many other critics were also put off by *Born to Kill*'s cynicism and unpleasantness, but there was praise for the performers, especially Tierney, who, wrote *Variety*, "plays his role straight and to the point, writers injecting psychosis angle by touching upon his utter lack of feeling in matters of murder if anyone stands in his way." In an unforgettable scene set late at night in a kitchen, Sam Wild (Tierney) confronts Danny (Tony Barrett), the guy his girlfriend Laury (Isabel Jewell) is seeing on the side. Sam quietly warns him to leave, and Danny makes the mistake of pulling a knife. Sam's violence, beating his competition to death, and then killing Laury when she walks in, is brutal and very disturbing, setting the tone for what's to follow. As Sam's pal Mart (Elisha Cook, Jr.) tells him, "You can't just go around killing people when the notion strikes you. It's just not feasible."

Claire Trevor's Helen Brent is drawn to Tierney's dangerous Sam Wild in the *film noir* classic *Born to Kill* (1947).

Tierney and co-star Claire Trevor make a strikingly nasty couple; he marries her foster sister (Audrey Long), but he and Trevor are two unsavory peas in a pod. "You're strength, excitement and depravity," Trevor breathlessly tells him. "You've a kind of corruption inside of you, Sam." She is conflicted about linking up with her murderous brother-in-law, but takes that path toward doom. Tierney is excellent and Trevor matches him (and then some) with her riveting, complicated portrayal. "Larry was a very interesting guy," said director Robert Wise. "You always felt a little edgy about him, and that quality came off on the screen, I think, that helped make the character he did in *Born to Kill*, and in other films like *Dillinger*...."

Shot in May-June 1946, *Born to Kill* was not released until May 1947, owing to censorship issues created by the violence. It was rejected by the Ohio Board of Censors, the first time they completely banned a film. The *Los Angeles Times*' John L. Scott called *Born to Kill* "subtle as a poke in the eye with a sharp stick."

Around this time, Tierney's brother Gerard, back from Navy service, began attending drama school. Larry gave him some advice and introduced him to his agent, who got Gerard little theater jobs.

It was announced that Tierney would play the main villain role in the Western *Trail Street*, but then Robert Ryan was cast in his place. Instead, Tierney was given a much better showcase: *The Devil Thumbs a Ride*, a noir in which he plays the quintessential

Lawrence Tierney role. As stickup man and forger Steve Morgan, a "slap-happy bird with a gun," he's bad to the bone, a sociopath with a lust to kill. The movie and Tierney get down to business immediately as he claims his first victim mere minutes into the proceedings. After that, he hitches a ride with nice-guy salesman Jimmy Ferguson (Ted North). They pick up two hitchhikers (Betty Lawford and Nan Leslie) and land at a beach house, where Morgan cannot control his rage. "Tierney is still one of the best young heavies that the screen has ever put forth," wrote the *Los Angeles Times*' Edwin Schallert. "He keeps *The Devil Thumbs a Ride* in high as a melodrama. He has a load of personality with a machine gun–like delivery of lines." While Tierney was more than believable, it was a role he disliked doing: "I resented all those pictures that they put me in," he told Rick McKay in a decades-later interview. "I never thought of myself as that kind of guy. I thought of myself as a nice guy who wouldn't do rotten things. But obviously that miserable son of a bitch in the film would! I hated that character so much, but I had to do it for the picture."

Tierney was then cast as reformed convict Jim Noland, just back from war duty, in 1946's *San Quentin*. Before the war, Noland helped found the San Quentin Inmates' Welfare League (based on a real group), an organization to educate and rehabilitate inmates. Of course, there's always one bad apple in the bunch, this time Nick Taylor (Barton MacLane). Risking his good rep and acting as a lone wolf (with some slight assistance from a pal), Noland must prove the League is a worthwhile venture by tracking down Taylor. The highlight comes at the conclusion as Tierney and MacLane square off with guns and fists. According to RKO publicity, they rehearsed the fisticuffs for five days, but considering the film's short shooting schedule, this is absurd. RKO also claimed that the Tierney-MacLane fight (less than two minutes) rivaled the scrap between William Farnum and Tom Santschi in *The Spoilers* (1914), then regarded by many as the best two-man film battle.

It's too bad Tierney didn't take the movie's reform message to heart; staying sober was just not in the cards. On August 18, 1946, during the making of *San Quentin*, Tierney fell off a glass-topped coffee table while fixing a light (or so he said). He arrived soaked in blood at Hollywood Receiving Hospital for treatment of neck gashes and a finger cut (which were "bleeding Scotch," joked one columnist). Fifteen stitches were needed to close his neck wound, four in his finger. At the hospital, he caused a disturbance and was arrested for violating his probation by being drunk. Tierney, booked under the alias Francis B. Moran, denied the charges, saying they "smelled brandy on his breath because a friend gave him a drink to revive him" after his fall. Two friends contradicted his "fixing the light" story by saying that Tierney was injured when he "fell on a bottle at a house party somewhere."

A week later, at his preliminary hearing, Larry pleaded not guilty. His RKO contract was in the balance, as they had warned Tierney they would can him after one more infraction. However, they did stand by him. He was found guilty and sentenced to 60 days; the judge, however, cut it down to five days with a warning: "You are one of those individuals who can't handle liquor. You and liquor don't get along and you might as well make up your mind to give it up or you will end up as one of the many derelicts in Lincoln Heights jail." He advised Larry to observe his fellow prisoners and to remember that "most of those men you are going to meet were once as good-looking, as square-shouldered and as healthy as you are today.... You're headed for the same fate that has overtaken them."

The following year, Tierney 'fessed up to *St. Louis Post-Dispatch*'s Myles Standish:

> I just fell into a coffee table at a party at a friend's house. The glass cuts a long gash in my neck—look, you can still see the scars—and cuts an artery in my right forefinger. They take me out to find an emergency hospital. The first one is being painted and the painters are all horrified to see me covered with blood. They don't like it, see, so we go into another emergency hospital. There are only two nurses there, and they are horrified, too. "Oh my," they say. "There isn't any doctor here. You're too badly hurt for us to do anything." So out we go, still looking for a doctor, me spouting blood like a fountain. All the time, I am taking nips out of a bottle, sort of medicine, see. So I'm pretty plastered when we get to a first-aid clinic at a police station.
>
> I make some remarks about not liking the Hollywood hospital system, and they tell me to shut up. I sound off and try to get the hell out of there. A bunch of cops jump me. There is quite a tussle. Then I find myself strapped down, and a surgeon taking stitches in my neck, zing, zing, like that.

A couple of days later, Tierney was again causing trouble. On October 16, police were called to three different nightclubs after there were complaints that Tierney was involved in minor scuffles. At the first two places, he had left before officers arrived. At the third, The Players, cops found him "acting belligerently," but they let him go with a warning to go straight home, which apparently, he did.

Tierney's "bad boy" image attracted the ladies, both in *and* out of show biz; from the "in show biz" group, he dated Jean Rickey (an Earl Carroll girl), Lina Romay, Jacqueline Dalya, Shelley Winters and more. Columnist Dorothy Kilgallen reported, "[He] quotes poetry, Shakespeare and the Scriptures during most of the evening when he dates local glamour girls—or so they breathlessly report." Virginia Mayo, who shared a few publicity dates with Tierney, told me that he was a "perfect gentleman," was never drunk, stayed with her all night at the function they attended and deposited her, unmolested, at her doorstep after the date was over.

The new year of 1947 began with a brawl with Henry Sturman, former Miami University intercollegiate middleweight boxing champ, at Manhattan's Empire Hotel. They charged each other with assault. Larry, appearing in court with a torn right ear and two black eyes, said the fight started when he "expressed concern over a very drunk young lady" who was sharing an elevator with them and another man. Sturman retorted that he was simply defending himself as Tierney had passed himself off as a house detective and then knocked him down. The drunk lady and other man left the scene before the cops arrived.

If this story wasn't bizarre enough, a witness appeared in court, so-called salesman Silvio Domenico, who testified that he saw Tierney kick Sturman. Tierney's attorney Saul Price pounced, accusing the witness of attempting to sell his testimony to Tierney for a couple of hundred dollars. "Didn't you say, 'If you want to do the right thing by me, I can have someone from the hotel testify that Sturman offered a bribe to a hotel employee for a passkey to a hotel room?'"

Fast-forward: In 1951, ex-con Pete Lombardo, hoping to wriggle out of a burglary charge, spilled about a gangland murder—and in the process, referenced Silvio "Slugs" Domenico, "one of the East Liberty racket mob" (*Pittsburgh Post-Gazette*'s Ray Sprigle), and Tierney:

> Slugs told me he had to appear as a witness for this movie actor, Lawrence Tierney, which is true because he showed me pictures. Lawrence Tierney was staying at the same hotel with

him and he had some trouble there and they were holding Lawrence Tierney for assault and battery and Slugs was to be a witness for him, and when he went there, he shook Lawrence Tierney down. He told me this. He said if he came through, he would witness for him, or else go talk to the prosecution.

Domenico wasn't as smart as he thought. Held on $10,000 bail, he was charged with perjury. (Tierney and Sturman eventually dropped their complaints against each other.)

Tierney told Myles Standish an expanded version of his hotel brawl story:

I come back to my hotel early in the morning pretty looped, and I see two guys getting off the elevator on the second floor with a girl between them, so stiff she could hardly walk. They sort of dragged her to a room. I said to myself, "Geez, what's going on here, I better help her." So I get off there too, though my room was on the fifth floor.

One of the guys comes out of the room and says, "What do you want, buddy?" I say, "What are you doing to that girl?" He says, "Who are you, a hotel dick or something?" Real tough. I say, "Yes." He looks me over and sees by my tuxedo I'm not a hotel dick. So he takes a swing at me.

We fight all over the hall. Then the elevator man opens the elevator door to see what all the noise is about, and we rassle into the elevator. "Going down," says the elevator man, and shuts the door. We're banging each other's brains out in the elevator, see? Down it goes to the first floor. The elevator man pulls open the door. "First floor," he says. "All out!" So we knock each other out into the lobby and continue to go at it.

Suddenly the other guy stops fighting and says, "I'm going to have you bumped off before the morning. I know the guys who can do it, too." He goes to a phone. I say to myself, "Geez, this is bad. He looks like he really means it." I don't want anybody pumping me full of bullets. That bullet stuff is all right in pictures. But not for me in real life. So I go up to a friend's room on the seventh floor to hide. The police come and get me there.

Larry was seen a lot with New York socialite Vivian Stokes Taylor and there were rumors the two would tie the knot.

In Baltimore, he got into a fistfight at the Lord Baltimore Hotel with the house detective who came to his suite to investigate loud noises in the wee small hours of the morning. Tierney was arrested, then bailed out right away to make a personal appearance at a local theater. Reportedly, the police had no idea that they'd had actor Lawrence Tierney (who was booked under an assumed name) in their lock-up.

He wasn't so lucky when he was arrested in California on a drunk charge. On April 16, 1947, he was ordered to spend the next four weekends in jail for violating probation.

Alas, after serving half of this sentence, he got into trouble yet again, this time with his 18-year-old brother Ed. On May 1, the brothers went to see a girl named Betty. An argument ensued and a "bloody brawl" started in her apartment and ended out in the street. Neighbors complained that the "language of the Brooklyn brothers was an education in gutterese." When cops arrived, they found the Tierneys swinging at each other in front of the building.

Larry explained, "We were just having a friendly quarrel, eh, Eddie?"

"That's right, Larry," Ed replied.

They were both arrested for intoxication and disturbing the peace. This time, Larry received a 90-day sentence and a lecture from the judge:

You are not only hurting the industry which you represent, but also your family. Your family has suffered a lot and when I gave you four weekends to spend in jail recently, I took pity on your family, not you. You have had four or five chances to straighten yourself out. Now I think you'd better spend about 90 days with a pick and shovel in a county road camp and see if that won't do you some good.

The Tierney family share a meal in their Brentwood home, circa 1947. Clockwise: father Lawrence Sr. (back to camera), Larry, brother Gerard (aka Scott Brady), mother Mary and brother Edward.

The *Los Angeles Times* remarked that this activity would be the "only elbow-bending" Tierney would get for a while. Brother Ed was released on $250 bail.

Despite Tierney's problems, RKO stuck with him; they promised that, upon his release, he'd get the lead in *Bodyguard*, in which he would play a good guy, and a pay raise to more than $1000 a week. The studio put out a statement that Tierney was to play heroes from then on, in an attempt to change his image. But Jimmie Fidler, once a Tierney supporter, threw up his hands at the actor's latest troubles: "The proper place for Lawrence Tierney is a sanitarium, not a carefully propped up pedestal." Erskine Johnson blamed Tierney's problems on RKO's soft treatment. "Movie stars are like kids," he wrote. "The only way you can really slap down a headstrong star is to take the camera away from him and stand him in a corner for a while without a spotlight. That hurts where it does some good, and has the same effect as a hairbrush."

Tierney wasn't getting preferred treatment in stir; he had to sleep on the floor of his cell because all the bunks were taken. (Larry told Tim Tierney that the guards taunted him, saying things like "Get your ass over here, Dillinger! Shovel this manure, Dillinger!") A week into his stay, he was put into solitary confinement because he didn't hear the six a.m. wake-up alarm. He was warned that if he missed another wake-up call, he would spend the rest of his sentence in solitary with no time off for good behavior.

Slightly good news came when the case involving his brother Ed went before a judge: Larry was fined $25, Ed $10; another 90-day sentence was suspended on the condition he refrain from drinking and from further run-ins with the law for a year after his release. But five days were tacked onto the 90 days he was currently serving.

On May 16, 1947, Tierney was moved from the county jail to the Sheriff's Honor Farm in Castaic where he served the rest of his time. There he delivered a series of half-hour lectures on the "evils of drinking."

On June 18, 1947, after a plea from his father, Tierney was paroled to start *another* program with Alcoholics Anonymous. He had served 48 days of his 90-day sentence.

He took up where he left off with Vivi Stokes Taylor, and his promises of reform prompted talk that they would marry. Vivi obviously had a thing for bad boys: At the time, she was also corresponding with a former flame who was now in a military prison. She ultimately left Tierney to reunite with him. Larry subsequently dated socialite Liz Whitney, Deanna Durbin ("We're just good friends," he said), Sara Spencer and a series of minor starlets.

Bad press accompanied Tierney's plan to set out on a cross-country tour to lecture about alcohol. "For sheer effrontery and bad taste, that one takes the proverbial cake," wrote Jimmie Fidler. The columnist, like many, thought this was a stunt, a way to gain publicity, and not "honest reform." Fidler felt the only way Tierney could re-establish himself with RKO and his fans would be to "buckle down, keep his mouth shut, his nose to the grindstone—and PROVE by his everyday life that he's cured himself of a persistent weakness. Until he does that, his lectures, I'm afraid, won't receive much serious consideration."

Tierney did make an effort to be good and control his drinking and violent tendencies, for a while at least. In fact, he remained on the sidelines during a September 10, 1947, battle at the Mocambo between two husky ex–college football players, which featured "fists, cocktail glasses and some bad, bad words" (*Los Angeles Times*). It was reported that Larry ("sipping milk") cheered the two on as they slugged it out.

In October '47, he was a "sensation" at the third annual Photographer's Costume Ball. Larry came dressed as Gargantua with his brother Gerard as his keeper. ("Even Orson Welles' mouth flew open at the sight," wrote Hedda Hopper.) Meanwhile, RKO wasn't assigning him any pictures. At the end of '47, they renewed his option, but he was forced to take a pay cut.

For about nine months after his release from the prison farm, Tierney kept his nose clean but, on February 24, 1948, he was arrested after a fight with bartender William Goldy at Barney's Beanery on the Sunset Strip. Goldy alleged that Tierney had knocked him down; Larry claimed Goldy called him a "sucker" and hit him first. It turned out that this was a rematch: Tierney claimed that, a year earlier, Goldy had "tried to push a lighted cigar in my eye."

Two weeks later, Goldy filed a $100,000 damage suit, alleging that Tierney had blackened his eye and impaired his vision and hearing before knocking him unconscious. The suit was later dropped and the charges against Tierney were dismissed.

In March, Tierney "opened a second front in Manhattan," wrote Dorothy Kilgallen, getting into some barroom fights before returning to the West Coast. He got a bit of good press when he joined some friends in financing a gym and sports center for underprivileged kids in his old Brooklyn neighborhood.

In April 1948, Tierney's next movie, the long-promised *Bodyguard*, was ready to roll; it was his first time in the front of the cameras since *San Quentin*. As homicide detective Mike Carter, who "uses his knuckles instead of his brains," Tierney is in his element. Clashing with his superior, Lt. Borden (Frank Fenton), he is thrown off the force for being hot-headed and disobeying orders, then framed for Borden's murder. With help from fiancée Doris (Priscilla Lane in her last movie), he seeks to clear his name. There are a couple of in-jokes that 1948 audiences probably snickered at: Tierney's character passes up booze for a glass of milk; and when Lane warns him to keep his temper in check, he remarks, "Now, you know me better than that, I never get into fights." Even so, Tierney has a doozy of a slugfest with Philip Reed in a dimly lit meat factory.

Due to his good showing in *Bodyguard*, RKO considered him for lead roles in the films noir *The Clay Pigeon* and *Follow Me Quietly*. Tierney was hoping his career was on the upturn and that bigger parts in bigger movies were in the offing. He was keeping his hands to himself after his experience with Goldy. There was an "almost" run-in with new-to-Hollywood Audie Murphy at a party. Murphy and his date Wanda Hendrix got into a spat, and Tierney came to Hendrix's defense. The volatile war hero Murphy ("as shy as a hand grenade with the fuse lit," wrote *Modern Screen*) looked Larry in the eye and growled, "If you don't get away from here, you'll be sorry." For once, Tierney backed down. In 1965, Murphy told John Cummings, "If somebody hadn't stopped me, I would very happily have killed him."

"If Lawrence Tierney is drinking again, as reported by a columnist, the news is certainly news to his bosses at RKO," Sheilah Graham wrote in June. "I saw Larry yesterday and he seemed perfectly sober. Why don't they leave this boy alone and give him a chance when he really is trying to overcome a craving?" As long as Tierney was making headlines and selling newspapers, he was a hot topic. He had hired a bodyguard to keep him out of trouble at nightclubs and bars, and ended up brawling with him instead.

In July '48, a couple of months before *Bodyguard* hit theaters, Tierney and RKO parted. The following month, he officially fell off the wagon, arrested on a drunk charge and for causing a disturbance at a Santa Barbara resort. Released on $10 bail, he put up another ten-spot for his 70-year-old cellmate, also jailed for intoxication. "Tierney's case is one of the saddest on Hollywood record," wrote Harrison Carroll. "Real talent being wasted there." According to Tim Tierney,

> Larry told me how he lived in Santa Barbara for a while in the late '40s, as it was a good place to lay low from the scene in Los Angeles 90 miles to the south. He would occasionally drive down to L.A. in his big Packard car and carouse around, sleeping on friends' sofas. His favorite drink at the time was the Stinger.

Actor-turned-producer John Shelton was interested in signing Larry and brother Gerard (now sporting the *nom de screen* Scott Brady) for the leads in an indie he was planning, *The Floyds of Oklahoma*, the story of gangster Pretty Boy Floyd and his law enforcer brother E.W. Floyd. This project never reached fruition. Nor did the fascinating idea of casting Tierney in the Peter Lorre role in a remake of 1931's *M*.

There was another arrest for intoxication and disorderly conduct (he was throwing things) on October 11, 1948, on Santa Catalina Island. The irony: He was cuffed by Andy Dobek, an officer who had once arrested the real John Dillinger.

It was announced that Tierney would play Robert Ford in the Western noir *I Shot Jesse James*, but that fell through when the producers decided they couldn't take a chance on him; John Ireland was given the part. Dorothy Kilgallen reported in December '48 that Larry was "so anxious to start movie work again," he offered to post a $5000 bond and to defer his salary as a guarantee that he'd stay sober throughout the making of a picture. There were no takers.

His actions did not exactly inspire confidence. On January 3, 1949, Tierney was booked on yet another drunk-and-disorderly charge when a cab driver claimed that Tierney tried to climb into the front seat with him, lunged repeatedly at the steering wheel, and threatened to throw him out of the vehicle. After Tierney passed out, the cabbie dumped him in front of the Hollywood sheriff's substation. He was freed on $50 bail the next day. The judge gave him a $150 fine, a suspended sentence and a lecture:

> You have come a long way in motion pictures. The public still maintains faith in you because of your portrayals in pictures. I am going to give you one more chance to demonstrate the faith the public has in you is not misplaced.

The new arrest cost Tierney a role in producer Harry Popkin's proposed *Inside Alcatraz*. Tierney wanted the part so much that, just hours before he started drinking that night, he promised Popkin he would go on the wagon. Larry left jail to find the deal called off.

When Tierney claimed to have signed for a movie in Italy, Jimmie Fidler sniped, "If that's true, may heaven help the Italians. They may still refuse to release United States coin, but after that picture is finished, I'll predict that they'll be mighty anxious to release Lawrence Tierney." Fidler expressed his disgust at all the chances Larry was getting:

> In my opinion, new "chances," in Tierney's case, are a public menace. Seemingly he can't get crocked without also getting belligerent, smashing things, insulting people and wanting to fight. If he's given enough chances, it will probably be some innocent bystander who will suffer.

The Italian film never happened. While Tierney was scrambling for work, brother Scott Brady was doing very well for himself. Inked to a contract with Eagle-Lion, he starred in the noirs *Canon City*, *Port of New York* and *He Walked by Night*. In 1949, he signed a seven-year pact with Universal-International. "There was no doubt [that Brady would] do everything in pictures that Lawrence has never been able to do," stated Louella Parsons. "Scott is a 'nice' boy and has never been in the headlines in the wrong way." In fact, there was friction between the Tierney brothers, with Scott disapproving of Larry's drinking and hellraising ways.

In February '49, Tierney was again in the news with three brawls. One of these brutal encounters "could have ended in tragedy," it was reported, "had it not been for the interference of bystanders. Tierney had his opponent down and was choking him when they were separated." The following month, he began work on director Max Nosseck's *Kill or Be Killed*, the first American-financed production to be filmed entirely in Portugal. "After this is finished," wrote Hedda Hopper, "Tierney is wanted for pictures in Paris and Italy. I guess if we don't want him, they do."

Nosseck, the director of *Dillinger*, got another good performance from Tierney, again portraying an innocent man wanted for murder. While trying to find the real culprit, he meets ex–concert pianist Maria Marek (Marissa O'Brien), the wife of a shady plantation owner (Rudolph Anders). Tierney's gentle scenes with O'Brien are among the most romantic he had played on film. *Kill or Be Killed* allowed him to show a lighter side to his personality: singing "Oh! Susanna," dancing and, in a nice moment, reacting to Maria's piano playing. But make no mistake: Tierney is his usual rough-and-tumble self and he has a helluva bloody fight with Anders.

Money was tight on *Kill or Be Killed* and Larry, along with other cast members, agreed to take salary deferments in exchange for a percentage of the box office. He ended up getting nothing—not even his salary.

Edith Gwynn relayed in her "Hollywood" column, "[R]eports from Europe where Hollywood's 'bad boy' [Tierney] had been picture-making are very good—and he may stay there indefinitely and appear in several more."

Reportedly nixing the foreign offers, Tierney was in New York City by June '49, dating Lady Iris Mountbatten (of all people) and entertaining a deal to star in summer stock. "He is presenting himself all nice and shined up ready for another chance in native movies or on the stage," wrote Dorothy Manners.

Days after that column item, Tierney was arrested in Weehawken, New Jersey, for engaging in fisticuffs with three men. Released on $50, Tierney also bailed out the others. A week later, in a courtroom "crowded with admiring teenagers," Tierney was acquitted on the charge of being drunk and disorderly due to lack of evidence. After the verdict was handed down, "more than 150 Tierney fans in the courtroom cheered, then mobbed him for autographs."

Promises of being good again had to be reinforced with a $3000 bond to summer theater owners that he would stay sober during an upcoming straw hat tour. But no theater dates materialized. There was talk of casting him in the Chicago company of *Detective Story* and a road tour of *Death of a Salesman*, but that's all it was … talk. Also not happening: a role in John Huston's *The Asphalt Jungle* and a picture deal at MGM. "I doubt that there could be a contract unless Larry cures himself of what ails him," reported Sheilah Graham.

To make matters worse, Vivi Stokes Taylor married Count Marco Fabio Crespi. Larry's reaction to the news was to go to P.J. Clarke's and drink—and then stick his head into an electric fan. Cholly Knickerbocker remarked that he was "scalped pretty badly. When alarmed customers rushed to his aid, Tierney wasn't a bit concerned about the gashes on his head. He wanted to repair the fan first." Recovering quickly from his injuries to head and heart, he dated, among others, Mary Rogers, the daughter of the late humorist Will. After Mary broke up with him, they "battled their way all over Manhattan" (Edith Gwynn), and Larry would continue to show up at restaurants to confront her and her dates.

In December '49, with no movie offers, Tierney accepted a starring role made to order for him: Death Row criminal Killer Mears in a revival of the stage play *The Last Mile* in Newark, New Jersey. This theater engagement—and his sobriety during it—piqued the interest of Hollywood once again, and he was back in Tinseltown at the beginning of 1950. Louella Parsons wrote (December 7, 1949), "Nothing makes me so happy as to report that a really fine actor, who once stumbled into a pitfall of temptation, is trying to regain his footing and win a new lease on life."

Universal wanted Tierney to co-star with brother Scott in *The Payoff*. He held out for top billing, an absurdity since he was lucky to be getting *any* screen jobs. "Some people, it seems to me, are very hard to please," wrote Jimmie Fidler. "Instead of holding out for top billing, [he] should be down on his 'hunkers,' thanking his lucky stars that he's getting another chance." Ultimately, there was no *Payoff* for either of the brothers.

Things looked up when Universal's William Goetz signed Tierney to a contract; as long as Larry behaved, Goetz said, he would get a buildup there.

His first movie for U-I was to be the lead heavy in the James Stewart Western *Winchester '73*; he was taken out (replaced by Dan Duryea) and cast as the lead in *Saddle Tramp*, which would have been a change of pace for him: a cowboy who adopts four children. Again, he was replaced, this time by Joel McCrea. It was as if Universal didn't know what to do with him. Then the lead in another Western, *Tomahawk*, passed from Tierney to Van Heflin.

By all accounts, Tierney seemed to be behaving himself and was working out to lose some weight. "I don't mind anything that is printed about me as long as it is the truth," he told Erskine Johnson. "I've nothing to hide and I've nothing to be ashamed of—except getting drunk a few times." Perhaps U-I was hesitant to assign him a role not because of things he did, but things he *failed* to do: On February 10, 1950, Sheilah Graham reported, "No one seems to know why Larry broke three studio appointments for wardrobe tests, etc., which is why he is out of *Winchester '73*."

On the personal front, he was still the Big Dame Hunter, dating Adele Mara and Joan Whitney plus socialite Belle Weil, Posey Judge and Selene Walters ("the girl who enchanted the Shah of Iran").

Universal assigned Tierney to the *noir Shakedown* (1950), about an unscrupulous news photographer (Howard Duff) who stops at nothing, not even blackmail, to get what he wants. Fourth-billed after Duff, Brian Donlevy and Peggy Dow, Tierney was cast as Harry Colton, a "one-man crime wave." Larry claimed not to be afraid of being typed, remarking to Bob Thomas, "Many stars have made a mint by being typed." He tackles this supporting role with gusto, and his presence is felt even during the stretches when he's off-camera.

He was confident that U-I would pick up his option after *Shakedown*, but when he nixed a part in *Wyoming Mail* ("My agent made me turn it down—too small"), Universal dropped him.

Tierney looked forward to touring in summer stock and the possibility of starring on Broadway. The whole Tierney clan, including their father, was offered the chance to appear together in an Allied Artists movie (never made) called *Police Story*.

On May 8, 1950, Tierney was arrested on a drunk charge at the Ocean Park boxing arena after a verbal altercation with a beer vendor who claimed that Larry had taken a beer without paying. When officers warned him to calm down, Tierney pointed the neck of a beer bottle at them and "playfully" said, "Stick 'em up!"

"I plead guilty to friskiness but not drunkenness," he told a judge the next day. "I did a lot of kidding. It might have been mistaken for drunkenness." The judge wasn't buying it. On May 24, after he pleaded guilty to disorderly conduct, he was fined $50 and put on two years' probation.Jimmie Fidler was customarily hard on Tierney after this latest brush with the law:

> Off-hand I can't remember the exact number of Tierney's arrests; I lost count somewhere, way back yonder, when he had made the pokey for the seventh or eighth times. Long, long ago, two things became perfectly apparent in his case. He was an incorrigible dipsomaniac, and he was a dipsomaniac of the dangerous type who, once in his cups, usually manages to get involved in a fight. First-hand accounts of several of his brawls (only a small percentage of which have made the headlines) make it clear that only the whims of Lady Luck have kept him from being involved in a tragedy, with someone else, in all probability, being the principal victim.

Fidler accused the studios that employed Tierney of being irresponsible: "[If] his career does end in tragedy, how can they be considered anything but accessories before the fact?"

Sheilah Graham was more sympathetic:

> When you talk to Larry, it's impossible to believe he's been such an alcoholic. He's very quiet, very intelligent, can quote good poetry by the hour. He's very charming and seems quite sincere in his desire to be a good boy....It's a shame to drown a good career in a bottle.

Tierney and a busty Ann Zika (aka Angela Stevens) in *The Hoodlum* (1951).

In August '50, Tierney went back to his old stomping grounds, RKO, for an eighth-billed role as Jesse James ("the quick, quiet one, who lived and slept with both eyes open") in *Best of the Badmen*. (He had previously played the outlaw in *Badman's Territory*, but there was no relation between the two movies.) His part was only incidental to the plot and he doesn't have much to do except supply atmospheric menace.

On October 14, 1950, on Normandie Avenue and Jefferson Boulevard in Los Angeles, a man and a woman in a parked Cadillac were, according to residents, yelling at each other, and the man was assaulting her. Police arrived and identified the couple as Tierney and actress Jean Wallace. She told officers she was not assaulted and did not want to press charges against Tierney. Larry, indignant and belligerent, demanded a sobriety test—which he failed. And he made things worse by trying to attack a photographer and reporter. He was later released on $20 bail. Wallace told Louella Parsons, "Larry called and asked if I would be interested in playing with him in a play, *The Respectful Prostitute*. We talked about the part and then I offered to drive him home. Suddenly he became wild and started to scream."

Jimmie Fidler tried to start a sort of boycott on Tierney's acting services. He felt Larry wouldn't be motivated into getting help for his anger and alcoholism as long as producers still sought him for work. "This time, in the interest of public safety and for his own good, he should be ruled out—not for a month or two, but for a sufficient length of time to effect a real cure. And he shouldn't be taken back until doctors offer certificates attesting the cure."

At a party, Tierney punched out a drunk who introduced him as "Scott Brady's brother." Remarked Dorothy Kilgallen, "Nobody could understand why the reference so incensed the flicker Dillinger."

"I finally discovered that alcohol can whip me," said Tierney, who began attending Alcoholics Anonymous meetings twice weekly. This led to the top spot in the very low-budget *noir The Hoodlum*, directed by his friend Max Nosseck. Scott Brady was reportedly set to play the part of Larry's screen brother, but then Ed Tierney was enlisted to take Scott's place. With its 12-day schedule (March 15–27, 1951), it looked cheap and seedy and ran the risk of succumbing to the usual clichés: a paroled career criminal returns home, finds he cannot keep on the straight and narrow and ends up destroying several lives. The Sam Neuman-Nat Tanchuck screenplay is tough, uncompromising, depressing and thoroughly original.

When I mentioned *The Hoodlum* to actress Allene Roberts, who played a young innocent impregnated and abandoned by Tierney's title character, she groaned, calling it a "very pitiful show." As for working with Larry, she said he "wasn't mean or anything" but "kind of aloof."

Tierney himself disliked *The Hoodlum*, but his intense performance ranks as one of his best. No one-dimensional crook is he: Tierney is able to movingly convey his frustrations about his poverty-stricken childhood. The adverse effect his criminality has on his mother (the superb Lisa Golm) brings out his shame and desperation in the two characters' stunning final scene. Their screen relationship in some ways reflects real life, as Larry's mother constantly fretted over his brushes with the law and, as in *The Hoodlum*, it did not end well.

As Ida Lupino and Collier Young planned their movie *The Hitch-Hiker* in April 1951, Tierney was their top choice to play the title psycho character; but this ideal role slipped away and it was given to William Talman. On April 30, 1951, in Santa Barbara, Larry headlined a stage production of *The Last Mile* that subsequently went out on a brief road tour. On May 14, at the Doll House in Palm Springs, he went toe to toe with a Texas oilman. Tierney explained,

> I have been on the wagon for nine months and I have been trying very hard to stay out of trouble. I was sitting at the bar drinking a Coke with Terry McGuire, a friend of mine, and a couple of girls. This stranger came up and pushed his way between the two girls. He offered to buy them a drink and butted into our conversation. It is very important to me to avoid trouble so I leaned over and asked the bartender who the man was. The fellow heard me and told me not to be a wise guy. He grabbed my coat collar and forced me back over the bar. I asked him not to start anything, but he cocked his other hand back as if he were going to hit me. I expect to start work soon and didn't want my face damaged so I let him have one left to the mouth. He fell away from me but started back to renew the fight. Then people separated us.

Witnesses corroborated Larry's story. Tierney's agent, Bill Shiffrin, explained to Erskine Johnson, "Larry thought of his career and everybody who believed in him for five minutes [as the oil man ran rampant]. Then he couldn't take it any longer and swung. I say that it's a good thing that not all Hollywood stars are cream puffs."

Cecil B. DeMille cast Tierney as a crook who wrecks the circus in his Oscar-winning film *The Greatest Show on Earth*. Impressed by his good conduct during the shoot, Paramount wanted to put him under contract and earmarked for him the lead in *Hurricane Smith* with Yvonne De Carlo and a vehicle called *The Story of Mrs. Murphy*. The latter was about an alcoholic who refers to his whiskey bottle as Mrs. Murphy; Thelma Ritter was to play his mother.

Even though DeMille had vouched for him, Larry botched the Paramount contract deal: At 5:30 a.m. on June 21, 1951, in West Los Angeles, college student John Naylor investigated a noise outside his house. He was greeted by two men who, according to Naylor, beat him unconscious and broke his jaw. From a photograph, he identified one of the men as Tierney. Tierney denied the charge.

Even though Larry was not supposed to leave California as he awaited trial, he accepted the role of Stanley Kowalski to Maria Palmer's Blanche DuBois and Jorja Curtright's Stella in a Santa Fe, New Mexico, stock production of *A Streetcar Named Desire*. (The name of the director seems appropriate: Jack Daniels.) When Tierney failed to show up for the July 26 performance, Arthur Franz, who had played the part in Australia, was tapped to sub for him. Tierney claimed he was suffering from appendicitis, but when he was found in a downtown Santa Fe bar, the producer fired him. Tierney explained that he "didn't have the vitality to go on. I was sober when I arrived at the theater, but I had been violently ill and couldn't go on." A couple of days later, a local warrant was issued when the Mayflower Café manager alleged that Tierney, drunk and disorderly, broke down a screen door and tore up some menus.

After a couple of delays, all Tierney's fault, the trial for battery on John Naylor was set for August 3. When Tierney was several hours late, he told the judge, "[M]y car battery went dead and I got a traffic ticket on my way here." The judge was not amused: "You've been treating this as a joke, but you're not going to be tried when you feel good and ready; you're going to be tried on the date set by the court." Larry's father backed up his son's story, but the judge wasn't having it: "In my opinion, this conduct is willful and deliberate and without justification. I declare the defendant in contempt." Trial was re-set for August 13. In the meantime, Tierney was sentenced to five days in the slammer for contempt of court and ordered to post $2500 bail upon his release.

On August 13, Tierney changed his story. He said that he and a friend were in the area visiting two girls. As they crossed a lawn, Naylor's mother turned her collie loose to attack them. Mrs. Naylor testified that after Tierney kicked the dog, she told her son to punch him in the nose. Larry's version of events was that he was defending himself from Naylor, who was brandishing a 12-inch butcher knife. Naylor asserted that Larry kicked him in the face, breaking his jaw in three places, and left him out cold. Tierney said he did not kick him. "I hit him with my hand. I hit him twice. When somebody has a knife, I'm going to hit as hard as I can." The jury, deliberating for four hours, found Tierney guilty of battery, but acquitted him of disturbing the peace.

Naylor filed a civil suit against Tierney for $30,587 because he said he had been unable to work for five weeks after the beating. (He eventually received $5000.)

Sentenced to 90 days in jail, Tierney asked for and received a stay pending an appeal. He told the judge at his August 30 probation hearing, "I realize that society must do something about a man like me. I am not a criminal, not a thief, and my actions have harmed only myself," but he added, "Before, I pleaded guilty because I was guilty. But this time it will be very difficult to go to jail because I am innocent." He said he was guilty only of defending himself.

Producer Jack Broder wanted to give Larry "another chance" on screen and gave him a part in the brutal low-budget Western *The Bushwhackers*. Third-billed over the title after John Ireland and Wayne Morris, Tierney is as mean as a snake as Sam Tobin, trigger-happy henchman of rancher Artemus Taylor (Lon Chaney). It was not a big role, but Tierney made the most of it.

Tierney sought solace in the Bible and there were reports that he turned "fanatically religious" (Harrison Carroll) at this time, spending hours praying and quoting Biblical verses.

At 6 a.m. on October 8, 1951, Santa Monica police officers were summoned to St. Monica Catholic Church by neighbors complaining of a "shabby, barefoot loiterer" on church grounds. The cops were met by the sight of Tierney, disheveled and belligerent but not drunk. He ran into the church, "approached the altar, made an obeisance and claimed sanctuary." His prayers, said one officer, were incoherent, the words gibberish, and he started raving to them about his fear of "being murdered like Robert Walker was." He also told a "disconnected story of alcoholism." After a "clawing, fist-swinging fight" with two cops, Tierney was finally restrained in leather straps. At the police station, his brother Ed tried to calm him, but Larry hit him. Larry was taken to Los Angeles Neurological Institute for treatment. Ed told the press, "Lawrence is a sick boy. He has been under treatment by doctors and psychiatrists at his home." Larry was released in Ed's care.

Two weeks later, Larry was back in jail, booked on suspicion of being drunk and disorderly—a matter of routine for Larry now. A shoeless Tierney entered a bar and "offered to whip anybody in the house." The arresting officers said Tierney had told them, "I can hold my liquor. I've been drinking double shots for three days without any sleep at all and I can still carry on a conversation." He refused to give his address and told police his occupation was "bum." Newsmen and photographers converged on him as he was being booked at the Lincoln Heights jail, and he spat in a reporter's face.

Due to this latest trouble, Tierney was sentenced to three days in jail on November 23, 1951. Put on three years' probation, he was ordered to attend Alcoholics Anonymous meetings on a regular basis—and to stay out of bars. "If I place you on summary probation," the judge asked, "will you give this court your word of honor that you will quit drinking? Just lay off the stuff—not even a short beer?" Tierney replied, "Your honor, I'll give you my word of honor on that."

At the end of 1951, producer Roger Kendall announced he had signed Tierney to act in two pictures for his newly formed indie company Kendall-Kirkwood Productions. Kendall told Aline Mosby,

> I don't feel I'm taking a chance. Tierney's convinced me of his sincerity to make good. I don't feel he has any worse problems than anybody who's down on his luck and doesn't know how to get back. He just needs a chance to show what he can do. He's a very good actor. That's why I chose him.
>
> We signed him to play a peace officer in one movie and a truck driver in another. They're all nice guys. After he gets a couple of good roles under his belt, people will forget that Dillinger legend and the heckling of him will stop. Before I signed Larry, I invited him to my home. When he's away from Hollywood and the Sunset Strip, he loses his tension and becomes a different, relaxed person. He's intelligent and has a sense of humor....When I offered him a drink, he stuck to orange juice. I don't think he'll be any problem.

The two films were not made.

Tierney wanted to check into the Menninger Clinic for treatment of his alcoholism, but he was unable to afford it.

Back to the John Naylor case: On March 13, 1952, Tierney got 90 days at the county honor farm. A model prisoner, he was released after serving 64 days. His lawyer said that Tierney had landed an important role in a picture.

The movie part did not happen, but in June '52 Larry was cast as Duke Mantee in a Miami Beach stage production of *The Petrified Forest*, with Franchot Tone as Alan Squier. (Tierney had already played Mantee on two radio versions of *Petrified Forest* in the '40s.) With Tone and Betsy von Furstenberg, Tierney toured with the show. Herb Rau of the *Miami News* wrote, "More down-to-earth, and fitting the role to the first letter of his last name, Lawrence Tierney played gunman Duke Mantee to the hilt. Bogart [who played Mantee on Broadway and the 1936 movie adaptation] couldn't have done better."

Betsy later told writer Rick McKay that Larry was a natural on stage and stole the show; with "his God-given, brilliant stage presence," no one would look at her or Tone. He "knew all of Shakespeare," she said, and taught her everything about acting. She also revealed a caring side to Tierney: When they were on the road, he sat up all night with her, helping her get off the drugs she said MGM had given her when she was under contract there.

He was sober for most of the tour, Betsy claimed, falling off the wagon only near the end. Columnist Vince Bird alleged that Larry "consumed more than a fifth between [the] matinee and evening show each afternoon and probably trebled the dosage from final curtain until the 1 a.m. curfew each night" when they were in Binghamton, New York. Although Betsy was reportedly Franchot Tone's fiancée, there were rumors that she and Larry had a love connection. Bird also wrote that, at the closing night's party in Binghamton, Tierney "paid a little attention to a local chick, and Von-watzername went into a paroxysm that was better than her emoting in the show."

Back at P.J. Clarke's in New York on August 8, 1952, Tierney met Philadelphia socialite Seward Heaton. For whatever reason, Heaton pestered him as Tierney tried in vain to ignore him ("Get away from me, ya crumb"). Finally, he flattened Heaton with a single haymaker between his eyes which resulted in a half-inch gash. Although the police were called, Heaton did not press charges.

Work was again scarce and it looked as if New York City was not the best place for him. Around this time, Tierney reportedly wrote a friend in Hollywood, "It's funny having kids stop you on the streets for autographs when you're wondering what the hell you're going to do next."

He could always count on getting into fights, and in November alone he duked it out on at least three separate occasions, as he made the rounds of the bars in the city. He also slugged a magazine writer outside P.J. Clarke's.

In January 1953, he was back in Hollywood and there was talk of the film *Brass Check* being a comeback vehicle for the wayward actor. That same month, he played a vicious convict in a segment for a proposed TV series called *Duffy of San Quentin* (based on the film of the same name). Starring Paul Kelly as Warden Clinton T. Duffy, three episodes were made but never aired; in 1954, they were edited together and released theatrically as *The Steel Cage*.

One of Tierney's most bizarre arrests came on February 10. Arriving by cab at Ocean Park, Tierney went over to a car and offered its occupants (three girls) a swig from his gin bottle. After they refused, he reportedly stood in front of the car and made faces at them. He then went over to two men on a bus bench and offered them a sip; they, too, declined. A cop, who had witnessed the whole thing, asked Larry where he lived, and Tierney replied, "I'm a pigeon and don't have a home." Arrested for drunkenness, he was released on $100 bail. After he no-showed in court a few days later, a warrant was issued. The judge declared the original bail forfeit; bail on the warrant was set at $500.

About a week later, Tierney entered the Blue Angel and began verbally abusing the waiters. "Two of them are good enough with their dukes to spar with Rocky Graziano," wrote Dorothy Kilgallen. "Luckily for the Hollywood bad boy, a couple of cooler heads rushed him out of the place just in time." Not long after this, he was back raising hell. Again at P.J. Clarke's, he knocked out a press agent; he later apologized, saying it was "just drunk stuff." The always unpredictable Tierney turned up the following night at Trader Tom's Steak House playing chess. At a cocktail party not long afterward, he kayoed a guy who called him "a star of gin-erama." In another case, reported Dorothy Kilgallen, he "took a stranger's girl away from him, slugged the fellow, and left in a cab with the girl before the police arrived." In June 1953, Earl Wilson said that Tierney had "retired as a barroom brawler" and was seen sipping orange juice and playing chess with a girl at the Shelburne Café.

In New York, he seriously dated showgirl June Kirby; they were spotted at various clubs drinking milk. Dorothy Kilgallen called Kirby a "brave girl" to be dating Tierney, although the columnist admitted that he "looked sober, amiable and unmenacing ... so maybe the reform wave is on."

On July 25, 1953, Tierney was arrested after he and an ex-boxer made "ferocious pugilistic gestures at each other" (Associated Press) in front of a Broadway restaurant. It was pretty much a stand-off, with the two exchanging words and menacing looks as 200 bystanders "watched curiously." The police arrived and escorted the duo to jail for disorderly conduct. Tierney was given a $25 fine, a suspended 30-day sentence and a lecture from the judge: "This is the sort of stuff that is grist for the Moscow propaganda mill. What is the sense of this thing? What is the trouble? Do you want to ruin a career?"

Three days later, in the Tiger Lily Lounge on 45th Street, Tierney asked pianist Benjamin Martini to play "I Wonder Where My Old Girl Is To-night?" Larry began singing, which prompted heckles from the other bar patrons, and somehow a microphone hit Martini, who was treated for scalp lacerations. Tierney was charged with felonious assault, but this was reduced. Calling it an accident, Tierney pleaded innocent; he was cleared. Months later, Martini sued Larry for $50,000.

Cutting a bloody swath through the New York bar scene, Tierney was not making many friends. In August '53, columnist Lee Mortimer claimed three thugs were being paid $250 each to rearrange Larry's face. Less than six hours after that item hit the papers, Tierney was hit by two chairs by a lady at P.J. Clarke's ("Does she get the dough?" asked Mortimer). As a result, Tierney was barred from that nightspot (finally!) and "practically every other saloon in town."

For most of 1954, Tierney was on the wagon and he was getting work. He was seen around New York with Diane Herbert, oil heiress Angela Lamb, actress Arlyn Roberts, photographer Lenore Lester and even Christine Jorgensen. He did the play *The Time of Your Life* with Franchot Tone and his (Tone's) newest love, Gloria Vanderbilt. She felt an instant connection:

> Images shot into my mind's eye the moment we met—eyes like steel found me, made me sense that I could be the stream to feed the roots, for his love seemed like a tree, needing a strange alchemy from my eyes—green moss, absorbing his eyes that shut me out.

Apparently not much of a devotee of the daily newspapers, Vanderbilt did not believe that Tierney had a bad rep:

> [He] scribbled poetry to me on paper napkins in coffeehouses as we sat philosophizing about this and that—obscure bits and pieces, passed wordlessly across the table like furtive notes

in school, strange and brilliant but making no sense. But what is "sense" coming from a poet, inarticulate and shut off from everyone save the few such as moi who had the sensitivity to understand him.

During *Time of Your Life* rehearsals, the play's director Sanford Meisner thought Larry was drunk and fired him; "It made him more fascinating than ever," Vanderbilt noted. His increasingly erratic moods soon dampened her ardor, especially when he telephoned her, "rattled, off-balance," right before she was to do a live sketch on *The Colgate Comedy Hour* with Tone. "I wasn't meant to be Florence Nightingale after all, nor did I want to be ... or did I? But no matter. Tierney had unsettled me, nothing more....I suspect he always found one Florence Nightingale or another who felt she was the one to save him...."

Tierney was offered the role of Charlie "The Gent" Malloy in Elia Kazan's *On the Waterfront* (1954), but for some reason, perhaps just his self-destructive streak, he demanded more money than was being offered. The chance-of-a-lifetime offer was promptly rescinded and in stepped Rod Steiger, who was Oscar-nominated. (Some sources claim Tierney was also in the running for the role that ultimately won Steiger an Oscar: the police chief in *In the Heat of the Night* [1967].)

In May 1954, Tierney had a supporting part as a gangster in director Max Nosseck's New York–lensed Holocaust musical-drama *Singing in the Dark*, produced by comedian Joey Adams. CBS took a chance on casting him on TV's *Man Behind the Badge*. In August, he acted on stage in Litchfield, Connecticut, in *Laura*, and there was talk of him starring as a New York detective in a series called *The Concrete Jungle*.

Producer Fred Finklehoffe sought to have Orson Welles direct and Tierney star in a Broadway adaptation of Nelson Algren's *The Man with the Golden Arm*; *Variety* opined, "Tierney, who has gotten himself straightened out after his recent personal difficulties, would be a natural for the title role of the card dealer in a Chicago gambling house." Yes, he would have, but it never came off.

Tierney began filming in November 1954 what would be his final lead role in a motion picture, *Girl Murdered*, actor Burt Kaiser's only film as an indie producer. The film's low production values and convoluted script (by Kaiser) work in its favor, producing a seedy, tawdry atmosphere that is completely noir. Tierney is given one of his best chances, playing Jack Stevens, a troubled, alcoholic police detective who suffers a blackout the same night as the strangulation murder of an actress. In this whodunit, Stevens wonders if *he* done it, and is determined to find the culprit.

Girl Murdered sat on the shelf for two years. During that time, a minor actress who had film-debuted in it, Jayne Mansfield, jumped to prominence, acting in movies and starring on Broadway in *Will Success Spoil Rock Hunter?* (1956). With the new title *Female Jungle* and special "Introducing" billing for Mansfield, it was released by American Releasing Corp (soon to become AIP).

Nineteen fifty-five found Tierney minding his ps and qs and off the sauce. Starting on June 27, at the Lakewood Theater in Lakewood Park, Pennsylvania, he starred in a week-long production of *Detective Story*. Marian Sheafer (*Pottsville Republican*) thought he did a "fine job in an unaccustomed role" as Detective James McLeod, "who has no warmth in his heart, who knows only that right is right and wrong is wrong."

The calm did not last. His 18 months of keeping a low profile ended in July when he was involved in a drunken brawl in a Fire Island, New York, pub with burly John "Shipwreck" Kelly over a girl they both fancied. (Dorothy Kilgallen: "She was Shipwreck's but eyewitnesses report she gave Tierney a bit of flirtatious encouragement just before the battle was joined.") "Shipwreck" later claimed he was never on Fire Island and never scuffled with Tierney. The following month, after yet another bar fight, Larry was ordered to leave Fire Island and never return. A restless Tierney wanted to land a part on Broadway, but this never happened, and he returned to Hollywood in October.

Life settled down a little bit after his Fire Island escapades. He was seen with another socialite, Barbara Gainsborough, and jazz singer Gayle Andrews. A movie called *Panic* with John Carradine was to be another screen comeback, but it never happened. In late February '56, he was involved in a brawl in the Old Knick in New York City and barred from the establishment. The following month, he was booked on a drunk and disorderly charge. At the police station, he took on two policemen. He pleaded guilty and received a suspended sentence. Shortly after midnight on April 9, at an Upper East Side intersection, a policemen tried to help Tierney, very unsteady on his feet, cross the street, Larry knocked him down. Taken to a local lock-up, Larry tried to hit another detective, was restrained, and put in a cell to sleep off his drunk. The next day, pleading guilty to disorderly conduct, he apologized and he was given a suspended sentence.

In 1956, there were no new acting assignments for him. In July, it was reported that he had a new career, selling stocks on Wall Street. With Tierney no longer making the headlines, Lee Mortimer asked in September, "Lawrence Tierney … and what became of him and who cares?"

Tierney was now being called a "former film star." Receiving his New York union work permit, he was employed as a construction laborer ("now cracking rocks instead of chins," noted Hy Gardner). Tierney admitted to Gardner,

> Yeah, I'm working as an iron man on construction jobs in New York City. If you think I'm going to tell you exactly where, you're crazy! Do you think I want crowds of people gaping at me? I've been at it for some weeks—I want to get in condition and lose a little weight for a movie role in the fall, a lead role. I play a man who comes out of prison and tries to reform himself.

Larry had also rejoined Alcoholics Anonymous.

A return to acting in October was short-lived: He walked out of a stage production of *The Last Mile* after an argument with its director.

On March 30, 1957, he was driving in Manhattan when he hit another vehicle. He got out of his car and proceeded to spit on the man in the other car and then punch him. He was arrested for driving intoxicated and without a license, and for assault; after a night in the jug, he was ordered by the judge to appear at an April 22 hearing. When he no-showed, the judge issued three warrants for his arrest. "I called this case three times," he said. "At his first appearance, I felt sorry for him, he looked so shabby. Now he is taking advantage of this court, so I will issue a warrant on each charge."

The next day, Tierney was in court brimming with apologies. He said he had been looking for work as a wire lather (building structural frameworks) and thought his lawyer had gotten an adjournment for him.

May 27, 1957, saw him in another jam involving a vehicle: After a brief pursuit, in which Tierney eluded two police cars through Queens, he was finally collared for running two red lights and reckless driving. On July 28, he was walking across Broadway when he was struck by a motorcycle; his minor injuries were treated at Knickerbocker Hospital. He was still brawling and being kicked out of bars.

He and his on again-off again girlfriend Georgette McDonald (the girl Cholly Knickerbocker claimed "makes Jayne Mansfield look like a boy") had a highly volatile relationship, and they often got into physical altercations at New York bars. If she dated other men, Tierney beat them up, and he would telephone her friends in search of her.

On August 25, 1957, Tierney, who had not heard from McDonald in a while, went to the apartment she shared with Eileen Keenan—unaware that she had moved out. Keenan was asleep when Larry began pounding on the door, demanding to be let in. When he broke down the door, a hysterical Keenan ran out onto the fire escape and called for help. Tierney left, but soon surrendered to police. They charged him with burglary, which surprised Keenan: "I just want him to stay away from me. He didn't take anything." Tierney said burglary was the farthest thing from his mind, and he had broken the door down because he thought she said it was stuck and needed help opening it! He was freed on $500 bail. The burglary complaint was reduced to unlawful entry, and then summarily dismissed by felony court magistrate Louis S. Wallach. "It seems unfortunate that a man of your talents has these things happen because of drinking," Wallach chided. "There's no reason why you can't stop this nonsense."

In mid–December 1957, Tierney got into a bar fight with Bill Wakeman over Georgette McDonald. He forgot about her by the following year, when it was rumored that he was headed to the altar with wealthy divorcée Hazel Kellogg. The rough-and-tumble Tierney was always catnip to socialites.

Someone had the bright idea of setting Tierney up in a private eye agency but, for once, wiser heads prevailed. For a while, he taught a drama class in Brooklyn. In April 1958, he was in Silver Springs, Florida, filming a TV series, *Civil Air Patrol*, with Sammy Petrillo. It was set at the local airport and Tierney learned to fly to play the role. Petrillo told Todd Rutt in *Psychotronic Video*,

> In the pilot I was ferrying in a bunch of rattlesnakes and I got bitten and had to crash-land. Then Larry comes and saves me....[The producers] told me I had to keep Larry busy, running track and playing cards with him so he doesn't drink. I said okay. So, I'm a little skinny kid. I'd be exhausted running track with him, before we'd shoot, after we'd shoot. Then we started playing cards, but he wanted to bet money. It cost me 800 bucks to keep the guy sober.

The pilot went unsold.

On July 24, 1958, back in New York City, Tierney was booked on a felonious assault charge brought against him by a Manhattan resident who claimed that on May 6, Larry broke his jaw in a fight. On October 13 into the 14th, Tierney "went on another of his periodic rampages": He and his friend Arthur Kennedy (not the actor) caused a disturbance in a midtown bar, "using boisterous language" and attacking bystanders outside. Two policemen arrived, one commenting that by that point Tierney and Kennedy "looked as though they had been in a half-dozen fistfights." Resisting arrest, Tierney kicked patrolman Louis Romano in the groin. Pacified via a billy club shot to the head and taken into custody, the bloody Larry was charged with disorderly conduct and felonious assault, the latter eventually changed to simple assault. Again, he was given another chance.

One Third Avenue bar had a sign out front that read, "Lawrence Tierney Fought Here." It was probably a given that New York City was happy to see him go back to California in 1959. He rejoined AA in hopes of revitalizing his dormant career.

On May 3, 1959, at about 9:30 a.m., Tierney stood in the middle of North Cahuenga

Blvd. verbally harassing three men who were headed to church. "He was pretty well loaded, but no force had to be used to bring him in," said the arresting officer. Tierney was released later that day; his bail money was forfeited when he didn't show up for court. On September 18, outside Hollywood High School, Tierney, reeking of whiskey, was pinched for trading punches with an elderly man.

Indie producer Medhat Mandour had an idea of casting Tierney as gangster Vincent "Mad Dog" Coll, but this potentially interesting project went nowhere. Tierney had aspirations to write for television, but this, too, never materialized. Television jobs trickled in, with appearances on such series as *New York Confidential, Naked City* and *The Detectives*.

On November 8, 1959, an intoxicated Tierney forced his way into an apartment looking for a woman who had been his date earlier in the evening. When he found another man there, he punched him out. For good measure, he also ripped the living room curtains to shreds. He was jailed on charges of drunkenness and battery. He pleaded not guilty and faced trial on January 7, 1960.

He didn't wait for the dust from this newest dust-up to settle before he was arrested again. On December 12, while heading to a bar, he and two men had a fistfight on a Los Angeles street corner. A drunken Tierney was bleeding from the mouth when the police took him away. There was a detour to the Central Receiving Hospital to care for Larry's split lip; an officer stuffed a towel in Tierney's mouth to stop him from yelling obscenities at the nurse attending him. A couple of days later, he got a one-day suspended sentence.

On January 7, 1960, the day Tierney went to court to answer to a battery charge, his 65-year-old mother was found dead in the Hollywood apartment where she resided with her son Ed. (By this time, both mother and son were divorced.) There was a bottle of sleeping pills next to her. Larry was so distraught, he got drunk and landed in jail that night. His brother Scott blamed Larry for her death and it was the start of an estrangement that lasted more than 20 years. "Things were sour between Larry and Scott since they were kids," said Tim Tierney, "and this was the final straw. They only started talking again when Eddie died in '83, but never really patched things up."

Tierney was seen in two TV episodes airing on the same night, January 25: Charles Bronson's *Man with a Camera*, where he played an ice cream vendor peddling narcotics at an amusement park, and *Adventures in Paradise*, portraying a grizzled, alcoholic sea captain. The series displayed Tierney's versatility, in two different types of roles, but no further work was made available to him.

Back on the wagon, but not for long: On May 30, 1960, he was arrested for attempting to force his way into the apartment of a gal pal. When Tierney was asked by police to identify himself, he pointed to the label on the bottle of Grand Macnish Scotch whiskey he was holding and replied, "Mr. Macnish." He remained in jail for five hours. The following day, he did not show up at Beverly Hills Municipal Court to answer to the charge of drunkenness. He was back in hot water on December 15 for driving under the influence in West Hollywood. The verdict on this case did not come until May of the following year, when he was fined $158, placed on probation and had his driver's license suspended for 30 days.

On December 26, 1960, Tierney guested on TV's *Peter Gunn* as a smooth operator who kidnaps a bank cashier and gets into a scuffle with Gunn (Craig Stevens). It was a small role, but Tierney showed his usual command in a part he could have done in his sleep by this point. The episode was co-written by ex-actor Tony Barrett, once an RKO contract player; Tierney had beaten him to death in *Born to Kill*.

His next acting job did not come until May 1961, when he was cast as a detective on *The Barbara Stanwyck Show* in the A.I. Bezzerides–written episode "The Assassin." Any good this admittedly small appearance could have done for him was negated when, on June 30, he tried to crash a private party Elizabeth Taylor and Eddie Fisher were hosting at Los Angeles' P.J.'s Restaurant for the touring Russian Moiseyev Dance Troupe of Moscow. When security guards and police tried to eject him, Tierney turned on them outside and was cuffed and charged with drunkenness and disturbing the peace. "Witnesses say he had nothing against the Russians," remarked one reporter, "he objected to not being served." At the police station, Tierney immediately fell asleep. Bail was set at $393.75. He pleaded innocent at a July 12 hearing. He was to go to trial on August 23, but the judge decided that this latest incident was a violation of the terms of his 1960 drunk-driving arrest, and he was ordered to serve 60 days behind bars. After his release, he returned to P.J.'s and apologized for creating the disturbance.

"Actor Lawrence Tierney, who has received so much unfavorable publicity with his drinking and barroom brawls, seems to be hitting the comeback trail instead of the bottle," wrote Dorothy Kilgallen in November '61. "Those who witnessed his first performance in the TV series *Follow the Sun* report that he was splendid." In fact, according to *Variety*, he "got a hefty round of applause from *Follow the Sun* set after a dramatic scene." The episode's highlight was the shootout between him and gravel-voiced tough guy Charles McGraw.

On November 30, 1961, Tierney entered the bar of a Hollywood bowling alley and approached accountant John A. Fox, demanding, "Where is my ten bucks?" before hitting the man. An arrest for battery was pending, but Fox decided not to prosecute. In December, a fight with an unidentified man left Tierney with abrasions on his knuckles and left knee. He was arrested on a drunk charge and released on $21.

Attending Alcoholics Anonymous three to five times a week, he was angling again for a comeback. Louella Parsons was pleased that Tierney was getting some work: "I have always liked Lawrence Tierney, and his mother used to talk to me about him. She had such faith in him. Lawrence is unfortunate that he has been accused often when he hasn't deserved it, and of course sometimes when he has."

On February '62, he appeared on an episode of TV's *Bus Stop*. He was to act in the *Dick Powell Theatre* episode "The Sea Witch" when it went before the camera in July 1962, but he was replaced at the last minute by Gerald Mohr. He did not get another TV role until he was signed for *The Lloyd Bridges Show* in the John Cassavetes–directed "A Pair of Boots," which aired in October.

He was considered for the role of Bobby Darin's father in Stanley Kramer's *Pressure Point* (1962). This did not happen, but producer Kramer soon gave him a part in *A Child Is Waiting* (1963) with Burt Lancaster, Judy Garland and Gena Rowlands, also directed by Cassavetes. "I loved [Cassavetes]. He liked me, too," Tierney told Rick McKay. The actor continued:

> It was a great experience to work with him. Gena Rowlands [Mrs. Cassavetes] was very snooty and very full of herself, like she was "*Miss* Gena Rowlands to you." John was very human, very warm, very down to earth. You tolerated her because you worshiped him. Judy Garland was … very nice. Easy to work with, no matter what they say.

The role appealed to Tierney because it was a change of pace: "I'm not a tough guy in this picture," he told Vernon Scott at the time. "Now maybe people will treat me like any other actor. I certainly hope so."

This was his first movie since 1954. "I've learned a number of important things in the last few years," Tierney told Scott. "One of them is that policemen don't like to get slugged." Claiming he was the last person in the world who wanted to get into a bar fight, he stated that sometimes it just can't be helped: "Every time I went into a bar, some guy wanted to take a poke at me so he could tell his friends about it. For a while I thought I had to uphold my reputation as a tough guy. So I fought 'em. But I finally realized I had nothing to gain, even if I won the barroom fight." These fights, he said, were a thing of the past, and he was looking forward to a calmer future and more acting jobs.

No such luck.

On June 1, 1962, at an all-night restaurant in Santa Monica, a "drunk and disorderly" Tierney argued with the night manager and cook, using "abusive and profane language" in front of the other patrons. Again, the long arm of the law reached out for him; he was released on $52.50 bail.

More arrests came in July and September '62. For the July incident, he was tried in October; he was facing accusations of throwing a cup of hot coffee and a glass of Scotch in the face of actor Dimitrios C. Georgopoulos. Georgopoulos claimed that Larry also tried to pull off his neck brace, and ripped the receiver out of a telephone when Georgopoulos tried to call the police. In court, the plaintiff did not appear and the charges against Tierney were dismissed.

Days later, Larry was arrested for being drunk and disorderly at a Sunset Blvd. apartment. A fight outside a bar on September 28 resulted in Tierney being cut with a beer bottle. Each time he was arrested, he insisted it would be the last, and he was trying to stop drinking with the help of AA. He received probation each time.

"Friends of Lawrence Tierney, who were hoping recent TV jobs would rehabilitate him, have been let down again," Eunice Field wrote in *TV Radio Mirror* (December '62). "The usual drunk charge ... but Hollywood keeps wishing on a could-be talented star."

May 1963 was a busy month, but the only *good* thing was his appearance as a gangland boss on *The Alfred Hitchcock Hour's* "Death of a Cop." That month, he was again pinched on a drunk charge. Soon after being released, there was another incident: His visit to a Hollywood lunch counter dissolved into insults and the wielding of objects. Witnesses told police that Tierney entered the establishment shouting obscenities. After he calmed down a bit, he ordered some coffee. As the counterman approached Larry, he was greeted by something decidedly not on the menu: a knuckle sandwich. The counterman "thanked" Larry with a slap across the face with a towel; Larry went berserk and began "throwing everything in sight" at the server. Tierney passed him the sugar—bowl and all—and the server passed Larry the cream dispenser—over his head. By the time police arrived, Tierney had fled; they found him passed out on the floor of his apartment and took him to the main jail medical section. Both men needed stitches to close up their wounds. The waiter sued for $65,000.

Still in the not-so-Merry Month of May, a woman claimed that Tierney had kidnapped her as she left a Sunset Blvd. restaurant. For seven hours, she related, they drove around Hollywood and Beverly Hills. She finally escaped when Tierney stopped at a hotel "to see someone." When the police arrested Larry, they said he was "highly confused and largely incoherent." His nephew Michael Tierney said,

> He had hundreds of fistfights with men but as far as I know he never hit a woman. I could be wrong, but so far, I have seen no evidence. He did stalk, bully, seduce, charm, etc. For example, he never hit my mother whom he had a child with. He would have her driving him all

over Los Angeles holding her captive in the car while he visited friends and drank in bars but that's about it. Harmless but exhausting.

On October 17, 1963, in New York City, Tierney got into a shoving match with two policemen who tried to arrest a friend of his for drunk driving. He was fined $25 for disorderly conduct.

Tierney's 72-year-old father died of a heart attack on February 13, 1964, in Hollywood. Four days later, in Manhattan, Larry was involved in a bizarre incident while riding in a taxi. He said the cabbie was "endangering my physical welfare" by arguing with the driver of another car over the right of way. Tierney reached from the back seat and turned off the cab's ignition and began choking the driver. Of course, Tierney was arrested: he was given a suspended sentence "on the condition that you try to help yourself." He told the judge he had stopped drinking.

His acting career had now fallen by the wayside. For the next few years, his name would only be mentioned in the newspapers in connection with his troubled personal life. Sheilah Graham wrote on May 6, 1964, "Lawrence Tierney was at it again in New York, in a rage in the lobby of an apartment house, smashing up things. But no one wanted to press charges. What a curse that firewater can be."

When the film *Young Dillinger* premiered in June '65, *Los Angeles Times* reviewer Kevin Thomas commented that Nick Adams' portrayal of the title gangster did not erase memories of Tierney's effort 20 years before. Thomas added, "Lawrence Tierney's classic tight-lipped, steely-eyed portrayal remains easier to accept as an accurate delineation of a vintage gangster."

If only there were more writeups of this type to help Tierney jumpstart his career. Around this time, he was trying to make a go of it in Italy, as an actor and a screenwriter for Spaghetti Westerns. If he had any credits as writer, they were under a pseudonym. He acted in *Assassino senza volto* (aka *Killer Without a Face*), playing a mute handyman.

While Tierney was in Europe, his activities went completely unreported for a lengthy stretch. His nephew Michael offers a possible explanation:

> Larry spent time in prison in Spain for manslaughter sometime in the '60s. I was told it was for two years but probably not that long. Apparently, he was in Italy on the set of [a Hercules-type film] and he borrowed Steve Reeves' Corvette. He got drunk and picked up a streetwalker and totaled the car, killing her. He fled the scene and ran to Spain and was captured and thrown in jail for a while. This is Larry's account yet there was virtually no press about it.

Earl Wilson wrote in October '66, "One-time movie bad guy Lawrence Tierney, who lost the battle to booze, is making a screen comeback—as a good guy." The movie in question, made in Spain, was *Custer's Last Stand*, directed by Robert Siodmak. It was produced by Philip Yordan, who later said that Tierney was "crazy" but completely sober during filming; he also said that Larry gave a brilliant performance. But Spanish officials aware of his reputation asked him to leave the country immediately after he finished his part. Shown in the U.S. as *Custer of the West* two years later, the film starred Robert Shaw as General George Custer with Tierney as his superior, General Phil Sheridan. Others in the cast included Robert Ryan, Jeffrey Hunter, Ty Hardin, Kieron Moore and Marc Lawrence.

Tierney was out of the news until January 6, 1967, when, in a Paris department store, he allegedly ripped a tag off a sweater and stuffed it into his jacket. His excuse: He intended to examine it by the light of day near the door and had no intention of stealing it. He was fined $80 and received a one-month suspended sentence.

By December '67, he was working for $7 an hour as a construction worker at the General Motors Building on Fifth Avenue in Manhattan.

Jack O'Brian, in his column "The Voice of Broadway," called Larry "a good actor whose life is a sad script." There were people in the industry willing to give him a chance, but he always seemed to scotch the deal. "[He] finally sobered up and wised up," Hy Gardner wrote in May 1969. "He got a job moving furniture to build himself up physically. Mickey Spillane just signed him to play the heavy in *The Delta Factor*, observing, 'Anyone who overcomes his alcoholic cancer deserves a break—and I'm giving one to Larry.'" But Tierney was not in the movie. He was cast in the title role in director John G. Avildsen's *Joe* but, two days before shooting commenced, Larry urinated on a Bloomingdale's escalator and hit a saleslady. In 2014, talking with *Screen Anarchy*'s Zach Gayne, Lloyd Kaufman, a production assistant on *Joe*, remembered the scene a little differently: "Lawrence Tierney! We were taking him in to get a fitting at Alexander's Department Store, and he pissed on my.... I felt this thing on my blue jeans, like that's a weird feeling. He was urinating on me. He was drunk! They got rid of him!" Tierney was replaced in *Joe* by Peter Boyle.

Tierney took to doing TV commercials, continuing in that field for many years. Around this time, Jack O'Brian wrote that Tierney was "happier as a construction hard hat than acting." Part of that "happy" was "blowing up to 235 pounds." The now-bald Tierney no longer had his leading man looks, but he retained his gruff, intimating presence, which made him useful in the few character parts and commercials he got between construction jobs and (*gasp*) bartending.

Jack O'Brian, "The Voice of Broadway," December 3, 1971: "Lawrence Tierney did a walk-on during the New York filming of Otto Preminger's *Such Good Friends* and upset a few people, including several pinched gals."

On January 18, 1973, Tierney was involved in a Manhattan street fight with Robert Rosado. They were brawling with their fists when Larry was stabbed in the stomach. He was rushed to St. Clare's Hospital. Rosado was charged with felonious assault and weapons possession. Tierney lost out on a stage role in *Gaslight* with Dawn Wells in Houston due to his injury.

Jack O'Brian, February 21, 1974: "Off- and on-screen tough guy Lawrence Tierney will have an acting go again: he said at Pete's Tavern he'll play Willy Loman in a Philadelphia revival of *Death of a Salesman*." To be directed by George C. Scott, no less! Actually, Larry did not star (Martin Balsam did), but he had a part in the production; and Scott was replaced by the playwright, Arthur Miller.

Also in 1974, Tierney began driving a hansom cab and, on the side, teaching a drama workshop in Manhattan. It was not an easy life. "There was a long time when he was just drinking and living in abandoned buildings and hoboing around the streets of New York," said nephew Michael. Former flame Gloria Vanderbilt saw him around: "He was almost unrecognizable slumped against a parked car in no condition to catch my eye. My impulse was to go to him. But I didn't. I walked on by. I knew there was nothing I could do to save him."

In June 1975, he was in the apartment of a 24-year-old secretary, drinking, when the nightgown-clad redhead jumped out of the fourth-floor window. Sustaining a fractured skull and internal injuries, she died in a hospital two hours later. Tierney, sobbing, explained,

We were sitting in her living room enjoying ourselves. Suddenly she said, "I'm going to jump." She put her drink of Scotch down, walked to the window, and went out. I couldn't believe it. I thought she was joking. For God's sake, if I knew she was serious, I could have grabbed her. I really loved the kid.

More small movie parts followed: *Abduction* (1975), *Andy Warhol's Bad* (1977), *The Kirlian Witness* (1979), *Bloodrage* (1979), *Gloria* (1980), *Arthur* (1981) and *The Prowler* (1981). Reportedly, he was up for the role of Perry White in Richard Donner's *Superman* (1978). In the late '70s, when schlock producer Sam Sherman was putting together a package of movies for TV, one of them was the 1966 English horror flick *Naked Evil*; he decided to "improve" it by retitling it *Exorcism at Midnight* and shooting new framing sequences with Tierney and another old-timer, cowboy star Robert Allen, as doctors.

Tierney had a sleazy but good role in John A. Russo's *Midnight* (1982) as a police officer who tries to force himself on his stepdaughter but later rescues her from Satanists. He had better material when he appeared with his friend James Cagney in the telemovie *Terrible Joe Moran*. That year (1984), Tierney was also seen in an Excedrin commercial as a construction worker; guested on TV's *Fame*, and played the driver of a horse-drawn carriage in the movie *Nothing Lasts Forever*. Tough as nails, he appeared fourteenth-billed in Stephen King's *Silver Bullet* (1985), wielding a bat called the Peace Maker against werewolves in a small town. His nephew Tim recalled:

[In 1983,] Larry came out to Los Angeles for [his brother] Eddie's funeral and ended up staying since he had nothing particular to return to in New York City, and decided to try to get back into Hollywood. I recall him coming to my house a few times during that period (it was always tense between him and my parents) and all of us turning on the TV show that was going to run his Excedrin commercial....

The upswing in Tierney's career started with John Huston's *Prizzi's Honor* (1985). It was a small role (as a police lieutenant) but in a high-profile movie. Ditto for his participation in Charles Bronson's *Murphy's Law* (1986). Between 1985 and '87, Tierney had a recurring role as Sgt. Jenkins on TV's *Hill Street Blues*.

He joined a good group of veteran actors for the 1987 indie *The Offspring*, aka *From a Whisper to a Scream*: Vincent Price, Clu Gulager, Cameron Mitchell. On a much larger scale, Norman Mailer's *Tough Guys Don't Dance* (1987) got Tierney a lot of attention. In it, he played one of his favorite roles, as Ryan O'Neal's "amusingly gravelly" (*Los Angeles Times*) father. At the time of its release, Tierney remarked, "I haven't had a drink in, oh, five years now. I finally wised up. I'd say it was about time. Heck, I threw away about seven careers through drink."

He guested on *Remington Steele*, *Tales from the Darkside*, *The Slap Maxwell Story* and *Star Trek: The Next Generation*, and gave a memorably tough performance as a police detective in a 1988 *Hunter* episode, "The Black Dahlia," which centered on the 1947 murder. There were more smallish film roles, too: *The Naked Gun: From the Files of Police Squad!* (1988), *The Horror Show* (1989), *Why Me?* (1990) and the Mark Harmon-starring TV movie *Dillinger* (1991), in which Tierney played a sheriff.

The television role everyone remembers is Tierney's turn in the *Seinfeld* episode "The Jacket" (1990). He played Elaine's (Julia Louis-Dreyfus) father, war veteran, adventurer and writer Alton Benes.

ALTON: Which one's supposed to be the funny guy?
GEORGE (*POINTING TO JERRY*): Ah! He's the comedian!

ALTON: We had a funny guy with us in Korea. Tail gunner. They blew his brains out all over the Pacific. There's nothing funny about that.

The crusty Tierney was absolutely brilliant; few, if any, actors could be as intimidating ("Pipe down, chorus boy!" he growls at George). The episode's priceless payoff, with Larry singing "Master of the House" (from *Les Misérables*), makes one wish he was allowed to do more comedy. This appearance was to be the beginning of a recurring role, but it didn't work out. The regular cast members admitted that his bizarre behind-the-scenes antics scared the hell out of them. On a kitchen set, Tierney surreptitiously took a butcher knife and hid it under his jacket, presumably intending to steal it. Confronted by Jerry Seinfeld, he cooked up an excuse and "kiddingly" did some *Psycho*-like downward thrusts with it. Needless to say, Alton Benes—who might have become a recurring *Seinfeld* character—never returned. We are poorer for that.

As an aside: In the next season's *Seinfeld* episode "The Boyfriend," Elaine sits in a car with baseball player Keith Hernandez (playing himself), winding up a date and chitchatting.

HERNANDEZ: You know, my mom's one-quarter Cajun.
ELAINE: My father's half-drunk.

Producers weren't breaking down Tierney's door but he kept fairly busy, certainly busier than he had been in the '60s and '70s. In addition to an episode of TV's *Equal Justice*, there were the 1991 features *The Runestone*, *City of Hope*, *The Death Merchant* and *Wizards of the Demon Sword*. Fred Olen Ray, producer-director of the latter, wrote of his first meeting with Tierney:

At a restaurant on Cahuenga, Larry Tierney went through the cafeteria line with a full tray, came to our table without paying and sat down, bypassing the cash register altogether.
I said, "Larry, do you need me to pay for that?"
Larry said, "You don't get it, kid. My middle name is crime, and crime does not pay."

Sometime later, Tierney's agent phoned Ray to see if there was a part for the actor in Ray's next picture. According to Ray, "I politely told the agent that Larry had threatened to kill me on our last picture and I didn't feel like we were a very good match."

The film that heralded Tierney's "comeback"—and proved once and for all that he was *the* man—was the heist movie *Reservoir Dogs* (1992). Tierney, as Joe Cabot, "with a voice like a tow-truck winch, is gruff as they get as the gang's rapacious boss" (*Los Angeles Times*). Director Quentin Tarantino inserted an in-joke for Tierney: Cabot says that one of his henchmen is "dead as Dillinger."

Norman Mailer had recommended Tierney to Tarantino, but with warnings. Still, Tarantino had his problems with Larry, calling him "insane": "He should not be walking the streets. He should be in Bellevue with constant medication....You can't talk to him. He's that far from having a nervous breakdown."

One night during the making of *Reservoir Dogs*, there was an incident at home: Larry took a .357 Magnum and started shooting at his nephew Michael. Tim revealed:

Michael had spent the afternoon pissing Larry off by lecturing him on spirituality. Mike saw Larry come out of his bedroom with a gun and ran out of the apartment, but Larry shot through the wall, trying to get him in the hallway. Mike went down to the street and phoned the cops to say there was an "accident," and made sure they didn't send the SWAT team after Larry, possibly saving his life.

Michael Tierney clarifies that the gun incident

had nothing to do with me lecturing him about spirituality. Larry was so tense during the early days of filming and actually earlier that day got into a fistfight with Quentin and was fired. Tempers calmed and a few hours later he was *re-hired* that afternoon. But Larry was still upset and stressed out and went out and got shit-faced drunk on whiskey at Boarder's and other Hollywood bars. I smelled trouble and called around and went looking for him that night and I finally found him passed out on his apartment floor, waking from time to time to flail his arms to guzzle from a big bottle of whiskey. When he tried to shoot me, he was in a full black-out yet surprisingly pulled it together enough to surprise me with the gun.

After I got him safely apprehended, he spent the weekend in jail, was bailed out by his agent, and the news of his arrest was kept from the director and producers until *after* shooting was over. The bullets pierced the walls of other apartments, going through two thick walls and a hallway, coming within inches of a Mexican family next door. That gun was huge and looked exactly like Clint Eastwood's long-barrel gun in Dirty Harry.

Reservoir Dogs cemented Tierney's badass rep and gained him a cult following. Unfortunately for the actor, it did not lead to better movies or roles: *Eddie Presley* (1992) and *Junior* (1994), the short films *Red* (1993) and *French Intensive* (1994) and the telefilms *Casualties of Love: The Long Island Lolita Story* (1993) and *A Kiss Goodnight* (1994). He was also seen on TV's *Silk Stalkings, L.A. Law* and *Pointman*.

In 1993, he was to have a major supporting part in the indie *Tollbooth* but, due to "scheduling conflicts" (*Variety*), he was replaced by Seymour Cassel. In April of that year, he was cast as a deputy prison warden in Oliver Stone's *Natural Born Killers* (1994), which was based on a story by Quentin Tarantino. Tierney later claimed that in rehearsals, Stone encouraged Woody Harrelson to ad-lib dialogue that caused the atmosphere on the set to "hit the boiling point." Tim Tierney picks the story up here: "Larry and Woody may have already had some bad blood between them, and their rehearsal quickly turned into a shouting and shoving match with Larry saying, 'Fuck you and your hemp pants!'"

Tierney was fired and replaced by Everett Quinton. Larry took the matter up with SAG and Stone responded by sending a letter telling his side of the story. *Variety* reported that Tierney claimed that Stone's version of events was untrue, libelous "and damaging to his career." Apparently, it was alleged that Tierney had been drinking, but he said he "has not had a drink in over two years." He filed a $2,550,000 suit against Stone and his company: $2,500,000 for libel plus $50,000 for the salary he claims was due him for the role.

Josh Weinstein, who worked behind the scenes on the animated TV sitcom *The Simpsons*, told writer Cydney Yeates that Tierney's 1995 appearance was "the craziest guest star experience we ever had." Reportedly, a temperamental Tierney yelled at and intimidated *Simpsons* crew members. But, Weinstein added, "He certainly delivered and he's one of my favorite characters we have had [on the show]."

His movie work was under the radar and got him no attention: *Starstruck* (1995), *Fatal Passion* (1995), *2 Days in the Valley* (1996), *Southie* (1998) and the unreleased *American Hero* (1997). In 1998's *Armageddon*, one of his rare mainstream movies, he played Bruce Willis' father. When Rick McKay told Tierney he had heard that Larry was "great" in the movie, Tierney dismissed him: "Baloney. I don't know how I am in it. I don't like to think too much or I die of chagrin when the movie finally comes out and I'm cut down to one second in it. I just take it as it comes." After more than 50 years in the business, Tierney knew the score.

A rare candid from the set of Tierney's comeback film *Reservoir Dogs* (1992). Despite the levity shown here with Michael Madsen (left) and Harvey Keitel (middle), the production was fraught with tension and Tierney even had a fistfight with the director.

"I was with Larry when the production company phoned him to do this picture, which he had no interest in," says Tim Tierney. "They paid him $10,000 for a one-day job and had to get some young girl on the phone to sweet-talk him into it. He later insisted they cut his scene because he overpowered Bruce Willis as an actor—which is probably true."

He did voice work in the straight-to-video 1996 releases *Toto Lost in New York, Who Stole Santa?* and *Christmas in Oz*. His last appearances on the small screen were in 1997 episodes of *EZ Streets* and *Star Trek: Deep Space Nine*.

His last film, *Evicted* (2000), was produced, written and directed by Michael Tierney, who also starred. According to Michael, when Larry returned to Hollywood, "he was much better behaved. He was still Larry for those people who knew him—he was still a tough guy, but not in jail all the time or anything like that. The people who knew Larry knew that wasn't all there was to Larry. He was a wacky, kind of quirky, comical guy, and a very nice man to a lot of people." Tim Tierney chimes in: "He was only better behaved due to old age slowing him down. Larry never got mellow."

And Larry remained tough until the end. His agent Don Gerler commented, "I was still bailing him out of jail. He was 75 years old and still the toughest guy in the bar!"

The last few years of Tierney's life were difficult, as he endured several strokes and had a pacemaker inserted, but he was cared for by Michael. There is some question whether or not Larry married, but he did have a couple of children. "I never heard of him being married," says Tim. "The only kid of his I know of is a daughter [Elizabeth, born August 19, 1961] that Eddie raised as his own."

"He has a couple of kids out there somewhere," says Michael. "I have a three-quarters sister by him [Elizabeth]. It's pretty confusing, but he met my mother first, before my dad, and had a kid by her, but my dad ended up marrying her. She's my sister, but we have the same mother, and her father is my uncle. Very *Chinatown*."

After a short stay in a Los Angeles nursing home, where he suffered from pneumonia, the 82-year-old Tierney passed away in his sleep on February 26, 2002. "No word on how many stitches Death needed after that collection," wrote one columnist.

On-screen and off-, no one could match Tierney's killer edge. He was typecast because he had that don't-mess-with-me attitude. His career was derailed by personal demons, but he continued to work almost up until the time he died. Anne Jeffreys, who complemented him well in *Dillinger* and *Step by Step*, felt he could have been a bigger star and a better actor if he had taken it seriously. She thought he was a smart, well-read and charming man when he was sober … but he rarely was. "Larry spoke passable Spanish and French and kept company with Sartre while in France and could discuss his philosophy," says Tim.

Still, we shouldn't take for granted what Tierney did bring to the screen. It is a testament to his overwhelming charisma that we still remember him as one of the best of the bad guys. "You're not a turnip, are you?" Claire Trevor remarks approvingly in *Born to Kill*.

Nope. That's something Tierney never was.

1943: *Gildersleeve on Broadway* (uncredited), *Government Girl* (uncredited), *The Ghost Ship* (uncredited).
1944: *The Falcon Out West* (uncredited), *Seven Days Ashore* (uncredited), *Youth Runs Wild*.
1945: *Birthday Blues* (short), *Dillinger*, *Those Endearing Young Charms*, *Back to Bataan*, *Mama Loves Papa*, *Sing Your Way Home* (uncredited).
1946: *Badman's Territory*, *Step by Step*, *San Quentin*.
1947: *The Devil Thumbs a Ride*, *Born to Kill*.
1948: *Bodyguard*.
1950: *Kill or Be Killed*, *Shakedown*.
1951: *The Hoodlum*, *Best of the Badmen*, *The Bushwhackers*.
1952: *The Greatest Show on Earth*.
1954: *The Steel Cage*.
1956: *Singing in the Dark*, *Female Jungle*.
1963: *A Child Is Waiting*.
1967: *Custer of the West*.
1968: *Assassino senza volto* (*Killer Without a Face*).
1971: *Such Good Friends*.
1975: *Abduction*.
1977: *Bad*.
1979: *The Kirlian Witness*.
1980: *Exorcism at Midnight*, *Gloria*.
1981: *Bloodrage*, *Arthur*, *The Prowler*.

1982: *Midnight.*
1984: *Terrible Joe Moran* (TVM), *Nothing Lasts Forever.*
1985: *Prizzi's Honor, Silver Bullet.*
1986: *Murphy's Law.*
1987: *The Offspring (From a Whisper to a Scream), Tough Guys Don't Dance.*
1988: *The Naked Gun: From the Files of Police Squad!*
1989: *The Horror Show.*
1990: *Why Me?*
1991: *Dillinger* (TVM), *Wizards of the Demon Sword, The Runestone, City of Hope, The Death Merchant.*
1992: *Reservoir Dogs, Eddie Presley.*
1993: *Red* (short), *Casualties of Love: The Long Island Lolita Story* (TVM).
1994: *French Intensive* (short), *Junior, A Kiss Goodnight* (TVM).
1995: *Starstruck, Fatal Passion, American Hero* (video game, voice).
1996: *2 Days in the Valley, Toto Lost in New York* (video, voice), *Who Stole Santa?* (video, voice), *Christmas in Oz* (video short, voice).
1997: *American Hero.*
1998: *Southie, Armageddon* (uncredited).
1999: *Ciao, Babe.*
2000: *Evicted.*

Sonny Tufts

"Mark Hellinger convulsed several of us with this true tale," Walter Winchell wrote at the start of an October 1945 column item. He went on to relate that on a recent *Screen Guild Players* program, Joseph Cotten was

> reading the closing spiel about the next week's show.... The script had been changed at the last moment and the new version was handed to Cotten (who hadn't had time to study it) at the mike. And so he orated as follows: "Until next week's program—at the very same time when we will offer another playlet starring one of Hollywood's truly great stars, one of the screen's finest heroes, one of the world's foremost actors," (at this point Cotten's eyes fell on the name of the "great actor" for the first time—and he shrieked in astonishment)—"SONNY TUFTS???"

Although he was a good actor, Sonny Tufts chose to hide behind a parody of himself.

This story would evolve through the years (the program given most often was *Lux Radio Theatre*) but one thing was constant: When Sonny's name was mentioned, it would be followed by a repeated "SONNY TUFTS???" with a rising, incredulous inflection.

In 1945, Tufts was at the height of his popularity and the above story served to mock Tufts in general and his acting in particular. It would be repeated by Sonny himself as fact and even Joseph Cotten "remembered" that it actually happened. But it never did. It was kept alive by Kermit Schafer, who produced popular *Pardon My Blooper!* albums (some of them recreated outtakes) starting in the '50s.

The much-vaunted "fact-checking" website Snopes.com joins the chorus of utterly ignorant voices and calls Sonny (who, after 1943's *So Proudly We Hail!*, was third-billed, second-billed or star-billed in all his '40s movies) "strictly a bit player in the 1940s film industry."

By the 1960s, Tufts was a parody of himself and the symbol of what a bad actor was. He later got his own chapter in Harry and Michael Medved's 1980 book *The Golden Turkey Awards*. The "SONNY TUFTS???" incident certainly contributed, but his offstage antics didn't help.

But in fact, he didn't deserve this treatment at all.

On July 16, 1911, Bowen Charlton Tufts III was born in Arlington, Massachusetts, into a prominent and wealthy family, and grew up in Winchester, Massachusetts. He was the second of four children (after firstborn Mary, he was followed by David and Jeanne). Their great-uncle Charles Tufts donated the land that became Tufts College (later Tufts University). Bowen Tufts, Sr., was a successful investment banker "identified with and director of about 50 business and other financial corporations" (*Boston Globe*).

From the first, Bowen Jr., or "Sonny" as he was nicknamed, was a bit of a reckless scamp—and highly accident-prone. In January 1922, the 12-year-old and his friend Elliott Court (son of dramatist-composer Ormsby Court) were sledding when they collided with a truck. Sonny suffered a fractured collarbone.

At a young age, he was interested in acting and performed in school plays and at the Old Beacon Club on Allerton Hill.

Breaking with the family tradition of going to Harvard, Sonny enrolled at Yale. He majored in anthropology, was on the rowing and football teams, sang in the Yale Glee Club, was on the editorial staff of the *Yale Record*, and wrote articles for the *Yale Weekly News*. He acted in plays and had the lead in the Yale Dramatic Association's comedy *Around the World in Eighty Days* in 1934. Sonny was also deemed to have "considerable musical talent" (*Boston Globe*) and independently studied music in New York City. His best pal, classmate and fellow hellraiser was Winthrop Rockefeller, who dropped out of Yale in 1934.

Sonny organized an orchestra in which he played drums and sang. In the summer months, he took the band "across the Atlantic 24 times," according to William C. Payette:

> Tufts said the band played for cruises and in Europe between looks at jails. He is familiar with the jails of most of occupied Europe, Tufts said, because of a difference in standards of humor. Tufts' humor was inclined toward the bag-of-water-out-the-window variety, while the European type, he said, was more the clapping-bandleaders-in-the-clink sort.

In May '34, Tufts fractured his pelvis while skiing on Tuckerman Ravine on Mt. Washington in New Hampshire.

On the morning of April 7, 1935, the body of 50-year-old Bowen Tufts, Sr., was found in his garage, a victim of carbon monoxide poisoning. A note addressed to a real estate rival was found in his pocket: "You told me that you would keep after me until you got me. Now you can take full credit for my death." His suicide came 24 hours after being named (as vice-president and director of Seaboard Utilities Shares Corporation) in a receivership petition filed in the Suffolk Superior Court. He and others in the company were going to be held accountable for the corporation's losses. Court documents claimed that the company's assets were only $1933, while the public had invested $16 million (over 300 million today).

Tufts Sr. was accused of "bucket shop" tactics, allegedly habitually utilizing unethical practices. After his death, three of his companies went into receivership. His financial empire was worth almost $100,000,000 but when the new investigations began, Tufts

Sr. realized his financial structure was in trouble. (One of Tufts Sr.'s disgraced business associates, Merton E. Grush, killed himself in 1936.)

In June 1935, Sonny graduated from Yale with a Bachelor of Arts degree. Bowen Sr.'s headline-making financial scandal did nothing to dampen his family's lifestyle. Sonny was comfortably taken care of via a trust fund.

He still had his stage ambitions. In 1936, he was tested by MGM, but nothing came of it. Reportedly, he had a desire to go into opera after hearing Italian tenor Tito Schipa. "I got the opera bug badly," Sonny later told Sheilah Graham, "and studied six months in Paris and three years in this country. I had an audition at the Metropolitan. But my friends kept saying, 'Why don't you do popular stuff like you used to at Yale?' All of a sudden, I became commercially minded."

When Sonny was offered a part in the Elsa Maxwell–produced Broadway revue *Who's Who* (1938), the "temptation was too great to resist," he told Sheilah Graham. In the show, he was billed as Bowen Charleton. Others in the cast: Imogene Coca, Jody Gilbert, Kirk Alyn and Rags Ragland. It lasted 23 performances.

Who's Who showgirl Leone Sousa introduced Sonny to Barbara Minot, a dancer who went under the name Barbara Dare. On December 5, 1938, Sonny and Barbara eloped to Fort Lee, New Jersey.

From April to June of 1939, Sonny was on Broadway in the revue *Sing for Your Supper*, produced by the Federal Theatre Project of the Works Progress Administration. Bowen Tufts (as he was billed) sang (with Bidda Blakeley) "Imagine My Finding You Here," a Ned Lehac-Robert Sour song the *Daily News'* Burns Mantle singled out as one of the production's best numbers.

Now using the Sonny Tufts moniker, he had his own nightclub act as a singer. In 1940, he headlined a long engagement at Philadelphia's 20th Century Tavern. "The gals must go for handsome Sonny Tufts," wrote columnist Rudolph Burlingame. "Sonny sings—and smoothly, too."

While he was in Philly, he and Barbara separated—and she was ready to make it a legal break. In May '40, she told a reporter that before she and Tufts had wed, he told her he didn't think he'd make a good husband. They went through with the nuptials anyway, but now, Barbara conceded, "I'm convinced he was right."

After his stint in Philadelphia, Tufts brought his show to New York's Glass Hat Club at the Hotel Belmont Plaza (their ads called him a "Musical Comedy Star") and the Jardin Royal at Whitehall in Palm Beach, Florida. The "romantic tenor," wrote the *Palm Beach Post*, "is already known to smart nightclub habitués in the metropolitan centers." By April, he was performing in Pennsylvania and in New York, where he sang and led the band at the Hotel Belmont Plaza.

Dorothy Kilgallen mentioned that it must be "maddening to be grown-up and be called by some tag that was all right when you were six, but is awfully silly now." The fact that the 6'4" Tufts would continue to be called by his childhood nickname Sonny certainly added to the later ridicule he had to endure.

His off-stage, immature antics just made things worse.

Although Tufts and his wife were separated, a divorce was not forthcoming and he played the field. In New York, he met the flamboyant Peggy Hopkins Joyce (who was 48 to Sonny's 29). She supposedly handed him a line about wanting him for a play she was contemplating and they ended up going around together. The much-married and -engaged Peggy was no stranger to publicity about her hectic love life. What happened (or didn't happen) in June '41 garnered both of them some unfavorable press. The *New York Daily News'* headline, "He Beats Peg and Peg Beats Him—Is It Love?," was followed by "Their idea of fun is to sock each other." The article quotes Tufts as saying, "You ought to see her. She's black and blue from head to foot. Sure, I did it. But she packs a mean wallop herself. I don't think I've got an unbruised spot on me." When Peggy became jealous of a woman paying attention to Sonny at the Stork Club (the "home of society brawls"—Paul Mallon), she gave Sonny a shiner. Scoffing at the idea of a breakup, Tufts told the *Daily News*, "She'll be around. Why, we've been socking each other regularly. Maybe that's why we get along so well." They both thought it good publicity. How times have changed. (Leonard Lyons later said that Sonny had been barred from the Stork Club.)

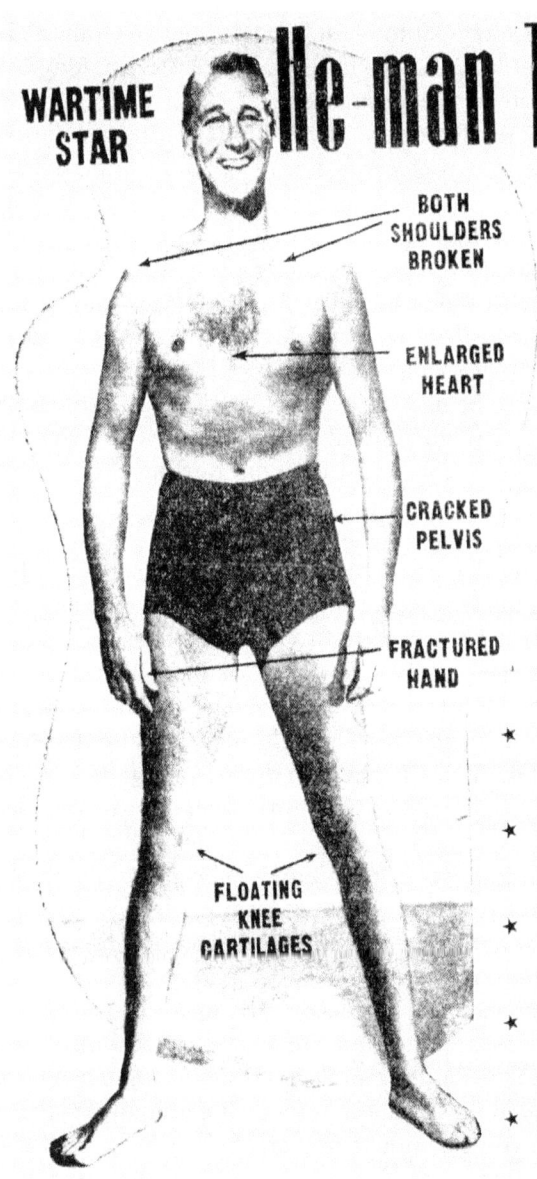

After his scuffle with Peggy, there were reports that he and Barbara had reconciled, but it was brief: By October they had reached an out-of-court settlement whereby Barbara would get 40 percent of Sonny's earnings (varying sources say his entire trust fund) and they obtained a legal separation.

Sonny, the "blond Tarzan" (Danton Walker), continued to sing and lead a band around New York: the Swing Club, the Hurricane Club, the Beachcomber, the Famous Door. (At the latter, he provided background music for Zorita and her boa constrictors.) An unnamed entertainer who appeared with Sonny at the Famous Door later told Danton Walker that after the show,

"Sonny Tufts is 6 feet, four inches tall and he weighs 200 pounds. But, despite his fine physique, above are some of the reasons why the draft board doctors passed up this handsome 'hunk-o'-Man.'"

"around 6 a.m.," a (presumably drunk) Tufts would "go out to Yorkville [a Manhattan neighborhood] looking for Nazis to slug." The informant also claimed that Lucille Malin was "so enthusiastic about Sonny that she guaranteed his salary of $75 a week, though he probably didn't know it." (Ex-showgirl Lucille, the widow of female impersonator Gene Malin, was an alleged madame who served jail time for running brothels.)

"Sonny Tufts, the 6-foot-4 café entertainer, has disappeared and not even his press agent knows his whereabouts."—Danton Walker, June 24, 1942

Whether he was out on a bender or not was never revealed. His name next showed up in the papers that September with the news that Warner Bros. had signed him for "adventure films." By this time, his friend Alexis Thompson, a former Yale classmate, now the millionaire owner of the Philadelphia Eagles, had begun representing him.

It wasn't Warners who had signed Tufts for films but Paramount. Thompson had a pal, hotelier Jack Donnelly, take Sonny to Paramount and introduce him to casting director Joe Egli. In a screen test, Sonny enacted a scene from the Charles Boyer starred movie *Love Affair*. "It was funny because it was not my style at all," Tufts remarked to Sheilah Graham. "I gagged it [up] all the way through." But it did the trick, and he was signed.

Producer-director Mark Sandrich liked Tufts' jokey test and signed the newcomer for the role of "Kansas" in *So Proudly We Hail!* with Claudette Colbert, Paulette Goddard and Veronica Lake. Sonny told Mayme Ober Peak that he was nervous his first time in front of the camera: "I thought I would never get on to the camera tricks. Everything I did was wrong. One day I asked Director Sandrich which was my worst angle and he said, 'You haven't any, they are all bad.'"

So Proudly We Hail! was a tribute to the brave Army nurses on Bataan, "an almost always authentic picture told against an extremely broad background," wrote the *Cincinnati Enquirer*. "At times ruthless and brutal in the telling, the story, nonetheless, is sincere and warming—almost at times inspirational." Lighter moments were handled by the romantic team of Goddard and Tufts. "Although Claudette Colbert got top billing, and although her love story with George Reeves is the main one, Paulette Goddard's attachment for the gangling newcomer is more attractive, and more believable," wrote the *Akron Beacon Journal's* Betty French.

Many agreed, and media attention centered on breakout star Tufts as the bashful ex–college football hero who wins the heart of flirty Goddard (who was Oscar-nominated for her performance).

"Well, girls, he's here," critic Belle Ayer wrote after viewing *So Proudly We Hail!*:

[We are] happy to report that Mr. Tufts lives up to his advance notices and that the Paramount enthusiasm is not just a product of some enterprising press agent's wishful thinking. True, Mr. Tufts isn't as tough as Alan Ladd, nor as pretty as Sterling Hayden, but as the big, soft-spoken marine, he proves he's got plenty on the ball.

The *Cincinnati Enquirer's* Ray Lanning commented that Sonny did "so well with his role that he's practically assured of a big following from now on in. He's sort of a Gary Cooper with looks—aping, in a way, Cooper's fumbling, off-hand, puppy-dog friendliness." Many liked his sincerity and warmth, even if his Boston accent belied his character name "Kansas."

Sandrich told Harold Heffernan: "He's the closest approach yet to Wally Reid. He has Wally's same easygoing, ingratiating manner. Barring accidents, or a call to service, he'll be a big star within two years."

Sonny was the "studio's answer to the male movie star shortage," wrote the *Des Moines Register*. "He's big, blond and a beautiful 4-F." Added the *Oakland Tribune's* Richard G. Harris, "Tufts is headed for stardom with Paramount, because handsome, blond, blue-eyed, tall, wide-shouldered men who can sing and act and are 4-F are pearls in Hollywood these days."

While most able-bodied men were off fighting in World War II, Paramount had to explain why the seemingly healthy, 6'4", 210-pound Tufts was not in uniform. "Skiing and playing football at Phillips Exeter and Yale have made a mess out of the Tufts chassis," explained Harrison Carroll. "He has had two broken knees, a broken hand, a cracked pelvis and a shoulder injury that causes his arm to always be popping out of the socket. Army doctors just laughed and told him to go home." Other injuries were added to this list and circulated in newspapers throughout the country and in the fan magazines with a chart showing damages to Tufts' body.

After just one film, Sonny became wildly popular and was second only to Alan Ladd in weekly fan mail at Paramount. Harold V. Cohen had anticipated bedlam when the ladies "get a load of his broad shoulders, wind-blown locks and handsome puss." During a personal appearance tour for *So Proudly We Hail!*, Sonny was mobbed by bobbysoxers. Screaming fans could be heard in the audience when he made radio appearances.

Tufts was in demand, at his studio and for loan-outs. The studio scrambled to find another vehicle for him and Paulette Goddard. Sheilah Graham thought the two should have been cast "indefinitely" after *So Proudly We Hail!*: "Paulette's essential toughness went well with Sonny's easygoing noninhibited personality." *Standing Room Only* (1944) seemed to be a possibility, but Fred MacMurray was assigned with Goddard instead.

Dudley Nichols requested Sonny be loaned out to RKO for *Government Girl* (1943), screenwriter Nichols' first as director. In the film, earnest, idealistic Tufts tries to cut through Washington red tape to build bombers for the war effort, and ends up playing straight man to an over-the-top Olivia de Havilland.

Government Girl was not the sparkling comedy it should have been, but it was not as bad as *The Golden Turkey Awards*—and Sonny himself—said it was. Sonny told Burt Prelutsky in 1970,

> After *So Proudly We Hail!* they thought they could put me in anything and make money. The material was just terrible....One night, my wife and I were driving down Hollywood Boulevard past Grauman's Chinese. The line for [*Government Girl*] went around the block. I wanted to stop the car and tell all those people that the movie stunk, but my wife wouldn't let me. I felt awful about those poor people waiting in line to see the worst movie ever made. Olivia and the director thought that it was very funny; I thought it was as funny as three caskets. I was right.

The movie made a profit.

Off-screen, there were rumblings that he was a troublemaker. "Sonny Tufts, Paramount's new baby, set himself a new high for hell raisin' on his New York visit," reported Hedda Hopper. "He thought it amusing to sign names of Paramount's executives to some of his better bills, and they're plenty happy that he's now safely home. But he was so good in *So Proudly We Hail!*, he got away with it."

He was reunited with Goddard in *I Love a Soldier* (1944), a comedy about wartime marriages. Reviewer Audrey Stanfield considered Sonny "one of Hollywood's better comedians. The total effect of his awkward charm and spontaneity of manner is utterly disarming." The Tufts-Goddard duo again exhibited good screen chemistry. Paramount brought them together just once more: a skit in the all-star *Duffy's Tavern* (1945).

Tufts and Paulette Goddard displayed a lot of chemistry in two wartime movies, *So Proudly We Hail!* (1943) and *I Love a Soldier* (1944), and in their *Duffy's Tavern* (1945) skit.

The Technicolor musical-comedy *Bring on the Girls* (1945) had a totally unexpected origin: Its story was based on Pierre Wolff's screenplay for the French film *L'homme qui cherche la vérité* (1940). Sonny was top-billed but the action revolved around wealthy Eddie Bracken and his efforts to be liked (and loved) for more than his money—even resorting to deafness to get at the truth. His family hires Tufts to be his guardian in the Navy.

"If you've ever had any doubts about Sonny as a comedian, toss them out the window," raved *Modern Screen*'s Virginia Wilson. "He's a wow. Wait till you get a load of him playing and singing 'Egyptian Ella'!" The song, written in 1913 by Walter Doyle, had been a staple in Tufts' nightclub act, but the lyrics had to be revised due to Breen Office objections. Sonny's slow, grimacing, casual performance of this song and "I'm Gonna Hate Myself in the Morning" are a little hard to take today but were deemed "cute" back in the '40s.

Sonny Tufts is being scolded by his movie employees for his off-screen didoes.—Dorothy Kilgallen, April 19, 1944

Filmed after *Bring on the Girls* but released first was the major Bing Crosby musical *Here Come the Waves* (1944), with Betty Hutton in a dual role as singing twins-turned-Waves Rosemary and Susie. Sonny played Bing's sailor pal Windy, a schemer who complicates Bing's relationship with Rosemary because he wants her for himself.

Tufts' opening screen moment would prove prophetic: He is seen backstage ogling the showgirls' legs. "What's the matter, son, drop your bridgework?" Bing asks him.

Near the conclusion, Sonny, with his high tenor, joins Bing in blackface to sing Harold Arlen and Johnny Mercer's Oscar-nominated song "Ac-Cent-Tchu-Ate the Positive."

In August 1944, Tufts headed the *Motion Picture Herald* "Stars of Tomorrow" poll. The runners-up: James Craig, Gloria DeHaven, Roddy McDowall and June Allyson.

Tufts never took himself seriously—at least not to the press. ("I'm no actor," he told *Modern Screen's* Jeanne Karr. "I just go to the studio at 9 and come home at 6. In between I say lines.") He came across as modest and developed a dull-witted, self-deprecating persona for himself. This would ultimately work against him.

In the beginning, there were a few jabs lobbed toward him, mostly having to do with his name. An example: "Sonny is an odd first name for anyone but a Dead End Kid, a polo player or a dog," wrote John Todd. "There's nothing impressive about it. You'd expect its owner to have freckles and buck teeth and maybe work in the 'Our Gang' comedies." Some deemed him a natural actor, but hardly worthy of note: "Is it true Olivia de Havilland asked for Sonny Tufts as her leading man in her next picture—and why?" remarked Dorothy Kilgallen.

His marriage to Barbara was always on rocky ground and they separated often. Reports of Sonny's accidents were frequent.

Sonny Tufts' arm in a sling, mangled by a washing machine.... Doing his own laundry?—Ed Sullivan, July 19, 1943

Paramount milked his popularity by stockpiling movies, but didn't give a thought to the image they wanted him to project. Bobbysoxers loved him but even they must have been confused by his solemn showing in *Miss Susie Slagle's*. Based on Augusta Tucker's novel, it was about a group of medical students who reside in a Baltimore boarding house run by the title character (Lillian Gish). The overly sentimental drama had many good moments (e.g., Joan Caulfield's scenes with Tufts) but was overlong and somber. Tufts' performance as an aspiring doctor (named Pug, no less) was quiet and sincere, but perhaps too quiet and sincere. Made in September 1944, the film was not released until March '46.

Another made in '44 but not released until two years later: *The Virginian*, fourth screen version of the classic Owen Wister novel. Joel McCrea essayed the title character and Sonny played his amiable friend Steve, who gets mixed up with cattle rustlers. Tufts' best scenes come after he is caught and waiting to be hanged. As often the case, he got no respect: "There is something unmercifully foolish about the sight of Mr. Tufts being hanged," opined the *New York Times*' Bosley Crowther. In fact, McCrea and Tufts' last scenes together, underlining their unspoken bond of friendship, are the film's highlight.

Cross My Heart was a loose reworking of *True Confession* (1937), itself an adaptation of the Louis Verneuil-Georges Berr play *Mon crime*. Betty Hutton starred as lawyer Tufts' fiancée, a compulsive liar he defends when she's charged with murder. Tufts plays second fiddle in this Hutton-fueled film; in his best scenes, crazed Michael Chekhov forces him to enact *Hamlet* with him. This noirish interlude seems out of place in the comedy. Filmed in late 1944 into early '45, it was not released until the beginning of 1947. In 1948, Hutton told Bob Thomas she considered it one of her worst films: "It stunk from start to finish."

Some reviewers were still stuck on Tufts' earlier image ("the fumbling hands, the

Sonny Tufts defends his compulsive liar fiancée Betty Hutton on a murder charge in *Cross My Heart* (1946).

slur voice and confused grin"—Dorothy Kilgallen), but Sonny had since dispensed with those mannerisms.

Paramount announced him for *Dear Ruth*, if "the studio clinches its near-half-million-dollar bid for the stage play," reported Sheilah Graham. Paulette Goddard and Diana Lynn were mentioned as his co-stars. (The movie ended up with Joan Caulfield, William Holden and Diana Lynn, and was a big hit.)

News of Tufts' brawls began leaking to the press, for instance a January '45 set-to at Lucey's Restaurant in Hollywood.

He had a supporting part in *The Well Groomed Bride* (made in February '45, released '46), a comedy about a battle over the last magnum of French champagne in San Francisco. Army lieutenant Tufts is set to marry Olivia de Havilland—that is, until she becomes jealous of his ex-girlfriend Constance Dowling and, of course, meets Navy lieutenant Ray Milland.

Tufts lost his discoverer and strongest booster at Paramount, Mark Sandrich, when the producer-director died suddenly of a heart attack on March 4, 1945. One wonders how this affected Tufts' standing at the studio.

On a personal appearance tour that July, Tufts was mobbed by Atlanta bobbysoxers and a car door was slammed on his hand. Local doctors did a hasty patch-up job so Sonny could continue his tour. During a stop in Ohio, reporter Marguerite Miller interviewed him for the *News Journal*:

What's he like? Well, tall, and blond, AND…! And besides that a very common, ordinary sort of person, with an air that makes you feel as if you had met him over a Coke somewhere before. In fact, his relaxed, casual manner probably kept him from being recognized in the restaurant. There was nothing affected about the athletic figure in the striped grey suit that slouched leisurely before the sandwich and beer on the counter.

When this yarn hit newspapers, Tufts was hospitalized in Cincinnati with an infected hand, wrist and forearm stemming from his hand injury. Girls camped outside the hospital to get a glimpse of him.

> We got a chuckle from Sonny Tufts' explanation of his "mysterious" week-long disappearance. He says he hid out in the Malibu Beach home of his secretary, then adds broodingly, "I had to get away from it all for a while—and think!"—Jimmie Fidler, October 4, 1945

Days later, Tufts started work on the horse-racing comedy *Easy Come, Easy Go* (another flick not released until 1947), co-starring Diana Lynn and Barry Fitzgerald. He considered the movie the low point of his stay at Paramount.

Also in October '45: the first mention of the "true story" of the "SONNY TUFTS???" incident attributed to Joseph Cotten. It took a while to catch on, but the seed was planted.

In April '46, producer Mark Hellinger (who, according to Winchell, started the "SONNY TUFTS???" joke) borrowed Sonny for his Universal drama *Swell Guy* (1947). (Tufts had turned down the part of "The Swede" in Hellinger's *The Killers*; the role made Burt Lancaster a star.) Hellinger's biographer and friend Jim Bishop claimed the producer was against Tufts for the *Swell Guy* role, but was "forced" by the William Morris Agency to cast him as the two-faced war correspondent with a mean streak. Harrison Carroll wrote, "It would be a strong dramatic role for Sonny, who is going like a house afire with the fans. He sent out 70,000 pictures this week to catch up on requests that have been piling up since Paramount quit handling his fan mail."

During the filming, more personal issues surfaced. "Sonny Tufts is worrying his friends—of whom I am one," Sheilah Graham vaguely informed her readers. Sonny again separated from his wife. There was an attempt to salvage the marriage by adopting nine-year-old Donald Devlin, who appeared in *Swell Guy*. But the promise of a $10,000 trust fund could not entice his family to part with him.

> Thieves stole $300 worth of stamps out of Sonny Tufts' car (he'd bought them for his fan mail), but overlooked two cases of Scotch. Don't ask me where he lined that up.—Harrison Carroll, June 25, 1946

By July '46, Tufts was trying (again) to clean up his act—and was excited about what the release of *Swell Guy* would do for his career. He called the role "like a breath of fresh air," adding to Erskine Johnson,

> I haven't had a good role since my first one in *So Proudly We Hail!* All I've been doing lately is following Bing Crosby around, laughing at his jokes, and chasing Betty Hutton up trees. Paramount didn't want me to do the role at first, because they said the bobbysoxers would get mad. But we finally talked the studio into it.
>
> I'm the new Sonny Tufts. I haven't been to a nightclub in weeks, and I'm even rehearsing my lines at home.

In October, after viewing a rough cut of *Swell Guy*, he and Hellinger reportedly agreed that if the picture was shown in its present form, Tufts would "be ruined as a film star," wrote Sheilah Graham. "So the movie is back on the soundstages for retakes, and

Sonny's character will be softened somewhat to leave him still a heel, but a heel with a better side to his heelishness." Robert Siodmak was in charge of retakes. In fact, censors were not happy with the sordid aspects of the movie, the nature of Tufts' personality and his relationships with the characters played by Ann Blyth and Ruth Warrick.

At Paramount, he did a guest spot in *Variety Girl*. He later said it was the sight of himself in that film that made him realize he had to lose weight. "I looked like the *Queen Mary* coming into dock," he told Gene Handsaker. He had a supporting part in *Blaze of Noon*, the story of four brothers (star William Holden, Tufts, Sterling Hayden and Johnny Sands) who go from barnstorming pilots to members of a pioneering air mail service in the 1920s. Holden's romance with Anne Baxter is the film's focal point.

Sonny and his wife Barbara at Ciro's in 1947.

Blaze of Noon's notoriously difficult director, John Farrow, had words with Tufts during filming. When Sonny said he didn't like the script, Farrow replied, "Who read it to you?" Farrow also told columnist Hubbard Keavy that he said to Tufts, "Sonny, there is a period in every actor's life when he must go gracefully from leading man to character actor." Who at Paramount thought this was good publicity?

In January '47, the release of *Swell Guy* was met with bewilderment. Hellinger may have blamed the casting of Tufts but even with Burt Lancaster (whom Hellinger wanted), the movie would still have tanked. The film, banned in Atlanta, was a story far ahead of its time; the original 1921 play (*The Hero*) also bombed. Sonny got good reviews, with the *New York Daily News* praising his "surprisingly versatile" performance. Still, it did a lot of harm—exactly what Paramount and Sonny had feared.

Sonny was growing tired of "playing roles where he's a big, good-natured doormat that everybody walks over," wrote Erskine Johnson. "He wants to be a tough guy and is trying to interest Paramount in a story in which he would play a bank robber."

But after *Blaze of Noon* wrapped in January '47, Paramount didn't seem interested in casting him in *any*thing. Sonny had far too much time on his hands and he overindulged in drinking and eating. His weight was often mentioned in the papers.

On a three-day junket for the Salt Lake City premiere for the Joel McCrea Western *Ramrod* (1947), Tufts whooped it up. "Sonny likes to celebrate," wrote Erskine Johnson, who was there and noticed that Sonny didn't sleep the entire time. Hedda Hopper, also in attendance, mentioned that Sonny "looked and acted like a ghost walking."

> Understand Sonny Tufts had such a good time on the Salt Lake City junket that he never did get to see the picture, *Ramrod*.—Harrison Carroll, March 3, 1947

> Twice in one week, Sonny Tufts got up on the bandstand at Ciro's and led and sang with Don Alfredo's orchestra. Sonny is just a lad who loves music, and the fact that he happened to have 12 Scotches under his belt had nothing whatsoever to do with it.—Jack Lait, Jr., May 28, 1947

Finally, in July '47, a possible role: Producer-director Roy Del Ruth sought Tufts for the lead in his independent production *The Babe Ruth Story*. You would think, with nothing on Tufts' schedule, Paramount would (pun intended) play ball. To Sonny's chagrin, the studio set his asking price at $150,000, too high for Del Ruth. (William Bendix was cast in the film, which was, second pun intended, a hit.)

Jimmie Fidler was "baffled" by the way Tufts was being handled by Paramount: "There's been every reason for the studio to boost Tufts' stock, and none that I can see to sell it short. The movie-going public went for him hook, line and sinker the first time he appeared in a featured role, indicating clearly thereby that he would be more than welcome as a star." Fidler admitted that he heard Tufts was hard to handle: "Maybe he is, but since when has that been enough to damn a potential box-office ace in Hollywood? Stars who are hard to handle CAN be handled if good judgment is used by their bosses; those who are forgotten through inactivity can seldom be revived."

In September '47, Paramount wasn't willing to try to revive Tufts and they said goodbye. Louella Parsons blamed the parting on Sonny, saying "he wouldn't diet and liked having a good time too well." Veronica Lake later alleged that Tufts was a pyromaniac, always setting fire to film sets—a claim that has never been substantiated.

> Just about everyone in Hollywood was sorry to hear that Paramount didn't pick up Sonny Tufts' option. I think Sonny should go into a huddle with himself and straighten himself out. When capable, he's one of the screen's best performers.—Erskine Johnson, October 16, 1947

There was interest in his services, and Fox was thinking of giving him a contract. MGM wanted him for the role of Porthos in *The Three Musketeers* (1948), but he foolishly turned it down because of the money; Gig Young was cast instead.

In February '48, Tufts was in the hospital, supposedly dealing with an old back injury. He again vowed to stop drinking and lose weight.

Producer Harry Joe Brown cast him in the leading role in The *Untamed Breed* (1948), where Tufts tries to get ranchers to buy a Brahma bull to help their depleted cattle strain. He also competes with William Bishop for the hand of pretty Barbara Britton. Sonny said he felt at home in the Western genre and hoped to do more. Brown wanted him for two others, but they never materialized.

> If Sonny Tufts isn't making the rounds of the Greenwich Village pubs these nites, he has a double.—Danton Walker, May 28, 1948

Through 1948, Sonny would insist he was on the wagon.

During July and August '48, Tufts played a supporting role (as "Pappy") in RKO's *Easy Living*, a drama in which he and Victor Mature played football players.

Whatever glow this good part gave him was overshadowed after production ended when Sonny's wife Barbara was rushed to the hospital for a ruptured appendix. She had been pregnant with what would have been the Tuftses' first child. She lost the baby.

> Aside to Sonny Tufts: He who makes much fuss about riding water wagon, looks better without champagne cocktail in hand.—Jimmie Fidler, October 21, 1948

Tufts and Victor Mature as football players in *Easy Living* (1949).

Sonny had ideas for producing films in Italy and doing a comedy TV series ("I'm laughing already. I haven't got a television set"—Erskine Johnson).

In November '48, Sonny was appearing at a state fair in Phoenix when he and actor Edward Troy got into some trouble. At a hotel, Tufts was giving Troy a piggyback (reasons unknown) when he dropped and injured Troy. Later that month, he began work on the film noir *The Crooked Way*. John Payne stars as war veteran Eddie Rice, an amnesia victim returning to his native Los Angeles hoping that he'll be spotted by someone who can tell him about himself. Unfortunately for Eddie, he's spotted by underworld types (Eddie was once one himself) who have a score to settle with him. Tufts had another change-of-pace part as Payne's onetime partner in crime, now his bitter enemy, a performance marked by frequent outbursts of violence. His portrayal of this murderous thug was one of the most convincing and effective of his career—and the critics noticed:

> Tufts gives the standout performance as a sadistic killer. He portrays as mean a brute as melodramatic devotees have hissed for some time.—John Scott, *Los Angeles Times*

> [Tufts] at last seems to have found his logical acting niche and definitely has won me over as a fan.—Shirle Duggan, *Los Angeles Examiner*

> [Give Tufts] the citation for the best supporting performance of the month....Sonny, the erstwhile charm boy, gives a sardonic, terrorizing authoritative performance.—Louella Parsons, *Cosmopolitan*

> A sensational performance from Sonny Tufts, who opens a new career to himself with his fantastic villainy and deadpan facial mimicry. Just spell it Sonny toughs from now on.—Red Porter, *Los Angeles Mirror*

In *The Crooked Way*, Payne's worst enemy was Tufts. In real life, Tufts' worst enemy was also Tufts: He gave out stories in 1949 about the "SONNY TUFTS???" blooper and how he thought it was funny—and that he bought a copy of the (non-existent) recording to keep!

The always accident-prone Tufts slipped in a fish pond and broke his ankle; and during a Texas personal appearance, he fell through an open manhole.

An inkling of things to come: "Sonny Tufts taking candid camera pictures of chorus girls' legs at Earl Carroll's café" (Erskine Johnson).

> The gradual disappearance of Mr. Sonny Tufts from the front line has been no great loss to the acting profession. One day somebody may be able to figure out how Mr. Tufts ever got as far as he did, but the person who does eventually put a finger on the reason or reasons will have to devote his entire lifetime to it.—Harold V. Cohen, July 3, 1949

In August 1949, in New Jersey, he was given a chance by producer-actor Harold J. Kennedy when he was cast as the lead in the play *Petticoat Fever*, getting paid $2000 a week. He proceeded to tour in it on the subway circuit with Sheila Bromley. They also performed the play in Pennsylvania. During its run, he hit himself in the eye playing the drums at Eddie Condon's jazz club in New York and then broke two ribs diving into a swimming pool in Connecticut.

And he was again barred from the Stork Club—reasons not mentioned.

After a short break, Tufts continued *Petticoat Fever* in Atlanta. There were some stage mishaps in this production but, according to reviewer Paul Jones, Tufts ad-libbed his way out "beautifully." Sonny "became so amused at himself on occasions that the audience began to giggle simply because Tufts was tickled." Many critics agreed that the play was not much, but Tufts' personality and the fun he seemed to be having was contagious and livened up the evening.

When he got back to New York, Sonny began misbehaving and it was reported that he and Paul Douglas almost had a brawl in a café. By all reports, he was having a great time—while his wife was elsewhere.

In November '49, he took *Petticoat Fever* to the Astor Theater in Connecticut. "As a comic," wrote the *Hartford Courant*, "Mr. Tufts has a casual, boyish style of funmaking which is very pleasant."

Apparently, something went wrong at this stop; M. Oakley Stafford mentioned in her column that Sonny

> fell down on Harold Kennedy's great hope for him.... More power to Harold, though, for trying. Anyone can take sure things. Harold gives chances to people who still have to prove themselves. Sometimes they don't come through.... Sonny had a name but apparently not the will to keep building that name up.

Back in New York, Sonny was doing things like helping bellhops carry other people's luggage at the Waldorf. In December '49, he started a run at Miami's Olympia singing on stage. The *Miami News* caught his act and called him "personable, and friendly, and looks mighty chic in a sharply-pressed dinner jacket." This was followed by a stint in Chicago.

At the beginning of 1950, he was slated to star in a Detroit Civic Light Opera production of *Good News*, but at the last minute he cancelled. "Some say because of illness," wrote the *Windsor Star*. "Some say because he wasn't up to the part assigned him."

Barbara Tufts, who had long been separated from Sonny, told Sheilah Graham that all was well: "The real good news is that 1950 will be the happiest for Sonny and me."

Poor Barbara.

In April, after a night of binge drinking at a Los Angeles bebop spot, Sonny was booked on a charge of drunkenness. He and three friends had staged an "impromptu foot race" at an intersection. Tufts was attempting to walk the white line in the middle of traffic. When approached by police, he was "staggering and antagonistic," and allegedly remarked to officers, "I could do handsprings on those double white lines. What does that do to you? Do you get a couple of bucks for every man you put in jail?" He then reportedly added, "I'll have your jobs for this." Sonny was released on $50 bail.

> In need of a good role to bolster waning prestige: Sonny Tufts.—Jimmie Fidler, November 22, 1950

Barbara finally had enough and announced her intention to divorce Sonny. This time, it took. For too many years she had tried to keep it together, but his promises to clean himself up were never kept. At the end of May '51, after Sonny was involved in two back-to-back drunken incidents at Ciro's and the Mocambo, she sued for separate maintenance. She told the judge that Sonny "loved the bottle more than home life," and that his addiction "to excessive use of alcohol" had resulted in "lavish spending" and dissipated their community property.

Two days later, Tufts was arrested as a "transient drunk" when he and Hawaiian actress Luukiana Kaeloa got into a scrap at an all-night café for failing to pay a $4.55 bill for fried chicken. He thought the whole thing pretty funny, and posed for photographers. At one point, he threw up his hands and cracked, "I'll wave to my mom in Boston." Tufts joked with the booking officer as he was fingerprinted, "I know how to do this. I've done it plenty of times."

> What a pity that Sonny Tufts doesn't realize that his fastest and best mode of travel, as far as his career is concerned, would be on the wagon.—Jimmie Fidler, June 6, 1951
>
> If Sonny Tufts' current spree lasts much longer, he's apt to run out of places to be tossed out of.—Jimmie Fidler, June 14, 1951

While Tufts was binging, his soon-to-be-ex Barbara held a four-day auction to sell their furnishings. Until their separate maintenance case came to trial, their assets were frozen.

> Sorry to report that SONNY TUFTS is following a *Lost Weekend* routine that can well pour him out of Hollywood for good. Last week, following an arrest for drunken driving, he was tossed out of the Palladium for starting a fight. Why, Sonny, why?—Harvey in Hollywood, June 26, 1951

Following a rough June '51, Tufts went back on the wagon and appeared on *Pantomime Quiz* and, more importantly, replaced Robert Stack in the British war movie *Gift Horse*, starring Trevor Howard and Richard Attenborough. It told of the Lend-Lease policy in the early days of World War II, whereby America (not yet in the fight) gave Britain 50 destroyers left over from the First World War. Third-billed as the good-natured but short-tempered Ordinary Seaman "Yank" Flanagan, Tufts is rarely on screen but he did enjoy a couple of sweet scenes with Dora Bryan. When released in the U.S., it was titled *Glory at Sea*.

In England, he was learning cricket at the home of actor Harry Green when he slipped in a gully, broke his wrist and gashed his forehead.

Before the start of this overseas trip, he said he would be a good boy in Blighty ... but he was up to his old tricks.

> Sonny Tufts' falling-down drunk scenes have London's upper crust wincing. One night recently his shenanigans, while with a party including Princess Margaret Rose, almost caused a fistfight.—Cholly Knickerbocker, November 17, 1951

Walter Winchell reported that Tufts had been barred from one establishment for going under the tables and giving hotfoots. The actor was having so much fun that he stayed in England well into 1952. Tufts toured in the play *Shadow of a Man* (1952), a thriller by Paul Erickson. Ads billed him as "The Celebrated Hollywood Star."

> Rumor or fact, I have it that Sonny Tufts became embroiled in a fistfight in London and narrowly escaped a jail visit. He lost his temper in a fashionable Hyde Park supper club, says Dame rumor, and he escaped arrest only through the intervention of a socially prominent society woman.—Jimmie Fidler, September 22, 1952

On October 21, 1952, in Santa Monica, Barbara Tufts received an interlocutory divorce and $10,000 from her share of the community property, plus alimony.

That November, Tufts finally gave England a break and returned to the U.S. He told Erskine Johnson, "I'm a quiet boy now living a healthy life. I really can't explain why I got so mixed up. It was a conflict of circumstances—partly personal. I was an unhappy character."

He was paired with another performer on the skids, Barbara Payton, in the low-budget indie *Run for the Hills*—a pairing Sheilah Graham called "the oddest casting of the year." It was an offbeat but engaging comedy with Sonny as an L.A. insurance actuary, obsessed with worries about the H-bomb, who announces his plans to move with his wife (Payton) into a cave in order to survive the eventual blast. As they live a stone's throw from the Stone Age, they earn money by charging visitors 50 cents a head and greeting them in leopard skins while wielding clubs. In one scene, Sonny envisions turning the place into a nightclub and, in a (day)dream sequence, pictures himself in top hat and leopard skin as its emcee, even sitting down at a piano to do a fast-paced rendition of "Frankie and Johnny." Both actors gave good performances—despite what has been reported elsewhere.

No Escape (1953) was screenwriter Charles Bennett's second of two directorial efforts. Bennett, best known for his work with Hitchcock and DeMille, never liked the threadbare production, but it is not a bad film noir. Again, Tufts contributed a solid performance as a complex police detective obsessed with girlfriend Marjorie Steele. The contrived storyline about who killed a playboy artist, Steele or jaded composer Lew Ayres, is boosted by an excellent cast amidst a seedy atmosphere.

During the summer of '53, Tufts went out on the straw hat circuit as the dimwitted boxer in *The Milky Way*. When it played East Rochester, New York, columnist Henry W. Clune commented on the 42-year-old Tufts' appearance:

> In the years since he left the Yale yard, he has acquired girth to add to his height; and Tuesday night there were times when the audience was not insensible of the heroic effort he was making to confine his abdomen in a T-shirt. He looked more like a retired than a current world's heavyweight champ; one who had known the good things in life, with heavy lunches at Club

If looks could kill: A jealous and overprotective Tufts (right) holds Marjorie Steele as he glares at Lew Ayres in *No Escape* **(1953).**

21 and ceremonial evenings at the Stork and El Morocco. But this may have added rather than lessened the comedy of the piece.

In August, he played the title role in *Mister Roberts* at the Monticello Playhouse in Kiamesha Lake, New York.

A top-billed Tufts portrayed the no-nonsense captain of the Moon Rocket 4 crew (Victor Jory, Marie Windsor, Bill Phipps and Douglas Fowley) in the 3-D sci-fi cult classic *Cat-Women of the Moon* (1953). Their ship lands on the moon where they discover an air-filled cave, a giant spider and Cat-Women (Carol Brewster, Susan Morrow, many more) living amidst set pieces from 1938's *The Adventures of Marco Polo* (both movies were made at Goldwyn).

Bill Phipps told Tom Weaver,

The day before we started shooting, [Victor Jory] and I happened to walk into a little coffee shop which was on the Goldwyn lot. I was very young at the time, and Victor Jory said, "Sonny Tufts is gonna do this picture, eh? Well, he'd better not take a drink while he's working, 'cause I'll knock him on his fuckin' ass!" I remember thinking at the time, and I still do, what a thing to say! And what a thing to say about a fellow actor, before he's done anything! Sonny Tufts was a known carouser and heavy drinker, but so were a lot of other people. But they worked! In other words, Victor Jory was trying to establish himself as top dog, but that didn't mean shit to me.

People ask me how we were able to keep a straight face making that movie. Well, we didn't!

Marie Windsor did, and so did Victor Jory, because they took themselves so seriously, but Sonny Tufts, Douglas Fowley and I had a ball. We were laughing and making fun of things all the time, trying to make the day as pleasant as possible.

Sonny Tufts is living it up again. This guy threw away a million-dollar career. When I saw him Sunday and asked, "What are you doing?" he wasn't quite sure.—Sheilah Graham, October 31, 1953

Customers at Ciro's last night got an eyeful of Carol Brewster walking out of the place *alone* at midnight—leaving her date, Sonny Tufts, sitting at [his] table to cry into his beer or whatever it was he was imbibing.—Don Hope, November 9, 1953

The headline writers missed a near-brawl involving Sonny Tufts, John Carradine and a belligerent bartender. The drink-mixer tongue-lashed the actors for a bit of horseplay that bystanders described as harmless.—Erskine Johnson, March 9, 1954

Dorothy Kilgallen claimed it was far from harmless, that the "hospital emergency ward out there knew all about it."

On March 13, 1954, Sonny and two friends were having dinner at the apartment of stripper Barbara Gray Atkins, 27, when Tufts wanted something not on the menu: He suddenly lunged at her and bit her upper left thigh. She said in her $25,000 damage suit that there was no provocation for the "vicious assault" and that it "caused her great agony, pain and shock and has prevented me from following my profession."

The following month, another woman, "interpretive dancer" Margarie Von, 22, came forward claiming that she was attacked by Tufts on a yacht that past February (while they were making the movie *Serpent Island*). Von said that she was sitting on a bunk below deck in her bathing suit when Tufts, who had just "breakfasted on beer," suddenly "pushed her back and sank his teeth into her right leg." The result was a three-inch contusion which cost her eight weeks' work. She was asking for damages of $26,000.

Tufts denied both charges, but settled with Von for $600. Atkins ultimately dropped her case when the defense started asking her questions about her personal relationship with Tufts. Embarrassed for herself and her family, she decided to bow out.

Will somebody pleeeze send Sonny Tufts a food-basket???!—Edith Gwynn, April 28, 1954

Sonny Tufts has written a song. We suggest as a title: "I Thigh for You."—Henry Vance, February 7, 1955

It is *not* anticipated that Sonny Tufts will join the American Dental Association.—Jerry Pam, January 2, 1961

Returning to the subject of *Serpent Island*, it starred Tufts as a San Pedro, California, marine engineer hired by a pretty Easterner (Mary Munday, wife of the film's director Tom Gries) to help her search for treasure buried in the Caribbean by her ancestors. It's the kind of movie where one shot shows man-of-the-seas Tufts scrutinizing the position of the sun in the sky to determine the time, and the next shot is a close-up of a wristwatch on someone's wrist. The ultra-cheapie may have gone straight to television with no previous theatrical release.

A comeback was mentioned when Tufts got a supporting role in director Billy Wilder's Marilyn Monroe vehicle *The Seven Year Itch* (1955). Tom Ewell played a Manhattanite whose wife (Evelyn Keyes) and son go to Maine for the summer, leaving him alone with his overactive imagination and a sexy upstairs neighbor (Monroe). Ewell is jealous when he hears that his wife went on a hayride with Sonny and he imagines all sorts of things. Tufts' comeback amounted to two scenes, but it was in a high-profile hit movie.

In January 1955, Sonny opened in St. Louis in the William Inge play *Picnic*. "You know," he told Louella Parsons, "I've been signed for 22 weeks to take the play out on the road. My notices in St. Louis were wonderful, and I was so happy that I was able to show what I can do on the stage." His notices might have been good but attendance was poor. In February '55, he was signed for the headed-for-Broadway musical *Ankles Aweigh* with Betty and Jane Kean.

> SONNY TUFTS???: At the Blue Angel they are chinning about Sonny Tufts, the male lead in *Ankles Aweigh*. "What a billing problem they are gonna have with him," said Trude Adams. "He's used to having his name PRONOUNCED in capital letters!"—Walter Winchell, February 18, 1955

> The reports of Sonny Tufts being on the wagon were greatly exaggerated, the town's bartenders will be glad to learn. Sonny quaffed double Scotches for lunch at Sardi's the other day.—Dorothy Kilgallen, March 9, 1955

Ankles Aweigh opened in New Haven on March 21, 1955. Sonny was singled out—but not in a good way. "Whatever his charms or abilities," wrote the *Hartford Courant*, "they are lost in musical comedy." Four days later, it was announced that he was withdrawing from the production and replaced by Mark Dawson.

He gave his best film performance of the 1950s in Republic's *Come Next Spring* (1956). Steve Cochran (who also produced) starred as a recovering alcoholic who returns to his wife (Ann Sheridan) and children on their Arkansas farm after a nine-year absence. Sonny vividly portrayed Cochran's loudmouthed, bullying rival. His constant needling of Cochran ultimately leads to a fistfight (*à la The Quiet Man*, which was compared to *Come Next Spring* in ads). If Sonny had worked at it, he would have been an excellent character actor during these later years, but as Marie Windsor later stated, "I don't think he ever cared much about acting."

On July 27, 1955, not long after *Come Next Spring* wrapped, Tufts was again accused of attacking a woman. This time, he went over to Adrienne Forman, a 22-year-old sitting with her mother in a Studio City restaurant, and insisted on joining them. When she objected, Tufts allegedly "struck, beat and bruised her" and then "ran his hand up her leg and pinched her on the upper thigh." After she screamed and told him to go away, Tufts reportedly replied, "You read too many *Confidential* magazines." Forman, who said she suffered from "serious and permanent injuries," sued for $10,000. Tufts denied the charges but settled for an undisclosed sum. (Not long afterward, Forman sued another man for beating her up.)

> Sonny Tufts has hired himself a press agent and is ready, willing and glad to show his notices in the Steve Cochran-Ann Sheridan starrer, *Come Next Spring*. What a chance Sonny had during the war to be a top star! Somewhere along the line, he lost it.—Sheilah Graham, February 25, 1956

Frontier legend claimed that Billy the Kid was not killed by Sheriff Pat Garrett, and producer Charles "Buddy" Rogers' *The Parson and the Outlaw* (1957) tells one version of that myth: Believed to be dead, Billy (Anthony Dexter) attempts to live in peace until circumstances and the titular parson (Rogers again) force him to pick up his guns and save a town. Tufts is Jack Slade, who is wary friends with Billy. In real life, Slade wasn't the hired gun (and notorious killer) portrayed in legend and in this film—in fact, he had a drinking problem. In any case, Tufts gave a strong performance as the conflicted gunslinger.

If Tufts had been interested in maintaining an acting career, he would have been pursuing more TV work. In addition to appearing as himself on series like *Pantomime Quiz*, he acted in *Damon Runyon Theater's* "A Tale of Two Citizens" (1956).

After columnist Hortense Morton attended the Hollywood premiere of the movie *Giant* (1956), she described for her readers

> one very low and horrifying incident.... After 2 a.m., when Eastern scribes had filed their stories to hometown papers, and were charging in to steak sandwiches and coffee at Ciro's, a tall figure barged in out of the night, took a stand in the dim lights of the dance floor and screamed "Sonny Tufts!," turned, and walked out into the night. It was Sonny Tufts! No longer do I think that old radio yarn is amusing.—Hortense Morton, October 19, 1956

> I hear it was a shiner that prompted Sonny Tufts to stay indoors for days on end.—Mike Connolly, October 19, 1956

In March 1957, Tufts took over for Wayne Morris as host of the local television program *Strange Lands and the Seven Seas*.

After Sonny's mother's death on March 9, 1957, he came into an inheritance. He instructed his lawyers to give him a small weekly allowance so he wouldn't burn through it. Six months later, an intoxicated Sonny was arrested outside a Sunset Strip nightclub. As two deputies approached, Tufts fell to the pavement and hit his head. His lady companion also fell—on top of Tufts. It took both officers to pick Tufts off the sidewalk. He was taken to Citizens Emergency Hospital where four stitches closed a gash over his eye. He was then booked on a drunk charge.

> Sonny Tufts is such a tragic person. He had the world in his hands and repeatedly has thrown it away. He looked pathetic in his latest drunk-charge.—M. Oakley Stafford, September 8, 1957

> Sudden thought: Whatever became of Sonny Tufts?—Jim Morse, July 20, 1958

In August '58, it was reported that Sonny was recovering from (a) a minor stroke, said to be the result of an overdose of arthritis medication, or (b) a mild heart attack stemming from an overdose of sleeping pills.

In June 1959, it was announced that he would star in a shot-in-Mexico TV series called *Gringo*, produced by Rondo Productions.

> Sonny Tufts slimmed down to 190 pounds and is so proud of his 33-inch waist. He hasn't touched liquor in more than a year and has no romantic involvements. He's thrilled over his coming TV series.—Hedda Hopper, June 6, 1959

> Sonny Tufts has his arm in a cast—and didn't dislocate it in a barroom! "I was working on this TV series, *Gringo*—just outside Mexico City," he told me. "Lee Van Cleef, the heavy, was to clip me. I was supposed to take a fall and make it look real. I zigged when I was supposed to zag and crashed into a stone wall."—Earl Wilson, December 19, 1959

Although there is no record that his TV series aired in the United States, Tufts repeatedly claimed he filmed it in Mexico.

According to Richard Lamparski, Sonny desperately wanted the role of Jim Bowie in John Wayne's production of *The Alamo* (1960). He lost the part to Richard Widmark.

> Sonny Tufts, who insists he was cold sober, stepped out of a cab before it stopped and wound up in St. Vincent's hosp.—Walter Winchell, January 25, 1960

> Sonny Tufts told friends in Armando's how he busted his arm: "I fell off the wagon and a ski lift the same weekend."—Robert Sylvester, January 27, 1960

By December '60, Sonny had dropped completely from sight.

Q: My husband says Sonny Tufts and Van Johnson are the same person, I say they aren't. Who is right?—G.M., East St. Louis, Ill.

A: Contrary to popular belief, there *is* a Sonny Tufts. They don't even have the same agents.—TV Mailbag, February 19, 1961

Reports stated that Tufts was independently wealthy; others that he was ranching in Helotes, Texas. Sometimes, Harold Heffernan wrote, he "phones old pals in the dead of night." He generally took it easy, "devoted his time to tinkering, riding, and taking trips to the Caribbean to go skin-diving" (*Orlando Evening Star*).

Sonny Tufts will leave ranching for another crack at a film career.—Earl Wilson, December 13, 1961

Wire from Sonny Tufts down in Helotes, Tex., concerning our item that he was giving up ranching for movies; "Dear Earl, I thank you. Old Paint and the doagies thank you."—Earl Wilson, December 18, 1961

In 1962, he and Marilyn Hinton were in talks to produce a movie called *Nylon Sky*, about the 82nd Airborne Paratroopers, written by Hinton's boyfriend Major Jim Corey.

Sonny Tufts, now seen only on the Late Show movies and other TV film programs, has turned down all offers to stage a comeback. He's quite content to rest on his laurels and his ranch in Texas.—Charley Channel, June 1, 1962

Not too content: In August '62, with TV City of Arizona Inc., he was looking to produce a Foreign Legion story. Another source said he was in discussions with the company to act in that or one of their other productions.

Sonny was still looking for financing for *Nylon Sky*, now retitled *All the Way*. He was to play a character called Jumping Joe in the production, and was looking for a leading man. Nothing came of the project.

Sonny Tufts is back on the wagon and anxious to get movie or TV work. There is a slight chance he'll co-star in Dean Martin's next movie.—Dave Freeman, January 1, 1963

Tufts wanted the role of Nevada Smith in the movie version of *The Carpetbaggers* (1964) but his old Paramount pal Alan Ladd got the part instead. On a May 14, 1963, *Tonight Show with Johnny Carson*, Sonny accompanied himself on the piano singing "Egyptian Ella."

Acting-wise, his comeback came in the September 18, 1963, episode of *The Virginian*, "Ride a Dark Trail." He played Trampas' (Doug McClure) gambler father. Several columnists made the same mistake that Tufts had previously portrayed the Trampas character in the 1946 movie of *The Virginian* (when actually, Brian Donlevy did). Tufts went along with it, stating to Terry Vernon, "This town is filled with handsome young men. An old galoot like me is lucky to get in the show at all. In fact, I'll be happy if they call me back 17 years from now and ask me to play the part of Trampas' grandfather."

Alex Freeman, July 15, 1963: "Sonny Tufts, who desperately wants a comeback, was a guest on *The Virginian* and delighted the cast and crew by turning in a flawless performance as Doug McClure's wayward father."

Tufts followed up with *Bob Hope Presents the Chrysler Theatre*'s "Have Girls, Will Travel," where he played a tough miner.

Sonny Tufts was offered to the Rainbow Room as a bandleader.—Earl Wilson, June 24, 1964

Sonny Tufts was not his smiling self when he phoned to tell me his former wife, Barbara, had died of cancer.—Hedda Hopper, August 12, 1964

Still the butt of a cheap joke: In a skit in the November 1964 episode of TV's satirical *That Was the Week That Was*, it was stated that Sonny was being groomed to oppose George Murphy in the next California Senatorial election.

To many, Tufts was the joke that kept on giving, whether he did anything or not. P.R. man Max Rosey called him a "household word, a national punchline, a celebrity just for joining the passing parade."

On the September 29, 1965, *Dick Van Dyke Show* ("Uhny Uftz"), Rob thinks he sees a flying saucer and that it said "Sonny Tufts" to him.

The notorious one-season TV series *My Mother the Car* was about a man (Jerry Van Dyke) whose mother (voiced by Ann Sothern) is reincarnated as a 1928 Porter automobile and speaks to him through the car radio. On the November 30, 1965, episode, "And Leave the Drive-In to Us," the family goes to the drive-in to watch *Surf Beach Drag Strip* starring Barrett Carmella and Tommy Bland, with special guest star Sonny Tufts. It's Mother's birthday and Sonny just happens to be her heartthrob. Throughout the episode, everyone repeats the "SONNY TUFTS???" joke ad absurdum. At the conclusion, when Sonny makes a brief appearance, Mother gets a bit overheated and speeds around, and doesn't want his fingerprints to be wiped off her hood.

On *Rocky and His Friends*, Boris Badenov steals Bullwinkle J. Moose's autographed picture of Tufts. Later, Boris saves his own life by giving the photo to Fearless Leader, who tells him, "You've found the chink in my armor."

On *The Monkees*, Micky Dolenz, posing as a movie producer, brags of a film he is doing, *The First Ten Days of Pompeii*, with "Gregory Peck, Elizabeth Taylor, Doris Day and Sonny Tufts." (The response: "Sonny T—?? What a production!")

Tufts (briefly) returned to Paramount for the eleventh-billed part in producer A.C. Lyles' Western *Town Tamer* (1965). He also did a segment of TV's *The Loner*, playing the father of 15-year-old Jeff Bridges.

> Q: Are Sonny Tufts of the late-night movies and Forrest Tucker of *F Troop* the same person? If so, why did he change his name? A.R.M., Tacoma.—The TV Mailbag, January 19, 1966

On the April 11, 1966, *Merv Griffin Show*, Sonny was so "thoroughly tufted he look[ed] like all the New Year's Eves since Prohibition rolled into one," wrote Jack O'Brian, who was at the taping.

> Merv Griffin is fuming at Sonny Tufts. Tufts showed up for a recent guest appearance on Merv's video show, whacked out his head on whiskey, and despite Griffin's frantic efforts to cover for Sonny Boy, Tufts took on an Alcoholier Than Thou attitude that threw the show into a state of offscreen bedlam.—John J. Miller, May 8, 1966

> Remember Sonny Tufts? Remember George Hamilton's mother, Anne Hamilton Spalding? Well, Anne and Sonny are getting away with it. They can prove they can swim, monkey and frug just like anyone else.—Mike Connolly, October 24, 1966

In November 1966, Sonny traveled to Lehigh Acres, Florida, to play a role in the indie *Cottonpickin' Chickenpickers* (1967), for which he received "Special Guest Star" billing. In addition to a group of country music "stars," the cast included Greta Thyssen, Slapsie Maxie Rosenbloom, Lila Lee and Tommy Noonan (hilarious as Bird-Dog Berrigan). It was a surprisingly funny comedy about drifters (Del Reeves and Hugh X. Lewis) hopping a train to Florida, getting arrested for stealing chickens, and then becoming fugitives. Tufts was Cousin Urie, a dirty, unshaven moonshine-guzzler telling jokes.

> Lately, I've been resorting to the slang of my youth when the teeny-boppers are around, and it confuses them utterly....They are completely undone when I shout "SONNY TUFTS????" and all my contemporaries double up with laughter. The kids have no idea why this is a guaranteed crack-up in my age group, and I'll never tell 'em.—Herb Caen, November 27, 1966

According to columnist Lou Cedrone, *Land's End*, a 1967 pilot produced by Desi Arnaz, with Sonny, Gilbert Roland, Rory Calhoun, Leigh Chapman and Martin Milner, was the worst unsold pilot of the year.

> George Brooks, the socialite, is negotiating for the rights to present a Sonny Tufts Film Festival in Detroit.—Hunter Hopwood, November 24, 1967

> My secret fear is: That Sonny Tufts will make a comeback.—Lee Pulos, April 5, 1968

That dreaded comeback, if you want to call it that, came in an ABC-TV special called *Romp!!!* (April 21, 1968), co-hosted by Ryan O'Neal and Michele Lee. It was about 1968 fads, with a curious guest list that included Jimmy Durante, Liberace, Casey Stengel, Sammy Davis, Jr., Barbara Eden and Sonny Tufts ("'Who?' most kids certainly cried"—James Doussard). Doussard described Tufts' participation: "Tufts said hello during the intros and smiled, 'and yours truly, Sonny Tufts.' That's what he said at the end. In between, like many old fogeys sent to Congress, he wasn't heard from at all."

In July '68, he was signed for continuing appearances on *Rowan & Martin's Laugh-In*. Trying to be a good sport, and desperate for any kind of exposure, Tufts parodied his image and revisited the "SONNY TUFTS???" joke.

At the end of '68, he guest-starred on Gary Owen's satiric Christmas play on radio station KMPC, "The Never Ending Story of the Christmas Clarvy," about a boy who wants to get his down-on-their-luck parents something they always wanted: a giant replica of Sonny Tufts carved out of chocolate.

> SONNY TUFTS?!? It's a sure-fire way of breaking up someone over 30. Just mention Sonny Tufts in an amazed sort of way and you'll have 'em rolling on the floor. It'll even bring tears to the eyes of some folks. People under 30 have no idea why this happens. And even many of those over 30 aren't exactly sure.—Bob Talbert, April 3, 1969

Funny thing: Talbert had no idea, either: He called Sonny an actor who "always just lost the girl to the main character—usually to Donald O'Connor—in movies of the late 1930s, 1940s and early 1950s." DONALD O'CONNOR???

Jack O'Brian reported in May 1969 that Sonny was "having rough going," but did not elaborate. O'Brian was one of the few columnists who never made fun of Tufts' acting, calling him an "unworthy target ... a remarkably unhammy and unpretentious transient star."

The following month, Sonny was taken to the hospital after he slipped on a restaurant floor and hit his head on a wooden railing. It took ten stitches to close the two-inch wound.

Burt Prelutsky interviewed Sonny early in 1970 and found him seemingly contented. Now retired, he was relaxing, "skin dives off Catalina and reads a lot and occasionally takes a nip."

On May 31, 1970, Tufts was hospitalized at St. John's Hospital in Santa Monica due to a "virulent organism." Five days later, the 58-year-old died of pneumonia. He is interred in his family's plot at Munroe Cemetery in Massachusetts.

"[Sonny] was a marvelous fellow, and he had the greatest sense of humor of anybody I've ever known," Bill Phipps related. "He should have been in vaudeville! They always made him like the amiable leading man or second leading man–type, but that wasn't really his nature at all. He was a funny, funny guy, and wonderful to be with. I loved him."

1943: *So Proudly We Hail!, Government Girl.*
1944: *I Love a Soldier, Here Come the Waves.*
1945: *Bring on the Girls, Duffy's Tavern.*
1946: *Miss Susie Slagle's, The Virginian, The Well Groomed Bride, Swell Guy, Cross My Heart.*
1947: *Easy Come, Easy Go, Blaze of Noon, Variety Girl.*
1948: *The Untamed Breed.*
1949: *The Crooked Way, Easy Living.*
1952: *Gift Horse.*
1953: *Run for the Hills, No Escape, Cat-Women of the Moon.*
1954: *Serpent Island.*
1955: *The Seven Year Itch.*
1956: *Come Next Spring.*
1957: *The Parson and the Outlaw.*
1965: *Town Tamer.*
1967: *Cottonpickin' Chickenpickers.*

Bibliography

Ross Alexander

Actor Fined as Drunk. *Buffalo Courier Express*, March 18, 1936.

Actor Tells Wife Death. *Los Angeles Times*, December 13, 1935.

Actress Charges Operation Made Her Barren. *Metropolitan Pasadena Star-News*, December 23, 1947.

Anne Nagel Asks $350,000 of Two Physicians. *San Francisco Examiner*, December 23, 1947.

Atkinson, Brooks. *New York Times*, January 4, 1934.

Bret, David. *Errol Flynn: Satan's Angel*. London: Robson Book Ltd., 2000.

Brown, John Mason. Two on the Aisle. *New York Post*, January 5, 1937.

Carroll, Harrison. *Monessen Daily Independent*, December 20, 1935.

_____. *Evening News*, January 14, 1937.

Collura, Joe. Beverly Roberts: A Thoroughbred from the Warners' Stable. *Classic Images*, November 1997.

Crews, Jr. Watson. Dr. Thorpe's Unhappy Year. *San Francisco Examiner*, May 16, 1948.

Dr. Freile Dies in Jersey. *New York Sun*, July 8, 1939.

Fidler, Jimmie. *Santa Ana Register*, June 29, 1936.

Film Tests Fail, Kills Self. *San Bernardino County Sun*, December 13, 1935.

Find Ross Alexander Fatally Shot. *Rochester Democrat Chronicle*, January 3, 1937.

Fonda, Henry, and Howard Teichmann. *My Life*. New York: New American Library, 1981.

Golden, John, and Viola Brothers Shore. *Stage-Struck John Golden*. New York: Samuel French, 1930.

Greene, Graham. A Midsummer Night's Dream. *The Spectator*, October 18, 1935.

Grief Drives Screen Actor to Kill Self. *Buffalo Courier Express*, January 4, 1937.

Hartley, Katharine. Ross Alexander the Great. *Movie Mirror*, October 1936.

Hermann, Ida. The New Talkie. *Courier-Post*, November 16, 1935.

Houghton, Norris. *But Not Forgotten: The Adventure of the University Players*. New York: William Sloane, 1951.

Hoyt, Caroline Somers. The Real Reason Why Ross Alexander Killed Himself. *Movie Mirror*, April 1937.

Lusk, Nobert. Screen in Review. *Picture Play*, February 1935.

Madden, George. Why Ross Alexander Married Again. *Movie Mirror*, February 1937.

M.H.K. The Ladder. *Brooklyn Daily Eagle*, October 23, 1926.

Mrs. Alexander is Prostrate. *The Times*, January 4, 1937.

Musset, Nina. Here Are Nice Young People Who Have Had Plenty of Fun. *Brooklyn Daily Eagle*, September 27, 1931.

New Films. *Boston Globe*, January 25, 1935.

Nugent, Frank S. Pigskin Parade, a Seasonal Musical Comedy, Opens at the Roxy—*Here Comes Carter*, at the Palace. *New York Times*, November 14, 1936.

Palmer, Gordon. They Discovered Friendship Through Heartbreak. *Photoplay*, June 1937.

Paroles' Gives Thought Upon Released Men. *Albany Evening News*, August 29, 1936.

Parry, Florence Fisher. On with the Show. *Pittsburgh Press*, June 26, 1936.

Parsons, Louella. *San Francisco Examiner*, August 6, 1935.

Peak, Mayme Ober. Story of a Sweater Behind Latest Hollywood Tragedy. *Boston Globe*, January 7, 1937.

Pollock, Arthur. Let Us Be Gay: ... The Theater. *Brooklyn Daily Eagle*, February 22, 1929.

Ross, George. *Times Herald*, May 15, 1936.

Ross Alexander Fined. *Newark Advocate*, April 28, 1936.

Ross Alexander, Movie Actor, Arrested. *Los Angeles Daily News*, March 11, 1936.

Sennwald, Andre. Warner Brothers Present the Max Reinhardt Film of A Midsummer Night's Dream at the Hollywood—*Pepo* at the Cameo. *New York Times*, October 10, 1935.

Sobol, Louis. The Voice of Broadway. *Logansport Pharos Tribune*, October 4, 1937.

Some Late Previews. *Hollywood Spectator*, February 13, 1937.

"That's Gratitude": Actor Fought Way Back to Health, *Daily Star*, August 25, 1930.

Thirer, Irene. *New York Daily News*, November 2, 1931.

Tildesley, Alice L. What Do You Know About Color? *Charleston Daily Mail*, September 6, 1936.

Under Glass. *Variety*, November 7, 1933.
Wales, Clarke. Bachelor Father. *Okland Tribune*, August 23, 1936.
Williams, Whitney. Reviews of the New Films. *Oakland Tribune*, November 11, 1934.
Young Film Actor in Drunken Row. *Daily Capital Journal*, March 12, 1936.

David Bacon

Actor, Stabbed in Back, Dies in Mystery Here. *Los Angeles Times*, September 13, 1943.
Amusing Plays at Summer Theatres. *Boston Globe*, August 6, 1940.
Belser, Lee. Old Crime Gains Life. *Lansing State Journal*, February 20, 1957.
Diary Enters Mysterious Actor Death. *Endicott Daily Bulletin*, September 15, 1943.
Diary of Marvel Studied by Police. *Pittsburgh Press*, September 15, 1943.
Extortion Note Reportedly Sent Bacon Checked. *Los Angeles Times*, September 20, 1943.
Extortion Slaying Clue. *Albany Times-Union*, September 21, 1943.
Gaspar G. Bacon Jr. Loses Car License. *Boston Globe*, June 24, 1935.
Gaspar G. Bacon Sr. Dies. *Boston Traveler*, December 26, 1947.
G.K. Gangster Opus Previewed. *Los Angeles Times*, October 8, 1942.
Hills Hide-out Enters Inquiry in Actor's Slaying. *Los Angeles Times*, September 18, 1943.
Hopper, Hedda. *Los Angeles Times*, September 24, 1940.
_____. *Idaho Daily Statesman*, January 29, 1941.
Jail Orderly for Bacon Case Story. *Albany-Times Union*, September 24, 1943.
Killer of Venice Boy Confesses. *Wilmington Daily Press Journal*, November 30, 1956.
Levins, Peter. What Has Happened to Justice? *New York Daily News*, May 21, 1944.
Mank, Gregory William. *Laird Cregar: A Hollywood Tragedy*. Jefferson, NC: McFarland, 2018.
_____. Email to Author, November 27, 2023.
Margo Lauds Hasty Pudding Men at Show's Rehearsal. *Boston Globe*, March 13, 1935.
Mines, Harry. Picturized Review. *Los Angeles Daily News*, June 26, 1942.
Mistaken in Identifying Slain Actor, Says Singer; Arrested. *Los Angeles Examiner*, September 21, 1943.
Murder in Hollywood: Will Newest Slaying Also Remain Mystery? *Tampa Tribune*, September 19, 1943.
Mystery Veils Actor's Death from Stabbing. *Vancouver Sun*, September 14, 1943.
One "Stranger" Mystery in Bacon Case Cleared. *Los Angeles Times*, September 19, 1943.
Othman, Frederick C. Masked Marvel Murder Case for Ellery Queen. *Boston Globe*, September 14, 1943.
Peak, Mayme Ober. I Cover Hollywood. *Boston Globe*, March 25, 1942.
Plays Out of Town. *Variety*, April 7, 1937.
Police Hold Youth, Arrested Twice, in Slaying of Bacon. *Los Angeles Times*, October 15, 1943.
Police Seek 2 Men in Actor's Slaying. *Philadelphia Inquirer*, September 18, 1943.
Radcliffe, E.B. Out in Front. *Cincinnati Enquirer*, July 16, 1943.
Schallert, Edwin. *Los Angeles Times*, January 12, 1942.
Seek Man in Mystery Murder. *Olean Times Herald*, September 11, 1943.
6th Lumbar Vertebrae—A Rare Spinal Abnormality. https://sciprogress.com/sixth-lumbar-vertebrae/
Stanton, Jeffrey. *Santa Monica Pier: A History from 1875 to 1990*. Los Angeles: Donahue Publishing, 1990.
Summer Plays in Review. *Boston Globe*, July 2, 1940.
Summer Plays in Review. *Boston Globe*, July 30, 1940.
Sweater Clue in Bacon Death, Extortion Report Sifted. *Los Angeles Daily News*, September 20, 1943.
Sweater New Clue in Mystery Murder of Masked Marvel. *Syracuse Journal*, September 20, 1943.
Tie as Prettiest Girl. *Bennington Evening Banner*, August 31, 1940.
Two Suspects Detained in Bacon Murder, Released. *Buffalo Evening News*, September 22, 1943.
Walker, Danton. Broadway. *New York Daily News*, December 25, 1939.
_____. Broadway. *New York Daily News*, January 12, 1940.
Young Gaspar Bacon May Be Film Actor. *Boston Globe*, December 29, 1939.

Bruce Cabot

Actress Again Asks Bruce Cabot Divorce. *Fresno Bee*, March 4, 1937.
Adrienne Ames Claims Hubby Not Family Man. *Medford Mail*, July 9, 1935.
American Actors Stranded in Rio Without Pay. *El Paso Herald Post*, December 25, 1963.
Ames III, Marshall. Hollywood Flashes. *Collyer's Eye and the Baseball World*, February 1, 1941.
Around Here. *El Paso Herald*, December 18, 1926.
Battling Artist Ignores Movie Rep, Takes Sock at He-Man Bruce Cabot in Night Spot. *Albuquerque Journal*, June 23, 1939.
Beebe, Lucius. Famous New York Columnist Tells of Reno's Film Event. *Nevada State Journal*, April 4, 1940.
_____. This New York. *St. Louis Post Dispatch*, August 8, 1943.
Behlmer, Rudy. *Henry Hathaway: A Director's Guild of America Oral History*. Lanham: Scarecrow Press, 2001.
Brigham, Ruth. Miami Medley. *Miami Herald*, February 2, 1947.

Brotherton, Jamie, and Ted Okuda. *Dorothy Lee: The Life and Films of the Wheeler and Woolsey Girl*. Jefferson, NC: McFarland, 2013.
Bruce Cabot Injured in Bel-Air Accident. *Ventura County Star Free Press*, May 1, 1939.
Bruce Cabot Named in Damage Suit. *Pasadena Independent*, February 1, 1946.
Bruce Cabot Ordered to Redeem Hot Checks. *Baytown Sun*, October 3, 1951.
Bruce Cabot Says Babies His Wife Names Aren't His. *Chicago Tribune*, June 8, 1955.
Bruce Cabot Sued. *Albuquerque Journal*, July 7, 1939.
Bruce Cabot Sued. *Santa Cruz Sentinel*, November 12, 1939.
Bruce Cabot Theft Brings Sentence. *Los Angeles Evening Citizen-News*, March 9, 1939.
Bruce Cabot Weds in Santa Barbara. *Santa Maria Times*, September 18, 1950.
Bruce Cabot's Arrest Ordered in Hassle on Child Support. *Long Beach Independent*, June 4, 1955.
Bruce Cabot's Salary Attached by Deputies. *Hollywood Citizen News*, October 26, 1939.
Bruce Cabot's Wife Asks Expected Baby's Support. *Los Angeles Times*, September 13, 1952.
Bustin, John. Show World. *Austin American*, May 24, 1967.
Cabot Heir. *Reading Eagle*, May 31, 1972.
Cabot Protégé Faces Court. *Hollywood Citizen News*, January 17, 1939.
Cabot-Radio Split. *Variety*, August 31, 1934.
Cabot Recalls University Days Here; Goes to Ranch. *Albuquerque Journal*, January 24, 1938.
Cabots Divide. *Dixon Evening Telegraph*, May 4, 1951.
Cameron, Kate. Audience at Rivoli Applauds *Dodsworth*. *New York Daily News*, September 24, 1936.
_____. Bruce Cabot Is Good in Rialto's *Bad Guy*. *New York Daily News*, August 26, 1937.
_____. Hell's Kitchen Film at Globe. *New York Daily News*, January 14, 1940.
Car Turns Over. *Carlsbad Current*, December 29, 1916.
Carmody, Jay. Politics, Just as Glamour, Is Raw Play Material. *Washington Evening Star*, December 3, 1940.
Carroll, Harrison. *Evening Independent*, December 22, 1938.
_____. *Morning Herald*, December 6, 1939.
_____. *Morning Herald*, July 22, 1942.
_____. *Press Democrat*, May 18, 1943.
_____. *Beatrice Times*, October 17, 1944.
_____. *Evening Herald*, August 19, 1949.
_____. *Evening Herald*, December 3, 1951.
_____. *Freeport Facts*, January 13, 1954.
_____. *Lancaster Eagle Gazette*, July 24, 1954.
_____. *New Castle News*, April 12, 1966.
Chapman, Tedwell. Cinema Lane. *Alton Evening Telegraph*, October 3, 1942.
Cohen, Harold W. The Drama Desk. *Pittsburgh Post Gazette*, August 13, 1936.
_____. The Drama Desk. *Pittsburgh Post Gazette*, February 3, 1943.
Connolly, Mike. *Pasadena Independent*, October 24, 1954.
Conrad, Harold. Gotham Grapevine. *Brooklyn Daily Eagle*, December 3, 1941.
Coons, Robbin. Bruce Cabot Sets Athletic Pace at Filmdom Capital. *Medford Mail Tribune*, March 8, 1933.
_____. *Warren Times Mirror*, January 27, 1941.
Crowther, Bosley. The Screen: *The Desert Song*, Modernized Version of the Old Operetta, with Dennis Morgan, Irene Manning, Opens at Hollywood. *New York Times*, December 18, 1943.
_____. Screen: *Goliath and the Barbarians* Sixth-Century Thriller from Italy Opens, *Jet Over the Atlantic* Also on Double Bill. *New York Times*, January 7, 1960.
De Bujac Plans to Marry Often Engaged Star. *Los Angeles Times*, August 2, 1929.
De Bujac-Smith Wedding is Brilliant New Year Event. *Orlando Sentinel*, January 2, 1927.
Denial by Bruce Cabot. *Kansas City Times*, Jun 8, 1955.
De Sabatino, Gabriel. Bruce Cabot Now Part Owner of Tourist Agency. *Corsicana Daily Sun*, May 5, 1958.
Dietrich, Marlene. *Marlene*. New York: Grove/Atlantic, 1989.
Dixon, Hugh. Hollywood. *Pittsburgh Post Gazette*, December 12, 1941.
Feature Reviews. *Boxoffice*, October 23, 1961.
Fidler, Jimmie. *Wilkes-Barre Record*, June 30, 1936.
_____. *The Tribune*, May 20, 1940.
_____. *San Pedro News Pilot*, July 11, 1940.
_____. *Evening Vanguard*, May 8, 1941.
_____. *Los Angeles Times*, August 14, 1941.
_____. *Indianapolis News*, August 6, 1942.
_____. *The Times*, August 11, 1942.
_____. *St. Louis Star and Times*, August 13, 1942.
_____. *Indianapolis News*, August 29, 1942.
_____. *Chronicle Telegram*, October 31, 1944.
Film Reviews. *Variety*, March 26, 1958.
Film Star Urges War Bond Purchase to Win "People's War." *Poughkeepsie Journal*, September 29, 1942.
Flynn's Kayo Punch May Have an Encore. *St. Louis Globe Democrat*, January 8, 1939.
Former Bellhop Here Is Jailed by Movie Stars. *Modesto Bee and News Herald*, January 17, 1939.
Freeman, Donald. Bruce Cabot Signs Up as Regular on Series. *Shreveport Journal*, May 18, 1966.
Friends Think Bujac's Death was Accidental. *Albuquerque Journal*, April 14, 1932.
Gardner, Hy. *Brooklyn Daily Eagle*, December 8, 1939.
Geurink, Bob. People in *WUSA* Are Real. *Atlanta Constitution*, November 28, 1970.
Goldrup, Tom, and Jim Goldrup. *The Encyclopedia of Feature Players of Hollywood, Volume 2*. Duncan, OK: BearManor Media, 2012.
Graham, Sheilah. Ex-Mrs. Gable Ranks Screen's Luminaries; March and Garbo Her Favorites; Raft Rates Last. *Star Tribune*, August 6, 1936.
_____. *Chattanooga Daily Times*, August 12, 1936.

_____. *Salt Lake Telegram*, January 3, 1939.
_____. *Hartford Courant*, December 9, 1939.
_____. *Hartford Courant*, December 29, 1939.
_____. *Hartford Courant*, February 28, 1941.
_____. *Tacoma News Tribune*, July 11, 1954.
_____. *Citizen News*, March 14, 1955.
Gwynn, Edith. *Pottstown Mercury*, February 18, 1948.
_____. *The Mirror*, September 2, 1952.
Hale, Wanda. Wholesale Murder at the Central Theatre. *New York Daily News*, October 31, 1940.
Harrison, Paul. *Evening Herald*, November 10, 1941.
Hopper, Hedda. *Los Angeles Times*, January 6, 1941.
_____. *Chicago Tribune*, March 6, 1944.
_____. *St. Louis Globe Democrat*, September 12, 1947.
_____. *Hartford Courant*, April 9, 1949.
Hutchinson, Tom. Rough Diamond. *London Guardian*, June 30, 1971.
James Bugg Just a Bug in Cabot's Ear. *Chico Record*, January 18, 1939.
Johnson, Erskine. *Daily News*, October 16, 1941.
_____. *Los Angeles Daily News*, September 21, 1942.
_____. *Los Angeles Daily News*, April 11, 1946.
_____. *Deadwood Pioneer-Times*, January 6, 1954.
Kilgallen, Dorothy. *Miami News*, June 24, 1940.
_____. *Star Tribune*, October 9, 1940.
_____. *Miami News*, November 17, 1940.
_____. *The Mercury*, September 15, 1942.
_____. *News Herald*, October 14, 1942.
_____. *News Journal*, October 17, 1942.
_____. *News Herald*, June 9, 1943.
_____. *Pittsburgh Post Gazette*, June 7, 1944.
_____. *Evening Herald*, June 15, 1944.
_____. *Wilkes-Barre Record*, November 8, 1944.
_____. *Pittsburgh Post Gazette*, November 24, 1944.
_____. *Times Tribune*, September 27, 1946.
Kinloch, John. In Review. *California Eagle*, March 10, 1938.
Kirkconnell, Robert. *American Heart of Darkness: Volume I The Transformation of the American Republic into a Pathocracy*. Bloomington, IN: Xlibris, 2013.
Kirkley, Donald. Adventure at Sea. *Baltimore Sun*, August 24, 1940.
Lyons, Leonard. Broadway Medley. *Shamokin News Dispatch*, November 18, 1940.
_____. Lyons Den. *Capital Times*, December 3, 1941.
_____. Lyons Den. *Escanaba Daily Press*, August 16, 1943.
_____. Lyons Den. *Daily Oklahoman*, July 6, 1948.
Mann, May. May Mann's Going Hollywood. *Ogden Standard Examiner*, April 1, 1942.
Masters, Dorothy. Divorce Goes to Brooklyn. *New York Daily News*, October 11, 1945.
McGilligan, Patrick. *Backstory: Interviews with Screenwriters of Hollywood's Golden Age*. Berkeley: University of California Press, 1986.

Merrick, Mollie. *Montana Butte Standard*, June 3, 1932.
Miss Ames of Films in Trial Separation. *St. Louis Globe-Democrat*, August 6, 1933.
Mrs. Bruce Cabot Gets a Divorce. *Winona Republican Herald*, November 28, 1951.
New Contract Won. *Los Angeles Times*. May 18, 1932.
News of Plays and Players of Stage and Screen. *Indianapolis News*, November 26, 1932.
Niemeyer, H.H. Movie Players in Unrehearsed Fights. *St. Louis Post Dispatch*, December 18, 1938.
Parsons, Louella. *Fresno Bee*, May 2, 1934.
_____. *The Courier*, December 30, 1940.
_____. *Fresno Bee*, April 28, 1941.
_____. *Fresno Bee*, March 16, 1942.
_____. *San Francisco Examiner*, November 9, 1942.
_____. *Sacramento Bee*, June 16, 1947.
_____. *Morning Call*, September 16, 1950.
_____. *San Francisco Examiner*, December 14, 1951.
_____. *Cumberland News*, July 7, 1962.
Peter Arno and Bruce Cabot Almost Mix with Blows in "Brutal" Café Society Brawl. *Los Angeles Times*, June 23, 1939.
Ratcliffe, David T. and L. Fletcher Prouty. *Understanding Special Operations and Their Impact on the Vietnam War Era: 1989 Interview with L. Fletcher Prouty Colonel USAF (Retired)*. Roslindale, MA: Rat Haus Reality Press, 1999.
Reviews of the New Films. *The Film Daily*, May 16, 1935.
Roales, Paul A. HEROES: Etienne de Pelissier Bujac, Carlsbad, NM. http://home.ionet.net/~heros/Bujachero.htm.
Roman Romances Just a Wife-Dream, Brice Cabot Claims. *Newsday*, June 9, 1955.
Ross, George. Broadway. *Pittsburgh Press*, November 19, 1942.
Salerno, Al. Brooklyn and Broadway Night Life. *Brooklyn Daily Eagle*, January 10, 1952.
The Shadow Stage. *Photoplay*, December 1941.
Sheaffer, Lew. Brooklyn and Broadway Night Life. *Brooklyn Daily Eagle*, March 28, 1947.
She's Cured! *Pottstown Mercury*, April 7, 1937.
S.J.B. At the Local Theaters. *Des Moines Tribune*, December 14, 1945.
Stevenson, L.L. New York Highlights. *Asbury Park Press*, November 6, 1942.
Sullivan, Ed. The Passing Show. *Hollywood Citizen News*, October 3, 1942.
_____. Little Old New York. *New York Daily News*, February 12, 1944.
_____. Little Old New York. *New York Daily News*, March 25, 1944.
Suspect in Bruce Cabot Home $1600 Theft Held. *Los Angeles Times*, March 23, 1945.
Tagging the Talkies. *Screenland*, October 1933.
Thirer, Irene. Screen Views and News. *New York Post*, January 21, 1936.
$30,000 Crash Suit Aimed at Cabot. *Hollywood Citizen News*, November 11, 1939.

Truesdell, John. *Courier Journal*, July 30, 1941.
⎯⎯⎯. *Beatrice Times*, December 19, 1942.
United Press. Meet the Folks Who Make News, Headlines. *Coos Bay Times*, February 24, 1939.
Wales, Clarke. Reviews of the New Films. *Democrat and Chronicle*, September 6, 1936.
Walker, Danton. *New York Daily News*, October 15, 1940.
⎯⎯⎯. *New York Daily News*, November 28, 1940.
⎯⎯⎯. *New York Daily News*, January 6, 1941.
What the Picture Did for Me. *Motion Picture Herald*, May 9, 1942.
Wilcox, Grace. The Hollywood Reporter. *Detroit Free Press*, November 15, 1936.
Winchell, Walter. *Scranton Republican*, July 16, 1929.
⎯⎯⎯. *Burlington Daily News*, August 16, 1937.
⎯⎯⎯. *Cincinnati Enquirer*, June 19, 1939.
⎯⎯⎯. *Pittsburgh Sun Telegraph*, November 29, 1939.
⎯⎯⎯. *Wilkes-Barre Times Leader the Evening News*, January 31, 1941.
⎯⎯⎯. *Lincoln Evening Journal*, June 28, 1944.
⎯⎯⎯. *St. Louis Post Dispatch*, July 11, 1946.
⎯⎯⎯. *Courier Post*, July 20, 1959.
Wister, Emery. Just Between Us. *Charlotte News*, November 19, 1970.

James Cardwell

Actor James Cardwell Ends Life by Shooting. *Shamokin News-Dispatch*, February 2, 1954.
Deidre's Diary. *Sunday Times*, June 10, 1951.
Flames Ate into the Spirit as Well as the Body of Luscious Cover-Girl. *Mirror*, December 26, 1953.
Jimmie Cardwell Acclaimed at Savar. *Courier-Post*, May 31, 1944.
Jimmy Cardwell Found Shot to Death in Auto. *Courier-Post*, February 2, 1954.
Junior Recreation Commission Elects. *Courier-Post*, June 21, 1939.
Parsons, Louella. *Scranton Tribune*, January 6, 1944.
Playcrafters Casts Gives Noted Drama. *Courier-Post*, December 16, 1939.
Schallert, Edwin. *Los Angeles Times*, January 14, 1944.
Shanghai Cobra Review. *Motion Picture Herald*, August 18, 1945.
Taylor, Clarice B. Community Players Delight First Nighters with Theater in the Round. *Honolulu Star-Bulletin*, October 6, 1949.
Wilson, Virginia. Movie Reviews. *Modern Screen*, October 1944.

William Eythe

Adams, Marjory. Warm Greeting Here 7 Years Ago Brings Eythe Back with His Play. *Boston Globe*, December 1, 1948.
Bill Eythe Has Eyes on Future. *Arizona Republic*, January 25, 1953.
Broomfield, Fred. Razzle Dazzle Revue Hot at Las Palmas. *Valley Times*, June 18, 1948.
Carl S. Eyth. *Pittsburgh Sun-Telegraph*, February 9, 1956.
Carroll, Harrison. Behind the Scenes in Hollywood. *South Bend Tribune*, June 3, 1948.
Chapman, John. Lend an Ear a Refreshing, Fast, Funny, Tuneful and Youthful Hit. *Daily News*, December 17, 1948.
Clark, Walter Van Tilburg. *The Ox-Bow Incident*. New York: Random House, 1940.
Cohen, Harold V. The Drama Desk. *Pittsburgh Post-Gazette*, July 17, 1940.
⎯⎯⎯. The Drama Desk. *Pittsburgh Post-Gazette*, September 5, 1941
⎯⎯⎯. The New Films. *Pittsburgh Post-Gazette*, February 14, 1946.
⎯⎯⎯. The Drama Desk. *Pittsburgh Post-Gazette*, June 18, 1949.
⎯⎯⎯. The Drama Desk. *Pittsburgh Post-Gazette*, September 20, 1949.
⎯⎯⎯. The Drama Desk. *Pittsburgh Post-Gazette*, November 17, 1949.
Daughtrey, Marcia. Terrific Trio! *Modern Screen*, May 1944.
Durgin, Cyrus. Lend an Ear, Charles Gaynor Intimate Revue at Wilbur, Very Funny. *Boston Globe*, December 3, 1948.
Eve of St. Mark. *LIFE*, October 19, 1942.
Eythe Sued for Divorce. *Pittsburgh Sun Telegraph*, January 10, 1948.
Eythe Tells About His New Revue. *Los Angeles Times*, June 13, 1948.
Fidler, Jimmie. *Knoxville Journal*, July 6, 1947.
Film Star in Tampa to Begin New Picture. *Tampa Tribune*, May 5, 1944.
Gaver, Jack. *The Liar* Thin Musical. *Pittsburgh Press*, May 23, 1950.
Graham, Sheilah. *Times Tribune*, February 28, 1945.
⎯⎯⎯. *Times Tribune*, July 12, 1945.
⎯⎯⎯. *Des Moines Register*, August 27, 1945.
Gwynn, Edith. Edith Gwynn's Hollywood. *Cincinnati Enquirer*, November 12, 1948.
Handsaker, Gene. Handsaker in Hollywood. *Valley Times*, June 12, 1946.
Hopper. Hedda. *Baltimore Sun*, December 31, 1944.
⎯⎯⎯. *Daily News*, Jul 30, 1948.
⎯⎯⎯. *Daily News*, Dec 28, 1948.
It's Swoony Stuff! Local Gals Meet Hollywood Stars. *Vidette Messenger of Porter County*, July 19, 1949.
J.H. The Note Book. *Berkshire Eagle*, August 14, 1941.
Kilgallen, Dorothy. On Broadway. *Pittsburgh Post-Gazette*, December 8, 1945.
Kirkley, Donald. Of Stage and Screen. *Baltimore Sun*, July 13, 1949.
Krug, Karl. On the Town. *Pittsburgh Sun Telegraph*, January 29, 1957.
Kubly, Herb. Fox Chapel Cast Excellent in Melodrama. *Pittsburgh Sun-Telegraph*, June 26, 1940.
Lyon, Herb. Tower Ticker. *Chicago Tribune*, June 25, 1956.

Man from Mars Jugged on Drunken Driving Rap. *Pittsburgh Press*, June 4, 1952.

M.B. *Royal Scandal* Is Pleasing Film. *Spokesman Review*, June 7, 1945.

McBrien, William. *Cole Porter*. New York: Knopf, 1998.

Monahan, Kaspar. Ex-Playhouse Revues Score Hit as Broadway Gaily "Lends an Ear." *Pittsburgh Press*, December 17, 1948.

Mosby, Aline. Movie Studios "Eating Crow." *Greenville News*, July 6, 1948.

O'Harra, Michaela. *Song of Bernadette* is Film of Beauty, Skillfully Directed. *Arizona Daily Star*, February 24, 1944.

Perry, Lawrence. Broadway Footlights. *Pittsburgh Press*, February 6, 1949.

Product Digest. *The Eve of St. Mark*. *Motion Picture Herald*, May 20, 1944.

Radcliffe, E.B. Out in Front. *Cincinnati Enquirer*, August 18, 1944.

Schallert, Edwin. *Los Angeles Times*, September 7, 1943.

_____. *Los Angeles Times*, June 17, 1948.

Shaffer, Rosalind. Bill Eythe Fears Being Typed as Film Weakling. *Knoxville Journal*, January 14, 1945.

Sheaffer, Louis. Curtain Time. *Brooklyn Daily Eagle*, May 22, 1950.

Standish, Myles. *Gramercy Ghost* a Weak Spook Comedy. *St Louis Post Dispatch*, January 30, 1952.

Straw Hat Reviews: Lend an Ear. *Variety*, September 3, 1941.

Tech Show Fails to Go on for First Time in 25 Years. *Pittsburgh Press*, March 13, 1941.

Thomas, Bob. *Indiana Gazette*, September 7, 1948.

Tudor, Ray. Improved Cast Sparks Play at Showcase. *Chicago Tribune*, November 19, 1953.

Walker, Danton. Broadway. *New York Daily News*, June 14, 1956.

Wilson, Earl. Nepotism But Nice: Tech Talent Crowds Broadway. *Pittsburgh Post-Gazette*, May 1, 1949.

_____. *Courier Post*, August 16, 1955.

Wister, Emery. Mars Loves Him: Bill Eythe Wanted to be a Director. *Charlotte Observer*, February 10, 1945.

Wallace Ford

Actor Freed in Drunk Driving Case. *Los Angeles Daily News*, May 1, 1947.

Actor Gets Thirty Days in L.A. Jail. *San Mateo Times*, August 17, 1943.

Actor Is Told of Lost Mother. *South Bend Tribune*, June 27, 1935.

Actor Testifies Barnett Beaten. *Hollywood Citizen News*, July 10, 1935.

Actor Wallace Ford Held on Suspicion of Hit-Run Felony. *Hollywood Citizen News*, January 3, 1947.

Actors Linked to Smuggling Quiz Involving Wife of N.Y. Jurist. *Racine Journal-Times*, December 6, 1938.

Another Actor Buys a Horse. *Los Angeles Daily News*, December 19, 1938.

Barnardo Boy Is Hollywood Star. *Brantford Expositor*, June 27, 1935.

Barnardo to Hollywood. *Sunday Mercury*, July 14, 1935.

Barnes, Eleanor. Truth Stranger Than Fiction in Wally Ford Case. *Los Angeles Illustrated Daily News*, January 17, 1934.

Baron, Michael. Wally Ford, of Films, Tells of Acting at Grand Here. *Winnipeg Tribune*, January 14, 1949.

Beast of the City Opens at Stanton. *Philadelphia Inquirer*, March 13, 1932.

Beautiful Acting in Court Charged to Wallace Ford. *Hollywood Citizen News*, April 17, 1947.

Benson, Jackson J. *John Steinbeck, Writer: A Biography*. New York: Penguin Books, 1990.

Bourke, George. On with the Show. *Miami Herald*, July 22, 1945.

British Army on Film Map. *Sunday Sun*, January 24, 1937.

Cameron, Kate. New Thriller at the Rialto. *New York Daily News*, September 20, 1940.

Carroll, Harrison. *Evening News*, September 17, 1937.

_____. *Holyoke Daily Transcript and the Holyoke Telegram*, October 25, 1937.

_____. *Covington Virginian*, October 11, 1938.

Carroll, Joseph. *Nebraskan* in 3-D and Color. *San Francisco Examiner*, December 19, 1953.

Charge Hit-Run Count on Actor. *Van Nuys News*, June 13, 1949.

Cohen, Harold W. The Drama Desk. *Pittsburgh Post Gazette*, April 30, 1940.

_____. The Drama Desk. *Pittsburgh Post Gazette*, February 3, 1943.

_____. New Film. *Pittsburgh Post Gazette*, December 10, 1948.

Conlon, Scoop. *Detroit Free Press*, November 8, 1931.

Court Clears Wallace Ford. *Los Angeles Times*. May 2, 1947.

CRIME: Chaperau's Way. *Time*, December 19, 1938.

Cummings, Ridgely. *Of Mice and Men* Given Good Production at Ivar. *Hollywood Citizen News*, March 3, 1953.

David, George L. On the Stage. *Democrat and Chronicle*, October 16, 1928.

Ex-Valet to Actor Freed of Gun Possession Count. *Detroit Free Press*, February 8, 1939.

Fawcett, Captain Roscoe. Screen Oddities. *Boston Globe*, April 4, 1932.

Fidler, Jimmie. *South Bend Tribune*, June 18, 1954.

Film Actor Clawed by Black Panther. *Brooklyn Times Union*, January 5, 1933.

Film Actor Dies After Attending Snow Festival. *San Bernardino County Sun*, January 27, 1950.

Foster, Ernest. Hollywood Film Shop. *El Reno Daily Tribune*, August 12, 1943.

Foundling Star Now Satisfied He Has Found His Mother. *Liverpool Echo*, December 23, 1936.

Francis, Robert. The Theater. *Brooklyn Daily Eagle*, November 24, 1937.

Garnier, Philippe. A Forgotten Director's Oddball Gem Screens at UCLA. *LA Weekly*, February 4, 2009.
Garrison, Maxine. Travelogue. *Pittsburgh Press*, December 28, 1945.
Gilmour, Clyde. Screening the Films. *Vancouver Sun*, July 8, 1952.
G.K. Beasts of Berlin New Screen Fare at Vogue. *Los Angeles Times*, February 25, 1943.
Gloss, Edward E. Mickey Mouse Makes Grade on Broadway. *Akron Beacon Journal*, February 25, 1932.
Graham, Sheilah. *Times Tribune*, July 8, 1943.
Greenberg, Abe. Voice of Hollywood. *Hollywood Citizen News*, June 14, 1966.
Gross, Ben. Listening In. *New York Daily News*, December 10, 1937.
_____. Listening In. *New York Daily News*, July 12, 1942.
Harrison, Paul. In Hollywood. *Messenger Inquirer*, November 15, 1935.
Heffernan, Harold. *Times Tribune*, September 1, 1939.
_____. *Times Tribune*, February 20, 1943.
Hopper, Hedda. *Los Angeles Times*, April 15, 1940.
_____. *Chicago Tribune*, December 2, 1958.
Hurtling Shaft Tears Shirt on Dick Powell. *Daily Clintonian*, February 23, 1951.
In the News. *Los Angeles Evening Citizen News*, May 31, 1951.
Johnson, Erskine. *Los Angeles Daily News*, September 19, 1941.
_____. *Daily Home News*, June 17, 1954.
Jones, Paul. Backstage. *Atlanta Constitution*, January 24, 1946.
Judge Commended by Actor He Sentenced to Jail While Presiding in Local Court. *Van Nuys News*, October 26, 1943.
Kendall, Read. *Los Angeles Times*, February 20, 1936.
_____. *Los Angeles Times*, July 1, 1937.
_____. *Los Angeles Times*, October 11, 1937.
_____. *Los Angeles Times*, October 15, 1937.
_____. *Los Angeles Times*, October 22, 1937.
Kirkley, Donald. The Screen Back East. *Baltimore Sun*, December 17, 1937.
_____. Broadway: The Stage. *Baltimore Sun*, March 15, 1938.
_____. Broadway Notes. *Baltimore Sun*, July 26, 1950.
Kofoed, Jack. The Night Watch. *Miami News*, October 28, 1941.
_____. Miami Story. *Miami News*, July 24, 1942.
_____. *Miami Herald*, February 22, 1951.
Levy, H.M. Of Mice and Men Stage Success. *Oakland Tribune*, April 25, 1939.
Littlefield, Joan. Wallace Ford Always Killed in His Movies. *Daily Province*, May 8, 1937.
Livingston, Lida. *Hollywood Citizen News*, Dec 3, 1941.
Los Angeles Briefs. *Los Angeles Times*, April 17, 1947.
Mantle, Burns. *New York Daily News*, November 13, 1938.
_____. Kindred Is a Poet's Plea for Idealism and a World Reformed. *New York Daily News*, December 27, 1939.
Martin, Boyd. James Cagney Hits Hard in Loew's Anti-Jap Film. *Courier-Journal*, June 21, 1945.
Martin, Mildred. Tale of T-Men Thrilling in New Documentary Film. *Philadelphia Inquirer*, January 11, 1948.
Masters, Dorothy. Marines Sabotaged at Brooklyn Strand. *New York Daily News*, July 9, 1943.
_____. Nebraskan Offered at the Brooklyn Fox. *New York Daily News*, February 6, 1954.
Mr. Manchester's Diary. *Manchester Evening News*, December 22, 1948.
Mosley, Glenn A. Henry Fonda and the Deputy: The Film and Stage Star and His TV Western. Albany, GA: BearManor, 2016.
Mystery Added to Thelma Todd's Death by New Clues. *Deseret News*, December 16, 1935.
Nathan, George Jean. The All-Broadway Second Team. *Atlanta Constitution Sunday Magazine*, February 13, 1938.
Oakley, Annie. The Theatre and Its People. *Windsor Star*, April 20, 1938.
Othman, Frederick C. Wally Ford Will Relive Hobo's Life. *Hollywood Citizen News*, October 16, 1937.
_____. Hollywood Day by Day. *Danville Morning News*, December 29, 1938.
Parham, Joe. *Macon News*, November 14, 1950.
Parsons, Harriet. *Courier Post*, August 24, 1937.
Parsons, Louella. *San Francisco Examiner*, October 22, 1937.
_____. *Scranton Tribune*, July 12, 1945.
_____. *Democrat and Chronicle*, September 22, 1949.
_____. *Philadelphia Inquirer*, September 30, 1949.
Percy, Eileen. *Pittsburgh Post-Gazette*, May 12, 1933.
Perry, Lawrence. Bellamy Rates Cities on Best in Which to Be Broke. *Indianapolis Star*, December 17, 1944.
Pinchot, Ann. Raised for Murder. *Atlanta Constitution*, January 2, 1938.
Play Review. *Variety*, April 7, 1939.
Police, Actor's Tale of Speed Do Not Jibe. *Chico Record*, June 28, 1939.
R.B. Runyon Comedy on Double Bill at the King. *Honolulu Star Bulletin*, August 1, 1938.
Previews: Tonight in Television. *Kokomo Tribune*, June 14, 1964.
Program Highlights. *Akron Beacon Journal*, June 14, 1964.
Redelings, Lowell F. The Hollywood Scene. *Hollywood Citizen News*, February 28, 1945.
Reviews and Previews. *Hollywood Filmograph*, January 13, 1934.
Richard Greene Seeks Army Leave to Make British Picture. *Hollywood Citizen News*, April 11, 1941.
Ross, George. Of Mice and Men Repeats Success in Stage Version. *Cincinnati Post*, December 1, 1937.
Schallert, Edwin. *Los Angeles Times*, September 12, 1934.

The Screen: *Night of Terror. Crowley Daily Signal*, October 23, 1933.
Seeks Dog Poisoner. *Wichita Evening Eagle*, January 3, 1936.
Self-Styled Valet of Stars Is Seized. *Detroit Free Press*, February 5, 1939.
Shaw, Len G. My Woman. *Detroit Free Press*, October 21, 1933.
Sloan, Lloyd L. The El Patio Reopens with Steinbeck Play. *Hollywood Citizen News*, January 28, 1948.
S.M. You'll Like Edith Fellows at Iowa. *Cedar Rapids Gazette*, April 6, 1938.
Smith, Darr. *Los Angeles Daily News*, March 16, 1951.
Soanes, Wood. Craven Curse Hits Star of *Our Town*. *Oakland Tribune*, April 30, 1939.
Sobol, Louis. The Voice of New York. *Press Democrat*, January 17, 1940.
Steinbeck Sees His Famous Production for First Time. *Los Angeles Times*, March 23, 1939.
Sullivan, Ed. Little Old New York. *New York Daily News*, June 28, 1941.
Summers, Bill. TV Comment. *Orlando Evening Star*, November 28, 1959.
Sympathy Went to Docs, Too, in Sizzling Week. *St. Louis Globe Democrat*, August 27, 1933.
Theaters' New Bills. *St. Joseph News-Press*, April 18, 1918.
Voss, Ralph F. *A Life of William Inge: The Strains of Triumph*. Lawrence: University Press of Kansas, 1989.
Wallace Ford, Actor, Ends Long Search for Mother. *Charlotte Observer*, December 24, 1936.
Wallace Ford Arrested in Hit, Run Case. *Valley Times*, January 3, 1947.
Wallace Ford Booked in Valley on Auto Charge. *Los Angeles Times*, August 17, 1943.
Wallace Ford Irked by Loss of Part. *Daily Olympian*, June 27, 1939.
Wallace Ford Pays Traffic Fines After Jail Sojourn. *Los Angeles Daily News*, June 28, 1939.
Wallace Ford Recovers from Blood Poisoning. *Fresno Bee The Republican*, August 16, 1933.
Wally Ford Fined on Driving Count. *Ogden Standard Examiner*, June 28, 1939.
Wear. Film Reviews. *Variety*, July 14, 1943.
Whisky vs. Whiskers Cause Recess in Ford Accident Trial. *Hollywood Citizen News*, April 18, 1947.
Williams, Whitney. Importance of Being Crazy. *Detroit Free Press*, September 8, 1935.
Wilson, Earl. Earl's Whirl. *Cincinnati Post*, October 9, 1953.
Wilson, Maggie. Tune In: Television Ends Technically Wonderful Week. *Arizona Republic*, April 2, 1955.

Billy Halop

Anderson, Nancy. No Dead End, Says "Kid" Billy Halop. *Cincinnati Enquirer*, August 26, 1974.
Biggers, Buck. Watch *Peter Pan* If Only to Compare to Mary Martin. *San Bernardino County Sun*, December 1, 1976.
Billy Halop Free on Drunk Count. *Long Beach Independent*, June 2, 1954.
Carroll, Harrison. Behind the Scenes in Hollywood. *Republican and Herald*, October 31, 1966.
Child Stars in Radio to Appear Here. *Hartford Courant*, March 29, 1935.
Dangaard, Colin. Billy Halop: Once a Busy Dead End Kid, Today He's a Part-timer on *All in the Family*. *Green Bay Press Gazette*, July 25, 1976.
David, George L. Century Marked by Acting of Billy Halop. *Democrat and Chronicle*, July 29, 1938.
Ex-Dead End Kid Granted Divorce. *Valley Times*. January 15, 1947.
Film Preview. *Variety*, July 30, 1937.
Forest Hills Actors at the Top. *Long Island Star-Journal*, July 1, 1953.
Graham, Sheilah. Meet the Transformed Dead End Kids. *Salt Lake Telegram*, August 6, 1938.
_____. The Dead End Kids Compete 2 Years in Hollywood But Think All Women There Are Wacky. *Long Island Daily Press*, October 1, 1938.
_____. Hollywood Today. *Hartford Courant*, August 23, 1939.
Hangover. *Independent*, November 30, 1967.
Harrison, Paul. *Kingsport Times*, July 6, 1941.
Helen Parrish and Dead End Kids Starred. *Daily Gazette*, July 22, 1938.
Hopper, Hedda. *Evening Sun*, March 27, 1951.
Johnson, Erskine. In Hollywood. *Dunkirk Evening Observer*, October 23, 1946.
Keefe, Willard. Dead End Is First Drama Hit of Stage. *Indianapolis Star*, November 3, 1935.
Life with Bogart Iowa Fare Friday. *Waterloo Courier*, April 23, 1939.
Mantle, Burns. Dead End as Alive as Steam. *New York Daily News*, October 29, 1935.
Marriage Reaches a Dead End. *Valley News*, November 30, 1967.
Parsons, Louella. *Albany Times-Union*, February 26, 1941.
_____. *Cumberland News*, July 19, 1947.
Reviews. *Tom Brown's School Days*. *Silver Screen*, September 1940.
Scott, John L. Dead End Kid Halop Stuck as Youngster. *Los Angeles Times*, December 13, 1966.
Sutton, Don. In New York. *Tallahassee Democrat*, November 20, 1935.
Thompson, Howard. SPOTLIGHT; Street Smarts. *New York Times*, January 18, 1998.
Turner, George. Flashbacks. *Amarillo Globe Times*, November 16, 1976.
Walker, Danton. *New York Daily News*, February 13, 1946.
Wilson, Arthur. Movie Talk. *New York Post*, December 12, 1941.
York, Cal. Gossip of Hollywood. *Photoplay*, October 1939.

Weldon Heyburn

Abie's Irish Rose (A Review). *Idaho Statesman*, October 22, 1925.

Abie's Irish Rose Proves to Be Real Treat. *Fremont Evening Tribune*, May 5, 1925.

Action Rules Both Capitol Feature Films. *Winnipeg Tribune*, August 8, 1936.

Actor Dies at Veterans' Hospital. *Long Beach Independent*, May 20, 1951.

Actor Sued by Ex-Fiancée: New York Actress Demands Return of Asserted Loan. *Los Angeles Times*, November 1, 1936.

Actress Sues Actor for "Nuptials" Loan. *Salt Lake Tribune*, November 1, 1936.

At the Movies. *Manitowoc Herald-Times*, July 20, 1943.

Atkinson, Brooks. THE PLAY; Elmer Rice's *Two on an Island* Is a Fable of Young People in Manhattan. *New York Times*, January 23, 1940.

Ballew, Harold. Greta Nissen Generous with Her Praise of St. Petersburg. *Tampa Bay Times*, August 16, 1933.

Carroll, Harrison. Behind the Scenes in Hollywood. *Daily Journal*, March 26, 1940.

_____. Behind the Scenes in Hollywood. *Bradford Era*, October 26, 1949.

The Critic on the Hearth. *Kansas City Star*, May 8, 1932.

Cromwell, John. Walter Winchell on Broadway. *The Gazette*, August 22, 1940.

Drama of Early Christian Period to Be Premiered. *Los Angeles Times*, October 17, 1943.

El Brendel Seen in Person at the Fox. *Philadelphia Inquirer*, February 20, 1932.

Famous Comedy Makes Bit Hit. *Vancouver Sun*, November 24, 1925.

Fidler, Jimmie. Jimmie Fidler in Hollywood. *Los Angeles Times*, March 30, 1940.

Field, Rowland. *Troyka*, A Gloomy Siberian Drama Comes to the Hudson. *Brooklyn Daily Times*, April 2, 1930.

Fiery New Bride of Society's Caveman Lover. *El Paso Times*, May 17, 1936.

Film Bulletin. *Independent Exhibitors Film Bulletin*, July 3, 1937.

Film Player Weds Eastern Debutante. *Los Angeles Times*, September 12, 1939.

Film Previews. *Variety*, January 20, 1933.

Freed, Greta Nissen Sees Love Holiday. *New York Daily News*, May 1, 1936.

Greta Nissen Marries Actor. *Windsor Star*, March 30, 1932.

Greta Nissen Sees Mate Swing Vainly at Escort. *Los Angeles Times*, October 15, 1932.

Greta Nissen to Sue for Divorce. *Piqua Daily Call*, March 9, 1934.

Greta Nissen's Ties Cut on Testimony of Mate. *Los Angeles Times*, April 30, 1936.

Hanifin, Ada. *Story to Be Whispered* Gets Premiere at Curran. *San Francisco Examiner*, August 20, 1937.

Heyburn in Bankruptcy. *Variety*, April 23, 1936.

Hobe. Film Reviews. *Variety*, August 25, 1937.

Hollywood and Los Angeles. *Variety*, June 21, 1932.

Home Robbed. *Long Beach Press Telegram*, May 8, 1936.

I Want a Policeman! Review. *Brooklyn Daily Eagle*, January 15, 1936.

Keavy, Hubbard. Screen Life in Hollywood. *Bluefield Daily Telegraph*, September 19, 1931.

_____. Screen Life in Hollywood. *Scranton Republican*, April 28, 1932.

Kilgallen, Dorothy. The Voice of Broadway. *Appeal-Democrat*, September 24, 1945.

Leading Man is Heyburn's Nephew. *Idaho Statesman*, October 22, 1925.

Martin, Linton. Simone Simon is *Emily* of New Play at Walnut. *Philadelphia Inquirer*, September 10, 1945.

M.B. *Careless Lady* Easy to Watch. *Spokesman Review*, April 23, 1932.

McCormick, Ella H. Film Industry Soft Pedals Talk of Stars' Big Salaries. *Detroit Free Press*, April 10, 1932.

Merrick, Mollie. What's What in Hollywood. *Winnipeg Tribune*, February 13, 1932.

_____. Actress' Husband Over Embankment. *Lincoln Journal Star*, June 20, 1932.

_____. Jean Ahead in Career. *Kansas City Star*, October 20, 1932.

Mines, Harry. Linger Long Greenwood. *Los Angeles Daily News*, December 23, 1939.

Outward Bound Thrills Pompton. *Paterson Evening News*, August 20, 1946.

Parsons, Louella. *Sacramento Bee*, December 10, 1933.

_____. *Fresno Bee*, March 18, 1936.

_____. *San Francisco Examiner*, October 11, 1943.

Pollock, Arthur. The Theater. *Brooklyn Daily Eagle*, January 15, 1936.

Porter, Reed. Edith Gwynn's Hollywood. *Los Angeles Mirror*, November 17, 1949.

Price, Edgar. The Premiere. *Brooklyn Citizen*, January 15, 1936.

Reviews. *The Film Daily*, September 20, 1937.

Sentence Is Suspended. *Daily Oklahoman*, May 9, 1943.

Sexes and Sevens Opens at Chestnut. *Philadelphia Inquirer*, October 16, 1934.

Temple Lead Formerly Starred on Teams at Alabama University. *Syracuse American*, March 18, 1928.

Trail Blazers, The. *Showmen's Trade Review*, November 2, 1940.

Very Convenient. *Los Angeles Times*, October 24, 1935.

Von Blon, Katherine. Rice's *Two on an Island* Given at Wilshire Ebell. *Los Angeles Times*, September 25, 1940.

_____. On Approval: What's Doing in Little Theaters. *Los Angeles Times*, November 16, 1941.

Weldon Heyburn May Be Real Name. *Spokane Daily Chronicle*, December 5, 1925.

Weldon Heyburn Supports Jeanne Eagels in Sketch. *Syracuse Herald*, May 26, 1928.

What the Picture Did for Me. *Motion Picture Herald*, November 27, 1937.
Winchell, Walter. On Broadway. *Courier Post*, September 8, 1933.
_____. On Broadway. *Courier Post*, January 9, 1939.

Ronald Lewis

Actor Banned for Three Years. *Chelsea News and General Advertiser*, February 13, 1970.
Actor "Conned" in King's Road. *Kensington News and West London Times*, February 6, 1970.
Actor Ronald's £21,000 Debts. *Daily Mirror*, July 1, 1980.
Actor Vanishes "to Take a Rest." *Western Mail*, January 9, 1959.
Back Again. *Worthing Herald*, March 6, 1959.
Barratt, Mark. *Ian McKellen: A Biography*. London: Virgin Books, 2006.
Belgrade Star Collapses. *Coventry Evening Telegraph*, September 15, 1979.
Bentley, Jack. *Sunday Mirror*, January 29, 1961.
Bryden, Ronald. *London Observer*, March 15, 1970.
_____. The McKellen Hamlet. *London Observer*, April 18, 1971.
Cardiff. *The Stage*, October 28, 1976.
Carry On Blogging Interview: Juliet Mills. January 18, 2019. https://carryonfan.blogspot.com/2019/01/carry-on-blogging-interview-juliet-mills.html
Carter, Nick. Palace at Its Best. *Harrow Observer*, October 28, 1977.
Carthew, Anthony. Anthony Carthew at the Films. *Daily Herald*, September 21, 1956.
Cat Nap but No Night Cap. *Motherwell Times*, August 17, 1956.
Connaught Cast Changes. *Worthing Herald*, January 12, 1951.
Davies, Russell, ed. *The Kenneth Williams Diaries*. New York: HarperCollins, 1994.
Dean, Peter. N.B.: Tomorrow Night at 7:30 Worthing Will be a Town of TV Clusterers. *Worthing Gazette*, October 1, 1958.
Edwards, Nadine M. Fans Left Grimacing by *Mr. Sardonicus*. *Los Angeles Evening Citizen News*, December 8, 1961.
Fabulous Moneymaker. *The Stage*, March 5, 1959.
Fellner, Chris. *The Encyclopedia of Hammer Films*. Lanham, MD: Rowman & Littlefield, 2019.
Findlater, Carole. Amateur Stage. *Nottingham Journal*, August 8, 1949.
Fraser, John. *Close Up: An Actor Telling Tales*. London: Oberon Books, 2006.
Hall, Edwin. Shows and People. *Worthing Herald*, March 16, 1956.
_____. Shows and People. *Worthing Herald*, September 5, 1958.
Hamlet. *The Stage*, April 18, 1946.
The "Hate" Man Has Arrived. *Peterborough Advertiser*, November 22, 1957.
Hearn, Marcus, and Alan Barnes. *The Hammer Story: The Authorised History of Hammer Films*. London: Titan Books, 2007.
His Majesty's R.A.D.A. Matinee. *The Stage*, March 30, 1950.
King's Road "Con." *Chelsea News and General Advertiser*, February 6, 1970.
Limelight. *The Stage*, July 7, 1955.
London Letter. *Western Mail*, January 16, 1957.
_____. *Western Mail*, September 11, 1958.
_____. *Western Mail*, September 24, 1959.
London Theatres: Power and Terror of Ibsen's Ghosts. *The Stage*, November 20, 1958.
Marriott, R.B. Ronald Lewis—Great Parts and Trivialities. *The Stage*, November 16, 1961.
_____. Obituary. *The Stage*, January 21, 1982.
Maxford, Howard. *Hammer Complete: The Films, the Personnel, the Company*. Jefferson, NC: McFarland, 2018.
McGarry, Peter. Star of Thriller Collapses at Curtain-up. *Coventry Evening Telegraph*, September 15, 1979.
_____. From One Hot Seat to Another…Ronald Takes It in His Stride. *Coventry Evening Telegraph*, September 21, 1979.
McKellen, Ian. Ian McKellen on Hamlet. https://mckellen.com/stage/00210.htm.
The Oresteia Is Saved by Ronald Lewis and Ruth Meyers. *The Stage*, November 9, 1961.
Our London Letter. *Western Mail*, October 23, 1952.
_____. *Western Mail*, June 11, 1955.
Peter Pan. *Birmingham Daily Post*, February 22, 1966.
Pigott-Smith, Tim. *Do You Know Who I Am? A Memoir*. London: Bloomsbury Continuum, 2017.
P.L.J. Triumph of Quality in Comedy. *Portsmouth Evening News*, May 5, 1953.
A Plum Part. *Manchester Evening News*, September 23, 1955.
Public Treated Like Imbeciles. *Aberdeen Evening Express*, January 28, 1975.
R.B.M. Jeans Steals the Show. *The Stage*, October 20, 1966.
_____. Lewis & Massey Save the Evening. *The Stage*, October 16, 1969.
_____. Not Good McCullers. *The Stage*, March 12, 1970.
Richards, Dick. Dick Richards at the Pictures. *Daily Mirror*, April 1, 1961.
Roberts, St. John. Drama. *The Stage*, August 13, 1959.
R.P.C. No Dreary Wastes at the Connaught. *Worthing Herald*, June 23, 1950.
_____. Theatre Company Turns to Farce. *Worthing Herald*, July 14, 1950.
_____. Family Plays at the Connaught. *Worthing Herald*, July 21, 1950
_____. Mrs. Warren's Argument No Longer Holds Good. *Worthing Herald*, December 8, 1950.
Showing Next Week. *Leicester Chronicle*, September 1, 1956.
Soft-hearted TV Actor Goes Broke. *Liverpool Daily Post*, July 1, 1980.

Sooty Inspires Murder Play! *Sunday Mirror*, August 2, 1959.
South Sea Bubble. Variety, April 11, 1956.
Star and Director Visit Leicester. *Leicester Chronicle*, February 10, 1961.
Students in Shaw Comedy. *Nottingham Journal*, August 4, 1949.
Swires, Steve. Merchant of the Magicks, Part Three. *Starlog*, March 1990.
Telecrit. *Liverpool Echo*, August 29, 1957.
Television Viewpoint. *The Stage*, March 3, 1955.
Thompson, Howard. Screen: Walt Disney's The Parent Trap Opens. *New York Times*, June 22, 1961.
Tragedy of The Nearly Man. *Daily Mail*, January 26, 1982.
Trewin, J.C. *Julius Caesar* at the Old Vic. *Birmingham Daily Post*, October 10, 1958.
_____. Insideout. *Birmingham Daily Post*, December 2, 1969.
Turney-Dann, Doreen. Arrested Cardinal's Interrogation Makes a Grim Prison Drama. *Bradford Observer*, April 22, 1955.
2 "Shiners" for a Film Actor. *Daily Mirror*, May 22, 1965.
What You Think. *Films and Filming*, March 1961.
Willis, Ray. New Films: A War Film But—The Conflict is Between Actors and Their Script. *West London Observer*, October 19, 1956.

Tom Neal

Abalone—No Baloney! *Corpus Christi Caller*, November 26, 1939.
Actor Tone Proposes and Blond Barbara Says "Yes." *Fort Worth Star Telegram*, September 17, 1951.
Actress Asks Divorce from Actor Mate. *Los Angeles Times*, July 7, 1949.
Adamson, Kent. Email to Author, April 8, 2022.
Allen Gets Neal Spot in *Fast and Loose* for Metro. *Variety*, December 28, 1938.
Altar with Inez Off Till Heir Finds Job. *New York Daily News*, September 13, 1935.
Barbara, Tone Row, She Takes Pills, Is Report. *Birmingham News*, March 20, 1952.
Belser, Lee. Tom Neal Has Become a Forgotten Person in Busy World of Movies. *Kingsport Times*, August 20, 1957.
Between You and Me: War Film Farce Should Stop. *The Tidings*, July 16, 1943.
Blonde Alibi and Western Thriller Provide Double Feature Entertainment. *Shamokin News Dispatch*, June 7, 1946.
Blonde Says Her Betrothed Struck Franchot Tone First. *Enid Daily Eagle*, September 15, 1951.
Bogdanovich, Peter. Edgar G, Ulmer Interview. *Film Culture* No. 58–60, 1970.
Carroll, Harrison. *Morning Herald*, November 1, 1944.
_____. *Lancaster Eagle Gazette*, July 16, 1951.
_____. *Evening Herald*, September 1, 1951.
_____. *Lancaster Eagle Gazette*, December 14, 1951.
_____. *Greensburg Daily News*, August 19, 1955.
_____. *Wilkes-Barre Times Leader*, January 16, 1956.
_____. *Kokomo Morning Times*, February 11, 1966.
Cassidy, Claudia. Stage *Laura* Fails to Equal the Book or the Movie. *Chicago Tribune*, June 23, 1946.
Coast Burglar Grabs $11,000. *Los Angeles Daily News*, February 4, 1952.
Cohen, Harold V. The Drama Desk. *Pittsburgh Post-Gazette*, February 22, 1951.
_____. New Season at Nixon Gets Started with an Old Drama. *Pittsburgh Post-Gazette*, September 29, 1953.
_____. *Pittsburgh Post-Gazette*, October 26, 1953.
Connolly, Mike. Hollywood Report. *Pasadena Independent*, June 18, 1952.
_____. Hollywood Report. *Pasadena Independent*, November 18, 1952.
_____. *Desert Sun*, April 28, 1956.
Coons, Robbin. Film Fare. *San Pedro News Pilot*, May 29, 1943.
Detour Tears Emotions. *Los Angeles Times*, October 30, 1945.
Dixon, Hugh. Hollywood. *Pittsburgh Post-Gazette*, November 14, 1945.
Elopement Denied by Barbara Payton. *News Press*, January 15, 1952.
Exhibitor Servisection. *The Exhibitor*, April 27, 1949.
Fearless. *Bonham (Texas) Daily Favorite*, May 28, 1944.
Ferrero, Lee. Tone Denies First Blow, Claims His Face Was Turned. *San Francisco Examiner*, September 16, 1951.
Fidler, Jimmie. *Chronicle Telegram*, July 17, 1944.
_____. *Quad-City Times*, October 30, 1944.
_____. *Sioux City Journal*, November 3, 1945.
_____. *Nevada State Journal*, March 2, 1946.
_____. *Valley Times*, October 4, 1951.
Flanagan, Barbara. Tone, Barbara Say "I Do" at Hasty Rites. *Minneapolis Morning Tribune*, September 29, 1951.
Forged-Letter Writer Sought by Cugat's Wife. *Los Angeles Times*, February 3, 1950.
Former Actor Tom Neal Booked in Slaying of Wife at Palm Springs. *Los Angeles Times*, April 3, 1965.
Franchot Tone In Coma Following Fight. *Charlotte News*, September 15, 1951.
Franchot Tone Is Sent to Hospital After Fist Fight. *Fresno Bee*, September 14, 1951.
Franchot Tone, Still in Serious Condition, Is Visited by Blonde Over Whom He Fought. *Daily Press*, September 16, 1951.
Franchot Tone's Face May Not Bear Closeups. *Green Bay Press-Gazette*, September 18, 1951.
Freeman Jr., Vernon. Crews Remove Maury Statue on Monument Avenue. https://www.wtvr.com/news/local-news/crews-to-remove-maury-statue-on-monument-avenue.

Friends Aiding Actor Tom Neal, Murder Suspect. *Reno Gazette Journal*, August 21, 1965.
Goldberg, Albert. Newest *Laura* Lacks Glamour of Old Versions. *Chicago Tribune*, June 11, 1946.
Graham, Sheilah. No Tommyrot for Maureen. *Spokesman Review*, April 24, 1940.
_____. *Times Tribune*, December 5, 1952.
_____. *Citizen News*, May 28, 1955.
Grange, Kenneth. Barbara Payton's Downbeat Diary. *Exposed*, April 1956.
Grant, Gloria. Assignment Hollywood. *West Los Angeles Independent*, August 23, 1951.
Gwynn, Edith. *Cincinnati Enquirer*, September 30, 1951.
_____. *Cincinnati Enquirer*, April 12, 1952.
_____. *Mercury Thu*, May 15, 1952.
Haas, Jim. Postman Always Rings Twice. *Evening Herald*, July 14, 1953.
Henshaw, Buck. Henshaw in Honolulu. *Honolulu Star Bulletin*, July 8, 1952.
Herbstman, Mandel. Reviews. *Motion Picture Daily*, May 13, 1949.
Herm. Film Review: Amazon Quest. *Variety*, May 11, 1949.
Hollywood Needs Great Revival, Graham Says. *Fort Worth Star Telegram*, September 17, 1951.
Hope, Bob. Hollywood. *The Mercury*, November 11, 1953.
Hopper, Hedda. *New York Daily News*, November 30, 1943.
_____. *St. Louis Globe Democrat*, February 1, 1950.
Houston, David. The Two Tom Neals: A Legacy. *Filmfax*, July 1988.
Independents. *Independent Exhibitors Film Bulletin*, December 20, 1948.
Irwin, Virginia. He's Taking Lessons in Love. *St. Louis Post Dispatch*, November 17, 1939.
Jaediker, Kermit, and Jim Bennett. Rockabye with a Bullet. *New York Daily News*, August 15, 1965.
Jealousy Charge Wins Decree for Vicky Lane. *Los Angeles Times*, August 9, 1949.
Johnson, Erskine. *Daily News*, September 19, 1951.
_____. *Daily News*, October 10, 1951.
_____. *Sioux City Journal*, November 7, 1951.
_____. *Los Angeles Daily News*, July 31, 1952.
_____. *Los Angeles Daily News*, October 9, 1952.
Katcher, Leo. Hollywood Hooligan. *The People*, December 9, 1951.
Kilgallen, Dorothy. *News Journal*, August 8, 1951.
_____. *Evening Herald*, September 24, 1951.
_____. *Star Gazette*, November 28, 1951.
_____. *The Gazette*, May 11, 1953.
_____. *Star-Gazette*, March 6, 1954.
_____. *News Journal*, October 16, 1965.
Korman, Seymour. Ex-Actor Jailed in Wife Slaying. *Chicago Tribune*, April 3, 1965.
_____. Neal Admitted Slaying Wife, 2 Friends Say. *Chicago Tribune*, April 17, 1965.
Kramer, Chuck. Neal's Life Threatened by Wife, Witness Says. *Desert Sun*, November 2, 1965.
_____. 15 Years Possible for Former Actor. *Desert Sun*, December 10, 1965.

Lewis, Jay. Books and Authors. *Norfolk Ledger-Dispatch*, January 12, 1939.
Lyon, Herb. Tower Ticker. *Chicago Tribune*, March 28, 1955.
Manners, Dorothy. *Cumberland News*, August 2, 1951.
_____. *San Francisco Examiner*, September 1, 1951.
Mason, Buddy. Behind the Movie Sets. *Shawnee American*, March 9, 1951.
Mate Too Jealous. *Wilmington Daily Press Journal*, August 8, 1949.
Mike McCauley Features Neal as Fem Heartthrob. *Santa Barbara News Press*, January 23, 1951.
Miss Payton and Neal Plan Trip Abroad. *Los Angeles Times*, June 18, 1952.
Miss Payton Gets Thick Again with Tom Neal. *Contra Costa Gazette*, September 21, 1951.
Monahan, Kaspar. Show Shops. *Pittsburgh Press*, September 29, 1953.
Moore, Bill. Film Fare. *West Carroll Gazette*, April 11, 1940.
Mortimer, Lee. New York Confidential. *Courier Post*, August 26, 1953.
Morton, Hortense. Don DeFore, Isa Miranda Head Fine Geary Comedy Case. *San Francisco Examiner*, January 31, 1951.
Mosby, Alice. Battle with Tone Brings Neal New Lease on Fame. *Los Angeles Daily News*, October 6, 1951.
Mrs. Neal Death Said Deliberate. *Santa Maria Times*, January 15, 1966.
Mrs. Tom Neal Found Shot Through Head. *Desert Sun*, April 2, 1965.
Muir, Florabel. *Los Angeles Mirror*, August 8, 1951.
_____. *Los Angeles Mirror*, September 24, 1951.
_____. *Los Angeles Daily News*, September 26, 1951.
_____. Tone Beats Babs to Divorce Punch. *Los Angeles Daily News*, November 21, 1951.
_____. Tom Neal Says He'll Marry Barbara Yet. *Columbia Record*, January 17, 1952.
Neal Caught with Babs, Warns Photog. *Pasadena Independent*, December 16, 1951.
Neal Confessed Killing Wife, Grand Jury Told. *Desert Sun*, April 15, 1965.
Neal Congratulates the Franchot Tones. *Minneapolis Morning Tribune*, September 29, 1951.
Neal Declares Engagement to Inez Norton Off. *Chicago Tribune*, September 22, 1935.
Neal Remains Silent During Murder Arraignment. *Desert Sun*, April 5, 1965.
Neal, Tone, Barbara Brawl Puts Franchot in Hospital. *Los Angeles Daily News*, September 14, 1951.
Neighbors Hint at Triangle Motive in Slaying of Ex-Actor Tom Neal's Wife. *Detroit Free Press*, April 5, 1965.
Neville, Lucie. Men Wanted! *Evansville Press*, August 20, 1939.
News Around the World. *Minneapolis Morning Tribune*, July 6, 1949.
Northwestern U. Graduate to Wed Racketeer Girl. *Belleville Daily News Democrat*, September 12, 1935.

O'Dowd, John. *Kiss Tomorrow Goodbye* (Second Edition). Albany, GA: BearManor, 2015.
The Palm Leaf Fan. *Fort Lauderdale News*, November 5, 1935.
_____. *Fort Lauderdale News*, May 8, 1939.
_____. *Fort Lauderdale News*, May 10, 1939.
Parsons, Louella. *Bakersfield Californian*, July 12, 1949.
_____. *San Francisco Examiner*, September 8, 1955.
_____. *Indianapolis Star*, January 11, 1956.
Plea by Ex-Actor Neal Is Dismissed. *Sacramento Bee*, August 5, 1966.
Previews. *Hollywood Review*, November 24, 1947.
Roland Young Cast for "Darling Daughter" Film at Warner Plant. *Hollywood Citizen News*, October 11, 1938.
Scandal-Ruined Actor Now an Ex-Con. *Progress Bulletin*, December 6, 1971.
Schallert, Edwin. *Los Angeles Times*, October 13, 1943.
_____. *Los Angeles Times*, June 27, 1944.
Scott, Vernon. Tough Tom Neal Finds Peace in Religion, Soil. *Boston Globe*, November 15, 1957.
Sentencing of Neal Set in Wife's Death. *Chicago Tribune*, November 20, 1965.
Simon, Leo. Stage and Screen. *Los Angeles Daily News*, March 26, 1940.
Skolsky, Sidney. *Los Angeles Evening Citizen News*, July 30, 1951.
_____. *Hollywood Citizen News*, July 19, 1955.
_____. *Hollywood Citizen News*, September 26, 1955.
_____. *Hollywood Citizen News*, January 31, 1956.
Sobol, Louis. New York Cavalcade. *Springfield News-Sun*, November 7, 1953.
Stafford, M. Oakley. Informing You. *Hartford Courant*, July 2, 1953.
Standish, Myles. *Postman* Lacking in Power, Tension. *St. Louis Post Dispatch*, October 13, 1953.
Steady Marksman. *St. Louis Star and Times*, August 17, 1939.
Stein, Herb. *Philadelphia Inquirer*, November 19, 1951.
Submarine Film is Showing at Embassy. *Cumberland News*, April 6, 1944.
Sullivan, Ed. Little Old New York. *New York Daily News*, January 4, 1941.
_____. Little Old New York. *New York Daily News*, December 3, 1951.
Sullivan, Ina. Your Film Star Neighbor: Doings of Valley Studio Players. *San Fernando Valley Times*, November 22, 1938.
Surmelian, Leon. To Outstay a Studio—Work! *Silver Screen*, June 1939.
Tom Neal, in Britian, to Call on Barbara. *San Bernardino County Sun*, September 13, 1952.
Tom Neal Sentenced to 1–15 Years in Jail. *Chicago Tribune*, December 11, 1965.
Tom Neal Tells How Wife Died. *Albuquerque Tribune*, November 3, 1965.
Tom Neal to Drop His Usual Villain Role in *Laura* Tonight. *Baltimore Sun*, May 20, 1946.
Tone Wins the Girl After Losing Fight. *Los Angeles Mirror*, September 17, 1951.
Two College Boys Get Job Kissing Actress in Revue. *South Bend Tribune*, May 9, 1937.
Under Age Review. *Harrison's Reports*, May 3, 1941.
Walker, Danton. *New York Daily News*, October 5, 1955.
Weaver, Tom. Neal-Payton-Tone: LaLaLand Love Triangle. *Films of the Golden Age*, Summer 2015.
Wife Shot in Struggle for Gun, Neal Claims. *Philadelphia Daily News*, November 3, 1965.
Wilson, Earl. *Miami News*, October 8, 1952.
Winchell, Walter. *Star Tribune*, October 5, 1951.
_____. *Des Moines Tribune*, October 16, 1951.
_____. *Scranton Tribune*, July 20, 1965.
Yank Who Became a Jap: *First Yank Into Tokyo*. *The Tidings*, November 23, 1945.
Zaiman, Bob. The Human Touch. *Hartford Courant*, July 16, 1953.

Allan Nixon

Actor's Wife Dies. *Kansas City Star*, October 1, 1958.
Allan, Nick. *Dynasty of Decadence: Hollywood's Lavender Casting Couch*. North Hollywood, California: Brandon House, 1966.
Allan Nixon Balks at Charge Against Wife. *Los Angeles Times*, January 21, 1958.
Allan Nixon's Bride Asks Annulment. *Los Angeles Times*, August 19, 1954.
Allan Nixon's Wife Dies of Blast Injuries. *Hollywood Citizen News*, October 1, 1958.
Barber Wins Over Katan in 3 Falls. *Richmond Times-Dispatch*, October 8, 1938.
Both Sutton, Nixon Are Lost to U.R.; Money Woes Cited. *Richmond News Leader*, October 1, 1936.
Carroll, Harrison. Behind the Scenes in Hollywood. *Gaffney Ledger*, December 16, 1948.
_____. Behind the Scenes in Hollywood. *Daily Clintonian*, December 30, 1948.
_____. Behind the Scenes in Hollywood. *Bradford Era*, February 23, 1949.
_____. Behind the Scenes in Hollywood. *Lancaster-Eagle Gazette*, February 7, 1950.
_____. Behind the Scenes in Hollywood. *Lancaster-Eagle Gazette*, March 2, 1950.
_____. Behind the Scenes in Hollywood. *Lancaster-Eagle Gazette*, January 1, 1951.
_____. Behind the Scenes in Hollywood. *Evening Independent*, March 8, 1951.
_____. Behind the Scenes in Hollywood. *Lancaster-Eagle Gazette*, January 30, 1954.
_____. Behind the Scenes in Hollywood. *News Messenger*, August 11, 1956.
Coates, Paul V. Tales of the Vine Street Woods. *Mirror News*, July 23, 1956.
Cops Find Actress' Husband Bit Tough. *Austin American Statesman*, December 15, 1948.
Doherty, Rosaleen. Movies' Dumb Blonde No. 1 in Coloroto. *New York Daily News*, November 10, 1946.

Drunk Count Jails Mate of Marie Wilson. *Los Angeles Mirror*, September 25, 1950.
Durden, Chauncey. The Sportview. *Richmond Times-Dispatch*, February 26, 1941.
_____. The Sportview. *Richmond Times-Dispatch*, March 7, 1941.
Durgin, Cyrus. The Stage. *Boston Globe*, September 3, 1946.
Ex-Husband of Marie Wilson Knifed by Wife. *Los Angeles Times*, January 19, 1958.
Famous Dumb Blonde Ministers to Husband. *Lebanon Daily News and the Lebanon Daily Times*, August 13, 1949.
Fisher, George. *The Mercury*, December 18, 1951.
Goldrup, Tom, and Jim Goldrup. *The Encyclopedia of Feature Players, Vol. 2*. Albany, GA: BearManor Media, 2012.
Goodman, Ezra. *Los Angeles Daily News*, November 29, 1949.
_____. Stage Review: *The School for Scandal*. *Los Angeles Daily News*, June 8, 1950.
Graham, Sheilah. *Times Tribune*, October 5, 1945.
_____. *Citizen News*, August 27, 1951.
_____. *Arizona Daily Star*, December 9, 1951.
Gwynn, Edith. Edith Gwynn's Hollywood. *Los Angeles Mirror*, August 10, 1950.
Hamilton, Chas. Looking at Sports with Chas. Hamilton. *Richmond News Leader*, September 8, 1936.
Hopper, Hedda. *New York Daily News*, December 20, 1948.
_____. *Los Angeles Times*, February 9, 1949.
_____. *Los Angeles Times*, November 22, 1950.
Husband of Marie Wilson Faces Drunk Rap in Car Crash. *Los Angeles Daily News*, September 25, 1950.
It's Too Early for Prophecy, Crane Claims. *Richmond Collegian* Vol. XXII, No. 5, September 24, 1935.
Johnson, Erskine. *Los Angeles Daily News*, May 8, 1950.
_____. *Portsmouth Herald*, December 19, 1951.
_____. *Los Angeles Daily News*, January 19, 1952.
Jones, Jimmy. Keeping Up with Jones. *Richmond Times-Dispatch*, February 20, 1938.
Kany, A.S. Let's Go Places. *Journal Herald*, January 25, 1951.
Kilgallen, Dorothy. *Miami News*, June 22, 1939.
_____. *Elmira Star-Gazette*, November 27, 1950.
_____. *The Gazette*, October 31, 1951.
_____. *Asbury Park Press*, November 19, 1958.
Kingsley, Grace. Novel Plays Begins Run. *Los Angeles Times*, January 9, 1952.
Lindeman, Edith. Dick Powell and Wife Costarred. *Richmond Times-Dispatch*, May 23, 1941.
Loeb, Theresa. Primeval Film Offers Surprise. *Oakland Tribune*, January 8, 1951.
Manners, Dorothy. *Courier Post*, September 10, 1945.
_____. *Fresno Bee*, August 23, 1949.
Maria Montez Tells Court About Astrology. *Los Angeles Times*, April 22, 1950.
Marie Wilson Bails Hubby Out of Jail. *New York Daily News*, December 15, 1948.
Marie Wilson Mate Slashed. *Hollywood Citizen News*, August 13, 1949.
Marie Wilson Pleads, but Police Get Hubby. *Los Angeles Times*, December 16, 1948.
Marie Wilson to Divorce GI Husband. *Evansville Press*, August 31, 1945.
Marie Wilson's Dog Credited for Her Dropping Divorce Suit. *Los Angeles Times*, February 8, 1949.
Marie Wilson's Ex-Mate Nixon Sued for Divorce. *Pasadena Independent*, August 20, 1954.
Martin, Mildred. Film at Studio Shows Women of Stone Age. *Philadelphia Inquirer*, December 30, 1950.
Masgay, Johnny. Hollywood Promenade. *Daily Calumet*, March 14, 1951.
Monk, Herbert L. *Come On Up* at American is Tailored to Maw West. *St. Louis Globe Democrat*, December 30, 1946.
Mosby, Aline. Cave-Women Tactics to Catch Your Man Urged by Actress. *Richmond Times-Dispatch*, June 10, 1950.
Mrs. Nixon Divorces Hollywood Actor. *Boston Globe*, March 28, 1940.
Muir, Florabel. Florabel Muir Reporting. *Los Angeles Mirror*, August 6, 1949.
Murphy, William S. The Pocket Reader. *Los Angeles Times*, February 25, 1968.
_____. The Pocket Reader. *Los Angeles Times*, April 17, 1966.
Nixon, Allan H. Movie Notes from a Former Richmonder. *Richmond Times-Dispatch*, April 25, 1943.
Nixon, Allan. *The Actor*. New York: Paperback Library, 1968.
_____. *Blessed Are the Damned*. New York: Paperback Library, 1963.
_____. *The Bitch Goddess*. New York: Paperback Library, 1969.
_____. *The Last of Vicky*. New York: Paperback Library, 1966.
_____. *Nikki*. Chicago: Playboy Press, 1977.
_____. *Power Man*. New York: Avon Books, 1972.
_____. *Shadow of a Man*. New York: Avon Books, 1979.
Oliver, John. Nixon Makes Good in Old Role as Pivotman at U.R. *Richmond News Leader*, October 2, 1935.
_____. The Right Angle. *Richmond News Leader*, October 1, 1937.
_____. Former U.R. Gridder Would Pursue Career as Wrestler; Appeals to Lewis for Match. *Richmond News Leader*, September 30, 1938.
Parsons, Louella. *Fresno Bee*, June 15, 1942.
_____. *Fresno Bee*, June 18, 1942.
_____. *Fresno Bee*, November 25, 1942.
_____. *San Francisco Examiner*, January 19, 1949.
_____. *The Tribune*, February 4, 1950.
_____. *Cumberland News*, February 10, 1951.
_____. *Pittsburgh Sun Telegraph*, June 22, 1951.
_____. *Fort Worth Star Telegram*, June 2, 1953.
Schallert, Edwin. School for Scandal Gay Circle Players' Venture. *Los Angeles Times*, June 9, 1950.

_____. *The Bear* Tops Series of Playlets at Circle. *Los Angeles Times*, October 6, 1950.

_____. Gladys George Vivid Sadie Thompson in *Rain*. *Los Angeles Times*, July 3, 1951.

Scheuer, Philip K. *Kitty Doone* Swings Haymaker at Hollywood. *Los Angeles Times*, December 8, 1949.

She Asks for Nothing. *Los Angeles Daily News*, February 1, 1949.

Skolsky, Sidney. Hollywood Is My Beat. *Hollywood Citizen News*, March 27, 1950.

Sloan, Lloyd L. O'Connor a Triple Threat, Chaplin Plans New Film. *Hollywood Citizen News*, December 8, 1949.

Thomas, Bob. Hollywood. *Denton Record Chronicle*, February 13, 1947.

Wife Wields Gift Steak Knives on Actor Allan Nixon. *Port Angeles Evening News*, January 18, 1958.

Williams, Dick. He Wants a Career of His Own. *Los Angeles Mirror*, September 25, 1950.

Craig Reynolds

Actor Planning Work in England. *Los Angeles Times*, October 6, 1934.

Barnes, Eleanor. Mae West Smashes Records. *Los Angeles Daily News*, September 25, 1934.

Burman, Sergeant Edward. War's Thrills Beat Movies, Says Player. *Seattle Star*, January 14, 1943.

_____. Young Actor Now Stars for Marines. *Cincinnati Post*, January 16, 1943.

Carroll, Harrison. Behind the Scenes in Hollywood. *Evening Independent*, March 31, 1943.

_____. Behind the Scenes in Hollywood. *Beatrice Times*, June 24, 1945.

_____. Behind the Scenes in Hollywood. *Daily Clintonian*, November 14, 1949.

Coons, Robbin. Hollywood. *Carthage Evening Press*, March 3, 1944.

Craig Returns to Hero Roles. *Lima News*, May 16, 1937.

Enfield, Dennis. Phone conversation with Author, 2007.

The Film Estimates. *The Footloose Heiress*. *The Educational Screen*, September 1937.

Hellman, Jack. Light and Airy. *Variety*, February 8, 1945.

Hopper, Hedda. *Chicago Tribune*, February 28, 1949.

Johnson, Erskine. *La Crosse Tribune*, July 2, 1955.

_____. *Decatur Daily Review*, April 29, 1967.

Jose. Queen of Burlesque. *Variety*, July 3, 1946.

Lady Chatterley's Lover Dull New Year's Eve Treat. *Los Angeles Times*, January 1, 1944.

Legit Opening: *All Women Are _____*. *Variety*, June 21, 1946.

May Be Fighter. *Saskatoon Star-Phoenix*, January 6, 1934.

Miller, Barbara. Romance and Melodrama Share Bills. *Los Angeles Times*, December 18, 1936.

Parsons, Louella. *Los Gatos Times-Saratoga Observer*, December 10, 1943.

_____. Reynolds, Home from War, Signed. *Wilmington Morning News*, February 1, 1944.

_____. *Tampa Bay Times*, April 12, 1946.

_____. *Miami Herald*, December 14, 1946.

_____. *Philadelphia Inquirer*, April 13, 1948.

Preview! Treachery Rides the Trail. *Variety*, February 28, 1936.

Schallert, Edwin. *Los Angeles Times*, August 17, 1933.

Von Blon, Katherine T. Vitality Seen in Community Drama Season. *Los Angeles Times*, October 14, 1934.

Danny Scholl

Alda Says Creation "Fighting for Life." *Cincinnati Enquirer*, April 10, 1975.

Alexander, Dick. Comeback Promise of Hero, Star. *San Francisco Examiner*, March 1, 1972.

Alexander, Pericles. On with the Show. *Shreveport Times*, May 30, 1961.

Annie Get Your Gun Scores Hit at Paper Mill Playhouse. *Bergen Evening Record*, November 4, 1959.

B.H.S. Have You Seen *Call Me Mister* at the Shubert. *Meriden Record*, March 16, 1946.

Boyar, Burt. *Philadelphia Inquirer*, September 18, 1959.

Bredemann, Dan. Ohioans Give Scholl a New Honor. *Cincinnati Enquirer*, January 16, 1974.

Brooks, Elston. Premiere No Calamity As Betty O'Neil Shines. *Fort Worth Star Telegram*, May 28, 1961.

_____. Don Wilson to Star in Casa's *Li'l Darling*. *Fort Worth Star Telegram*, July 11, 1961.

Carroll, Harrison. Behind the Scenes in Hollywood. *Evening Herald*, February 19, 1949.

Cassidy, Claudia. On the Aisle. *Chicago Tribune*, June 16, 1955.

Collins, William. *Top Banana*'s Scholl So Very Near his Goal. *Cincinnati Enquirer*, March 25, 1954.

Corinne Griffith-Scholl Marriage Short-Lived. *Cincinnati Enquirer*, April 1, 1965.

Evans, Lee. Ex-GIs Come Up with Socko Musical That Looks Like Broadway Long Termer. *Cincinnati Enquirer*, April 23, 1946.

Ex-Star Must Pay Husband $200 Support. *Fresno Bee*, December 24, 1965.

Feck, Luke. For Scholl. *Cincinnati Enquirer*, April 14, 1960.

Former Star Danny Scholl Plans Return. *Dayton Daily News*, September 19, 1979.

Free-for-All Halted. *Cincinnati Enquirer*, April 14, 1932.

Gaver, Jack. Latest Farrell "Folly" Better Than Others. *Dayton Daily News*, November 26, 1949.

George, Stewart. Danny Scholl's Disc of "Shrimp Boats" a Hit. *Richmond News Leader*, December 28, 1951.

Gerhard, Inez. Star Dust. *Ralston Recorder*, May 11, 1950.
Graham, Sheilah. Hollywood. *Times Tribune*, February 18, 1949.
_____. Hollywood. *Spokesman Review*, March 18, 1949.
Hornbaker, Alice. Danny Scholl Hits the Road Marked for Comeback Trail. *Cincinnati Enquirer*, May 29, 1983.
Ill Husband Stalls Actress' Divorce. *Pasadena Independent*, May 5, 1966.
Lait, Jr., Jack. Hollywood. *Brooklyn Daily Eagle*, February 21, 1949.
Lanning, Ray. Night Club Notes. *Cincinnati Enquirer*, July 30, 1944.
Martin, Mildred. *A Gentleman at Heart* Packs Wallop at Earle. *Philadelphia Inquirer*, February 14, 1942.
McHarry, Charles. On the Town. *New York Daily News*, December 26, 1960.
McPartlin, R.F. TV Diary. *Boston Globe*, February 19, 1951.
Mesmer, Marie. Gals!—The Line Forms on the Right. *Los Angeles Daily News*, June 16, 1953.
New Stars to See *Music Man*. *Fort Worth Star Telegram*, July 23, 1961.
O'Brian, Jack. Broadway. *Sandusky Register*, January 17, 1947.
Parsons, Louella. *San Francisco Examiner*, February 24, 1965.
Radcliffe, E.B. *Cincinnati Enquirer*, July 7, 1962.
_____. *Cincinnati Enquirer*, March 7, 1964.
Rose, Sydney. Casa's Musical Gets Top Rating. *Big Spring Daily Herald*, August 8, 1961.
Rosenburg, John. Films, Young Star Snub Each Other. *Columbia Record*, May 18, 1950.
Ryan, Hunt. New Records. *Baltimore Sun*, January 27, 1952.
Scholl Honor. *New York Daily News*, December 27, 1949.
Scholl Loses Alimony Bid. *St. Joseph News-Press/Gazette*, March 14, 1966.
Seeks Alimony. *Cincinnati Enquirer*, August 7, 1965.
Smith, Darr. *Los Angeles Daily News*, December 3, 1948.
Smith, J. Frazier. Danny Scholl's Condition Serious After Fall from Ramp. *Cincinnati Enquirer*, June 19, 1983.
Starr, Eve. Inside Television. *The Mercury*, April 20, 1964.
Stophlet, Jeanne M. Letter. *Cincinnati Enquirer*, July 2, 1983.
Tombstone in Court. *Cincinnati Enquirer*, August 7, 1932.
Traffic Hurts Fatal to Roselawn Man, Andrew Rub, 74. *Cincinnati Enquirer*, June 17, 1956.
TV-Radio Briefs. *Cincinnati Enquirer*, September 3, 1970.
Use for Fists with Corinne. *Kansas City Times*, May 11, 1966.
Valentine, Carole. Benefit Concert. *Cincinnati Enquirer*, March 3, 1975.
VFW Awards Makes Deputy "Most Proud." *Cincinnati Enquirer*, September 26, 1976.
What Age? Corinne Hits Record. *Pensacola News Journal*, May 6, 1966.
Wife Wields Pitcher. *Cincinnati Enquirer*, August 6, 1932.
Wilson, Earl. It Happened Last Night. *Courier Post*, August 28, 1954.
_____. It Happened Last Night. *Winona Daily News*, July 7, 1956.
_____. It Happened Last Night. *Evening Standard*, November 19, 1957.
Winged Pigeons, Air Forces Show, to Tour Forward Areas. *Honolulu Advertiser*, June 26, 1945.
With the Military. *Cincinnati Enquirer*, September 5, 1942.
Women Fined; Men Dismissed. *Cincinnati Enquirer*, April 15, 1932.
W.P.M. *Vanities* a Good Argument for Return of Vaudeville. *Ottawa Citizen*, April 25, 1942.

Lawrence Tierney

Actor Acquitted of Assault on Piano Player. *Austin Daily Herald*, August 18, 1953.
Actor & Ex-Boxer Charged in Quarrel. *Minneapolis Star*, July 25, 1953.
Actor Charged in Bar Brawl. *Orlando Sentinel*, December 3, 1961.
Actor Claims He Was Frisky but Not Drunk. *Brownsville Herald*, May 11, 1950.
Actor Is Facing Burglary Charge. *Spokane Chronicle*, August 26, 1957.
Actor Lands in Jail Again. *Tampa Bay Times*, October 15, 1950.
Actor Tierney Gets Jail Term. *Los Angeles Times*, October 9, 1946.
Actor Tierney Gets 90 Days; his Probation is Revoked. *Los Angeles Daily News*, May 1, 1947.
Actor Tierney Guilty in Cabbie Assault. *Salt Lake Tribune*, April 21, 1964.
Actor Tierney Will Face New Charges. *Stockton Evening and Sunday Record*, May 13, 1963.
Barefoot Actor Seized in Church. *San Bernardino County Sun*, October 9, 1951.
Bird, Vince. Bird's Eye View. *Scrantonian Tribune*, October 17, 1954.
_____. Bird's Eye View. *Scrantonian Tribune*, April 10, 1955.
Boggs, Johnny D. *Jesse James and the Movies*. Jefferson, NC: McFarland, 2011.
Bottled Dillinger Decanted into Jug. *Los Angeles Mirror*, January 4, 1949.
Carroll, Harrison. Behind the Scenes in Hollywood. *Vidette-Messenger of Porter County*, October 9, 1945.
_____. Behind the Scenes in Hollywood. *Beatrice Times*, September 8, 1948.
_____. Behind the Scenes in Hollywood. *Portage Daily Register*, October 16, 1951.
Court Tames "Tough Guy" of Movies. *Daily Oklahoman*, November 21, 1946.

Court to Tierney: Behave. *New York Daily News*, August 30, 1957.
Crowther, Bosley. The Screen: *Born to Kill*. *New York Times*, May 1, 1947.
Cummings, John. Celluloid Heroes Revisited: Part II. *Newsday* (Suffolk Edition), April 14, 1965.
Doherty, Rosaleen. Charge of Perjury Enlivens Film Dillinger Court Drama. *New York Daily News*, January 15, 1947.
Ex-Grid Players Jailed After Mocambo Brawl. *Los Angeles Times*, September 11, 1947.
Fidler, Jimmie. *Sioux City Journal*, May 12, 1945.
_____. *Sioux City Journal*, November 29, 1945.
_____. *Sioux City Journal*, February 13, 1946.
_____. *Minneapolis Daily Times*, May 12, 1947.
_____. *Durham Sun*, July 9, 1947.
_____. *Monroe News-Star*, January 11, 1949.
_____. *Quad-City Times*, January 24, 1949.
_____. *Joplin Globe*, February 27, 1949.
_____. *Sioux City Journal*, January 17, 1950.
_____. *Quad-City Times*, May 17, 1950.
_____. *Indianapolis News*, October 25, 1950.
Field, Eunice. East West Gossip. *TV-Radio Mirror*, December 1962.
Film Dillinger Booked on Drunk Charge. *Los Angeles Times*, March 11, 1946.
Film Stars' "Most Notable" Fight. *Oakland Post Enquirer*, January 19, 1946.
Film Tough Guy Tries It for Real. *Atlanta Journal*, October 14, 1958.
Gardner, Hy. *Oakland Tribune*, September 5, 1956.
_____. Glad You Asked That. *Jersey Journal*, April 24, 1969.
Gayne, Zach. Interview: Lloyd Kaufman, Decades Deep into the American Film Market. *Screen Anarchy*, November 23, 2014. https://screenanarchy.com/2014/11/interview-lloyd-kaufman-decades-deep-into-the-american-film-market.html
Graham, Sheilah. *Boston Globe*, May 3, 1946.
_____. *Tampa Times*, June 3, 1948.
_____. *Pittsburgh Post-Gazette*, October 15, 1949.
_____. *Tacoma News Tribune*, February 10, 1950.
_____. *St. Louis Globe-Democrat*, June 6, 1950.
_____. *Honolulu Star-Bulletin*, December 11, 1950.
_____. *Durham Morning Herald*, May 7, 1964.
Gwynn, Edith. *Philadelphia Inquirer*, May 29, 1949.
_____. *St. Louis Post-Dispatch*, September 16, 1949.
Hopper, Hedda. *St. Louis Globe-Democrat*, October 22, 1947.
_____. *Los Angeles Times*, May 29, 1948.
_____. *Chicago Tribune*, February 9, 1949.
_____. Mistakes They Never Confess. *Modern Screen*, January 1950.
"I'm a Pigeon, Coos Tierney"; Wings Clipped. *Los Angeles Evening Citizen News*, February 11, 1953.
Jack La Rue Hurt in Brawl Growing Out of Hollywood Party. *Los Angeles Times*, January 19, 1946.
Jeffreys, Anne. Phone conversation with Author, January 13, 2011.
Johnson, Erskine. *Lancaster Eagle-Gazette*, April 19, 1946.
_____. *Kingsport Times*, May 14, 1947.
_____. *Dixon Telegraph*, April 6, 1950.
_____. *Johnson City Press*, June 26, 1951.
_____. *Memphis Press-Scimitar*, July 28, 1951.
_____. *Los Angeles Daily News*, November 9, 1952.
Judge Gives Tierney One More Chance. *Lexington Herald*, January 6, 1949.
Kidnap Charge Filed; Tierney Held as Drunk. *Chicago Tribune*, May 24, 1963.
Kilgallen, Dorothy. *Pittsburgh Post-Gazette*, November 29, 1946.
_____. *Pittsburgh Post-Gazette*, March 29, 1948.
_____. *Fort Worth Star-Telegram*, December 2, 1948.
_____. *Pittsburgh Post-Gazette*, April 20, 1950.
_____. *Shamokin News-Dispatch*, December 26, 1950.
_____. *Greensboro Record*, February 26, 1953.
_____. *Fort Worth Star-Telegram*, March 8, 1953.
_____. *Greensboro Record*, June 11, 1953.
_____. *Fort Worth Star-Telegram*, July 9, 1953.
_____. *Pottstown Mercury*, July 27, 1955.
_____. *Philadelphia Daily News*, November 9, 1961.
King, Martin. Drink with Actor Tierney Ends in Leap to Her Death. *New York Daily News*, June 21, 1975.
Knickerbocker, Cholly. *San Francisco Examiner*, July 19, 1949.
_____. *Philadelphia Inquirer*, October 4, 1957.
Larry Tierney in Dutch Again. *New York Daily News*, May 28, 1957.
Lawrence Tierney Arrested as Drunk. *Record American*, September 19, 1959.
Lawrence Tierney Booked as Drunk. *Los Angeles Times*, August 19, 1946.
Lawrence Tierney Jailed as Drunk. *Indiana Gazette*, October 24, 1951.
Lawrence Tierney Put on Liquor Probation. *Los Angeles Times*, November 24, 1951.
Lawrence Tierney Stabbed in Brawl. *Orlando Sentinel*, January 19, 1973.
Lawrence Tierney Wins Nightclub Tiff. *The Independent*, May 16, 1951.
Lyons, Leonard. The Lyons Den. *Montgomery Advertiser*, June 13, 1949.
Manners, Dorothy. *Albuquerque Journal*, June 7, 1949.
Mayo, Virginia. Phone conversation with Author, 1998.
McClure, David. They Want to Get Married. *Modern Screen*, September 1948.
McKay, Rick. Crack Up: The True Story of a Hollywood Tough Guy. *Scarlet Street* #29, June 1998.
Midnight Palace with Gary Sweeney. Radio show, 2011.
Mortimer, Lee. *Scranton Tribune*, August 14, 1953.
_____. *Scrantonian Tribune*, September 2, 1956.
Mosby, Aline. Hollywood. *Durham Morning Herald*, December 28, 1951.
Motion Picture Actor Held on Drunk Charge. *Hanford Sentinel*, August 19, 1946.

Movie Dillinger Socks Stars in Predawn Hollywood Brawl. *Miami News*, January 19, 1946.

Movie Tough Guy Freed of Drunk Charge. *Pittsburgh Press*, June 14, 1949.

Movie Tough Guy Jailed for Contempt. *San Bernardino County Sun*, August 4, 1951.

Movie Tough Guy Tierney is Arrested at Eddie-Liz Party. *Stockton Evening and Sunday Record*, June 29, 1961.

O'Brian, Jack. Voice of Broadway. *Jersey Journal*, April 29, 1969.

_____. Voice of Broadway. *Jersey Journal*, May 3, 1969.

_____. Voice of Broadway. *Asbury Park Press*, August 18, 1971.

_____. Voice of Broadway. *Wilkes-Barre Record*, October 2, 1971.

_____. Voice of Broadway. *Fort Worth Star-Telegram*, December 14, 1971.

_____. Voice of Broadway. *Asbury Park Press*, February 21, 1974.

Parsons, Louella. *The Morning News*, October 4, 1944.

_____. *Galveston Daily News*, February 22, 1949.

_____. *San Francisco Examiner*, December 7, 1949.

_____. *San Francisco Examiner*, October 16, 1950.

_____. Hollywood's Most Tragic People. *Modern Screen*, February 1952.

_____. *Indianapolis Star*, February 19, 1962.

Party of Film Notables Ends in Fisticuffs. *San Francisco Examiner*, January 19, 1946.

Peary, Gerald. Lawrence Tierney. http://www.geraldpeary.com/interviews/stuv/tierney.html

Police Beat. *Des Moines Register*, November 9, 1959.

Police Hunt Tierney, Bad Man of Films. *Los Angeles Mirror*, June 22, 1951.

Police Seize Actor. *Kansas City Star*, July 24, 1958.

Police Soften Up Film "Tough Guy." *Salt Lake Tribune*, May 4, 1959.

Rau, Herb. Beach Debuts Summer Stock. *Miami News*, June 10, 1952.

Rutt, Todd. Those Two Fireballs of Fun: Interview with Sammy Petrillo. *Psychotronic Video* #11, 1992.

Santa Fe Issues Tierney Warrant. *Albuquerque Tribune*, July 28, 1951.

Schallert, Edwin. Jungle Fury, Cityfied Crime Vie in Dual Bill. *Los Angeles Times*, April 26, 1947.

Scott, John L. Contrasting Movie Fare Served Up. *Los Angeles Times*, July 3, 1947.

Scott, Vernon. Comeback for a Tough Guy. *Memphis Press-Scimitar*, February 27, 1962.

Screen Actor Cleared. *Cincinnati Enquirer*, June 14, 1949.

Sheafer, Marian. *Detective Story* Lakewood Hit. *Pottsville Republican*, June 29, 1955.

Sprigle, Ray. Lombardo Puts Finger on Valenti in Evans Murder. *Pittsburgh Post-Gazette*, April 5, 1951.

Standish, Myles. Movie Actor Tells of Battles On and Off Screen. *St. Louis Post-Dispatch*, February 13, 1947.

Table, Not "Wagon" He Fell Off, Actor Says. *Cincinnati Post*, August 20, 1946.

Thomas, Bob. *Asbury Park Press*, April 27, 1950.

Thomas, Kevin. *Young Dillinger* Right on Mark. *Los Angeles Times*, June 11, 1965.

Threat of Knife Told by Tierney. *Los Angeles Times*, August 15, 1951.

Tierney Again Finds Trouble. *Hanford Sentinel*, October 17, 1946.

Tierney Arrested. *Shreveport Journal*, July 21, 1962.

Tierney Charged After New Brawl. *The Independent*, February 25, 1948.

Tierney Clips N.Y. Socialite in Bar. *Valley Times*, August 9, 1952.

Tierney Delivers Own Lecture at Sentencing. *Los Angeles Times*, August 31, 1951.

Tierney Fights Brother; Gets 90 Days in Jail. *Los Angeles Times*, May 2, 1947.

Tierney Gets Break in Court. *New York Daily News*, April 23, 1957.

Tierney Goes on Wagon. *San Francisco Examiner*, November 24, 1951.

Tierney Jailed Again, Fights Police. *Los Angeles Mirror*, December 12, 1959.

Tierney to Stand Trial. *Los Angeles Evening Citizen News*, June 2, 1962.

Tierney, Michael. E-mails to Author, January 7, 2016, October 10, 2018.

Tierney, Tim. E-mails to Author, September 30, 2015.

Tierney Transfers His Escapades to New York Scene. *San Bernardino County Sun*, January 13, 1947.

Tough Guy of Films Is Taken to Nerve Clinic. *Modesto Bee*, October 9, 1951.

Toughie Tierney Gets $25 Tap and a New Rap. *New York Daily News*, August 1, 1953.

Turan, Kenneth. *Reservoir Dogs*, Tarantino's Brash Debut Film, Announces a Director to Be Reckoned With. *Los Angeles Times*, October 23, 1992.

Vanderbilt, Gloria. *It Seemed Important at the Time: A Romance Memoir*. New York: Simon & Schuster, 2009.

Wagner, Laura. Allene Roberts: True to Her Roots. *Films of the Golden Age* #58, Fall 2009.

_____. Lawrence Tierney: Tough Guy. *Films of the Golden Age* #83, Winter 2015.

Walker, Danton. Broadway. *New York Daily News*, June 11, 1947.

The Week in Review. *Los Angeles Times*, June 5, 1960.

Wilmington, Michael. *Tough Guys Don't Dance*. *Los Angeles Times*, September 17, 1987.

Wilson, Earl. It Happened Last Night. *Winona Daily News*, March 31, 1953.

_____. It Happened Last Night. *Delta Democrat-Times*, June 22, 1953.

_____. Show Time. *Richmond Times-Dispatch*, June 8, 1959.

_____. *Evening Standard*, October 4, 1966.

Yeates, Cydney. *The Simpsons* Writer Marks 25 Years of Episode with Crazy Behind-The-Scenes Story of Cameo Star. *Metro*, December 18, 2020.

https://metro.co.uk/2020/12/18/the-simpsons-writers-crazy-behind-the-scenes-story-of-cameo-star-13771417/#:~:text=The%20Simpsons%20writer%20Josh%20Weinstein,the%20late%20actor%20Lawrence%20Tierney.

Sonny Tufts

Actor Sonny Tufts Arrested as Drunk. *Lubbock Evening Journal*, September 2, 1957.
Actor Sonny Tufts, 58, Is Dead of Pneumonia. Miami News, June 6, 1970.
Actor Sonny Tufts Nabbed as Drunk. *Statesville Daily Record*, April 25, 1950.
Ayer, Belle. Film Fanfare. *Rock Island Argus*, September 3, 1943.
Banker Ends Life in Garage. *Boston Globe*, April 8, 1935.
Barleycorn Splits Sonny Tufts, Wife. *Miami News*, May 30, 1951.
Burlingame, Rudolph. Slim and Sam Return After Long Separation. *Philadelphia Inquirer*, April 5, 1940.
Caen, Herb. Out of My Mind. *San Francisco Examiner*, November 27, 1966.
Cannel, Ward. It Helps to be a Has-Been. *Lansing State Journal*, November 29, 1964.
Carroll, Harrison. Behind the Scenes in Hollywood. *Wilkes Barre Record*, July 3, 1943.
_____. Behind the Scenes in Hollywood. *Beatrice Times*, April 23, 1946.
_____. Behind the Scenes in Hollywood. *Wilkes Barre Record*, June 25, 1946.
_____. Behind the Scenes in Hollywood. Bradford Era, March 3, 1947.
Channel, Charley. TV Alley Tells Me… *Daily News*, July 1, 1962.
Clune, Henry W. Seen and Heard. Democrat and Chronicle, August 1, 1953.
Cohen, Harold V. Hollywood. *Pittsburgh Post-Gazette*, August 5, 1943.
_____. Drama. *Pittsburgh Post-Gazette*, July 3, 1949.
Connolly, Mike. *Desert Sun*, October 19, 1956.
_____. Hollyw'd Reporter. *Arizona Republic*, October 24, 1966.
Crowther, Bosley. The Screen. *New York Times*, April 18, 1946.
Doherty, Rosaleen, and Warren Hall. He Beats Peg and Peg Beats Him—Is It Love? *New York Daily News*, June 17, 1941.
Doussard, James. Television Review. *Courier Journal*, April 22, 1968.
Fidler, Jimmie. *The Mercury*, October 4, 1945.
_____. *Monroe News Star*, September 15, 1947.
_____. *News Press*, November 20, 1950.
_____. *Valley Times*, December 20, 1950.
_____. *Press Democrat*, June 6. 1951.
_____. *South Bend Tribune*, June 14, 1951.
_____. *Town Talk*, September 22, 1952.
Freeman, Alex. TV Time. *Daily Oklahoman*, July 15, 1963.
Freeman, Dave. TV Close-Up. *Hartford Courant*, January 1, 1963.
French, Betty. On with the Show. *Akron Beacon Journal*, September 13, 1943.
Graham, Sheilah. *Indianapolis Star*, July 6, 1943.
_____. *Miami News*, February 14, 1945.
_____. *Courier Journal*, October 14, 1945.
_____. *Kingsport News*, April 27, 1946.
_____. *Times Tribune*, October 5, 1946.
_____. *Times Tribune*, January 14, 1950.
_____. *Dayton Daily News*, December 29, 1952.
_____. *Honolulu Star Bulletin*, October 31, 1953.
_____. *Indianapolis Star*, February 25, 1956.
Gwynn, Edith. *The Mercury*, April 28, 1954.
Handsaker, Gene. Hollywood Finds Sonny is a Reformed Character. *Cedar Rapids Gazette*, September 5, 1948.
Harris, Richard G. Sonny Tufts, Tough Marine in Picture, is Only 4-F in Draft; He's a Find. *Oakland Tribune*, September 10, 1943.
Harvey in Hollywood. *Council Grove Republican*, June 26, 1951.
Heffernan, Harold. Hollywood Today. *Winnipeg Tribune*, January 12, 1943.
_____. What Ever Happened To…? *Pittsburgh Press*, March 28, 1962.
Hope, Don. Hollywood. *The Mercury*, November 9, 1953.
Hopper, Hedda. *Chicago Tribune*, September 25, 1943.
_____. *Detroit Free Press*, June 15, 1946.
_____. Seeing the Sights at Salt Lake City. *The Times*, March 3, 1947.
_____. *Chicago Tribune*, June 6, 1959.
_____. *Los Angeles Times*, August 12, 1964.
Hopwood, M. Hunter. Hoppin' Around. *Detroit Free Press*, November 24, 1967.
Investigating Firms Controlled in Past by Tufts. *Burlington Free Press*, April 10, 1935.
Johnson, Erskine. *Dunkirk Evening Observer*, July 25, 1946.
_____. *Daily Home News*, January 29, 1947.
_____. *Dunkirk Evening Observer*, February 27, 1947.
_____. *Journal Gazette*, October 16, 1947.
_____. *Dunkirk Evening Observer*, November 9, 1948.
_____. *News Herald*, June 2, 1949.
_____. *Elmira Advertiser*, December 17, 1952.
_____. *Journal Gazette*, March 9, 1954.
Jones, Paul. Penthouse Theater Scores. *Atlanta Constitution*, October 12, 1949.
Karr, Jeanne. Big Boy. *Modern Screen*, January 1944.
Keavy, Hubbard. Director John Farrow Acts His Part Right to the Hilt. *Courier Journal*, November 24, 1946.
Kilgallen, Dorothy. *News Journal*, June 3, 1941.
_____. *News Journal*, June 26, 1943.
_____. *Republican and Herald*, April 19, 1944.
_____. *Shamokin News Dispatch*, January 3, 1945.
_____. *Pittsburgh Post-Gazette*, January 23, 1945.

_____. *The Mercury*, April 6, 1954.
_____. *News Journal*, March 9, 1955.
Knickerbocker, Cholly. Cholly Knickerbocker Observes. *San Francisco Examiner*, November 17, 1951.
Lait, Jr., Jack. Hollywood. *Brooklyn Daily Eagle*, May 28, 1947.
Lanning, Ray. Movie Reviews. *Cincinnati Enquirer*, September 3, 1943.
Mallon, Paul. Behind the News. *Evening Sun*, June 21, 1941.
Mantle, Burns. *Sing for Your Supper* Gives the Federal Theatre a Break. *New York Daily News*, May 7, 1939.
Masters, Dorothy. Hellinger *Swell Guy* Vivid Tale of a Heel. *New York Daily News*, January 26, 1947.
Miller, John J. Memo from John J. Miller. *San Francisco Examiner*, May 8, 1966.
Miller, Marguerite. Sonny Tufts Was in Town, Girls! *News Journal*, July 18, 1945.
Morse, Jim. TV Topics. *Star Gazette*, July 20, 1958.
Morton, Hortense. Play by Play. *San Francisco Examiner*, October 19, 1956.
New Comedy at Shubert is Colorful. *Hartford Courant*, March 22, 1955.
O'Brian, Jack. Voice of Broadway. *Glens Falls Times*, April 6, 1966.
_____. Voice of Broadway. *Wilkes-Barre Times Leader*, May 7, 1969.
_____. Voice of Broadway. *Daily Journal*, June 24, 1969.
On the Aisle. *Miami News*, December 1, 1949.
Palm Beach Notes. *Palm Beach Post*, January 16, 1941.
Pam, Jerry. Laughs for 1961. *Valley Times Today*, January 2, 1961.
Parsons, Louella. *The Tribune*, May 15, 1948.
_____. *Albuquerque Journal*, January 15. 1955.
Payette, William C. Very Easy to Crash the Movies. *Pittsburgh Post-Gazette*, July 17, 1943.
Peak, Mayme Ober. Boston's Sonny Tufts, Hollywood's New Rave. *Boston Globe*, October 10, 1943.
Pulos, Lee. Me. *Vancouver Sun*, April 5, 1968.
Randolph, Nancy. Society. *Daily News*, May 1, 1940.
Restaurant Fall Hurts Actor Sonny Tufts. *Fresno Bee*, June 29, 1969.
Rosemary La Planche Likes What Hollywood Says in Her Ear. *Des Moines Register*, April 25, 1943.
Scheuer, Steven H. His Tack Changes the Site. *The Record*, February 14, 1956.
Skolsky, Sidney. Columnist's Mail Bag. *Valley Times*, December 16, 1967.
Smathers, Craig. The Know-It-All. *Indianapolis Star*, October 26, 1968.
Sonny Tufts Booked for Drunk. *Town Talk*, May 31, 1951.
Sonny Tufts Breaks Wrist. *Evening Sun*, September 24, 1951.
Sonny Tufts Stars Play in East Hartford. *Hartford Courant*, November 22, 1949.
Stafford, M. Oakley. Informing You. *Hartford Courant*, November 30, 1949.
_____. *Hartford Courant*, September 8, 1957.
Stanfield, Audrey. Down the Aisle. *Dayton Daily News*, December 6, 1944.
Stripper Puts Bite on Sonny. *Miami News*, April 21, 1954.
Strip-Teaser Sues Sonny Tufts, Says He Bit Her. *Star Tribune*, March 31, 1954.
Sullivan, Ed. Little Old New York. *New York Daily News*, July 19, 1943.
Sylvester, Robert. Dream Street. *Morning Herald*, January 27, 1960.
Talbert, Bob. Bob Talbert's Detroit. *Detroit Free Press*, April 3, 1969.
The Theatre and Its People. *Windsor Star*, January 11, 1950.
Thomas, Bob. Hollywood's Top Movie Stars List Worst Films. *Town Talk*, July 29, 1948.
Todd, John. Sonny Tufts Turns Out to Be Blond Giant. *Tampa Bay Times*, June 25, 1943.
TV Mailbag. *Hartford Courant*, February 19, 1961.
The TV Mailbag. *Evening Sun*, January 19, 1966.
Two Boy Coasters Hurt in Winchester. *Boston Globe*, January 5, 1922.
Two Dancers Bitten on Thigh Sue Sonny Tufts for $50,000. *Escanaba Daily Press*, April 21, 1954.
United Press. Around the Clock. *Daily News Journal*, August 7, 1955.
Vance, Henry. The Coal Bin. *Birmingham News*, February 7, 1955.
Vernon, Terry. Tele-Vues. *Independent*, September 18, 1963.
Walker, Danton. Broadway. *New York Daily News*, November 21, 1941.
_____. *New York Daily News*, June 24, 1942.
_____. *Philadelphia Inquirer*, September 2, 1942.
_____. *Philadelphia Inquirer*, July 25, 1947.
_____. *New York Daily News*, May 28, 1948.
Walker, Paul. Reviews and Previews. *Harrisburg Telegraph*, April 1, 1941.
What Ever Happened to Sonny Tufts? *Orlando Evening Star*, December 8, 1962.
Wilson, Earl. It Happened Last Night. *Courier Post*, December 19, 1959.
_____. *Arizona Republic*, December 13, 1961.
_____. *Morning Call*, December 18, 1961.
_____. *Philadelphia Daily News*, June 24, 1964.
Wilson, Virginia. Movie Reviews. *Modern Screen*, April 1945.
Winchell, Walter. *Cincinnati Enquirer*, October 17, 1945.
_____. *Des Moines Tribune*, November 13, 1951.
_____. *Courier Post*, March 8, 1954.
_____. *Pottsville Republican*, February 18, 1955.
_____. *New York Daily News*, January 25, 1960.
Winchester Man Again Honored at Yale. *Boston Globe*, January 17, 1934.

INDEX

Numbers in ***bold italics*** indicate pages with illustrations

Abbey Players 22
Abbott, George 86
Abbott and Costello 55
Abduction 275, 279
Abel, Walter 134, 235
Aberdeen Evening Express 162
Abie's Irish Rose 92, 96, 133
About Faces 129
Abraham Lincoln 92
Absent Minded 94, 119
Absolute Quiet ***101***, 101, 119
Academy Award Theatre 112
"Ac-Cent-Tchu-Ate the Positive" 288
Accent on Youth 11
The Actor 211, 213
Actors Company 162
Adair, Yvonne 83
Adam, Trude 299
Adam and Eva 133
Adam-12 130
Adams, Joey 267
Adams, Marjory 80–81
Adams, Nick 273
Adams, Peter 208
Adamson, Kent 170, 171, 172, 191
Addams, Dawn 56, 162
Addiss, Jus 208
"Adelaide" 239
Adler, Jerry 231
Adventures in Paradise 270
The Adventures of Marco Polo 297
The Adventures of Ozzie and Harriet 130, 227
Adventures of Wild Bill Hickok 185, 210
Aeschylus 155
After Tomorrow 8
Agnew, Spiro T. ***242***
Air Force 170, 194
Air Strike 129, 131
The Akron Beacon Journal 118, 285
The Alamo 300
The Alarm Clock 133
The Alaskans 213
Albany Evening News 15
Albarelli, Jerald 130
Albert, Abbey ***235***
Albuquerque Journal 40

The Alcoa Hour 212
Alda, Alan 242
Alex Joseph and His Wives 242, 244
Alexander, Dick 241
Alexander, John 88
Alexander, Pericles 239
Alexander, Ross 5–18, ***5***, ***10***, ***11***, ***12***, ***13***, ***14***, ***17***
Alexandra Theatre 162
Alfred Cramer Junior High 61
The Alfred Hitchcock Hour 272
Alfredo, Don 292
Algieri, Sal 59
Algren, Nelson 267
All in the Family 120, 130
All-Out Arlene 74
All the Way see *Nylon Sky*
"All Through the Day" 78
All Women Are— 223–225
Allan, Anthony see Hubbard, John
Allan, Nick 214
Allegheny Uprising 44
Allen, Fred 233
Allen, Irving 53
Allen, Robert 275
Allotment Wives 223
Allyson, June 288
"Along with Me" 231
Alta Lodge 53
Altman, Ruth 145
Alvarado Hotel 40
Alyn, Kirk 283
L'amante di Paride 186
Amazon Quest 177–178, 194
The Amazons 162
Ameche, Don 74
American Hero 277, 280
Americans All 93
Ames, Adrienne 36, ***36***, 38, 44, 143, 221
Ames, Harriet 181
Ames, Marshall III 48
Ames, Michael 201
Ames, Stephen 36
Ammidon, Phil 50
Amphitryon 86
"And Leave the Drive-In to Us" 302
Anders, Rudolph 258

Andersen, Arthur 164
Anderson, Anne 82
Anderson, Maxwell 10, ***10***, 69, 73, 93
Anderson, Nancy 127
Andrews, Dana ***23***, 23, 74, ***75***, 76
Andrews, Gayle 268
Andrews, Nancy 86
Andrews, Dr. V.L. 16
The Andy Griffith Show 118, 130
Andy Hardy Meets Debutante 170
Andy Warhol's Bad 275, 279
Angel and the Badman 53, 60
The Angels Wash Their Faces 124, 131
Angels with Dirty Faces 123, ***124***, 130
Anhalt, Edward 53
Ankers, Evelyn 225
Ankles Aweigh 299
Ankrum, Morris 133
Ann Vickers 36, 37, 60
Anna Karenina 37
Anna Lucasta 148, 203, 232
Annapolis Naval Academy 36
Anne Bronaugh Players 133
Annie Get Your Gun 237, 238
Another Face 98, 119
Another Thin Man 168, 193
Ansara, Michael 117
Apache Chief 178, 194
Apache Warrior 212, 215
Apartment Hunters 193
The Ape Man 110, 119
Applesauce 133
"Are These Our Children?" 246
Are You Decent? 139
Are You Listening? 96, 119
Arizona Daily Star 72
Arizona Republic 88
Arlen, Harold 288
Arlen, Richard 81
Arlington National Cemetery 145
Armageddon 277–278, 280
Armando's 300
Armchair Mystery Theatre 160
Armchair Theatre 150, 151, 153, 154, 157, 160, 161
Armida 111
Arms and the Man 148

325

Armstrong, Robert 114, 201
Armstrong Circle Theatre 55, 87, 116
The Army Speaks 128
Arnaz, Desi 303
Arno, Peter 43
Arnold, Gen. Benedict **22**, 22
Around the World in Eighty Days 282
Arthur 275, 279
Arthur, Jean 8
Arthur, Johnny 25
Arthur Godfrey's Talent Scouts 232
Arts Theatre 149
As You Like It 148
Asher, Jerry 17
Ashley, Sylvia 56, 57
Asner, Ed 243
The Asphalt Jungle 259
"The Assassin" 271
Assassino senza volto 273, 279
Associated Film Productions 9
Associated Press 28, 266
Astaire, Fred 44
Astor Theater 294
Astoria Hotel 162–163
Atkins, Barbara Gray 298
Atkinson, Brooks 9
Atlanta Constitution 59
Atlanta Constitution Sunday Magazine 104, 105
Atlantic Flight 141, 145
Attenborough, Richard 295
Atwater, Gladys 175
Atwill, Lionel 135
Aubert, Jeanne 138
Aubert, Lenore 64
Aumont, Jean-Pierre 201
Austin, Glenn 190
Austin Daily Texan 217
Autry, Gene 141, 178
Avalanche 53, 60
Avildsen, John G. 274
Avonde, Richard 209
Ayckbourn, Alan 161–162
Ayer, Belle 285
Ayres, Lew 296, **297**

Babbs, Dorothy 82, **84**
The Babe Ruth Story 292
Babes in the Woods 66
The Baby Cyclone 93
Bacall, Lauren 57
Bachelor, Stephanie 143
Bachelor of Hearts 152, 153, 162, 163
Back Door to Heaven 105, 119
Back to Bataan 248, 279
Baclanova, Olga 96
Bacon, "Bunty" 46
Bacon, David 19–31, **20**, **22**, **23**, **24**, **25**, **26**, **27**
Bacon, Gaspar G., Sr. 19
Bacon, Robert 19, 21, 30
Bacon, Robert Low 19
Bacon, Rod 31
Bacon, William 19, 21, 30

Bad Blonde see *The Flanagan Boy*
Bad Girl 94, 95, 97
Bad Guy 40, 60
The Bad Man of Brimstone 40, 60
The Bad Samaritan 149
Badman's Territory 248, 261, 279
Bailey, Ray 177
Baker, Diane 118
Baker, George 150
Baker, Mimi 44
Baker, Stanley 154
Balenda, Carla 209
Ball, Lucille 54, 219, 226, 227, 238
"The Ballad of the Betty Lou" 239
Ballard, Kaye 235
Ballard, Tina 180
Ballew, Harold 137–138
Balsam, Martin 274
The Baltimore Sun 45, 83, 104, 116, 176, 235
Balzer, Robert Lawrence 190–191
El Bandido 151
Bane, Paula 231
Banjo Eyes 71
Bank Club 45
Bankhead, Tallulah 75–76, **76**, 77, 79, 81, 140
Bankside Players 148
Bannon, Jim **226**
Bar of Music 232
The Barbara Stanwyck Show 118, 271
Barclay, Joan 63, **65**
Bard, Katharine 21
Bari, Lynn **64**
Barker, Jess 171
Barker, Lex 201
Barnardo, Dr. Thomas John 91, 99, 102
Barnes, Eleanor 94–95, 99–100, 218
Barnett, Genevieve 100
Barnett, Vince 100
Barney, John 24
Barney's Beanery 256
Baron, Lita 174, 238
Baron, Michael 113
Barratt, Mark 161
Barrett, Judith 108
Barrett, Tony 250, 270
Barrie, Wendy 122, 140, 141
Barry, Philip 87, 166
Barrymore, Diana 44, 249
Barrymore, Ethel 89, 249
Bartholomew, Freddie 102, 127
Bartlett, Hall 213
Bass Rocks Theatre 21
The Bat 70
Bathsheba 80
Batman 59
Bautzer, Greg 79, 82
Baxes, Jim 178
Baxter, Anne 23, 72–73, **73**, 75, 291
Baxter, Warner 136, 223, 225
"Beach House" 89
Beach Playhouse 165

The Beachcomber 149, 163
Beal, John 85
Beale, Jack 156
The Beast of the City 95, 119
Beaton, Cecil 160
Beatty, Clyde 97
Beatty, Robert 149
Beaumont, Hugh **173**
Beddows, Alfred 91
Beddows, Mary 91, 98
Beebe, Lucius 45
Beggar on Horseback 136
The Beggar's Opera 70
Behind the Mask 63, **65**, 68
Behind the Rising Sun 171–172, 173, 194
Belasco Theater 222
Belgrade Theatre 162
Belita 250
Bellamy, Ralph 94
Belle Starr's Daughter 114, 119
Belmont, Terry *see* Bonnell, Lee
Belmont Hote 87
Belser, Lee 31, 92, 189
Ben Casey 240
Ben-Hur 150
Bendix, William 207, 292
Benedict, Billy 126
Bengal Tiger 218
Bennett, Charles 296
Bennett, Constance 35, 48, 50, 128
Bennett, Joan 77, 98
Bennett, Richard 93
Benny, Jack 15, 105, 106, 227
Benson, Jackson J. 107
Bentley, Jack 155
Bergen Evening Record 238
Berger, David Garrison 105–106
Berger, Harris 126
Berger, Senta 213
Bergmann, Bus 166
Berkshire Eagle 71
Berle, Milton 49, 243
Bernerd, Jeffrey 223
Bernstein, Morton 140
Berr, Georges 288
Berry, Michael 230
Best of the Badmen 54, 60, 261, 279
The Best People 133
Between Friends 88
Betz, Carl 70
The Beverly Hillbillies 227
Beverly Hills Country Club 230
Beverly Hills Hotel 115, 200
Beverly Summer Theatre 81
Beyond Glory 177, 194
Bezzerides, A.I. 271
Bickford, Charles 41, 53, 111
Big Boy Now! 161
The Big Broadcast of 1936 11
The Big Cage 97, 119
The Big Game 39, 60
Big Jake 58, 60
"Big Joe's Comin' Home" 117
"The Big Movie Show in the Sky" 233

The Bigelow Theatre 129
Biggers, Buck 130
Billings, Sam 112
Billy Budd 157, ***157***, 163
Billy the Kid 21, 299
Biltmore Theatre 217, 235–236
Bird, Vince 265
Birdwell, Russell 35
Birmingham Daily Post 153, 160
Biró, Lajos 75
The Birth of a Nation 104
Bishop, Jim 290
Bishop, William 64, 292
Bissell, Whit ***67***
The Bitch Goddess 202, 214
Black Chiffon 148
"The Black Dahlia" 275
The Black Knight 158, ***158***
Black Legion 39
Black Limelight 223
The Black Panther 210
Black Spurs 58, 60
Blackfriar Players 133, 246
"Blackjack" 54
Blackmer, Sidney 115
Blackouts 200, 202
Blaine, Vivian 77
Blake, Pamela 177
Blakeley, Bidda 283
Blane, Sally 97
Blaze of Glory 187
Blaze of Noon 291, 304
Blessed Are the Damned 213
Blessed Sacrament Church 89
Block, Martin 235
Blonde Alibi 174, 194
Blondell, Joan 11, ***11***, 89
Blood on the Moon 218
Blood on the Sun 111, 119
Bloodrage 275, 279
Bloomer Girl 74, 236
The Blue Angel 266, 299
Blues in the Night 119, 127, ***127***, 131
Blyth, Ann 291
Blythe, Betty 94, 241
Boarder's 277
Bob Hope Presents the Chrysler Theatre 301
Bob, Son of Battle 80
Bodyguard 255, 256–257, 279
Boehnel, William 97
Bogarde, Dirk 152
Bogart, Humphrey 15, 45, 49, 112, 122, 123, 124, ***125***, 248, 265
Bogdanovich, Peter 175
Boland, Mary 134, 235
Bolden, William 13–14
Bombay 232
Bonanza 59
Bond, Ward 37, 114
Bonham (Texas) Daily Favorite 169
Bonnell, Lee 143
Booth, Shirley 115–116
Born to Kill 1, 245, 250–251, ***251***, 270, 279
Borton, Esther 62, 63
Borzage, Frank 197, 248

The Boss of Big Town 23, 31
Boston Blackie 129, 183
The Boston Globe 10, 16–17, 20, 21, 83, 235, 282
Boston Lying-in Hospital 30
Boston Music Festival 237
Boston Traveler 19
Boulder Dam ***13***, 13, 18, 228
Le Bourgeois Gentilhomme 235
Bourke, George 112
Bow, Clara 102
Bowery at Midnight 171, 194
Bowie, Jim 300
Boxoffice 56
The Boy from Oklahoma 116, 119
The Boy with a Cart 148
Boyar, Burt 238
Boyd, Bill 35
Boyer, Charles 75, 285
"The Boyfriend" 276
Boylan, Malcolm Stuart 85
Boyle, Peter 274
Boys Town 167
Bracken, Eddie 287
Bradford Observer 149
Bradley, Grace 101
Bradley, Truman 82
Brady, Alice 8, 217
Brady, John P. 203
Brady, Scott 3, ***67***, 245, 246, 247, 251, ***255***, 256, 257, 258, 259, 261–262, 270
Braggiotti, Francesca 21
Brahm, John 201–202
Brandstatter, Eddie 34
Brantford Expositor 91
Brass Check 265
The Brat 133
Braun, Bob 241, 243
Brave Eagle 211
Break It Up 86
The Breaking Point 115, 119
Breen, Johnny 113
Bren, J. Robert 175
El Brendel 111
Brent, Earl 232
Brent, George 49
Breslin, Patricia 84
Bret, David 12, ***12***
Brewster, Carol 297, 298
Brian, Mary 36, 46
Bricker, George 174
Bride of the Gorilla 180
Brides Are Like That ***5***, 13, 18
The Bridge of Estaban 148
Bridgend Grammar School 147
Bridges, Alan 148
Bridges, Jeff 302
The Brigand of Kandahar 159, ***159***, 163
Bright, John 105
Bright Shadow 148
Bring on the Girls 287–288, 304
Britton, Barbara 81, 292
Broadway 93, 94
Broadway Is My Beat 128
Broccoli, Albert "Cubby" 44, 53, 59

Broder, Jack 180, 263
Broken Branches 92
Bromley, Sheila 294
Bronco 213
Bronson, Charles 270, 275
Bronston, Samuel 62
Brooklyn Citizen 139
Brooklyn Daily Eagle 7, 93, 104
Brooklyn Daily News 55
Brooklyn Daily Times 134
Brooks, David 74
Brooks, Elston 239
Brooks, George 303
Brooks, Geraldine 114, 117
Brooks, Jean 23
Brooks, Phyllis 45, 98
Broomfield, Fred 82
Brother Rat 166
Brotherton, Jamie 37
Brown, Clarence 95, 191
Brown, Harry Joe 292
Brown, Joe E. 10, 66
Brown, John Mason 8
Brown, Johnny Mack 134
Brown, Merrill 192
Brown, Capt. Thad 28, 31
Brown, Wally 117
Browne, Coral 160
Brownfield, Harry 227
Browning, Tod 95, ***96***
Bruce, Carol 236
Bruce Gentry, Daredevil of the Skies 177, 194
The Brute Man 174, 194
Bryan, Dora 160, 295
Bryant, James McKinley 44
Bryden, Ronald 161
Brynner, Yul 212
The Buccaneer 212, 215
Buckland, Wilfred, Jr. 29
Bugg, Jimmy 42
Il bugiardo 85
Bujac, Adele 32
Bujac, Étienne de Pelissier, Sr. 32, 33, 35, 40
Bujac, Grace Julie (Jennifer) 33, 57
Bujac, James N. 35
Burgess, Dorothy 34
Burke, James ***122***
Burke's Law 59
Burleigh, Fred 70–71, 89
Burlingame, Rudolph 283
Burman, Edward 221
Burn 'Em Up O'Connor 167, 193
Burns, David 86
Burns, Eleanor 44
Burns, George 105, 106
Burr, Mary Neal 164, 188, 193
Burr, Raymond 117, 227
Burr, Walter 164, 169, 180–181, 192
Burroughs, Helen 7
Burton, Richard 161
Bury, Sean 161
Bus Stop 271
Bushkin, Joe 231
The Bushwhackers 263, 279
Bustin, John 58

Butler, David 116
Buttons, Red 202
Buttram, Pat 118
Byrd, Ralph 43

Cabot, Alphonsine 56, 57
Cabot, Bruce 1, 32–60, **32**, **34**, **36**, **41**, **47**, **51**, **58**
Cabot, Brucie 56–57, 59
Caen, Herb 303
Caesar and Cleopatra 6
Café Montmartre 34
Café Pierre 45
Cagle, Bob 126
Cagney, James 10, 24, 62, 103, 111, 123, 180, 275
Cagney, William 180
Cahn, Edward L. 40
Cain, James M. 186, 187, 213
Calamity Jane 239
Calhoun, Rory 117, 238, 239, 240, 303
California Eagle 40
California State Prison in Chino 192, 193
Call a Messenger 126, 131
Call Her Savage 136, 145
Call Me Mister 231–232
Call of the Klondike 178, 194
Calleia, Joseph 48
Cambridge 161
Camden Drama Guild 62
Cameron, Kate 109
Camp Blanding 50
Camp Wood 128
Campbell Summer Soundstage 116
Cannady, Mona 95
Canon City 258
Cantillon, James 190
Cantor, Eddie 71
Canyon Passage 64, 68
El Capitan Theatre 107, 143, 202, 218
Capone, Al 94
Caprice 21, 71
Captain Blood 11–12, **12**, 18
Captain Blood: His Odyssey 11
Captain Brassbound's Conversion 6
Captain Carvallo 148
Captain Caution 45, 60
Captain China 81
The Captives 153
Cardwell, James 1, 61–68, **61**, **63**, **64**, **65**, **66**, **67**
Care, Ralph 234
Careless Lady 136, 145
Carey, Harry 44
Carey, Harry, Jr. 114
Carey, Macdonald 110
Cargill, Patrick 156
Carlisle, Mary 97
Carlsbad Cemetery 59
Carlsbad Current 33
Carlton, Jack *see* Moore, Clayton
Carmody, Jay 46
Carnegie Tech 69, 70, 71

Carney, James M. 203
Carousel 239
The Carpetbaggers 301
Carr, Andrew 162
Carr, Joseph L. 113
Carradine, John 210, 268, 298
Carrillo, Leo 116
Carroll, Harrison 14, 42, 44, 49, 50, 52, 54, 55, 56, 59, 82, 102, 104–105, 143, 145, 174, 180, 181, 184, 188, 192, 202, 203, 204, 207, 210, 212, 222, 223, 226, 232, 248, 257, 264, 286, 290, 292
Carroll, Nancy 141, 143
Carroll, Paul Vincent 108
Carry on Nurse 156–157
Carson, Doris 21
Carson, Jack 127, **127**, 235, 237
Carson, Johnny 301
Carten, Kenneth 153
Carter, Nick 162
Carter Hall 42
Carthew, Anthony 150
Caruso, Anthony 118, **173**
Cary, Falkland 150
Casa Mañana 239
Casablanca Hotel 211
Case, Allen 118
The Case of the Baby Sitter 177, 194
The Case of the Frightened Lady 148
"Casey at the Bat" 236, 237
Caspary, Vera 176
Casper, Bill 100
Cassavetes, John 271
Cassel, Seymour 277
Cassel, Walter 221
Cassidy, Claudia 236, 276
Casson, Ann 147
Castle, William 155, **156**
Casualties of Love: The Long Island Lolita Story 277, 280
Cat Ballou 58, 60
Cat-Women of the Moon 297–298, 304
Caulfield, Joan 288, 289
The Cavalcade of America 83, 86
Cavanagh, Paul 174
CBS Playhouse 49
Cedar Rapids Gazette 104
Cedars of Lebanon Hospital 14
Cedrone, Lou 303
Celebrity Club 67
Celestin, Jack 135
Centennial Summer 78, 90
Central Park 96, 119
Central Receiving Hospital 270
"Champion" 117
Champion, Gower 82
Chance of a Lifetime 236
Chandler, Raymond 83–84
Chandu the Magician 3, 136, **137**, 145
Chaney, Lon 107, 110, 263
Channel, Charley 301
Channing, Carol 82, 83, 84, 85, 89, 236

Chaperau, Albert 105–106
Chaplin, Charlie 177, 203
Chaplin, Sydney 203, 206
Chapman, Frank 79
Chapman, the Rev. Gordon C. 140–141
Chapman, John 83
Chapman, Leigh 303
Chapman, Patrizia Cobb *see* Cobb, Buff
Chapman, Tedwell 49
Chapman College 80
Chapman Park Chapel 23
Charles, Ezzard 230
The Chase 58, 60
Chatterton, Ruth 71, 77
Checco, Al 82, 83
Chekhov, Michael 288
Chelsea News 161
Chester, Hally 123, 126
Chestnut Street Opera House 139
Chetwyn, Robert 161
Cheyenne 213
Chicago Seals 165
Chicago Tribune 88, 94, 176, 188, 236
A Child Is Waiting 271, 279
Children's Professional School 121
China Clipper **14**, 15, 18
China Girl 170, 194
Chinatown 279
The Chinese Cat 144, **144**, 146
Chisum 58, 60
Choque de Sentimentos 58, 60
Christian, Linda 174
Christian, Paul *see* Hubschmid, Paul
Christians, Mady 21
Christmas in Oz 278, 280
Churchill, Marguerite 7
Churchill, Sarah 235
Ciannelli, Eduardo **247**
"Cibola" 118
Cilento, Diane 154, **154**
Cincinnati Conservatory of Music 230
Cincinnati Enquirer 25, 229, 230, 231, 236, 237, 239, 241, 242–244, 285
Cincinnati Post 104
Cincinnati Veterans Hospital 243
Cintrón, Conchita 48
The Circle 6
Circle Theatre 203, 206
Ciroette Room **199**
Ciro's 46, 49, 54, 55, 127, 182, 184, **291**, 292, 295, 298, 300
The Cisco Kid 129
Citizens Emergency Hospital 300
City Detective 67
City of Hope 276, 280
Civil Air Patrol 269
Clair, René 46
Clark, Bobby 235
Clark, Dane 114
Clark, Walter Van Tilburg 71

Index

Clark, Wilbur 55
Clary, Wilton 237
Claudia and David 62
The Clay Pigeon 257
Climax! 117
Clinton, Frank 141
Cloud, Roger 241
Club Casanova 24
Club Havana 174, 194
Club New Yorker 136
Club 21 297
Clune, Henry W. 296–297
Clyde, June 98
Coast to Coast on a Bus 120
Coates, Irene 160
Coates, Paul V. 210, 211
Cobb, Buff 79, 81–82, 83, 86
Cobb, Elizabeth 79
Cobb, Irvin S. 79
Coburn, Charles 76–77
Coca, Imogene 283
Cochran, Steve 299
Coffee, Lenore 95
Cohan, George M. 93
Cohen, Albert J. 204, 206
Cohen, Harold V. 38, 39, 70, 71, 77, 82, 84, 85, 109, 110, 179, 187, 286, 294
Cohn, Harry 171, 207, 208
Colbert, Claudette 8, 53, 285
Coleman, Nancy 207
Coletti, Frank 107
The Colgate Comedy Hour 55, 235, 267
Coll, Vincent "Mad Dog" 38, 270
Colleano, Maurice 67
College Humor 166
The Collier Hour 15
Collier's 176
Collins, Joan 149
Collins, Michael 116
Collins, Ray **226**
Collins, William 236
Collura, Joe 15
Colman, Ronald 85
Colonel Effingham's Raid 76–77, 90
Colt, Sammy 249
Colt .45 213
Columbia Theater 218
Columbia University 166
The Comancheros 57, 60
Come Across 20
Come Back, Little Sheba 115–116
Come Next Spring 299, 304
Come on Up 201
Comics Scene 110
Common Clay 92
Compliments of the Season 134, 145
Compson, Betty 137
Compton, Fay 149
The Concrete Jungle 267
Condon, Eddie 294
Confidential 56, 189, 210, 299
Conlon, Scoop 91
Conn, Maurice 201
Connard, Phyllis 133

Connaught Theatre 148, 153
Connell, Roland *see* Schaum, Franklin
Connery, Sean 59
Connolly, Mike 56, 185, 186, 188, 300, 302
Connolly, Walter 24
Conrad, Harold 49
Conroy, Frank 71
Conspiracy of Hearts 153–154, 162, 163
Convention Girl 139, 145
Coogan, Jackie 182, 184, 209
Cook, Elisha, Jr. **247**, 250
Cook, Tommy 117
Cook County Jail 86
Coons, Robbin 32, 46, 171, 221, 222
Cooper, Gary 180, 285
Cooper, Jackie 136
Cooper, James Fenimore 38
Cooper, Merian C. 24, 35
Coquette 8, 134, 218, 228
Corey, Jim 301
Corio, Ann 73
Cornell University 171
Coroner Creek 113, 119
Coronet Theater 82, 209
Cort Theater 94
Cosmopolitan 97, 293
Costello, Diosa 169
Cotten, Joseph 110, 281, 290
Cotton Follies 242
Cottonpickin' Chickenpickers 302, 304
County Players 148
County Theatre 81
The Courageous Dr. Christian 170, 193
Courier-Post 11, 61, 62
Court, Elliott 282
Court, Hazel 80
Court, Ormsby 282
Courtney, Inez **140**, 141
Coventry Evening Telegraph 162
Coward, Noël 29, **150**, 151
Cowl, Jane 71
Cox, Morgan 167
Coy, Johnny 235
Coy, Walter 176
Crack-Up 112, 119
Cradle Snatchers 93
Craig, James 183, 288
Crain, Jeanne 76, 78, 79
Crane, Richard **25**, 74
Crane, Russ 196
"Crash Detective" 81
Crash Dive **23**, 23, 31
Crashout 210, 215
Craven, John 24
Crawford, Broderick 52, 104, 107
Crawford, Joan 95, 121–122, 145, 167, 169, 170
Cregar, Laird 3, 22, 30
Crespi, Count Marco Fabio 259
Crime Doctor 223, 225
Crime, Inc. 174, 194
Crime Does Not Pay 167, 168, 169

Crime School 122–123, 130, 142, 145
Crist, Judith 118
Croker, June 66, 67
Cromwell, John 141, 143
Cromwell, Richard 98
The Crooked Way 293, 294, 304
Crooks Square 133
Crosby, Bing 209, 232, 287–288, 290
The Crosby Case 174
Cross Country Cruise 217, 228
Cross My Heart 288, **289**, 304
The Cross of Lorraine 110, 119
Crossley, Hella 250
Crowley, Ann 235
Crowley, Timothy Francis 246
Crowley Daily Signal 97
Crown Court 161
Crowther, Bosley 49, 57, 250, 288
Cruze, James 37
Crystal Room 115
Cugat, Lorraine 178–179
Cugat, Xavier 178–179
Cumberland News 173
Cummings, John 257
Cummings, Ridgely 117
Cummins, Peggy 152
Cuppett, Katherine 43
Curran Theatre 142
Currie, Louise 110
Curtis, Tony 116
Curtiz, Michael 12, 42
Curtright, Jorja 263
Cushing, Peter 149
Custer, George 273
Custer of the West 273, 279
Custer's Last Stand see Custer of the West
Customs Agent 85, 90
Cymbeline 148

Daily Clintonian 116
Daily Gazette 120
Daily Herald 150
Daily Mail 147, 148, 158, 163
Daily Mirror 155
Daily Province 102
The Daily Star 7
Dakota Lil 114, 119
Dalton, Audrey 155
The Daltons' Women 178, 194
Dalya, Jacqueline 253
Damita, Lili 42
Damn Yankees 237, 238
The Damned Don't Cry 145, 146
Damon, Cathryn 238
Damon Runyon Theater 300
Danch, William 116
Danger Zone 178, 194
Dangerous Years 128, 131
Daniel Boone 59, 118
Daniel Mayer Company 160
Daniels, Bebe 229
Daniels, Jack 263
Danny Larkin 83
Danny Scholl Memorial Music Scholarship 243

Index

Dano, Royal 118
Darcel, Denise 180
Darcy, Jacques 139
Dare, Barbara *see* Tufts, Barbara Minot
Dare, Dorothy 138
Darin, Bobby 271
Dark City 204
Darling Enemy 138, 145
Darnell, Linda 53, 62, **64**, 78
Darrow, Paul G. 43
Darwell, Jane 201
D'Assunta, Rocco 56
Datig, Fred 168
Daughter of the Jungle 64, 66, 68
Daughters of Atreus 166
Daughtrey, Marcia 79
Dauphin, Claude 154
David, George L. 91, 123
David O. Selznick Company 22

Davis, Bette 17
Davis, Edgar B. 7
Davis, J. Frank 7
Davis, Sammy, Jr. 303
Dawson, Mark 299
Day, Doris 239, 302
Days of Glory 128
Dayton Daily News 243
Dead End 120, 121–122, **122**, 123, 130
Dead End Kids 1, 109, 120, 121–124, **121**, **112**, **123**, **124**, **125**, 126, **126**, 127, 128, 129, 130, 142, 288
Dead Reckoning 112, 119
Deadlier Than the Male 250
Dean, Peter 152
Dear Evelyn 148
Dear Ruth 81, 289
Dearden, Basil 149
The Death Merchant 276, 280
"Death of a Cop" 272
Death of a Salesman 259, 274
Death Takes a Holiday 62
Death Valley Days 116, 209
Death Valley Manhunt 143, 145, 146
Deauville Beach Club 208
De Carlo, Yvonne 262
Decision 93
Decker, John 249
de Cordoba, Pedro 174
Dee, Frances 37
Deerfield Academy 20
Deering, Olive 166
DeFore, Don 179, 207
DeHaven, Gloria 288
De Havilland, Olivia 10, 286, 288, 289
Dehner, John 174
Dekker, Albert 238
De La Motte, Marguerite 97
De Leon, Jack 135
Delilah 29, 236
Dell, Gabriel 121, 122, **122**, 123, **124**, 126, 130
Delmar, Kenny 233
Delmar, Viña 94

De Loqueyssie, Paul 250
Del Ruth, Roy 292
The Delta Factor 274
Deltgen, René 178
De Mille, Agnes 86, 236
DeMille, Cecil B. 38, 45, 50, 143, 212, 262, 296
Democrat and Chronicle 39, 91, 93, 123
Dempsey, Jack 88, 133, 139
Denison, Leslie 28
Denning, Richard 129
Denny, Reginald 97, 111
Denny, Roger Quayle 110
The Deputy 118
De Rochemont, Louis 77
Des Moines Register 286
Des Moines Tribune 53
De Sabatino, Gabriel 57
De Scaffa, Francesca 55–57
De Schauensee, Baroness 19
Desert Inn 55
The Desert Song 49, 60
Desmond, William 217
Destry 117, 119
Detective Story 259, 267
The Detectives 270
Detour 164, 174–175, **175**, 177, 189, 193, 194
Detroit Civic Light Opera 294–295
Detroit Free Press 39, 91, 97, 106, 136
De Veuster, Father Joseph Damien 167
The Devil Thumbs a Ride 1, 245, 251–252, 279
Devine, Andy 97
Devlin, Donald 290
Dewey, Tom 143
De Wolfe, Billy 230
Dexter, Anthony 299
D'Harcourt, Countess Zina 183
Diamond, David 103
Diamond, Margaret 148
Diamonds Are Forever 59, 60
Díaz, Alicia 72
DiCicco, Pat 44, 53, 55
The Dick Powell Show 239
The Dick Powell Theatre 118, 271
Dick Tracy 185
The Dick Van Dyke Show 239, 302
Dieterle, William 11
Dietrich, Marlene 46–48, **47**
"A Different Drummer" 88
Digges, Dudley 134
Dillinger 245, **247**, 247–248, 249, 249, 250, 251, 258, 252, 264, 273, 279
Dillinger (1991) 275, 180
Dillinger, John 245, 247–248, 249, 255, 257, 262, 264, 276, 279
Dillon, Josephine 35, 39, 134
Dinner for 3 144
Disgraced 36, 60
Divorce 53, 60, 223, 228
Divorce Bait 214
The Divorce Question 143

Dix, Richard 35, 37, 63, 64, 246
Dixon, Hugh 49, 175
Dixon, Jean 218
Dixon, Lee 18
Dmytryk, Edward 170, 171
Dobek, Andy 257
Dock Players 70
Dr. Kildare 239
Dodge, Ray 45
Dodge City 41, 42, 60
Doherty, Lindy 235
Doherty, Rosaleen 201
Dolan, Robert 233
Dolenz, Micky 302
Doll Face 77
The Doll House 188, 262
Domenico, Silvio "Slugs" 253–254
Domergue, Faith 49
Dominick's 188
Don Q, Son of Zorro 74
Donahue, Jack 93
Donlan, Yolande 157
Donlevy, Brian 49, 98, 260, 301
The Donna Reed Show 70
Donnelly, Jack 285
Donner, Richard 275
Donovan, Warde 232
Donovan's Reef 58
Don't Bet on Love 217, 228
Don't Gamble with Love 38, 60
Don't Turn 'Em Loose 38–39, 60
Dorn, Faith *see* Domergue, Faith
Dors, Diana 57
Douglas, Don 174
Douglas, Kirk 117
Douglas, Melvyn 8, 24, 231
Douglas, Paul 294
Doussard, James 303
Dow, Peggy 260
Dowler, Josephine Marie 217
Dowling, Constance 289
Dowling, Doris 81
Downing, Joseph 121
Doyle, Michael 109
Doyle, Walter 287
Dracula 137
Dragnet (1947) 201, 215
Dragonwyck 77
Drake, Alfred 85, 86
Drake, Dona 169
Drake University 166
Drama Art Workshop 216
Draper, Allen 87
Dressler, Eric 134
Dressler, Marie 96, 136
Drew Field 75
Dreyfuss, Randy 66
Drums in the Deep South 183
The Drunkard 66
Duane, Michael 64
Dubinsky, Edward 92
Dude Ranch 116
Duel in the Sun 159
Duff, Howard 260
Duff, Warren 95
Duffy, Albert 109

Index

Duffy of San Quentin see *The Steel Cage*
Duffy's Tavern 286, **287**, 304
Duggan, Shirle 293
Duke, Doris 44
Duke Street Cemetery 116
Dunbar, Dixie 169
Dunn, J. Colvin 21
Dunn, James 97, 103
Dunne, Irene 36
Duquesne Spy Ring 77
Durante, Jimmy 303
Durbin, Deanna 256
Durden, Chauncey 197, 198
Durgin, Cyrus 83, 201
Duryea, Dan 259
Dust Be My Destiny 124, 131
Dvorak, Ann 203
Dynamite Delaney see *Highway Patrol*
Dynasty of Decadence: Hollywood's Lavender Casting Couch 214

Eagels, Jeanne 134
Earhart, Amelia 40
Earl Carroll's Vanities 231
Earles, Harry 96
East of Fifth Avenue 97, 119
East of Sudan 158
Eastwood, Clint 277
Easy Come, Easy Go 290, 304
Easy Living 292, **293**, 304
Eaton, Shirley 150
Eck, Johnny **96**
Eckert, Stuart 143
Economic Cooperation Administration 128
Ecstasy see *Ekstase*
The Ed Sullivan Show 234
Eddie Presley 277, 280
Eddington, Nora 54
Eddy, Nelson 169
Eden, Barbara 303
Edge of Darkness 49
Edge of Hell 56
Edinburgh Festival 161
The Educational Screen 219
Edwards, Blake 117, 190
Edwards, James G. 42
Edwards, Nadine M. 155
Egli, Joe 285
"Egyptian Ella" 287, 301
Egyptian Theatre **233**
Eichelberger, Jane 140–141, 142, 143
Ekstase 167
Ellerbe, Harry 144
Elliott, Cecil 203
Elliott, Gordon 15
Elliott, Laura 82
Elliott, William 54
Ellis, Mary 149
Ellis, Patricia **13**, 13, **219**
Embassy Club 34
Embraceable You 114, 119
Emergency Ward 213
Emerson, Faye 87, 203

Emerson, Hope 117
Emily 145
Empire Hotel 253
Employees' Entrance 97, 119
Empress Theater 87
The End Zone 214
Endicott Daily Bulletin 29
Endore, Guy 222
Enfield, Andree 216
Enfield, Dennis 3, 216, 217, 221, 222, 223, **224**, 225, 226–228
Enfield, John 216, 226–227
Enfield, Leila 216, 226, 227
Enfield, Oscar 216, 226, 227
Enfield, Rollin 216, 227
Enright, Ray 15
Enter Madame 6
The Entertainer 162
Entwistle, Peg 6
Epstein, Jerry 203, 206
Equal Justice 276
Equus 162
Eric, Elspeth 121
Erickson, Leif 82
Erickson, Paul 296
Erickson, Vincent N. 179
Ernst, Hugh "Bud" 41
Errol, Leon 25
Evans, Lee 231
Evanston Showcase Theater 88
Evanston Township High School 164
The Eve of St. Mark 73–74, **73**, 89
Evening Herald 187
An Evening with Danny Scholl 243
Everett, Chad 243
Every Day's a Holiday 142, 145
Evicted 246, 278, 280
Ewell, Tom 298
Excess Baggage 93
The Exhibitor 178
Exiled to Shanghai 102, **103**, 103, 119
Exorcism at Midnight 275, 279
Exploring the Unknown 81
Exposed 180
Eyerman, Richard 243
Eythe, Howard 69
Eythe, William 2, 69–90, **70**, **72**, **73**, **75**, **76**, **78**, **84**
EZ Streets 278

F Troop 302
"The Fabulous Money Maker" 153
The Fabulous Texan 225, 228
The Face of Love 149, 163
Faerber, Matthew J. 51
Fain, Sammy 239
Fair and Warmer 133
Fair Park Auditorium 235
Fairbanks, Douglas 56, 86
Fairbanks, Douglas, Jr. 96
The Faithful Heart 7
The Falcon Out West 246, 279
Falkenburg, Jinx 171, **171**
Fallen Angel 53, 60

Fallon, Robert 207, 209
Fame 275
Family Portrait 62
The Family Upstairs 148
Famous Door 284–285
Fancy Pants 54, 60
Fantastic Summer 149, 163
Farber, Burt 231
Farmer, Frances 44
Farnum, William 177, 252
Farrell, Anthony Brady 233
Farrell, Charles 96
Farrell, Eve 139
Farrell, Glenda 172
Farrow, John 291
Fast and Loose 167
"Faster Gun" 189
Fatal Passion 277, 280
Father Knows Best 117
Fay, Frank 112
Faylen, Frank 118
Feck, Luke 238
Fellner, Chris 155
Female Fugitive 222, 228
Female Jungle 267, 279
Fenton, Frank 256
Fenton, Patricia 188, 189
Ferrero, Lee 182
Fibber McGee and Molly 117
Fidler, Jimmie 14, 45, 48, 49, 52, 81, 117, 143, 173, 174, 175, 184, 248, 250, 255, 256, 258, 259, 260, 261, 290, 292, 295, 296
Field, Betty 127
Field, Charlotte 142
Field, Eunice 272
Field, Rowland 134
Field, Virginia 143
"Fifth Floor People" 154
The Fifty Worst Films of All Time 66
The Fighting Chump see *Highway Patrol*
The Fighting Sullivans see *The Sullivans*
Film Culture 175
The Film Daily 37, 94, **101**, 141
Films and Filming 157
Finch, Peter 151
Findlater, Carole 148
Finian's Rainbow 83
Finishing School 37, 60
Finklehoffe, Fred 267
Fireside Theatre 210
First Day of a New Season 160
First Motion Picture Unit 200
First Yank into Tokyo 175, 176, 194
The First Year 133
Fisher, Eddie 271
Fisher, George 209
Fitzgerald, Barry 108, 290
Fitzgerald, Geraldine 22
The Flame of New Orleans 46, **47**, 48, 60
Flame the Dog 177
Flanagan, Barbara 183
The Flanagan Boy 186
Fleischmann's Yeast Hour 24

Flesh and Fury 116, 119
Fletcher, Bramwell 135
Fletcher Stock Company 92
Flight Command 170, 193
Flint, Helen 7
The Flip Side 160
Flirtation Walk 9, 10, 12, *12*, *17*, 18
Floyd, E.W. 257
Floyd, Pretty Boy 257
The Floyds of Oklahoma 257
Flying Devils 35, 60
Flying Tigers 170, 194
Flynn, Errol 1, 11–12, *12*, 32, 40, 41–42, *41*, 44, 45, 49, 50, 52, 54, 55, 56, 59, 124, 202, 246, 249
Flynn, Nora see Eddington, Nora
Foch, Nina 85
Folies Bergère 44
Follow Me Quietly 257
Follow the Sun 271
Fonda, Henry 7, 8, 9, 13, 14, 73, 105, 118
Fonda, Jane 58
Fong, Benson *65*, *144*
Fontaine, Jacqueline 209, *211*, 211
The Footlighters 241
The Footlighters Workshop 126
The Footloose Heiress 219, *222*, 228
"Footnote to the Conspiracy" 161
"For All We Know" 139
Foran, Dick 9, 109, *126*, 218
Forchheimer, Landon L. 230
Ford, Glenn 44, *226*
Ford, John 44, 97, 98, *99*, 111–112, 114, 166, 200
Ford, Patricia 93, 112
Ford, Robert 257
Ford, Wallace 2, 91–119, *92*, *96*, *99*, *101*, *103*, *108*, *115*
Fore 94, 119
Forest Lawn Memorial Park 17, 226
Forman, Adrienne 299
Fort Lauderdale News 166, 168, 169
Fort Pitt Orchestra 33
Fort Thomas Veterans Administration Hospital 244
Fort Worth Star Telegram 239
Foster, Ernest 92
Foster, Norman 7, 96
Foster, Preston 227
Foster, Silvers A. 112
Foster, Stephen 231
Foster, Susanna 193
The Four Feathers 150
Four Girls in White 167, 193
Four Hours to Kill! 218, 228
Four Sided Triangle 186
4:20 A.M. 188
Fowley, Douglas 113, 297–298
Fox, John A. 271
Fox Chapel Players 70
Fox Chapel Playhouse 70
Fox Valley Playhouse 236
Foy, Bryan 97, 225

Foy's Supper Club 110
Francine, Anne 144
Francis, Kay 53, 223
Francis, Robert 104
Frankie and Johnny 237
"Frankie and Johnny" 296
Franz, Arthur 263
Fraser, John 151, 152, 163
Fry, Christopher 148
Frazee, Harry 28, 29
Frazier, Brenda 42, 43, 44
Freaks 95–96, *96*, 119
Frederick, Pauline 52, 53
Free for All 201
Freed, Arthur 232
Freel, Aleta 8, 9, 13–14, 15, 16, 17
Freeman, Alex 301
Freeman, Dave 301
Freeman, Donald 59
Freeman, Vernon, Jr. 167
Freile, Aleta see Freel, Aleta
Freile, Dr. William 17
Fremont, Harry 27
Fremont Evening Tribune 133
French, Betty 285
The French Connection 214
French Hospital 226
French Intensive 277, 280
French Without Tears 81
Friends 161, 163
Fritz 52
From a Whisper to a Scream see *The Offspring*
"From This Moment On" 86
Frontier Gunlaw 145, 146
The Fugitive 130
The Full Treatment 154–155, *154*, 163
Fuller, Dolores 209
The Furies 114, 119
Furnace Creek Inn 100
Furness, Betty 46
Fury 38, 60

Gable, Clark 1, 17, 35, 37, 38, 40, 46, 48, 56, 95, *132*, 132, 134–135, 136, 137, *138*, 139, 141, 143, 145, 168–169, 172, 174, 218
Gaines Little Theater 185
Gainsborough, Barbara 268
Gaither, Gant 231
The Gallant Legion 54, 60
Gals, Incorporated 25, *26*, 31
Gang Busters 128, 188
Garbo, Greta 35, 77, 106, 169
Gardiner, Betty 153
Gardiner, Reginald 48
Gardner, Bella 21
Gardner, Hy 268, 274
Garfield, John 62, 115, 124, *125*, 170
Gargan, William 35, 107, 218
Garland, Bill, Jr. 186
Garland, Judy 123, 127, 271
Garnier, Philippe 105
Garrett, Betty 231, 232
Garrett, Pat 299
Garrison, Maxine 112

"Garrity's Gamble" 214
Gas House Kids 128, 131
Gaslight 274
Gassman, Vittorio 57
Gates, Walter S. 113
Gathering Storm 148
Gaver, Jack 85, 234
The Gay Caballero 136, 145
Gayne, Zach 274
Gaynes, George 86
Gaynor, Charles 70, 82, 88
Geary Theater 95, 107, 179, 222
The Gene Autry Show 178
General Advertiser 161
General Electric Theater 116
Gentlemen Are Born 9–10, 18
Gentlemen Prefer Blondes 84
George, Gladys 208
George, Stewart 235
George Washington Slept Here 71
George Washington University 133
George White's Scandals 33
Georgopoulos, Dimitrios C. 272
Gerhard, Inez 234
Gerler, Don 278
Gerson, Hal 83
Get Garrity 214
Get It First 218
Get That Man 98, 119
Geurink, Bob 59
The Ghost Ship 246, 279
Ghosts 151, 153
G.I. Jane 178, 194
Gibbons, Floyd 209
Gibson, Harry (The Hipster) 201
Gibson, Hoot 43
Gibson, Wynne 44
Giesler, Jerry 55
Gifford, Frances 170
Gift Horse 295, 304
Gilbert, Franklin 82, 85
Gilbert, Jody 283
Gilbert, Ricardo 135
Gilbert, Walter 139
Gildersleeve on Broadway 246, 279
Gill, Robert 70
Gillette, Priscilla 86
Gillette Safety Razor Co. 42
Gilmore, Virginia 81
Gilmour, Clyde 116
A Girl, a Guy, and a Gob 45
Girl Crazy 238
A Girl in Every Port 207
"Girl in the Window" 232
Girl Murdered see *Female Jungle*
Gish, Lillian 208
Git Along Little Dogies 141, 145
Give Us a Break see *They Shoot Horses, Don't They?*
Give Us Wings 109, 119, 131
The Gladiator see *The Square Ring*
"The Gladiola Girl" 83, 89
Glasmon, Kubec 37–38
Glass Hat Club 283
The Glass Menagerie 81, 82

The Glass Palace 118
Gleason, Jackie 235
Glen Group Players 128
Glenn Miller's Army Air Force Band 231
Glenn Rendezvous 231
Gloria 275, 279
Glory at Sea see Gift Horse
Go for Garrity 214
Goddard, Paulette 40, 49, 232, 285, 286, ***287***, 289
Godfrey, Peter 143
Godfrey, Renee 143
Goetz, William 259
Going Highbrow 11, 18
The Gold and Glory Guy 214
Goldberg, Albert 176
Golden, John 7, 9
Golden, Ray 88
Golden Boy 128, 167
The Golden Turkey Awards 282, 286
Goldoni, Carlo 85
Goldrup, Jim 40, 197, 200, 202, 205, 207, 209, 214
Goldrup, Tom 40, 197, 200, 202, 205, 207, 209, 214
Goldsmith, Martin M. 174
Goldwyn, Samuel 72, 111, 122, 166, 201, 297
Goldy, William B. 256, 257
Goliath and the Barbarians see *Il terrore dei barbari*
Golm, Lisa 262
Gomer Pyle, U.S.M.C. 130
Gone with the Wind 143, 170
Good, John ***25***
Good Luck, Mr. Yates 171, 194
Good Men and True 139
Good News 295
Good Night Garrity 214
Good Samaritan Hospital 89
Goodbye Again 70, 97, 119
Goodhart, Al 101
Goodliffe, Michael 161
Goodman, Benny 62
Goodman, Ezra 203–204, 206
Goodrich, Marcus 29
Goodyear Playhouse 116
Goold, Leila 216, 226–227
The Goose Hangs High 133
Gorcey, David 123, 126
Gorcey, Leo 121, 122, 123, ***124***, 126, 128, 129
Gordon, Gale 166
Gordon, Michael 176
Gordon, Vera 217
Gordon of Ghost City 217, 228
Gorsen, Norah 147, 148
Gould, Sandra 232
Government Girl 246, 279, 286, 304
Grable, Betty 39
Graham, Billy 182
Graham, Fred 31
Graham, Sheilah 38, 42, 44, 48, 56, 77, 111, 123, 126, 169, 186, 188, ***199***, 200, 208, 209, 232, 238,

250, 257, 259, 260, 273, 283, 285, 286, 289, 290–291, 295, 296, 298, 299
Grahame, Margot 112, 139
Grahame-White, Claude 52–53
Gramercy Ghost 87
Grand Central Players 94
Grand Hotel ***101***
Grand Theatre 160
"The Grandma Bandit" 153
Grange, Kenneth 180
Granlund, N.T. 166
Grant, Cary 44, 46, 47, 48
Grant, Gloria 181
Grant, Kirby 128
"The Grass Is Singing" 161
Grauman's Chinese 286
Graves, Julia Armandine 32, 40
Gray, Charles 151
Graziano, Rocky 266
The Great Adventure 118
The Great Heart 167, 193
The Great Jasper 35, 60
The Great Jesse James Raid 186, 194
The Great Jewel Robber 145, 146
The Great John L. 111, 119
The Great Love Stories 186
The Greatest Show on Earth 262, 279
The Greeks Had a Word for It 8
Green, Harry 296
Green Acres 227, 228
The Green Beetle 133
The Green Berets 58, 60
The Green Years 112, 119
Greenberg, Abe 118–119
Greene, Graham 11
Greenwood, Charlotte 86, 87, 143
Grey, Virginia 168
Grey, Zane 142
Gries, Tom 298
Griffin, Merv 302
Griffith, Corinne 240–241
Griffith, D.W. 104
Grinde, Nick 198, 199–200
Gringo 300
Gross, Ben 110
Groton School 19, 20
Gruen Guild Theater 55
Grundy, Samuel 91
Grush, Merton E. 283
Guadalcanal Diary 222
Guardatele ma non toccatele! 57, 60
Guest, Val 154, 155, 157
Guild, Minda 58
Guinness, Alec 149
Gulager, Clu 275
Gulliver and the Little People 209
Gunfighters 54, 60
Gunga Din 104
Gunn, James 250
Gunsmoke 130, 212
Guy Bates Post Theater 143
A Guy Could Change 112, 119
Gwynn, Edith 55, 83, 145, 183, 185, 206, 259, 298

Gwynne, Anne ***126***
Gypsy 93
Gypsy Jim 93

The H-Bar-O Rangers 120
Haal, Renee *see* Godfrey, Renee
Haas, Hugo 56, 204
Haas, Jim 187
"Hacienda in Hawaii" 54
Hackett, Hal 82, 83
Hadley, Reed 77
Hale, Alan 41, 97, 114, 115
Hale, Barbara 175
Hall, Eddie 172, 174
Hall, Edwin 151, 152
Hall, Flo ***41***
Hall, Huntz 120, 121, ***122***, ***124***, 126, 129
Hall, John 154
Hall, Jon 166
Hall, Lois 66
Hall, Mordaunt 95
Hall, Norma 44
Hall, Raymond 129
Halop, Benjamin 120, 122, 123, 124, 129, 130
Halop, Billy 1, 120–131, ***121***, ***122***, ***124***, ***125***, ***126***, ***127***
Halop, Florence 120, 126
Halop, Lucille 120, 122, 123, 129, 130
Hamilton, Chas. 196
Hamilton, George 302
Hamilton, Margaret 88
Hamilton, Shirley 189
Hamlet 147, 161, 288
Hammer Complete: The Films, the Personnel, the Company 155
Hammett, Dashiell 49
Hammond, Alma Christina 210
Hampstead Theatre Club 160, 162
Hampton, Orville H. 211
Handsaker, Gene 78, 291
Hanford, A.C. 20
Hanifin, Ada 142
Hanratty in Hell 162
Happy Family 160
Hard to Kill see *Mr. Reckless*
Hardie, Russell 134
Hardin, Ty 273
Harding, Ann 93
Hardy, Betty 151
Hardy, Oliver 114
Harleigh Cemetery 68
Harlow, Jean 95, 136, 137, ***138***
Harmon, Mark 275
Harper's Bazaar 44
Harrelson, Woody 277
Harriet's Back in Town 161
Harrington, Bill 234
Harris, Jed 166
Harris, Richard G. 286
Harris, Sam H. 197
Harris Theatre 179
Harrison, Dennis 85
Harrison, Paul 49, 98, 127
Harrison, Tom 188
Harrison's Reports 86, 170

Hart, Gordon *219*
Hartford, Huntington 88
Hartford Courant 105, 120, 186, 294, 299
Hartley, Katharine 8, 9, 15
Hartman, Elizabeth 118
Hartman, Grace 117
Harvard Architecture School 20
Harvard University 20, 22, 24, 165, 282
Harvey 66, 112, 115, 119
Harvey in Hollywood 295
Haskin, Byron 213–214
Hastings, Charlotte 153
Hasty Pudding Club 20
The Hat-Box Mystery 177, 194
Hatari! 57, 60
Hatcher, Mary 233
Hathaway, Henry 22–23, 48, 77
Hatton, Rondo 174
Have Girls, Will Travel 59, 301
Haver, June 74
Hawaiian Eye 213
Hawkins, Jack 154
Hawkins, William 85
Hawkins Falls: A Television Novel 188
Hawks, Howard 59
Haworth, Joseph 93
Haworth, Martha 92–93, 99, 100, 107, 109–110, 116, 117, 118
Haworth, William 93
Hayden, Harry *219*
Hayden, Russell 142
Hayden, Sterling 285, 291
Hayes, Peter Lind 231
Haymes, Dick 232
Hayward, Louis 222
Hayworth, Rita 40
He Ran All the Way 115, 119
He Walked by Night 64, *67*, 68, 225, 258
Heaton, Seward 265
Heavenly Express 8
Hedgerow Theater 62
Hedgerow Theater Group 62
Hedin, Eda 143
Heffernan, Harold 108, 285, 301
Heflin, Van 259
Heir to the Flesh 209
Helen of Troy 149, 163
Hell Fighters 58, 60
Hellinger, Mark 281, 290, 291
Hellman, Jack 223
Hellman, Lillian 122
Hellman, Marcel 85
Hell's Angels 136
Hell's Kitchen 124, 131
Help Wanted 168, 193
Henderson, Florence 235
Hendley, Opal 198, 214
Hendricks, Dr. Charles 28
Hendrix, Wanda 257
Henning, Linda 227
Henry Jewett Repertory Theater 6
Henshaw, Buck 185
Hepburn, Katharine 39, 85

Hepburn, Richard Houghton 85
Her Cardboard Lover 134
Herbert, Diane 266
Herbstman, Mandel 178
Here Come the Marines see *Marines Come Thru*
Here Come the Waves 146, 287–288, 304
Here Comes Carter 15, 18, 228
Hermann, Ida 11
Hernandez, Keith 276
Hernández, Tom 58
Herne, Chrystal 133
The Hero 291
Herrera, John 190
Hersholt, Jean 170
Hervey, Irene *101*
Heston, Charlton 212
Hey, Teacher! 118
Heyburn, Weldon 1, 132–146, *132, 135, 137, 138, 140, 142, 144*
"Hialeah" 54
Hickman, Darryl *126*
Hickman, Dwayne 118
High Pressure 14
High Sierra 49
"Higher Than a Hawk" 239
Highway Patrol (TV) 212
Highway Patrol 139, 145
Hildegarde Withers 37
Hill, Arthur 228
Hill, Paula 209
Hill, Virginia 127
A Hill in Korea 150, 163
Hill Street Blues 275
Hilliard, Harriet 25
Hillyer, Lambert 37, 177
Hinds, Samuel S. 167, *168*
Hine 161
Hinton, Marilyn 301
Hired Wife 137–138, 145
Hirliman, George A. 39, 109
His and Hers 161
His Greatest Gamble 37, 60
"His Old Man" 231
"His Rightful Heritage" 110
The Hitch-Hiker 262
Hitchcock, Alfred 110, 111, 272, 296
Hitler, Adolf 52, 77, 105, 161, 218
Hitler's Children 171
H.M.S. Pinafore 236
Hobart, Rose 139
Hoch, Homer 62
Hodiak, John *73*, 75
Hoffman, Al 101
Holden, William *226*, 289, 291
Holiday 8
"The Hollow Crown" 151
Hollywood Bowl 10, 182
Hollywood Citizen-News 109, 113–114, 117, 155, 167
Hollywood Filmograph 97
Hollywood High School 270
Hollywood Hotel 15
Hollywood Jackpot 232
Hollywood Opening Night 87
Hollywood Receiving Hospital 252

The Hollywood Reporter 9, 38, 210
Hollywood Review 177
The Hollywood Spectator 18
Hollywood Stadium Mystery 222
Hollywood Star Time 80
Hollywood Talent Scouts 240
Hollywood Theatre Time 180
Hollywood Went Thataway 59
Holm, Celeste 74
Holmes, Stuart *219*
Holmes, William A. 223
Holy Communion Lutheran Church 62
Holy Cross Cemetery 118
Holzman, Ethelyne 6
Home, William Douglas 149
Home or Away 148
Home, Sweet, Home 120
Homicide Bureau 40, 60
L'homme qui cherche la verité 287
Honeymoon 8
Honolulu 167, 193
Honolulu Advertiser 231
Honolulu Community Theatre 66
Honolulu Star-Bulletin 66, 102
The Hoodlum *161*, 262, 279
Hook, Line and Sinker 228
Hooray for Hollywood 242
"Hootin' Owl Trail" 233
Hopalong Cassidy 143, 213
Hope, Bob 54, 59, 187, 209, 238, 239, 243, 301
Hope, Don 187, 298
Hope Rubber Co. 139
Hopkins, Miriam 44, 93, 176, *176*
Hopper, Hedda 21, 46, 54, 75, 82, 83, 109, 112, 117, 129, 172, 178–179, 202, 207, 225, 245, 256, 258, 286, 291, 300, 301
Hopwood, Hunter 303
Hornbaker, Alice 229, 230, 243
The Horror Show 275, 280
"Horseshoes Are Lucky" 233
Horton, Edward Everett 11
Hostages 49
Hot Money *14*–15, 18
Hotel Belmont Plaza 283
Hotel Stadler *235*
Hotel Sutton Plaza 54
The Hottentot 21
Houghton, Norris 8
Hour of Mystery 151
The Hour of Power 243
House of Chedworth 74
House of Horrors 174
The House on 92nd Street 77, *78*, 79, 82, 85, 89
Houseboat 228
How the Other Half Loves 162
Howard, Leslie 137
Howard, Shemp 139
Howard, Trevor 295
Howard, William K. 105
Hoyt, Caroline Somers 5–6
Hubbard, John 82, 167
Huber, Harold *125*
Hubschmid, Paul 56

Hudson, Rochelle 37
Hudson, Rock **58**
Hughes, Howard 21, 22, 30, 44, 49, 136
Hughes, James 160
Hughes, Russell S. 85
Hull, Henry 93
Humphrey Takes a Chance 178, 194
Hunt, Terry 226
Hunter 275
Hunter, Jeffrey 273
Hunter, Kim 85
Hunter, Ross 232
Huntington Hartford Theater 88
Hurlbut, William 142
The Hurricane 166
Hurricane Club 284
Hurricane Smith 262
Hurst, Lloyd 27
Hussey, Ruth 167, **168**
Huston, John 259, 275
Huston, Walter 95
Hutchinson, Josephine 14
Hutchinson, Tom 57–58, 59
Hutton, Barbara 48
Hutton, Betty 236, 238, 239, 287, 288, ***289***, 290
Hyams, Leila **96**
Hyde-White, Wilfrid 160
Hymer, Warren 141
Hypnotized 96, 119

I Came Back 222
I Hate Women 98, 119
I Love a Soldier 286, ***287***, 304
I Love Lucy 227
I Married a Doctor 14, 15, 18
I Shot Billy the Kid 178, 194
I Shot Jesse James 257
I Take This Oath 221, 228
I Want a Policeman! 139, 143
I Wanted Wings 45
"I Wonder Where My Old Girl is To-night?" 266
Ibsen, Henrik 151, 153, 162
Idaho Statesman 133
"An Ideal Husband" 161
If 217
If This Be Error 148
If This Be Treason 166
I'll Tell the World 217, 228
"Imagine My Finding You Here" 283
Immortal Girl 144
Immortal Sergeant 73
In Harm's Way 58, 60
"In Love in Vain" 78
In Love with Love 133
In Old Colorado 143, 146
In Spite of Danger 98, 119
In the Heat of the Night 267
Independent Exhibitors Film Bulletin 141, 177
Indianapolis News 35
Indianapolis Star 94
The Informer 98, **99**, 111, 112, 119
Inge, William 115, 116, 299

Ingham, Barrie 161
Inglehart, Wendy 44
Inner Sanctum 117
Inside Alcatraz 258
Inside the Law 110, 119
Insideout 160–161
International News Service 43
"The Invader" 87
Invitation for a Murder 70
Ireland, John 257, 263
Irish Eyes Are Smiling 74
Irvin, Frances 232
Irwin, Deedy 239
Irwin, Virginia 166
Isabelita *see* Baron, Lita
Isle of Destiny 107, 119
It Could Only Happen Here 126
It Might as Well Be Spring: A Musical Autobiography 79
It Pays to Advertise 7
"It's Good to Be Alive" 233
ITV Sunday Night Theatre 160
ITV Television Playhouse 155, 157
Ivar Theater 117
Ivarene Café 115
"I've Confessed to the Breeze (I Love You)" 235
Ivoryton Playhouse 81, 86

The Jack Benny Program 227
The Jack Paar Show 238
Jack Pot 169, 193
Jack Straw 217
"The Jacket" 275–276
Jackie the Jumper 157
Jaffe, Sam 104
Jagger, Dean 102
Jailbreak **218**, 218–219, 228
Jamaica Plain High School 195
James, Dennis 236
James, Gordon 133
James, Jesse 116, 119, 186, 194, 248, 257, 261
Jane Wyman Presents the Fireside Theatre 117
Jardin Royal 283
The Jazz Singer 136
Jealousy 198
Jeans, Isabel 160
Jeffreys, Anne 3, 248–249, **249**, 279
Jenkins, Allen 122, 177
Jericho 101, 119
Jewell, Isabel 102, 107, 111, 250
Jewett, Henry 6
Jigsaw 157, 163
Jingle-Bob Jones 213
Joe 274
Joe and Ethel Turp Call on the President 168, 193
Joe Hale 128
Joe Palooka 178, 194
Joel and Garda Stone 167
Johann, Zita 134
John B. Mack Players 133
John Paul Jones 57, 60
The John Sullivan Story 162, 163
Johnny Concho 117, 119

Johnson, Choo Choo *see* Lynch, Sheila
Johnson, Erskine 48, 49, 53, 109, 117, 128, 184, 186, 204–205, 209, 227, 255, 260, 262, 290, 291, 292, 293, 294, 296, 298
Johnson, Noel 161
Johnson, Rita 165, 167
Johnson, Susan 235
Johnson, Van 301
Jones, Carolyn 209
Jones, Catharine 91, 98, 99, 101–102, 109, 114, 116
Jones, Gordon 221
Jones, Jennifer 72, **72**
Jones, Jimmy 196
Jones, Paul 111, 294
Jonesy 94
Jordan, Bobby 121, 122, ***123***, ***124***, 126, 129
Jordan, Jim 117
Jordan, Marian 117
Jorgensen, Christine 266
Jory, Victor 10, 16, 297–298
Josey, Lenoir 55
Joy Ride 88
Joyce, Dianne 198
Joyce, Peggy Hopkins 283–284
Judge, Posey 260
Judge Roy Bean 211
Juke Box Jury 116
Julius Caesar 153
June Night 166
The Jungle Captive 174
Jungle Girl 66, 170, 194
Junior 94, 277, 280
Junior G-Men 127, 131
Junior G-Men of the Air 127, 131
Juran, Nathan 158
"Just a Quiet Evening" 16
Just Before Dawn 223, 228

Kaeloa, Luukiana 295
Kahn, Gordon 95
Kahn, Ivan 217
Kaiser, Burt 267
Kandel, Aben 14, 201, 203–204
Kany, A.S. 206
Karloff, Boris 97, 106, 176
Karr, Jeanne 288
Katcher, Leo 184
Katzell, William R. 83, 85
Katzman, Sam 177
Kaufman, George S. 104, 107
Kaufman, Lloyd 274
Kautschuk 178
Kaye, Buddy 234
Kaye, Danny 86
Kazan, Elia 127, **127**, 267
Kean, Betty 299
Kean, Jane 231, 299
Kearns, Jack "Doc" 139
Keavy, Hubbard 134, 136, 291
Keefe, Willard 37, 121
Keel, Howard 239
Keeler, Ruby 9, 11, 16, **17**, 18

Keeling, W.A. 144
Keenan, Eileen 269
Keene, Tom 221
Keighley, William 94
Keitel, Harvey **278**
Keith, Brian 207
Keith, Ian 222
Kellam, James 190
Keller, Greta 3, 23–24, **24**, 26, 28, 29, 30, 31
Kellogg, Hazel 269
Kelly, John "Shipwreck" 267–268
Kelly, Nancy 49, 73, 201
Kelly, Paul 265
Kendall, Cy 123
Kendall, Kay 149
Kendall, Read 102–103
Kendall, Roger 264
Kenley, John 187
Kennedy, Arthur (actor) 210
Kennedy, Arthur 269
Kennedy, Douglas 170
Kennedy, Harold J. 294
Kent, William 249, 250
Kent's High Academy 195
Kern, Jerome 78
Kerr, John 237
Kerrigan, J.M. 112
Keyes, Evelyn 172, 298
Kibbee, Guy 11
Kick In 133
Kid Galahad 196
Kid Monk Baroni 55, 60
Kilgallen, Dorothy 45, 46, 49, 50, 52, 54, 79, 126, 127, 145, 181, 184, 186, 188, 190, 197, 207, 208, 213, 253, 256, 257, 262, 266, 267–268, 271, 283, 287, 288, 289, 298, 299
Kilgallen, Helen 127
Kilian, Victor **126**
Kill or Be Killed 258, 279
Killer Without a Face see *Assassino senza volto*
The Killers 290
Kind Lady 208
Kindred 108
King, Philip 150
King, Stephen 275
King Brothers (Frank and Maurice) 86, 247, **247**, 248, 250
King Carol II of Romania 24, 49
King Farouk 57
King Kong 32, **34**, 35, 59, 60
King of the Bullwhip 178, 194
King of the Khyber Rifles 159
The King's Maid 71
Kingsley, Grace 23, 110, 209
Kingsley, Sidney 105, 121, 122
Kinloch, John 40
Kirby, June 266
Kirke, Donald 222
Kirkland, Alexander 9
Kirkley, Donald 45, 83, 104, 116
The Kirlian Witness 275, 279
A Kiss Goodnight 277, 280
Kiss Me, Kate 86

Kitty Doone see *You Twinkle Only Once*
Kleefeld, Travis 186
Kloke, Gail Lee 189–192
Klondike 118
Klondike Kate 172, 194
Knapp, Evalyn 217
Knapp, Robert 203, 209
Knickerbocker, Cholly 259, 269, 296
Knickerbocker Hospital 268
Knickerbocker Hotel 198
Knox, Alexander 74
Knox, Elyse 201
Kofoed, Jack 109, 110
Kokomo Tribune 118
Kramer, Stanley 271
Krasna, Norman 47–48
Kreuger, Ivar 153
Krug, Karl 89
Kruger, Hardy 152
Kruger, Otto 176
Kubly, Herb 70

L.A. Law 277
LA Weekly 105
Labarr, Marta 44
Lacey, Catherine 153
Ladd, Alan 52, 110, 158, **158**, 177, 205, 285, 286, 301
The Ladder 6–7
Ladies in Retirement 71
Lady Chatterley's Lover 222
Lady Esther Screen Guild Theatre 111
Lady in the Dark 209
A Lady Mislaid 148
Lady Windermere's Fan 160
Lafayette Theater 94
Laff That Off 133
Laguna Beach Playhouse 201
Lait, Jack, Jr. 232, 292
Lake, Arthur 138
Lake, Florence 138
Lake, Veronica 285, 292
Lake Forest Academy 164
Lake Shore Drive Hotel 33
Lakewood Theater 187, 267
Lamarr, Hedy 44, 56, 167, 169, 186
Lamb, Angela 266
Lamb, Gil 236
Lamb, Sybil 236
Lambert, Gerard B. 42
Lambert, Paul 82
Lambie, Jack 141
Lamour, Dorothy 44, 209
Lamparski, Richard 129, 300
La Muro, Pierre 55
Lancaster, Burt 212, 245, 271, 290, 291
Lancelot and Guinevere 158
Land, Lillian 141
Land of the Giants 130
Landis, Carole 44
Landon, Judy 207
Land's End 303
Lane, Lenita 134, 218
Lane, Priscilla 49, 127, **127**, 257

Lane, Vicky 172–174, 178, 184
Lang, Fritz 38, 105
Lang, June 44, 107
Langan, Glenn 77
Lanning, Don 109
Lanning, Ray 231, 285
Lardner, Ring 117
Larsen, Curtis D. 21
La Rue, Jack 249
La Rue, Lash 178
Las Palmas Theater 82, 232
Lassie 118
The Last Flight 134
The Last Mile 259, 262, 268
The Last of Mrs. Cheyney 70
The Last of the Mohicans 38, 60
The Last of Vicky 197, 214
The Last Rose 81
The Late Edwina Black 148
Lauer, Edgar J. 105, 106
Lauer, Elma N. 105, 106
Laura 66, 80, 176, 267
Laurel Avenue Workshop Theater 126
La Verne, Lucille 217
Lavery, Emmet 171
Law, Jenny Lou 83, 87
The Law in Her Hands 218
Law of the Lawless 58, 60
Lawford, Betty 252
Lawford, Peter **25**
Lawman 213
Lawrence, D.H. 222
Lawrence, Marc 174, **247**, 273
Lawrence, the Rev. William A. 133
Lawrence Collegians 196
Leave It to Beaver 227
LeBeau, Madeleine 73
Lebedeff, Ivan 141
Le Borg, Reginald 186
Lecours, Meg see Magda, Maria
Lee, Anna 101
Lee, Belinda 151
Lee, Christopher 155
Lee, Dorothy 37
Lee, Lila 302
Lee, Michele 303
Lee, Sharon 212
Legion of Terror 39, 60
Lehac, Ned 283
Leicester Chronicle 150, 154
Leigh, Janet 232, **233**, 243
Leigh, Marjorie 44
Leigh, Vivien **150**, 151
Lembeck, Harvey 238
Lemmon, Leonore 45
Lend an Ear 70, 71, 82, 85, **81**, 86, 87, 88, 89
Lengyel, Melchior 75
Leonard, Sheldon 172
Leonard Appliance Company 129
Lerner, Samuel 101
LeRoy, Mervyn 122
Leslie, Nan 252
Lesser, Sol 80, 201
Lessing, Doris 161
Lester, Ann 172

Lester, Lenore 266
Let 'Em Have It 37, 60, 220
Let Us Be Gay 7, 8
Let's Be Ritzy 217, 228
Let's Go Navy! 178, 194
Let's Pretend 120
Levin, Herman 231
Levins, Peter 19–20, 30
Levy, H.M. 107
Levy, Parke 46
Lewis, Bill 197
Lewis, Diana 170
Lewis, George J. 217
Lewis, Hugh X. 302
Lewis, Jerry 117, 227, 228
Lewis, Ronald 1, 147–163, **147**, **150**, **154**, **156**, **157**, **158**, **159**
Lewis, Sinclair 14
Lewton, Val 246
The Liar 85–86
Liberace 303
Liberty Weekly 134
Life magazine 73
Life with Father 21
Life with Linkletter 241
Light, Robert 9
Light Up the Sky 66
Lights Out 86, 87
Li'l Abner 238
Liliom 70
Linda, Be Good 201, 215
Lindeman, Edith 198
Linden, Eric 35, 37
Linder, Alfred **78**
Lindsay, Margaret **138**, 174
Lippert, Robert 177, 178, 180, 186, 189
Lipscott, Alan 46
Listen, Kids 54
Litel, John 23
The Little Minister 6
The Little Sister 83–84
Little Tough Guy 120, 123, 130
Little Tough Guys 126, **126**
Littlefield, Joan 102
The Live Wire 88
Liverpool Echo 151
Livingston, Lida 110
The Lizard on the Rock 154
Lloyd, Harold 218
Lloyd, Sue 161
The Lloyd Bridges Show 271
Lobero Theatre 22, 179
Lockheed 22
Loder, John 176, 203
Lodge, John 21
The Lodger 30
Loeb, Theresa 205
Loew's State Theatre 166
Logan, Ella 230
Logan, James 208
Logan, Joshua 8, 88
Logan, Stanley 144
Loma Linda University Medical Center 59
Lombardo, Pete 253–254
London Bankruptcy Court 162
London Guardian 57–59, 162

The London Observer 161
The Loner 302
Long, Walter 231
Long Island Star-Journal 120
Longstreet, Stephen 89
Loo, Richard 175
Look magazine 246
Lord, Marjorie 144
Lord Baltimore Hotel 254
Lord Jeff 102
Lorenzon, Livio 57
Lorre, Peter 257
Lorring, Joan 82, 83
Los Angeles County Nursing Home Association 118
Los Angeles Daily News 23, 143, 170, 181, 202–204, 206, 229, 232
Los Angeles Evening Citizen News 116
Los Angeles Evening Express 95
Los Angeles Evening Post-Record 94
Los Angeles Examiner 28, 29, 293
Los Angeles Illustrated Daily News 94–95, 99
Los Angeles Mirror 182, 197, 294
Los Angeles Neurological Institute 264
Los Angeles Times 23, 35, 43, 82, 95, 98, 102–103, 107, 110, 113, 136, 139, 143, 144, 172, 175, 176, 202, 203, 206, 209, 217–219, 222, 251, 252, 255, 256, 273, 275, 276, 293
Lost in Alaska 55, 60
The Lost Patrol 97, 104, 119
The Lost Weekend 223, 228, 248, 295
Lottie Dundas 22
Louis-Dreyfus, Julia 275–276
Louise, Anita 10, 13, 15
Love Affair 285
Love Birds 217, 228
Love, Honor and Oh-Baby! 109, 119
Love Is Not Important 8
Love Is Not So Simple 166
The Love Specialist see *La ragazza del palio*
Love Takes Flight 39–40, 60
The Love Test 133
The Love Trap 214
Loves of Three Queens see *L'amante di Paride*
Lovett, Dorothy 170
Lowe, Edmund 247, **247**, **137**
Lowell, Helen 93, 94
Loyalties 6
Lubitsch, Ernst 75, 77
Lucas, John 42–43
Lucas, Wilfred 42
Luce, Claire 107
Lucey's Restaurant 289
Lucky Devils 35, 60
Luez, Laurette 205, **205**
Lugosi, Bela 97, 110, **137**, 171
Lupescu, Magda 49
Lupino, Ida 74, 262
Lusk, Nobert 10

Lux Radio Theatre 281
Lux Video Theatre 55, 87
"Luxury Liner" 239
Lyceum Players 93
Lyden, Pierce 145
Lydon, Jimmy 105, 118
Lyles, A.C. 58
Lynch, James 102
Lynch, Sheila 109
Lynch, Violet see Lynch, Sheila
Lynn, Diana 289, 290
Lynn, Judy 235
Lynn, Mara 205
Lyon, Ben 101
Lyon, Herb 88, 188
Lyons, Leonard 46, 49, 50, 54, 284
Lyric Hammersmith 148
"Lysette" 153

M 257
Macayo 207
Macbeth 62, 162
MacDonald, Jeanette 169
Machatý, Gustav 167
Machine Gun Mama 111, 119
Machris, Elsinore 188
Mack, Helen 42, 53
Mackey, William 190, 192
MacLane, Barton 54, 252
MacMahon, Aline 105, 108
MacMurray, Fred 53, 286
MacRae, Gordon 235
Madame X 133
Madden, George 6, 15–16
Madden, Jeanne 141
Madison, Guy 183
Madsen, Michael **278**
Mae Desmond Players 134
Mafia: Operation Cocaine 214
Mafia: Operation Hit Man 214
Mafia: Operation Porno 214
Magda, Maria 213
Maggard, Virginia 143
The Magical World of Disney 118
Main, Marjorie 121, 122
Make Me Sing It 234
Make Mine the Tall One 54
Makley, Charles 105
The Male Animal 71
Malibu Pick-Up 214
Malin, Gene 285
Malin, Lucille 285
Mallon, Paul 284
The Maltese Falcon 49
Mama Loves Papa 248, 279
Mamma's Affair 7
Man Behind the Badge 267
The Man from Colorado 225, **226**, 228
The Man from Laramie 117, 119
Man from Texas 113, 119
The Man of the World 161
The Man Who Reclaimed His Head 98, 119
Man with a Camera 270
The Man with the Golden Arm 267

Manchester Evening News 114, 150
Mander, Miles 201
Mandour, Medhat 270
Manhattan College 246
Mank, Gregory William 3, 30
Mann, the Rev. Cameron 33
Mann, Daniel 115
Mann, May 49
Manners, Dorothy 181, 200, 203, 259
Manning, Irene 49
Mansfield, Jayne 267, 269
Il mantello rosso 56, 60
Mantle, Burns 105, 121, 283
Many a Slip 94
Mara, Adele 260
March of Time 120
March or Die 218
Margo 69–70, 171
Marin, Edwin L. 141
The Marines Come Thru 109, 110, 119
Marion, Frances 136
Mark Hellinger Theater 233
The Mark of Zorro 74
Marlow, Elizabeth 158
Marlowe, Hugh 176
Marlowe, Marion 238
Marlowe, Philip 83–84
Marquess of Bath 152
Marriott, R.B. 156, 163
Marsh, Carol 148
Marsh, Marian **108**
Marshall, E.G. 117
Marshall, Peter 232
Marshfield Players 196
Martel, June 11
Martin, Boyd 111
Martin, Dean 117, 301
Martin, Heloise 166
Martin, John 211
Martin, Mary Lambie 164
Martin, Mildred 113, 206, 231
Martini, Benjamin 266
Marx, Groucho 207
Mary Burns, Fugitive 98, 119
Mary Stuart 153
Masgay, Johnny 207
The Masked Marvel 25–26, **27**, 28, 30, 31
Masks and Memories 138, 145
Mason, Buddy 179
Mason, James 80
Mason, LeRoy 217
Massey, Anna 160
Massey, Raymond 82, 239
Master of Arts 148
"Master of the House" 276
Masters, Dorothy 53, 110
Mather-Smith, Charles Frederic 33
Mather-Smith, Grace 33
Mather-Smith, Grace Mary 33
Mathews, Carole 178
Mature, Victor 45, 205, 292, **293**
Maugham, W. Somerset 76, 161
Maury, Matthew Fontaine 167–168

Maverick 213
The Maverick Queen 117, 119
Max Liebman Presents 236
Maxford, Howard 155
Maxine Elliott's Theatre 108
Maxted, Daniel 101, 102
Maxwell, Elsa 283
Maxwell, Kate 229
Mayan Theatre 218
Maybe It's Love 10, **10**, 18
Mayer, Louis B. 39, 96, 169, 170
Mayer, Ray 102
Mayflower Café 263
Mayo, Mary 237
Mayo, Virginia 3, 253
McBrien, William 86
McBurney's School for Boys 121
McCallister, Lon 2, 78–80, 83, **84**, 86–89
McCallum, David 151
McCarey, Leo 96
McCarter Theatre 46, 81
McCarthy, Charlie 106
McCarthy, Glenn 54
McCarthy, Mary Eunice 98
McCarty, Mary 236, 237
McClure, Doug 301
McCormick, Ella H. 136
McCormick, Myron 8
McCoy, Horace 108, 109
McCrea, Joel 122, 259, 288, 291
McCullers, Carson 161
McDonald, Georgette 269
McDonald, Grace 25, **26**
McDonald, Marie 49
McDonald, Sheriff W.L. 35
McDonogh School 69
McDowall, Roddy 288
McEwan, John A. 33
McGarry, Peter 162
McGavin, Darren 189
McGee, James Vincent 83
McGilligan, Patrick 47–48
McGraw, Charles 271
McGuire, Dorothy 62, 73, 74
McGuire, Terry 262
McGuire, William Anthony 143
McHarry, Charles 238–239
McHugh, Frank 93
McIntyre, Christine **65**, 143
McIntyre, Archbishop J. Francis 115
McKay, Rick 252, 265, 271, 277
McKellen, Ian 161
McKenna, Virginia 149
McLaglen, Victor 97, 98
McLintock! 58, 60
McMahill, Betty 230
McNulty, Dorothy *see* Singleton, Penny
McPartlin, R.F. 235
McTurk, Joe 201
Meadow Players 155, 156
The Meal Ticket 214
Medina, Patricia 56
Medved, Harry 66, 282
Medved, Michael 282
Meeker, George 97

Meet Buddy Rogers 234
Meet Me at Dawn 80, 90
Meisner, Sanford 267
Melford, George 137
Melly, Andrée 148
Melody for Two **219**, 228
Melville, Herman 157
Men in White 97, 119
Men of the Hour 98, 119
Men of the Night 37, 60
Menninger Clinic 264
Mercer, Johnny 16, 233, 234, 288
The Merchant of Venice 147, 148
Merchantville Players 62
Meredith, Burgess 69–70, 107
Meredyth, Bess 42
Meriden Record 231
Merkel, Una 93, 116, 140
Merrick, Lynn 63
Merrick, Mollie 132, 136
Merrill, Dick 109, 141
The Merv Griffin Show 302
Mesa of Lost Women 209, **210**, 215
Mesmer, Marie 229, 233, 235
Messinger, Gertrude 141
Methinks the Lady 80
Methot, Mayo 93
Meyer, Johnny 49
Miami Herald 112
Miami News 265, 294
Miami University 253
Michael, Gertrude 174
Michaels, Beverly 204, **204**
Mickey the Kid 43, 60
Midnight 275, 280
Midshipman Jack 36, 60
A Midsummer Night's Dream 10–**12**, 18, 120, 148
"The Mighty Casey" 236, **237**
Mike Hammer 189
Mike Lyman's 200
Mike McCauley 179
Mikels, Ted V. 242
Milestone, Lewis 62, 106, 107
The Milky Way 218, 296–297
Milland, Ray 289
Millar, Ronald 160
Miller, Arthur 274
Miller, Barbara 218–219
Miller, John J. 302
Miller, Kristine 174
Miller, Llewellyn 94
Miller, Marguerite 289–290
Miller, Maurice 211
The Millerson Case 225
Million Dollar Ransom 217, 228
Mills, John 101
Mills, Juliet 157, 160
Milner, Martin 303
Mines, Harry 23
Minick 6
Minneapolis Morning Tribune 178, 183
The Miracle Kid 170, 194
The Mirage 95
Miranda 208
Miranda, Isa 56, 179
Les Misérables 276

Miss Susie Slagle's 288, 304
The Missing Lady 63, 68
Mr. Manchester 114
Mr. Reckless 81, 90
Mister Roberts 297
Mr. Sardonicus 155, **156**, 163
Mr. Watson 14
Mitchell, Cameron 117, 275
Mitchell, Thomas 8
Mitchell, Yvonne 154
Mitrovich, Marta 144, 209
Mix, Tom 59
Mob Town **126**, 131
Mocambo 48, 54, 180, 205, 249, 250, 256, 295
Modern Screen 62, 79, 245, 257, 287, 288
Moffitt, Deke 230
Mohawk Showroom 233
Mohr, Gerald 271
Mohr, Hal 222
Moiseyev Dance Troupe of Moscow 271
Molière 235
Molnár, Ferenc 71
Mon crime 288
Monahan, Kaspar 83, 187
Money Means Nothing 98, 119
Money to Loan 167, 193
Monk, Herbert L. 201
The Monkees 302
Monmouth County Players 8
Monroe, Marilyn 128, 298
Montalbán, Ricardo 127
Montez, Maria 201
Montgomery, Douglass 94
Montgomery, Robert 17, 24
"A Month of Sundays" 233
Monticello Playhouse 297
The Moon Is Down 71, 72, 89
Mooney, John 117
Mooney, Martin 174
Moore, Aubrey Malin 129
Moore, Bill 170
Moore, Clayton 166, 167
Moore, Colleen 9
Moore, Dennie 46
Moore, Kieron 273
Moore, Sam 234
Moran, Polly 96
The Morey Amsterdam Show 234
Morgan, Butch 52
Morgan, Charles 148
Morgan, Dennis 49
Morgan, Frank 24
Morgan, Harry **23**
Morgan, Jack 231
Morgan, Read 118
Morgan Wallace Players 92
Morley, Karen 221
El Morocco 49, 50, 52, 54, 55, 297
Morris, Chester 24
Morris, Dorothy 25, 174
Morris, Mary 70, 71, 149
Morris, Wayne 15, 196, 263, 300
Morrison, Charlie 249
Morrow, Susan 297
Morse, Jim 300

The Mortal Storm 197, 214
Mortimer, Lee 187, 266, 268
Morton, Hortense 179, 300
Mosby, Alice 82, 183, 205, 264
Mosley, Glenn A. 118
The Most Dangerous Game 35
Moten, Etta 236
Motherwell Times 151
Motion Picture 231–232
Motion Picture and Television Country House and Hospital 59, 118, 119
Motion Picture Daily 178
Motion Picture Exhibitor 78
Motion Picture Herald 48, 63, 73, 141, 288
Motion Picture Relief Home 118
The Motorola Television Hour 116
Moulin Rouge 55
Mount, Peggy 150
Mount Sinai Memorial Park 130
Mourning Becomes Electra 149
Movie Mirror 5–7, 15, 16
Mrs. Cook's Tour 134
Mrs. Partridge Present 6
Mrs. Warren's Profession 148
Much Ado About Nothing 6
Mug Town 128, 131
Muir, Florabel 181–185, 203
Muir, Jean 10
Mullen, Margaret 121
Mummy's Boys 220
The Mummy's Hand 109, 110, 119
The Mummy's Tomb 110, 119
Munday, Mary 298
Muni, Paul 124
Munn, Fernanda 46
Munroe Cemetery 303
Munshin, Jules 231
Murder by Invitation **108**, 109, 119
Murder in the Surgery 42
Murder on the Blackboard 37, 60
Murphy, Audie 257
Murphy, Dudley 108, 136
Murphy, George 302
Murphy, Ralph 114
Murphy, William S. 213, 214
Murphy's Law 275, 280
Murray, Barbara 161
Murray, Ken 200, 202
Murray Funeral Home 68
Murray Hill 196
Music Box Theatre 104
Musical Comedy Time 235
My Darlings: A Memoir 33
My Dog Shep 177, 194, 225, 228
My Friend Irma 201, 206
My Friend Irma Goes West 204, 206
My Mother the Car 302
My Son Is Guilty 44, 60
My Three Sons 227
My Woman 97, 119
The Mysterious Kiss 138, 145
The Mysterious Mr. Wong 98, 119
The Mysterious Rider 142–143, 145
The Mystery Man 133

Mystery Monthly 214
The Mystery of Mr. Wong **220**, 228
Mystery of the White Room 42, 60

Nagel, Anne 15–17, 141, **142**, 221
Nagel, Conrad 39
Naish, J. Carrol 112, 141
Naismith, Laurence 151
Naked City 270
Naked Evil see *Exorcism at Midnight*
The Naked Gun: From the Files of Police Squad! 275, 280
Nancy Ann 93
Nancy Goes to Rio 233, **234**, 244
Narayan, Jagaddipendra 54
Nash, Stephen 31
Nathan, George Jean 104
National Student Drama Festival 153
National Theatre 46, 83
Natural Born Killers 277
Navy Bound 178, 194
Naylor, John 263, 264
The NBC Children's Hour 120
Neal, Dorothy 164, 165, 166
Neal, Thomas Carroll 164
Neal, Tom 2, 3, 66, 164–194, **164**, **168**, **171**, **173**, **175**, **180**, **192**
Neal, Tom, Jr. 188, 189, 193
Neal's Nursery 188
Nebenzal, Seymour 201–203
The Nebraskan 116, 119
Needles, Ellanora 203
Negri, Pola 30, 139
Neilan, Marshall 9
Nelson, Gene 82, 83
Nelson, Robert 117
Neuman, Sam 262
"Neurotic You and Psychopathic Me" 83
Nevada 222, 228
"The Never Ending Story of the Christmas Clarvy" 303
Neville, Lucie 168
The New Breed 130
New Century Theatre 87
New Mexico Military Institute 33
The New Moon 169
New York Aqueduct 246
New York Confidential 270
New York Daily News **13**, 19–20, 29, 30, 38, 40, 44, 53, 83, 93, 94, 95, 109, 110, 116, 184, 201, 238–239, 284, 291
New York Herald-Tribune 45, 118
New York Post 85, 127
New York Sun 17
New York Times 9, 11, 15, 37–38, 49, 57, 95, 143, 154, 250, 288
New York World-Telegram 85, 97
Newfield, Sam 209
Newill, James 16
Newman, Nanette 157
Newman, Paul 59
News in the Air see *Exiled to Shanghai*

News Journal 289–290
Newton, Theodore 121
Next Time We Love 140
Ney, Marie 151
Nichols, Dudley 98, 286
Niemeyer, H.H. 42
Niesen, Gertrude 138, 219, 230
Nigh, Jane 179
Night Alarm 37, 60
Night Hostess 7
Night Must Fall 148, 151
Night of Terror 97, 119
Nightingale's Boys 161
Nikki 134
Nikki (novel) 195, 201, 213–214
"Nikki and Her War Birds" 134
Nimoy, Leonard 55
Nissen, Greta **135**, 135–136, 137–138, 139, 140, 143
Nixon, Allan 1, 195–215, **195**, **199**, **204**, **205**, **208**, **210**, **211**
Nixon, Annette 214
Nixon, Richard 242
Nixon Theater 187
No Escape 296, **297**, 304
"No Man Is an Island" 241, 242, 243, 244
No More Blondes 7
"No! No! Nanette" 235
No Questions Asked 9
No Time for Comedy 21
No Time for Love 170, 194
No Way Out 226
Nobody Hides Forever 214
Nobody's Business 93
"Nobody's Chasing Me" 87
Noel, Jimmy 193
Nolan, Lloyd 127
"The Nomad" 238
Noonan, Tommy 302
Norden, Christine 238–239
Norfolk Ledger-Dispatch 174
Norfolk Shamrocks 197
Norris, Edward 37, 40
North, Ted 252
North American Aviation 111
The North Star 72
North West Mounted Police 45, 143, 145
Northwestern University 164
Norton, Inez 165–166
Nosseck, Max 258, 262, 267
Nothing Lasts Forever 275, 280
Nottingham Journal 148
Noyes, Helen 209
Nugent, Frank S. 15
Nurse on Wheels 157, 163
The Nut Farm 93, 94, 98, 119
Nylon Sky 301

Oakie, Jack 100, 218
Oakland Tribune 9–10, 107, 204, 286
Oakley, Annie 104
Oakman, Wheeler 171
O'Brian, Jack 231–232, 274, 302, 303
O'Brien, Edmond 115, 166

O'Brien, George 114
O'Brien, Marissa 258
O'Brien, Pat 15, 93, 105, 111, 112, 114–117, 119, 123, **124**, 134
O'Connell, Hugh 46, 218
O'Connell, Patrick 162
O'Connor, Carroll 130
O'Connor, Donald 303
"October" 240
O'Donnell, Judson 181
O'Dowd, John 3, 164, 169, 180–181, 189, 192
O'Driscoll, Martha 174
Of Mice and Men 103–104, 106–110, 113–114, 117
O'Farrell, Bernadette 149
Off the Record 46
The Offspring 275, 280
"Oh! Susanna" 258
Oh, Susanna 231
O'Hara, Maureen 22, 114, 169
O'Harra, Michaela 72
Ohio Board of Censors 251
O.H.M.S. see *You're in the Army Now*
O'Keefe, Dennis 113, 201
Oklahoma! 235, 236
Olay, Valentina Asterman Garcia de 52
Old Beacon Club 282
Old Knick 268
"The Old School Noose" 161
The Old Soak 133
The Old Vic 153, 155, 156
Olean Times Herald 26
Oliver, John 195–197
Olympia 294
O'Malley, John 206
Omnibus 88, 236, **237**
On Dress Parade 124, 131
On Stage Everybody 112, 119
On the Waterfront 267
The One Day a Year Man 152
One Frightened Night 98, 119
One Million B.C. 205
One Sunday Afternoon 45
O'Neal, Ryan 275, 303
O'Neill, Betty 239
O'Neill, Eugene 149
Only Yesterday 217, 228
"Open, Parachute!" 234
The Oresteia 149, 155, 156
Orlando Evening Star 301
Orlando Sentinel 33
Ormond, Ron 178, 208–211
Ormskirk County Hospital 114
Orr, William T. 213
Osborne, John 162
O'Shaughnessey, Patrick 166
O'Shea, Michael **66**, 73, 176
Othman, Frederick C. 26, 27, 91, 106
Ottawa Citizen 231
Our Daily Bread 220–221
"Our Love Story" 234
Our Town 21
Ouspenskaya, Maria 166
Out of the Unknown 160

Out of This World 86–87
Out West with the Hardys 167, 193
The Outlaw 21
Outlaw Women 208–209, **208**, 215
Outward Bound 145
The Outward Room 105
Overture Players 148
Owen, Bill 149, 153
Owen, Gary 303
The Ox-Bow Incident 71–72, 89, 117
Oxford Playhouse 155, 156

Paar, Jack 237–238
Packard Theatre Institute 6
Pagan Lady 134
Page, Anita 96
Paid 167
Paige, Mabel 24, **26**
Painting the Clouds with Sunshine 116, 119
"A Pair of Boots" 271
Paiva, Nestor 81
The Pajama Game 237, 238
Palm Beach Post 283
Palm Springs Racquet Club 188, 189
Palmer, Gordon 16
Palmer, Lilli 153
Palmer, Maria 263
Pam, Jerry 298
Panama Hattie 236
Panic 268
Panic in the Parlor see *Sailor Beware*
Pantomime Quiz 55, 295, 300
Paper Mill Playhouse 238
El Paraiso Lodge 115
Pardon My Blooper! 281
Paris in Spring 218, 228
Park Open Air Theatre 148
Parker, Cecilia 170
Parker, Jean 109, 169
Parker, Phyllis 29
Parker, Willard 186
Parole, Inc. **66**, 68
Parrish, Helen 127
Parry, Florence Fisher 13
The Parson and the Outlaw 299, 304
Parsons, Harriet 102
Parsons, Louella 12, 37, 46, 48–50, 53, 55, 58, 62, 103, 112, 115, 123, 128, 135, 139, 144, 178, 188, 198–200, 202, 204, 207, 208, 210, 222–223, 225, 240, 245, 247, 258, 259, 261, 271, 292, 293, 299
The Party's Over 8
Pasadena Community Theatre 217
Pasadena Playhouse 66
Pasternak, Joe 46, 233
A Patch of Blue 118, 119
Paterson Evening News 145
El Patio Theater 113, 114
The Patsy 133
Patterson, Blakely Clifford 29

Patton, Virginia 64
Paul and Michelle 161, 163
Payette, William C. 282
Payment Due 248
Payne, John 62, 81, 293–294
Payne, Laurence 149
The Payoff 259
Payton, Barbara 3, 180–183, *180*, 184–189, 191, 192, 296
Payton, John 180
Peak, Mayme Ober 16–17, 20, 22–23, 285
Pearl, Jack 105, 106
Peck, Gregory 114, 180, 302
Peck, Steve 190
Peg o' My Heart 133
Peil, Paul Leslie 211
Pemberton, Brock 6, 7
"Penelope" 155
Penn, Leonard 209
Penny Wise 70
Pepper, Barbara 3, 100, 219–222, 223, ***224***–228
Pepper, Dennis *see* Enfield, Dennis
Peppermint West 239
The Pepsi-Cola Playhouse 55
Percy, Eileen 95, 97
The Perfect Gentleman see Lord Jeff
Perils of Pauline 217, 228
Perona, John 49, 54
Perry, Lawrence 80, 94
Perry, Mary 82
Perry Mason 130
Peter Gunn 270
Peter Loves Mary 118
Peter Pan 160
Peterborough Advertiser 151
Peters, Brock 236
Peters, Don 81
Peterson, Marjorie 94
Peterson, Ralph W. 148
Pete's Tavern 274
The Petrified Forest 265
Petrillo, Sammy 269
Petticoat Fever 88, 294
Petticoat Junction 227, 228
Pétursson, Jóhann 205
The Phantom 211
The Phantom of the Air 217, 228
Philadelphia Eagles 54, 285
Philadelphia Inquirer 95, 113, 135, 139, 231, 238
Philco Television Playhouse 83–84, 85
Phillips Exeter 286
Phipps, William 179, 297–298, 303–304
Photographer's Costume Ball 256
Photoplay 16, 48
Physical Culture 165
Piano Portraits 232
"Picket Fence" 105
Pickford, Mary 134, 136–137, 218, 225
Pickup 204, ***204***, 206, 215

Picnic 299
Picture Play 10
Pierre of the Plains 49, 60
Pigg, Joseph 160
Pigott-Smith, Tim 161
Pigs 93, 133
Pinchot, Ann 102, 105
Pine-Thomas 81, 82
Pistols 'n' Petticoats 59
Pitts, ZaSu 11, 37
Pittsburgh Art Institute 70
Pittsburgh Playhouse 70, 83, 88
Pittsburgh Post-Gazette 82, 114, 187, 253
Pittsburgh Press 13, 85, 187
Pittsburgh Sun-Telegraph 70, 89
Pivar, Ben 174
P.J. Clarke's 259, 265, 266
P.J.'s Restaurant 271
The Plainsman 38
Platt, Louise 45
The Players 253
Playhouse Company 148
Playhouse 90 117
Pleasence, Donald 149, 158
Pointman 277
Police Story 260
Pollack, Sydney 109
Pollock, Arthur 7, 108, 139
Polyclinic Hospital 7
Pompton Lakes Summer Theater 145
Poor Bito 157, 158
The Poor Nut 86
Popkin, Harry 258
The Poppy God 92
Port of New York 258
Porter, Cole 86–87
Porter, Red 294
Portsmouth Evening News 149
Possessed 95, 119
Post Road 70
The Postman Always Rings Twice 186–187
Pottsville Republican 267
Poughkeepsie Journal 50
Powell, Dick 9–11, 16, ***17***, 118, 239, 271
Powell, Jane 233
Powell, Robert 230
Powell, Wayne 27
Powell, William 170
Power Man 214
Power, Tyrone ***23***, 23, ***70***, 71, 74, 76, 78, 80, 85, 165
Powers, John 197
Prehistoric Women 204–206, ***205***, 207, 215
Prelutsky, Burt 286, 303
Preminger, Otto 75, 274
Pressman, Dr. Joel 53
Pressure Point 271
Price, Edgar 139
Price, Saul 253
Price, Vincent 77, 275
The Pride of the Yankees 170, 194
Prince, William 73
Princeton 74

Prinsep, Anthony 139
The Prisoner 149, 163
Private Lives 81, 82
Prizzi's Honor 275, 280
"Prodigal's Mother" 24
Producers' Showcase 236
"The Promise" 85
Prophet Without Honor 167–168, 193
Prospect Theatre Company 161
Prosperity 96–97
Prouty, Jed 109
Prouty, L. Fletcher 52
The Prowler 275, 279
Pryor, Roger 109
Psycho 276
Psychotronic Video 269
The Public Enemy 37
Public Eye 161
Pulos, Lee 303
Punsly, Bernard 121–122, ***122***, 123, ***124***, 126, 129
Purcell, Bob 115
Purcell, Dick ***219***
The Purple Fig Tree 148
Pursuit of Happiness 196

Quayle, Anthony 160
Queen Christina 35
Queen Elizabeth Slept Here 148
Queen of Angels Hospital 116
Queen of Burlesque 225, 228
The Quiet American 57, 60
The Quiet Man 299
Quinlan, Roberta 233
Quinn, Anthony 212, 249
Quinn, Tandra ***210***
Quinton, Everett 277
Quirk, Lawrence 17

Rachevsky, Zina *see* d'Harcourt, Countess Zina
The Racket Man 172, ***173***, 194
Racket Squad 129, 183
Radar Secret Service 178, 194
Radcliffe, E.B. 25, 74, 239–240
Radio City Matinee 71
Raft, George 98
La ragazza del palio 57, 60
Ragland, Rags 283
Rain 133, 134, 208
Rainbow Room 301
Rains, Claude ***125***
Ralph's 238
Rambeau, Marjorie 133, 142
Ramrod 291–292
Randolph Air Force Base 20
Random Harvest 148
Rangeley Lakes Summer Theatre 128
Rathbone, Basil 24, 235
Rau, Herb 265
Rawhide 213
Ray, Fred Olen 276
The Razor's Edge 76, 80
Reading High School 230
Ready, Willing and Able 16, ***17***, 18
Reagan, Ronald 241

Red 277, 280
The Red Cloak see *Il mantello rosso*
Red Desert 178, 194
"The Red Dress Case" 188
Red Dust 137, **138**
Red Harvest 49
The Red House 80
Red Ryder 198
Red Stallion in the Rockies 114, 119
Redelings, Lowell F. 111
Redfield, William 86
Redhead 37, 60, 146
Redwood School and Rehabilitation Center 242
Reed, Donna 70, 177
Reed, Florence 133
Reed, Luther 139
Reed, Maxwell 149
Reed, Oliver 159, **159**
Reed, Philip 257
Rees, Lanny 177
Reeves, Del 302
Reeves, Ellanora *see* Needles, Ellanora
Reeves, George 45, 82, 203, 285
Reeves, Steve 57, 273
"The Regal Rustler" 54
Reid, Wallace 285
Reinhardt, Max 10, 11
Reisman, Leo 24
Remick, Lee 236
Remington Steele 275
Reservoir Dogs 276–**278**, 280
The Respectful Prostitute 261
Rest Haven Memorial Park 243
The Return of the Whistler 64, 68
Reunion in France 24
Reunion Theatre Association 147
Reynolds, Craig 2, 3, 216–228, **216, 218, 219, 220, 222, 224, 226**
Reynolds, Quentin 50
Rice, Elmer 143
Rice, Florence 23, 167, 169
Richards, Addison 15
Richards, Alun 161
Richards, Dick 155
Richmond, Kane 63
Richmond Arrows 197
Richmond College Messenger 196
Richmond Collegian 196
Richmond News Leader 195, 196
Richmond Spiders 196
Richmond Times-Dispatch 196, 197–198
Rickey, Jean 253
"Ride a Dark Trail" 301
Rieser, Marianne 144
Right to Happiness 144
Ring for Catty 156–157
"Ring Twice for Laura" 176
Ringling Bros. and Barnum & Bailey Circus 121
Ripley, Arthur 201
Rippy, Robert 236
Ritter, Thelma 262
The Rivals of Sherlock Holmes 161

Riverside County Jail 190
Riverside County Superior Court 190
Riviera 237
Riviera Country Club 42
Riviera Girl 206
Roach, Hal 45, 107, 200
Roach, Margaret 169
Road to Bali 209, 215
The Roadhouse Murder 35, 59
Roar of the Press 109, 119
Roark, Aidan 41–42
Robbery Under Arms 51, 163
Rober, Richard 209
Roberta 238
Roberts, Allene 3, 262
Roberts, Arlyn 266
Roberts, Beatrice 39
Roberts, Beverly 14–15, **14**
Roberts, Donald 26
Roberts, Kenneth 45
Roberts, St. John 153
Robertson, Dale 189
Robertson, Elizabeth Jean 216
Robeson, Paul 101
Robin Hood of El Dorado 38, 60
Robinson, Alan 148
Robinson, Frances 44, 249
Robinson, Jane Geraldine 32, 40
Robson, Flora 153
Rochester Democrat and Chronicle 93
Rock, Felippa 208
Rock Golf Course 62
Rock Island Trail 54, 60
Rockefeller, Winthrop 282
Rocky and His Friends 302
Rodeo 116, 119
Rodeo Dough 170, 193
Roe, Suzanne 129–130
Rogers, Charles "Buddy" 225, 234, 229
Rogers, Ginger 21
Rogers, Kasey *see* Elliot, Laura
Rogers, Mary 44, 259
Rogers, Will 44, 259
The Rogues Tavern 100, 119
Roland, Gilbert 303
Rolfe, Guy 155, **156**
Rolfe, Mary 73
Roll, S. Ernest 182–183
Romain, Yvonne 159
Romance Road 221, 228
Romano, Don 214
Romano, Louis 269
Romanoff, Mike 55
Romanoff's 55
Romay, Lina 253
Rome, Harold 231
Romeo and Juliet 120, 148
Romero, Cesar 37
Rommel, Erwin 56
Romp!!! 303
The Rookies 120
Rookies on Parade 198, 214
Room for Two 148
Room Service 70

Rooney, Mickey 10, 179, 184, 190, 217, 225
Roosevelt, Franklin D., Jr. 19, 42–44
Roosevelt, Theodore 19
Roosevelt Hospital 238
Roosevelt Theatre 81
Rosado, Robert 274
Rose, George 149
Rose, Princess Margaret 296
Rose, Sydney 239
Rose Marie 235
Rosedale Dance Academy 230
Rosenberg, Leon 190, 191
Rosenbloom, Slapsie Maxie 302
Rosenburg, John 232, 234
Rosey, Max 302
Ross, George 50, 104
Ross, Stuart 24
Roth, Lillian 138
Rothstein, Arnold 165
The Round Up 143, 146
Rowan & Martin's Laugh-In 303
Rowland, Betty 207
Rowlands, Gena 271
Rowles, Polly 70
Royal Academy of Dramatic Art (RADA) 148
A Royal Scandal **73**, 75–76, **76**, 77, 89
Royal Theatre 148
Rub, Andrew 230, 236–237
Rub, Louisa 230, 231, 236, 237
Rudolph Wurlitzer Company 230
Rumba 218, 228
Run for the Hills 186, 296, 304
The Runestone 276, 280
Russell, Rosalind 8, 223
Russo, John A. 275
Rutherford, Ann 185
Rutt, Todd 269
Ryan, Fran 228
Ryan, Hunt 235
Ryan, Ray 54, 59
Ryan, Robert 251, 273
Ryan, Sheila 180
Ryan, Tommy 43

Sabatini, Rafael 11
Sabu 210
Saddle Tramp 259
Sailor, Beware! 98, 150, 163, 179
St. Clair, Lydia **78**
St. Clare's Hospital 274
Saint Joan 62, 147
St. Johns, Adela Rogers 97
St. John's Hospital 129, 303
St. Joseph News-Press 92
St. Louis Municipal Opera 236
St. Louis Post-Dispatch 87, 166, 253
St. Luke's Cathedral 33
St. Martin of Tours Roman Catholic Church 118
St. Monica Catholic Church 264
St. Stephen's Episcopal Church 133
St. Vincent's Hospital 203

Sale, Virginia 177
Salerno, Al 55
Saleslady 141, **142**, 145
Salty O'Rourke 52, 60
Salute to Heroes see *Ten Gentlemen from West Point*
San Bernardino County Sun 115, 130, 186
San Francisco 38
San Francisco Examiner 142, 167, 179, 241
San Juan Hotel 33
San Quentin 252, 256, 279
Sanders, George 48
Sandrich, Mark 285, 289
Sands, Johnny 291
Sangster, Jimmy 155
Santa Barbara News Press 279
Santell, Alfred 106
Santschi, Tom 252
Saporito, Joe 188
Sardi's 299
Sargent, Joe 24
Saskatoon Star-Phoenix 217
Satins and Spur 236
The Saturday Evening Post 196
Saturday Night Bandwagon 128
Saturday Night Theatre 161
Saturday's Children 10, **10**
Saturday's Millions 217, 228
Saunders, John Monk 134
Savage, Ann 3, 169, 172, 174–175, **175**, 188, 191, 193
Savar Theatre 61
Savoir, Alfred 139
Sawtelle Veterans Hospital 210, 241
Sayers, Jo Ann 168, 169
Sayonara 202
Scala 160
Scarlet River 35
The Scavengers 214
Schaaf, Ed 196
Schafer, Kermit 281
Schallert, Edwin 22, 62, 74, 82, 98, 172–173, 207, 208, 217, 252
Schallert, William 203, 206
Schaum, Franklin 106
Scheuer, Philip K. 176, 203
Schipa, Tito 283
Schlitz Playhouse of Stars 87
Schmeling, Max 136
Schneer, Charles H. 158
Scholl, Arthur 229, 230
Scholl, Danny 2, 229–244, **229**, **233**, **234**, **235**, **237**, **242**, **244**
The School for Scandal 148, 206
School for Soldiers see *Ten Gentlemen from West Point*
Schrock, Raymond L. 174
Schuller, the Rev. Robert H. 243
Schuman, William 236, **237**
Schwartz, Charles 87
Scofield, Paul 163
Scotch and Soda 70
Scott, George C. 274
Scott, Janette 158, **158**
Scott, John 95, 293

Scott, Martha 88
Scott, Randolph 38, 54, 74, 113, 248
Scott, Ridley 160
Scott, Vernon 189, 271–272
Scream of Fear see *Taste of Fear*
Screen Anarchy 274
Screen Directors Playhouse 117
Screen Guild Players 281
Scudda Hoo! Scudda Hay! 80
The Sea Hawk 45
Sea Racketeers 141, 145
"The Sea Witch" 271
Sea Wolf 188
Seaboard Utilities Shares Corporation 282
Seaton, George 73
Sebold, William G. 77
Secret Command 111, 119
"Secret Love" 239
The Secret Place 151, 163
Secrets 137
Seegar, Miriam 144
Seidel, Tom **25**
Seinfeld 275–276
Seinfeld, Jerry 276
Sekely, Steve 178
Sellars, Elizabeth 151
Seltzer, Leo A. 209
Selwyn, Edgar 95
Selznick, David O. 22, 34–35
Sennett, Mack 96
Sennwald, Andre 37–38
September Tide 148
Sepulveda's Veterans Administration Hospital 243
Sergeant Preston of the Yukon 213
Serlin, Oscar 71
Serling, Rod 117, 239
Sernas, Jack 149
Serpent Island 298, 304
The Set-Up 114, 119
Seven Days Ashore 246, 279
The Seven Year Itch 298, 304
Seventeen 92
Seventh Heaven 79
77 Sunset Strip 57, 130, 213
Sewanee Military Academy 33
Sex Hygiene 200, 215
Sexes and Sevens 139
Seyferlich, Frank 189-190
Seymour, Helena 238
Shadow of a Doubt 110, 119
Shadow of a Man 212, 214
Shadow of a Man (1952) 296
Shadows of Sing Sing 36, 60
Shaffer, Anthony 162
Shaffer, Peter 162
Shaffer, Rosalind 69
Shakedown 260, 279
Shakespeare, William 6, 10, 149, 253, 265
Shamokin News Dispatch 177
Shamrock Hotel 54, 116
The Shanghai Cobra 63, **65**, 68
Shantytown 136–137
Sharp Players 134
Shaum, Glenn Erwin 29

Shaw, George Bernard 1, 148
Shaw, Irwin 39
Shaw, Len G. 97
Shaw, Robert 273
She Couldn't Say No 116, 119, 143
She Couldn't Take It 98, 119
She Has What It Takes **171**, 171, 194
Sheafer, Marian 267
Sheaffer, Louis 86
Shed No Tears 114, 119
The Sheik 137
Shelburne Lounge 234
Shelton, John 257
Sheridan, Ann 41, 50, **51**, 54, 59, 219, **222**, 299
Sheridan, Gen. Phil 273
Sheridan, Richard Brinsley 206
The Sheriff of Fractured Jaw 57, 60
Sherman, George 198
Sherman, Harry 49, 143, 213
Sherman, Lynn 213
Sherman, Sam 275
Shields, Arthur 108
Shiffrin, Bill 262
Shipmates Forever 11, **17**, 18
Show Boat 236
The Show-Off 133
Show Them No Mercy! 37–38, 40, 60
Showmen's Trade Review 143
Shreveport Times 239
"Shrimp Boats" 235
Shubert Theatre 86, 88, 230
Sidney, Sylvia 122, **122**
Siege of the Saxons 157, 158, **158**, 159, 163
Siever, Velda May 212–213
Sifton, Claire 218
Sifton, Paul 218
"Silent Night" 231
The Silent Service 212
The Silent Witness 135, 145
Silk Stalkings 277
Silver, Bill 106
Silver, William Clay 136
Silver Bullet 275, 280
Silver Queen 49, 60
Silver Screen 126, 165
The Silver Theatre 203
The Silver Whistle 66, 86
Silvers, Phil 57, 235
Simms, Ginny 223
Simon, Leo 170
Simon, Simone 145
The Simpsons 277
Sing for Your Supper 283
Sing Your Way Home 248, 279
Singing in the Dark 267, 279
Single Lady 134
Singleton, Penny 141
Sinner Take All 38, 60
Sinners in Paradise 40, 60
Siodmak, Curt 180
Siodmak, Robert 273, 291
Sioux City Journal 93
Siren of Atlantis 201–202, 215
Sister Kenny 223, 234

"Sisters of Shadow" 86
"Sitting Duck" 162
6,000 Enemies 168, 193
60 Minutes 83
Skidding 134
Skinner, Edith Warman 70
Sklar, George 176
Skolsky, Sidney 180, 188, 204
Sky Murder 170, 193
Sky Raiders 126, 131
Skyscraper Souls 96, 119
Slade, Jack 299
Slander House 221, 228
The Slap Maxwell Story 275
Sleuth 162
Sloan, Lloyd L. 113–114, 204
Sloman, Ernest 43
The Slowest Gun in the West 57, 60
Small, Edward 38, 53
Smashing the Racket 40, 60
Smilin' Thru 133
Smith, Cyril 150
Smith, Darr 116, 232
Smith, Grace 33
Smith, Harold Jacob 85
Smith, Kate 71
Smith, Lorraine 26
Smith, Maggie 155
Smith, Maude 5, 16
Smoky 53, 60
Snow White and the Seven Dwarfs 6, 226
The Snowdropper 161, 162
So Proudly We Hail! 281, 285–**287**, 290, 304
Soanes, Wood 107
Sobol, Louis 17, 108, 187
Social Register 9, 18
"Solid Citizen" 177
Solow, Eugene 106
Sombrero Playhouse 179, 209
Some Girl 133
Someone to Remember 24–25, **25**, 31
A Son Comes Home 101, 119
The Son of the Sheik 202
The Song of Bernadette 72, **72**, 89
Sorrowful Jones 54, 60
Sothern, Ann 38, 233, **234**, 302
Sour, Robert 283
Sousa, Leone 283
"South America, Take It Away" 231
South Pacific 237
South Sea Bubble **150**, 151
South Shore Players 71, 81
Southio 277, 280
Southside 1-1000 86
The Spa 54
Spain, Fay 58
Spalding, Anne Hamilton 302
"Sparkin'" 207
Special Agent 82, 90
The Spectator 11
Speed 140, 141, 145
Spellbound 111, 119
Spencer, Sara 256

Sperry, Ray 79
Spillane, Mickey 188, 274
The Spoilers 117, 119, 252
Spokane Daily Chronicle 133
Spokesman Review 76, 136
Spotlight 154
Spotlight Theater 217
Spreckels, Geraldine 26
Spreckels, Gloria 44
Sprigle, Ray 253
Spring Dance 166
Spring Song 217
The Square Ring 148–149, 151, 153, 163
The Square Root of Wonderful 161
Stack, Robert 197, 295
Stafford, M. Oakley 187, 294, 300
The Stage 147–149, 153, 156, 160–163
Stage 7 227
Stagecoach 44
Stahl, John M. 217
Stamp, Terence 157, **157**
Standing Room Only 286
Standish, Myles 87, 253, 254
Stanfield, Audrey 286
Stanford Hall People's Festival 148
Stanton, Jeffrey 31
Star Time 234
Star Trek: Deep Space Nine 278
Star Trek: The Next Generation 275
Stardust 101, 119
Starlog 158
Starr, Eve 240
Starr, Irving 42
Starrett, Charles 145
Stars Over Hollywood 55, 110
Starstruck 277, 280
State Fair 76
Steel, Anthony 151
Steel, Jane 139
Steele, Marjorie 296, **297**
The Steel Cage 265, 279
Steel Pier 139
Steele, Tom 25, 31
Stehli, Edgar 87
Steiger, Rod 267
Stein, Herb 184
Steinbeck, John 71, 103, 106, 107, 117
Steiner, Max 98
Stengel, Casey 303
Stengel, Patricia 172
Step by Step 248–249, **249**, 279
Stephenson, Cornelius 16, 17
Stephenson, Henry 15
Sterke, Jeanette 149
Sterling, Robert 198
The Steve Allen Show 234
Stevens, Angela **261**
Stevens, Craig 198, 270
Stevens, Inger 212
Stevens, K.T. 176
Stevens, Naomi 206
Stevenson, L.L. 50
Stewart, Bruce 161

Stewart, James 8, 115, 140, 197, 259
Stewart, Martha 236
Stick to Your Guns 143, 146
Stockdale, Julian 231
Stocking, Laila 56, 57
Stoloff, Benjamin 97
Stone, George E. 104
Stone, Lewis 39
Stone, Milburn 141
Stone, Oliver 277
Stone, Paula 141
The Stone Jungle 201
Stop Me Before I Kill! see *The Full Treatment*
Stophlet, Jeanne M. 243–244
Stork Bites Man 225
Stork Club 45, 284, 294, 297
The Stork Is Dead 8
Storm Over the Nile 150, 163
Storm, Gale 87
The Story of a Guy 74
The Story of Dr. Wassell 50
The Story of Mrs. Murphy 262
"The Story of the Birth of Christ" 66
The Story of William Tell 56
Story: The Magazine of the Short Story 201
Story to Be Whispered 142
The Strange Affair of Uncle Harry 223, 228
Strange Cargo 169
Strange Lands and the Seven Seas 300
Strasberg, Susan 155
Strategy for Murder 89
Stratton, Ron 238
The Stratton Story **233**
Street, David 87, 212
A Streetcar Named Desire 263
Stromberg, Hunt, Jr. 176
Stronger Than Desire 168, 193
Stroud, Ruby 185
Stuart, Gloria 10, **10**
Student Players of Toynbee Hall 147
Studio One 87, 117
Sturges, Allen T. II 52–53
Sturman, Henry 253–254
Such Good Friends 274, 279
Suffolk Superior Court 282
Sugarfoot 213
Sullavan, Margaret 8
Sullivan, Barry 250
Sullivan, Ed 50, 51, 83, 169, 184, 234, 288
Sullivan, Ina 167
Sullivan, John L. 111, 119
The Sullivans 61, 62, **63**, 68
Summer in St. Louis 236
Summers, Bill 118
Summerville, Slim 37
Sunday Dinner for a Soldier **73**–75
Sunday Mercury 98–99
Sunday Mirror 154–155
Sunday Sun 101

Sunday Times 66
Sundown 48, 60
Sunset Inn 34
Sunset Plaza Apartments 180
Superman 275
Supper Serenade 231
"Suppressed Desires" 207
Surfside 6 213
Surmelian, Leon 165, 166
Susan and God 45, 60
Susann, Jacqueline 196
Suspense 128, 250
Sutton, Don 121–122
Sutton, John 62
Swarthout, Gladys 79
Sweeney, Gary 246
Sweet and Low-Down 62, **64**, 68
Swell Guy 290–291, 304
Swellhead 97, 119
Swing Club 169, 284
Swing It, Sailor! 102, 103, 119
Swiss Family Robinson 112
Sydney, Basil 151
Sylvester, Robert 300
Syms, Sylvia 153, 160
Syracuse American 134
Syracuse Journal 28
Syracuse Theater Guild Empire Players 134

T-Men 113, 119
Tabbert, William 83
Taft Theatre 231
Take a Tip 70
Take It or Leave It 74
Talbert, Bob 303
Talbot, Lyle **13**, 94, 209
"A Tale of Two Citizens" 300
Talent Parade 234
Talent Scout 218, 228
Tales from the Darkside 275
Tales of the Texas Rangers 211
Tales of Tomorrow 55, 87
Tales of Unease 161
Tales of Wells Fargo 118, 189
Tallas, Gregg G. 202
Talman, William 262
Tamba the chimp 204
Tamber, Selma 86
The Taming of the Shrew 219
Tampa Bay Times 137
Tampa Club 54
Tampa Tribune 75
Tanchuck, Nat 262
Tani, Yôko 152
Tarantino, Quentin 276, 277
Tarantula see *Mesa of Lost Women*
Tarzan 38, 170, 201, 204, 249, 284
Taske, Robert 105
Taste of Fear 155, 162, 163
Taylor, Clarice B. 66
Taylor, Elizabeth 271, 302
Taylor, Laurence 151
Taylor, Robert 167, 168, 170, 213
Taylor, Vivian Stokes 254, 259
Tedrick, Hazel 130
Ted's Rancho 130

Telephone Time 129
Temple Players 134
Tempo 158
Ten Gentlemen from West Point 22, **22**, 30, 31, 170, 194
Tenderloin 238
Tenth Avenue Kid 40, 43, 60
Terrible Joe Moran 275, 280
Il terrore dei barbari 57, 60
Il tesoro di Rommel 56, 60
Tess of the Storm Country 118, 119
Tevos, Herbert 209
The Texan 238
Texas, Li'l Darlin' 235, 237, 239
Thalberg, Irving 96
"Thanks America" 242
That Was the Week That Was 302
That's Gratitude 8
Theatre Guild 166
Theatre Guild of the Air 85, 234
Theatre Musart 198
Their Big Moment 37, 60
Them! 67, 68
There's No Dead End 130
There's Something About a Soldier 172, 194
Thesiger, Ernest 153
They All Come Out 167, 193
They Don't Grow on Trees 160
They Made Me a Criminal 123–124, **125**, 131
They Sell Sailors Elephants see *A Girl in Every Port*
They Shoot Horses, Don't They? 108, 109
They Were Expendable 111–112, 119
The Third Visitor 148
Thirer, Irene 8, 34–35
Thirteen Against Fate 160
13 Rue Madeleine 80
The 13th Man **140**, 141, 145
This Is My Best 79
This Is Your FBI 79, 128
This Space Is Mine 160
Thistlethwaite, Glenn 196
Thomas, Bob 82, 201, 260, 288
Thomas, Dan 36
Thomas, Dylan 162
Thomas, Frankie 118
Thomas, Kevin 273
Thompson, Alexis 49, 50, 51, 54, 285
Thompson, Howard 122, 154
Thorn, Ronald Scott 154
Thoroughbreds 174, 194
Thorpe, Dr. Franklyn 16
Those Endearing Young Charms 248, 279
Three Cornered Moon 97, 119
Three Live Ghosts 133
Three Mesquiteers 143
The Three Musketeers 292
The Three New Yorkers 24
Three on a Match 37
Three Out of Four 206–207
3 Ring Circus 117, 119
Three Wise Fools 148

The Three Wise Guys 38, 60
Three Wishes 118
Thunderbird 67
Thurston, Carol 73
Thyssen, Greta 302
The Tidings 171–172, 176
Tidyman, Ernest 214
Tierney, Ed 245, 246, 254, 255, **255**, 262, 264, 270, 275, 279
Tierney, Gene 48, 80
Tierney, Lawrence 1, 3, 245–280, **245**, **247**, **249**, **251**, **255**, **261**, **278**
Tierney, Lawrence, Sr. 245–246, 250, **255**, 256, 260, 263, 273
Tierney, Marion "Mary" Alice Crowley 245, **255**, 262, 270, 271
Tierney, Michael 3, 246, 272–273, 277, 278
Tierney, Tim 3, 246, 247, 255, 257, 270, 277, 278
Tiger Lily Lounge 266
"'Til Death Do Us Part" 203
Tildesley, Alice L. 9
Tilton, Martha 174
Time 105, 106
"Time After Time" 232
"Time and Time Again" 233, **234**
The Time of Your Life 266–267
A Time to Live 188
Tinney, Lester 118
The Tirol 190
To Step Aside: Seven Long Short Stories 29
To Tell the Truth 243
To What Red Hell 217
Toast of the Town 83
Tobacco Road 210
Todd, Ann 155
Todd, John 288
Todd, Mike 231
Todd, Thelma 44, 100
Tognazzi, Ugo 57
Toland, Gregg 122
Toler, Sidney 65, **144**
Tollbooth 277
Tom Brown's School Days 126, 131
Tomahawk 259
Tommy 93
Tone, Franchot 2, 9, 49, 121, 134, 180–187, 189, 190–193, 265–267
Tongue in Cheek 232–233
Tonight on Broadway 83
Tonight Show 237–238, 301
Tonight's the Night 207
"Too Marvelous for Words" 16
Too Young to Marry 148
Top Banana 235–236, **235**, 244
Topping, Bob 54
Tormé, Mel 86
The Torso Murder Mystery see *Traitor Spy*
Tosatti, Mario 43
Totò lascia o raddoppia? 56, 60
Toto Lost in New York 278, 280
Tough Guys Don't Dance 275, 280
Toumanoff, Princess Marusia 239
Tourneur, Jacques 167

Town House 188
Town Tamer 58, 60, 302, 304
Towne, Hugh W. 6
Tracy, Lee 103
Tracy, Spencer 38, 103, 167
Trader Tom's Steak House 266
The Trail Blazers 143, 145
Trail Street 251
Train to Tombstone 178, 194
"The Traitor" 85
Traitor Spy 44, 60
The Travels of Jaimie McPheeters 118
Travers, Bill 149
Travis, June 102, ***103***, **218**
Travis, Tony *see* Kleefeld, Travis
Treacher, Arthur 21
Treachery Rides the Range 218, 228
Tree, Dorothy 97
A Tree Grows in Brooklyn 74
Tremayne, Les 144
Trent, John 40
Trent, Sheila 121
Treves, Frederick 148
Trevor, Claire 8, 44, 94, 122, 171, ***251***, 251, 279
Trewin, J.C. 153, 160
Trocadero 14, 100, 196
Troilus and Cressida 149
Trouble Over the Pacific see *Isle of Destiny*
Troup, Bobby 193
Troy, Edward 293
Troy, Eleanor 169
Troyka 134
True Confession 288
Truesdell, John 48, 50
Tucker, Augusta 288
Tucker, Forrest 54, 113, 302
Tudor, Ray 88
Tufts, Barbara Minot 283, 284, 288, ***291***, 292, 295, 296, 301
Tufts, Bowen, Sr. 282–283
Tufts, Charles 282
Tufts, Sonny 1, 186, 281–304, ***281, 284, 287, 289, 291, 293, 297***
Tufts University 282
Tully, Jim 105
Tupper, Helen 128
Turner, George 123
Turner, Lana 173
Turney-Dann, Doreen 149
"Turning the Town Upside Down" 101
Turpentine Boy 62
TV Radio Mirror 272
Twelvetrees, Helen 36
The 20th Century-Fox Hour 117
20th Century Tavern 283
Twice Round the Daffodils 156–157, 163
Twitchell, Archie 68
2 Days in the Valley 277, 280
Two Fellows and a Girl 7
Two Girls on Broadway 109, 119
Two in the Dark 98, 119
Two-Man Submarine 172, 194
Two on an Island 143

Tyers, John 231
Tyler, Tom 217

"Uhny Uftz" 302
Ulmer, Edgar G. 174, ***175***, 175, 186
Ulric, Lenore 134
The Undefeated 58, **58**, 60
Under Glass 8
Under Milk Wood 162
The Unexpected 129, 177
Union Pacific 213
United Press 27, 42, 92, 189
Universal Studio Tours 59
University of Alabama 133, 134
University of New Mexico 33
University of Pennsylvania 62
University of Richmond 195, 197
University of the South 33
University of Tours, France 33
University Players 7–8, 19
The Untamed Breed 292, 304
Untamed Mistress 210–211, **211**, 212, 215
The Unwritten Code 172, 194
Ustinov, Peter 157

Vail, Lester 139
Vaile, David 205
Valentine, Carole 240
Valentine, Paul 82
The Valentines 85
Vallee, Rudy 24
Valley Times 82
The Vamp see *Delilah*
Van Brunt, Barbara 128–130
Vance, Henry 298
Van Cleef, Lee 300
Vancouver Sun 116
Vanderbilt, Gloria 44, 266–267, 274
Van Dyke, Dick 239, 302
Van Dyke, Jerry 302
Van Eyck, Peter 72
Van Nuys News 111, 114
Van Wyck Players 81
Varconi, Victor 38
Variety 5, 8–9, 20, 37, 71, 107, 110, 122, 136, 137, 141, 143, 151, 167, 178, 218, 223–225, 248, 250, 267, 271, 277
Variety Girl 291, 304
Veiller, Bayard 167
Velez, Lupe 101
Venable, Evelyn 222
Verdugo, Elena 185
Verneuil, Louis 288
Vernon, Glen 209
Vernon, Terry 301
Veterans Administration Hospital 145, 243, 244
Veterans' Canteen 223
Veterans' Hospital 210
Veterans of Foreign Wars Convention 243
Vetry's Den 250
The Vigil 148
Vince Lombardi National Youth Football League 242

Vincent, June 114
Virginia City 45
Virginia Military Institute 33
The Virginian 55, 288, 301, 304
"Vivat Rex" 161
Voice of the Whistler 63, 68
Von, Margarie 298
Von Blon, Katherine 143
Von Borsody, Eduard 178
Von Furstenberg, Betsy 186, 265
Voss, Ralph F. 115–116

Wadsworth Veterans Hospital 243
Wagenheim, Charles **78**
Wagner, Robert 117
Wagon Train 130
Waikiki Tavern Orchard Room 66
Wakeman, Bill 269
Wald, Jerry 9
Wale, Terry 162
Wales, Clarke 6, 39
A Walk in the Sun 62, 68
Walker, Danton 24, 45, 46, 88, 128, 188, 284–285, 292
Walker, Robert 264
Wallace, Francis 196
Wallace, Jean 261
Wallace, Mike 83
Wallach, Louis S. 269
Wallis, Hal B. 204
Walsgrave Hospital 162
Walsh, Raoul 52, 101
Walters, Selene 260
Walthall, Henry B. 104
Wanamaker, Richard 120
Wanger, Walter 48, 49, 64
Wanted: Dead or Alive 130
The War Wagon 58, 60
War Wife 246
Ware, Irene ***137***
Ware, Linda 82
Warner, Jack 149, 157
Warpath 115, ***115***, 119
Warren, Annette 232
Warren, Fran 235
Warrick, Ruth 291
Warship 161
Warwick, Robert 7
Warwick University Arts Centre Theatre 162
Washington Evening Star 46
Washington Redskins 196
Waterloo Courier 124
Watford Palace Theatre 162
Watson, Betty Jane 238
Watterson, Mrs B. 26
Watts, Richard 85
Wayne, Fredd 235
Wayne, John 44, 45, 47, 53, 57, 58, **58**, 59, 114, 300
We Proudly Present 148
Wead, Frank "Spig" 15
Weaver, Tom 3, **20**, 110, 164, 179, 297–298
Webb, Clifton 80
Webb, Dr. Frank R. 28

Weber, Elise 236
Weber, Rosa 105–106
Webster, Paul Francis 239
The Wedded Blisses 238
Weil, Belle 260
Weinstein, Josh 277
Weissmuller, Johnny 201
The Well Groomed Bride 289, 304
Welles, Orson 256, 267
Welliver, Andy M. 45
Wellman, William 71
Wells, Dawn 274
Wells, Jacqueline 44
Wells, Robert 86
Welsh, Jean C. 61–62
Welsh Drama Company 162
Welsh National Theatre 162
Wenham, Jane 161
Werba's Flatbush 134
We're in the Money 11, **11**, 18
"We're on the Road to Athens" 86
Werfel, Franz 72
West, DeDe 214
West, Mae 93, 142, 201
West London Observer 150
West Los Angeles Independent 181
West of Singapore 137, **138**, 145
Westchester Music Theater 237
Westerby, Robert 149
Western Mail 149, 151, 153
Westinghouse Playhouse 239
The Westland Case 220
Westman, Nydia 93
Westmoreland Country Club 164
Westwood Methodist Episcopal Church 141
The Wet Parade 96, 119
Whale, James 40
Whalen, Michael **66**
Whalen, Father Will 246
What Anne Brought Home 148
What Price Glory? 73, 114, 133
What Price Hollywood? 35
Whedon, John 234
Wheeler, Jim 74
Whelan, Tim 144
Where's Charley? 236
While, Charles R. 29
Whirlpool see *Methinks the Lady*
Whirlybirds 117
Whispering Wires 7
The Whistler 117
Whitaker, David 152
White Collars 133
Whitehall 283
Whitehead, O.Z. 22
Whitelaw, Billie 154
Whiteman, Paul 230
Whiting, Margaret 78–79
Whiting, Richard 16
Whitney, Joan 260
Whitney, Liz 40–42, 45, 48, 256
Whitney, Peter **127**
Who Stole Santa? 278, 280
The Whole Town's Talking 98, 119
Whorf, Richard 127, **127**
Who's Who 283
Why Me? 275, 280

Why Men Leave Home 133
Wide Country 118
Widmark, Richard 300
Wilcox, Grace 39
Wilcoxon, Henry 38
Wild Bill Hickok Rides 48, 60
The Wild Duck 6, 162
Wildcat 238
Wilde, Cornel 78, 166
Wilder, Billy 298
Wilder, Pat 44
Wilder, Thornton 21
Wilder, W. Lee 188
Will Success Spoil Rock Hunter? 267
Willett, James 190, 191
William Beaumont Veterans Hospital 35
William, Warren 48, 97
Williams, Ben Ames 24
Williams, Dick 197, 198, 206
Williams, Emlyn 151
Williams, Esther 54, 173
Williams, Frances 33
Williams, Guinn "Big Boy" 41, 44
Williams, Kenneth 163
Williams, Robert 92, 96, 100
Williams, Tennessee 81
Williams, Wade 193
Williams, Whitney 9–10, 99
Willis, Bruce 277, 278
Willis, Ray 150
Wilshire Ebell Theatre 143, 144, 243
Wilson 74, 89
Wilson, Arthur 127
Wilson, Carey 167
Wilson, Don 239
Wilson, Dorothy 37
Wilson, Earl 70, 76, 88, 116–117, 186, 236–238, 266, 273, 300, 301
Wilson, George 197
Wilson, Maggie 117
Wilson, Marie 1, 15, 195, 198–201, **199**, 202–210
Wilson, Roland 190
Wilson, Virginia 62, 287
Wilson, Woodrow 74
Winchell, Walter 33, 40, 43, 44, 46, 50, 53, 57, 95, 138, 141, 143, 183, 190, 281, 290, 296, 299, 300
Winchester '73 259, 260
The Wind Cannot Read 151–152, 163
Windsor, Claire 241
Windsor, Marie 209, 297–298, 299
Windsor Star 104, 295
Wing, Toby 109
Wing and a Prayer: The Story of Carrier X 74, **75**, 89
Winged Pigeons 231
Winged Victory 231, 244
Wings of Steel 170, 194
The Winnah! 138, 145
Winnipeg Kiddies 92
Winnipeg Permanent Players 92

Winnipeg Tribune 113, 133
Winsett, Betty 236
Winters, Shelley 113, 115, 118, 253
Winterset 69–70
Wise, Robert 251
The Wiser Sex 8, 18
Wishbone Party 234
Wister, Emery 59
Wister, Owen 288
With a Song in My Heart 243
With the Marines at Tarawa 222
Withers, Grant 109
Within the Law 167, **168**, 193
Without Children 37, 60
Wizards of the Demon Sword 276, 280
Woideman, Mignon 44
Wolcott, the Rev. P.C. 33
Wolff, Pierre 287
Wolfit, Donald 153
The Woman in Room Thirteen 7
A Woman's Man 97, 119
A Women Rebels 39
Wonderful Town 87
Wood, Sam 21, 96
Woodbury, Joan 144, **144**
The Wooden Slipper 9
Woodrow Wilson High School 61
Woods Hole Village Cemetery 30
Woodside, J.B. 92
Woodward, Joanne 59
Woolley, Monty 110, 113
The World Our Stage 152
Worth, Irene 153
Worthing Gazette 152
Worthing Herald 148, 151–153
Worthing Theatre Company 148
The Would-Be Gentleman 235
Wray, Fay **34**, 35, 134
Wray, Ted 113, 115
Wright, Cobina, Jr. 44
Wright Players 7, 133
W.T. Johnson Circus Rodeo 121
Wurtzel, Sol M. 128
WUSA 59, 60
Wyler, William 122
Wynn, Keenan 118
Wynters, Charlotte 222
Wyoming Mail 260

X Marks the Spot 95, 119
Xavier University 243
The XYY Man 161

Yale Dramatic Association 282
Yale Record 282
Yale University 74, 282, 283, 285, 286, 296
Yale Weekly News 282
Yeates, Cydney 277
Yes, My Darling Daughter 70
Yordan, Philip 247, 273
York, Al 224
York, Cal 126
Yothers, Jean 33
You Can't Get Away with Murder 124, **125**, 131
You Can't Take It with You 70

You Only Live Once 105
You Twinkle Only Once 201, 203–204
Young, Carleton G. 225
Young, Collier 262
Young, Georgiana 127
Young, Gig 292
Young, James R. 171
Young, Loretta 97, 127, 243
Young, Robert 62
Young Dillinger 273

Young Sinners 94
Younger, Cole 54
The Youngest 87
Your Show of Shows 236
You're in the Army Now 101, 119
You're Not So Tough **126**, 131
Youth Runs Wild 246, 279
Yurka, Blanche 6

Z Cars 161
Zachary, Peter Nicholas 112, 115

Zachary, Stephanie 112
Zachary, Zeno 112
Zaiman, Bob 186
Zanuck, Darryl F. 41, 71, 74, 76, 79, 80, 82
Zarak 159
Die Zarin 75
Zika, Ann *see* Stevens, Angela
Zinnemann, Fred 168
Zorita 284

www.ingramcontent.com/pod-product-compliance
Lightning Source LLC
Chambersburg PA
CBHW060335010526
44117CB00017B/2833